the
psychology
of
adolescence

Arthur T. Jersild
Columbia University

Judith S. Brook
Columbia University

David W. Brook
Mount Sinai School of Medicine

the
psychology
of
adolescence

3rd
edition

Macmillan Publishing Co., Inc.
New York

Collier Macmillan Publishers
London

Macmillan Publishing Co., Inc.
866 Third Avenue, New York, New York 10022

Collier Macmillan Canada Ltd.

Library of Congress Cataloging in Publication Data

Jersild, Arthur Thomas, (date)
    The psychology of adolescence.

    Bibliography: p.
    Includes index.
    1. Adolescent psychology. I. Brook, Judith S.,
joint author. II. Brook, David W., joint author.
III. Title.
BF724.J4   1978   155.5   76-51737
ISBN 0-02-360610-X

Printing: 1 2 3 4 5 6 7 8   Year: 8 9 0 1 2 3 4

To
Pamela and David
Adam and Jonathan

preface

This third edition has been revised to reflect new research findings and theories pertaining to the development and behavior of adolescents and to keep it in step with changing attitudes and social forces that influence the views and conduct of youth. A new chapter and new sections in other chapters deal with the following issues:

- Changes in sexual mores and the impact of these changes on youth.
- The consequences of increasingly strong demands for equality between the sexes, including revised ideas about masculinity and femininity and the effect such ideas might have on the self-image and vocational aspirations of boys and girls.
- Drug use among adolescents, including the increasing use of alcohol in early and middle adolescence.
- The problem of delinquency as seen from the points of view of the delinquents themselves and their apprehensive elders.
- Militancy and social activism, notably at the college level.

We discuss the objective features of growth and behavior traditionally associated with the psychology of adolescence, and we also explore the subjective aspects of adolescence. We emphasize the concept of the self and experiences that flow through the private lives of adolescents: love, joy, anger, fear, and anxiety; self-esteem and self-reproach; fantasies and dreams. This psychological approach was warmly received by those who used earlier English language and foreign language editions of the book.

In our discussion of physical development we note the effect of genetic factors, and also discuss the ways in which adolescents' physical characteristics and personal appearance, whether influenced by genetic or environmental factors, affect their views of themselves and the way they are appraised by others.

In the area of intellectual development, we first examine recent findings regarding cognitive development, and then discuss mental ability as measured by intelligence tests.

In various chapters we emphasize the role of the family in personality development, and also note that from the time of infancy children's own qualities influence their interactions with their parents. We further draw attention to social factors outside the home, notably peer relationships, that play an important part in determining an adolescent's values and conduct.

In our account of adolescents at school we describe aspects of conceptual development that determine a young person's potential readiness for mastering new ideas. We discuss the dropout situation, especially at the high school level, and consider aspects of the school program, as well as competing out-of-school forces, that influence young people's attitudes toward education. We also cite reasons and findings to support our view that students should be encouraged to learn about themselves in the educational program, from kindergarten through college.

We are fortunate in having had the help of Professor Mary Sue Richardson, who wrote the chapter on vocational development. Her wide-ranging knowledge of the literature is complemented by her association with a historic longitudinal study of vocational choices and adjustments.

Many people have contributed to the contents of this book. We have drawn heavily on the research and theoretical papers listed in the bibliography and are greatly indebted to their authors. We owe a debt of gratitude to a great number of high school and college students, teachers, and parents. Their help has come by way of formal research, personal interviews and consultations, anonymous self-report essays, and observations in classrooms, workshops, and volunteer discussion groups designed to help participants mutually examine their perception of themselves and others.

We are also much indebted to Eleanor Balka and Dr. Judith Lukoff for their help in reviewing the literature. We are grateful to Ann Scovell Gordon for help in reviewing the literature and for reading the manuscript and to Dr. Robert Muser for his constructive criticism. Dr. Irving F. Lukoff has been generous in allowing us to use data from a longitudinal study of adolescents and their parents. Mrs. Barbara Robinson provided a challenging discussion of the legal aspects of delinquency and drug behavior. The final typing of the entire manuscript was done with unusual care by Carrie Macaulay.

The people at Macmillan have, as usual, been very genial and helpful. We are grateful to Pat McConahay for his encouragement, to Mollie Horwitz for help in steering the book from manuscript into print, and to Clark Baxter for his invaluable support.

Arthur T. Jersild
Judith S. Brook
David W. Brook

contents

the
psychology
of
adolescence

part one

INTRODUCTION

1

the place of adolescence
in the life span:
the transitional years

There is a saying: "If youth but knew, if old age but could." It has also been said that youth is so wonderful it is a shame to waste it on young people. Although these statements sound like an old person's lament over the inroads of age, they express a truth, though only the part of a truth, concerning the adolescent period of life. It is true that youth is a time of great possibility. But for many it is also a time of trial.

One of the authors once asked a number of adults whether they

3

would do anything differently if they could live their adolescence over again. All of them said yes. Then they were asked whether they would like to relive this period of their lives, if given a chance to do so, with the benefit of all that they had learned during and since their adolescence. All of them gave an emphatic no.

When seen from the perspective of the life span, adolescence appears as the time when the surge of life reaches its highest peak. The adolescent's life is, or might be, full of opportunities to enter into new experiences, to explore new relationships, to feel new resources of inner strength and ability. Adolescents have, or might have, more freedom to explore than when, as children, they were bound close to home. Older adolescents usually also have more freedom to venture than they will have at a later age when they must carry the responsibilities of a job and a family. Adolescence is also for many a time when youthful dreams of love and power have not been disturbed by the realities of life. One might ask—as many do at a later time of life—"Why don't they make the most of it?"

Although adolescence is a time of great possibility, it is also a time when most young people must pay a price for the privilege of growing up. Their freedom to seize what life offers is curtailed both from without and from within. The outer restraints—the rules they must follow, the conditions they must conform to—are obvious, and they are strong.

The limits imposed from within are not so visible, but in many respects they are even stronger. The new vistas that open before adolescents do not clear away old habits of thinking and feeling, especially thoughts and feelings about themselves.

Even if all has gone well in their earlier development, adolescents face a promised land that is also a strange land. No matter how much help their elders try to give them, the adults cannot fully open the way or prepare a place for them. It is the adolescents themselves who must find a path and build a settlement of their own. They must seek to discover themselves, their reaches and limits, their identity, and their role in the adult world.

Why study the adolescent?

We might study adolescence because it is a crucial period in the life span; adolescence represents the culmination of childhood and an intimation of the adult who is to be. Scholars have long pondered the meaning of the many changes that occur during this phase of life. We might also have a practical interest in studying adolescents to give us wisdom in dealing with them. Yet another motive in studying adolescence might be a desire to learn about oneself. Such a desire is quite understandable if the student is of adolescent age, but it is also a sound motive for an older person. There is much of the adolescent left in all of us, no matter how old we are. Anything that helps individuals to face the adolescents they once were gives them a better understanding of the kind of persons they now are. Indeed, any effort to understand human development at any stage of life is likely to be most fruitful if combined with an effort to understand oneself.

The older person who studies the adolescent has within himself a potential source of insight into issues facing the person of adolescent age—issues that he once had to face and perhaps still faces. Perhaps he lived under unduly rigid controls of his own making. If so, perhaps these still govern his life. Perhaps he had ideas about himself and inner conflicts which, as he now sees it, kept him then from living life to the full. If so, these, in similar or disguised ways, may still be a burden.

It is also important to note the role that adolescents, notably the older ones, play in the origin and maintenance of patterns of cultural change. As expressed by Eisenberg (1965), adolescence as a distinct developmental stage is critical in terms of its impact on a changing society as well as the effect it has on the development of the individual.

The adolescent period

The term *adolescence* is used in this book to denote a period during which the growing person makes the transition from childhood to adulthood. Although it is not linked to any precise span of years, adolescence may be viewed as beginning roughly when young people begin to show signs of puberty and continuing until most of them are sexually mature, have reached their maximum growth in height, and have approximately reached their full mental growth as measured by intelligence tests. The period as covered in this book includes the years from about the age of eleven to the early twenties.

Goals of adolescent development

The main goals we expect the young person to achieve during the adolescent period of development are easy to see, but it is worthwhile to look at them briefly. In later sections of this book we will discuss them in more detail, and thereby get a picture of society's demands on the adolescent.

The goals of adolescent development are determined to an important degree by the young person's innate capacities and by the pattern of relationships that has developed within the family. Goals are determined also by the cultural demands placed on the individual. Cultures differ in the support given to adolescents and in the demands made on them (Mead, 1953).

The basic changes that occur during adolescence spring mainly from the individual's genetic endowment. The timing and course of these changes, and the stature of mind and body the young person eventually achieves, are determined to an important degree by heredity.

Physical Maturity

The most obvious outcomes of development in adolescence appear in physical stature and proportions and in primary and secondary sex characteristics. We will note these in greater detail in Chapters 4 and 5. During this period young persons reach—or almost reach—their full height. We say "almost" for there are some young people who keep getting taller well beyond the time we usually think of as adolescence.

Progress Toward Mental Maturity

Dramatic changes in cognitive development occur during adolescence. During this period the adolescent achieves or almost achieves full growth of the mental capacities that are measured by mathematical reasoning tests and tests of verbal ability. We say "almost achieves" because, as we will see later, some people continue to "grow" mentally into their twenties and beyond in certain areas (Schaie and La Bouvie-Vief, 1974). Some grow not only in knowledge and understanding, but also in verbal ability and ability to deal with symbols and abstractions after they have reached an age when we usually consider adolescence to be over. In separate chapters we will deal with cognitive development and mental ability as measured by intelligence tests.

Progress Toward Emotional Maturity

Another goal in adolescent development is to make some progress toward achieving emotional maturity. Again, we must speak of "progress toward," for emotional maturity is not a fixed condition that is established at any one period of life. There are two aspects of maturing emotionally that are linked psychologically with physical maturity. If all goes well, the older adolescent and young adult are capable of physical intimacy with the opposite sex. To realize the fullest personal meaning of this development it is important for them also to be ready for emotional intimacy, tenderness, and the ability to give and receive affection.

Furthermore, when young people are able physically to beget children it is important for them to be able to assume the emotional responsibilities and to enjoy the emotional satisfactions of parents. This also calls for tenderness and the ability to feel affection. It further requires that the young persons who are heading for parenthood must eventually be able to allow their young children to be emotionally dependent on them, just as they, during childhood, were emotionally dependent on their parents.

Finding the Self

The heading of this section is borrowed from Leta S. Hollingworth's classic book on adolescence (1928). She viewed adolescence as a period when, more than at any other time of life, it is important for young people to establish convictions about their identity. They must, as far as possible, find themselves. More recently, Erikson (1959, 1968) has similarly emphasized that a principal task of adolescence is the achievement of what he calls ego identity.

Ideas and attitudes pertaining to the self have been evolving since earliest childhood. They show considerable stability before a person reaches adolescent years, but much happens in the course of adolescence that makes it necessary for adolescents to take a fresh look at themselves. Many go through a phase of being physically awkward and self-conscious about the properties and proportions of their bodies. They must even become accustomed to hearing a change in the sound of their voices.

The task of "finding the self" has many other facets. Not only is it essential that adolescents become concerned with viewing themselves as they are, but they must also be able to project themselves into the future. They are in a state of being and also as in a process of becoming. As older adolescents make the transition to young adulthood it is important for them, at least vaguely, to anticipate what lies before them—to have some expectation of what is yet to be.

When adolescents are in the process of "self-discovery" they face many alternatives—at least in theory. According to Erikson (1965), in order to achieve integration of the ego the young person must "from all possible and imaginable relations, make a series of ever-narrowing selection of personal, occupational, sexual, and ideological commitments [Erikson, 1965, p. 13]."

In the process of establishing an identity as a distinct self, many adolescents face questions about their origins and endowments. This aspect of finding the self may be very difficult for orphans, adopted children, and members of minority groups against whom there is prejudice.

Adolescents are deeply involved in the timeless search to discover who they are, what they are, and what they might become. [Charles Harbutt/Magnum.]

One important part of the adolescent's establishment of an identity is to define and accept one's sex role. As we will note in a later chapter, in the past it has appeared to be more difficult for girls to accept their femininity than for boys to see themselves in a masculine role. However, the trend in recent years has been to encourage women to assert themselves and to enter occupations and positions previously dominated by males. Actually, the percentage of women entering the professions and the work force in general has steadily been increasing. In a recent, somewhat limited, study, 45 per cent of a group of male college students, when interviewed, expressed varying degrees of anxiety about their inability, in relationships with women, to demonstrate the traditional ideal of masculinity (assertiveness, independence, determination) when faced with stress (Komarovsky, 1973).

Another aspect of finding the self is to begin to formulate, more or less clearly, a hierarchy of goals. Instead of being torn by a mass of inconsistent aspirations, it is important for adolescents to establish some degree of order in their aspirations for the future.

Adolescents who are on the way to finding themselves have the rudiments of a philosophy of life. This philosophy is rarely formulated in the neat logic of a philosopher's book. Much of it is not articulated. However, adolescents who have the beginnings of a philosophy of life have principles of conduct, an inner guide, as it were. They will be puzzled, baffled, and bewildered at times, but they are not unscrupulous opportunists one day and passionate idealists the next; they do not constantly waver between moral responsibility and irresponsibility, even though they are likely to be doubtful at times and continue to face moral conflicts.

Emancipation from Parents

One of the tasks an adolescent faces in establishing an identity of his own is to outgrow dependency on his parents, to achieve what has been called emancipation from his parents. This frequently involves a struggle that is mixed with rebellion. But when adolescents satisfactorily cross this hurdle, they will be capable of self-direction, without feeling a continuing need, as they grow older, either to depend on their parents or to defy them.

Currents in the lives of adolescents

Faith

A number of adolescents profess a faith formulated in terms of religious beliefs, but they also have a faith that usually is unspoken. If spoken it might be phrased in the conviction that life is worth living. This faith is usually not carefully thought out. In a sense it is imposed on every human being: one is alive and the natural thing is to go on living. But there are other elements.

The Search for Meaning

Imbedded in the striving of an adolescent who feels the throb of life is a search for meaning. From the time adolescents as children first acquired the power to sense and to reason they sought to explore and to know the meaning of things. As they matured they asked questions about the what and why. If their questioning was not suppressed they would ask: What does it matter? What difference does it make?

As children grow older many of them become subdued in their quest for meaning. By the time they have reached adolescence, many seem convinced that it is not good to inquire too deeply into the meaning of things. The answers they get at school when they ask, for example, "Why should we learn all about the French Revolution?" may be quite elaborate, but they are likely to boil down to a simple, "You'd better, there will be questions about it on the exam." Most adolescents become resigned to the idea that they should learn what is assigned whether it has much or little personal significance.

Yet, in all adolescents, as in all human beings, a search for meaning is linked with the fact of being alive, and it goes on in many ways.

Choice

The adolescent who is moving into life is constantly faced with the necessity of making choices. Most individuals, old or young, have the conviction that they have the power to choose. The range within which they can choose may be limited. The idea of freedom may be an illusion from all logical and scientific points of view. But, from the *point of view of the person himself,* it is he who chooses. It is he who feels he is free to say yes or no, to turn right or left, to plan for tomorrow or go fish today.

Common sense tells us that our freedom is restricted. But adolescents, like their elders, cannot avoid making choices, taking the consequences, and then feeling responsible for the choices they have made. Jean Paul Sartre has spoken of this in its starkest form: The freedom to choose is the only freedom an individual does not have the freedom to renounce. It has been called dreadful freedom. Philosophers may argue about the freedom of the will and deny it. But internally each person is likely to feel differently: I made a choice. I might have chosen something else. Now I am stuck with it, or proud of it.

Investigators from many diverse disciplines have long been concerned with an individual's ability to take responsibility for his or her decisions. A construct labeled internal-external control of reinforcement has received much attention in recent years. *Internal control* refers to an individual's belief that rewards follow or are contingent on one's behavior; *external control* denotes an individual's belief that rewards are controlled by forces outside oneself, such as "luck," "fate," or "chance." *Locus of control* (internal versus external) has been found to be predictive of motivation and performance, learning, and differences in social behavior, as will be noted in a later chapter. According to research findings, persons who are the object of prejudice and discrimination face a more difficult task in acquiring internal controls than those who are not so encumbered.

Purposes and Goals

Related to the search for meaning and the making of choices is the establishment of goals and purposes. When all goes well, adolescents are engaged in a continual process of defining goals, determining the means by which to achieve these goals, evaluating the effectiveness of the means used to attain these goals, and selecting the most effective way of achieving these goals as well as changing them when necessary.

The purposes underlying an adolescent's acts may be clearly conceived or they may be only dimly recognized. Adolescents may have goals of which they are hardly aware. The purpose individuals believe they are following may not be the purpose they really are pursuing; the purpose may, to an extent, be a false one. However, even if the purpose they give for their acts is not the real one, it still—as far as they are concerned—is a purpose, and their acts, instead of being aimless, have a purpose and logic of their own.

Hope

Much of an adolescent's life is built on hope—a clearly defined or dim, but dogged, assurance of what is yet to be. Hope is a precious element in the lives of all persons (it "springs eternal in the human breast"), but there are many aspects of the adolescent's career that make hope especially essential. Many of the adolescent's labors, especially at school, are geared to the future. In much of what they do they must defer immediate reward for the hope of greater future gratification. Self-imposed delay of reward has been thought of as an antecedent condition for normal social behavior.

The hopeful adolescents go on with their labors, confident that their present endeavors will bear fruit at a later time. Others, who are not sustained by such hopes, muddle along, just manage to squeak through high school, and then live as much as possible for the passing moment. They do not desire to defer until tomorrow the things they can grasp today. Such adolescents must manage as best they can to mark time in school. Many of them cease preparing for a distant future, quit school, and get a job if one is to be had. It appears that persons of low socioeconomic levels are more likely to be oriented to immediate rewards than those from the middle class (McCandless, 1967). In a recent study of ninth-grade students, Zytkaskee et al. (1971) found that black adolescents are less likely to choose delayed rewards than white subjects. Actually, there are many circumstances, including greater unemployment among blacks than among whites, that provide fewer incentives for black adolescents to look forward to a promising future.

Trends and stresses in adolescent development

Earlier Onset of Puberty

At present adolescents mature physically earlier than their forebears. They also show certain interests and claim certain privileges at an earlier age than was true a generation or more ago.

Several American and European studies indicate that the average age at which girls reach the menarche has declined during the past hundred years. In a review of these studies, Tanner (1955) reports that the trend in studies of various populations is "remarkably similar . . . with the age at menarche getting earlier by one-third or one-half year per decade over the period 1850–1950 [p. 92]." However, in 1968 Tanner reported that the age of menarche is leveling off in the United States and may level off elsewhere in ten to twenty years. It is also possible that earlier findings may have been inexact, having been based largely on retrospective data that are subject to error (McCammon, 1965). Even with this reservation, there is sufficient evidence to indicate that the menarche occurs earlier today than a few generations ago.

In many regions of the world children and adolescents are taller and heavier, age by age, than they were several generations ago (Tanner, 1955, 1970). Moreover, the adolescent growth spurt comes earlier, and at maturity boys and girls are taller and heavier.

Earlier Onset of Sexual Interests and Activities

Present-day adolescents show an earlier overt interest in the opposite sex and in the right to date than they did some decades ago. In the 1950s American city girls were found to have their first dates earlier than was true in the 1920s (Smith, 1952).

In a comparison between interests and activities reported by ninth-grade students in 1935, 1953, and 1959, Jones (1960) found that the more recent generations of ninth-graders indicate greater maturity of heterosexual interests, as well as some other notable changes. A larger proportion of the youngsters in 1953 and 1959 than in 1935 expressed such interests as talking about having dates, talking about boy- or girlfriends, and approving of love scenes in movies. There was a sharp increase in the number of boys and girls who approved of girls' wearing lipstick.

An earlier expressed interest in social relations, love, and marriage was also noted by Harris (1959), who compared problems and interests expressed by high school boys in 1957 with those expressed in another study in 1935. In more recent years there has also been an increase in marriages among teenagers (Burchinal, 1959a, 1959b, 1960).

Several studies indicate that a larger proportion of adolescents and young men and women are sexually active before marriage than was the case when the famous Kinsey studies were published in the 1950s (Dreyer, 1975).

The evidence does not consistently indicate that earlier physical maturing and more precocious heterosexual interests are accompanied by accelerated maturity of the personality as a whole. The young people in a study by Jones (1960) showed more serious purpose and a more tolerant attitude than an earlier generation of adolescents toward social issues; however, Hetzer (1959) reports, on the other hand, that, while showing a considerably earlier appearance of heterosexual interests, young people lagged behind the children of 1926 in "maturity of self-evaluation."

Stresses and Dislocations

In every period of development, from birth onward, a person may face difficulties in moving from one stage to the next along life's way. There are, however, some aspects of adolescence that make it different from other phases of growth.

The adolescent is in many ways a marginal character: too old to be treated as a child, too young to have the rights of an adult. There are several facets of this marginal existence. As was true of earlier generations, today's youths are concerned with resolving conflicts relating to sexual adequacy, interpersonal power, autonomy of beliefs, and acceptance by their peer group. However, youth must now deal with an unpredictable future, bizarre headlines, and the questioning of simple truths that once were easily accepted.

ECONOMIC UNEMPLOYMENT

Even though an increasing proportion of young people are represented in the work force, unemployment rates are higher for young people, having exceeded one million in 1971.[1] Individuals are counted as unemployed if they are looking for or are available for work—regardless of whether they are in school. The usual problems faced by youngsters in a modern society, where social and technological changes are pronounced, are intensified when there is an economic slowdown such as had been taking place in the American economy when this was written. In an advanced technologic society, a large proportion of young people have not yet acquired the technical skills necessary for higher-paying jobs. Unemployment rates have also been found to vary by age, sex, color, and school enrollment status.[2] Moreover, youngsters are usually not paid on the same scale as older employees doing comparable work.

[1] *Employment of School-Age Youth*, Labor Force Report 147 (Washington, D.C.: U.S. Department of Labor, Bureau of Labor Statistics, 1971).

[2] *Employment of School-Age Youth*, Labor Force Report 135 (Washington, D.C.: U.S. Department of Labor, Bureau of Labor Statistics, 1971).

Even when adolescents are not earning money, they might still find a reward in being useful. This was easier in earlier generations when adolescents did essential work on the farm, in the shop, or around the home. Often such work gave them a feeling of ownership and responsibility.

Many present-day adolescents have difficulty in feeling useful. They have no cows to milk, no calves to feed. When they wash the dishes or wash the car they know they are doing something that must be done, but they are not contributing to a growing economy. They are not watching a calf grow into a fine heifer or a promising young bull.

LEGAL OBLIGATIONS WITHOUT
LEGAL PRIVILEGES

Adolescents are reminded of their marginal citizenship when they must accept the legal obligations of adults without having adults' rights. Up until 1974 young men could be drafted into the armed services. They were old enough to fight, old enough to die, old enough to pay taxes, but too young to vote in many localities. When earning their own keep before they are legally of age, they are adults until they come to places marked "No minors allowed." Laws have recently been liberalized in many places, but the problem still remains.

Some inequalities in the treatment of adolescents are of their own making. There is a higher rate for automobile insurance for adolescent boys due to their higher accident rates. However, in some communities boys in late adolescence notice that the police are notoriously more rude to them when they drive the car alone than when their fathers are along. The police often are exasperated by adolescents. But, in situations such as these, adolescents with good records will not get much comfort from the fact that they are discriminated against because the cops are angry at other adolescents.

SEXUAL BEHAVIOR

In many areas of the world adolescents are sexually mature and have strong sexual urges prior to the usual age of marriage. A period of lack of sexual expression in the past had been inevitable for a large number of young persons in a complex society. It was tied in with financial circumstances, the long period of preparation necessary for some vocations, and the moral attitudes of the adult population. As we have already noted, the percentage of individuals engaging in premarital intercourse has increased markedly in the last decade, especially among females (Christensen and Gregg, 1970). There is an increasing moral acceptance of premarital intercourse. But this does not remove the problem or solve the moral issues it involves. Problems about sexual activities are still common among adolescents. With increasing sexual activity has come an increased incidence of venereal diseases, which has reached epidemic proportions, according to some accounts. According to data of the Department of Health, Education, and Welfare (HEW) gathered for 1974, a large per cent of the total illegitimate births occurred among unmarried females under twenty years of age. Moreover, the increasing frequency of early marriage and giving birth to children soon after marriage raise issues of autonomy and intimacy earlier in the adolescent's life (Gordon, 1971).

Storm and Stress

In our society adolescence has traditionally been viewed as a time of greater storm and stress (*Sturm und Drang*) than other periods of life. But some authors claim that the extent of adolescent turmoil has been exaggerated. There is no exact measure that will compare the stresses of an adolescent with those of a six-year-old who is beginning school or with those of an adult. (Many parents of adolescents, if free to be outspoken, would claim it is they, more than anyone else, who are passing through a period of Sturm und Drang.)

It is clear, however, that there are conspicuous signs of tension in adolescence: the delinquency rate is higher than in earlier years and higher than the crime rate in later years. There is an increase in rebellion against authority at home and at school. There is some evidence also that many adolescents are more troubled than they were previously, or will be somewhat later, about their own identity—who and what they are, their sex roles, and their place in the scheme of things.

Several investigators have studied the rebelliousness that occurred in the late 1960s in colleges and high schools throughout the nation. Lipset and Ladd (1972) put at 350,000 the number of student radicals during the late 1960s. Feuer (1969) maintains that student activists acted on hostility to the older generations with which they were in conflict. Generational conflict is thought by Bengtson et al. (1974) to be a transient part of adolescence. Some adolescents "find it difficult to separate from dependent or affectionate childhood ties; they may exhibit an exaggerated sense of independence to convince themselves and others that they can stand on their own feet" [Group for the Advancement of Psychiatry, 1966, p. 27].

As distinguished from the rebelliousness of the 1960s, it appears that more recently there has been a trend toward conservatism. According to the American Council of Education, a survey directed by Alexander Astin of 1974–1975 college freshmen showed a decline in the number of students favoring legalization of marijuana (a reversal of a six-year trend), in the number calling themselves liberal, and in the number favoring job equality for women.

Evidence that adolescence is a time of acute stress for some (such as delinquents) does not mean that it is a stressful time for all. But it is reasonable to assume that a time that is fiery for some is at least smoky for others.

The ideas adults have concerning the carefreeness or turbulence of the adolescent period are greatly influenced by (1) the ideas they would like to regard as true and (2) the extent to which they look at or beyond the more superficial aspects of the adolescent's life. When we judge typical adolescent boys and girls (leaving out delinquents and serious troublemakers) by their public conduct in a high school, the picture is, on the whole, quite optimistic. They go about their work without much fuss. They seem to have absorbing academic or extracurricular interests. They look healthy and handsome, despite occasional skin blemishes and extremes of dress. Although they have their foibles, they are nice people and it is a pleasure to work with them.

Such a picture of adolescents is comfortable for adults to have in the typical school where little or no attention is given to children's emotional problems or personal concerns. It also helps to justify the kind of education that is offered.

A different picture emerges when we look not only at adolescents as they appear in public, but when we try to fathom their inner lives. When investigators attempt this they must first find a way to push aside the veil of secrecy behind which the adolescent ordinarily lives. In a study of presumably normal high school and college girls, Frank et al. (1953) noted that adolescents usually are afraid to reveal their thoughts and feelings and to let adults gain access to their reveries, their worries, and aspirations. Even when preoccupied with their personal problems and eager to know what they should do, they will ordinarily not confide their troubles to adults, even when they urgently need help.

The picture of adolescents is somber in studies that have been conducted by means of projective techniques (described in Chapter 8). Frank et al. (1953) found evidence of more frequent and severe emotional disturbances than they had anticipated. They also report that girls in their study had a general fear of sex in ways the girls did not always consciously recognize.

Emotional problems of adolescents that have been studied extensively include those connected with obesity, anorexia nervosa, depression, and schizophrenia.

As will be discussed in Chapter 16, drug abuse—including the use of marijuana, heroin, LSD, amphetamines, barbiturates, and others—has in recent years become widespread among adolescents of all social classes and in all areas of the country. There also has been an increase in alcoholism.

Adolescence in retrospect

In the informal study mentioned at the opening of this chapter, many persons claimed they would do things differently if they could relive their adolescence. However, they also gave an emphatic no when asked whether they would care to go through the adolescent period again, even if they could do so with all that they had learned since. Perhaps another, or a larger, sampling would give another answer. However, these observations suggest that an older person who has scaled the adolescent hurdle is glad to be done with it. This does not apply to adolescence alone, however. In another inquiry (unpublished) by Jersild, parents were asked whether they would rear their children differently if they could have another try. Most of them said yes. But when asked, "Would you like to have a chance to try again?" all of them replied with a fervent no.

The episodes older people view as being most satisfying center to a very large degree on happenings that are most likely to occur after a person has reached the middle twenties or so: marriage, the birth of children, home and family life, and satisfactions connected with occupation.

Contending forces

During adolescence, as in every period of life, there are forces that work against each other. There are conditions that push young persons forward and others that hold them back, especially in the early adolescent years. Adolescents have a desire to assert their individuality and also a great need to conform. They want to be big and yet also to be protected. They harbor many conflicting motives and feelings: loyalty and an impulse to rebel; aggressive impulses and fears and guilt regarding them. There is something radical about being an adolescent, yet something conservative. The impulse to grow is strong. The impetus to venture into the new and untried is powerful, too. But while adolescents anticipate the new, they are also bound by the past.

Conflicting and Confusing Pressures in the Culture

Adolescents face many conflicting moral and cultural pressures. They are supposed to be wholeheartedly generous, yet they see savage competition all about them. They should be ambitious but also modest. They should stand up for their rights but also turn the other cheek.

One condition in present-day society that adds to the difficulty of adolescents is that many adults, both at home and at school, are themselves confused about issues pertaining to the discipline, teaching, and rearing of young people. Much of their confusion stems from the difficulty in resolving the issue between authority and freedom. In many schools and homes there is a conflict between being strict or lenient, autocratic or democratic. For some decades it has been emphasized that the good school is a democratic school and the good parent is a democratic parent. For many decades the prevailing view among "experts" was that an authoritarian approach is bad.

It would be easier in many ways if all adults who deal with young people were consistently democratic or if all were arbitrary and laid down the law consistently. If treated in an authoritarian way the youngsters might conform or rebel, but at least they would know what to expect of others and what others expect of them.

Some confusion in the discipline of youngsters is, of course, bound to occur, even under the most settled conditions. Circumstances of life are such that it is not humanly possible for an adult to be consistent in everything he does. But there is reason to believe that today there are many adolescents who have been exposed to more than the usual amount of confusion and inconsistency. In a study directed by the senior writer (Jersild et al., 1949) a number of years ago, many parents told of their conflicts and confusions. Some said, for example, that they had been authoritarian at an earlier time, or with an older child, and now were shifting to more democratic ways. Such shifts—even if in theory they are in the right direction—are likely to involve tension both for parents and children. A parent or teacher who has been brought up according to one theory of child-rearing cannot easily turn about and apply another.

References

Astin, A. Personal communication, 1976.
Bengtson, V. L., Furlong, M. J., & Laufer, R. S. Time, aging, and the continuity of social structure: Themes and issues in generational analysis. *Journal of Social Issues*, 1974, **30**(2), 1–30.
Burchinal, L. G. Adolescent role deprivation and high school marriage. *Marriage and Family Living*, 1959, **21**, 378–384.a.
Burchinal, L. G. Does early dating lead to school-age marriage? *Iowa Farm Science*, 1959, **13**(8), 11–12.b.
Burchinal, L. G. Research on young marriage: Implications for family life education. *The Family Life Coordinator*, 1960, **9**(1–2), 6–24.a.
Christensen, H. T., & Gregg, C. F. Changing sex norms in America and Scandinavia. *Journal of Marriage and the Family*, 1970, **32**, 616–627.
Dreyer, P. H. Changes in the meaning of marriage among youth: The impact of the "revolution" in sex and sex role behavior. In R. E. Grinder (Ed.), *Studies in adolescence* (3rd ed.). New York: Macmillan, 1975.

Eisenberg, L. A developmental approach to adolescence. *Children*, 1965, **12**, 131–135.

Employment of school-age youth (Labor Force Report No. 135, U.S. Department of Labor. Bureau of Labor Statistics). Washington, D.C.: 1971.

Employment of school-age youth (Labor Force Report No. 147, U.S. Department of Labor. Bureau of Labor Statistics). Washington, D.C.: 1971.

Erikson, E. H. Identity and the life cycle. *Psychological Issues*, 1959, **1**, 1–171.

Erikson, E. H. Youth: Fidelity and diversity. In E. H. Erikson (Ed.), *The challenge of youth*. New York: Anchor, 1965.

Erikson, E. H. *Identity: Youth and crisis*. New York: Norton, 1968.

Feuer, L. *The conflict of generations*. New York: Basic Books, 1969.

Frank, L. K., Harrison, R., Hellersberg, E., Machover, K., & Steiner, M. Personality development in adolescent girls. *Monographs of the Society for Research in Child Development*, 1953, **16**(53).

Gordon, C. Social characteristics of early adolescence. *Daedalus*, Fall, 1971, 931–960.

Group for the Advancement of Psychiatry. *Sex and the college student*. New York: Atheneum, 1966.

Harris, D. B. Sex differences in the life problems and interests of adolescents, 1935 and 1957. *Child Development*, 1959, **30**, 453–459.

Hetzer, H. Der Körper in der Selbstdarstellung von Kinder im Jahre 1926 und im Jahre 1957 (The body in self-descriptions of children in 1926 and 1957). *Zeitschrift für Experimentale und Angewandte Psychology*, 1959, **5**, 15–21.

Hollingworth, L. S. *Psychology of the adolescent*. Englewood Cliffs, N.J.: Appleton, 1928.

Jersild, A. T., Woodyard, E. S., & del Solar, C. *Joys and problems of child rearing*. New York: Bureau of Publications, Teachers College, Columbia University, 1949.

Jones, M. C. A comparison of the attitudes and interests of ninth-grade students over two decades. *Journal of Educational Psychology*, 1960, **51**, 175–186.

Komarovsky, M. Presidential address: Some problems in role analysis. *American Sociological Review*, 1973, **38**, 649–662.

Lipset, S. M., & Ladd, E. C., Jr. The political future of activist generations. In P. G. Altbach & R. S. Laufer (Eds.), *The new pilgrims: Youth protest in transition*. New York: McKay, 1972.

McCammon, R. W. Are boys and girls maturing physically at earlier ages? *American Journal of Public Health*, 1965, **55**, 103–106.

McCandless, B. R. *Children: Behavior and development*. New York: Holt, 1967.

Mead, M. *Growing up in New Guinea*. New York: Mentor Book, 1953.

Schaie, K. W., & Labouvie-Vief, G. Generational versus ontogenetic components of change in adult cognitive behavior: A fourteen year cross-sequential study. *Developmental Psychology*, 1974, **10**, 305–320.

Smith, W. M. Rating and dating: A re-study. *Marriage and Family Living*, 1952, **14**, 312–317.

Tanner, J. M. *Growth at adolescence*. Springfield, Ill.: Thomas, 1955.

Tanner, J. M. Earlier maturation in man. *Scientific American*, 1968, **218**, 21–27.

Tanner, J. M. Physical growth. In P. H. Mussen (Ed.), *Carmichael's manual of child psychology* (Vol. 1). New York: Wiley, 1970.

Zytkaskee, A., Strickland, B., & Watson, J. Delay of gratification and internal versus external control among adolescents of low socioeconomic status. *Developmental Psychology*, 1971, **4**, 93–98.

2

the adolescent self

The ideas and attitudes adolescents have regarding themselves influence, and are influenced by, their responses to everything that happens in their lives. In this chapter we will consider aspects of self-appraisal that must be taken into account when, in later sections, we discuss the personal meanings of physical, mental, emotional, and social development during adolescent years. We will also discuss conditions that influence adolescents' outlooks on life in ways they themselves do not perceive.

Selfhood is the essence of a person's existence as it is *known* to him or her. It is in the subjective world of the self that the adolescent is aware of the substance of his or her humanity.

The self as known includes all the ideas and feelings an individual has regarding the properties of his or her body, qualities of mind, and personal characteristics. The beliefs, values, and convictions of a person are included in the self, as are conceptions of a person's past life, background, and future prospects. The components of the self range from neutral details of self-perception to attitudes that are charged with feeling, such as pride or shame, inferiority, and self-esteem or self-reproach.

When we use the modifier *known* in describing the self, we imply that the views persons have of themselves do not give a full accounting of what they are and how they came to be that way. The self is a person's subjective evaluation. The views individuals have of themselves represent their convictions—what they know or think they know—about their make-up—not what they have forgotten. It may encompass ideas concerning their motives that they may revise. Their convictions may include self-appraisals that, according to all standards except their own, are incorrect. But to them they are real. The self may seem shadowy to others, but for each person it is a rock as long as he or she maintains it.

Aspects of the known self

The "Actual Self"

Adolescents have ideas and attitudes about what they "really are like." When questioned, they can (if they are candid) describe themselves in detail as they think they are. Such descriptions may include attitudes of self-approval or disapproval, ranging from serene self-acceptance to bitter self-rejection.

The "Ideal Self"

Adolescents are also more or less aware of differences between what they are and what they wish they might be, think they ought to be, or are trying to become.

The sum of a person's views of what he or she wishes to be or ought to be has been called the ideal self, as distinguished from the real, or actual, self. The ideal self has many facets and includes aspirations a person is vigorously striving to attain, or hopes dimly someday to realize.

All adolescents or adults who calmly assess things, see some things unfinished in themselves, perhaps weaknesses yet to be overcome or improvements yet to be achieved. The elements of the ideal self may range from unrealistic dreams to goals and improvements that are within reach.

Irrational Ideas About Self

Individuals may have views of themselves that are irrational in the light of their own later insights or in the light of all that can be known about them by others. The label *self-idealization* has been used to denote a system of irrational ideas and attitudes regarding self. A conscious element of this idealized image of self is, from the person's own standpoint, a reality, a constituent of the "actual" self and not just a fiction.

Self-idealization is a form of self-deception.[1] We have examples of self-idealization when adolescents who are afraid of their sexual impulses adopt attitudes of extreme prudishness but regard their prudishness as elements of strength in their characters, not as defenses built upon fear. Adolescents who are driven by compulsions to compete have "idealized" these facets of themselves when they view competitiveness as signifying noble ambitions, not as expressions of needs to vanquish others.

Self-idealization may take the form of regarding a weakness as a strength, as in the preceding examples, and also of masking admirable qualities with self-imputed weaknesses. This happens, in another example, when adolescents with good potentials disavow them with stubborn "I'm no good" attitudes. It occurs also if they repudiate their capacities for winning affection with rigid poses, such as "No one could like me."

Adolescents who have self-deprecating attitudes of this sort disavow their latent good qualities. When they do this hidden reasons are present that we will consider in another section. It seems incredible that adolescents would cripple themselves in this way. Yet, when we look around us we can see young people who act out disparaging views of themselves that, as seen by others, produce needless suffering and failure.

The unknown dimension

The fact that there are important influences in adolescents' mental lives that are not comprehended within the image they have of themselves does not minimize the importance of the self as known. From an adolescent's

[1] An extreme example of this appears in a delusion, such as when a person is convinced that he is Napoleon. Such a delusion is abnormal. Persons who generally are regarded as normal also deceive themselves, but in less spectacular ways.

point of view, the known self is the core of his or her existence. But to understand an adolescent, or another person, or oneself, it is also essential to inquire into conditions that lie, as it were, outside the known self. This is one of the elementary facts of life, but it raises some thorny questions: What are these conditions and influences? What should we call them? Just to name them presents a problem.

According to Freudian theory, the psychic apparatus, a hypothetical construct, has three main components: the id, which comprises the basic drives, such as sexual or aggressive feelings; the ego, which includes the executive and integrative aspects of the personality and mediates between the id, the superego, and the demands of external reality; and the superego, which represents the conscience and embodies parental commands and restrictions. A feeling of guilt ensues when the demands of the superego are ignored or disobeyed by the ego. These mental functions occur both in our awareness and at levels of which we are unaware.

The label *the unconscious* was used by Freud and has since been used by Freud's adherents, to designate psychological processes that ordinarily lie beyond the reach of a person's self-awareness. The concept of the unconscious has also been adopted by many psychoanalysts and psychologists who have been influenced by Freud but who do not fully accept Freudian theory. However, there are many who object to the use of the term *the unconscious* on the ground that, in their judgment, the label is imprecise.

It is beyond the scope of this book to delve into the pros and cons associated with what has been called the unconscious. It is understandable that many people are reluctant to speak of the unconscious. One reason is that it refers to aspects of mental life and motivation that some of us prefer to ignore. The idea that individuals might harbor irrational notions or be swayed by motives they do not comprehend is distasteful to those who prize their intellects and believe that reason reigns supreme.

Another, and better, reason for the reluctance to use the label *the unconscious* is that it has often been used loosely and thus has had vague connotations assigned to it. The unconscious is often discussed as though it were a separate he or she, a person within a person, a character endowed with faculties for planning and outwitting the person in whom this he or she resides.

One expedient that has been used in dealing with the problem of terminology is to speak of the *phenomenal self*, implying that there is a nonphenomenal self. The phenomenal self, in free translation, means the self that shows forth, is apparent—that is, is observable from a person's own point of view.

The position taken in this book can be made by summarizing some points already discussed here and by adding a few statements. What adolescents know about themselves is, from the adolescents' standpoint, an indisputable reality. To understand them we must take account of this solid fact. It is as important in assessing them as the details we can see or measure with objective tests. Their explicit rational ideas about themselves rest on realistic premises of self-assessment. Their irrational ideas are based on misapprehensions, but they are not aware of this. Furthermore, the motives that govern the acts, thoughts, and attitudes of adolescents range from those they clearly perceive to those they do not recognize.

In this book we will frequently take note of factors that enter into thinking, feeling, and motivation in ways that a person is able knowingly to identify or is unable knowingly to identify. Due to the ambiguous connotations associated with the label *unconscious*, we will favor variations in terminology, such as unrecognized, unwitting, and unknowing, to name but a few other labels.

Ways of knowing the adolescent self

Although adolescents, as a rule, are silent about their private thoughts and feelings, they disclose themselves in a variety of ways. An adult who works with them has many opportunities to get glimpses of how they regard themselves. When adults use these opportunities wisely, they can begin to know the adolescent as a living person rather than as just another youth or a nameless character in a textbook.

In day-to-day contacts, most of our judgments about how adolescents regard themselves are inferred from their behavior. We assume that they are confident in themselves if they look self-assured and that they are unsure of themselves if they show off. An accurate judgment about the adolescents' self-assessment from their conduct is not easy to obtain, however, especially if they are skillful in putting on a good "front" or are retiring individuals. But, in working with adolescents, we constantly and unavoidably form judgments.

Adolescents also reveal themselves in their own words, and when we deal with them we are constantly noting and drawing inferences from what they say. The most common self-descriptions appear in what adolescents express in ordinary conversation. A more systematic account can be obtained from what they reveal in a personal conference. Such a conference may be brief and limited to what the adolescent talks about on the spur of the moment. Or it may be an "interview in depth" conducted over a period of time, in a setting that encourages the interviewee to elaborate and rethink what he or she has said before and to bring in new material.

Interviews may be structured with a set of questions prepared in advance that encourage the interviewees to speak in an ordered sequence. Or they may be casual and free, allowing the interviewees to let their minds wander, to select what they want to say in any way they please. When thus free to roam, a person will bring up seemingly disconnected thoughts, feelings, and fantasies. Some of the most revealing information comes when an adolescent expresses a thought and then catches himself or herself on the wing, so to speak, and asks, "Now why did I think that? I wonder what it means?" and then, by a process of free association, goes on to explore the statement.

Ordinarily, adolescents do not let their minds wander in this way when talking to an adult. They are likely to think the adult will regard what they say as nonsense. To perceive meaning in what adolescents confide in this way, adults must be able to let their own minds drift along with what adolescents say. They must listen with "the third ear."

It is possible at times to achieve a remarkable degree of communication when two persons allow their minds to drift in this way. However, there are strong barriers against this kind of communication. To overcome them it is necessary for adolescents to trust the adults in whom they are going to confide. It is necessary also for both adolescents and adults to have the courage to risk what might happen, for when persons venture into processes of free association they are likely to express thoughts and sentiments that they ordinarily would not disclose to others and that others might prefer not to hear.

Although this form of communication is rarely employed, we mention it here to underscore two points. First, the stream of consciousness that constitutes a person's self-awareness often is quite different from the logical order of ideas that appears in concentrated moments of thinking.[2] The reader needs only to catch himself or herself in moments of seemingly "aimless" thoughts to verify this. Second, adolescents cannot freely reveal these streams of thought and feeling if they are required to fit them into logical structures.

Direct self-description may also be obtained through written compositions on themes such as "What I Like About Myself" or "What I Don't Like About Myself." The meaning of such compositions will vary according to the degree adolescents are willing and able to reveal themselves. Compositions of this sort serve better as a starting point for further inquiry than as statements that can be regarded as complete.

Diaries and autobiographies offer a more extensive means of self-description. They range from brief accounts written on request to personal diaries that young people have felt an urge to write.

Lengthy diaries and autobiographies frequently reveal intimate and poignant information, especially if they were kept in secret but then

[2] Even the thoughts that occur to a student or teacher while listening attentively to a lecture are likely to flit hither and yon, away from and then back to the ordered sequence of what the lecturer is saying.

entrusted to someone else. The accounts are notably revealing when adolescents have written them without intending to impress others. Some of the most revealing glimpses into the lives of individual adolescents have come from diaries and autobiographies. We cannot, however, assume that those who keep such records speak for all adolescents. Those who keep diaries are a minority. They have some characteristics not found to the same degree in adolescents at large: an interest in recording and examining their own thoughts and feelings combined with a desire to express them in words and a resolve to take time out to do so.

Among the adolescent autobiographies the senior writer here has had the privilege to examine were many that expressed yearnings, heartaches, and feelings of loneliness. Diarists often seem to seek solace in their own company. They confide, as it were, in themselves (sometimes using the word *confide* or its equivalent).[3]

An example of a diary that provides unique insight into the nature of adolescent thinking is the diary of Anne Frank (as cited by Scarlett, 1975). In the words of Anne Frank:

> "For in its innermost depths youth is lonelier than old age!" I read this saying in some books and I've always remembered, and found it to be true. Is it true then that grownups have a more difficult time here than we do? No. I know it isn't. Older people have formed their opinions about everything, and don't waver before they act. It's twice as hard for us young ones to hold our ground, and maintain our opinions, in a time when all ideas are being shattered and destroyed, when people are showing their worst side and do not know whether to believe in truth and right and God [Scarlett, 1975, p. 71].

Although Anne is referring to conditions during World War II in this illustration, her concern perhaps portrays a universal condition associated with adolescence.

Self-description Inventories

Many tests have been devised to measure aspects of the known self (also frequently referred to as the self-concept or the phenomenal self). These commonly are built on a list of adjectives or statements pertaining to such attributes as cheerfulness, generosity, irritability, and attractiveness. Although many techniques have been devised to measure the known self, none of them fully captures the concept of the self. "Indeed, this would be an

[3] These sentiments are often captured in popular lyrics, as in the lines (probably more characteristic of an adult than an adolescent): "Me and my shadow . . . no one else to tell my troubles to."

impossibility, since by definition the self concept is private [McCandless, 1970, p. 452]." Many of the existing techniques are vulnerable to a desire to give socially acceptable answers.

Nevertheless, self-reports may be as valid as indirect techniques, such as projective measures (discussed in Chapter 8) of personality characteristics.

In one procedure the descriptive items are listed one by one on a single form preceded by such phrasing as "I am" or "I would like to be" and followed by modifiers such as *not at all, to some degree,* and *to a great degree.* For example, an adolescent boy marks the response to each item that best describes what he thinks he is—presumably, his actual self. He can then also mark each item as he thinks he ought to be or desires to be (presumably his ideal self). According to further instructions, he may be asked to mark each item as he thinks others would rate him or to use the items to rate other persons who are specifically named.

THE Q-SORT TECHNIQUE

The Q-sort technique has been used to obtain reports from the individual about the self (e.g., as used by Block, 1961). Items can be placed on separate cards that people can sort into piles ranging from those that mention characteristics they regard as most descriptive of themselves to those they regard as least descriptive. The cards may contain statements such as "I am an aggressive person," "I am anxious," and "I am a friendly person."

The person who takes this test (whether to describe his or her actual self or ideal self) is instructed to sort the cards that contain the descriptions of personality qualities or traits into an arbitrarily prearranged distribution that usually approximates a normal distribution.[4] (See figure 2.1.)

One of the problems of the Q-sort is that individuals are required to place a majority of statements in the middle range.

THE SEMANTIC DIFFERENTIAL

Still another procedure that has been used is the *semantic differential.* Various scales are used to rate the meanings of words, phrases, or concepts (Osgood et al., 1957). For example, adolescents may be presented with the phrase "my self" and asked to rate it on a seven-point scale with an adjective such as "strong" on one end of the scale and "weak" at the other extreme.

---

[4] Stephenson has reviewed studies using the Q-sort technique (1952). Self-assessments by means of a Q-sort technique that includes a hundred statements have been reported by Rogers and Dymond (1954).

Other self-assessment instruments have been described by Jervis (1958), Mischel (1976), and Spivack (1956).

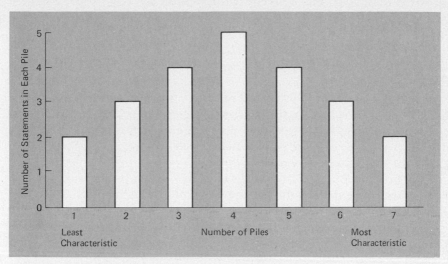

Figure 2.1. A prearranged Q-sort distribution of personality descriptions.

Adolescents are asked to mark the point that represents the meaning of the phrase on one of several scales. (See figure 2.2.)

Uses of Self-descriptions or Self-ratings

The information obtained from such descriptions or ratings of self (and others) can be used to compare:

1. The individuals' claimed views of themselves as they are with what they say they would like to be. It is possible to note how frequently and to what extent there are similarities or discrepancies between what they profess they are and think they ought to be.

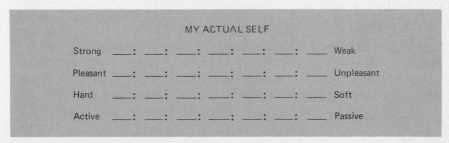

Figure 2.2. Selected rating scales of the semantic differential and phrase to be rated. The scales seem to tap three semantic factors: evaluative (good–bad), potency (strong–weak), and activity (active–passive).

2. Individuals' ratings of themselves with their ratings of others. This comparison has been used to measure the relationships between self-acceptance and acceptance of others.

3. Individuals' ratings of themselves with the ratings they think others will apply to them.

4. Individuals' ratings of themselves with the ratings others actually apply to them. These show the degree of correspondence between individuals as they appear to themselves and as they appear to others.

5. Individuals' self-ratings with the ratings others think they will apply to themselves.

6. Individuals' (a) approval of themselves and (b) their approval or acceptance of others with (c) the extent to which others accept or reject them.

Such comparisons, if based on authentic data, give an indication of the correspondence between self-acceptance, acceptance *of* others, and acceptance *by* others.

The results obtained from self-descriptive evaluations and the evaluations of others are very interesting, especially when applied, with the consent of all concerned, to people one knows.[5] It is fascinating to compare the qualities students attribute to themselves with the impressions one has of them and with the impressions fellow students have of them. Some students, as judged by others, are very realistic in assessing themselves, whereas others seem to be way off base.

Although interesting, findings from tests of this kind are useful mainly as a point of departure for further study. The information they yield cannot be accepted at face value or as a final diagnosis, for the responses are influenced by personal factors the tests do not assess. We will discuss some limitations of these tests because in doing so we will touch on facets of the self and of self-appraisal that are of general significance.

Adolescents' responses to a self-assessment inventory, like their responses to any opportunity for revealing themselves, will be influenced by their *candor*. They may respond with tongue in cheek or answer all items as candidly as they can.

Responses will also be influenced by attitudes regarding the propriety of the questions that are asked. The responses will also be influenced by a person's willingness to reveal him- or herself to the person asking the questions. For example, when adolescents in a study by Rivenbark (1971) were asked to rate the extent to which they would reveal themselves to their parents, females reported that they revealed more to their mothers than

---

[5] In several studies it has been found that self-ratings on tests such as those mentioned here show a considerable degree of consistency when scores on one rating are compared with scores obtained on the same test administered a few days or a few weeks later. (*Reliability coefficients* have ranged from the .50s to the .90s.)

males reported they would reveal to their fathers. However, the males and females were similar in the extent to which they would reveal themselves to the parent of the opposite sex. The extent to which adolescents are willing to reveal themselves may also be influenced by age. In a study of Indian girls aged twelve to eighteen years, Sinha (1972) found that as girls advanced from age twelve to age fourteen they tended to limit their self-disclosure; however, as they advanced from mid- to late adolescence (defined as a period ranging from fourteen to eighteen years), they were more likely to disclose their innermost thoughts.

Responses to inquiries concerning individuals' views of themselves as compared with their views of others will be influenced to an undetermined degree by a desire to appear *consistent*. This can produce spurious results. For example, if I claim I am a friendly person it would be necessary, for the sake of consistency, to say that other people, similarly, tend to be friendly. To accuse *them* of being unfriendly would belie my own claim of being friendly.

The most serious problem in interpreting results from self-assessment instruments (or any kind of self-revelation) is that they will be influenced to an undetermined degree by a person's *insight*. No matter how frank adolescents are in revealing themselves they will differ greatly in the depths of their self-knowledge. They will differ in the degree to which they have tended to rationalize or critically examine their views of themselves. For example, adolescents who are vengeful and are aware of it may report that they are vengeful. Others, who are equally vengeful, may perceive themselves as individuals with a strong sense of justice and deny any taint of vengefulness. (The interplay between thinking and feeling involved in insight into self is discussed at some length in Chapter 6.)

Major Themes in Self-description

When young people describe themselves in their own words, the characteristics they mention range from details of their physical appearance to sweeping descriptions of their personalities.

Adolescents frequently name the following characteristics in assessing themselves:

1. Physical: height, weight, body build, and facial features, such as the eyes, nose, and hair
2. Intellectual: having or not having a good ability to learn, think, reason, and remember; having or lacking curiosity
3. Special talents: ability or lack of ability in music, dancing, the arts, and mechanics

4. Interest and skill, or lack of skill, in sports and games
5. Clothes and grooming, including taste in choosing clothes, hairdo, and the like
6. Performance in school and attitudes toward school
7. Character traits and temperamental qualities: being easygoing or having a sense of humor
8. Social attitudes and relationships: the ability to get along with others

The characteristics most frequently named by over a thousand adolescents in a study by the senior writer here (Jersild, 1952) fell under the headings of (1) *personality and character*, including moral qualities, inner resources, humor, poise, and emotional tendencies, and (2) *social attitudes and relationships*, including feelings about other persons. Self-descriptions under these headings were most numerous at all levels from the elementary grades through college. Students at the college level mentioned their intellectual qualities more often than those at the high school level, and this is to be expected. But even at the college level references to intellectual qualities were far less frequent than references to character and social attitudes.

The major themes adolescents emphasize cut across differences in age, sex, socioeconomic status, and intellectual ability. In describing themselves young people differ in the particular words they use and in the specific qualities they name, but they emphasize conditions people share in common much more than characteristics that set people apart. We have here what the senior writer has called the universal language of self. As we move away from outer appearances and distinctions toward the inner dimensions of experience we enter a realm of fellowship such as seldom is achieved in overt conduct. The deeper adolescents penetrate into the reaches of all that constitutes their experiences of themselves, the more they will identify qualities that they share with others. The more adolescents realize the nature of their own existence, the more potentially capable they will become of feeling compassion for others.

Factors Related to Adolescents' Views of Themselves

As youngsters approach and pass through adolescence dramatic changes occur in their physical and psychological development. Physical changes (which will be discussed in Chapters 3 to 5) will have an impact on the adolescent's body-image and probably also on the adolescent's self-image.

Changes that occur in the process of cognitive development will also have an effect on adolescents' views of themselves. As we will note in

Chapter 6, adolescents become capable of formal operational thinking and are considerably more able than they were at an early age to examine their own thinking. This ability, if cultivated with the aid of others, opens the way for them to view themselves more objectively than was formerly possible. They also are better able to take account of the perspectives of others. Their perceptions of other peoples' views of them, if taken seriously, may have a profound impact on their perceptions of themselves. "Moreover, the ability to think about thinking allows the adolescent to discover the privateness of his thoughts and the social isolation of his reflective self [Elkind, 1975, p. 55]."

When faced with a need to make major decisions concerning their careers and their future lives, to establish their independence and to form relationships with members of the opposite sex, they also are likely, if they are realistic, to feel impelled to take stock of themselves.

Individuals in the adolescents' environment can have a tremendous impact on adolescents' views of themselves. Parental factors have long been known to have an effect on a person's self-evaluation. The noted psychiatrist Harry Stack Sullivan is one of many who have emphasized the powerful influence a parent, notably the mother, may have on the development of what he calls the "self-system." Even in infancy, according to him, a child's feeling of security may be enhanced or undermined by the degree to which a mother (or mothering person) is self-accepting, securely self-confident and warmly accepting of her child or is self-rejecting, insecure, and anxious. A parent's subtle or overt approval or disapproval, according to Sullivan, can have a decisive effect on a child's self-approval or self-rejection. The influence of parental attitudes and practices will be discussed from several angles in later sections of this book.

Sullivan's account of the influence of parents, and many other discussions regarding parent-child relationships, do not adequately recognize that the action does not flow in one direction—from parent to child. There is interaction. The stamina and temperamental qualities of children influence the interplay between them and their parents. Indeed, the anxiety a "bad" mother communicates to a child, according to Sullivan's account, may have been engendered in part by her inability to soothe and pacify a sickly or "difficult" child. A distraught mother may feel that she is not a good mother, and to that extent she has an attitude of self-rejection. The child's role in the parent-child relationship will be documented in Chapter 12. It must be recognized, of course, that even though the child's role is important, the parents obviously are more powerful and resourceful. It is the parents who dispense praise and blame, approval or disapproval; regardless of what the child's role may be, parents can be warmly accepting or coldly rejecting in a way that has a crucial influence on the child's own attitudes of self-acceptance or self-rejection.

Studies of boys by Coopersmith (1967, 1968) are among the numerous investigations that have been made in recent years of factors influencing self-acceptance. The youngsters were given a variety of tests of personality and ability. In general the boys who seemed to be more competent regarded themselves more positively. By virtue of their achievements in a variety of areas, they received greater recognition from others, which contributed to a positive picture of themselves. Boys with high self-esteem more often had mothers who rated them positively than boys with low self-esteem. Their parents also tended to manifest high self-esteem. Specific parental child-rearing practices were also found to be related to the level of esteem displayed by the boys. For example, Coopersmith found that mothers of boys with high self-esteem believed that reward and praise were more efficacious than punishment.

In another study, Sears (1970) reported that sixth-grade children whose parents displayed "warmth and affection" were more often found to have positive self-esteem.

From an early age peers influence a child's self-regard, and with the onset of adolescence the peer group has increasing importance as a means of providing adolescents with evaluative information regarding their worth. Among numerous studies dealing with this factor is an investigation of adolescents' sensitivity to peer approval as related to the adolescents' self-consciousness by Fenigstein et al. (1975). Other studies in this area will be discussed in later chapters.

Among the many environmental factors that may affect adolescents' views of themselves are those connected with school. Among studies dealing with this subject, which will be discussed in greater detail in Chapter 17, is an investigation by Simmons et al. (1973), who found that when youngsters enter junior high school there may be a disturbance in their self-image. Twelve-year-olds in junior high school as compared with twelve-year-olds remaining in elementary school reported lower self-esteem and greater self-consciousness. Moreover, the adolescents in junior high school more often reported that other individuals held negative opinions of them.

These factors are only a few of the myriad social influences that affect adolescents' views of themselves.

Stability and Change in Self-views

Several investigators have studied the changes that occur with the passage of time in an adolescent's self-image. In a longitudinal study Engel (1959) tested youngsters when they were in the eighth and tenth grades and then again when they were two years older. She found that as a group the youngsters exhibited considerable continuity in their self-concepts over the two-year period. Adolescents with favorable self-concepts were more stable in their views of themselves than adolescents with unfavorable self-concepts. In a study of youngsters when in grade six and then again when in grade twelve, Carlson (1965) also found considerable stability in adolescent self-concepts, although approximately one third of the adolescents showed some instability in their conceptions of themselves.

In contrast to the two previously mentioned studies, which used a longitudinal approach (using the same subjects at an earlier and then at a later age), Simmons et al. (1973) made cross-sectional studies of third- to twelfth-grade students. To obtain a measure of the "stability of the self" they asked questions such as: "A kid told me: 'Some days I like the way I am. Some days I do not like the way I am.' Do your feelings *change* like this?" Eight- to eleven-year-olds showed greater stability of self-image than twelve- to eighteen-year-olds. But significant differences appeared in self-image stability between twelve and fourteen years and between fifteen and eighteen years of age. Thus, the greatest change in the stability of the self-image occurred during the period between 12 and 14. Several other dimensions of the self-image were studied by these authors, namely the individuals' feelings of "self-consciousness" and self-esteem and their perceptions of how others viewed them. The results suggest that twelve- to fourteen-year-old adolescents, as compared with eight- to eleven-year-olds are more self-conscious, have less positive attitudes toward themselves, and view others (parents, peers, and teachers) as seeing them more unfavorably. The fifteen- to eighteen-year-old adolescents were similar to the twelve- to fourteen-year-olds with one important exception: there was a positive increase in their global self-esteem scores. In concluding, the authors state: "A definite disturbance in self-image has been shown to occur in adolescence, particularly early adolescence. In some respects this disturbance appears to decline in later adolescence, while along other dimensions it persists [p. 342]."

Monge (1973), in a factor analytic study of students in grades six through twelve, studied the self-concepts of adolescents. The adolescents were to rate the concept "My Characteristic Self" in terms of twenty-one adjectives on a seven-point scale, using one scale for each adjective (semantic differential scales). He found considerable consistency among the adolescents of varying ages in their self-concepts. Males showed greater consistency of self-concepts than females. Monge's study was cross-sectional. It would be of interest to determine whether similar findings would emerge in a longitudinal study.

With the exception of a few studies, attention has not been given to the stability of the self-concept from early childhood through later adult years. One such longitudinal study of females is that of Sears and Barbee (1975). These investigators did a follow-up study of the classic study by

Terman of gifted children (IQ 135 or above) who were originally seen in 1922–1928. The average age of these women when last studied in 1972 was sixty-two years. In general the findings suggest that there was considerable stability in the self-concepts of the women over the years. An interesting finding of this study is that those females who reported positive self-ratings when younger also reported greater general satisfaction with life in later years. It is as though those youngsters who are self-confident at an early age are prone to create situations for themselves at later ages that are likely to promote satisfaction.

Signs of Self-acceptance

Adolescents who realistically accept themselves, while still employing their potentialities for learning and growth, have a treasure. Within their own worlds the ones with meager talents who forthrightly appreciate what they have are richer than the ones who are bountifully endowed but deplore themselves.[6]

Self-accepting individuals have a realistic appraisal of their resources combined with appreciation of their own worth; assurance about standards and convictions of their own without being slaves to the opinions of others; and realistic assessments of their limitations without irrational self-reproach.

Self-accepting adolescents recognize their assets and are free to draw on them even if they are not all that could be desired. They also recognize their shortcomings without needlessly blaming themselves. A male adolescent basketball player might wish he were three inches taller. But he plays

---

[6] Criteria for measuring self-acceptance and self-rejection have been described by Spivack (1956) and in a number of other studies reviewed by Wylie (1961).

In many studies it has been assumed that individuals are self-accepting to the degree that their professed actual self corresponds with what they claim as their ideal self. If they say they are lazy and then claim that, for them, laziness is an ideal state, they are self-accepting on that item. On the other hand, they would receive a maximum self-rejection score on this item if they rated themselves at one extreme in one response (he is lazy *all of the time*) and at the other extreme in the other (he wishes he were *never* lazy). This, however, is a superficial way of assessing self-acceptance. It suffers from the underlying limitations of self-concept inventories that were discussed earlier in this chapter. It also rests on the dubious assumption that degree of self-acceptance can be computed by a simple process of arithmetic—so many points for each item on the test—as though items that are arithmetically equal are also psychologically equal. An adolescent male might, for example, say that he is very inartistic and wishes he were very artistic. He might also say that he is very unattractive to girls and wishes he were very attractive. He will receive the same maximum nonacceptance score on both of these items, as though they counted equally, even though he does not give a second thought to his lack of artistic ability but is very much concerned about what he regards as his lack of attractiveness to girls.

the game with the stature he has, without kicking himself for being unable to outjump the giants on the opposing team. He does not blame himself unreasonably by assuming he could be several inches taller if he had eaten the right foods, as though his height were entirely of his own making. A bright short adolescent boy who told his peers when being teased about his height, "It's not how high your head is from the ground but what's in it," appeared to recognize his assets as well as his liabilities. Similarly, the self-accepting adolescent girl who is very tall will see advantages in being shorter; but she comes forth gracefully, she does not stoop as though apologizing for her height.

Among the outstanding characteristics of self-accepting adolescents are spontaneity and responsibility for self. They accept the qualities of their humanity without condemning themselves for conditions beyond their control. They do not see themselves as persons who should be above anger or fear or devoid of conflicting desires, free of human fallibility. They feel they have a right to have ideas, aspirations, and wishes of their own. They do not begrudge themselves the satisfactions of being alive.

Symptoms of Self-rejection

Self-rejection includes chronic attitudes of self-disapproval, self-disparagement, and self-distrust and feelings of being unworthy—of not being deserving of satisfactions, reward, or success. In one of its cruelest forms, self-rejection includes severe guilt, viewing oneself as among the damned.

One sign of self-rejection is severe self-criticism, although self-criticism is not in itself an evidence of rejection. One mark of self-accepting persons is that they can detect and acknowledge their faults. Self-criticism is a sign of self-rejection when individuals feel inferior according to a standard of appraisal that is patently incorrect, or when they deplore themselves for failing to reach standards of perfection no one could achieve.

We may suspect that adolescents are self-rejecting if they say all others are against them, view them unfairly, and belittle and disapprove of them. Such attitudes attributed to others may be a projection of attitudes they hold regarding themselves.[7]

Adolescents reject themselves when they automatically bow to the opinions and decisions of others, even though there is no basis for believing

[7] However, such a judgment about others is not necessarily a sign of self-rejection. An adolescent may correctly perceive that others are prejudiced against him and still remain convinced of his own worth (although this is not an easy thing to do). This conviction occurs, for example, when bright adolescents who ask penetrating questions in class are called oddballs by their associates but still cling to their right to raise questions.

that the others are wiser. They show symptoms of self-rejection when they persistently judge themselves by a competitive standard as though they can feel worthy only if they surpass others.

Self-rejection also prevails when adolescents habitually strike a pose by pretending to be what they are not or by going out of their way to boast or to impress others. They reject themselves when they are self-destructive, plunge recklessly into one scrape after another, and invite punishment or disgrace when there is nothing to gain and everything to lose.

The tragic thing about adolescents who severely reject themselves is that they often do things that cause others to confirm the low opinion they have of themselves. Deeper even than the tragedy of severe self-rejection is its pathos. Severely self-rejecting adolescents are their own enemies. They have taken unto themselves what might be the unkindness of their heredity and all the harshness of their environment, and they have added something more: everything is their fault and they are no good.

Sex Differences in Attitudes Toward Self

Because females in America tend to be devalued in comparison with men, it has been alleged that females have fewer positive feelings about themselves than men (Bardwick, 1971). Interestingly enough, evidence regarding sex differences in adolescents' views of themselves does not always support this conclusion.

In a study of stability and change in eleven- and seventeen-year-olds, Carlson (1965) found that at both ages no sex differences appeared in either the level or the stability of the adolescents' self-esteem. However, Bohan (1973), using Coopersmith's self-rating self-esteem inventory, did find one sex difference: Bohan reported that tenth-grade females had lower self-esteem scores than fourth-, sixth-, and eighth-grade females and males and tenth-grade males.

Silverman et al. (1970) found that female college students were similar to male college students in the percentage of favorable adjectives they checked in describing themselves. In an experimental study Skolnick (1971) informed one group of students that they had failed and a second group that they had succeeded on certain performance tasks. Members of a third group were left uncertain as to their success or failure. All the college students were then asked to rate their performances retrospectively on seven-point scales. The males and females in all three groups were found to be similar in their levels of self-esteem. Having reviewed the literature in this area, Maccoby and Jacklin (1974) concluded that when sex differences in self-esteem do appear they are no more likely to favor one sex than the other.

Although similarities do appear to exist between the ways in which males and females rate themselves over all, there do appear to be sex differences in their approaches to certain specific tasks and the ways in which they define themselves. In a study by Crandall (1969), college students were asked to indicate the grades they expected to achieve in several courses. Their expected grades and actual grades were then compared. Although there were no differences in the actual scores the students achieved, college men claimed they expected to receive higher scores than college women. In general the males tended to overestimate the grades they would receive, whereas females tended to underestimate their expected grades.

Males are more individualistic than females, and females are more socially oriented than males in their own self-descriptions, according to Carlson (1971). College students were given a check list and instructed to check ten adjectives that best described them. The "personal" or "individualistic" cluster included such adjectives as ambitious, idealistic, and energetic, whereas the "social" domain included items such as friendly, persuasive, and attractive. The males rated themselves higher on the individualistic items and lower on the social items. In contrast the females rated themselves higher on the social than on the individualistic items. There is the suggestion, then, that females consider themselves more socially oriented, and males see themselves as more concerned about their personal status.

Even though it appears from the foregoing that males and females may be similar in their overall positive evaluations of themselves, beyond the high school level, present-day males tend to be more confident than females of their abilities to perform at high levels on certain tasks.

The Balance Between Self-acceptance and Self-rejection

Do adolescents typically tend to view themselves favorably or unfavorably? How do they view adolescents as a group? Do they tend to give themselves higher or lower ratings than they give to others? Do they, in general, view themselves more favorably or unfavorably than they are viewed by adults?

Several studies have dealt with these questions. Unfortunately, the answers are inconclusive. Differing methods applied to differing populations have produced conflicting findings. Available findings indicate that the typical adolescent views himself or herself with a blend of approval and disapproval, but the balance is more on the side of approval than disapproval (Engel, 1959; Offer, 1969; Wiggins, 1973).

Some studies show that young people tend to compare themselves more favorably with others in connection with some traits than in connection with other traits. Students who took part in a study conducted by Zazzo (1960) saw their peers as being socially more at ease, more stable, and generally more relaxed than themselves. Musa and Roach (1973) reported that most adolescents rated their physical appearance as favorably as they rated the appearance of their peers. On the other hand, Collignon (1960) found that a large proportion of youngsters, notably boys in an age range from eleven and a half to fifteen years, tended to view themselves as taller than they really were. Youngsters who attached the greatest importance to size as a feature of their total make-up tended to make the greatest errors in estimating their height. The relationship between self-esteem and self-acceptance by others will be discussed further in Chapters 3, 4, and 5.

Although adolescents value some traits more than others and tend to overestimate or underestimate themselves on some traits more than on others, their self-ratings of particular traits generally regarded as desirable are likely to be more similar than dissimilar. For example, if they give themselves favorable ratings in assessing their mental characteristics, they also are likely to give themselves favorable ratings when assessing their personality traits or their social relationships (Taschuk, 1957). However, ratings are more similar in some areas of self-perception than in others. In a study of ninth-graders, there was a higher degree of correspondence between self-ratings of mental and social traits than between self-ratings of mental and physical characteristics. Gray and Gaier (1974) found a positive association between the way adolescents see themselves and the way their parents and friends think they view themselves.

In a study by Brandt (1958) sixth-graders and eleventh-graders estimated how well they would do on a variety of academic and physical tasks and also estimated how well they were regarded by their peers. These estimates were then compared with their actual performances on a number of tests and their social reputations as rated by their peers. Brandt found that if youngsters are biased in one direction (such as overestimating themselves) in their self-ratings in one area (such as academic achievement) they tend to be biased in the same direction in other areas. "Whether an individual is accurate or inaccurate seems to depend more on his self-structure than on the specific nature of the perceived characteristic [p. 87]." Although a majority of the youngsters gave themselves higher ratings in one performance (such as spelling) than in another (such as strength of grip), one fourth of them consistently either overrated or underrated themselves. According to Brandt (1958) this finding emphasizes the need for considering "major aspects of the total self-concept, rather than isolated bits of it" when we try to understand youngsters.

Available evidence also suggests that trends in self-evaluation will vary among people in different segments of the population and will be influenced by circumstances that require them to take a critical look at themselves.

Thompson (1974) studied the self-concepts of high school students identified by teachers as being well adjusted, maladjusted, and delinquent. As first-year students, the maladjusted group viewed themselves less positively than the adjusted or delinquent groups, but by the time these students were seniors there were no differences in their views of themselves. It appears that the adjusted group became less positive in terms of their self-evaluation when they were seniors. The adolescents were also asked to rate themselves as they thought others might rate them. Among the seniors, the maladjusted rated their fathers' and teachers' perceptions of them less positively than the well-adjusted adolescents. The delinquents, in comparison with the well-adjusted adolescents, reported that their mothers, fathers, and teachers viewed them less favorably.

Nine- to seventeen-year-old girls were asked to tell if they were much better than, a little better than, a little poorer than, or much poorer than girls their own age on a number of items such as being quick to learn, good in sports and games, well dressed, good looking, and having many friends. Ratings of these items did not vary according to their socioeconomic backgrounds. However, on several items such as sports and physical appearance, black females, on the average, rated themselves higher than white females (Prendergast et al., 1974).

An interesting study of a selected sampling of young people is reported by Sanford (1957), who obtained data regarding Vassar girls as they moved from the freshman through the senior year and beyond. Sanford states that at the time of his research Vassar College seniors were on the average more unstable or "upset," and more uncertain about themselves and about life than the freshmen. The seniors reported more disturbance than the freshmen in a variety of ways, such as more depression, self-criticism, anxiety and doubt, and consciousness of conflict. But the picture of greater instability in seniors might be due in part to their greater ability to recognize and report their difficulties, in keeping with their better education and greater maturity. On the other hand, as compared with freshmen, according to Sanford, seniors were more "liberated"; more assertive, rebellious, and adventurous; less passive and less submissive; and they had greater breadth of consciousness, more self-insight and familiarity with their inner life. The seniors also were confronted with the near prospect of having to leave the protection of academic life and having to get ready to "face the world" and to make important decisions. They faced this prospect at a time when they had to let go of the external controls they relied on as freshmen and while inner controls were being established.

These observations regarding college seniors cannot be regarded as applying to the typical young woman, or the typical college woman, as she moves from late adolescence into early adulthood.[8] However, they do emphasize the differences between the objective and subjective dimensions of a young person's life. From an objective point of view, the college seniors in Sanford's study had many reasons for feeling complacent about themselves: they were bright; they were about to graduate from a college that ranks high in prestige; and the main hurdles of adolescence were behind them. For almost four years they had weathered rigorous academic requirements. But, instead of feeling serene about these things, many of them apparently were challenged to examine themselves. A person who has enough insight to question herself but has not yet found the answers is not likely to be very complacent. Her score on one of the conventional self-concept tests quite likely will be less favorable than the score of one who has less insight and is not inclined to question.

Viewpoints of Adolescents and Adults

Tomé's analysis of the self-concept of adolescents, as summarized by Elkind (1975), provides new insights into an understanding of the nature of

[8] Elsewhere in this book (Chapter 17) we will review findings indicating that the effects of four years in college seem to vary considerably in different colleges and do not generally lead to as much soul-searching as Sanford found in his group.

the adolescents' conceptions of themselves and others. Three relatively independent dimensions were delineated by Tomé: "egotism (for example, the tendency to feel superior); self-control (for example, the ability to solve problems without help); and sociability (for example, confidence)."

In this study, adolescent boys twelve to eighteen years of age and girls twelve to twenty-one years old described themselves as less egotistical and more self-controlled than did their parents. In general, parents agreed in their evaluations of their adolescents. An interesting aspect of this study was Tomé's comparison of the adolescents' perceptions of their parents' evaluations of them with their parents' perceptions of what the adolescents thought of themselves. Surprisingly, the adolescents had a better idea of what the parents thought of them than the parents had of the adolescents' own views of themselves.

EMPHASIS ON CONFORMITY AND SOCIAL STEREOTYPES

Typical adolescents place great emphasis on social conformity when assessing themselves. This is not surprising. Adolescents who are nonconformists run the risk of being outcasts. They are not alone in this, for adults also emphasize conformity. Even such concepts as emotional adjustment and mental health are frequently defined primarily in terms of social conformity.[9]

To achieve the status of independent adults, it is necessary for adolescents to conform within prudent limits, but it is also necessary for them to be nonconformists. Nonconformity linked with a healthy course of development is a form of courage: the courage to be and to become. When adolescents are rebellious because that is the only way they can grow in self-direction, they are showing courage. But adolescents (reflecting the attitudes of adults around them) are more likely to view such rebellion as a fault than to feel proud about being a rebel in a good cause.

There are other facets of their worth that adolescents commonly regard in subrosa fashion. The course of their sexual development is filled with vexations, but much happens also that they properly can regard with pride. Some of them do so in the privacy of their own thoughts. Many girls feel pride, for example, when they have their first menstruation (Landis et al., 1940). But few report feeling proud when they tell about themselves.

A policy of keeping their self-professed weaknesses within the bounds of respectability appears in what adolescents report about their attitudes toward sex. When over a thousand adolescents of junior, senior, and college age told what they liked or disliked about themselves in a study

[9] The tests and inventories that have been devised for self-description similarly, to a large degree, measure claimed conventionality rather than psychological insight.

done by Jersild (1952), not a single one directly professed any self-deprecation in the area of sex. Yet we know from other sources that most adolescents have had sexual experiences of one sort or another and that at least some of them feel guilty or uneasy about their sexual desires.[10]

There are other ways in which the accounts adolescents give of themselves echo social stereotypes. Many adolescents mention their tendency to get angry when reporting what they deplore in themselves. But rarely do adolescents (unless closely questioned) express pride in their freedom to feel angry and to show it when anger is justified. When describing what they regard as their faults they are far more likely to name specific manifestations than to acknowledge a more pervasive condition of weakness. In this respect, again, they reflect their elders.[11]

The foregoing discussion is not meant to belittle what adolescents *do* say about themselves; what they say is significant as far as it goes. It is meant rather to point to what they ordinarily *do not* report when they informally tell about themselves or when they respond to the typical self-assessment inventory. What they report is patterned on the conventional, censored, and rather superficial model of self-assessment that prevails among adults. No one in particular can be blamed for this. We cannot expect adolescents to be more profound than their elders. However, in the process, adolescents do themselves an injustice, both in not disclosing the nature of the predicaments of life that underlie their limitations and in not revealing the depths of their resources.

Sex-role identity and learning

In the past, probably more than at present, there have been deeply rooted notions (some more stereotyped than others) as to what are properly boyish or masculine attitudes and forms of behavior as distinguished from what are properly girlish or feminine attitudes and forms of conduct. Boys have received tools and toy vehicles as gifts; girls have received dolls and toy furniture. It has been assumed that boys are more aggressive, girls more compliant; that girls may cry but boys should not be crybabies, and so on. Actually, so-called sex-typed behavior is more in conformity with examples set in the past by males and females. Maccoby and Jacklin (1974) point out,

---

[10] Inventories that have been used in studies of the self-concept usually touch on sex obliquely, if at all. The main reason for this is not that the psychologists who devise such instruments are sexless creatures, but that a self-assessment inventory dealing frankly with sex would probably be banned.

[11] In a study by Jersild et al. (1962), it was noted that many teachers acknowledged several symptoms of anxiety, but then denied that they were "anxious"; many reported symptoms of a competitive attitude but then denied they were "competitive."

for example, that although boys traditionally play with trucks and cars, today they observe that their mothers drive the family car more often than their fathers do. Increasingly, boys and girls are seeing women in occupations formerly regarded as masculine and men cooking in the kitchen or minding the baby.

In a study of cross-cultural differences in sex-role stereotypes, Block (1973) found a similarity of sex-role stereotypes in five northern European countries and the United States. There were, however, some differences between Americans and Europeans; for example, American men emphasized "adventurous," "assertive," "ambitious," and "competitive" stereotypes in their portrayal of the masculine ideal more than European men.

The "degree to which an individual regards oneself as masculine or feminine" has been referred to as sex-role identity [Kagan, 1964, p. 144]. A number of investigators have studied the processes through which individuals gain an awareness and, in the end, an assurance of their identity as independent, mature adults. Some of these proposals will be presented in the following section.

Biological Correlates

In discussing the etiology of psychological sex differences, Maccoby and Jacklin (1974) call attention to genetic factors that might affect the development of sex differences. For instance, boys may be biologically more inclined than girls to learn aggression. It is possible that differences in sex hormones in males and female are related to sex differences in behavior. Although biological factors may have an effect on sex-role characteristics, many psychologists have noted that cognition, emotions, and socialization also are influential.

Cognition, Learning, and Identification

Kohlberg (1966) espouses an internal, cognitive view and believes that (1) the child's increasing cognitive awareness of its sexual identity plus (2) the child's increasing cognitive awareness of the culturally determined sex-roles influence his or her repertoire of sex-role behavior (cognitive-developmental theory). Cognitive growth, rather than external reinforcement, is emphasized, although reinforcement is not excluded as a factor influencing cognitive development. Kohlberg refers to this cognitive awareness as "gender constancy" and believes it underlies more complex sex-role behaviors. He states that this occurs by ages five or six, when the child becomes readily able to sort and group together people (and the self) according to sex. Thus, young children have learned the meaning of concepts of masculinity and femininity.

According to Kohlberg (1966), "The child's sexual identity is maintained by a motivated adaptation to physical social reality and by the need to preserve a stable and positive self-image [p. 88]."

According to social learning theory, the learning of sex roles depends on cognitive and observational processes. Sex-typed behavior on the part of adolescents is affected by motivational and situational factors as well. For instance, adolescents are aware of those sex-typed behaviors that are viewed as appropriate by their peers. At the same time they recognize the consequences of engaging in sex-type behavior that is not approved by their peers. For instance, if an adolescent boy were to wear dresses to school, he would not receive approval from his peer group, and he would be ostracized by them for his inappropriate sex-typed behavior. Social learning theorists focus attention on the process of imitation, and note that children and adolescents are more likely to have their behavior reinforced when they imitate a model of the same sex rather than a model of the opposite sex.

In a summary of several studies conducted with adolescents or adults, in which some models were more similar to the subjects than other models, Mischel (1970) concluded that individuals who perceive a model as similar to themselves are more likely to match their behavior to that of this model.

Another process through which individuals gain an awareness and, in the end, an assurance of their identity as independent, mature adults is identification. According to theoretical accounts, varying motives may operate when children are in the process of establishing their identity. Children may pursue these motives knowingly or unknowingly. As pointed out by Kagan and Havemann (1976), they may, for example, emulate their parents or heroic figures in order vicariously to share their strengths. Or, according to psychoanalytic theory, they may seek to be like the parent of the same sex as they struggle to overcome an Oedipus complex. Or, they may identify with another person or a group as a defense mechanism in order to cope with their own conflicts and anxieties. At the present time there is some debate about the process of identification. Identification, when firmly established, is not the same as imitation, although imitation may serve as a basis for the beginning of the process of the development of one's identity. Identity formation requires the ability to distinguish between oneself and others and involves the integration of an individual's drives, feelings, abilities, conscience, and view of self with the realities of the external world. When children have the ability to distinguish between themselves and others, which according to Piaget (1970) is established quite early in childhood, they are on their way to separating themselves psychologically from their parents and are prepared for further stages in the development of their identity.

Parental Influences

Maccoby and Jacklin (1974) suggest that direct parental socialization pressure may account for some sex differences in behavior, and they believe that the child's identification with the same-sex parent and other same-sex models is important. In addition they stress, as do others who have studied the matter, that, with increasing age, children increasingly form ideas regarding what presumably is masculine and what is feminine. They then attempt to match their behavior to these ideas.

Many investigators have studied the amounts of positive and negative reinforcement given to boys and girls. According to Maccoby and Jacklin (1974), who have reviewed many recent studies in this area, boys receive from parents and significant others more of both positive and negative reinforcement than girls do. They speculate that perhaps this finding is related to the greater "attention-getting" propensity of school-aged boys.

As noted earlier there are characteristics, or qualities, generally regarded as masculine or feminine. The common stereotype of masculinity includes such traits as achievement, independence, competence, dominance, and rationality; femininity includes dependence, warmth, possessiveness, and abasement (Kagan and Moss, 1962).[12] The father and mother to varying degrees embody these stereotypes and deliberately or unknowingly the parent encourages sex-linked sex-role behavior in the child. Heilbrun (1968) states that different sex-role behaviors may result, depending on which parent acts as the primary model for identification. For example, if the father acts as the primary model for identification, the daughter's feminine behavior contrasts with the father's masculine behavior, but the daughter may also show certain masculine-type traits, such as more assertiveness. Heilbrun (1965) believes that the father's masculinity is particularly important for the sex-role learning in both sexes, more so than the mother's femininity. In a study done by Heilbrun and Hall (1964), both sexes tended to use the mother as the primary identification model if they believed she exerted more control over them. The implications of these findings for the

---

[12] These findings are confirmed by Broverman et al. (1972), who comment on the widespread stereotyped thinking about sex-role behavior, with more favorable traits indicating competence being assigned to men.

"controlling" mother's influence on her children's sex-role behavior indicate possible strengthening of the daughter's feminine sex-role learning and weakening of the son's masculine sex-role learning.

As concerns personal adjustment, Heilbrun (1973) notes that adolescent males who identified with the appropriate parent model showed the most effective behavior. In females, identification with a feminine-type mother tended to lead to poor adjustment, whereas identification with a masculine-type mother tended to produce better personal adjustment. Further studies reported by Heilbrun also show that adjusted males were more similar in specific ways to father, and maladjusted males to mother. Adjusted females showed similarity with both parents, whereas maladjusted females showed poor similarity.

The work of Lynn (1959, 1966, 1969) has been useful in examining the overall vicissitudes of sex-role learning in an integrated fashion. According to Lynn, dissimilarities between people in general, parents, and same-sex children may occur for several reasons: identification may be disturbed by the parents' own inadequate or inappropriate sex-role learning, or there may be difficulties in the parent-child relationship that foster the desire to be unlike the parent. Lynn found that males and females both identify with the mother at first, but boys shift to masculine identification later.

Lynn (1966) believes that a critical period of the male's life involves the change from identification with mother to masculine sex-role identification. The male learns first what not to do, but must figure out for himself more independently what to do to fill masculine sex-role behavior. This and later difficult tasks may have the effect for a time of producing more anxiety in males about sex-role behavior than in females. Female "tomboys" are more accepted than male "sissies," and feminine-type behavior is severely disapproved in males.

At adolescence, because of the greater rewards given by male-dominated society to males, sex-role learning is easier for males than for females. The early greater stress on masculine behavior for males increases the ease of masculine identification during adolescence. This may contribute to the increasing preference for masculine behavior expressed by many females with increasing age. Lynn states that sex-role identification problems are fewer in adolescence for males than for females.

According to Mischel (1970), a prominent writer in this area, children see same-sex models, especially parents, as similar to themselves, and so tend to imitate them and their sex-typed behaviors more than dissimilar models. Mischel (1976) also notes that adolescents' sex-role behaviors are influenced by factors outside the family including the particular culture in which they live.

Changes in sex-role preferences

According to Dreyer (1975), the sex-role preferences of adolescent females, and of males, to some extent, are changing. Young women today more often express interest in careers than women years ago who emphasized the traditional role of homemaker. In comparing young women in the 1970s with women in the 1950s, Komarovsky (1973) noted that young women today are less likely to conceal their abilities. For instance, in response to the question: When on dates how often have you pretended to be intellectually inferior to the man? in 1950, 58 per cent said at least once, as compared with 45 per cent in 1971. More young American women are attempting to combine the "traditional feminine role" with the "modern role" by combining careers and going to school with getting married and raising families. In order to achieve both roles successfully, these young women probably will have to be assertive, goal-directed, and highly flexible.

Some changes in the sex-role preferences of present-generation men have occurred; however, their attitudes toward the roles played by their future wives appear to be full of inconsistencies. In a study of men at an Ivy League college, more than half of the students reported they wanted their future wives to combine a family and career. However, only 7 per cent reported that they would change their own behavior by sharing in homemaking and childrearing in order to assist their future wives in attaining a career. In summary, Komarovsky (1973) noted: "The ideological support for the belief in sharp sex-role differentiation in marriage has weakened, but the belief has not weakened [p. 897]."

References

Bardwick, J. M. *Psychology of women: A study of bio-cultural conflicts.* New York: Harper, 1971.

Block, J. *The Q-sort method in personality assessment and psychiatric research.* Springfield, Ill.: Thomas, 1961.

Block, J. H. Conceptions of sex role: Some cross-cultural and longitudinal perspectives. *American Psychologist,* 1973, **28**, 512–526.

Bohan, J. S. Age and sex differences in self concept. *Adolescence,* 1973, **8**, 379–384.

Brandt, R. M. The accuracy of self-estimate: A measure of self-concept reality. *Genetic Psychology Monographs,* 1958, **58**, 55–99.

Broverman, I. K., Vogel, S. R., Broverman, D. M., Clarkson, F. E., & Rosenkrantz, P. S. Sex role stereotypes: A current appraisal. *Journal of Social Issues,* 1972, **28**, 59–78.

Carlson, R. Stability and change in the adolescent's self-image. *Child Psychology,* 1965, **36**, 659–666.

Carlson, R. Sex differences in ego functioning: Exploratory studies of agency and communion. *Journal of Consulting and Clinical Psychology*, 1971, **37**, 267–277.

Collignon, M. Conquête de l'autonomie et taille d'après les appréciations de garçons et de filles de 12 à 15 ans (Conquest of autonomy and height according to the judgments of boys and girls 12 to 15 years of age). *Enfance*, 1960 (3), 291–319.

Coopersmith, S. *The antecedents of self-esteem.* San Francisco: Freeman, 1967.

Coopersmith, S. Studies in self-esteem. *Scientific American,* 1968, **218**, 96–106.

Crandall, V. C. Sex differences in expectancy of intellectual and academic reinforcement. In C. P. Smith (Ed.), *Achievement related motives in children.* New York: Russell Sage Foundation, 1969.

Dreyer, P. H. Changes in the meaning of marriage among youth. The impact of the "revolution" in sex and sex role behavior. In R. E. Grinder (Ed.), *Studies in adolescence: A book of readings in adolescent development* (3rd ed.). New York: Macmillan, 1975.

Elkind, D. Recent research on cognitive development in adolescence. In S. E. Dragastin & G. H. Elder, Jr. (Eds.), *Adolescence in the life cycle: Psychological change and social context.* New York: Wiley, 1975.

Engel, M. The stability of the self-concept in adolescence. *Journal of Abnormal and Social Psychology,* 1959, **58**, 211–215.

Fenigstein, A., Scheier, M. F., & Buss, A. H. Public and private self-consciousness: Assessment and theory. *Journal of Consulting and Clinical Psychology*, 1975, **43**, 522–527.

Gray, D. F., & Gaier, E. L. The congruency of adolescent self-perceptions with those of parents and best friends. *Adolescence*, 1974, **9**, 299–303.

Heilbrun, A. B., Jr., & Hall, C. L. Resource mediation in childhood and identification. *Journal of Child Psychology and Psychiatry*, 1964, **5**, 139–149.

Heilbrun, A. B., Jr. Sex differences in identification learning. *Journal of Genetic Psychology*, 1965, **106**, 185–193.

Heilbrun, A. B., Jr. Sex role identity in adolescent females: A theoretical paradox. *Adolescence*, 1968, **3**, 79–88.

Heilbrun, A. B. Parent identification and filial sex-role behavior; the importance of biological context. *Nebraska Symposium on Motivation* (Vol. 21). Lincoln: University of Nebraska Press, 1973.

Jersild, A. T. *In search of self.* New York: Bureau of Publications, Teachers College, Columbia University, 1952.

Jersild, A. T., Lazar, E., & Brodkin, A. *The meaning of psychotherapy in the teacher's life and work.* New York: Bureau of Publications, Teachers College, Columbia University, 1962.

Jervis, F. *The meaning of a positive self-concept.* Unpublished doctoral dissertation, Teachers College, Columbia University, 1958.

Kagan, J. The acquisition and significance of sex typing and sex role identity. In M. Hoffman & L. Hoffman (Eds.), *Review of child development research* (Vol. 1). New York: Russell Sage Foundation, 1964.

Kagan, J., & Havemann, E. *Psychology: An introduction* (3rd ed.). New York: Harcourt, 1976.

Kagan, J., & Moss, H. A. *Birth to maturity: A study in psychological development.* New York: Wiley, 1962.

Kohlberg, L. A cognitive-developmental analysis of children's sex role concepts and attitudes. In E. E. Maccoby (Ed.), *The development of sex differences.* Stanford, Calif.: Stanford U.P., 1966.

Komarovsky, M. Cultural contradictions and sex roles: The masculine case. *American Journal of Sociology*, 1973, **78**, 873–884.

Landis, C., Landis, A. T., & Bolles, M. M., et al. *Sex in development.* New York: Paul B. Hoeber, 1940.

Lynn, D. B. A note on sex differences in the development of masculine and feminine identification. *Psychological Review*, 1959, **66**, 126–135.

Lynn, D. B. The process of learning parental and sex-role identification. *Journal of Marriage and the Family*, 1966, **18**, 466–470.

Lynn, D. B. *Parental and sex-role identification: A theoretical formulation.* Berkeley: McCutchan, 1969.

Maccoby, E. E., & Jacklin, C. N. *Psychology of sex differences.* Stanford, Calif.: Stanford U.P., 1974.

McCandless, B. R. *Adolescents: Behavior and development.* New York: Holt, 1970.

Mischel, W. Sex-typing and socialization. In P. H. Mussen (Ed.), *Carmichael's manual of child psychology* (rev. ed.). New York: Wiley, 1970.

Mischel, W. *Introduction to personality* (2nd ed.). New York: Holt, 1976.

Monge, R. H. Developmental trends in factors of adolescent self-concept. *Developmental Psychology*, 1973, **8**, 382–393.

Musa, K. E., & Roach, M. E. Adolescent appearance and self-concept. *Adolescence*, 1973, **8**, 385–394.

Offer, D. *The psychological world of the teen-ager: A study of normal adolescence.* New York: Basic Books, 1969.

Osgood, C. E., Suci, G. J., & Tannenbaum, P. H. *The measurement of meaning.* Urbana, Ill.: The University of Illinois Press, 1957.

Piaget, J. Piaget's theory. In P. H. Mussen (Ed.), *Carmichael's manual of child psychology* (Vol. 1). New York: Wiley, 1970.

Prendergast, P., Zdep, S. M., & Sepulveda, P. Self-image among a national probability sample of girls. *Child Study Journal*, 1974, **4**, 103–114.

Rivenbark, W. H. III. Self-disclosure patterns among adolescents. *Psychological Reports*, 1971, **28**, 35–42.

Rogers, C., & Dymond, R. *Psychotherapy and personality change.* Chicago: U. of Chicago, 1954.

Sanford, N. The uncertain senior. *Journal of the National Association of Women Deans and Counselors*, 1957, **21**, 9–15.

Scarlett, G. Adolescent thinking and the diary of Anne Frank. In J. J. Conger (Ed.), *Contemporary issues in adolescent development.* New York: Harper, 1975.

Scott, W. A., & Johnson, R. C. Comparative validities of direct and indirect personality tests. *Journal of Consulting and Clinical Psychology*, 1972, **38**, 301–318.

Sears, P. S., & Barbee, A. H. *Career and life satisfaction among Terman's gifted women.* Paper presented at the Lewis M. Terman Memorial Symposium on Intellectual Talent. Baltimore: Johns Hopkins, November 6, 1975.

Sears, R. R. Relation of early socialization experiences to self-concepts and gender roles in middle childhood. *Child Development*, 1970, **41**, 267–289.

Silverman, I., Shulman, A. D., & Wiesenthal, D. L. Effects of deceiving and debriefing psychological subjects on performance in later experiments. *Journal of Personality and Social Psychology*, 1970, **14**, 203–212.

Simmons, R., Rosenberg, F., & Rosenberg, M. Disturbance in the self-image at adolescence. *American Sociological Review*, 1973, **38**, 553–568.

Sinha, V. Age differences in self-disclosure. *Developmental Psychology*, 1972, **7**, 257–258.

Skolnick, P. Reactions to personal evaluations: A failure to replicate. *Journal of Personality and Social Psychology*, 1971, **18**, 62–67.

Spivack, S. A study of a method of appraising self-acceptance and self-rejection. *Journal of Genetic Psychology*, 1956, **88**, 183–202.

Stephenson, W. Some observations on Q-technique. *Psychological Bulletin*, 1952, **6**, 483–498.

Taschuk, W. A. An analysis of the self-concept of grade nine students. *Alberta Journal of Educational Research*, 1957, **3**(2), 94–103.

Thompson, B. Self-concepts among secondary school pupils. *Educational Research*, 1974, **17**, 41–47.

Wiggins, R. G. Differences in self-perceptions of ninth grade boys and girls. *Adolescence*, 1973, **8**, 491–496.

Wylie, R. C. *The self-concept.* Lincoln: University of Nebraska Press, 1961.

Zazzo, B. L'image de soi comparée à l'image de ses semblables chez l'adolescent (The self-concept compared with the conception of peers among adolescents). *Enfance*, 1960 (2), 121–141.

part two

PHYSICAL ASPECTS
OF DEVELOPMENT

3

the genesis and course
of growth

The most important single event in adolescent development occurs in the changes that take place in the young person's body. In general the rate of growth prior to puberty (with the exception of the first two years after birth) proceeds by way of regular continuous increments. In contrast, at puberty, a considerable change in the growth rate is evident. Dramatic changes in body size and shape (the adolescent growth spurt) are accompanied by the rapid development of the reproductive system. Physical changes during the

55

adolescent period are the result of hormones secreted for the first time or in greater amounts than before.

Some of the physical changes are spectacular. A boy may grow as much as four inches or more in a single year (Stolz and Stolz, 1951). Some changes are dramatic. One day the girl is a child; the next day she has her first menstruation, and she is physically nearly a woman. Although her first menstruation is the culmination of changes that have been going on for a long period of time, for her it is a sudden occurrence.

The timing and extent of these changes are unpredictable, from the adolescent's point of view. An authority on physical growth may be able to foretell, with considerable accuracy, how long young adolescents will continue to grow. But adolescents themselves seldom have such knowledge. And even with a great amount of knowledge, much would remain unforeseeable—the profile of the new face, the pitch and timbre of the boy's voice, the distribution and texture of the boy's beard, the size of the boy's buttocks and genitals, and the size and contours of the girl's breasts.

The aura of the unknown is increased by the fact that body changes are extremely variable when youngsters are compared with each other. One boy's body may have completed its adolescent development, whereas that of another boy of the same chronological age may hardly have begun. In the meantime the late-maturing boy may worry and wonder what is wrong with him. One girl may reach the menarche at eleven, whereas one of her friends may not face the event until five years later.

Even though there are many findings showing that physical changes occur earlier in adolescent development today than they did years ago, the sequence of biological events remains quite constant. As was true years ago, girls as a group outpace boys in physical development by approximately two years. The typical eighth-grade girl is physically more nearly on a par with a tenth-grade boy than with the boys in her own class. Even here, however, there is a further complication, for although the average girl in the early teens is biologically more mature than the average boy (Frisch and Revelle, 1971), the boy is more precocious in his sexual behavior.

Physical changes have important psychological repercussions as youngsters adapt themselves to their changing bodies and to the surge in their sexual capacities. The boy, although still so young that it seems incongruous to picture him as a father, becomes a potential mate. The girl has the figure of a woman although she is scarcely accustomed to her new clothes. It takes time for adolescents to get used to their new equipment and to adjust to changes in their body proportions. Some adolescents go through a period when they cannot walk "naturally," and it is as though they once more have to learn the skill of locomotion.

Even attributes that normally are regarded as desirable may cause embarrassment. The girl with a shapely bosom is likely for a time to be self-conscious about it. Her self-consciousness is increased when she thinks the boys are staring at her (and when she thinks this, she probably is right). A boy whose genitals have grown rapidly may be embarrassed at the thought that others are noticing them.

Adolescent endocrinology: the hormonal basis for the growth spurt

The adolescent growth spurt also is seen in the various endocrine glands, which secrete hormones particularly important in the sexual changes of adolescence. Increased secretions of the "master gland," the pituitary, have the effect of stimulating the growth and functions of the organs that develop reproductive cells: the female ovaries and the male testes. These secretions are called gonadotrophic hormones, particularly the follicle-stimulating hormone, or FSH, which stimulates both the growth of the eggs in the ovaries and the growth of testicular sperm-producing cells. Cells in the ovary and the testicle produce female and male sex hormones, respectively. Estrogen (female hormone) secretion in the ovary increases sharply with the onset of adolescence and becomes cyclical as regular menstruation is established.

The secretion of adrenal androgens (male sex hormones) also increases greatly at puberty in both sexes. The adrenal production of androgens is probably similar in both sexes. Adrenal androgens are responsible for the growth of pubic and axillary hair in girls, whereas these secondary sex characteristics in boys are caused by testosterone, produced by the testicles. Some minor estrogen secretion is also noted in males, probably from the adrenal cortex. It is of interest to emphasize that both sexes produce both male and female sex hormones.

The sex difference in the adolescent growth spurt is affected by the presence of testosterone, an anabolic (or growth-producing) hormone, in boys, which leads to increased muscle and bone development in males. Probably, an increase in growth-hormone secretion by the pituitary combined with the increased adrenal androgens also affect the adolescent growth spurt.

The part of the brain structure known as the hypothalamus affects the functioning of the pituitary gland, indicating that brain maturation has a role in the onset of puberty. There may be a feedback mechanism involving the differential sensitivity of hypothalamic cells to sex hormones (Donovan and van der Werff ten Bosch, 1965). The cause of this change in hypothalamic sensitivity is unknown.

This outline of the endocrine changes in adolescence is, of course, simplified in presentation, and much is still unknown in this area.

Changes in height and weight

All boys and girls show a spurt in growth during adolescence. Height velocity curves (height gain per year) for boys and girls are presented in Figure 3.1.

The velocity of growth doubles during approximately the first year of the typical pubertal phase of growth. During this period of time the peak height velocity (PHV) is approximately 10.5 centimeters a year in boys and 9 centimeters in girls (within a standard deviation of 1 centimeter a year). This growth spurt is followed by a period of diminished rate, with gradually lower increments until mature height is achieved in the typical adolescent. (See Figure 3.1.)

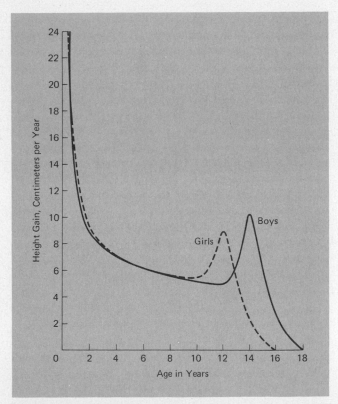

Figure 3.1. Typical individual velocity curves for supine length or height in boys and girls. These curves represent the velocity of the typical boy and girl at any given instant. [From "Standards from birth to maturity for height, weight, height velocity, and weight velocity; British children, 1965" by J. M. Tanner, R. H. Whitehouse, and M. Takaishi, *Archives of the Diseases of Childhood*, 1966, *41*, 455-471. Reprinted by permission.]

The velocity of change in height for boys reaches a peak, on the average, at fourteen years of age in this country, whereas for girls the peak occurs, on the average, at the age of twelve. Several investigators (see, for example, Tanner, 1962), have reported that 98 per cent of growth stops in boys at 17.75 years ± 10 months, and in girls at 16.25 years ± 13 months. These figures indicate that a small percentage of nontypical adolescents continue to grow past the age of eighteen (and possibly up to the early twenties). In contrast to highly developed countries, growth tends to be prolonged in developing countries (Prokopec, 1970). Similar differences in the growth pattern are apparent between higher and lower social-class groups within the same population. The nature of the growth spurt in adolescence results from a complex of genetic, environmental and organismic factors (including physical activity).

Some relationships between the rate of growth and comparative size and the onset of menstruation in girls are shown in Table 3.1. Some of these groups of girls underwent a considerable shift in average height. An indication of rate of growth in height as related to menarcheal age is given in Figure 3.2. Examples of patterns of growth in height are given in Figures 3.3 and 3.4.

One question that frequently concerns parents as well as growing children (especially boys who are short and girls who fear they will grow too tall) is what their ultimate height is likely to be. Individual variations in the pattern of growth are so pronounced that it is hazardous to generalize from averages to individual cases, yet there are some trends that are of interest in connection with the issue.

On the average, girls who are tall as preadolescent children tend to reach the menarche at an earlier age than girls who are short. They also enter the adolescent growth spurt at an earlier age (Tanner, 1970). At least for a

Table 3.1. Comparative average height of girls, grouped according to age of first menstruation when measured at the age of ten, thirteen and a half, and seventeen years.

Age at first menstruation	Rank order in average height from tallest to shortest		
	10 yrs.	13½ yrs.	17 yrs.
A: before 11.5 years	B	B	E
B: 11.6–11.11	C	C	C
C: 12.0–12.5	A	E	B
D: 12.6–12.11	E	D	F
E: 13.0–13.5	D	A	D
F: 13.6–13.11	F	F	H
G: 14.0–14.5	G	G	G
H: After 14.5	H	H	A

Source: From "Sexual maturation and the physical growth of girls age six to nineteen" by F. K. Shuttleworth, *Monographs of the Society for Research in Child Development,* 1937, **2**, No. 5. Reprinted by permission.

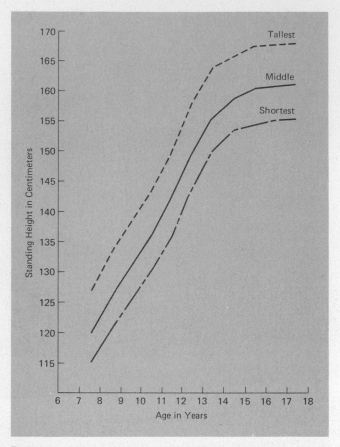

Figure 3.2.   Growth trends in average standing height of girls with the same menarcheal age, 13–0 to 13–5. [From *Sexual maturation and the physical growth of girls, age six to nineteen* by F. K. Shuttleworth, Monographs of the Society for Research in Child Development, 1937, *2*, No. 5. Reprinted by permission.]

time, accordingly, such girls are tall compared with many other girls of their own age. However, ultimate stature cannot be predicted with any assurance on the basis of the height a girl happens to have reached at a particular time while the growth process is continuing. A relatively tall girl of twelve who is sexually mature (has reached the menarche) may be outdistanced in height by a girl of similar age and size, or even by a somewhat shorter girl of similar age who is immature (has not reached the menarche) and not yet had the full benefit of the growth spurt.

Among girls who reach the menarche at the same age, those who were tallest during earlier years are likely to continue to be taller through the adolescent years and at maturity (Tanner, 1970).

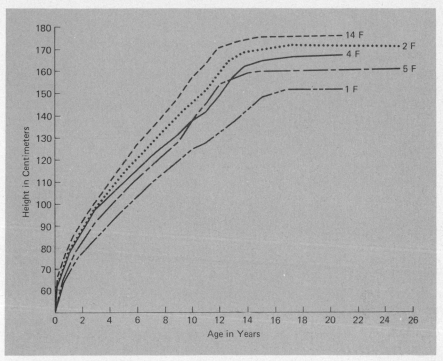

Figure 3.3. Curves of stature by age for five girls in the Berkeley Growth Study, including the tallest female in the group (14F), the shortest, and three girls of intermediate height. [From "Individual patterns of development" by N. Bayley, *Child Development*, 1956, *27*, 45–74. Reprinted by permission.]

There is a high correspondence between the comparative height of boys at the beginning and at the end of the pubertal growth cycle. Stolz and Stolz (1951) found a correlation of .819 between the height of boys at the onset, and at the end, of the pubertal period. Tanner (1970) also found a similar correlation. Although this is an impressive correlation, it is important to note that 33 per cent of the variance of final adult height results from variations in the size of the adolescent growth spurt. In other words, shifts would occur if the boys were arranged in the order of their height, from the tallest to the shortest at the beginning of the period, and rearranged again in order of height at the end. The fact that boys nonetheless show a very marked tendency to remain tall or short appears from other data in the Stolz study. For example, there were thirteen boys (in one group of eighty-three) who were shorter at the end of the pubertal growth cycle than some of the other boys in the group were at the beginning.

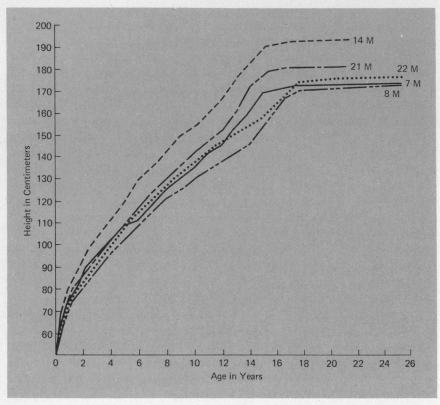

Figure 3.4. Curves of stature by age for five boys in the Berkeley Growth Study, including the tallest male in the group (14M), the shortest, and three boys of intermediate height. [From "Individual patterns of development" by N. Bayley, *Child Development*, 1956, *27*, 45–74. Reprinted by permission.]

The Secular Trend in Physical Growth

There has been a long-term trend over a number of decades toward an increase in height and weight. This has been referred to as the secular trend in physical growth. It has appeared in various populations. Several investigators have reported secular trends in increasing size in Great Britain (see, for example, Weir, 1952). In comparing the height and weight of schoolboys at a secondary school in Sweden with boys' measurements in earlier investigations, Abramson and Ernest (1954) found increases in height and weight. The secular trend in physical growth has also been documented in Canada and Japan (see, for example, Gruenwald et al., 1967; Insull et al., 1968).

Within the United States many investigations dealing with the white population suggest that boys and girls of today are larger than they were years ago (see, for example, Knott and Meredith, 1963). Tanner (1968) has reviewed several investigations dealing with the secular trend in physical growth, paying particular attention to the adolescent. In a review of growth studies of urban North American black youths, Moore (1970) reports that weight and height have increased over the past seventy-eight years. According to Tanner (1960), the secular trend in physical growth is leveling off, particularly within the white population. (Due to bibliographic space limitations, a selection of a single reference or two has been made when a number of studies report similar findings.) Hamill (cited in Schmeck Jr., 1976), chairman of a government group studying American growth trends, reported that the trend of increasing size with each new generation of American children may have ceased or nearly ceased. The group based its conclusions on an analysis of data on 20,000 American children varying in age from infancy through adolescence. It has been suggested that the leveling off may indicate that environmental factors in human growth, such as good nutrition and decreases in infectious diseases of childhood, are making their maximum contribution in the United States. Moreover, it may be that American youngsters have reached their genetic potential regarding growth.

Sex Differences in Height and Weight

During the early years of life boys slightly surpass girls in height and—as a matter of common observation—the average adult male is several inches taller than the average female. However, there is a period in adolescence during which girls are slightly taller than boys of similar age and family background. The average girl for a time also is heavier than the average boy, but then the growth curves cross each other and boys continue to make large gains after the curve for girls has begun to taper off. The adolescent height spurt is greater in boys than girls, and boys are taller than girls at the start of the growth spurt (Tanner, 1970).

Girls become taller and heavier than boys in early adolescence because the growth spurt starts in girls about two years earlier than in boys. However, after their growth spurts, boys surpass girls in height and weight. (See Figure 3.5.)

Ethnic and Social-Class Differences in Physical Growth

To recognize physical differences between groups of people with different genetic pools is not to claim that one group is either inferior or

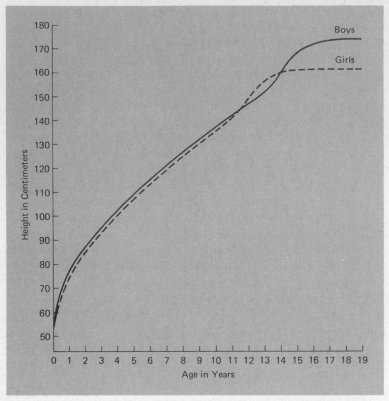

Figure 3.5. Typical-individual height-attained curves for boys and girls (supine length to the age of 2). [From "Standards from birth to maturity for height, weight, height velocity, and weight velocity: British children, 1965" by J. M. Tanner, R. H. Whitehouse, and M. Takaishi, *Archives of the Diseases of Childhood*, 1966, *41*, 451–471; 631–635. Reprinted by permission.]

superior to another. It is, of course, difficult to differentiate between environmental (mainly nutritional) and genetic factors in interpreting such differences.

In a longitudinal study of normal, healthy Philadelphia black and white children, Krogman (1970) obtained physical growth data of each adolescent's head, face, trunk, and limbs. The heights in centimeters of males and females are presented in Figure 3.6.

An examination of Figure 3.6 indicates that, until the age of eleven, black and white boys are similar in height. At this time the white boys accelerate rapidly and continue to be taller than black boys. A different pattern of racial differences emerges for the girls. Until the age of fifteen, black females are taller than white females. At the age of fifteen, white females are similar in height to black females and continue to be so during the rest of their growth in height. It is interesting to note that, between the

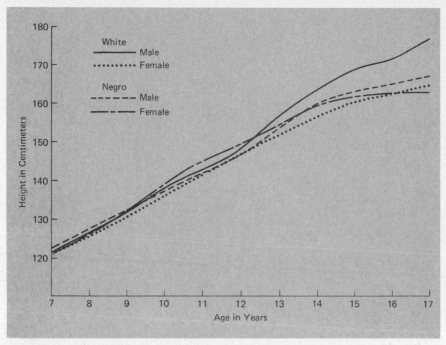

Figure 3.6. Height of Philadelphia children. [From *Growth of head, face, trunk, and limbs in Philadelphia white and Negro children of elementary and high school age* by W. M. Krogman, Monographs of the Society for Research in Child Development, 1970, *35*, No. 136, Copyright 1970 by The Society for Research in Child Development, Inc. Reprinted by permission.]

ages of nine and twelve, black girls are taller than white girls and both black and white boys.

The weights of black and white girls and boys are illustrated in Figure 3.7.

As shown in Figure 3.7, white boys are heavier than black boys. After age twelve the difference between white and black boys increases. Until the age of fifteen, black girls are slightly heavier than white girls. After this age white girls are slightly heavier. Blacks have relatively shorter trunks and longer legs than whites in North America (Moore, 1970).

Social class also has been found to be related to physical development. Upper-class children tend to be larger than those from lower social classes (Tanner, 1962, 1970). Children in families where the fathers had attained higher education were taller than children whose fathers had completed only a few years of schooling, in a sampling studied by Prokopec (1970). Upper-class girls have menarche two to three months earlier than lower-class girls in European countries except Great Britain (Tanner, 1970). It is interesting to note that Czechoslovakian youths from families with only a few children are of higher average stature than children who have many

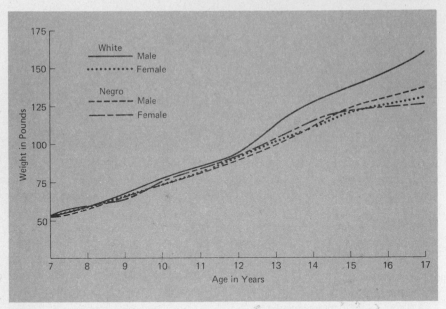

Figure 3.7. Weight of Philadelphia children. [From *Growth of head, face, trunk, and limbs in Philadelphia white and Negro children of elementary and high school age* by W. M. Krogman, Monographs of the Society for Research in Child Development, 1970, *35*, No. 136. Copyright 1970 by The Society for Research in Child Development, Inc. Reprinted by permission.]

siblings (Prokopec, 1970). Causes of social-class differences in physical development are complex and include nutrition, exercise, and general home conditions, which may reflect parental care.

Children whose mothers were Japanese and whose fathers were American whites (J–W) were compared, in a study by Hoshi (1970), with children whose mothers were Japanese and whose fathers were American blacks (J–B). The children, who had entered an institution at an early age, were reared there under similar environmental conditions. In comparing the J–Ws with the J–Bs, ages six to fifteen, Hoshi (1970) found differences in body build that reflect the differences between American whites and American blacks. Many of the differences in body proportion were evident at an early age. These findings imply the dominance of genetic factors in body proportions. With respect to stature and weight, evidence of genetic influence became more pronounced after puberty.

Changes in body proportions

Different parts of the body grow at different rates and achieve their maximum size at different times. At the time of birth, for example, a child's head length constitutes a far longer proportion of his total body length than it will at maturity. At birth his legs are comparatively shorter than they will be at maturity. The trunk is relatively longer at birth than are the thighs and the legs. Similarly, the trunk is relatively longer than the arms. Such differing growth rates illustrate two principles that can be observed in a child's development almost from the time of conception: growth tends to proceed in a *cephalocaudal* direction (from the head toward the tail) and in a *proximodistal* direction (from the main stem to the extremities). At adolescence the dimensions of the body proceed to develop in a fairly regular order. The peak for leg length is reached first, followed by body breadth. The shoulder width reaches its peak last. "Thus, a boy stops growing out of his trousers (at least in length) a year before he stops growing out of his jackets [Tanner, 1970, p. 94]."

Relation of Body Build to Rate of Sexual Maturation

Early maturing boys tend to have broad hips and narrow shoulders, whereas late-maturing boys tend to be characteristically slender-hipped and (comparatively) long-legged (Bayley, 1943). Late-maturing girls tend to have broad shoulders. In other words, the boy who matures early veers toward the body build of girls (who, as a group, mature earlier than boys), whereas the late-maturing girl veers toward the masculine build (broad shoulders). Bayley points out that this does not mean, however, that the early maturing boy is more feminine or the late-maturing girl more masculine in the total trend and direction of their development. However, Mussen and Jones (1957) found that late-maturing boys are late also in establishing heterosexual behavior.

Skeletal growth

X-rays are used to evaluate skeletal maturity, or bone age—the most useful of several possible measures of physiological maturity. The degree to which the bones of a particular area have advanced toward maturity in degree of ossification is referred to as skeletal maturity. Bone shape and the relative positions of bones to one another also play a role in evaluating skeletal maturity.

Bone growth starts as a primary ossification center, which then grows and becomes structured and shaped. Bone growth also occurs at the ends of bones (epiphyseal centers), especially the long bones of the limbs, where epiphyseal growth centers then form. Ossification proceeds from there and eventually the epiphyses fuse with the body of the bone in the mature adult bone. Skeletal maturity is evaluated from the number and development of the growth centers present. There are interesting relationships between the development of the skeleton and other physical developments at the onset of puberty. As a child matures, bone structures that at first were soft and cartilaginous become more osseous, more "bony"—dense, hard, and brittle. Among areas that have been singled out for X-ray pictures in studies of ossification are the wrist, hand, foot, elbow, knee, ankle, hip, and shoulder (Tanner, 1970).

Examinations of bone development provide ratings of what is called skeletal age. The typical six-year-old has a "skeletal age" of six. A child of the same chronological age may have a bone structure that is characteristic of a seven-year-old. His chronological age is six, but his skeletal age is seven. Another six-year-old's bone development may not have gone beyond what is normal at age five. His skeletal age is five.

An assessment of skeletal maturity is made by comparing a given radiograph (X-ray picture) against a set of standards of children who vary in age. The skeletal age then is indicated by the age of the standard that is closest to that of the radiograph. A more recent method assigns skeletal age in terms of the age at which the given score lies at the median or 50th percentile (Hiernaux, 1970).

Skeletal age is closely related to growth in size. According to Bayley (1943): "At a given skeletal age we may say that a child has achieved a given proportion of his eventual adult body dimensions. Consequently, mature size can be predicted with fair accuracy if a child's present size and skeletal age are known [p. 45]." Bone age is more reliable than chronological age as a measure of "biological" age.

Skeletal age similarly gives a better prediction than chronological age of the onset of puberty in girls, as indicated by first menstruation (Schonfeld, 1969). Whereas the range of chronologic age when menarche occurs is approximately ten to sixteen and a half, the range of skeletal age of menarche is smaller—twelve to fourteen and a half. The correlation between menarcheal age and skeletal age is .85 (Tanner, 1970). Dental maturity—that is, the eruption of adult teeth—is also partly related to general skeletal and body maturity. (Children who enter adolescence early also show an early eruption of permanent teeth.) It would appear that those physiological processes that are related to the development of the skeletal system are also related to the events of adolescence. A general consistency in the advancement or retardation of physical maturation has been observed, even though some variability occurs.

Girls are more advanced in skeletal and nervous system development at birth, and they continue to be more advanced during childhood. On the average, the growth spurt in girls occurs at an earlier skeletal age than that of boys (Schonfeld, 1969). The same hormones that are responsible for the spurt in skeletal and muscle dimensions cause a spurt in growth of the limbs and heart. The spurt in these dimensions occurs at approximately the same time.

There also is a positive relationship between skeletal maturity and a variety of other factors, such as strength, motor ability, and body build (Tanner, 1970). The increase in strength at adolescence is a result of the increase in muscle size. Boys are stronger than girls at this time, partially as a result of their larger muscles. Boys also have proportionately larger hearts and lungs, with a slower heart rate. Systolic blood pressure tends to be higher in boys, as does the oxygen-carrying capacity of the blood. Boys are also more able to metabolize the end products of exercise, including lactic acid.

The growth of different tissues and organs

Muscles, bones, kidneys, liver, and spleen all follow the growth curve for height. Reproductive organs grow slowly prior to adolescence but show a great adolescent growth spurt, compared to the "general" growth curve. The central nervous system and the skull grow rapidly in the early years of life, with only a small adolescent growth spurt, if any. There is a slight adolescent spurt for the eye, which probably causes the increase in short-sightedness (myopia) sometimes noted at puberty. Lymphoid tissue (glands and vessels conveying lymph or tissue fluid and producing white blood cells) grows maximally at about the ages of ten to eleven, with its own particular growth curve declining under the influence of sex hormones. (See Figure 3.8.) At adolescence boys lose limb fat, whereas the growth of limb fat in girls stops temporarily; body fat slows in boys but keeps increasing until adulthood in girls.

The head and face continue to grow slowly throughout life, as do the widths of bones in the leg and hand. The vertebral column grows until about age thirty.

Fatty tissues and fat deposits

Several investigators (Cheek, 1968; Hampton et al., 1966) have reported that between 10 and 20 per cent of adolescents are obese. Assessments of "fatness" vary depending on the particular investigator. However, one approach often used is to calculate the weight that normally goes with a given height. More recent methods have been described by Mellits and Cheek (1970) for estimating total body water and body fat.

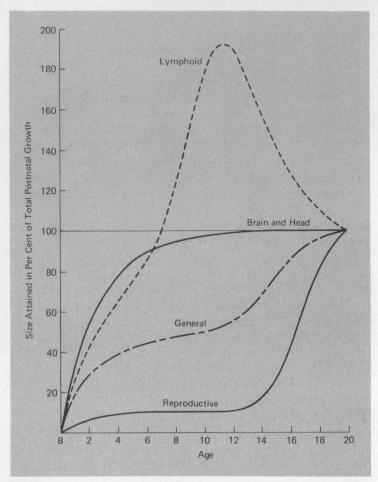

Figure 3.8. Growth curves of different parts and tissues of the body, showing the four chief types. All the curves are of size attained—plotted as per cent of total gain from birth to 20 years—so that size at age 20 is 100 on the vertical scale. *Lymphoid type:* thymus, lymph nodes, intestinal lymph masses. *Brain and head type:* brain and its parts, dura, spinal cord, optic apparatus, cranial dimensions. *General type:* body as a whole, external dimensions (except head) respiratory and digestive organs, kidneys, aortic and pulmonary trunks, musculature, blood volume. *Reproductive type:* testis, ovary, epididymis, prostate, seminal vesicles, Fallopian tubes. [From "Physical growth" by J. M. Tanner. In P. H. Mussen (Ed.) *Carmichael's manual of child psychology*, 1. New York: Wiley, 1970. Reproduced by permission from Tanner, *Growth of Adolescence*, Oxford, Blackwell, 1962.]

Obesity in children can then be evaluated in terms of its deviation from the expected norm. The balance between energy input (nutrition) and output (including physical activity) modifies the trends in the development of body fat (Pařízková, 1970).

For a time during adolescence boys and girls differ considerably in the development of adipose (fat-bearing) tissue. With increased height females show a more marked growth of fat than males. A study by Reynolds (1951) offers interesting information on this subject. Reynolds obtained repeated X-ray measurements of the thickness of fat layers in various areas of the bodies of boys and girls during a twelve-year period beginning when the children were six and a half years old. During a period prior to, and including, the middle teens (12.5 to 15.5 years) boys showed a drop, whereas girls showed a continuing gain in cumulative volume of fat in six areas of the body. In the period from 15.5 to 17.5 years, boys showed a gain, and girls a loss, in these same areas. But girls maintained a considerably higher ratio of fat into the late teens (using averages at 6.5 years as a standard of 100, the total breadth of fat layers in six areas of the body rose to 136 in boys and 162 in girls at the age of 17.5 years).[1]

The differences between boys and girls when at their peak rate of growth are especially marked in some areas of the body: where the upper thigh has its largest girth and on the chest at the nipple level. Beyond the middle teens the differences become less marked, although the average mature girl has a larger proportion of fat than the average mature boy (Tanner, 1970).

Girls show this "rounding of the figure" more than boys, but many boys for a time have increased deposits of fat in various areas of their bodies. In some boys not only is there a transient swelling of the breasts, but there may be a slight secretion (Greulich et al., 1938). Enlarged breasts, if noticeable, may be embarrassing to boys (Schonfeld, 1962). If they are so large that they bob up and down when a boy walks or runs they are acutely embarrassing. Wattenberg (1955) gives a poignant example of a boy with this difficulty; the boy was jeered by his schoolmates and was so mortified that he had himself excused from physical education classes.

A large proportion of boys have, for a time, what Stolz and Stolz (1951) have called male-inappropriate fat deposits in the breasts, thighs, and lower part of the trunk. They estimate that for a time at least 50 per cent of boys show an increase in girdle fat. Temporary fat deposits in the genital area, which make a boy's penis seem shorter than it actually is, are likely to contribute to a boy's feeling of inadequacy about his manliness.

The amount and distribution of fat in an adolescent's body are complicated from both a physical and a psychological point of view. An

[1] The correlations between total fat breadth and total weight were as follows at 11.5 and 15.5 years:

Age Level	Boys	Girls
11.5	.74	.71
15.5	.69	.91

obvious cause of being fat is eating too much fat-producing food. But there is not a one-to-one relationship between food intake and fatness. Some people "eat like a horse" and stay slim, others get fat. Moreover, a person cannot control where he will bulge the most just by eating more or less food. Some people get fat all over. Some lay on fat in the midriff, others in the thighs. Some have an "underslung" build and others an "overslung" build. Some are slim but have fat legs. It should be noted that the characteristic inactivity of many adolescents probably plays a role in their being overweight (Herald, 1960).

Differences in contours appear among people whether they eat a lot or a little. These are probably due to genetic factors. Because of this, an adolescent who tries to control his or her weight faces a complicated problem. When a girl who has fat thighs but is slim elsewhere goes on a diet, she may impair, rather than improve, her general appearance—while she is reducing her thigh girth her face may develop a thin and drawn look.

There is a further complication because the size of a particular part of the body that seems "fat" may be due not to fat but to the size of other tissues. This is brought out in the study by Reynolds (1951). The body contours are determined to varying degrees by fat, muscle, bone, and the shape of the skeleton; and adolescents vary in the proportions of total body weight consisting of fat, muscle, and bone. Due to differences in bone structure, a girl who looks very "hippy" may actually have a thinner layer of fat than another girl who has a narrower bone structure and looks slimmer. As a result of varying proportions of muscle, fat, and bone tissue, standard height-weight tables can be very misleading when applied to a given individual. "There are fat 'underweight' children and lean 'overweight' children [Garn, 1960, p. 31]."

Psychological Implications of Obesity

Obesity (body size that is enlarged as a result of an excessive accumulation of fat tissue) has many psychological as well as biochemical facets. In our culture, and in many others, slimness is admired and obesity is deplored. The idea that a roly-poly person is jovial and serene is probably more a fiction and pretense than a fact. Someone expressed this view by saying, "Imprisoned in every fat person a thin one is signaling wildly to be let out."

In our culture, obese adolescents may have difficulty in establishing social relations because of derogatory cultural attitudes concerning being overweight. Rightly or wrongly, the fat person is likely to blame himself for being the way he is—he eats too much; he should control his diet. Then, when he keeps on devouring food and remains as fat as ever, he is likely to have feelings of guilt and self-contempt.[2] There is nothing jovial about that.

The remedy does not seem to be simply to prescribe a rigid diet or reducing pills, which may be dangerous. The propensity for overeating may have profound psychological roots that no simple prescription will remove. Overeating has many psychological meanings in which food is used for non-nutritional reasons. Some people apparently overeat to allay anxiety. For some girls obesity is a kind of protection. While deploring their unattractiveness they also may use this unattractiveness as a means of shielding themselves from men and sex and the responsibilities of adult womanhood. Some apparently overeat as a way of grasping all they can get. Some seem to be resigned to the idea that the only gratification life can offer them is the pleasure of eating. Eating may also be a means of disguising and discharging hidden rage.

When these influences prevail, a young person is not simply facing the transient problem of a temporary increase in fat deposits during adolescence, but a more basic personality problem. A condition of obesity that is linked with self-contempt is rooted in compulsions that perpetuate the self-contempt. Instead of being the butt of jests and jokes, such a person needs understanding and help.[3]

Our present-day society, with its emphasis on thinness and beauty, also may encourage many adolescents to attempt to be thinner than their optimal weight (Bruch, 1969).

Heredity and adolescence

The course and outcomes of an adolescent's development are determined by an interaction between the genetic endowment and the nurturing and experiences provided by the environment. Beginning life as a single cell one possessed the biochemical substances, known as genes, that are the basis of heredity. These genes play a crucial role in determining the nature and course of one's development. Interaction between a person's genetic endowment and the environment begins at the moment of conception. An individual's nature requires nurturing from the beginning, in the womb.

[2] According to Garn (1960) there are six chances out of ten that the fat adolescent "will eat a broad path directly into fat adulthood [p. 27]."

[3] The plight of the excessively fat person from a psychological point of view has been discussed in a revealing way by Bruch (1940, 1969) who has been investigating this problem for many years. She describes life situations and emotional experiences that provoke an increased desire for food, thus leading to obesity. She (1940) notes that unfortunate experiences may lead genetically predisposed persons to face their problems by overeating.

Although heredity has a vital bearing on each person's life, it has been far more often ignored than emphasized in studies of adolescents. One reason perhaps is that investigators regard a person's genetic endowment as something belonging to the past, about which not much can be done. Another reason is that the influences of genetic and environmental factors are so intertwined, notably in the psychological sphere, that it is difficult to disentangle them. The fact that it is difficult to trace the influence of heredity helps to explain, but obviously does not justify, the widespread policy of ignoring genetic factors.

Genotypes and Phenotypes

In addition to all that shows forth in their appearance and conduct, adolescents have latent genetic potentialities. Some of these may become apparent at a later time. Some never become apparent but can be transmitted to their children. The term *phenotype* denotes all that shows, all that is manifest, in an individual's make-up. The term *genotype* denotes the person's total genetic endowment, both manifest and latent.

A person's phenotype represents the outcome, in each particular case, of the action of the genes, their interaction with each other, and their interaction with the environment. Some aspects of the phenotype are unchanging, others are fluid, modifiable, and compounded by many forces. At a given time a person's phenotype may include long legs, because genes that produce long legs were inherited; a body that is thin because of not eating enough; and a sour disposition due to having just failed to get something one wanted. One's genotype is usually more stable and permanent.

The genetic factors that can produce a discrepancy between an adolescent's phenotype and genotype are complex and intricate. To describe them would fill a whole book, but we will touch briefly on some of them.

The genes that generate hereditary characteristics may be *dominant* or *recessive*. Dominant genes usually prevail over the recessive ones, but the recessive ones are not lost. Their effects may appear in a later combination. Among the genes that determine eye color, for example, the brown determiners are usually dominant over those genes that might produce blue. Accordingly, when the father has a pure strain of brown and the mother a pure strain of blue, the child probably will have brown eyes. But this child will have the genes for blue eyes in his or her germ plasm. Now if this person mates with another of similar hereditary background, several combinations are possible in *their* offspring. The child might inherit brown elements from both parents. Then the resulting phenotype and genotype will be brown. Or the child might inherit only brown from one parent and blue from the other.

Then the resulting phenotype will be brown, but the genotype will contain both brown and blue. Or the child might inherit elements of blue from both parents. Then the phenotype and genotype both will be blue.

In connection with many other traits, there similarly may be an exact, or a close, correspondence or a discrepancy between the genotype and the phenotype.

The concordance or discrepancy between phenotype and genotype is influenced by many factors. Many characteristics are determined by multiple genes. In the case of height, for example, the ramifications are quite complicated, for an individual's total height is influenced by sets of genes that determine the length of the legs, thighs, trunk, neck, and head. Through various chance combinations of these genes it is possible for parents and their children, and for brothers or sisters, to have exactly the same height or to differ considerably.

The element of chance is diminished somewhat by the fact that height is influenced to some degree by "selective breeding." A child with a tall mother is more likely than not to have a father who also is tall, because tall women generally prefer mates as tall as themselves.

Such selective mating during several generations would tend to produce "pure" strains of tallness and shortness and a close correspondence between phenotypes and genotypes. But other conditions that produce diversity are at work, including the fact that persons of all statures are not completely averse to choosing mates who are shorter or taller than themselves.

A diversity between the genotype and the phenotype can be serious if a person has a phenotype that is "normal" and healthy but a genotype that includes hereditary weaknesses.

Genes differ not only in dominance and recessiveness, and in their interaction with one another, but also in their degree of dominance and recessiveness. There are some genes, or sets of genes, that almost invariably dominate and others that do not.

Among the special conditions that genes produce with varying degrees of dominance and recessiveness are certain allergies, certain blood types and blood deficiencies, many conditions connected with the hair (such as patterns of baldness), susceptibility to certain forms of mental illness, predisposition to rheumatic fever, and several kinds of mental retardation.

The inheritance of sex-chromosome abnormalities leading to personality disturbance is a controversial area in genetics now. Males have an X and a Y sex chromosome, whereas females have two X chromosomes. There are several types of sex-chromosome disturbances. An XYY sex-chromosome abnormality has been linked to violent and criminal behavior in tall men (Hook and Kim, 1971). This finding is not accepted by many workers, and it is feared that XYY children who are labeled as prone to violence may, in a self-fulfilling prophecy, be treated as violent and become violent because of the expectations of others.

The Biochemical Basis of Heredity

In the last two decades much has been discovered about how information is transmitted by the genes from one cell to the next so that each can build the protein molecules necessary for life. A detailed account of the biochemistry of genetics may be found in such modern works as *Human Genetics* by McKusick (1969).

There are some twenty types of amino acids that make up protein molecules, arranged in each molecule in a chain of from 100 to 500 amino acid units, in a specific arrangement for each protein molecule. Each protein molecule is manufactured by the cell based on the genetic instructions located in the cell's *deoxyribonucleic acid* (DNA), which consists of two strands of DNA arranged in a double helix. DNA and *ribonucleic acid* (RNA) take part in complex operations inside the cell to ensure the proper production of proteins in the cell from one generation to the next. Protein synthesis itself occurs in the cell's cytoplasm. A description of these operations can be found in the specialized literature dealing with intracellular metabolism and physiology. During cell division, each of the two strands of DNA is replicated, so that each daughter cell has the full genetic information of the parent cell.

It is possible that expanding our recently acquired knowledge of the biochemical aspects of genetics will result in laboratory-controlled protein synthesis. Whether such control can benefit mankind remains to be seen. Furthermore, this type of research and its possible future use in the control of protein synthesis in man raise profound moral and ethical questions. Certain other dangers are involved in doing this type of research: for example, working with particularly virulent or possibly cancer-producing microorganisms requires extremely careful techniques.

Interactions Between Genetic and Environmental Factors Prior to Adolescence

Many lines of evidence support the dictum that "The child is the father of the man." When we ask how this fatherhood comes about, we face the fact that each adolescent's personality emerges from the interaction of heredity and environment. In this interaction there is a threefold influence: first, the environment can enhance or impair development; second, inher-

Like parent, like child—through the interaction of heredity and environment. [Bruce Davidson/Magnum.]

ited qualities influence one's response to the environment; and third, inborn tendencies influence the way others respond to us.[4]

From the time of birth babies show distinct marks of individuality: differences in the way they react to stimuli as well as differences in the way they cope with stress (Ribble, 1943). During their first few days they show characteristic differences in the intensity and tempo of their responses to stimulation (Barten et al., 1971). A genetic component in activity level has been reported by Willerman (1973) in his study of same-sexed twins.

Twins may be *monozygotic* (identical or one-egg), derived from the same fertilized egg cell, or *dizygotic*, derived from two separate fertilized eggs. Monozygotic twins are always of the same sex and usually look so much alike as children that a casual observer cannot tell them apart. They have the same set of genes. Dizygotic twins are, genetically, no more alike than siblings of unlike age. They may be of the same or opposite sex.

Congenital characteristics (reaction tendencies appearing at birth or shortly thereafter) have been studied by Thomas et al. (1963). Longitudinal

[4] Controversy has surrounded studies of the relationship between heredity and intelligence. These reports will be discussed in Chapter 7.

studies of children beginning in infancy and some other studies will be discussed in later chapters.

In early infancy, and frequently during the first days of life before leaving the maternity hospital, children show individual differences in temperamental qualities and reaction patterns. These temperamental qualities may be so distinctive and persistent that they seem to be due to genetic factors. Actually, it is difficult to tell whether they are mainly hereditary or due to environmental factors. As described by Shirley (1933), each baby is born with a "tough core" of temperamental qualities.[5]

Whatever their origin might be, a child's temperamental qualities are not only manifested in response to the environment, but they also shape the environment. Bell (1968) describes the role the child plays in influencing the behavior of each parent. The mutual shaping of parent and child responses has been noted also in a study by Osofsky and O'Connell (1972). We see such an influence when a baby who is actively responsive elicits a smile from others (who thus reinforce the child's seeming good cheer), whereas a fretful and fussy baby elicits concern and perhaps even anxiety in the mother (who thus may reinforce the child's fretfulness).

By the time youngsters reach adolescence, their original tendencies may become so overlaid with the outcomes of their interaction with the environment that it becomes very difficult for one who does not know their family background, and has not studied them since infancy, to surmise what these original tendencies might have been.

Interaction Between Genetic and Environmental Factors During Adolescence

Many facets of the adolescent's heredity do not appear until adolescent years. Genetic factors influence an adolescent's physical development (for example, the rate of skeletal development, the onset of the menarche, the profusion of body hair, the timing and pattern of the "growth spurt," height, physique, the distribution of fatty tissue).[6] These physical changes influence the adolescent's self-perception and the way others react to that adolescent.

HEREDITY AND HEIGHT

Tables 3.2 and 3.3 show findings obtained in comparisons between the heights of parents and children. Table 3.2 is based on repeated measurements of the same children over a period of many years by Bayley

[5] For studies dealing with this, see Shirley (1933), Thomas et al. (1963), and Willerman (1973).
[6] Numerous studies dealing with genetic factors in physical development have been reviewed by Davenport (1923) and by Tanner (1970).

Table 3.2. Correlation between mid-parent heights and heights of their children

Age	Boys		Girls	
	Number	Correlation	Number	Correlation
6 months	32	.35	29	.61
2 years	27	.36	23	.66
10 years	24	.60	24	.59
18 years	21	.58	17	.76
	(father-sons)	.52	(father-daughters)	.64
	(mother-sons)	.44	(mother-daughters)	.52

Source: From "Some increasing parent-child similarities during the growth of children" by Nancy Bayley, *Journal of Educational Psychology*, 1954, **45**, 1–21. Reprinted by permission.

(1954). "Mid-parent" height was computed by a formula that expressed, in one measure, the heights of both parents. In a study of Czechoslovakian children seven to eighteen years of age, Prokopec (1970) reported that the difference in the average height between children whose parents were tall and those whose parents were short was approximately nine centimeters.

Table 3.3, from a study by Eichorn (1959), offers a kind of information that is very rare in developmental psychology, and it is included even though it deals with young children and adults rather than adolescents. The parents in her study had been measured repeatedly from the time they were children until they were adults, and their children were measured repeatedly in infancy and during a five-year period.

The findings by Bayley and Eichorn indicate the importance of heredity as a factor in determining height. Bayley's study showed that the resemblances between parents and children in relative height are likely to be larger at the time the youngsters reach childhood and adolescence than at the time of infancy. Garn (1966) also reported that mother-daughter correlations in height are greater than mother-son correlations in height up to puberty.

Table 3.3. Two-generation similarities in height during the first five years

Age (in months)	No.	Correlation: children and parents as children	Correlation: children and parents as adults	Correlation: parents as children and as adults
3–8	30	.18	.29	.61
9–14	29	.19	.12	.66
15–20	17	.52	.49	.69
21–30	24	.31	.40	.65
31–42	27	.27	.40	.66
43–53	18	.22	.39	.68
55–66	18	.67	.67	.83

Source: From "Two-generation similarities in weight, height and weight/height during the first five years" by Dorothy H. Eichorn. Reported at Twenty-fifth Anniversary Meeting, Society for Research in Child Development, National Institutes of Health, Bethesda, Md., March 10, 1959. Reprinted by permission.

OTHER MANIFESTATIONS OF HEREDITY

More directly, in the psychological sphere, there is evidence that certain forms of mental illness, which are not, in many cases, clearly manifested until a person begins to undergo the stresses of adolescent or adult life, may be influenced by heredity,[7] although some authors who espouse a strong environmental point of view have disputed this conclusion.

As we will note in Chapter 7, there are also certain intellectual attributes that more clearly show the influence of genetic factors when youngsters reach adolescence than was true in earlier years.

The Importance of Taking Account of an Adolescent's Heredity

There are several reasons why it is essential to consider the influence of heredity in adolescent development. Although we cannot change the seeds from which adolescents sprang, much can be done to help them to maximize their potentialities. Much can also be done to help young people—and their parents and teachers—acquire a realistic attitude toward inherited resources and limitations.

It is far more humane to have wholesome respect for heredity than to pretend it does not exist. Such respect can help to spare adolescents from blaming themselves, or being blamed by others, for conditions over which they have little or no control—such as maturing early or late, physique, or height. A proper regard for heredity may also help to relieve adolescents with inborn physical handicaps from the severe self-reproach some of them visit upon themselves.[8]

Today there undoubtedly are many afflictions, including afflictions in the sphere of personality development for which people blame themselves and are blamed by others, that eventually may be found to be rooted in the inherited biochemical make-up of those who suffer. Therefore, it is important to recognize the role an adolescent's genetic endowment might have played and continues to play in determining what one is able to take from the

[7] A predisposition to the psychological illness diagnosed as schizophrenia, for example, which often is not clearly manifest until the teens or later, appears to be influenced by genetic factors. When one member of a twin pair is afflicted, the chances are many times greater that the other also will be afflicted if the twins are identical—uniovular, or sharing the same genetic substance—than if the twins are nonidentical—springing from two separate fertilized eggs (Kallman, 1953). The greater likelihood that identical twins will be afflicted similarly prevails even if the identical twins have been separated and have lived in different environments. See also Gottesman (1962). Manic-depressive psychosis may also have a genetic factor in its etiology.

[8] Youngsters suffering from physical disabilities or ailments, whether due to genetic weaknesses or unavoidable misfortunes, frequently blame themselves for their afflictions (Gips, 1956).

environment and what one is able to bring to it. It is essential also to have a deep respect for what the environment can do to further or to impair the adolescent's welfare. Such respect is far more realistic and compassionate than an extreme environmentalist or an extreme hereditarian point of view. It helps to ward off heartless judgments, such as "This person sprang from 'bad seed' and is beyond hope of repair," or "This person is mentally ill because of being reared by a 'schizogenic' mother."

The Significance of Knowledge of Genetics for Adolescents

Some adolescents are interested in genetics for a personal reason: They can relate some of the information to themselves and can weigh its meaning when they are looking for a prospective mate. The interplay between genetics and environmental factors is so intricate that no adolescent can foresee what a merger between his or her genes and those of another might bring forth. However, information about genetics may be helpful in assessing obvious signs of genetically influenced strengths or weaknesses.

The body image and self-evaluation

Traditional beliefs about body build date back to Aristotle, who stated that body build and facial features are related to personality functioning. These beliefs are exemplified in Shakespeare's portrayal of Cassius as expressed by Caesar:

> Let me have men about me that are fat;
> Sleek-headed men, and such as sleep o'nights:
> Yond Cassius has a lean and hungry look;
> He thinks too much: such men are dangerous.

The influence of body build on personality and behavioral development is likely to operate indirectly by way of positive or negative attitudes individuals may have regarding their bodies, the perception they have of themselves, and the manner in which they think they are perceived by others. Physical attractiveness is valued both by males and females and may indirectly have an influence on personality development.

The body image as described by Schilder (1935) is the "picture of our own body which we form in our mind [p. 11]." The idea of body image has been further elaborated on and differentiated by Kolb (1959). This image plays an important role in a person's evaluation of himself, whether the image is sketchy or comprehensive, and whether it comes close to being a mirror image or is a distorted picture.[9]

From early childhood an adolescent is often reminded by others of the significance of size, physical appearance, and physical ability. According to Staffieri (1967): A person's body configuration has an influence on social interactions, and the effects of these interactions on a person's self-concept play an important role in the total process of personality development. Thus, those individuals who deviate from their peers by being smaller or fatter may feel inferior. This may result in their being either shy or troublesome in an effort to avoid notice or to gain attention. The image adolescents have of themselves is likely to be influenced by the way they are appraised by their peers. Ruff (1951) has pointed out that to be acceptable to one's peer group during adolescence one must not differ too much from others in physical appearance. If youngsters differ considerably they are likely to be avoided by others or to receive derogatory nicknames (Orgel and Tuckman, 1935). Some other nicknames that call attention to a boy's masculinity may be a source of pride. Most nicknames are likely to make adolescents keenly aware of the attitudes others have regarding their physical appearance.

Several investigators (see, for example, Kleck et al., 1974; Walster et al., 1966) have reported a positive relationship between physical attractiveness and the degree to which one is liked by others. Adolescents also prefer to date individuals whose appearance is considered to be attractive. Moreover, socially desirable personality traits are more often attributed to the physically attractive than the physically unattractive (Dion et al., 1972). However, it may be that physical attractiveness is only significant at the onset of a relationship between two people and that its role decreases with the duration of the relationship. Nevertheless, Kleck et al. (1974), in a study of boys 9 to 14 years of age, found attractive physical appearance to be related to sociometric status, which was measured after intense social interaction during a period of several weeks at a camp. Sociometric status refers to peer acceptance as shown by who chooses whom and who is most and least chosen in a group of peers.

When adolescents respond positively or negatively to those regarded as physically attractive or unattractive, it is possible that they are reacting to the behavior associated with high or low attractiveness rather than attractiveness *per se*.

The evaluations individuals give of their body (hair, body build, skin, and so on) are more likely to resemble, than to differ from, their

[9] There are many features of a person's physical make-up of which he or she is consciously aware, but there also are many that are not clearly recognized or that have special meanings for reasons one does not apprehend. The elements in a person's physical being that influence behavior and attitudes, but of which one is not consciously aware, have sometimes been called the unconscious body image.

feelings concerning other aspects of themselves such as morals, first name, popularity, life goals, and moods (Secord and Jourard, 1953).

Among a selected group of adolescents who stated they cared "very much" about whether they were good-looking, only 13 per cent of twelve- to fourteen-year-olds and 6 per cent of fifteen-year-olds or older adolescents rated themselves very favorably on this quality.

Some of the features young people report as having favorable or unfavorable effects on their self-esteem are shown in Table 3.4. This table shows the percentages[10] of youngsters from the fourth grade through college who, when asked to write compositions on the subjects "What I Like About Myself" and "What I Dislike About Myself" mentioned physical characteristics. Among the characteristics named most frequently were size, weight, and features of the face and head. At all grade levels from the sixth through the twelfth, the number of girls who complained about their physical characteristics was larger than the number who spoke favorably about such characteristics.

Those parts of the face that adolescents refer to as important include the following: hair, 53 per cent; eyes and teeth, 47 per cent; mouth, 40 per cent; lips, 26 per cent; and ears, 20 per cent (Kleck et al., 1974).

In a growth study conducted at the Institute of Child Welfare at the University of California it was found that of 93 boys, at least 29 were definitely disturbed by their physical characteristics at one time or another during an eight-year period (Stolz and Stolz, 1944). Five of the youngsters apparently faced a major problem of adjustment because of difficulty in accepting their physical characteristics. In a group of eighty-three girls, there were thirty-eight who gave evidence of being disturbed by their physical characteristics. The investigators regard this as a minimum accounting, for some of the young people might have been disturbed without bringing it to the attention of the physician who was in charge of the physical measurements.

Adolescents regard their appearance in complicated ways. We might expect that a girl would be pleased to be pretty and that a boy would be glad to see himself as handsome. However, one impressive quality in some young people, when one gets beyond a surface acquaintanceship with them, is that they can be disturbed by their good looks. The extremely pretty girl faces certain hazards and problems her plainer looking sister does not. Others may try to exploit her or to gain prestige by being associated with her. She may become the object of competition for favor that is not founded on appreciation of her personality but rather on appreciation of the glamor of her looks. The pretty girl may also from an early age become a means of satisfying parental ambition by being "shown off." She will notice also that

[10] The percentages probably would be much higher if the young people had been asked specifically to name physical characteristics instead of being questioned in general terms.

Table 3.4. Percentage of boys and girls at various grade levels from the fourth grade through college who mentioned certain physical characteristics when writing compositions on the subject of what they liked and disliked about themselves

"What I Like About Myself"

Category	Elementary grades						Junior high school						High school						College			
	IV		V		VI		VII		VIII		IX		X		XI		XII		Fresh-Soph.		Jr.-Sr.	
	B	G	B	G	B	G	B	G	B	G	B	G	B	G	B	G	B	G	B	G	B	G
	N220	206	147	142	171	172	96	77	134	151	170	204	151	157	112	124	137	122	50	50	50	50
I. Physical characteristics	15	19	22	30	12	30	14	13	29	42	23	35	25	37	17	19	15	20	40	28	20	38
A. General appearance	3	5	3	3	2	4	7	3	5	5	3	4	10	8	13	6	11	6	36	18	18	38
B. Size, weight	1	1	2	3	5	5	1	1	8	7	6	11	6	13	6	2	3	4	0	0	0	0
C. Body build	0	1	0	1	1	2	1	0	4	1	5	2	3	4	5	4	2	2	6	10	4	4
D. Features of face and head	10	14	14	25	8	23	6	13	13	35	11	25	9	26	4	12	4	14	2	6	4	4
E. Upper extremities	1	3	3	6	1	1	0	0	1	3	1	1	2	2	0	2	0	0	0	4	2	0
F. Lower extremities	2	2	2	1	1	1	1	0	1	3	2	3	3	5	2	2	0	1	0	2	0	0
II. Clothing and grooming	16	27	12	26	12	28	14	12	13	25	13	23	17	11	10	15	9	6	10	34	24	20
A. Clothes	13	22	5	15	8	19	11	8	7	17	6	11	13	6	5	10	5	4	6	32	20	20
B. Grooming	5	5	8	11	2	8	5	4	4	8	3	9	3	4	4	4	7	2	4	4	8	4
C. Make-up, hairdo, haircut	5	6	1	3	4	5	2	1	3	5	4	4	4	3	1	2	1	0	0	0	0	0
III. Health and physical soundness	6	2	8	8	7	5	8	0	8	5	4	3	5	5	8	2	4	2	4	0	6	0

"What I Dislike About Myself"

Category	Elementary grades						Junior high school						High school						College			
	IV		V		VI		VII		VIII		IX		X		XI		XII		Fresh.-Soph.		Jr.-Sr.	
	B	G	B	G	B	G	B	G	B	G	B	G	B	G	B	G	B	G	B	G	B	G
	N220	205	147	142	171	172	96	77	134	151	170	204	151	157	112	124	137	122	50	50	50	50
I. Physical characteristics	11	16	17	30	17	41	17	26	24	48	32	53	27	44	13	32	10	30	12	20	8	12
A. General appearance	0	2	1	2	2	1	5	5	2	7	7	5	3	8	3	6	6	11	6	6	0	6
B. Size, weight	4	2	2	4	5	10	8	9	10	15	19	17	11	18	8	12	5	8	2	12	4	4
C. Body build	0	0	0	3	2	3	0	1	2	7	2	13	4	5	1	6	1	4	4	2	0	0
D. Features of face and head	6	11	10	20	6	20	4	12	8	26	12	35	13	24	4	11	3	11	2	4	4	8
E. Upper extremities	2	3	3	6	1	7	0	1	1	3	2	7	3	8	0	1	1	1	0	0	0	0
F. Lower extremities	0	0	0	4	1	6	0	1	2	5	4	8	3	9	2	1	2	3	0	2	0	0
II. Clothing and grooming	4	10	7	5	4	9	2	8	4	7	3	10	1	3	3	3	4	2	0	0	2	2
A. Clothes	2	5	1	2	1	3	2	3	1	3	1	5	1	1	2	2	1	1	0	0	2	2
B. Grooming	0	0	4	2	1	0	0	0	1	1	1	0	0	1	1	0	1	0	0	0	2	0
C. Make-up, hairdo, haircut	1	7	2	1	2	6	0	5	3	5	2	5	0	1	1	2	1	1	0	0	0	0
III. Health and physical soundness	2	3	3	4	5	4	4	1	4	1	6	2	3	3	0	6	1	2	6	2	0	2

Source: From In search of self by A. T. Jersild, Bureau of Publications, Teachers College, Columbia University, 1952. Other categories pertaining to mental and emotional characteristics, personality traits, etc., are included in the complete table but are not reproduced here. Reprinted by permission.

at times she gets special favors (such as special consideration from male instructors and traffic cops), and she may feel uneasy about this or even a little guilty. Nevertheless, in spite of such complications, most girls would probably prefer to be pretty.

Hazards such as these are perhaps not as prominent among boys, but boys too build on precarious ground if their appraisals of their own worth rest to an important degree on the effects of their good looks on others.

Interplay of Psychological and Physical Factors in Personal Appearance

Just as an adolescent's physical development has a psychological effect on attitudes regarding the self and on the attitudes others have toward him or her, psychological attitudes can have an influence on a person's physical appearance. In everyday speech we note that a person has a "hang-dog look" or looks "cranky," "harassed," "worried," "gay," "happy," "twinkling," and so on.

The relationship between attitude and physical appearance is apparent when a person clearly is trying to falsify his or her appearance, as happens when a girl's dyed hair or false eyelashes give her an artificial look. Even though many females are successful in camouflaging their appearance, they are probably still aware of the discrepancy between what they are and their ideal body image. Such a discrepancy may prevail in those who try to enhance their appearance, but it also exists for those who are sloppy in appearance. It happens also in more subtle ways when, for example, tightly set lips, tightly braided hair, and a prim facial expression go with a stiff manner of acting and talking. We see it again when a girl, seemingly unable to accept her own femaleness, selects styles that are most likely to cover her body from view, such as high-necked blouses or loosely cut clothes that conceal the shapeliness of her body.

The attention adolescent girls give to their appearance, including clothes and cosmetics, is related to other personal characteristics (Silverman, 1945). While girls in the age range from twelve to eighteen show a strong tendency to conform to prevailing fashions and to dress alike, there are many individual differences. The motivations most commonly underlying girls' efforts to look well include a desire for approval, a desire for the internal satisfaction of feeling well-groomed, and a wish for sexual attractiveness. Silverman states that concern about appearance is purposive and is rooted in a girl's past history. Girls who were rated as giving much attention to appearance seemed to have a higher estimate of themselves than girls who were rated low in appearance. Financial considerations do not seem to be of primary importance in influencing clothing and grooming practices, except that wealthier girls are better able to afford luxury items, such as Gucci shoes and fur-trimmed coats.

In their dress and grooming, adolescent girls are usually quite style conscious and try to conform to the fashions of the day. However, within this framework, they often try to modify current styles according to their own tastes and ideas of what is most becoming. Through varying her dress, hairdo, and make-up, a girl expresses her individuality and experiments to discover effects that in her judgment are most fitting.

Some girls not only adopt current fashions, but exaggerate them. This, at times, creates conflict between a girl and her elders. At a time when hemlines are rising and necklines are falling, parents and school officials may feel they should interfere. Although a girl may need to be advised, it is important for her own development to have freedom of choice within the limits of propriety.

Adolescent boys, too, are style conscious, although usually they are less likely than girls to admit it. Many boys go through a phase when it is stylish to have no style. The boy scorns a nice suit and even a decent shirt. He cherishes old pants his mother would gladly burn. If none such are around he abuses a good pair of pants until they are battered to a fine point of fashion. But times change. Soon the boy who once looked like he owned only one pair of jeans will deck himself in the best clothes he can get.[11]

Discrepancy Between Self-image, Photo Image, and Judgment of Appearance by Others

One may view oneself as being far less physically attractive than others see one without being aware of what has led to this view. Sometimes there is a considerable discrepancy between a person's self-image and a photographic image. It is a revelation for some people to observe a TV view or a home movie of their appearance, posture, gestures, and facial expressions. Some people have trouble reconciling themselves to the appearance they make on the screen even after several viewings.

Discrepancies also appear in connection with still pictures. Some adolescents and adults never seem able to get a photograph of themselves that is "just right." One of the writers once questioned a group of students who had just received copies of pictures that would appear in their high school yearbook. Some thought the likenesses were fine; others did not. One good-looking boy pointed to a picture that was an exceptionally good

[11] Psychological repercussions of early and late maturing and of physical characteristics associated with sexual development and motor development are discussed in Chapters 4 and 5.

likeness, except in his own eyes, and said: "I don't look that good—just see for yourself. It doesn't show my freckles." Apparently the thing he had noticed most about his image in a mirror was his freckles. To him they were unbecoming and blurred his eyes to the handsome features of his face. A girl who disapproved very much of her picture pointed to it and said: "I don't look like that!" But at that instant her face showed an unbecoming expression of annoyance and distaste—almost the exact duplicate of what the camera had caught. When looking at herself in the mirror, she apparently had not duplicated this sour expression.

References

Abramson, E., & Ernest, E. Height and weight of schoolboys at a Stockholm secondary school, 1950, and a comparison with some earlier investigations. *Acta Paediatrica*, 1954, **43**, 235–246.

Barten, S., Birns, B., & Ronch, J. Individual differences in the visual pursuit behavior of neonates. *Child Development*, 1971, **42**, 313–319.

Bayley, N. Body build in adolescents studied in relation to rates of anatomical maturing with implications for social adjustment. *Psychological Bulletin*, 1941, **38**, 378. (Abstract)

Bayley, N. Skeletal maturing in adolescence as a basis for determining percentage of completed growth. *Child Development*, 1943, **14**, 1–46.

Bayley, N. Some increasing parent-child similarities during the growth of children. *Journal of Educational Psychology*, 1954, **45**, 1–21.

Bayley, N. Individual patterns of development. *Child Development*, 1956, **27**, 45–74.

Bell, R. Q. A reinterpretation of the direction of effects in studies of socialization. *Psychological Review*, 1968, **75**, 81–95.

Bruch, H. Obesity in childhood. III. Physiologic and psychologic aspects of the food intake of obese children. *Americal Journal of Disturbed Children*, 1940, **59**, 739.

Bruch, H. Obesity in adolescence. In G. Caplan & S. Lebovici (Eds.), *Adolescence: Psychosocial perspectives.* New York: Basic Books, 1969.

Cheek, D. B. *Human growth: Body composition, cell growth, energy, and intelligence.* Philadelphia: Lea and Febiger, 1968.

Davenport, C. B. *Body-build and its inheritance.* Washington, D.C.: Carnegie Institution, 1923.

Dion, K., Berscheid, E., & Walster, E. What is beautiful is good. *Journal of Personality and Social Psychology*, 1972, **24**, 285–290.

Donovan, B. T., & van der Werff Ten Bosch, J. J. *Physiology of puberty.* Baltimore: Williams & Wilkins, 1965.

Eichorn, D. H. Two-generation similarities in weight, height and weight/height during the first five years. Reported at the Twenty-fifth Anniversary Meeting, Society for Research in Child Development, National Institutes of Health, Bethesda, Md., March 10, 1959.

Frisch, R. E., & Revelle, R. Height and weight at menarche and a hypothesis of critical body weights and adolescent events. *Human Biology*, 1971, **43**, 140.

Garn, S. M. Growth and development. In E. Ginzberg (Ed.), *The nation's children* (Vol. 2, *Development and education*). New York: Columbia U.P., 1960.

Garn, S. Body size and its implications. *Review of Child Development Research*, 1966, **2**, 529–561.

Gips, C. How illness experiences are interpreted by hospitalized children. Unpublished doctoral dissertation, Teachers College, Columbia University, 1956.

Gottesman, I. I. Differential inheritance of psychoneuroses. Paper read at the annual meeting of the American Institute of Biological Sciences, Corvallis, Ore., August 30, 1962.

Greulich, W. W., Day, H. G., Lochman, S. E., Wolfe, J. B., & Shuttleworth, F. K. A handbook of methods for the study of adolescent children. *Monographs of the Society for Research in Child Development*, 1938, **3**(2).

Gruenwald, P., Funakawa, H., Mitani, S., Nishimura, T., & Takeuchi, S. Influence of environmental factors on fetal growth in man. *Lancet*, 1967, **I**, 1026–1028.

Hampton, M. C., Heunemann, R. L., Shapiro, L. R., Mitchell, B. W., & Behnke, A. R. A longitudinal study of body composition and body conformation and their association with food and activity in a teen-age population—anthropometric evaluation of body build. *American Journal of Clinical Nutrition*, 1966, **19**, 422–435.

Heald, F. Obesity in the adolescent. *Pediatric Clinics of North America*, 1960, **7**, 207.

Hiernaux, J. Interpopulational variation in growth, with special reference to sub-saharan Africa. In J. Brožek (Ed.), Physical growth and body composition. Papers from the Kyoto symposium on anthropological aspects of human growth. *Monographs of the Society for Research in Child Development*, 1970, **35**(7, Serial No. 140).

Hook, E. B., & Kim, D. Height and antisocial behavior in XY and XYY boys. *Science*, 1971, **172**, 284–286.

Hoshi, H. Physical growth of Japanese-American hybrids from 6 to 15 years of age, with special reference to genetic-environmental relationships. In J. Brožek (Ed.), Physical growth and body composition. Papers from the Kyoto symposium on anthropological aspects of human growth. *Monographs of the Society for Research in Child Development*, 1970, **35**(7, Serial No. 140).

Insull, W., Jr., Oiso, T., & Tsuchiya, K. Diet and nutritional status of Japanese. *American Journal of Clinical Nutrition*, 1968, **21**, 753–777.

Jersild, A. T. *In search of self*. New York: Bureau of Publications, Teachers College, Columbia University, 1952.

Kallman, F. J. *Heredity in health and mental disorder*. New York: Norton, 1953.

Kleck, R. E., Richardson, S. A., & Ronald, L. Physical appearance cues and interpersonal attraction in children. *Child Development*, 1974, **45**, 305–310.

Knott, V. B., & Meredith, H. V. Body size of U.S. schoolboys at ages from 11 years to 15 years. *Human Biology*, 1963, **35**, 507–513.

Kolb, L. C. Body image in the schizophrenic reaction. In A. Auerbach (Ed.), *Schizophrenia*. New York: Ronald, 1959.

Krogman, W. M. Growth of head, face, trunk, and limbs in Philadelphia white and Negro children of elementary and high school age. *Monographs of the Society for Research in Child Development*, 1970, **35**(5, Serial No. 136).

McKusick, V. *Human genetics* (2nd ed.). Englewood Cliffs, N.J.: Prentice-Hall, 1969.

Mellits, E. D., & Cheek, D. B. The assessment of body water and fatness from infancy to adulthood. In J. Brožek (Ed.), Physical growth and body composition. Papers from the Kyoto symposium on anthropological aspects of human growth. *Monographs of the Society for Research in Child Development*, 1970, **35**(7, Serial No. 140).

Moore, W. M. The secular trend in physical growth of urban North American Negro schoolchildren. In J. Brožek (Ed.), Physical growth and body composition. Papers from the Kyoto symposium on anthropological aspects of human growth. *Monographs of the Society for Research in Child Development*, 1970, **35**(7, Serial No. 140).

Mussen, P. H., & Jones, M. C. Self-conceptions, motivations, and interpersonal attitudes of late and early maturing boys. *Child Development*, 1957, **28**, 243–256.

Orgel, S. Z., & Tuckman, J. Nicknames of institutional children. *American Journal of Orthopsychiatry*, 1935, **5**, 276–285.

Osofsky, J. D., & O'Connell, E. J. Parent-child interaction: Daughters' effects upon mothers' and fathers' behavior. *Developmental Psychology*, 1972, **7**, 157–168.

Pařízková, J. Activity, obesity, and growth. In J. Brožek (Ed.), Physical growth and body composition. Papers from the Kyoto symposium on anthropological aspects of human growth. *Monographs of the Society for Research in Child Development*, 1970, **35**(7, Serial No. 140).

Prokopec, M. Growth and socioeconomic environment. In J. Brožek (Ed.), Physical growth and body composition. Papers from the Kyoto symposium on anthropological aspects of human growth. *Monographs of the Society for Research in Child Development*, 1970, **35**(7, Serial No. 140).

Reynolds, E. L. The distribution of subcutaneous fat in childhood and adolescence. *Monographs of the Society for Research in Child Development*, 1951, **15**(2).

Ribble, S. A. *The rights of infants.* New York: Columbia U.P., 1943.

Ruff, W. K. A study of some aspects of personal adjustment common to high school boys, with implications for physical education. Unpublished doctoral dissertation, Teachers College, Columbia University, 1951.

Schilder, P. The image and appearance of the human body: Studies in the constructive energies of the psyche. *Psyche Monographs* (4). London: Kegan Paul, Trench, Trubner, 1935.

Schmeck, H. M., Jr. Trend in growth of children lags. *New York Times*, June 10, 1976, p. 13.

Schonfeld, W. A. Gynecomastia in adolescence, effect on body-image and personality adaptation. *Psychosomatic Medicine*, 1962, **24**, 379.

Schonfeld, W. A. The body and the body image on adolescents. In G. Caplan & S. Lebovici (Eds.), *Adolescence: Psychosocial perspectives.* New York: Basic Books, 1969.

Secord, P., & Jourard, S. M. The appraisal of Body-cathexis: Body-cathexis and the self. *Journal of Consulting Psychology*, 1953, **17**, 343–347.

Shirley, M. M. The first two years: A study of twenty-five babies. III, Personality manifestations. *Institute of Child Welfare Monographs* (Series No. 8). Minneapolis: University of Minnesota Press, 1933.

Shuttleworth, F. K. Sexual maturation and the physical growth of girls age six to nineteen. *Monographs of the Society for Research in Child Development*, 1937, **2**(5).

Silverman, S. S. *Clothing and appearance: Their psychological implications for teen-age girls.* New York: Bureau of Publications, Teachers College, Columbia University, 1945.

Staffieri, J. R. A study of social stereotypes of body image in children. *Journal of Personality and Social Psychology*, 1967, **7**, 101–104.

Stolz, H. R., & Stolz, L. M. Adolescent problems related to somatic variations. In N. B. Henry (Ed.), *43rd Yearbook of the National Society for the Study of Education* (Part I, *Adolescence*). Chicago: U. of Chicago, 1944.

Stolz, H. R., & Stolz, L. M. *Somatic development of adolescent boys: A study of the growth of boys during the second decade of life.* New York: Macmillan, 1951.

Tanner, J. M. *Growth at adolescence* (2nd ed.). Oxford: Blackwell, 1962.

Tanner, J. M. Earlier maturation in man. *Scientific American*, 1968, **218**(1), 21–27.

Tanner, J. M. Physical growth. In P. H. Mussen (Ed.), *Carmichael's manual of child psychology* (3rd ed.). New York: Wiley, 1970.

Tanner, J. M., Whitehouse, R. H., & Takaishi, M. Standards from birth to maturity for height, weight, height velocity and weight velocity: British children, 1965. *Archives of Diseases in Childhood*, 1966, **41**, 454–471; 613–635.

Thomas, A., Birch, H. G., Chess, S., Hertzig, M. E., & Korn, S. *Behavioral individuality in early childhood.* New York: New York U.P., 1963.

Walster, E., Aronson, V., Abrahams, D., & Rottmann, L. Importance of physical attractiveness in dating behavior. *Journal of Personality and Social Psychology*, 1966, **4**, 508–516.

Wattenberg, W. W. *The adolescent years.* New York: Harcourt, Brace, 1955.

Weir, J. B. de V. The assessment of the growth of schoolchildren with special reference to secular changes. *British Journal of Nutrition*, 1952, **6**, 19–33.

Willerman, L. Activity level and hyperactivity in twins. *Child Development*, 1973, **44**, 288–293.

4

sexual maturation:
onset of puberty
and sexual behavior

Adolescents reach an important milestone in their sexual development when they are able to produce live germ cells.

Several terms are commonly used to describe the events that take place in the process of sexual maturation. One term is *puberty*, derived from *pubes*, which, in one of its meanings, pertains to hair. One meaning of the term *pubescent* is to grow hair, or to grow hairy. Puberty refers to the appearance of hair in the genital area. In ordinary usage puberty denotes not simply the beginning of the process of sexual maturation, but the whole process or completed process. It denotes the earliest age at which "the generative power becomes established." Another term in common use is *menarche*, which denotes the beginning of menstruation. Still another term is *sexual maturity*, which sometimes is used as though it were synonymous with puberty and menarche in girls, although it is not. The menarche, or first menstruation, is an important event in a girl's life, but it does not necessarily mean that she is sexually mature in the sense of being able to produce fertile egg cells.

In boys there is no clearly defined event corresponding to the menarche in girls that can be used as a criterion of puberty. The basic criterion is the ability to produce well-formed, mobile, and fertile spermatozoa. There have been observations of the onset of puberty as judged by this criterion, but obviously it is difficult to conduct such studies on a large scale. In lieu of this, other criteria have been used: changes in the velocity of growth of certain dimensions of the body, changes in the velocity of growth of the penis and testes, and ratings of the characteristics of pubic hair, including the amount of such hair, its color, distribution, texture, and the eventual development of the kink, or twist.

As noted in an earlier chapter, adolescence begins at about eleven (sometimes at age ten or even earlier in girls), and lasts until about the age of twenty or even a little later. The age of onset of adolescence is influenced more by genetic and socioeconomic factors and nutrition than by climate or race (Tanner, 1962; Zacharias et al., 1970). Through the influence of both genetic and environmental factors, there is a wide variation possible within the range of normality.

Physical changes preceding and associated with sexual maturation

Many of the physical changes associated with the growth of adolescents are familiar to any casual observer, but students of adolescence will be interested in examining these in some detail.[1]

The chronological age at which any given development appears and the interval between the appearance of one feature and another vary considerably from individual to individual. Tables 4.1 and 4.2 from Schonfeld (1969) show the approximate time order of some changes associated with sexual maturation in boys and in girls.

The menarche in girls and the development of sexual maturity in boys are a culmination of developments in the endocrine system (ductless glands)

[1] Shuttleworth (1949) has provided a very instructive pictorial atlas of physical development in adolescence.

Table 4.1. Normal maturational sequence in boys

Phase	Appearance of sexual characteristics	Average ages	Age range
Childhood through preadolescence	*Testes* and *penis* have not grown since infancy; no *pubic hair*; growth in *height* constant. No spurt.		
Early adolescence	*Testes* begin to increase in size; *scrotum* grows, skin reddens and becomes coarser; *penis* follows with growth in length and circumference; no true *pubic hair*, may have down.	12–13 yrs.	10–15 yrs.
Middle adolescence	*Pubic hair*—pigmented, coarse, and straight at base of penis becoming progressively more curled and profuse, forming at first an inverse triangle and subsequently extends up to umbilicus; *axillary hair* starts after pubic hair; *penis* and *testes* continue growing; *scrotum* becomes larger, pigmented and sculptured; marked spurt of growth in *height* with maximum increment about time pubic hair first develops and decelerates by time fully established; *prostate* and *seminal vesicles* mature, spontaneous or induced *emissions* follow, but *spermatozoa* inadequate in number and motility (adolescent sterility); *voice* beginning to change as *larynx* enlarges	13–16 yrs.	11–18 yrs.
Late adolescence	*Facial* and *body* hair appear and spread; *pubic* and *axillary hair* become denser; *voice* deepens; *testes* and *penis* continue to grow; *emission* has adequate number of motile *spermatozoa* for fertility; growth in *height* gradually decelerates, 98 per cent of mature stature by $17\frac{3}{4}$ yrs. ± 10 months; indentation of frontal *hair line*.	16–18 yrs.	14–20 yrs.
Postadolescence to adult	Mature, full development of *primary* and *secondary* sex characteristics; *muscles* and *hirsutism* may continue increasing	onset 18–20 yrs.	onset 16–21 yrs.

Note: Normal range was accepted as 1st to 9th decile (80 per cent of cases).
Source: Table 4–1 in "The Body and the Body-Image in Adolescents," by William A. Schonfeld, Chapter 4 in *Adolescence: Psychosocial perspectives,* edited by Gerald Caplan and Serge Lebovici, © 1969 by Basic Books, Inc.

that begin several years before puberty (Tanner, 1969). This observation is based on studies of the secretion of sex hormones as determined by the analysis of urine. Such analysis revealed a small excretion of androgens (male sex hormones) and of estrogens (female sex hormones) by both boys and girls many years before puberty. At about nine years of age there begins a differentiation in the hormonal excretion of boys and girls, with an increase in the ratio of androgens in the boys and of estrogens in the girls.

Table 4.2. Normal maturational sequence in girls

Phase	Appearance of sexual characteristics	Average ages	Age range
Childhood through preadolescence	No *pubic hair*; *breasts* are flat; *growth* in height is constant, no spurt.		
Early adolescence	Rounding of *hips*; *breasts* and nipples are elevated to form *"bud"* stage; no true *pubic hair*, may have down	10–11 yrs.	9–14 yrs.
Middle adolescence	*Pubic hair:* pigmented, coarse, straight primarily along labia but progressively curled and spreads over mons and becomes profuse with an inverse triangular pattern; *axillary hair* starts after pubic hair; marked *growth* spurt with maximum *height* increment 18 months before menarche; *menarche: labia* become enlarged, *vaginal secretion* becomes acid; *breast:* areola and nipple elevated to form "Primary" breast	11–14 yrs.	10–16 yrs.
Late adolescence	*Axillary hair* in moderate quantity; *pubic hair* fully developed; *breasts* fill out forming adult-type configuration; *menstruation* well established; *growth* in height is decelerated, ceases at $16\frac{1}{4} \pm 13$ months.	14–16 yrs.	13–18 yrs.
Postadolescence to adult	Further growth of *axillary hair*; *breasts* fully developed	onset 16–18 yrs.	onset 15–19 yrs.

Note: Normal range was accepted as 1st to 9th decile (80 per cent of cases).
Source: Table 4–2 in "The Body and the Body-Image in Adolescents," by William A. Schonfeld, Chapter 4 in *Adolescence: Psychosocial perspectives*, edited by Gerald Caplan and Serge Lebovici, © 1969 by Basic Books, Inc.

Girls show a cyclic excretion of estrogens about a year and a half before the onset of the menarche. Thus, the rhythm of menstruation is foreshadowed in the chemistry of the body before the first experience of menstruation and the establishment of the menstrual cycle. The increase in female sex hormones is more drastic and occurs within a shorter time span than the corresponding changes in boys.[2]

Interesting findings concerning the relationship between behavior and the presence of the male hormone (androgenic material) are reported by Sollenberger (1940). Information was obtained concerning male hormone content and also concerning the interests and attitudes of several boys. There was a high correlation between hormone content and maturity of interests. As a further check, ten boys with high hormone content were

[2] For recent literature on sexual development and its association with the changing hormonal secretory activity of the gonads and pituitary, see Root (1973).

compared with thirteen boys with low hormone content. A higher proportion of boys with a high male hormone content expressed interest in heterosexual activities, personal adornment, and strenuous competitive sports.

Findings such as these are not surprising. They represent a line of inquiry dealing with the important relationship between psychological and physiological phenomena and give an indication of the complex forces that operate in the conduct of the individual adolescent. Two adolescents may be very much alike in the upbringing they have received but differ considerably in the physiological factors that influence the intensity of their sexual drive. As a result, they differ in the extent to which they have a problem in managing that drive.

The Onset of Puberty in Girls—Menstruation

Investigators dealing with different groups of American children have reported somewhat different averages concerning the age of onset of menstruation. The average girl reaches the menarche at about the age of 12.5 years, but this "average" does not mean much in view of the wide variations. A small proportion of girls reaches the menarche before the end of the tenth year, whereas a small proportion has not reached the menarche before the age of sixteen, seventeen, or even eighteen years. Menarche occurs after the peak of the height spurt has passed.[3]

Prior to menstruation the ovary becomes enlarged, and follicular ripening begins. Secondary sex changes also begin, including the rounding of the hips and growth of the breast "bud," in which the areola is elevated; this will be discussed further later in this chapter.

Pubic hair, which is initially downy, grows along the labia and becomes coarse, pigmented, and straight or curly (middle adolescence). The pubic hair becomes curlier and grows over the mons to form the female triangular pattern, spreading over the inner thighs by late adolescence. Axillary (armpit) hair commences growth about two years after pubic hair, in middle adolescence.

The Menarche and Fertility

The beginning of the menstrual cycle does not necessarily mean ability to conceive a child. Evidence suggests that there may be a lag of as

[3] The relationship between height, weight, and age at menarche has been discussed by Frisch and Revelle (1970) and Johnston et al. (1971).

much as six years at one extreme to possibly no time lag at all between the menarche and fertility. The findings also suggest, although not conclusively, that the lag between the menarche and capacity to conceive is shorter for girls who reach the menarche at a later age than for those who begin to menstruate at an early age. In a review of the literature bearing on this point, Ford and Beach (1951) point out that menstruation starts in most girls before their ovaries are capable of producing ripe eggs and that egg production begins before the uterus is mature enough (sometime in the late teens) to support the bearing of a child. They report that relatively few girls are capable of reproduction before the age of fifteen years, and even then reproductive capacity will not be as great as it will be at a later time. This does not, however, change the fact that in individual instances pregnancy may occur at age eleven or twelve or even earlier.

Limited findings also suggest the possibility that there is less variability in the age of onset of fertility than in the age of onset of menstruation.[4] In recent decades most adolescent girls have become fertile at earlier ages than in the past, as shown in a review of studies of fertility from 1870 to 1968 (Cutright, 1972).

Even though first menstruation does not provide an unquestionable criterion of puberty, it obviously is an important landmark in a girl's sexual development. It usually occurs several years before she marries or assumes the responsibilities of an adult. Moreover, the time lag between the menarche and adulthood has increased by virtue of the menarche coming earlier in the present generation than was true fifty or one hundred years ago. It is a part of the secular trend to earlier maturation described in Chapter 3.

During the past five to ten decades, youngsters have reached puberty progressively earlier (Muuss, 1970). According to Tanner (1968) "girls have experienced menarche progressively earlier during the past 100 years by between three and four months per decade [p. 25]". Compared with females of 100 years ago, today's girls attain puberty 2.5 to 3.5 years earlier. The average age of menarche for females from middle and upper socioeconomic groups is 12.8 years. Although all of the causes of earlier onset of menarche are not known, environmental changes, such as better nutrition, are probably responsible, to an important extent, for the change in menarcheal age. It is interesting to note that in the United States, where economic conditions are better than in many other parts of the world, the trend toward earlier menarche appears to be leveling off.

In contrast to previous studies indicating that girls are experiencing their menstrual period earlier than girls many years ago, Zacharias et al. (1976), based on a ten-year study of American females, reported that

[4] For a discussion of this subject, see Montagu (1946).

American females are no longer attaining sexual maturity at a younger age. She found that the average age of menarche has remained stable for the past thirty years. Moreover, the age of menarche of these girls was similar to that of their mothers. The results further indicate that the present generation of Americans is not any taller or heavier than the last generation.

THE PSYCHOLOGICAL IMPACT OF MENSTRUATION

Girls differ greatly in the extent to which they are prepared for their first menstruation and in their emotional response to it.

It is likely that a girl's response to first menstruation will be affected by factors in her past life that have influenced her personality as a whole, such as her attitude toward herself as a female, her feelings about her mother, and her outlook on life in general (see, for example, Newton, 1955).

Girls differ too in their psychological reactions to menstruation after the menstrual cycle has become established. They vary in the extent to which they experience physical pain or discomfort or changes in mood, such as depression, listlessness, and irritability. One theory about psychological reactions to menstruation is that they are related to the woman's acceptance or rejection of her status and role as a woman. According to this view, a woman who finds menstruation difficult may also be a woman who has difficulty in reconciling herself to other features of the feminine role, such as the thought of giving birth to children, caring for them, "mothering" them, and breast-feeding them (see Newton, 1955).

There have been, in the past, many misconceptions and superstitions about menstruation that have not been at all flattering to womankind. The vernacular referring to menstruation as a "curse" suggests that it is a symbol of unworthiness or punishment for sin. Hollingworth (1914) has given an interesting account of views that had been held by laymen and by scholars on this subject. Views ranged from statements that meat is likely to become tainted if handled by a woman during her menstrual period (construed, incidentally, as an argument against allowing women to become doctors or midwives) to the view that a woman is subject to periods of physical incapacity and weakness that would prevent her holding a responsible position outside her home. In writings reviewed by Hollingworth it was even suggested that criminal law should take into consideration that a woman, during a considerable part of her life, should be looked on as abnormal and subject to natural feeblemindedness.

Such views are no longer accepted. The scientific literature on the subject refutes the idea that a woman is less consistently efficient or reliable because of the menstrual cycle. However, emotional lability increases in many women during menses; the effect of this on efficiency and reliability needs further investigation.

Table 4.3. Premenstrual syndrome

Symptoms	%
Diarrhea	12
Constipation	12
Headaches	15
Breast swelling	73
Backaches	41
Nausea	26
Change in sleeping habits	34
	(12 less, 22 more)
Stomach swelling	65
Change in eating habits	46
	(20 less, 26 more)
Irritability	65
Physical sensitivity	40
Spotting	7
Weight gain	40
Dream about sex	12
Feel sexy with boyfriend	31
Cramps	42
Skin eruptions	40
Depression	12

Note: N = 26. Percentage of population reporting a given symptom.
Source: From "Patterns of affective fluctuation in the menstrual cycle" by
M. Boufford and J. Bardwick, *Psychosomatic Medicine*, 1968, **30**, 336–345.
Reprinted by permission.

Several investigators have shown the impact of physiological changes associated with menstruation on the emotions. Feelings of helplessness, anxiety, and a desire for love have been found to be associated with low estrogen and progesterone levels just prior to menstruation (Shainess, 1961). Premenstrual depression and irritability also have been found to be related to a number of unpleasant physical symptoms.

In a study of female college students, Boufford and Bardwick (1968) found that the girls experienced more anxiety two or three days prior to the onset of their menses than at the time of their ovulation. The number of symptoms reported by the girls prior to menstruation appears in Table 4.3.

All the girls reported at least one symptom. It appeared that those girls who received gratification when sick as youngsters or experienced rejection in childhood tended to experience the most symptoms.

Contrasts between reproductive functions of males and females

There is no regular happening in the sex life of a postpubescent boy comparable to the menstrual cycle in girls. Approximately every four weeks the girl is reminded that she is a potential mother. One (sometimes more than one) of the thousands of egg cells contained in her ovaries ripens, and nature makes elaborate preparations for the conception of a child. When nothing happens, nature "empties the room" that has been prepared for a guest that did not come, and the process of ripening and preparation begins anew.

In the meantime the boy's reproductive apparatus is also active, but in a more helter-skelter way. He becomes tumescent and detumescent several times a day; he has experiences with nocturnal emissions and masturbation. But the activities of his reproductive organs are erratic compared with those of a girl. One day, or week, or month is for him biologically much the same as the one before. There is no periodic crescendo of preparation for parenthood, no cycle to remind him each month that he is a potential father.

From a strictly biological point of view, a particular male is dispensable, but the individual female is indispensable in the process of reproduction. A single robust man could supply enough sperm to artificially impregnate thousands of women. But it is not possible (not yet, at least) to hire a substitute for the individual woman's egg bank, or to take care of the process of ovulation, or to supply a substitute uterus for bearing her child.

These considerations should enhance the sexually mature girl's pride in her sex and the developments that have occurred during her adolescence. But, as noted in several parts of this book, many studies have found that young women seem, on the whole, to have more difficulty in accepting their femininity than men have in accepting their masculinity. The reason for this probably is that many girls perceive more disadvantages than advantages in the reality of their biological nature, and they perceive that in spite of their biological indispensability in our culture men have more power and privileges than women. Also, girls have a more complex psychological path to maturity than boys, and parental reactions to daughters differ from reactions to sons.

Development of the Breasts

Breast development is the most important and most apparent of the secondary sex characteristics in the developing girl. There is considerable variability in the timing and outcome of this development (Reynolds and Wines, 1948). The breasts of most girls have progressed from the beginning bud stage to a more mature stage before the menarche. Breast development more often precedes than follows the appearance of pubic hair, but in some girls pubic hair appears first, and in some the two occur together.

In a group of girls studied continuously over a period of years by Reynolds and Wines (1948), the breasts developed from bud to mature size in about three years between the ages of eleven and fourteen. At any stage of development, breast size ranged from small to large. Breasts were classified as small, medium, or large in size and as flat, hemispherical, or conical in shape. Hemispherical contours were the most frequent classification.

Growth of the Male Genital Organs

In boys growth of the testicles and enlargement and reddening of the scrotum is apparent earlier than growth of the penis. Penile growth is rapid from age fourteen to sixteen, and there is a close correspondence between the timing of rapid growth in height and rapid growth of the penis (Stolz and Stolz, 1951).

Marshall and Tanner (1970) studied the development of changes in the genitalia and pubic hair using whole-body photographs. Genitalia and pubic hair were classified into six developmental stages (Tanner, 1969):

- Stage 1: Preadolescent; genitals as in childhood; no pubic hair
- Stage 2: Enlargement of the scrotum and testes; reddening of scrotal skin; sparse, downy hair at the base of the penis
- Stage 3: Penis growth, especially in length, with further testes and scrotum growth; darker, coarser, and curly pubic hair
- Stage 4: Glans of penis grows; further growth in breadth and darkening of scrotal skin; adult hair type, but smaller hairy area than in adults
- Stage 5: Adult genitalia; adult pubic hair; with growth on the medial surface of the thighs
- Stage 6: Into the mid-twenties; hair growth up to the umbilicus and beyond the inverse triangle

A review of several studies by Marshall and Tanner shows that there is considerable agreement between investigators as to the mean ages at which boys reach the different stages of genital and pubic hair development, even though the samples studied varied.

With testicular growth the seminiferous tubules enlarge, Leydig's cells appear and produce androgens, and this leads to the formation (in later adolescence) of spermatozoa.

As already noted, middle adolescence makes its appearance with the growth of pubic hair, which becomes pigmented and curly at the base of the penis. The amount of pubic hair increases and it becomes curlier, forming the characteristic male pattern as it spreads up to the umbilicus. The testes, scrotum, and penis become larger. Pigmentation of the nipples occurs, and the voice deepens, secondary to laryngeal growth. Axillary hair growth starts about two years after the appearance of pubic hair, and concomitantly, hair growth on the upper lip occurs. The final distribution of face and body hair varies in racial and ethnic groups.

There is great variation in the beginning and end of each of the physical events that occurs in adolescence. For instance, the acceleration of growth of the testes begins at age eleven and a half on the average, but sometimes as early as nine and a half and sometimes as late as thirteen and a half. The completion of testis development occurs on the average at fifteen, but in some boys it is as early as thirteen and one half and in others as late as seventeen years of age. Thus, for thirteen-, fourteen- and fifteen-year-old boys, there is considerable variability in terms of maturity of their reproductive system.

In a longitudinal study of the physical changes at puberty in normal boys, Marshall and Tanner (1970) found that some normal boys between the ages of thirteen and fourteen had not entered the second stage of genital development (when scrotum and testes begin to enlarge), whereas the genitals of other boys were adult in size and shape.

While the timing of particular events varies considerably, the sequence of events varies less. Indeed, some boys take more time to pass through a particular stage of genital development than others take to complete the entire process of genital development (Marshall and Tanner, 1970).

Table 4.4 (based on a study by Ramsey, 1943) shows some results that were obtained when boys between the ages of ten and sixteen were questioned about developments associated with adolescence, including ejaculation, voice change, nocturnal emission, and pubic hair. Two hundred and ninety-one histories were obtained by personal interviews; 85 per cent of the boys were between the ages of twelve and sixteen. The data are not complete, for some of the boys were questioned before they had reached the age when the development in question would occur. Yet, it is interesting to observe that about 2 per cent of ten-year-olds and about 7 per cent of eleven-year-olds reported that they had experienced ejaculation. From this

Table 4.4. Percentage at every age-group showing phase of sexual development

Age group (in yrs.)	Ejaculation (in %)	Voice change (in %)	Nocturnal emission (in %)	Pubic hair (in %)
10	1.8	.3	.3	.3
11	6.9	5.6	3.7	8.4
12	14.1	20.5	5.3	27.1
13	33.6	40.0	17.4	36.1
14	30.9	26.0	12.9	23.8
15	7.8	5.5	13.9	3.3
16	4.9	2.0	16.0	1.0

Source: From "The sexual development of boys" by G. V. Ramsey, American Journal of Psychology, 1943, 56, 217–233. Reprinted by permission.

it would seem that the capacity to have ejaculation appears, at least in some boys, very early in the adolescent period and before other prominent features of adolescent development have been clearly established. Ordinarily, ejaculation occurs about one year after the onset of the penile growth spurt.

According to Ramsey, the first ejaculation occurred as a result of masturbation (as distinguished from nocturnal emission or other kinds of stimulation) in 75 per cent of the cases. The findings in Table 4.4, indicating a capacity for ejaculation at a rather early age in some boys, is in keeping with findings made by Kinsey, Pomeroy, and Martin (1948) in their study of sexual behavior in the human male.

PSYCHOLOGICAL REACTIONS TO GENITAL DEVELOPMENT

Many boys are sensitive to the size of their genital organs, especially if they think they are small. Some boys with small organs stay away from athletics because they do not want to appear naked before others in the public showers. It is possible that adolescent concern about genital size is a remnant from childhood competitiveness with the father, when the boy compares his small size (and the size of his penis) with his father's adult size and feels inferior. A feeling of inferiority may linger in some boys whose psychosexual development was impaired because of serious strains in the early relationship with the father if they were subject to Oedipal rivalry for the mother's affections.

Differences in the size of the penis are especially conspicuous at ages thirteen through fifteen, when many boys have reached the postpubescent stage and many have not. In a study of penile size by Schonfeld and Beebe (1942), it was found that at ages thirteen and fourteen the boys in the upper 10 per cent had organs that were at least twice as long as those in the lowest 10 per cent. But at the fifteen- to eighteen-year levels the difference was about 50 per cent. The difference between the largest and smallest is more marked in the early and middle teens than in the late teens and early twenties.

Large variations such as these no doubt contribute to an important degree to the "feeling of being different" that afflicts many boys. A study of thirty-six men and twenty-four women revealed that a large penis and hairy chest were considered (incorrectly) as indicating greater potency than a nonhairy chest and a small penis (Verinis and Roll, 1970).

Although boys freely comment among themselves on this feature of their anatomy, they hesitate to discuss it with adults.[5] Yet, it could be very

[5] Some boys have concern about their genitals that seems to parallel the concern some girls have about their breasts. But a girl has reminders of publicly accepted normal variations each time she looks at brassiere advertisements or goes shopping for lingerie. Boys have no corresponding open reminders that wide variations are not abnormal.

reassuring to boys to discuss this with an understanding teacher. (Some physical education teachers encourage such discussion.) The mere fact of having an opportunity to reveal worries on this subject could be helpful.

It should be reassuring to boys to know that there is a wide normal variation in size; that the difference between them and others is not likely to be as large when they reach full growth as it is in the middle teens; that "manly men," regardless of body size and height, differ greatly in this respect; that there is no demonstrated relation between normal variations in the size of the male organ and attractiveness to the opposite sex (if there is any relation, it is more likely to be due to the young person's attitudes toward himself and women than to the actual size of his organ); that the boy's capacity, as a future husband, for love, tenderness, and thoughtfulness will be far more important in marital sex relationships than the size of his genitals.[6]

Apart from viewing his male organ as a symbol of manliness, a normal adolescent boy is frequently reminded of his genitals because he has erections. These may occur at embarrassing moments in class or other times. Some adolescents attempt to control their erections by turning their thoughts to somber channels. But, often, tumescence cannot be consciously controlled.

Other pubertal changes

Hair Growth

Changes in hair growth associated with puberty include not only the appearance of pubic hair and hair in the armpits but also in the amount and distribution of hair on other parts of the body. Hair growth is notable especially in boys, who show a rapid development of hair on limbs and trunk during adolescence.

Another change is connected with the shape of the hairline of the forehead. In immature boys this line is a bowlike curve, as in girls, but in most mature males the hairline is broken by a wedge-shaped (bi-temporal) indentation on each side. These indentations are a mark of maleness. In many men, as they grow older, the wedges become deeper and wider.

---

[6] Statements such as these will not touch on the core of a boy's difficulty if he has deep-seated attitudes of self-rejection and then "attaches" these to a notion that his organ is not as large as he would like it to be. But with a teacher who has a talent for counseling, a discussion of this problem may become a point of departure for exploring the boy's attitudes regarding himself.

...at and Sebaceous Glands

A ... the activity ... f pubertal change is increased activity of the ... glands in ... h the typical odor of perspiration. The glands ... areas ... of ... ound in other limited areas of the body (the ... ary ... ain, genita... anal regions), but they differ from the sweat glands that ... tributed over the body as a whole. The ... of these ... ds (known as apocrine) begins at about the ... of the ... h of ... hair and appears to be related to the status of ... repro... sys... glands do not reach full development until ... is ... he time enlargement of the sebaceous glands ... the gland ... ome plugged and easily infected. A common ... ... nown as acne results from this condition.

... ... n boys is a commonly recognized feature of ... scen ... op ... ... esults from the enlargement of the larynx. ... ... not occur at any fixed age but frequently ... con ... dly ... ... wth of the penis. Usually, a deepening of the ... ... ntil several other signs of sexual maturation ... appear ... ... ows the range of tones correctly sung by ... ... ough the age of ten, and by men and women.

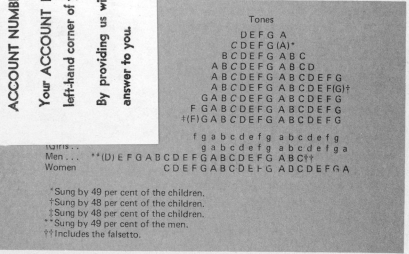

Tones

	D E F G A
	C D E F G (A)*
	B C D E F G A B C
	A B C D E F G A B C D
	A B C D E F G A B C D E F G
	A B C D E F G A B C D E F(G)†
	G A B C D E F G A B C D E F G
	F G A B C D E F G A B C D E F G
	‡(F) G A B C D E F G A B C D E F G
	f g a b c d e f g a b c d e f g
	g a b c d e f g a b c d e f g a
Men ...	**(D) E F G A B C D E F G A B C D E F G A B C††
Women	C D E F G A B C D E F G A D C D E F G A

*Sung by 49 per cent of the children.
†Sung by 48 per cent of the children.
‡Sung by 48 per cent of the children.
**Sung by 49 per cent of the men.
††Includes the falsetto.

Figure 4.1. Tones sung by 50 per cent or more of children and by adults. A few tones reproduced by slightly less than 50 per cent are shown in parentheses. [From "A study of the development of children's ability to sing" by A. T. Jersild and S. Bienstock, *Journal of Educational Psychology*, 1934, *25*, 481–503. Reprinted by permission.]

The voices of girls also usually deepen somewhat during adolescence. Women could sing several low tones that ten-year-olds could not, but they continued to be able to sing as high in the scale as the ten-year-olds. On the other hand, the men, although they had become able to sing a large number of low tones that ten-year-old boys could not sing, had also lost the ability to sing some of the high tones the younger males could sing. The gain in the low register is larger, however, than the loss in the high end of the scale.

The change of voice causes embarrassment to some boys. They go through a period when their voices are unstable; "breaks" may occur, with the voice suddenly rising or falling a whole octave. Changes may also be preceded by huskiness (Curry, 1946). Some who have enjoyed singing become self-conscious about it when their voices are in the process of changing. Some youngsters drop out of the school chorus or glee club while in the process of getting accustomed to the new qualities of their voices, and boys who once sang lustily in assembly or in church may, for a time, refuse to sing at all.

Some psychological effects of early and late sexual maturation

The timing of body changes during adolescence has an important psychological impact,[7] and differences in rate of growth may have different effects on boys and girls, especially in the early teens. A series of inquiries conducted in connection with a long-term growth study at the University of California (Berkeley) offers interesting findings on this subject. Jones (1949) found that it is in many ways a disadvantage for a time for a girl to mature early, whereas for a boy early maturing brings several advantages. On the other hand, Faust (1960) reports that neither accelerated nor retarded physical development in girls can consistently be regarded as an advantage.

The early maturing girl is likely to be relatively big and physically conspicuous. Although still a child of ten or eleven years, she has to anticipate and deal with the responsibilities involved in menstruation. Her size and proportions and the other characteristics that go with being more mature may make it difficult for her and other girls of her age to accept each other on equal terms. Moreover, she is physically advanced at a time when most of the boys of her age are still childish and unable to appreciate her

[7] Psychological aspects of sexual development, heterosexual relationships, and other urges and practices related to sex are also discussed in later chapters. Ways in which attitudes toward self and others are expressed through sexual interests and practices are discussed in several sections of this book, including those dealing with anxiety, personality development, and heterosexual relationships.

physical qualities. The boys may even be wary in their attitude toward her. In addition, when her physical maturing is very precocious, she is not likely to have corresponding social or intellectual maturity. In that event, she will not be ready to associate with older girls who are similar to her in physical development. She may also have special conflicts, for her parents are likely to regard her as still a very young girl and to restrict her dating and her desire to dress like "older" girls.

The situation is not, however, always bleak for the girl who matures early. In a certain group it may be an advantage for a girl to mature early if the most popular and most influential members of the group are early maturers. Indeed, a girl who matures late may actually feel left out of things and even begin to be concerned about herself if other girls with whom she likes to associate mature early and she does not. In one such situation, a twelve-year-old girl had a difficult time. The half-dozen twelve-year-old girls with whom she had associated were blossoming as young women. They told her they did not want her to go with them on the bus to the movies for she could not "look like fourteen." In their view it was harder for them to act convincingly in public as though they were at least fourteen- or fifteen-year-olds when this "girlish"-looking person was with them.

In a later study in the California series (Jones and Mussen, 1958), early maturers and late maturers were studied at the age of seventeen. Few differences were found, at that later age, between the two groups, except that early maturing girls showed "more favorable self-concepts," and early maturing girls rated higher in popularity at age seventeen than they had rated in their earlier teens.

As already noted, the early maturing boy is more likely to have an advantage than a disadvantage, both in the early and later teens. For a time he is relatively bigger and stronger than many other boys, even though, later, some of these boys will reach him or outstrip him in both height and strength. As a bigger and stronger person he is likely to have a considerable advantage in competitive sports. At the junior high school level it has been found that boys who are sexually more mature are more likely to be chosen as athletic leaders (Latham, 1951), and are likely to be less neurotic. Moreover, the rapidly maturing boy has an earlier assurance of his maleness and a basis for feeling confident about his masculinity. He is also expected to behave in a more adult manner (Money and Clopper, 1974).

The psychological reactions to early and late maturing present an interesting illustration of the interplay between genetic factors, attitudes that prevail in the social environment, and attitudes toward self. Repercussions of having what boys regard for a time as an "inadequate masculine physique" associated with later maturing have been discussed by Schonfeld (1950). He notes that many of the variations in pubertal development that are frequently regarded as abnormal are "genetically determined" physiological variations in the process of development. But many slow-maturing boys whose organic development is well within the limits of normal are not free to wait for nature to take its course because the attitudes of others encourage prepubescent boys to take pride in their masculinity and frequently do not show proper consideration for basic differences among individuals.

During the second decade of life, the attitudes of the companions of the boys in Schonfeld's study had a decisive role in formulating standards of masculinity. At this age all the boys had a great need for acceptance by their peers. Not only could the late-maturing boys see for themselves that they differed from what the group regarded as normal, but in addition they became targets for criticism and disapproval.

A youngster's attitudes play an important role in the way he reacts to the standards set by others. "Being different to a child usually implies being inferior. . . . It is inadequate adjustment to being different [Schonfeld, 1950, p. 50]." Schonfeld noted that feelings of inadequacy persisted in some slow-maturing boys even when the physical differences that had made them feel inferior no longer existed.

Some boys build defensive "compensatory mechanisms" to avert the anxiety that would arise from a full awareness of their self-contempt. A common defense was to swing toward "compulsive drives for dominance, mastery, and power [Schonfeld, 1950, p. 51]." However, when boys who were striving to attain superiority set goals for themselves that were impossible to achieve, their failures reinforced their convictions of being worthless.[8]

In a study by Jones and Bayley (1950) of ninety boys, the sixteen who were earliest in maturing were compared with the sixteen who were latest in maturing. Boys in the early maturing group were rated as physically more attractive, less affected, and more relaxed when judged by observations of their behavior. When the boys rated one another on various traits, the early maturers tended to be regarded as more grown-up, more assured, and more likely to have older friends. In a later inquiry (Mussen and Jones, 1957), in the same long-term study, the sixteen boys who had been consistently accelerated in their physical development were compared at age seventeen with seventeen who had been consistently retarded, on the basis of their responses to a projective test. (See Chapter 8.) More of the late maturing than the early maturing boys gave evidence of an unfavorable view of themselves, were less popular, and showed more feelings of inadequacy and negative self-concepts (Jones, 1958). In responding to pictures in the Thematic Apperception Test (TAT), a larger proportion of the late maturers told stories in which the hero was rejected by parents or authority figures

[8] A study by Dimock (1937) also showed that boys below average in physical development had less wholesome attitudes toward themselves than boys with superior or average development.

(Jones, 1958). The investigators point out that some parents may have been disappointed in their physically retarded sons, and the boys might have interpreted this as rejection. Moreover, late maturing boys are more likely to experience guilt, low self-esteem, and depression, according to Weatherley (1964). In some cases, also, parents may have been reluctant to allow the slow-maturing boy to establish his independence, with resulting tension and increased parent-child conflict. A larger proportion of late maturers than early maturers also showed negative attitudes toward their parents. Relatively few of the early maturing boys manifested feelings of being inadequate, rejected, or dominated or showed feelings of rebellion against their families.[9] Late maturers also preferred to be with younger children as a consequence of peer rejection (Money and Clopper, 1974).

Behavioral, attitudinal, and moral aspects of sexual development

In the adolescent's sexual development there is an interplay of all the important forces that affect human existence. Sex has an urgency of its own, but it is also intimately tied to nearly all other aspects of a person's strivings and relationships with others. Sexual development is a meeting ground of the biological, psychological, and moral influences that shape an adolescent's life. It is also a meeting ground of the present and the past, for sex behavior has a history that goes back to early childhood. The biological features of an adolescent's sexuality are present at birth. In early infancy there are evidences of special sensitivity in the genital zones. Because of the psychophysical interrelation between anatomical and physiological aspects of sexual maturation on the one hand, and sexual behavior on the other, we will include a discussion of sexual behavior in this chapter. A later chapter (Chapter 14) dealing with dating, courtship, and marriage will consider the more distinctly interpersonal and sentimental aspects of sexual development.

The most direct and specific way in which sex enters into the adolescent's experience is in the form of a body hunger, or drive. Back of this hunger, in the process of evolution, is a blind urge of life to beget life.

[9] Fortunately, not all boys who are slow maturers are deeply disturbed about it, and, according to Schonfeld (1950), those who are disturbed can benefit greatly from psychological help if it is made available. The picture, however, is so somber that it calls for sympathetic conern by all who are responsible for the upbringing and education of adolescents. This is one reason why Jersild (1951) has maintained that those who can profit most from a study of adolescent development are adolescents themselves. A course dealing with adolescence will not dispel the more severely ingrained personality problems. But good instruction and class discussion can help to dispel the mystery, the mistaken ideas about what is normal and abnormal, and the self-reproach based on false premises.

However, there is an additional large and complicated cluster of meanings connected with sex. Sex obviously is associated in the boy's mind with his concept of his role as a male, and in the girl's mind with her concept of herself as a female.

Attitudes Toward Sexual Behavior

Since the 1940s there has been a considerable change in attitudes toward sex and the constraints conventionally related to marriage and family life. According to a survey done by Yankelovich (1972), 43 per cent of college students do not feel extramarital sexual relations are morally wrong. Fifty-eight per cent of the students reported that having children without a formal marriage was not morally wrong. While one third of the students reported marriage was obsolete, 61 per cent expressed interest in attempting a marriage relationship at a later date.

Recent longitudinal data suggest that sexual standards have become more liberal for males, and to a greater degree, for females (Croake and James, 1973; Perlman, 1974). In general, women are becoming liberated from the "double standard" of sexual morality; however, perpetuation of the double standard is more frequent in the United States than in parts of Europe (Luckey and Nass, 1969). Permissive attitudes toward premarital intercourse have increased more markedly than actual changes in behavior. Whereas the percentages of males and females at a midwestern university reporting approval of premarital sexual intercourse in 1958 were 47 and 17, respectively, the corresponding percentages in 1968 were 55 and 36 (Christensen and Gregg, 1970). The females in this study showed the greater change with regard to more permissive attitudes toward premarital coitus.

In a study of Temple University coeds, 65 per cent in 1958 and 36 per cent in 1968 reported that they had "gone too far" by having premarital intercourse in a dating relationship. Among the students engaged to be married, 41 per cent in 1958 and 20 per cent in 1968 stated they had "gone too far" by having premarital intercourse (Bell and Chaskes, 1970). Findings regarding the trend toward relaxation of sexual morals among college students have also been confirmed in surveys of high school students (Sorenson, 1973).

Upper- and middle-class blacks have less accepting attitudes regarding premarital coitus than blacks of the lower class, but among whites social class differences are minimal. Since the 1940s, upper- and middle-class whites have become more accepting of premarital sex relations (Reiss, 1971). A permissive attitude regarding premarital sex appears most marked among black males; ranking next in permissiveness are white males, followed by black females and, lastly, white females (Reiss, 1964).

Sexual Behavior

EARLY MANIFESTATIONS

When boys and girls reach adolescence, all of them have had experiences of one sort or another relating to sex. These experiences, when the adolescents were children, included discovery of the anatomical differences between the sexes, an interest in childish forms of sex play, and curiosity about sex and reproduction. Boys begin to have erections almost from the time they are born. According to evidence presented by Kinsey et al. (1953), there are children, both boys and girls, who are capable of true sexual response before they reach adolescence.

SEXUAL BEHAVIOR DURING PREADOLESCENCE AND EARLY ADOLESCENCE

There are large individual as well as group differences in expressed sexual interests and activities that must be taken into account when we read findings regarding the prevalence of any particular form of sexual behavior. Nevertheless, there are some experiences and practices that are very widespread. In a study by Ramsey (1943) it was found that 73 per cent of the boys had had experience with masturbation by the age of twelve years, and 98 per cent had had such experience by the age of fifteen. Over half the boys in Ramsey's study had experienced nocturnal emissions, or "wet dreams,"

The beginnings of sexual behavior often appear in play. [AlexWebb/Magnum.]

by the age of fifteen. Nocturnal emissions during sleep come about without any deliberate action by the dreamer. A large percentage of boys had had ejaculations brought about by themselves or through sex play with others before they experienced wet dreams. By the age of thirteen, 38 per cent of the boys had been involved in homosexual play. Preadolescent sex play with girls or women appeared in two thirds of their histories. The proportion of girls reporting masturbation during adolescence is smaller than that of the boys (Pomeroy, 1969).

Recent data tend to confirm Ramsey's findings (Simon and Gagnon, 1970). The significant finding is that a substantial number of boys and a large number of girls are active sexually in one way or another just prior to, or at the onset of, adolescence. Because attitudes toward masturbation have become more permissive in recent years, previous feelings of guilt accompanying masturbation have probably declined.

SOME MISLEADING ASPECTS OF STATISTICS REGARDING SEXUAL ACTIVITY

Before proceeding with a survey of findings pertaining to sexual behavior, it is necessary to point out that some of the statistics may be misleading. First, changes in the direction of more permissive attitudes toward sex, as indicated previously, do not necessarily denote a corresponding change in overt behavior. More importantly, even statistics regarding overt sexual behavior may be confusing. Take the matter of virginity (the term *virgin* has increasingly been applied to both males and females); a person ceases to be a virgin if he or she impulsively just once has had intercourse and then abstains or if he or she embarks on a deliberate plan to have intercourse occasionally or often. A substantial decline in the incidence of virginity does not necessarily mean a commensurate breakdown in scruples about sex. Many of the percentages pertaining to sexual activity represent "cumulative incidence"—namely, the proportion of persons who, up to a given age, have had this or that sexual experience at one time or another, only once or regularly and often over a long period of time. In several studies, including Kinsey's, the investigators not only report this "whether or not" statistic, but also include statistics on how much or how often. The latter statistics show that within the group that has had sexual intercourse there are large numbers who have had the experience only once or a few times, indicating that there were periods of months or years during adolescence when no such sex activity took place.

RECENT CHANGES IN SEXUAL BEHAVIOR

Greater sexual freedom may mean liberation from age-old taboos, but it may also, in many instances, entail anxiety and suffering. Many adults have, to a great extent, condoned or supported the drift toward greater sexual freedom. There are coeducational dormitories for young people who are still in their teens. There has been a rash of pornography, which once would have been treated as a criminal offense, and a good deal of the literature now available to young people would once have been banned as obscene. Abortion has been sanctioned, within legal limits, although it remains a source of conflict and controversy (Stycos, 1974). The "pill" is widely available, and other methods of contraception are discussed with an openness that once would have been regarded as scandalous. Among older persons there are some who view the so-called sexual revolution with alarm. Some look upon "liberated" youth with envy. Some openly or secretly acknowledge that their major regrets about their past lives were the temptations they successfully resisted.

But what about the young people themselves? The data bearing on this question deal more with the incidence of overt forms of behavior than with the extent to which sexual behavior is spontaneous and joyful, or enmeshed in conflict and confusion, or impelled by an awkward need to conform. At any rate, for some young persons, notably girls, freedom exacts a price. One price, faced by the girl herself or her parents or social agencies, comes with the bearing of an illegitimate child. In spite of widespread publicizing of methods of contraception, many adolescents do not use any method of contraception (Boyce and Benoit, 1975). There has been a great increase in births by unmarried teen-agers, according to Campbell (1975). Illegitimate births, according to this source, have increased 50 per cent among teen-agers as contrasted with a drop of 30 per cent among non teen-agers, during the years from 1963 to 1973. These statistics do not take account of marriages, eagerly or reluctantly entered into, by pregnant teen-agers. Whatever the latter statistics might be, there remains the sobering thought, as noted later in this book, that early marriages face a greater chance of divorce than marriages entered into by people in their twenties or older. The outcome, for better or for worse, of being a child of an unmarried mother or of a divorced mother is also a pertinent consideration. Through the generations, the taboos and restraints imposed on the burgeoning sexuality of young persons have, to varying degrees, been harsh and cruel (witness, for example, Hawthorne's *Scarlet Letter*). But whether cruel or tempered by compassion, they have had an impact not only on the contemporary generation but on children yet unborn.

A further consideration should be added. Although, as mentioned in this chapter, recent changes in attitudes toward sexual behavior have been quite marked among adolescent girls, the premarital sex experiences of a large proportion of girls, notably among those who go to college, may be limited to relations with boys whom they plan to marry.

SEXUAL ACTIVITIES IN MIDDLE AND LATE ADOLESCENCE

There is a great accumulation of findings regarding sexual interests and activities during adolescent years, but, unfortunately, many of these deal with sex in a fragmented way. The monumental and well-known studies by Kinsey and his associates deal almost entirely with the physical (one might almost say the mechanical) aspects of sexual experience. Kinsey and his associates give elaborate statistics about sexual "outlets" with little or no attention to the personal meaning of these outlets, their emotional and moral significance, and the interpersonal relationships (other than physical) existing between persons who mutually engage in sex activities.

Studies dealing with other facets of heterosexual behavior—such as dating, courtship, falling in love, early marriage—which will be discussed in Chapter 14, usually cover a broader personal and social context; but even some of these give more attention to statistics than to underlying psychological motivations.

In the early teens there is a sharp upswing among boys, and a much more gradual increase among girls, in various practices and experiences.[10] The chief types of sex activity are masturbation, nocturnal sex dreams (mainly in males), petting, and sexual intercourse.

At the end of the teens it has been found or estimated that over 90 per cent of boys (unmarried) have practiced masturbation and that a majority carry on the practice regularly one or more times per week.[11]

The incidence of this practice among girls is smaller. Studies in which female adults have reported about their adolescent activity have given percentages clustering from about 30 to 60 per cent, although some investigators have reported a much higher or lower figure. Kinsey reports that by late adolescence about two fifths of girls have had experience with masturbation, but only about half of these are actively pursuing the practice at any particular time.

During recent decades there has been a marked change in what is being said and written about masturbation. The horrid and brutal threats of depravity, sterility, and hell-fire once repeated in books on "What Every Boy Should Know" have largely been removed. But there probably still is

[10] Findings showing the incidence of various sex activities should be interpreted with some caution, for the findings obviously depend on the veracity of those who are questioned and (in retrospective accounts) on their ability to remember accurately. However, several recent investigations, employing varying methods and involving different populations, have shown a high degree of agreement on the points here under review.

[11] This statistic is from Kinsey (1948). Various other studies within the past few decades have reported that from about 90 to practically 100 per cent of males have engaged in the practice more or less regularly for shorter or longer periods of time (see Kinsey, 1948; Sorenson, 1973).

some guilt and fear associated with masturbation. It seems that the more guilt adolescents feel about sexual behavior, the more restricted their levels of intimacy in premarital sexual experiences are likely to be (Mosher and Cross, 1971).

There is probably less guilt and fear associated with masturbation among adolescents today than in the past. Masturbation may be the result of anxiety over fantasied sexual activity with another person; it may serve to protect one from threatening physical intimacy with the opposite sex and from establishing an emotionally intimate relationship with a member of the opposite sex.

Petting is one of the most common erotic activities during adolescence. Kinsey (1948) has defined petting as any sort of physical contact that does not involve a union of the genitalia but in which there is a deliberate attempt to effect erotic arousal. Petting will be discussed in a later chapter.

In an international survey of male and female college students, Luckey and Nass (1969) found that students in the United States and Canada have more conservative views regarding sexual behavior than students in Europe, including England and Norway. As shown in Tables 4.5 and 4.6, females are more conservative than males in each country.

Table 4.5. Per cent of males reporting experiencing various forms of sexual behavior

Type of sexual behavior	U.S.	Canada	England	Germany	Norway
Light embracing or fond holding of hands	98.6	98.9	93.5	93.8	93.7
Casual goodnight kissing	96.7	97.7	93.5	78.6	86.1
Deep kissing	96.0	97.7	91.9	91.1	96.2
Horizontal embrace with some petting but not undressed	89.9	92.0	85.4	68.8	93.6
Petting of girl's breast area from outside her clothing	89.9	93.2	87.0	80.4	83.5
Petting of girl's breast area without clothes intervening	83.4	92.0	82.8	69.6	83.5
Petting below the waist of the girl under her clothing	81.1	85.2	84.6	70.5	83.5
Petting below the waist of both man and girl, under clothing	62.9	64.8	68.3	52.7	55.1
Nude embrace	65.6	69.3	70.5	50.0	69.6
Coitus	58.2	56.8	74.8	54.5	66.7
One-night affair involving coitus; didn't date person again	29.9	21.6	43.1	17.0	32.3
Whipping or spanking before petting or other intimacy	8.2	5.7	17.1	0.9	5.1
Sex on pay-as-you-go basis	4.2	4.5	13.8	9.8	2.5
(N)	(644)	(88)	(123)	(112)	(75)

Note: N = number.
Source: From "A comparison of sexual attitudes and behavior in an international sample" by E. Luckey and G. A. Nass, Journal of Marriage and Family, 1969, 31, 364–379. Copyright 1969 by National Council on Family Relations. Reprinted by permission.

Table 4.6. Per cent of females reporting experiencing various forms of sexual behavior

Types of sexual behavior	U.S.	Canada	England	Germany	Norway
Light embracing or fond holding of hands	97.5	96.5	91.9	94.8	89.3
Casual goodnight kissing	96.8	91.8	93.0	74.0	75.0
Deep kissing	96.5	91.8	93.0	90.6	89.3
Horizontal embrace with some petting but not undressed	83.3	81.2	79.1	77.1	75.0
Petting of girl's breast area from outside her clothing	78.3	78.8	82.6	76.0	64.3
Petting of girl's breast area without clothes intervening	67.8	64.7	70.9	66.7	58.9
Petting below the waist of the girl under her clothing	61.2	64.7	70.9	63.5	53.6
Petting below the waist of both man and girl, under clothing	57.8	50.6	61.6	56.3	42.9
Nude embrace	49.6	47.6	64.0	62.1	51.8
Coitus	43.2	35.3	62.8	59.4	53.6
One-night affair involving coitus; didn't date person again	7.2	5.9	33.7	4.2	12.5
Whipping or spanking before petting or other intimacy	4.5	5.9	17.4	1.0	7.1
(N)	(688)	(85)	(86)	(96)	(56)

Note: N = number.
Source: From "A comparison of sexual attitudes and behavior in an international sample" by E. Luckey and G. A. Nass, *Journal of Marriage and Family*, 1969, **31**, 364–379. Copyright 1969 by National Council on Family Relations. Reprinted by permission.

In a large national sample of adolescent students, 59 per cent of the boys, and 45 per cent of the girls (thirteen to nineteen years of age) reported that they had had premarital intercourse (Sorenson, 1973). The Sorenson report of adolescent behavior has received a great deal of attention because it presents findings relating to sexual behavior of students representative of the entire United States. However, the reader should be cautious when reading the prevalence data presented, as only 47 per cent of the adolescents contacted agreed to be interviewed. In this study a higher percentage of sixteen- to nineteen-year-olds reported premarital intercourse than younger adolescents.

Variations in Sexual Behavior

Recent studies have found that religion, education, race, sex, and personality factors influence sexual behavior. A higher percentage of whites than blacks report they were virgins (the term *virgin* as here used refers to both males and females) in their teens (McCary, 1973). The incidence of premarital intercourse is far higher among those who leave school at the end of the elementary school period than among those who are headed for college or actually are attending college.[12] Adolescents with strong religious commitment more often report they are virgins than adolescents who do not feel committed (McCary, 1973; Sorenson, 1973). Among students attending eastern colleges and universities, a higher percentage reported having premarital intercourse than students attending midwestern schools (Packard, 1970). According to a Gallup poll (1973) conducted in 1970, over one half of political conservatives, but only one fifth of political liberals, stated it was important to marry a virgin.

In a cross-cultural study of male and female students, Luckey and Nass (1969) found that more European than American men reported that females were "willing to go farther." In general, men and women from both America and Canada were more conservative than Europeans, particularly in terms of premarital intercourse.

One of the most impressive longitudinal studies of the correlates of virginity and nonvirginity has been reported by Jessor and Jessor (1975), whose investigations cover high school as well as college students. In their study the Jessors attempted to explore the transition from the status of virginity to nonvirginity as well as explore the differences between virgins and nonvirgins. Questionnaires were administered to high school students in ninth grade and during the following four years. A similar procedure was used with the college sample. Jessor and Jessor report a nonvirginity rate at the sixteen- to eighteen-year levels of 38 and 27 per cent for males and females, respectively. This is considerably lower than Sorenson's rates for sixteen- to nineteen-year-olds—72 and 57 per cent for males and females, respectively. The differences in rates may be due to the fact that the Jessors' high school sample consisted of middle-class Anglo-American students. (According to Kinsey's earlier studies, heterosexual activity is more common among persons at the lower socioeconomic levels.)

As might be expected, virgins were found to be more conventional in their beliefs, attitudes, and values than nonvirgins. The virgins' parents and particularly their peers provided an environment for the virgin adolescent characterized by control and less approval of nonconventional behavior. These factors were also "shown to obtain prior to the initiation of sexual intercourse experience and to constitute therefore a transition-proneness that significantly predicts becoming a nonvirgin during the subsequent year [Jessor and Jessor, 1975, p. 480]." The nonvirgins, as well as the virgins who are likely to have intercourse in the subsequent year, place more importance on the role of independence, are closer to their friends than to their parents, and are more likely to engage in other nonconventional behavior. Moreover, among the high school male students, 61 per cent of the nonvirgins had tried marijuana more than once, compared with 28 per cent

[12] The percentages bearing on this situation have varied somewhat in different investigations (see, for example, Ehrmann, 1952; Sorenson, 1973).

of the virgins. The corresponding percentages for the females were 67 and 21 per cent, respectively. Similar findings in other studies conducted by the Jessors were found with respect to drinking. On the basis of their findings with respect to marijuana, excessive drinking, and nonvirginity, the Jessors emphasize that the onsets of many of these behaviors are frequently concurrent, or that the onset of one behavior increases the probability of the onset of another.

In the college sample the correlates of premarital sexual relations were less pronounced. One of the reasons for this may be that to engage in premarital sexual relations at the college level is less of a departure from what conventionally have been regarded as age-appropriate norms than at the high school level.

Several investigators have reported that many young people are more concerned with the personal relationship between the two people who are involved than in cultural standards of right or wrong (Luckey and Nass, 1969). In one study of college women, coeds expressed a more permissive attitude toward premarital sexual relations if the couple involved had developed a deep emotional commitment or became engaged (Bell and Buerkle, 1961).

As we have noted, adolescent boys are much more active sexually than adolescent girls. By the age of seventeen, according to Kinsey (1953), practically 100 per cent of boys had experienced orgasm, whereas about 35 per cent of girls had had a sexual climax. Boys and girls are more alike in petting—by age twenty-one practically all members of both sexes have had experience with petting—but the practice is less frequent, on the average, and more sporadic, among girls.

Undoubtedly there are cultural reasons for this difference. It reflects, at least in part, the double standard that still prevails, although not as rigorously as it did in the past. Boys have more freedom; girls are more carefully supervised; girls are warned against (and often frightened by) the threat of pregnancy out of wedlock. Both boys and girls tend to regard a girl's forbidden sex behavior as a more serious offense than a boy's behavior. Boys are conventionally regarded as the ones who take the initiative in sex conduct (McCary, 1973). In a study by Ehrmann (1952) of the dating behavior of college students, behavior ranging from holding hands to intercourse or attempted intercourse was initiated by the boys in about three fourths of the instances when such behavior occurred (according to the boys themselves, 75.3 per cent, and according to the girls, 78.9 per cent of such advances). The boys and girls also agreed, to a marked degree, in their reports that when advances were stopped at a certain point it was the girl, far more often than the boy, who was responsible. To a large extent a girl is required to be "a conscience for two" in her dealings with boys. Bell and Blumberg (1960) reported that whereas over one half of teenage girls experienced guilt feelings if they went "too far" in petting with their dates, the corresponding percentage for boys was 25 per cent.

Although cultural factors undoubtedly account for much of the difference between the sex behavior of boys and girls it also appears that there are physical differences in the timing of the sex drive. According to Kinsey et al. (1948, 1953), males apparently reach their peak sexual capacities in the mid-teens, whereas the female peak does not come until later. Even when there is freedom and opportunity for sex experience, it appears that the young male's drive is stronger. By the average age of fifteen the girls in the Kinsey group reported that they were having orgasm every two weeks if they were having any at all, whereas the average boy of the same age reported about five orgasms every two weeks.

Differences between boys and girls appear not only in connection with actively initiated sex behavior, but also in connection with more passive sex experiences. Kinsey found that nocturnal emissions (wet dreams) were far more frequent among boys than sex dreams that resulted in a sexual climax among girls. A person cannot deliberately bring about a sex dream. Undoubtedly, strong inhibitions that may be at work even when a person is asleep can prevent them. But this difference between boys and girls suggests that the sexual mechanism can be triggered more readily in boys than in girls, especially in early and middle adolescence.

Parent-Adolescent Disparity in Sexual Attitudes

Within recent years there have been a number of studies designed to examine the differences between generations in attitudes, values, and beliefs as well as to assess the social and psychological factors affecting generational conflicts.

Children's attitudes regarding sexual permissiveness tend to resemble the attitudes held by their parents. However, how adolescents perceive or interpret their parents' sexual permissiveness is related to their own permissiveness (Walsh, 1972). Several investigators have shown that some women who have had premarital coitus without regrets expect their daughters to conform to a more conservative ethic (Cuber and Harroff, 1966).

Whereas only a small percentage of mothers in a recent study had a permissive attitude toward premarital coitus for their daughters and sons, approximately one third of these same mothers had experienced premarital coitus (Wake, 1969). One explanation for this difference may be that a mother in her premarital sexual experiences was aware of the importance of an emotional commitment as a necessary condition for sexual contact;

however, she may question whether her daughter is governed by such a commitment. Differences in attitudes toward sex between parents and their teenage child may also reflect the parents' feelings of responsibility for their children (Reiss, 1968, 1971).

Social Issues Raised by Findings Regarding Sex Practices

It is apparent that in the sphere of sex there is considerable discrepancy between what society conventionally demands or condones and what individuals actually do. In commenting on this, after the first Kinsey report, MacIver (1948) states that 95 per cent of the male population engage with some regularity, or have engaged, in sexual practices that are criminal offenses. If the laws were invariably enforced by males who do not break the law, this would mean that 5 per cent of the male population would have to send the remaining 95 per cent to jail.

One issue that arises from findings concerning sexual practices is the question as to what might be the effect on adolescents when they read about these findings. Several studies dealing with the response of college students to the Kinsey reports were reviewed by Ellis in 1953. One group of college students expressed the view that the Kinsey report on men had more of an effect on their attitudes than on their sex practices (Crespi and Stanley, 1948–1949). Other studies do not convincingly indicate that awareness of the Kinsey findings would substantially change attitudes or have an appreciable effect on overt behavior.[13]

Homosexuality in Adolescence

Considering the upsurge of sexual feelings at puberty, it is not surprising that many young adolescents have had some homosexual experiences. According to Kinsey et al. (1948, 1953), over 50 per cent of males and over 33 per cent of females remembered some homosexual activity either before or in early adolescence. However, 70 per cent of preadolescent boys reported some such activities, as did about 10 per cent of preadolescent girls. These activities including showing the genitals and mutual masturbation. Probably more homosexual feelings occur among females than has been reported, because warm and loving feelings between females are more

[13] The Kinsey and similar reports probably offer far less erotic excitement than many other influences to which young people are constantly exposed, including movies, novels, and even illustrated advertisements in Sunday newspapers, not to mention the sex talk adolescents carry on with one another.

socially acceptable in our culture than such feelings among males and these feelings may be disguised and unrecognized. Kinsey et al. (1948) stated that about 25 per cent of males of age twenty had had homosexual orgasm, with a higher incidence among early maturing boys and among boys who did not attend college. The percentage of girls reaching homosexual orgasm was much lower [1953, p. 454], with a higher percentage of homosexuality among better-educated girls. Most of the adolescents engaging in homosexual activity do not become overt, active homosexuals in adult life, so that a distinction must be made between transient homosexual interests and more lasting homosexual identity and behavior.

The development of homosexual identity is complex, differs in boys and girls, and remains a controversial subject. Many psychiatrists still consider homosexuality a developmental disturbance, although some do not. The American Psychiatric Association recently removed overt homosexuality from a list of sexual deviations by vote, but some groups of psychiatrists want to reopen the vote. (In a straw poll of New York psychiatrists [1975], 57.6 per cent favored the reopening of the vote, 38.5 per cent opposed it, and 3.9 per cent had no opinion.) If it is regarded as a disturbance of sexual development, as it has traditionally, it should be noted that homosexual activity is found among people with many different kinds of psychiatric problems, and it probably should be investigated as a fixation at, or a regression to, a particular period of emotional development. Although causal factors are disputed, it may be noted that homosexual activity may be associated with a variety of circumstances, such as underlying needs for closeness and support, anxiety about competition with the parent of the same sex, low self-esteem, difficulties in relating to the parent of the opposite sex (absence or emotional inaccessibility included), and difficulties in giving up early sadistic impulses.

In some instances men appear to show a characteristic parental background involving overprotective, dominant mothers and emotionally absent or hostile fathers. With such a background, the parental relationship is often poor, and such mothers tend to underrate the fathers; feminine activities may be pushed, and the mothers may be seductive to their sons while distant from their husbands. It is possible, of course, that the child's characteristics lead to these reactions of the parents, and there are homosexuals with a history of satisfactory relationships with both parents. There is some evidence that homosexual women experience opposite patterns of relationships with their parents to those stated here for men. Some homosexual women show a jealousy of men and a wish to be like men.

Homosexual activity is more prevalent in situations of limited contact with the opposite sex, such as in prisons or all-male or all-female boarding schools of various types.

There does appear today to be an increasing tolerance of homosexuality, and homosexuals are more openly organized to protest discrimination and also to justify and rationalize their sexual preferences. There are, however, many difficulties, both interpersonal and social, that are part of the homosexual's life.

Moral and Emotional Aspects of Adolescent Sex Behavior

When adolescents tell about their sex activities many justify them with the remark, "Everybody does it." However, in view of the pervasive moral and religious restrictions and sanctions surrounding sex,[14] it is unlikely that anyone can avoid conflicts concerning sex by this bland announcement. Such conflicts do not arise only in those who overtly violate the moral code, but also in many young people who covertly do forbidden things in their fantasies. The conflict is likely to be especially acute, however, when it is compounded by fear of public disgrace and fear of disapproval by others. Conflict combined with fear apparently is more prevalent among girls than boys, for under a double standard of morality the girl is the one who is more likely to meet disapproval. Moreover, it is mainly she who must bear the burden of pregnancy out of wedlock. Statistics concerning illegitimate births give only a meager indication of how justified such fears may be, for such statistics do not include pregnancies that have been terminated or that have been legitimized by marriage. (In one group of girls who married before finishing high school, Burchinal [1959] found that about 40 per cent were pregnant before marriage.) Even if complete statistics were available, these would give only a small part of the story, for they would not tell of girls who feared they might have become pregnant as a result of an indiscretion but did not, nor of those who are discreet but fear the thought of extramarital pregnancy.

In a study of the interests of 2,000 high school boys and a similar number of girls in problems relating to marriage and parenthood, Lantagne (1958) found that the subject of pregnancy rated highest in interest among the girls (it was eleventh on the boys' list). An interest in pregnancy

[14] There are codes regarding sex conduct even among those whose codes seem most unconventional (see, for example, Whyte (1943) "A Slum Sex Code"). Actually, when young people make the statement, "Everybody does it," they may express not simply an excuse for sex behavior but, in some instances, a state of being unable to resist the social pressures brought to bear on them. In a study by Smith (1924) a large proportion of girls said they petted because of a desire to do so, but 30 per cent said they petted because others did it, 12 per cent said they lacked courage to resist, 12 and 11 per cent, respectively, said their motive was a desire to please the man or a fear of being unpopular. (These percentages are not mutually exclusive, for some girls gave several answers.)

problems cannot be interpreted as meaning fear of premarital pregnancy, but it is apparent, and quite understandable, that girls are considerably more concerned about pregnancy than boys.

Three fifths of a group of single women and about half of a group of married women who took part in an investigation by Landis et al. (1940) reported that they had been the object of aggressive sexual advances by boys or men prior to the time they reached puberty. Over half of those who had had this experience reported emotional distress, including shock, worry, shame, fear of being found out, guilt, and extreme fright.

In a study by Jameson (1941), 21 per cent of a group of girls, juniors in college, reported that they had had shockingly undesirable experiences with boys during their college years. Although these girls did not hesitate to report that they had been shocked by the kind of advances men made to them, very few of them offered to describe these experiences.

Apart from acute emotional stresses, such as those just described, conflicts regarding sex arise when people feel compelled, in spite of strong scruples, to have sex relations in order to be popular or to conform or to "prove" their masculinity or femininity. Emotional conflict is likely to arise, whether consciously recognized or not, whenever a person uses sex "dishonestly" to satisfy devious needs, such as a need for conquest, a desire to defy authority, a desire for revenge, a need to overcome feelings of inferiority, or a need to hurt others, or when one pretends a love one does not feel in order to persuade another to gratify one's sexual desires.

Sex in Relation to Attitudes Toward Self and Others

As noted, there are complicated interrelationships between attitudes toward sex and attitudes toward self and others. If a child's elders are anxious about sex, regard it as dirty, shame the child when, for example, the child plays with its genitals, the child is being taught to regard a part of its own person as something dirty and objectionable. When a child is taught to view sexual feelings with shame, the child is being taught to view a normal part of itself as shameful.

Sex may become entangled in other ways with attitudes the adolescent has about himself and others. A person's sex behavior (including fantasies) may reflect other trends or traits in the personality: a tendency to be responsible or irresponsible; a tendency to be considerate, thoughtful, and tender in one's relations with others or a tendency to be callous; or a tendency to be compliant and conforming or rebellious.

The fact that sex is interwoven with all that goes into the making of a personality renders it difficult to interpret many of the research findings dealing with sexual behavior. To what extent, it might be asked, do the various forms of behavior reported by Kinsey and more recent research workers indicate what is "natural" from a purely sexual point of view, and to what extent and in what ways do they reflect a mixture of motives? We need a more comprehensive approach to sex in relation to the personality as a whole to answer this question.

References

Bell, R. R., & Blumberg, L. Courtship stages and intimacy attitudes. *Family Life Coordinator*, 1960, **8**, 60–63.

Bell, R. R., & Buerkle, J. V. Mother and daughter attitude to premarital sexual behavior. *Marriage and Family Living*, 1961, **23**, 390–392.

Bell, R. R., & Chaskes, J. B. Premarital sexual experiences among coeds, 1958 and 1968. *Journal of Marriage and the Family*, 1970, **32**, 81–84.

Boufford, M. I., & Bardwick, J. M. Patterns of affective fluctuation in the menstrual cycle. *Psychosomatic Medicine*, 1968, **30**, 336–345.

Boyce, J., & Benoit, C. Adolescent pregnancy. *New York State Journal of Medicine*, 1975, **75**, 872–874.

Burchinal, L. G. Does early dating lead to school-age marriages? *Iowa Farm Science*, 1959, **13**, 11–12.

Campbell, A. Personal communication, 1975.

Christensen, H. T., & Gregg, C. F. Changing sex norms in America and Scandinavia. *Journal of Marriage and the Family*, 1970, **32**, 616–627.

Crespi, L. P., & Stanley, A. E. Youth looks at the Kinsey Report. *Public Opinion Quarterly*, 1948–1949, **12**, 687–696.

Croake, J. W., & James, B. A four year comparison of premarital sexual attitudes. *Journal of Sex Research*, 1973, **9**, 91–96.

Cuber, J. F., & Harroff, P. B. *The significant Americans*. New York: Appleton, 1966.

Curry, E. T. Voice changes in male adolescents. *Laryngoscope*, 1946, **56**, 795–805.

Cutright, P. The teenage sexual revolution and the myth of an abstinent past. *Family Planning Perspectives*, 1972, **4**, 24–31.

Dimock, H. S. *Rediscovering the adolescent*. New York: Assn. Pr., 1937.

Ehrmann, W. Dating behavior of college students. *Marriage and Family Living*, 1952, **14**, 322–326.

Faust, M. S. Developmental maturity as a determinant in prestige of adolescent girls. *Child Development*, 1960, **31**, 173–184.

Ford, C. S., & Beach, F. A. *Patterns of sexual behavior*. New York: Harper, 1951.

Frisch, R. E., & Revelle, R. Height and weight at menarche and a hypothesis of critical body weights and adolescent events. *Science*, 1970, **169**, 397–399.

Gallup. Tolerance on sex is found growing. *New York Times*, August 12, 1973.

Hollingworth, L. S. Functional periodicity, an experimental study of the mental and motor abilities of women during menstruation. *Contributions to Education* (No. 69). New York: Teachers College, Columbia University, 1914.

Jameson, S. H. Adjustment problems of university girls arising from the urge for recognition and new experience. *Journal of Social Psychology*, 1941, **144**, 129–144.

Jersild, A. T. Self-understanding in childhood and adolescence. *American Psychologist*, 1951, **6**, 122–126.

Jersild, A. T., & Bienstock, S. F. A study of the development of children's ability to sing. *Journal of Educational Psychology*, 1934, **25**, 481–503.

Jessor, S. L., & Jessor, R. The transition from virginity to nonvirginity among youth: A social-psychological study over time. *Developmental Psychology*, 1975, **11**, 473–484.

Johnston, F. E., Malina, R. M., & Galbraith, M. A. Height, weight and age at menarche and the "critical weight" hypothesis. *Science*, 1971, **174**, 1148.

Jones, H. E. Adolescence in our society. From anniversary papers of the Community Service Society of New York, in *The family in a democratic society*. New York: Columbia U.P., 1949.

Jones, M. C. A study of socialization patterns at the high school level. *Journal of Genetic Psychology*, 1958, **92**, 87–111.

Jones, M. C., & Bayley, N. Physical maturing among boys as related to behavior. *Journal of Educational Psychology*, 1950, **41**, 129–148.

Jones, M. C., & Mussen, P. H. Self-conceptions, motivations, and interpersonal attitudes of early and late-maturing girls. *Child Development*, 1958, **29**, 491–501.

Kinsey, A. C., Pomeroy, W. B., & Martin, C. E. *Sexual behavior in the human male*. Philadelphia: Saunders, 1948.

Kinsey, A. C., Pomeroy, W. B., Martin, C. E., & Gebhard, P. H. *Sexual behavior in the human female*. Philadelphia: Saunders, 1953.

Landis, C., Landis, A. T., & Bolles, M. M. *Sex in development*. New York: Paul B. Hoeber, 1940.

Lantagne, J. E. Interests of 4,000 high school pupils in problems of marriage and parenthood. *Research Quarterly of the American Association for Health, Physical Education and Recreation*, 1958, **28**, 407–416.

Latham, A. J. The relationship between pubertal status and leadership in junior high school boys. *Journal of Genetic Psychology*, 1951, **78**, 185–194.

Luckey, E., & Nass, G. A comparison of sexual attitudes and behavior in an international sample. *Journal of Marriage and the Family*, 1969, **31**, 364–379.

MacIver, R. M. Sex and social attitudes. In D. P. Geddes & E. Curie (Eds.), *About the Kinsey Report*. New York: New American Library, 1948.

Marshall, W. A., & Tanner, J. M. Variations in the pattern of pubertal changes in boys. *Archives of Disease in Childhood*, 1970, **45**, 13–23.

McCary, J. L. *Human sexuality—physiological, psychological and sociological factors*. New York: Van Nostrand, 1973.

Money, J., & Clopper, R. R., Jr. Psychosocial and psychosexual aspects of errors of pubertal onset and development. *Human Biology*, 1974, **46**, 173–181.

Montagu, A. *Adolescent sterility*. Springfield, Ill.: Thomas, 1946.

Mosher, D. L., & Cross, H. J. Sex guilt and premarital sexual experiences of college students. *Journal of Consulting and Clinical Psychology*, 1971, **36**, 27–32.

Mussen, P. H., & Jones, M. C. Self-conceptions, motivations, and interpersonal attitudes of late- and early maturing boys. *Child Development*, 1957, **28**, 243–256.

Muuss, R. E. Adolescent development and the secular trend. *Adolescence*, 1970, **5**, 267–284.

Newton, N. *Maternal emotions*. New York: Harper, 1955.

Packard, V. The sexual attitudes of 2200 young adults. In V. Packard (Ed.), *The sexual wilderness. The contemporary upheaval in male-female relationships*. New York: Pocket Books, 1970.

Perlman, D. Self-esteem and sexual permissiveness. *Journal of Marriage and the Family*, 1974, **36**, 470–473.

Pomeroy, W. B. *Girls and sex*. New York: Delacorte, 1969.

Ramsey, G. V. The sexual development of boys. *American Journal of Psychology*, 1943, **56**, 217–233.

Reiss, I. L. The scaling of premarital sexual permissiveness. *Journal of Marriage and the Family*, 1964, **26**, 188–204.

Reiss, I. L. Premarital sexual standards. In C. E. Vincent (Ed.), *Human sexuality in medical education and practise*. Springfield, Ill.: Thomas, 1968.

Reiss, I. L. Premarital sex codes: The old and the new. In D. Grumnon & A. M. Barclay (Eds.), *Sexuality: A search for perspectives*. New York: Van Nostrand, 1971.

Reynolds, E. L., & Wines, J. V. Individual differences in physical changes associated with adolescent girls. *American Journal of Diseases of Children*, 1948, **75**, 329–350.

Root, A. W. Endocrinology of puberty: I. Normal sexual maturation. *Journal of Pediatrics*, 1973, **83**, 1–19.

Schonfeld, W. A. Inadequate masculine physique as a factor in personality development of adolescent boys. *Psychosomatic Medicine*, 1950, **12**, 49–54.

Schonfeld, W. A. The body and body-image in adolescents. In G. Caplan & S. Lebovici (Eds.), *Adolescence: Psychosocial perspectives*. New York: Basic Books, 1969.

Schonfeld, W. A., & Beebe, G. W. Normal growth and variations in the male genitalia from birth to maturity. *Journal of Urology*, 1942, **48**, 759–777.

Shainess, N. A re-evaluation of some aspects of femininity through a study of menstruation: A preliminary report. *Comprehensive Psychiatry*, 1961, **2**, 20.

Shuttleworth, F. K. The adolescent period. A pictorial atlas. *Monographs of the Society for Research in Child Development*, 1951, **14**(50).

Simon, W., & Gagnon, J. H. Psychosexual development. In W. Simon & J. H. Gagnon (Eds.), *The sexual scene*. Chicago: Trans-action Books, 1970.

Sollenberger, R. T. Some relationships between the urinary excretion of male hormones by maturing boys and girls and their expressed interests and attitudes. *Journal of Psychology*, 1940, **9**, 179–189.

Sorenson, R. C. *Adolescent sexuality in contemporary America: Personal values and sexual behavior, ages 13–19*. New York: World, 1973.

Stolz, H. R., & Stolz, L. M. *Somatic development of adolescent boys*. New York: Macmillan, 1951.

Stycos, J. M. Some dimensions of population and family planning: Goals and means. *Journal of Social Issues*, 1974, **30**, 1–29.

Tanner, J. M. *Growth at adolescence*. Oxford: Blackwell, 1962.

Tanner, J. M. Earlier maturation in man. *Scientific American*, 1968, **218,** 21–27.

Tanner, J. M. Growth and endocrinology of the adolescent. In L. Gardner (Ed.), *Endocrine and genetic diseases of childhood*. Philadelphia: Saunders, 1969.

Vener, A., & Stewart, C. Adolescent sexual behavior in middle America revisited: 1970–1973. *Journal of Marriage and the Family*, 1974, **4**, 728.

Verinis, J. S., & Roll, S. Primary and secondary male characteristics: The hairiness and large penis stereotypes. *Psychological Reports*, 1970, **26**, 123–126.

Wake, F. R. Attitudes of parents towards the premarital sexual behavior of their children and themselves. *Journal of Sex Research*, 1969, **5**, 170–177.

Walsh, R. H. The generation gap in sexual beliefs. *Sexual Behavior*, 1972, **2**, 4–10.

Weatherley, D. Self-perceived rate of physical maturation and personality in late adolescence. *Child Development*, 1964, **35**, 1197–1210.

Whyte, W. F. A slum sex code. *American Journal of Sociology*, 1943, **49**, 24–31.

Yankelovich, D. *The changing values on campus*. New York: Simon & Schuster, 1972.

Zacharias, L., Rand, W. M., & Wurtman, R. J. A prospective study of sexual development and growth in American girls: The statistics of menarche. *Obstetrical and Gynecological Survey*, 1976, **31**, 325–336.

Zacharias, L., Wurtman, R. J., & Schatzoff, M. Sexual maturation in contemporary American girls. *American Journal of Obstetrics and Gynecology*, 1970, **108**, 883–886.

5

physical abilities and their
psychological meanings

During late childhood and adolescence there is a more pronounced gain in muscular strength than in physical size. Measurements of the strength of a group of young people over a span of years from age eleven to eighteen showed that four fifths of an adult's strength, but hardly more than one third of his height, is acquired after the age of six years (Jones, 1949a).

Through gains in strength, speed, and capacity for coordinated movement that occur during adolescence, the body reaches, or almost

128

reaches, the maximum development of its physical powers. The peak of ability in some performances may be reached even before the period usually covered by the term *adolescence* has been completed.

During adolescence many persons reach not only their peak performance in several motor activities, but also the peak of their desire to be active. Many begin to show a strong decline in their desire for being physically on the go at the middle and toward the end of adolescence. This differs from their behavior in the early childhood years. One mark of childhood is a strong desire to be active. One of the most stable marks of maturity is a strong inclination to sit down.

Girls "mature" in this fashion earlier than boys—except, perhaps, in their interest in dancing. As we will see later, girls also reach their maximum capacity for physical activity earlier than boys (Tanner, 1970). But boys begin to slow down a bit and to curtail the number of their play activities as they reach the end of the teens. They are likely to confine their activities or to specialize much more than they did when they were ten or twelve. Even the boy who still knocks himself out on the college football field (while the girls, seated, look on) is likely to be much more sedentary between games and practice periods than he was in high school or in the elementary grades. (Men, as a group, seem to cling more to the memory of their active childhood years than women do, but most of them do so vicariously by watching others play the games they used to play.)

Growth trends in motor performances of boys and girls

Some measurements of motor development are shown in Figures 5.1 through 5.4. These measurements were made by Espenschade (1940) in a study in which the same boys and girls were tested repeatedly over a period of several years. Figure 5.1 shows performances in a test of jump and reach. Figure 5.2 is based on a test of the distance those tested could throw a 12-ounce ball. Figure 5.3 shows speed of running a 50-yard dash, and Figure 5.4 shows distance of a broad jump. In all these performances the boys excelled the girls, and in most of them the boys were still showing appreciable gains from one half-year to the next. The girls, instead of improving from one half-year to the next, made a poorer record in three of the performances when tested at age sixteen, or a short time thereafter, than they had made in tests when they were younger. Differences between boys and girls were less marked, however, in a test for accuracy in throwing at a target.

In other words, the superiority of boys is less when it involves precision of movement. Moreover, in dealing with performances that call for

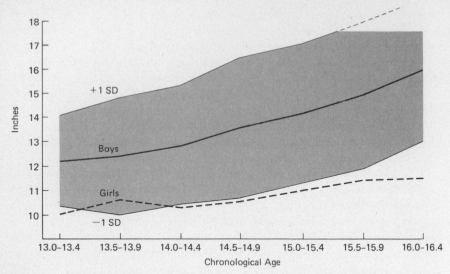

Figure 5.1. Measurements in motor development: Jump and reach. [From *Motor performance in adolescence* by A. Espenschade, Monographs of the Society for Research in Child Development, 1940, *5*, No. 1. Reprinted by permission.]

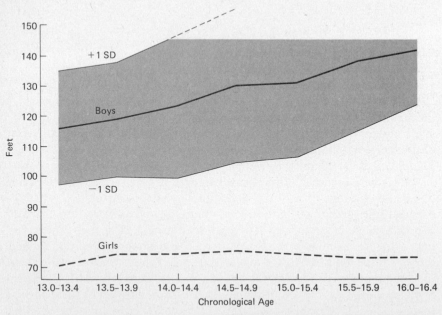

Figure 5.2. Measurements in motor development: Distance throw. [From *Motor performance in adolescence* by A. Espenschade, Monographs of the Society for Research in Child Development, 1940, *5*, No. 1. Reprinted by permission.]

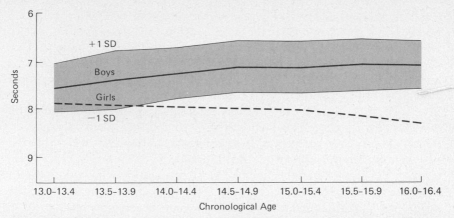

Figure 5.3. Measurements in motor development: Fifty-yard dash. [From *Motor performances in adolescence* by A. Espenschade, Monographs of the Society for Research in Child Development, 1940, *5*, No. 1. Reprinted by permission.]

skillful coordination rather than speed or vigor of movement, it is likely that the difference between boys and girls, if there is a difference, will depend more on the amount of practice they have had than on any special advantage that goes with being a boy or girl. This is illustrated in a study by McFarlane (1925). Tests designed to measure "practical ability" were given. Some of the tests called not only for manual skill in fitting various mechanical parts

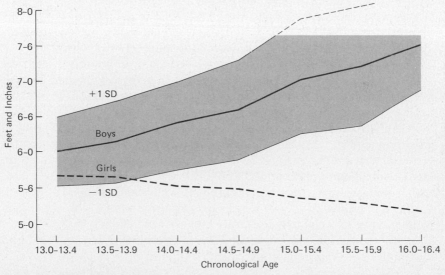

Figure 5.4. Measurements in motor development: Broad jump. [From *Motor performance in adolescence* by A. Espenschade, Monographs of the Society for Research in Child Development, 1940, *5*, No. 1. Reprinted by permission.]

together, but also for the ability to perceive or to grasp what the parts added up to or what could be made of them. Two tests involved pieces of wood that, when fitted together, produced a wheelbarrow and a wooden cradle. Two tests required the fitting together of pieces of cloth to produce a girl's dress and a boy's coat. Another test called for speed and precision in inserting a steel plunger into a succession of sockets.

The boys were superior to the girls in putting together a cradle and wheelbarrow, but the girls were superior to the boys (and to a greater degree) in all comparisons in making garments out of pieces of cloth. In the test with the plunger there was little difference. In other words, in activities in which the girls presumably had had more practice than the boys, they not only equaled, but surpassed, the boys. This suggests that many of the sex differences that are found in motor and mechanical activities are due not so much to a genuine sex difference as to a difference in amount of interest, experience, and practice.

In general, boys manifest greater speed and coordination of gross body movements, whereas girls excel in manual dexterity. Several investigators have reported that girls score higher than boys in finger dexterity and perceptual speed and accuracy (Droege, 1967; Backman, 1972; and Strutl et al., 1973). These findings point to the significance of the distinction between small and large muscle movements, or fine versus relatively gross movements.

The tendency of boys to participate in activities that involve large muscle or gross motor activity more often than girls has been observed even at the preschool level (Emmerich, 1971). One might speculate that this difference is related to the greater interest manifested by boys in both informal and formal sports (Maccoby and Jacklin, 1974).

We have noted that boys continue to show an interest in physical activities after many girls have begun to show a sharp falling off in such interests. In junior and senior high school, girls frequently ask to be excused from gym classes. In one large school population studied by Lund (1944) there was an increase of 400 per cent from the seventh to the twelfth grade in girls' requests for excuses due to alleged physical disability. However, this increase was due to changes in interest and motives rather than to an increase in illness or other kinds of physical disability. The social interests of the girls apparently were not in accord with what was demanded or offered on the gymnasium floor. Among the reasons given were a lack of physical inclination to take the exercise, concern about the effect gym work might have on the hairdo and make-up, fear of developing big muscles, and unwillingness to change clothes.

Sex differences in strength were also noted by Goss (1968), who measured the grip of third-, sixth-, ninth-, and twelfth-grade students using a dynamometer. Boys were found to increase their strength much more than girls as they entered adolescence. The difference in strength between twelfth-grade girls and boys was much greater than that between third-grade girls and boys. It is likely that at least some of these differences resulted from the lessened interest and esteem placed on strength by girls that has already been noted.

Interestingly, according to Rarick (1973), the level of physical performance in adolescent girls is not affected by the menses; where effects are cited in the literature, performance is poorer premenstrually, with improved performance during the period and the best performance post-menstrually.

Asmussen (1973), using a dynamometer, found that boys tended to be stronger than girls at every age. It was conjectured that male sex hormones might play a role in influencing muscular growth, leading to an "extra gain of strength" in boys at adolescence. Espenschade (1947) found similar results using the Brace Motor Ability Test: girls' performances decreased after age fourteen, whereas boys showed increasing ability to perform the tests.

Rarick and Smoll (1967) examined the stability of growth in muscular strength (using a dynamometer) and motor performance from childhood into adolescence, using twenty-five boys and twenty-four girls (from the Wisconsin Growth Study). Data were obtained annually from age seven to twelve and again at seventeen. The conclusion was that the strong child or the child who performed motor tasks well did not necessarily retain that superiority in adolescence, although a child who was both strong and showed good motor skills would probably rank high among his or her peers in adolescence. Growth in height, weight, and physique was relatively stable, but growth of muscle strength was variable, more so in the arms than in the legs.

In a study of boys retested annually from ten to sixteen, Carron and Bailey (1974) found that there were small but significant correlations between strength and both height and weight. Individual differences in strength remained stable, and early maturers showed greater strength than late maturers, perhaps because of greater body weight. Maximum increase in strength was found to occur one year after both peak height velocity and peak weight velocity.

In a summary of studies relating to ethnic differences in physical ability, Malina (1973) concluded that black boys are similar to white boys in strength and performance, except in consistently better vertical jumping performance by black boys. The data comparing black and white girls were inconclusive.

Hereditary factors appear to play an important role in individual differences in motor abilities and activity levels according to twin studies done by McNemar (1933) and Willerman (1973). The correlations between the motor abilities of fraternal twins were significantly lower than between identical twins (McNemar, 1933).

Relationships between mental and physical growth

At practically all age levels the individual who is above average in one major feature of his make-up is more likely to be above than below average in other features. Positive correlations have been found between mental ability and certain physical measurements. However, among normal children the correlations between mental ability and body size, and between intelligence and motor ability, while positive, are low (Abernethy, 1936).

Lauten (1968) found a correlation of .15 between motor abilities and intelligence. Asmussen (1973) reported no correlation between IQ and strength in the normal range of IQ, but found that boys of lower IQ (70–90) showed lower strength than normals at similar heights. Within the normal range of intelligence, the correspondence between mental and physical growth is so low that youngsters who are homogeneous in mentality will be very heterogeneous physically.

Sexton (1973) compared measures of masculinity and academic achievement in 1,000 ninth-grade boys and girls and found that less masculine boys had better marks in most school subjects, with the exceptions of physical education and science, and that the boys rated as most masculine usually received their worst grades in English. Low-achieving boys were found to spend more time on sports and with girls than high-achieving boys.

Relationships between physical ability and popularity

Relationships between motor performance and other traits, as shown by a group of California boys who cooperated in a growth study in which various measurements were made at half-yearly intervals from age eleven to age eighteen, are shown in Tables 5.1 and 5.2. The gross motor scores were based on a series of athletic performances such as are commonly involved in playground games. Popularity was based on a measure of reputation with classmates. "Good looks" were also determined by classmates' ratings.

Popularity was more closely linked with physical strength and skill in athletic activities than with intelligence and school achievement. Also, there was a higher correspondence between strength and popularity than between popularity and socioeconomic status. An athletic boy from the "wrong side

Table 5.1. Motor performance correlations with other developmental traits in boys

	Total strength (grip, pull, thrust)	Gross motor scores (track events)
Chronological age	.39 ± .06	.18 ± .07
Skeletal age	.50 ± .055	.36 ± .06
Height	.65 ± .04	.40 ± .06
Popularity	.30 ± .07	.39 ± .06
"Good looks"	.21 ± .07	.38 ± .06
Intelligence	−.17 ± .07	.05 ± .08

Source: From *Motor performance and growth* by P. A. Bower and H. E. Jones, University of California Press, 1949. Reprinted by permission.

Table 5.2. Correlations of strength and other traits with popularity (boys)

Variable	Correlation
Dynamic strength	.39 ± .06
Static strength	.30 ± .07
Maturity (skeletal age)	.15 + .07
Height	.07 ± .08
Social status (home rating)	.05 ± .08
Intelligence	.04 ± .08
School achievement	.03 ± .08
Chronological age	.00 ± .08

Source: From *Motor performance and growth* by P. A. Bower and H. E. Jones, University of California Press, 1949. Reprinted by permission.

of the tracks" was likely to be more popular than a nonathletic boy from the right side.

Popularity has also been found to be related to interest in sports and information about sports (Horowitz, 1967). In a study of leadership and interests among adolescents, Marks (1957) reported that boys who were male clique leaders were interested in social activities, were popular, and displayed athletic prowess. Among adolescent girls, leaders were attractive, popular, and were interested in either scientific matters or athletic skills. Among college students, athletic ability plays a role in maintaining a leadership position in some groups but not in others (Maccoby and Jacklin, 1974).

Observations such as the foregoing are significant from the point of view of understanding adolescents and the way they appraise one another. Adults rating adolescents are likely to give more weight to intelligence and school achievement and less to strength and athletic ability than young people do. In the view of some adults, therefore, adolescents follow a superficial system of values.

The preceding observations do not, of course, show anything approaching a perfect correspondence between social acceptance and strength or athletic ability. Other characteristics obviously are important.

For instance, Jones (1949a) points out that the prestige boys attach to physical characteristics, especially to strength and the masculine meaning of strength, is likely to vary in different social groups. However, the high value placed on athletic ability stands out sharply in quite diverse communities.[1]

Values attached to athletic ability

In a study conducted in a large high school in Brooklyn, New York, Tannenbaum (1959) asked eleventh-graders to record their attitudes toward hypothetical students with various combinations of (1) athletic ability, (2) brilliance, and (3) studiousness.

The eleventh-graders were asked to mark each hypothetical student on the basis of a list of fifty-four traits. (Twenty-seven of these traits had been rated as desirable by a large percentage of high school students in a preliminary study; nineteen had been rated as undesirable, and eight had received a divided vote and were treated as neutral.)

Table 5.3 shows that the hypothetical nonathletic model was consistently rated lower than the athletic model by girls and boys. Students who had good scholastic records, or whose parents were above average in education, did not differ significantly from other students in placing a high value on athletic ability.[2]

Table 5.3. Average ratings made by eleventh-graders of the social acceptibility of 8 hypothetical students

	305 Girls		310 Boys	
	Average	*Rank*	*Average*	*Rank*
Brilliant, nonstudious, athletic	31.36	1	25.28	1
Average, nonstudious, athletic	29.04	2	23.14	3
Average, studious, athletic	26.10	3	22.27	4
Brilliant, studious, athletic	23.66	4	23.83	2
Brilliant, nonstudious, nonathletic	14.27	5	9.24	6
Average, nonstudious, nonathletic	10.68	6	10.61	5
Average, studious, nonathletic	8.86	7	8.02	7
Brilliant, studious, nonathletic	1.58	8	2.83	8

Note: The maximum possible range of scores was from +46 to −46.
Source: From "A study of verbal stereotypes associated with brilliant and average students," by A. J. Tannenbaum, unpublished Doctor of Philosophy dissertation, Teachers College, Columbia University, 1959. Reprinted by permission.

[1] Tannenbaum (1959) has reviewed a number of studies on this subject, including writings by Americans and Europeans who have discussed evidences of "anti-intellectualism" in the United States.

[2] In the same study, results from small samplings of adolescents with varying ethnic backgrounds in other urban and rual communities did not differ significantly from those shown in Table 5.3.

When adolescents place a very high value on athletic ability and a low estimate on studiousness, they are reflecting attitudes common in adult society. The athletic star is honored more than the hard-working scholar. However, individual adolescents have varying motives for upgrading the athlete and downgrading the bright, studious nonathlete. Some perhaps envy the diligent student, especially if he or she is bright. It is likely also that some young people who give a low rating to studiousness are knowingly or unknowingly expressing rebellion against teachers and the meaninglessness, to them, of what they have to memorize at school. Whatever the varying motives might be, however, it is clear that the athlete has high prestige. This finding is true cross-culturally and for both sexes. For many past generations of adolescents athletic "stars" have predominantly been boys or young men. In recent years there has been a strong push to give girls and young women a more equitable and honored position in the athletic program. At present, tennis is one sport in which girls in their teens or many years beyond their teens have especially achieved prominence. Gymnastics is another area, among many, in which adolescent and postadolescent girls are encouraged and often win distinction. Even baseball has been opened to girls to a greater extent than in the past, in spite of the doubts and resistance manifested by many males. It is likely that, as we move into the future, the field of sports and leisure-time activities requiring motor skills will be considerably less dominated by males than it has been in the past. However, males undoubtedly still will be better able than females to deliver a crushing uppercut in a prize fight or to execute (or survive) a powerful tackle in football.

In a study done by McCandless and Ali (1966) investigating the effects of culture on the relationship between athletic skills and popularity, it was found that athletics was more important to girls in all-girl schools than in coeducational schools. Athletic girls in all-girl schools were significantly more popular than nonathletic girls, perhaps filling the niche held by athletic boys in a coeducational school.

On the other hand, even though the high esteem accorded to physical ability and athletic skill is impressive, there is something artificial about it. The athlete is honored more than he is emulated. Educators who are interested in promoting physical fitness, rather than simply in whipping a small minority of students into a winning team, frequently deplore the general unfitness of a large proportion of young people. In a study of 1,000 students entering a midwestern university, Cureton (1943) found that a large proportion were lacking in ordinary physical skills. Fourteen per cent were classified as soft and flabby with an undeveloped physique; 24 per cent could not jump a waist-high obstacle; 26 per cent could not chin themselves five times; 42 per cent could not skin the cat; and 64 per cent could not swim fifty yards. In another, larger, college group of 2,628 men, 40.5 per cent

Girls increasingly participate in sports once dominated by boys. [Abigail Heyman/Magnum.]

could not run a mile in seven minutes;[3] and 52 per cent could not do twenty leg-lifts and sit-ups in succession.

There are many schools in which, from the viewpoint of some adults, the prestige system is dominated too much by athletics (Coleman, 1961). An athletic program (or any other program) that throws the spotlight on a few stars can do an injustice to those who do not make the grade.

The value adolescents place on athletic ability may, however, have a democratizing effect if it is not the dominant or only standard applied in judging the worth of the individual student. In a school where scholastic ability is an important criterion for judging a student's worth, there will be many students who will be judged unworthy by that standard even though, in other respects, they are very worthy. If, however, in this school students are judged also by athletic ability, there will be an opportunity for a larger proportion of students to have their abilities recognized. In the group of good scholars there will be some who belong to the group of good athletes; but it is more likely that many students will belong to only one of the groups,

[3] Older readers might wonder why anyone would *want* to run a mile in less than seven minutes. But speed in running is very important in most of the sports that bring athletic acclaim. Moreover, other skills in the above list are advantageous in other ways. Ability to jump a waist-high hedge might be very handy for an enterprising young man, and ability to swim fifty yards could make the difference in staying alive or drowning.

PHYSICAL ASPECTS OF DEVELOPMENT **138**

for there is only a low correlation between motor ability and academic ability.

Motor ability does not seem to be distributed according to social class or socioeconomic status to the same extent as intellectual ability. Jones (1949a) compared children of high socioeconomic status within his total group with children of low status. The first three years of the study coincided with three years of severe economic depression when many of the "low" families lived on drastically reduced budgets and some depended on public relief. Although, as Jones points out, other studies have shown that children of higher socioeconomic status tend to have an advantage in height and weight (Sanders, 1934), the findings in Jones's study still indicate that motor ability cuts across socioeconomic lines to a greater extent than does intellectual ability.

As everyone who follows the sports events, including the Olympics has observed, blacks, who might be subject to discrimination in other areas, are winning much acclaim in athletics.

Personal implications of physical ability

Not only are young adolescent boys with athletic skill more popular, but administrators and teachers perceive them as having more desirable personality traits (Clarke and Clarke, 1961). The positive association between personality ratings and athletic ability in young adolescents may reflect the fact that involvement in sports facilitates socialization.

The meaning of having or lacking the kind of strength and athletic ability that is highly valued in a group has been brought out in very personal terms by Jones (1949a) in the study already cited. Jones compared the ten boys who stood lowest in ability with the ten who stood highest.

The boys selected as "strong" were, more often than not, well favored when evaluated in terms of other aspects of their personalities. The group of boys who were poor in tests of strength presented a different picture. The lower ten were socially, as well as physically, weak; usually they were not so much disliked as ignored by their classmates. When records of their personal adjustment were examined, only one of the ten showed up in a distinctly favorable light. Three had approximately average scores in "total adjustment" but showed evidence of persisting tension and conflicts seemingly associated with feelings of inferiority. Six of the boys had records that seemed definitely to reveal maladjustment, especially at the end of adolescence. One boy, for example, fell from being about average in popularity to a very unpopular position at a time when physical differences between him and his associates were most marked. At age fourteen and a half he was regarded by his classmates as unfriendly, listless, lacking in humor about himself, immature, inactive in games, and unwilling to take a chance. He did not easily accept this loss in social esteem. Although he took no part in games, he showed an increase in restlessness; and although he was judged to be less friendly, he was more talkative and attention seeking. Actually, he did not want to be less friendly, but he was immature and ineffective in his use of social techniques.

Another boy described by Jones (1949a) also suffered a decline in prestige, but the decline in his case came later, partly because he had a natural buoyancy that helped him for a time. At the age of fourteen and a half he was still above average in popularity, but three years later he was rated low in popularity. He was no longer regarded as friendly by his classmates; he no longer stood out as a person who seemed to enjoy himself in most situations; he had less humor; and he was looked upon as immature. His reaction, like the reaction of the other boy mentioned, was to become bossier, restless, and more talkative in an effort to gain attention. But, as described by Jones, he was not one to be held down by adversity, so he also showed a tendency to become more aggressive ("enjoys a fight") and more daring ("always ready to take a chance at things that are new and unusual"). Both these boys, Jones points out, were exposed to similar adolescent stresses from causes that were in part the same, but their reactions to these stresses were an outgrowth in part of their earlier personality tendencies. One of them, who already was a fighter, became the "fightingest" boy in the group. The other, who was previously timid, became the least aggressive of the group in situations that required initiative and physical enterprise.

The fact that physical skills have great prestige value suggests that troubled and unaccepted adolescents might benefit from a systematic program to improve skills. Although this is probably true, it is stated too simply. More would be required than merely to patch certain skills onto an already existing personality structure. A person's tendency to join in activities or to stay passively on the sidelines is not determined simply by the factor of skill. Whether one enters into sports will be influenced by one's willingness to rub elbows with others, one's ability to enter easily and freely into social contacts, one's aggressiveness, and one's willingness to face the possibility of being roughed up a bit. The tendency to enter in vigorously or to stay on the fringe is influenced also by the person's ability to tolerate being tested, being defeated, and making mistakes.

Team sports involve close cooperation among team members, a subordination of the individual's desire to be the center of attraction, and fierce competitiveness between opposing teams. Discipline within a team is often achieved through an inflexible dominance hierarchy (Fiedler, 1954) that results in greater cooperation and subordination of the player. In contrast, one-to-one sports (tennis) allow the player to compete as well as "show off" (Maccoby and Jacklin, 1974). Thus, different sports involve varying degrees of aggression and cooperation. An individual's personality will determine which sports suit his or her particular needs and interests.

In one study in which "actives" and "fringers" were compared (Cowell, 1935), it was observed that lack of desire or ability to take part in the physical education program may be tied to characteristics such as shyness and sensitivity and a tendency to be upset by defeat and to shrink from new ventures. In another study, Fauquier (1940) cites findings and opinions that support the theory set forth by Adler (1929) that it is not just by chance that a person joins in this or that game or sport. According to this theory, one's choice of a certain activity, one's approach to it, and the importance one attaches to it tell something about one's attitudes regarding the self and one's relationships with others. From findings in a study comparing "aggressive" and "submissive" boys, Fauquier (1940) concluded that play habits are not isolated and disconnected elements in a boy's personality that can be molded and manipulated at will. Rather, play habits are symptoms reflecting a larger and more complicated system of thinking, feeling, and acting.

Play activities may give expression to a desire for novelty, adventure, and excitement. They may express a need for social approval, attention, status, and recognition, or they may spring from an urge for a sense of mastery, power, success, and achievement (Dimock, 1937).

In view of the fact that participation in physical activities is linked with pervasive tendencies within the personality, it is apparent that a program designed to help individual youngsters must be varied and flexible. This would hold true especially in a program designed to help shy and troubled youngsters. Instead of demanding a standard of excellence that is beyond the reach of a large number of youngsters, such a program would recognize levels of ability so that youngsters would be aware of achievement and improvement even though they were far from a "perfect" performance. It would not have a lopsided emphasis on a few sports, such as football and basketball; nor would it center entirely on competitive activities. This would require teachers or leaders who are sensitive to differences in interest and temperament and who are able to tolerate a wide range of achievement. It would require teachers who can identify with individuals at various levels of skill and who are not seeking by proxy to work out some of their own unmet needs to be glamorous stars.

This would mean, among other things, that the instructor might encourage one youngster to strive to reach a peak of form while trying to get other youngsters to participate regardless of form. Also it would mean that in an activity such as square dancing the immediate goal might be to help some people improve their timing and rhythm while helping other people to grip their partners as though they really meant business, even though they were still somewhat inept in going through the steps. There is perhaps no other single department of the high school that offers greater opportunity than the physical education program for studying individual students, their styles of life, their potentialities for being spontaneous and free, their hesitancies and lack of self-confidence, their need to vanquish, or their need at all costs to avoid defeat or a contest in which they might look awkward.

But to realize the potentialities for helping young people in the quest for self-discovery we need an emphasis different from the one students often see as prevailing in most schools.

References

Abernethy, E. M. Relationships between mental and physical growth. *Monographs of the Society for Research in Child Development,* 1936, **1**(7).

Adler, A. *Understanding human nature.* Garden City, N.Y.: Doubleday, 1929.

Asmussen, E. Growth in muscular strength and power. In G. L. Rarick (Ed.), *Physical activity—human growth and development.* New York: Academic, 1973.

Backman, M. E. Patterns of mental abilities: Ethnic, socioeconomic, and sex differences. *American Educational Research Journal,* 1972, **9**, 1–12.

Bower, P. A., & Jones, H. E. *Motor performance and growth.* Los Angeles: U. of California Press, 1949.

Carron, A. V., & Bailey, D. A. Strength development in boys from 10 through 16 years. *Monographs of the Society for Research in Child Development,* 1974, **39**(4, Serial No. 157).

Clarke, H. H., & Clarke, D. H. Social status and mental health of boys as related to their maturity, structural, and strength characteristics. *Research Quarterly,* 1961, **32**, 326–334.

Coleman, J. S. *The adolescent society.* New York: Free Press, 1961.

Cowell, C. C. An abstract of a study of differentials in junior high school boys based on the observation of physical education activities, a study of "fringers" vs. "actives." *Research Quarterly,* 1935, **6**(4), 129–136.

Cureton, T. K. The unfitness of young men in motor fitness. *Journal of the American Medical Association,* 1943, **123**, 69–74.

Dimock, H. S. *Rediscovering the adolescent.* New York: Assn. Pr., 1937.

Droege, R. C. Sex differences in aptitude maturation during high school. *Journal of Counseling Psychology,* 1967, **14**, 407–411.

Emmerich, W. Structure and development of personal-social behavior in preschool settings. Educational Testing Service–Head Start Longitudinal Study, November, 1971.

Espenschade, A. Motor performance in adolescence. *Monographs of the Society for Research in Child Development,* 1940, **5**(1).

Espenschade, A. Development of motor coordination in boys and girls. *Research Quarterly. American Association of Health,* 1947, **18**, 30–44.

Fauquier, W. The attitudes of aggressive and submissive boys toward athletics. *Child Development,* 1940, **11**, 115–125.

Fiedler, F. E. Assumed similarity measures as predictors of team effectiveness. *Journal of Abnormal and Social Psychology,* 1954, **49,** 381–388.

Goss, A. M. Estimated versus actual physical strength in three ethnic groups. *Child Development,* 1968, **39,** 283–290.

Horowitz, H. Prediction of adolescent popularity and rejection from achievement and interest items. *Journal of Educational Psychology,* 1967, **58,** 170–174.

Jersild, A. T., Telford, C. W., & Sawrey, J. M. *Child psychology.* (7th ed.). Englewood Cliffs, N. J.: Prentice-Hall, 1975.

Jones, H. E. *Motor performance and growth.* Berkeley: University of California Press, 1949.

Jones, H. E. Adolescence in our society. Anniversary papers of the Community Service Society of New York. In *The family in a democratic society.* New York: Columbia U.P., 1949.

Lauten, D. A. Relationships between intelligence and motor proficiency in the intellectually gifted child. Unpublished doctoral dissertation, University of North Carolina, 1968.

Lund, F. H. Adolescent motivation: Sex differences. *Journal of Genetic Psychology,* 1944, **64,** 99–103.

Maccoby, E. E., & Jacklin, C. N. *The psychology of sex differences.* Stanford, Calif.: Stanford U.P., 1974.

Malina, R. M. Ethnic and cultural factors in the development of motor abilities and strength in American children. In G. L. Rarick (Ed.), *Physical activity—human growth and development.* New York: Academic, 1973.

Marks, J. B. Interests and leadership among adolescents. *Journal of Genetic Psychology,* 1957, **91,** 163–172.

McCandless, B. R., & Ali, F. Relations among physical skills and personal and social variables in three cultures of adolescent girls. *Journal of Educational Psychology,* 1966, **57,** 366–372.

McFarlane, M. A study of practical ability. *British Journal of Psychology Monograph Supplement,* 1925, 3(8), 35–36.

McNemar, Q. Twin resemblances in motor skills and the effects of practice thereon. *Pedagogical Seminary and Journal of Genetic Psychology,* 1933, **42,** 60–99.

Rarick, G. L. *Physical activity—human growth and development.* New York: Academic, 1973.

Rarick, G. L., & Smoll, F. L. Stability of growth in strength and motor performance from childhood to adolescence. *Human Biology,* 1967, **39,** 295–306.

Sanders, B. S. *Environment and growth.* Baltimore: Warwick and York, 1934.

Sexton, P. C. Play, games and sport in the psychosocial development of children and youth. In G. L. Rarick (Ed.), *Physical activity—human growth and development.* New York: Academic, 1973.

Strutl, G. F., Anderson, D. R., & Well, A. D. Developmental trends in the effects of irrelevant information. Paper presented to the *Society for Research in Child Development,* Philadelphia, 1973.

Tannenbaum, A. J. A study of verbal stereotypes associated with brilliant and average students. Unpublished doctoral dissertation, Teachers College, Columbia University, 1959.

Tanner, J. M. Physical growth. In P. H. Mussen (Ed.), *Carmichael's manual of child psychology* (Vol. 1). New York: Wiley, 1970.

Willerman, L. Activity level and hyperactivity in twins. *Child Development*, 1973, **44**, 288–293.

part three
THOUGHT AND FANTASY

6

mental growth:
cognitive aspects

This chapter and some that follow deal with various facets of thought, concept formation, and other intellectual processes that have an important role in the mental life of adolescents. The focus in this chapter will center primarily on thinking. In the next chapter, which also is entitled "Mental Growth," intellectual abilities as measured by mental tests will be considered. Mental processes will again enter the discussion in later chapters dealing with adolescent fantasies and dreams, the development of moral

147

Jean Piaget (1896–), Swiss-born psychologist, teacher, and author. [The Bettmann Archive, Inc.]

concepts and attitudes, and ideas that enter into adolescents' concepts pertaining to themselves and their evaluation of themselves. Various facets of intellectual orientation will also be considered in Chapter 17 dealing with young people's response to high school and college.

To describe thinking at the adolescent level it is necessary to give some attention to earlier cognitive development and changes in various other intellectual operations.

Piaget's contributions to knowledge of the growth of understanding[1]

The most comprehensive descriptive and theoretical account of the development of perceptual and cognitive functions has been offered by Jean Piaget, director of studies of the Institut Jean-Jacques Rousseau in Geneva,

[1] For a review of Piaget's early work, see *The Child's Conception of the World* (1926), *The Child's Conception of Physical Causality* (1960), and *Judgment and Reasoning in the Child* (1928). Two books dealing with studies of infancy are *The Construction of Reality in the Child* (1937) and *The Origins of Intelligence in Children* (1936). Several books are devoted to the development of conceptions of number, measurement, logical classes, and geometry (Piaget et al., 1960). For more recent presentations of his theory, see Piaget, 1970a, b,; 1972.

Switzerland. In numerous books and articles Piaget has traced the forerunners of processes that appear in thinking at the adolescent level. These processes include, among others, the ability to center one's attention on a given event or topic; to formulate an intention or objective that includes an outcome that may be anticipated but has not yet been achieved; to deal effectively with the concepts of cause and effect, number, quantity and measurement; to classify things or ideas according to a logical system; to view things, thoughts, feelings, and relationships not only from one's own standpoint (an egocentric orientation), but also from the standpoint of someone else's perspective (someone whose view may be different from, or contrary to, one's own); and, as a crowning intellectual feat, to back off, so to speak, and examine one's thoughts and attitudes, making them objects of scrutiny rather than taking them for granted.

Much of Piaget's work has been replicated in the United States, Great Britain, Canada, and elsewhere (see, for example, Almy et al., 1970; Brook, 1970; Chapman, 1975; Keating, 1975; and Kramer et al., 1975).

Biological Attributes Underlying Mental Activity

According to Piaget, intellectual functioning rests on two biological attributes common to all living creatures: *organization* and a *capacity for adaptation.*

Among the elements in a person's organization are those involved in the function of the intellect. Normal children are so organized that they are destined to become thinkers. At first they respond to circumstances encountered in the process of living to a large extent by way of reflex action. But as time passes, the cerebral cortex increasingly intervenes in a manner that eventually leads to an elaborate mental organization.

Children's capacity for adaptation includes two complementary processes: *assimilation* and *accommodation.* Assimilation occurs, for example, when a youngster notices that a spherically shaped piece of candy placed before him on a flat surface rolls when he inadvertently gives it a push, and a marble, similarly placed before him, also rolls when pushed. The child may now be on the way toward forming the idea that things that are spherical are also rollable. (Later on, a rolling rubber ball is likely to be assimilated into this incipient thought structure.) He puts the candy in his mouth: it is sweet and chewable. With a gleam in his eyes he puts the marble in his mouth: it is neither sweet nor chewable. So now (or in time), by a process of accommodation, he must adapt himself to the fact that objects similarly round and rollable are not necessarily edible. When he deliberately pushes a ball to see if it will roll, or puts a marble in his mouth expecting it to be sweet, he is, in a rudimentary way, testing a theory, foreshadowing the day, many years hence, when in a chemistry laboratory he will make a test of a theory he has formed. The processes of assimilation and accommodation are involved not only in the thinking of young children, but also, at the adult level, in the profound thinking of scientists.

Stages and Qualitative Changes in Cognition

While Piaget maintains that intellectual behavior manifests a basic continuity from infancy to adulthood, he also emphasizes that there are qualitative differences in the individual's thought processes at various stages of development. It should be pointed out that although Piaget presents a broad age range in which various behaviors can be observed, he is not concerned with the absolute level of age norms. The thrust of his theory is that the individual progresses through a series of ordered, invariant stages and cannot skip a particular stage in development. "By stages Piaget refers to the lawful succession of relatively stable structures of knowing which characterize the behavior of the organism [Furth, 1969, p. 17]." Furthermore, later stages incorporate earlier ones and "enrich the earlier structures by their reconstruction and extension on a higher plane [Furth, 1969, p. 18]."

According to Piaget, three operational structures can be distinguished in the individual's cognitive development. Each of these represents the attainment of a significant stage of development with its accompanying substages.

STAGE I: SENSORY-MOTOR OPERATIONS

From birth through the middle of the second year the infant uses his sensory and motor equipment to know his immediate spatial surroundings. During this period the child comes to recognize that objects have permanence and a separate existence of their own.

An increasing capacity to act purposively, to elaborate, to differentiate, and to examine causes and effects, as well as to distinguish between means and ends eventually occurs during the sensory-motor stage of development. By the end of this stage the child recognizes that events occur in a temporal order (one event leads to another event), which puts him on the trail of the idea of cause and effect. According to Piaget, the learning that occurs during this period of life provides the basic foundation for all later meaningful learning.

In his study of the formation of concepts of intellectual operations, Piaget emphasizes that the child is not a passive recipient of, but actively interacts with, his environment.

STAGE II: CONCRETE THINKING OPERATIONS

The second developmental stage begins at approximately eighteen months and lasts until about the beginning of adolescence (eleven or twelve years of age). During this period, until about the age of seven, an elaboration of mental operations takes place. This process is then followed by an equally long process of "structuration" (Inhelder, 1962). At first during this period, thought processes are not reversible. Thus, the younger child is not aware that a change in form does not change the total amount of matter (conservation of matter). A classical Piagetian experiment involves presenting the youngster with two identical balls of plasticine. The youngster is then asked to flatten or make a sausagelike form of one of the balls or break it into small pieces. The child is then asked whether the changed ball of plasticine is smaller than, larger than, or identical to the original ball. Whereas five- or six-year-olds are likely to maintain that a change in form involves a change in total size or dimension, the older child is able to relate different dimensions to each other simultaneously. Thus, the older child is likely to say that there must be the same amount of plasticine all the time; that you only have to make the sausage into a ball again and you can see right away that nothing is added and nothing is taken away (Inhelder, 1962). Although elementary mathematical thought structures make their appearance at about seven, it takes several years before the child can apply these structures to a variety of concrete contents. Thus, the ability to "conserve" quantity (judging that the quantity remains the same even if transformed) occurs before conservation of weight, which precedes conservation of volume.

At the beginning of stage II, children have difficulty in distinguishing among mental, physical, and social reality. Thus, at early stages of development, the word used to designate a thing appears to the child as an essential and inherent attribute or property of the thing, rather than simply an arbitrary designation. The replies of young children that the sun is named sun because it *is* a sun indicate that for young children the name is inherent within the object and is not just a label used to identify the object (Brook, 1970). However, older children in the study by Brook were more successful in their ability to differentiate between the symbol and the referent and were better able to recognize the arbitrariness of names. This would explain their readiness to state that names can be changed. Moreover, the findings in this study indicate that thinking does not progress in a uniform fashion but does so very unevenly, so that "childish" and "mature" ideas exist side by side (Brook, 1970).

During the sensory-motor (stage I) period of development, children's orientation is described by Piaget as *egocentric*. They view the world from the standpoint of their own perspective. This, of course, is about all one might expect. But the beginning of a somewhat modified view of things occurs, for example, when children begin to grasp the idea that objects, whether in view or not, have a permanence of their own: a ball with which they have been playing disappears when a screen is placed between the ball and their immediate field of vision, but it still exists—it can be seen again if they are able to remove the screen or reach behind the screen to lay hold of the ball.

However, a marked degree of egocentricity still persists beyond stage I and well into the period encompassed by stage II. A familiar example may be cited: A child who has learned to recognize which of his hands is the left and which the right correctly points to his right hand when someone facing him says to him, "Please show me your right hand." But when asked, "Please show me *my* right hand," the child will, while still retaining an egocentric orientation, point to the hand directly opposite his own—actually the other person's left hand—not realizing that the right-left relationship is not confined to his own stance.

A decline in egocentricity, with a corresponding increase in the ability to see things from a point of view other than one's own, occurs, according to Piaget, at about age seven or eight. The ability to perceive or contemplate another's intentions or feelings increases by the age of eleven or twelve, as we will note later in this chapter. However, remnants of infantile egocentricity may persist throughout life, even in the thinking of an erudite scholar.

STAGE III: FORMAL THINKING OPERATIONS

By Piaget's account, the third stage of cognitive development occurs at approximately eleven or twelve years of age when formal, abstract thought operations develop. According to Inhelder and Piaget (1958), the young adolescent's interest in spinning theories, speculating, and expressing ideas about various and sundry issues in the world about him represents an important phase in his transition from childhood to adulthood. "Each one has his own ideas (and usually he believes they are his own) which liberate him from childhood and allow him to place himself as an equal with adults [p. 341]." Inhelder and Piaget view the early teens as a period when decisive changes occur or have occurred in the nature of children's thinking. Some other investigators view these changes in thinking as occurring in many children before adolescence. But, whatever their timing, it is instructive to examine them.

When children reach the adolescent period, most of them are able to think not only in general terms, but also in abstract terms to a greater degree than was true earlier. They are capable of a greater amount of learning involving *symbols* rather than *concrete things*.

The younger child is likely to prefer to deal with a type of problem that goes like this: "In Farmer Brown's barn there are two horses and four cows. How many animals are there in the barn?" At a later age he will tackle a problem that involves the same quantities, but more abstractly: "If X is two and Y is four, how much is X plus Y?" This increased ability to deal with abstractions is recognized by practices in teaching that have to do with quantities. It has been customary, for example, to assume that the typical child becomes ready for thinking in the abstract terms of algebra by about the age of thirteen or fourteen.[2]

The ability to deal with the abstract appears in connection with qualities as well as quantities. It is especially important in connection with the growing person's search for meaning. Much that goes into the convictions and commitments that constitute a person's view of life must be formulated in abstract, intellectual terms, if formulated at all. Note the phrasing here: if formulated at all. A person can have an effective philosophy of life without being able to define it precisely in intellectual terms. He can be loyal, for example, without being able to give an abstract definition of loyalty. However, to the extent that a person wants to grasp, in general terms, his own beliefs and values or wants to clarify for himself some of the meanings he holds, an ability to think abstractly about qualitative concepts is essential. And if he is seeking to communicate his thoughts and feelings to others, to share them, and to catch the meaning of the values others embrace, it is necessary to be able to comprehend the meaning of abstract concepts and to express such meanings in words.

As has been previously noted, the normal adolescent is able to generalize far better than he could when he was a young child. The younger the child, the more his thinking is likely to be restricted to specific things. As he grows older, he is able to think in more inclusive terms. This was illustrated in a study (Jersild and Tasch, 1949) in which children were asked to name "three wishes." In grades one through three, 80 per cent of all wishes dealt with specific material objects or possessions. In grades seven through twelve, only about 30 per cent of the wishes were of this nature. A young girl wished, for example, for a new dress, a new hat, and new shoes. An older girl included a "whole new spring outfit" in one wish and then had two wishes to spare.

As children increase in age, they may wish for more abstract things. Having interviewed seven- to twelve-year-old boys and girls concerning the three wishes they would make, Ables (1972) found that with increasing age there is an increase in wishing for some personal skill, attribute, or self-identity. The greater prevalence of girls wishing for another person to relate to as compared with boys wishing for money and material possessions may reflect the orientation of boys toward assuming the breadwinner's role.

[2] This assumption works out pretty well in practice, although there are some youngsters who are unable to handle the more difficult problems in algebra at the age of fourteen who probably could do so if given a little more time to mature, say until sixteen or seventeen; and there are some youngsters who are never ready to handle algebra.

These findings may have to be modified at some time in the future, now that women's roles in society are changing.

While the younger child views things on a *perceptual* level, the older child views them more on a *conceptual* level. For instance, in studies (Preston, 1942; Jersild and Meigs, 1943) of children's reactions to a war situation (World War II), it was observed that younger children described war in terms of specific happenings, such as the damage that had been done by bombing. Children near adolescence, on the other hand, saw the war in terms of larger concepts: the damage from a particular bombing was not just an isolated episode, but a sign of danger yet to come.

According to Piaget, by the time adolescents are fourteen or fifteen years of age, their operations are likely to acquire a firmly fixed system of thought structures. Whereas the youngster in the concrete-operation stage is limited to the concrete, adolescents are able to form hypotheses and subject them to empirical tests. The use of language reflects this mode of thought; logical syllogisms and constructs are seen (Inhelder, 1962). Piaget (1970a) presents an interesting experiment to demonstrate that adolescents are capable of combinatorial, or formal, logic. The experimenter presents the child with five bottles of colorless liquid. If the adolescent combines the contents of the first, third, and fifth bottles, a brownish color will appear. The second bottle contains liquid that is neutral and the fourth bottle contains a solution that is color reducing. The child is then requested to produce a colored solution. It is not until stage III, when adolescents become aware of the combinatorial method (constructing a table of the total number of possible combinations as well as determining the consequences of each factor), that they are capable of finding a solution to this problem.

How universal are formal operations? Several recent investigators have indicated that adolescents attain formal operational thinking in some areas but not in others.

In studies of eleven- and twelve-year-olds, junior and senior high school students, and college students (Elkind, 1961a; 1961b; 1962), Elkind found that only 27, 47, and 58 per cent of these students, respectively, had attained conservation of volume. In the typical conservation of volume experiment, the adolescent is presented with a glass container with water in it. The adolescent is then shown that each ball of clay when placed in the water causes the water to rise to an identical height. The material in one of the balls is then altered by the experimenter and the adolescent is asked if the water will rise to the same height. The findings did not support the view that 75 per cent of eleven- and twelve-year-olds could conserve volume. In a study of seventh through twelfth graders, Hobbs (1973) presented adolescents with volume and weight tasks varying in difficulty. Whereas 96 per cent of the adolescents realized that a ball of clay remained constant in weight when its shape was changed (conservation of mass), only 40 to 50 per cent of the males and 20 per cent of the females gave evidence of conservation of volume. Hobbs's findings as well as those of Elkind suggest that Piaget may have overestimated the extent to which eleven- and twelve-year-olds have mastered the idea of the conservation of volume.

Tomlinson-Keasey (1972) obtained cross-sectional data on the cognitive development of sixth-grade girls, college coeds, and older women. The subjects were presented with pendulum, balance, and flexibility problems taken from Inhelder and Piaget. In the Inhelder and Piaget (1958) study, a person's ability to exclude extraneous factors from a list of possible causal factors is tested by "presenting a pendulum in the form of an object suspended from a string; the subject is given the means to vary the length of the string, the weight of the suspended objects, the amplitude, etc. The problem is to find the factor that determines the frequency of the oscillations [p. 67]." Another possible factor is the push given the object. Only the length of the string is actually causally related to the frequency of oscillation. The subjects' abilities to determine this relationship vary with age. In the Tomlinson-Keasey study using these Piaget tasks, 32 per cent of the girls' responses, 67 per cent of the coeds' responses, and 54 per cent of the older women's responses were at the formal level of cognitive development. Moreover, attainment of the highest level of cognitive development was rare.

The findings of these studies, together with those of Bynum et al. (1972), would seem to raise the question of how universal formal operations are at adolescence. According to Elkind (1975), more research in this area is greatly needed. It may be, as Laurendeau and Pinard (1962) and Brook (1970) found in their investigations of child thought, that the adolescent does not necessarily attain the same level in all areas of logical development simultaneously. Moreover, thinking may not progress in a uniform fashion but in a very uneven one, so that "childish" and "mature" ideas may exist side by side.

What factors are related to performance on formal-operational tasks? Several studies have examined the relationship between ability as assessed by standardized tests and Piagetian operational thinking at the concrete level of cognitive development (DeVries, 1974); however, research at the formal operational stage of development is scarce indeed. In a study of boys at the early adolescence level, Keating (1975) reported that precocious boys, as assessed by standardized tests, showed the ability to reason at the formal operational stage earlier than their peers, who were of average ability. These findings have recently been confirmed with bright and average girls (Keating and Schaefer, 1975).

Both mental age and IQ have been found to be positively associated with formal operational thinking (Neimark, 1975). Among individuals classified as dull-normal (60 to 80 IQ range), no evidence of formal operational thinking was apparent in two studies (Inhelder, 1966; Stephens et al., 1971).

Although intelligence is related to formal operational thinking, other factors known and unknown at the present time are also of significance. One such factor is cognitive style. Neimark (1972) found that individuals who were reflective, as measured by Kagan's Matching Familiar Figures (MFF) Test, tended to score higher on a number of cognitive tasks. Another factor that has been thought to play a role in cognitive development is that of education. Generally speaking, the results from a number of studies seem to suggest that large differences in education are related to differences in cognitive functioning (Goodnow, 1962). For example, Papalia (1972) reported that amount of schooling was related to the ability to perform on volume-conservation tasks. However, at the present time, specific kinds of training, such as science training, have not been found to have an effect on performance (Neimark, 1975).

Consequences of the Cognitive Changes of Adolescence

The changes that sooner or later occur in the cognitive abilities of adolescents have far-reaching consequences. These changes enable adolescents, potentially, to grasp the logic of science, to assimilate the discoveries made by others and, if they are bright, to launch discoveries of their own. It enables them, potentially, to view ideas and issues in the human area from the standpoint of another person. It enables them, potentially, to question their own ideas and attitudes from an objective point of view. The human mind reaches supreme heights when it is able to examine its own operations.

From a strictly cognitive or intellectual point of view, intelligent adolescents possess a latent capacity for taking a thoughtful view of their own subjective experiences. They are not likely to employ this capacity effectively, however, unless it is nurtured and cultivated.

Sex Differences

The majority of studies using Piaget's tasks find few or no sex differences, whether the tasks involve conservation, class inclusion and other grouping problems, or more complex operations made by adolescents (see, for example, Brainerd, 1973).

Children's Conceptions of Time

Piaget (1970) has designed numerous studies relating to the child's conception of time. These investigations were undertaken at the urging of Albert Einstein. According to Piaget, children's concepts about time develop as a result of their interaction with the environment. Whereas the young child confuses concepts of time with those of distance and velocity, the adolescent is likely to move toward an abstract, or adult, conception of time. To cite one study, Piaget presented young children with an hourglass with levels marked at $\frac{1}{4}$, $\frac{1}{2}$, and $\frac{3}{4}$ full. The children were asked to transfer marbles from one container to another and to relate the time it took them to perform this task to the flow of sand in the hourglass. Then they were asked to describe the movement of the sand when they worked more quickly and more slowly. The young children maintained that the movement of sand changed depending on whether they worked slowly or quickly. Older children, adolescents, and adults, however, are aware that time moves at a uniform rate and is not dependent on the activities in which one is engaged. Nevertheless, Elkind (1974), when noting the psychological dimension of time, presents an "updated old story (used to explain relativity) to the effect that when Raquel Welch sits on your lap an hour seems like a minute but when you sit against a hot stove a minute seems like an hour."

In early childhood it is apparently easier for children to comprehend the idea of the immediate past, such as yesterday, than to comprehend the near future, such as tomorrow (Friedman, 1944a). Even so, it is not until approximately the ages of eleven to thirteen that the majority of children grasp the abstract idea of the historic past (Oakden and Sturt, 1922; Bradley, 1947). At the sixth-grade level (which is close to the beginning of adolescence for many children), the understanding of time concepts is still incomplete.

Understanding time concepts has been measured by tests of the meaning of terms descriptive of time (*medieval, B.C., prehistoric*); locating historic events on a time line; and placing in proper sequence the times of Lincoln, Washington, Columbus, and the mother of the person taking the test (Friedman, 1944b). Responses to such tests show a gain in understanding time until the tenth grade, when young people reach about the same level of understanding as that shown by the average adult.

Although the ability to anticipate the future, to imagine what might happen in it, and to plan for it begins to develop in childhood, it comes into play especially during the adolescent years. Building a perspective about the future requires greater mental maturity than building a perspective concerning the past.

Adolescents' ability to grasp and apply the concept of the future in a personal way has not been studied systematically. However, the ability is revealed indirectly when adolescents plan for vocational careers and show a realistic appreciation of how their present activities serve goals that cannot be realized until a future time.[3]

The ability to deal with the concept of the future is especially important as adolescents make the transition from childhood to adulthood. In making this transition the enterprising adolescent anticipates adult status long before he or she actually is an adult. Adolescents show evidence of anticipating this future status as adults when they make idealistic plans for bettering the society in which they live.

Understanding of the Social World and the Viewpoints of Others

Within recent years psychologists interested in the growth of understanding have been concerned with the development of children's ability to take the role of another person as well as their increasing sensitivity to the motivations of others. According to Flavell (1970), a real literature in the area of social-cognitive development is beginning to emerge, stimulated in part by the work of Piaget (see, for example, Flavell et al., 1968; Turnure, 1975; Whiteman et al., 1974).

The ability to perceive or interpret the feelings, thoughts, motives, and intentions of others was studied by Flapan (1967) in an investigation that compared twelve-year-old girls with girls at ages nine and six selected to represent youngsters of average or near-average intelligence. Sound-motion filmstrips from commercial movies (very impressive as judged by adults) were used to portray quite obvious expressions of feeling, such as crying, anger, and less obvious states of mind or situations, such as guilt, remorse, sorrow, indecision, forgiveness, misunderstanding, and what adults would regard as unduly severe punishment by a parent, followed by regret and an effort to make amends.

Twelve-, nine-, and six-year-olds were quite similar in their accounts of the clearly depicted actions, such as crying, fighting, or depriving a girl of a pair of roller skates she recently received as a gift. On the other hand, twelve-year-olds were far more sensitive than six-year-olds in identifying correctly (from an adult point of view) less obviously portrayed motives, thoughts, and intentions. The differences between girls aged twelve and girls aged nine were not so pronounced, but they favored the older girls. When a rating scale, designed by two psychologists to measure sophistication in inferring thoughts, feelings, and intentions, was applied to verbatim accounts by the girls of what they had seen or heard (with a maximum

[3] Much of what the adolescent is required to learn has meaning only if he is able to view it as an investment in the future.

possible score of 106), the following average scores emerged: 36.5 at age six, 61 at age nine, and 73.7 at age twelve. In other words, there were impressive gains from ages six to twelve, but the twelve-year-olds were, on the average, substantially less sophisticated than the adult investigators who devised the scale deemed themselves to be.

Twelve-year-olds were compared with younger children in a study by Dimitrovsky (1964) of ability to identify the intended meaning of vocal expressions of emotion. The youngsters listened to three random recordings of adult male and female voices intended to express each of four emotions: anger, happiness, love, and sadness. Stick-figure drawings designed to depict these emotions were shown to the younger children to help them indicate which of the various emotions each sound recording might represent. Twelve-year-olds identified the simulated emotion considerably more frequently than the younger children, although the gains from year to year were uneven.

Differences in the identification of the various simulated emotions were more interesting (and more disconcerting, in some respects) than age differences. At all ages, a voice intended to depict sadness was identified more often than a voice designed to represent an expression of happiness or love. At all ages, similarly, the "correct" scores for anger were higher than the correct identifications of simulated happiness or love. It would, of course, require a more complex set of clues (such as seeing as well as hearing) to determine whether youngsters as a rule are more likely to perceive an adult as angry or sad than as joyful or affectionate. But, in any event, in everyday life, the young person's perception or interpretation of an adult's feelings may be more important, psychologically, than the feelings the adult is actually experiencing or trying to communicate.

Using a modified version of a test designed to assess the individual's ability to take the role of another, Turnure (1975) found an increase with age in this ability to take the role of the other person among seven- to twelve-year-olds.

A review of the social-cognitive literature confirms the already noted finding that the ability to infer the motivations, feelings, intentions, and cognitions of others changes with development. Rothenberg (1967) and Gollin (1958) have found an increase with age through middle childhood and adolescence in the ability to explain overt behavior in terms of underlying psychological states. Whiteman et al. (1974) also found that eight- and ten-year-olds have a more complete understanding than younger children of the actions of others.

In a study of children in grades one, three, and six, Whiteman et al. (1977) studied the development of ability to surmise what might be the motives underlying behavior that is incongruous. For example, the children were told: "A lady gives a party and is mean to her guests. Why?" The results show an increase with age in naming possible underlying psychological motivations. For example, one of the older children said: "She had an argument with her husband that morning and was taking it out on her guests." In contrast, the response of a young child was, "She was a mean lady."

The occurrence of an increase with age in interpreting behavior in terms of underlying motives is in accord with Piaget's emphasis on the abstract, hypothetical quality of formal operations and its onset at about eleven years of age.

The Relationship of Adolescent Cognition to Affective Changes in Adolescence

According to Piagetian theory, several other important cognitive changes occur during adolescence (1958). As already suggested, adolescents become able to think about thinking and to formulate theories about their own mental processes. Adolescents also use theory formation to build ideals, which in turn are used to help them adapt to society. While adolescents become more perceptive about the reactions of others, they also become increasingly self-conscious and introspective.

As the adolescent's thinking ability and interpersonal skills increase, the demands of reality in relating to others more and more take precedence over personalized fantasy.

Qualities and varieties of intellectual functioning

Two people with similar IQs may differ greatly in their intellectual performances and in the way they apply their minds. This holds true even among adolescents with very high IQs. One is glib, one is profound. One scintillates, another is unimaginative. One can excel all contestants on a TV quiz program—"throw the book," so to speak; another responds in a clumsy fashion to a rapid-fire quiz but comes forth with novel ideas of his own. One moves in a conventional, logical way toward finding the correct answer to a problem; another speculates, introduces new ideas of his own, and evolves novel solutions.

Creativity

In the early 1950s Guilford and his colleagues contributed greatly to the identification of thinking processes that can be described as creative.

Guilford's distinction between *convergent* and *divergent* thinking is especially noteworthy. According to Guilford (1959), in divergent thinking, as compared with convergent thinking, there is more flexibility, originality, a greater flow of ideas, and more ingenuity. The course of divergent thought is not confined to the information at hand; it goes beyond what is obvious and apparent. In convergent thinking, thought is channeled, or controlled, more in the direction of finding one correct solution. In divergent thinking there is less conformity to a fixed pattern, more freedom to strike off in new and different directions, more of a disposition to consider several possible answers and novel solutions. Divergent thinking draws more on creative abilities than does convergent thinking. Guilford has developed a number of measures designed to tap both convergent and divergent thinking.

Creativity may involve such attributes as being venturesome, with some or several of these varying qualities: the creative person takes risks, makes novel assumptions, questions rules and authority, enjoys trying out a hunch, takes the risk of venturing into what others regard as absurd or silly (see, for example, Getzels and Jackson, 1962). When Wallach and Kogan (1965) asked a number of creative people to describe their thought processes when they were engaged in artistic or scientific productivity, they found that the creative process included an abundance of unique "associative content" and a "playful and permissive" attitude.

Seventh-grade boys were administered a battery of creativity tests adapted from Wallach and Kogan in a study published by Cropley (1972). Five years after taking the tests, data relating to their achievement in nonacademic life in art, drama, literature, and music were obtained. More specifically, the adolescents were asked about the degree of their involvement in these areas. The results of this study indicate that scores on creativity tests are positively related to creativity in nonacademic life.

The interplay of thinking and feeling in insight into self

One of the finest tributes one can pay an adolescent (or an older person) is that he or she is "wise to himself or herself"—that is, "doesn't fool himself or herself." Although insight into self is generally held in high regard, our knowledge concerning how much insight the typical adolescent attains, or *might* attain, is very meager. Nonetheless, the subject is so important that it deserves attention here.

Insight means to see into, to be aware of. The writers of this book have searched widely to get a simple definition of insight, but the search has not been fruitful. One reason probably is that insight is a very personal kind of enlightenment, with many individual variations that cannot be covered by a single general definition.

Insight is usually something a person possesses to a greater or lesser degree, rather than something one either has or has not. It may be very articulate in the sense that a person can "intellectualize" and express it fluently in words, or it may operate as a canny form of unspoken self-appraisal. It may spring from a sudden jolt or surprising discovery, but it is more likely to come through a slow process of exploration. It may even come as an incidental afterthought, or seemingly from out of nowhere, when least sought.

Cognitive and Noncognitive Aspects of Insight

When insight into self is formulated as an explicit idea it involves cognition—an intellectual comprehension of an inner state. However, an adolescent cannot acquire insight by the sheer intellectual effort one uses in learning a logical syllogism.

This is one of the baffling and oftentimes exasperating aspects of insight. People may be intellectually aware of facets of themselves—personal assets they might use or faults they would like to correct—and still not be able to do anything about them. Acquiring an insight involves a mobilization of emotion as well as thought, and the emotional involvement may range from acute agony to an uneasy, but unshakable, state of perplexity. The emotional component will also include great satisfaction when a person makes what to him or her is an important self-discovery.

It is absorbing to observe, as sometimes with good luck one can, that an adolescent may get a thrill of satisfaction even when he or she discovers a facet of himself or herself that, per se, usually is regarded as unfavorable, such as a characteristic that has offended his or her peers. A junior high school student from a poor neighborhood, who seemed to have gained much from a course dealing with adolescent problems, once told the senior writer with a pleased grin, "I ain't learned nothin' in this class but I sure get along better with other kids." And then he told how he was "on" to characteristics that had made others dislike him, but that he previously had attributed to others.

The fact that the process by which people acquire insight into themselves involves a complicated blend of thought and feeling makes it very difficult to predict when insight might occur or how it came about when it did occur. Studies that have explored insight by experimental methods have, in general, been quite unrevealing.[4]

The Advantages of Insight and Lack of Insight

A temporary advantage of a *lack* of self-insight is that it makes a person free to *externalize* his or her problems. One can regard one's difficulties, and even one's aspirations, as residing in outside circumstances or in other people. One has many grievances, let us say, but this does not mean that one is hostile—"they" or "it" or "life" give offense. If one is adept at this, one is able to disavow responsibility for oneself.

There are conditions under which lack of insight is a blessing. One prevails when adolescents' limitations are so dire that to realize them fully would leave them in a state of complete despair. It is better for them to live with an illusion than to go into a state of hopelessness; for the possibility remains that on a future day they might have more strength to face realities.

The major advantage of self-insight for a person who has the courage and strength to acquire it is that one's resources can be used in a realistic way. Such insight may even enable one to regard as assets qualities that were once regarded as faults. Adolescents who once blamed themselves for not trying to be best at everything may discover that they are wise in not trying to knock themselves out by competing with everyone.

Even when insight does not dispose of a problem it can do much to soften its effects. This happens, for example, when people make a discovery about the nature of their moods. A boy who has had unaccountable spells of feeling depressed or a girl who now and then has weeping spells may discover that these moods are most likely to occur at some time after occasions when their feelings were hurt but they pretended there was nothing to be angry about. Having gained insight into this sequence, the person might anticipate a melancholy mood—and thereby blunt it. Or, one might take steps to prevent it by deliberately trying to be alert to one's feelings at the moment they are aroused, instead of ignoring or swallowing them and then feeling miserable afterward.

Insight consists not only in recognition of personal limitations or faults, but also in awareness of assets. This needs to be emphasized, for often in everyday life (and sometimes even in psychological literature) insight is regarded as primarily denoting that one perceives faults in oneself that

[4] A number of studies in this area have been reviewed by Wylie (1961). Experimental studies of insight are not likely to be fruitful if insight is regarded as a form of logic or clever divination or is defined primarily as a person's awareness of faults that others see in him, as the equivalent of "adjustment," or as something that can be assessed by a jury.

others also perceive. Actually, an adolescent's sagacity in realizing his or her good qualities is just as important, and in many ways more productive, than the ability to discern only frailties.

Adolescents who are wise to their assets and limitations avoid the error of constantly overestimating or underestimating themselves. Their expectations are likely to be reasonably realistic. This spares them from being carried away by hopeless dreams. It also spares them from setting their sights so low that they do themselves an injustice.

In informal interviews with adults about their adolescence the senior writer has found many persons who regretted that they underrated themselves during middle and late adolescent years. One person, for example, recalled that at about age nineteen he calculated that it would take him ten years to complete his professional education while earning his own way. It took only five. He figured that at thirty he might be earning $3,000 a year. When that time came (before the inflation of recent years) he actually earned several times that much. He did not try to date the girls who attracted him most, believing he would not be attractive to them.

This young person, who thus underestimated himself, was pleased, of course, when his fortunes turned out much better than he had foreseen. But, as he moved into adult life, he was slow in making a more realistically favorable self-estimate, and he lost thereby. His undervaluation of himself was costly even in financial matters. His first car was a poor secondhand one (the best he thought he could afford), and when he had to turn it in soon after for a better one, he lost money that he could have saved had he bought a better car at the start. Later he built a house, planning it on a small scale; but soon thereafter he had to spend much more to get it enlarged than it would have cost had he planned a larger house from the beginning.

Difficulties in Achieving Self-insight

We might expect that adolescents would know themselves well for they have had a long time to get acquainted. However, self-knowledge seems to be more difficult to acquire than other forms of knowledge. Persons with brilliant intellects can encompass vast areas of learning and still have little insight into their own motives or habits of thought.

The barriers to achieving self-insight reside in the culture as well as in each individual. In the intellectual climate of most schools it is not easy to pursue a search for knowledge of self.

Apart from cultural barriers to the idea of self-examination there are conditions within each individual that make self-examination difficult.

FLUCTUATING ABILITY TO HANDLE ONE'S
EMOTIONS REASONABLY

Adolescence is marked by surges of strong emotions combined with equally strong and sometimes rigid defenses: It is this fluctuation that gives adolescence its stormy character. If an adolescent is going through a period of asceticism in an effort to control unconscious sexual feelings, self-examination is difficult to pursue. The hyperidealism of adolescence is well known, encouraged by the development of formal modes of thinking during adolescence (Inhelder and Piaget, 1958). Because adolescents potentially can think about their own thinking, the recourse to philosophizing to explain away their conflictual feelings may come easily. This, in turn, hinders the development of emotional awareness. A good capacity for thinking can be used as an aid to self-enlightenment—or self-deception.

SLOW DEVELOPMENT OF THE ABILITY TO
VIEW THE SELF OBJECTIVELY

In their childhood adolescents did not, as a rule, use their intellect to reflect on the nature of their feelings or their thoughts. They were likely to be swept by anger and fear long before they could detach themselves from their emotions to ask, "What's going on here?" They were likely to reach opinions or conclusions without trying to retrace the steps in their thinking that led to these conclusions. Young children obviously have less capacity for reflective thinking than older people. However, it also appears that young children vary greatly in their ability to view themselves objectively.[5]

GAPS IN RECALLING EARLIER DEVELOPMENT

Another obstacle to self-understanding in an adolescent (or older person) is the gap between what one remembers and what actually happened in one's earlier life. The typical adolescent does not have conscious memories of happenings in life prior to about the age of three and a half years (Dudycha and Dudycha, 1933). By that time youngsters have had a vast number of experiences that might influence their mental outlook and ideas and attitudes regarding themselves and others. Even memories an adolescent can trace back to the years after three and a half are fragmentary. And they may be erroneous. For, as we have noted earlier, a person's memories are likely to be *selective*. They give more of an indication of what one now is—and the rationale one has built to justify or explain one's present state—than of actual happenings in one's earlier life that determined what one now is.

---

[5] One of the present writers once heard a tired four-year-old child, just home from nursery school, announce: "Don't bother me, I'm in a bad mood." This seemed to show a certain amount of self-scrutiny.

This is a barrier to self-knowledge, although it is not in itself an insurmountable barrier. As long as the effects of past experience persist in the present there still remains a possibility of examining them, even though all persons have a strong disposition to preserve, rather than to question and revise, their interpretations of their past.

Incentives for Self-examination

Although there are barriers to self-examination there also are incentives for breaking down these barriers. Persons who deal with troubled individuals repeatedly emphasize that they can count on a strong impulse to grow, a striving toward wholeness and health even in persons who, at the same time, are resistant to such strivings (see, for example, Rogers, 1942; Horney, 1945, 1950).

In Chapter 11 we note how people, in spite of being committed to "strategies" that protect them from facing the nature and meaning of their anxiety, still feel promptings to get rid of these strategies. The person who is compulsively competitive feels an urge, at times, to relax, to join in spontaneous fellowship with others. The person who has tried to protect himself or herself by withdrawing, by remaining aloof, still possesses an urge for intimacy with others. Such promptings and urges give a person a glimpse of something that might be. Such a glimpse is, in itself, a nascent form of insight. It may lead to a more profound insight if a person ventures to examine it.

References

Ables, B. Three wishes of latency age children. *Developmental Psychology*, 1972, **6**, 186.

Almy, M. C., Dimitrovsky, L., Gordis, F., Hardeman, M., & Elliott, D. L. *Logical thinking in the second grade.* New York: Teachers College Press, 1970.

Bradley, N. C. The growth of the knowledge of time in children of school-age. *British Journal of Psychology*, 1947, **38**, 67–78.

Brainerd, C. J. Order of acquisition of transitivity, conservation, and class inclusion of length and weight. *Developmental Psychology*, 1973, **8**, 105–116.

Brook, J. S. A test of Piaget's theory of "Nominal Realism." *Journal of Genetic Psychology*, 1970, **116**, 165–175.

Bynum, T. W., Thomas, J. A., & Weitz, L. J. Truth–functional logic in formal operational thinking: Inhelder and Piaget's evidence. *Developmental Psychology*, 1972, **7**, 129–132.

Chapman, R. H. The development of children's understanding of proportions. *Child Development*, 1975, **46**, 141–148.

Cropley, A. J. A five-year longitudinal study of the validity of creativity tests. *Developmental Psychology*, 1972, **6**, 119–124.

De Vries, R. Relationships among Piagetian, IQ, and achievement assessments. *Child Development*, 1974, **45**, 746–756.

Dimitrovsky, L. The ability to identify the emotional meaning of vocal expressions at successive age levels. In J. R. Davitz (Ed.), *The communication of emotional meaning*. New York: McGraw-Hill, 1964.

Dudycha, G. J., & Dudycha, M. M. Adolescents' memories of preschool experiences. *Journal of Genetic Psychology*, 1933, **42**, 468–480.

Elkind, D. Children's discovery of the conservation of mass, weight and volume. *Journal of Genetic Psychology*, 1961, **98**, 219–227.a.

Elkind, D. Quantity conceptions in junior and senior high school students. *Child Development*, 1961, **32**, 551–560.b.

Elkind, D. Quantity conceptions in college students. *Journal of Social Psychology*, 1962, **57**, 459–465.

Elkind, D. *Children and adolescents*. (2nd ed.). New York: Oxford U.P., 1974.

Elkind, D. Recent research on cognitive development in adolescence. In S. E. Dragastin & G. H. Elder, Jr. (Eds.), *Adolescence in the life cycle: Psychological change and social context*. New York: Wiley, 1975.

Flapan, D. Children's understanding of social interaction. New York: Teachers College Press, 1967.

Flavell, J. H. Concept development. In P. H. Mussen (Ed.), *Carmichael's manual of child psychology* (Vol. 1). New York: Wiley, 1970.

Flavell, J. H. (in collaboration with Botkin, P. T., Fry, C. L., Wright, J. W., & Jarvis, P. E.). *The development of role-taking and communication skills in children*. New York: Wiley, 1968.

Friedman, K. C. Time concepts of elementary school children. *Elementary School Journal*, 1944, **44**, 337, 342.a.

Friedman, K. C. Time concepts of junior and senior high school pupils and of adults. *School Review*, 1944, **52**, 233–238.b.

Furth, H. G. *Piaget and knowledge*. Englewood Cliffs, N.J.: Prentice-Hall, 1969.

Getzels, J. W., & Jackson, P. W. *Creativity and intelligence: Explorations with gifted students*. New York: Wiley, 1962.

Gollin, E. S. Organizational characteristics of social judgment: A developmental investigation. *Journal of Personality*, 1958, **26**, 139–154.

Goodnow, J. J. A test of milieu differences with some of Piaget's tasks. *Psychological Monographs*, 1962, **76**(36, Whole No. 555).

Guilford, J. P. Three faces of intellect. *American Psychologist*, 1959, **14**, 469–479.

Hobbs, E. D. Adolescents' concepts of physical quantity. *Developmental Psychology*, 1973, **9**, 431.

Horney, K. *Our inner conflicts*. New York: Norton, 1945.

Horney, K. *Neurosis and human growth*. New York: Norton, 1950.

Inhelder, B. Some aspects of Piaget's genetic approach to cognition. In W. Kessen & C. Kuhlman (Eds.), *Monographs of the Society for Research in Child Development*, 1962, **27**(2, Serial No. 83).

Inhelder, B. Cognitive development and its contributions to the diagnosis of some phenomena of mental deficiency. *Merrill-Palmer Quarterly,* 1966, **12**, 299–319.

Inhelder, B., & Piaget, J. *The growth of logical thinking from childhood to adolescence.* New York: Basic Books, 1958.

Jersild, A. T., & Meigs, M. F. Children at war. *Psychological Bulletin,* 1943, **40**(8), 541–573.

Jersild, A. T., & Tasch, R. J. *Children's interests.* New York: Bureau of Publications, Teachers College, Columbia University, 1949.

Keating, D. P. Precocious child development at the level of formal operations. *Child Development,* 1975, **46**, 276–280.

Keating, D. P., & Schaefer, R. A. Ability and sex differences in the acquisition of formal operations. *Developmental Psychology,* 1975, **11**, 531–532.

Kramer, J. A., Hill, K. T., & Cohen, L. B. Infants' development of object permanence: A refined methodology and new evidence for Piaget's hypothesized ordinality. *Child Development,* 1975, **46**, 149–155.

Laurendeau, M., & Pinard, A. *Causal thinking in the child.* New York: International University Press, 1962.

Neimark, E. D. Longitudinal development of formal operations thought. Report No. 16, 1972, as reported in Neimark, E. D. Intellectual development during adolescence. In F. D. Horowitz (Ed.), *Review of Child Development Research* (Vol. 4). Chicago: U. of Chicago, 1975.

Neimark, E. D. Intellectual development during adolescence. In F. D. Horowitz (Ed.), *Review of Child Development Research* (Vol. 4). Chicago: U. of Chicago, 1975.

Oakden, E. C., & Sturt, M. Development of the knowledge of time in children. *British Journal of Psychology,* 1922, **12**, 309–336.

Papalia, D. E. The status of several conservation abilities across the life-span. *Human Development,* 1972, **15**, 229–243.

Piaget, J. *The child's conception of the world.* New York: Humanities Press, 1951. (Originally published 1926.)

Piaget, J. *Judgment and reasoning in the child.* New York: Humanities Press, 1952. (Originally published 1928.)

Piaget, J. *The origins of intelligence in children.* New York: International Universities Press, 1952. (Originally published 1936.)

Piaget, J. *The construction of reality in the child.* New York: Basic Books, 1954. (Originally published 1937.)

Piaget, J. *The child's conception of physical causality.* Patterson, N.J.: Littlefield, Adams, 1960. (Originally published 1927.)

Piaget, J. *The child's conception of time.* New York: Basic Books, 1970.a.

Piaget, J. *Structuralism.* New York: Basic Books, 1970.b.

Piaget, J. Intellectual evolution from adolescence to adulthood. *Human Development,* 1972, **15**, 1–12.

Piaget, J., Inhelder, B., & Szeminska, A. *The child's conception of geometry.* New York: Basic Books, 1960.

Preston, R. C. Children's reactions to a contemporary war situation. *Child Development Monographs,* 1942, **28**.

Rogers, C. R. A study of the mental health problems in three representative elementary schools. A study of health and physical education in Columbus public schools. Monographs of the Bureau of Educational Research (25). Columbus: Ohio State University Press, 1942.

Rothenberg, B. B. Children's ability to comprehend adults' feelings and motives. Paper read at the *Society for Research in Child Development.* New York, March, 1967.

Stephens, B., McLaughlin, J. A., & Mahaney, E. J. Age at which Piagetian concepts are achieved. *Proceedings of the 79th Annual Convention of the American Psychological Association,* 1971, 203–204. (Summary).

Tomlinson-Keasey, C. Formal operations in females from eleven to fifty-four years of age. *Developmental Psychology,* 1972, **6**, 364.

Turnure, C. Cognitive development and role-taking ability in boys and girls from 7 to 12. *Developmental Psychology,* 1975, **11**, 202–209.

Wallach, M. A., & Kogan, N. *Modes of thinking in young children: A study of the creativity-intelligence distinction.* New York: Holt, 1965.

Whiteman, M., Brook, J. S., & Gordon, A. S. Children's motivational perception as related to the instrumentality and effect of action. *Developmental Psychology,* 1974, **10**, 929–935.

Whiteman, M., Brook, J. S., & Gordon, A. S. Perceived intention and behavioral incongruity. *Child Development,* 1977, In press.

Wylie, R. C. *The self-concept.* Lincoln: University of Nebraska Press, 1961.

7

mental growth as measured by intelligence tests

With the publication of a test of intelligence by Binet and Simon in France in 1905, a systematic method for appraising the development of mental abilities became available. Binet's first tests were devised to measure children's ability to do schoolwork. These tests were the forerunners of the well-known Stanford–Binet Test, which, in common with a number of other measures of intelligence, has had a marked impact on theories of intelligence as well as on research on the area of intellectual development. Lewis M.

170

Alfred Binet (1857–1911), French psychologist who originated the intelligence test. [Bettmann Archive, Inc.]

Terman was the person mainly responsible for revising and publishing the Binet tests in this country. Roughly 800,000 persons a year were tested on the Stanford–Binet Test during the period from 1960 to 1972 (Thorndike, 1975).[1]

The meaning of intelligence

Because "intelligence" is a hypothetical construct, it has been defined in different ways by different theorists. Generally speaking, intelligence is regarded as encompassing what falls under the general heading of mental ability—ability to pay attention, to perceive, to learn, to remember, to think, to recognize relationships, to form generalizations, to reason inductively and deductively, and to comprehend abstractions.

Theorists have differed in viewing intelligence as a general unitary function or as comprised of a number of specific independent abilities (Thurstone, 1947).[2]

[1] For a review of the area of mental testing see Thorndike and Hagen (1977).

[2] Spearman viewed intelligence as encompassing a general factor (g) common to all forms of intellectual behavior as well as specific (s) factors.

Stanford-Binet Intelligence Scale

The latest revision of the Stanford–Binet appeared in 1960, but it was renormed in 1972. This intelligence test is individually administered at childhood and adolescent levels. In the construction of the Stanford–Binet Scales, an attempt has been made to select problems that would be familiar to children, adolescents, and adults. The difficulty levels are adjusted to suit progressively older children in order to yield a mental age score. The tests are both statistically reliable and valid (they measure what they purport to measure). An overall appraisal of functioning, the intelligence quotient (IQ), is computed from knowledge of the adolescent's mental and chronological ages.

$$IQ = \frac{100 \, MA \, (\text{mental age})}{CA \, (\text{chronological age})}$$

Thus, if twelve-year-old (CA) Jane receives a mental age of thirteen (equal to that of a normal thirteen-year-old), she would receive an IQ score of 108. In the latest revision of the Stanford–Binet, deviation IQs (standardized scores with a mean of 100 and standard deviation of 16 at each age level) are presented. Knowledge of a particular individual's score will provide information concerning his or her standing as compared with peers.

Although the reliabilities of several intelligence tests are satisfactory, one should be cautious in interpreting the scores, as chance errors do occur. Thus, if an adolescent receives a score of 100, it is best to think of his or her score as somewhere between 95 and 105, and quite probably between 90 and 110. Even though the Stanford–Binet has been found to be very useful in predicting how children will do in school, it is not very useful for older adolescents, as the ceiling (the upper limit of measurement set by the test items) decreases with age. The difficulty level is more appropriate for early, than for late, adolescence.

In a recent analysis of the Stanford–Binet Intelligence Scale and other Binet tests, Smith (1974) reported that some items on the Binet are more responsive to cultural influences than others. According to Thorndike and Hagen (1977), intelligence tests should not be biased by cultural factors. Several attempts have been made to construct tests that are suited to individuals with varying socioeconomic status, but these attempts have not been completely successful. It is claimed that individuals from impoverished environments are at a disadvantage when tested with the Stanford–Binet and Wechsler Intelligence Scales for children and adults. Therefore, in interpreting test scores of individuals it is essential to take into consideration their past and present environments. According to Thorndike (1975), the use of inflexible "levels of test performance as the basis for decision or action...seems unwise and perhaps pernicious. Binet's test—or any other—must guide, and not replace, informed judgment [p. 7]." In concluding his presidential address to the American Educational Research Association, Thorndike stated that the challenge for the next seventy years, beginning in 1975, was the use of the Binet test, or others, to "facilitate constructive adaptations of educational programs for individuals [Thorndike, 1975, p. 7]."

While ability tests (that is, intelligence tests) focus on items designed to show the individual's ability to learn new material, achievement tests are designed to measure performance in areas in which training has occurred. However, the distinction between achievement and ability measures is far from clear, as it is often difficult to differentiate the products of past learning from the capacity for new learning (Maccoby and Jacklin, 1974).

Growth in ability as measured by intelligence tests

With increasing age, adolescents are able to deal with increasingly complex material. Development in mental abilities, particularly verbal knowledge, continues through adolescence and later (Bayley, 1970).

Table 7.1 is based on a study by Freeman and Flory (1937) of boys and girls who were tested annually from the age of eight to the age of seventeen. The table shows the annual increase in scores on four parts of the intelligence test through age seventeen. As can be seen, each succeeding year showed a gain over the preceding year, but the gains became smaller as the young people moved on into the teens. It is also apparent, however, that the young people were still gaining at the age of seventeen, when most of them dropped out of the study. Some of the individuals represented in Table 7.1 were retested after they had left high school and had spent a year or more in college. The average score at seventeen years of fifteen boys was 245.7; on a later test at an average of 18.7 years, the average was 277.5. There were eleven girls who earned an average score of 246 at the age of seventeen and an average of 278.8 when tested at an average age of 18.7 years. These limited findings indicated that mental ability, as measured by these tests, continued to increase at the college level.

Other findings dealing with trends in the growth of intelligence are shown in a study by Thorndike (1948), based on two or more tests and retests of about 1,000 persons ranging in age from thirteen and a half to twenty. The findings indicate that in individuals still attending school, "Ability to achieve on a standard type of paper and pencil test of intelligence or scholastic aptitude continues to increase at least until age twenty and probably beyond [p. 15]."

Table 7.1. Annual increments on the four parts of test and on the total test administered to the same group of children annually from age eight to age seventeen

Tests	Ages								
	8–9	*9–10*	*10–11*	*11–12*	*12–13*	*13–14*	*14–15*	*15–16*	*16–17*
Vocabulary	6.25	5.81	6.23	4.89	3.72	3.31	3.85	3.95	2.01
Analogies	3.62	5.35	4.83	3.90	4.67	4.56	2.91	1.16	.38
Completion	5.31	6.84	6.31	8.05	6.45	5.99	6.95	4.78	2.96
Opposites	3.59	3.90	4.90	4.53	3.80	2.22	3.59	2.47	.34
Total test	18.85	21.62	22.27	22.20	18.17	15.80	18.26	11.61	5.58

Source: From "Growth in intellectual ability as measured by repeated tests," by F. N. Freeman and C. D. Flory, *Monographs of the Society for Research in Child Development*, 1937, **2**, No. 2. Reprinted by permission.

In a review of the literature on the development of mental abilities, Bayley (1970) cites several studies that suggest that adolescents who are mentally retarded, as well as those who are gifted or average, continue to make gains during their teen years.

Changes in Intellectual Functions
After Adolescence

Use of the longitudinal method (repeated measures of the same people over a period of time) in recent studies of the intelligence of adults has provided information at variance with earlier findings with respect to the age of greatest ability and the extent to which intelligence levels decline with age. In earlier cross-sectional studies, in which the test scores were based on samples of adults at increasing ages, the highest scores typically occurred in the early twenties, after which a decrease occurred (Jones and Conrad, 1933; Wechsler, 1944). The conclusion that there is a general pattern of intellectual decrement in adulthood and old age has been documented in several studies but has been questioned in other investigations (Schaie and Labouvie-Vief, 1974). Several investigators have maintained that samplings of individuals at different ages in a cross-sectional study may differ not only in age, but also in environmental background. A decisive measure would require a longitudinal study with tests and retests of the same population over a span of years. In a study using both cross-sectional and longitudinal methods (Schaie and Labouvie-Vief, 1974), the longitudinal findings did not indicate a decisive intellectual decrement during the adult life span. They administered the Primary Mental Abilities Test to adults twenty-one to seventy-seven years of age in 1956 and 1963 and to adults twenty-one to eighty-four years of age in 1963 and 1970.

In a study by Owens (1953), 127 men who had been tested with the Army Alpha (developed in World War I) as a college entrance test in 1919 were tested again about thirty years later, from 1949 to 1950. The individuals in Owens's study showed an increase in the total Alpha score. The increases in some subtests were substantial, and there was no significant decrease in score on any subtest.

Owens (1966) tested these same men again when they were sixty-one years of age. He reported that arithmetic scores decreased with age. However, with increased age there was an increase in the scores on items measuring reasoning ability—reasoning ability being highest at age sixty-one. Verbal ability was considerably higher at age fifty than at age nineteen, and only slightly higher than at age sixty-one.

Owens raised many questions as to the meaning and interpretation of these results. Among other things, it may be noted that his population consisted of persons who went to college (80 per cent of them finished four or more years of college). It is possible that those who went to college and who were interested in cooperating in such a study thirty years later had a stronger motivation to do well on the test than those in a random sampling of the population. It is possible that they were involved in daily intellectual activities of a kind that might keep them mentally alert and in better trim to do the kinds of tasks required by an intelligence test.

Interesting findings concerning the level of mental ability persons maintain as they grow older have been reported by Bayley and Oden (1955). Over a thousand adults, who were above average in intelligence when tested at an average age of about thirty years, were retested several years later. There was a high correlation between the test and retest scores, and all groups who took part in the study showed an increase in the average scores on the retest. The findings indicate that in this large group of superior adults there was strong evidence that the kind of intelligence tested by means of a "concept-mastery" scale continues to increase at least through fifty years of age.

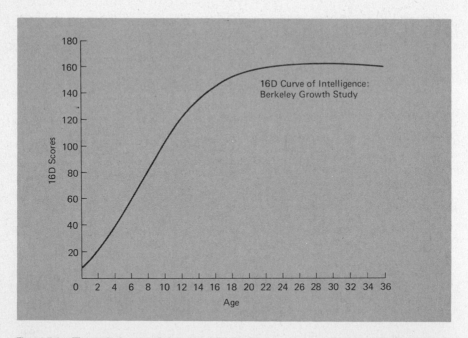

Figure 7.1. Theoretical curve of the growth of intelligence, based on data from the longitudinal Berkely Growth Study. The units of growth (16D scores) are derived from a modification of Thurstone's method of absolute scaling. [From "Development of mental abilities" by N. Bayley. In P. H. Mussen (Ed.), *Carmichael's manual of child psychology* (3rd ed.). New York, Wiley: 1970. Reprinted by permission.]

Bayley (1966, 1968a, 1968b) reported results of intelligence tests given to individuals varying in age and found their scores increased through age twenty-six, after which their scores remained unchanged through the age of thirty-six years.

Bayley (1968a) also found increases in scores among the lowest-scoring individuals as well as those who were average and above average.

In a review of studies of multiple mental abilities, Bayley (1970) concludes that some abilities, such as verbal facility and knowledge, increase in adults to age thirty or older. Other abilities, such as arithmetic and speed, reach their peak in the twenties. In general, measures of flexibility and speed of perception (memory and psychomotor coordination) decline more quickly than measures that depend more on experience, such as general information, comprehension, and vocabulary.

According to Jarvik (1975), there is likely to be a decrement in mental ability in persons who are physically and mentally inactive. Jarvik (1975) also believes, based on his research, that the greater the individual's "initial" ability as a youngster the less likely he or she is to undergo a decline in mental functioning in later life. Future research in this area is greatly needed to determine the ontogenetic components of change in various mental functions. Research and knowledge concerning the interaction of psychosocial and biological factors in producing age-correlated changes are also greatly needed according to Jarvik.

Implications of the Continuation of Mental Growth into the Late Teens and Twenties

The fact that young people continue to grow in intelligence up to and beyond the age of twenty-five has important implications for education and for planning a vocation or a career. One implication is that there is a long period during which young people might test their abilities as far as academic learning is concerned. If a boy does not have the mental ability to master algebra at the age of fourteen, it does not follow that he is forever barred from learning algebra. As a result of continuing mental growth, he may have the ability to master the subject at sixteen or eighteen. On the other hand, if we assumed that mental growth ceased at about fourteen, fifteen, or sixteen (as was assumed in the past), we would pretty much have to conclude that if he did not have the necessary ability at about the middle teens he would never possess it.

The same implication probably holds with respect to many other school subjects, including the learning of subject matter in the areas of physics, chemistry, biology, and other branches of science. Some individuals, who were not fully able to master these subjects in the early or middle teens, might later be able to do so by virtue of the mental growth that continues into the late teens, for even if their IQ remains constant, their mental age will increase.

The full implications of findings in recent years to the effect that growth in intelligence continues until the age of twenty-five and beyond, instead of ceasing at the age of sixteen, if not before, have not yet been explored. It is quite possible that there are many young people who do not seem to be "ready" for the conventional college program at the age of seventeen or eighteen, or who give up or are thrown out, who might be ready to tackle this program at twenty or twenty-one or later.[3]

Consistency and Change in Rates of Mental Growth

Several longitudinal studies using repeated tests of children over time have questioned the commonly held assumption of the "constant IQ" (Bayley, 1970). Little or no correlation exists between scores received during the first two years and scores earned at four years of age or later (Hindley, 1960), although the scores are valid measures of the children's intellectual abilities at the time they were obtained. In contrast, after six years of age, several investigators have reported that children's IQs are relatively stable, even though individuals differ in their pattern of growth and large shifts in the IQ score can occur (Honzik et al., 1948; Sontag et al., 1958).

How accurately can the intelligence of a person during the early, middle, and late adolescent years be predicted from tests given at an earlier age? How consistent is a person's rating on intelligence tests likely to be during the adolescent years? These queries touch on the general question of the constancy of the IQ.

Evidence bearing on these questions has been offered by Thorndike (1947) and others. In an analysis of several thousand test records, Thorndike compared scores obtained by young people at the end of high school and scores obtained by the same group at varying intervals prior to that time. In 600 cases the data provided comparisons with tests given ten or more years prior to the test given at the end of the high school period. Thorndike concluded that tests given at various times during a child's high school career are about equally accurate in foretelling what his score will be at the end of the high school period. In other words, a test given in the freshman year of high school seems to give practically as accurate a

[3] Many college instructors have maintained that young people who enter military service after high school and then go to college gain more from college after this delay than they would have gained at an earlier age.

prediction of a person's score at the end of the senior year as does a test given, say, at some time during the junior or senior year. A test administered in the ninth grade gives almost as accurate a forecast of scores that will be obtained at the end of the senior year as do tests administered only a few months before the end of the senior year. Tests administered during upper elementary grades also give a reasonably accurate statistical prediction of scores at the end of the high school period, but the accuracy of the predictions is somewhat lower. The correspondence between test results at one age and at a considerably later age is influenced both by the length of time elapsing between the two tests and by the particular tests that are used.

The findings in Thorndike's study imply that as far as the factor of general intelligence is concerned, it might be possible to give a student substantially as accurate guidance concerning his educational plans at the beginning of his high school course, and perhaps even in the upper elementary grades, as at the end of the course.[4] Such consistency means that substantial changes in score are the exception rather than the rule. However, as indicated earlier in this chapter, there are individual variations in growth rate and potentials in particular areas of ability. Although there is likely to be a high degree of similarity between a person's rank in total or composite score at age fourteen and at age eighteen or twenty, there may be significant variations in the rank one attains in specific areas of aptitude at one age as compared with a later age. Moreover, as noted above, when a person's IQ remains constant during the teens there is an increase in mental age.

Although there is consistency in group trends in mental growth there also are individual variations in pattern of growth. This was brought out in an investigation by Bayley (1949) in which forty children were tested and retested from early infancy through most or all of eighteen years. Bayley's findings show, as other findings have shown, that the scores children earn on tests given before the age of two do not at all provide an accurate prediction of what the same children will do later on. But test scores become more stable and consistent as children move beyond the preschool period. In the span of years from eleven to eighteen, the correlations between tests separated by an interval of three or more years were not materially or consistently different from correlations obtained between tests separated by an interval of only a year or two. The correlation between IQs at adolescence and adult status has been found to be .85 (Bayley, 1970).

Bayley advances the theory that as the individual approaches a mature level, or as he comes nearer to the limits of growth in a particular process, fluctuations are likely to be less marked than during an earlier period. As children approach the ceiling, their rate of growth tends to

[4] See, also, Goodenough and Maurer (1942).

become more stable. In general, measures of IQ obtained during adolescence are good predictors of the IQs of adults.

There were some young people in Bayley's study who, during the eighteen-year span of the investigation, tended to be *labile*: they varied from time to time, showing a heightened quickening or a slowing in rate of growth. Other children tended to be relatively *stable*, manifesting fairly steady progress without spurts and lulls in the growth process. There were other children who, at different periods and for varying lengths of time, appeared to be both labile and stable. For example, a child might be very stable in his intelligence test ratings for several years and then become labile, showing considerable change from test to test. Just what trends such as these might mean Bayley does not have sufficient evidence to tell, but she does point out that, at least within her limited population, the tendency toward lability or stability did not seem to be tied to adult intelligence level. Sontag et al. (1958) have reported that children who are assertive and show signs of independence and competitiveness are more likely to be in the group that shows increases in IQ scores.

Using data from a Fels Foundation longitudinal study of middle-class children between two and one-half and seventeen years of age, McCall et al. (1973) examined developmental changes in IQ with age. The data indicate that between the ages of two and one half (considered by some as too early to get a reliable predictive measure) and seventeen years of age, the average individual changed 28.5 IQ points. Furthermore, one out of seven individuals changed more than 40 points and rare individuals shifted as much as 74 points. The changes in IQ with age reported by McCall and his colleagues are quite substantial. There is also the suggestion that girls are less likely to show increases in IQ than boys. However, with the changes that are occurring in the role of women in society, these findings may have to be altered in the future. The findings of this study also indicate that low-income and minority groups manifest little or no change in IQ with age.

Sex differences in specific abilities

From age three until adolescence there are small differences between boys and girls in verbal ability (France, 1973; Routh and Tweney, 1972). In contrast one of the most widely documented findings is the general superiority of adolescent girls on verbal tasks (Droege, 1967; Svensson, 1971). In a longitudinal study of sex differences in aptitude measurement during high school, Droege (1967) found that the girls' superiority on tasks of a verbal nature increased from grades nine to twelve. This study used a large number of tests to measure verbal ability: spelling, verbal comprehension, and comprehension of difficult logical relations presented in verbal terms.

A review of the literature indicates that there are no differences between young boys and girls in quantitative ability—that is, ability to deal with arithmetic, algebra, and mathematics (Maccoby and Jacklin, 1974; Svensson, 1971). During adolescence, boys tend to receive higher scores on mathematical ability tests (Backman, 1972). Some investigators suggest that boys score higher than girls in mathematical ability because of differential interest in this area. Nevertheless, when they take a similar number of math courses during high school, boys are still superior in math (Flanagan et al., 1961). Adolescent boys' superior performance in math parallels their better performance on science tests. According to Maccoby and Jacklin (1974), differences in mathematical and scientific ability are related to different cognitive skills and ways of attacking problems in these areas. In a review of studies on spatial ability, they conclude that there are few, if any, sex differences until adolescence. During adolescence, boys move ahead and the sex differences on this factor increase with age through high school (Droege, 1967; Flanagan et al., 1961).

Developmental asynchronies

Eichorn (1975) discusses asynchronies in adolescent development. By this she means the differential growth rates of the various parts or functions of an individual (intraindividual asynchronies) as well as the differences in growth rates among members of a group (interindividual asynchronies). Much of the literature refers to asynchronies in physical rather than psychological development; the work of Stolz and Stolz (1951) and Tanner (1970) is noteworthy in this regard. Growth spurts have been charted for each dimension in physical growth. Psychological and cognitive asynchronies are only rarely discussed in the literature. Physical asynchronies can be caused by both hereditary and environmental factors. Psychological asynchronies also can have hereditary or environmental causes—that is, the brain structure may not develop properly, or parent-child interaction may lead to distortions in psychological or cognitive growth. Asynchronies may not be abnormal; they may be normal occurrences of transitional periods (such as adolescence). In discussing behavior, some authors have stated that prolonged emotional and economic dependence asynchronous with physical and cognitive growth can have harmful psychological and social effects. Eichorn (1975) states, "That retardation in one ability may have far-reaching consequences is documented in research on school dropouts, whose educational failure is accompanied by personality problems and difficulties in social relationships [p. 90]." Considering all the variables possible in physical and psychological growth, asynchronies in some areas are present in everyone to some degree. In adolescence especially, with its important psychophysiologic changes, asynchronies may play a major role in determining the course of the adolescent's future life. There are many research difficulties in obtaining data on asynchronies, particularly "the inadequacies of the instruments available for measuring most developmental characteristics [Eichorn, 1975, p. 93]," especially when dealing simultaneously with two variables. It is also necessary to distinguish between the effects of intraindividual and interindividual asynchrony, which sometimes is a difficult task.

Superior and gifted youths

Young people with IQs of 120 or 125 and above, who are commonly labeled as superior, comprise from 5 to 10 per cent of their age group. Persons within this group with IQs of 135 to 140 and above, who are commonly labeled as gifted, represent from 1 to 3 per cent of the total population. According to Albert (1971), children with IQs above 155 should be considered exceptionally gifted.

A bright adolescent is an important asset to society. The present age of science, technology, and complicated social engineering requires good brains. It requires a high level of intellectual ability to master higher mathematics, nuclear physics, electronics, advanced chemistry, and certain aspects of economics, sociology, or medicine. Whether because of innate limitations or limitations in training, large numbers of persons in the population are unable to take responsibility for managing the scientific and technological demands of a modern society. This highlights the social importance of mental ability.[5]

Intelligence is obviously also an important personal asset, although many adolescents, when evaluating themselves, emphasize other qualities more than their intelligence. They are more likely, for example, to mention their emotional and social characteristics than their mental abilities when describing what they admire in themselves (Jersild, 1952). There are, however, two qualifications that should be made. First, young people who go to college (and probably also high school students who are bound for college) place a higher premium on intelligence than those who do not intend to go to college. Second, many young people probably attach more importance to intelligence than they openly admit.

Even when young people do not express pride in being bright, they are likely to go to great lengths in resisting the idea that they may not be as bright as they would like to be. This appears indirectly in a study in which students and their teachers gave their opinion as to why students fail in high

[5] There are those who believe that much latent talent remains undiscovered and uncultivated, especially in underpriviledged sections of the population. (See, for example, Bond, 1960.)

school subjects (Gilbert, 1931), cited in Chapter 17. In making a check list of reasons for failure, teachers gave the highest rating to "lack of brains." By contrast, "lack of brains" ranked eighth in the students' accounts.

Many facts have been established concerning typical gifted adolescents.[6] Most of them were "gifted children," whose brightness showed forth at an early age (Bradley and Earp, 1970). Most of them come from homes that are above average or at least average in socioeconomic status, although there also are many very bright youngsters in lower socioeconomic groups (Drews, 1961). They are above average in size and health. Compared with other youngsters, they usually have more favorable attitudes toward school. They are more concerned than the average with abstract ideas, and they are curious and have long memories. They have more interests and hobbies than children of average intelligence (Feldhusen, 1966). They are above average on tests of emotional adjustment and moral judgment (Bradley and Earp, 1970), although not as measured by all investigators. Chambers and Dusseault (1972) found that gifted college students were significantly less well adjusted than their peers in many areas. Many of the personal and social qualities in which they excel are characteristic of persons in the socioeconomic level from which a majority of the gifted come. The good showing they make in a number of characteristics may, therefore, be linked with their family background rather than solely with their high IQ (Groth, 1971). But the gifted also produce unique work and new ideas (Bradley and Earp, 1970). They have unusual abilities in the organization of ideas and are more able to integrate and evaluate ideas critically (Isaacs, 1971).

Gifted young people demonstrate the principle that in human development "correlation rather than compensation is the developmental rule": to him that hath, much is given. But there are many exceptions. Bright adolescents, on the average, do superior schoolwork, but many are "underachievers" (Goldberg et al., 1959). The correlation between IQ and academic achievement in high school is about .60 (Thorndike and Hagen, 1961)—a respectable correlation, but far lower than would prevail if each youngster's schoolwork were on a par with his intelligence test score. Although they are, on the average, superior in tests of adjustment, some bright children bear the scars of old wounds, acquired when they were resented or misunderstood by their teachers and rejected by their schoolmates.[7] Many suffer from feelings of inadequacy in spite of their high ability (Smith, 1932). In Terman's classic long-term study, it was found that at age forty or fifty, individuals who had been in the gifted group excelled the average to a more marked degree in scholastic and vocational success than in social and emotional adjustment (Terman and Oden, 1959).

[6] See Goldberg (1962); Jacobs (1972); and Terman and Oden (1940, 1959).
[7] Hollingworth (1939) gives an illustration of this.

Sears and Barbee (1975) studied the Terman gifted females at age sixty-two. Many of the women reported great satisfaction in life, particularly in their work. For those women who were homemakers, generally satisfying life situations were also reported.

Extremely bright youngsters may actually appear to be misfits and oddballs when thrown in with an average group of peers (or teachers), especially when they are aggressive in asserting their cleverness or have interests others can neither understand nor share. They cannot help but become aware that they are in some ways different from others.

Gifted young people face many hurdles. They face the boredom and monotony of the usual school situation. They run the risk of developing poor work habits in high school that will plague them when they face stiffer competition in college. They face the difficult task of acquiring harmony between their intellectual precocity and their social and emotional development.

For some, the greatest problem is to avoid selling out, as it were, to the intellect while sacrificing their capacity for feeling. In one study this problem was mentioned by many bright persons, and more often by women than by men (Jersild et al., 1962). A person who easily masters the usual academic skills, and is honored for this ability, can be lured, so it seems, into placing his or her chips on this success while neglecting other resources.[8]

The Bright "Underachiever"

The so-called underachiever is one whose work at school is distinctly poorer than might be expected from his or her score on an intelligence test. The problem of underachievement becomes especially baffling when bright students fail, or are constantly on the margin of failure, or show a sharp discrepancy between their mental test ratings and academic performance. Underachievement among gifted youngsters frequently becomes most apparent early in the high school years (Terman, 1947).

The first question that might be raised about the underachiever is "According to what standard, and whose standard, is one an underachiever?" Maybe one is so labeled because one is not eager to meet the usual academic requirements but is using one's mind in one's own way. If so, the idea of underachievement exists primarily in the minds of

[8] One of the women in this study expressed her regret about having gone "all out" for the intellectual by saying, "From now on I want to be a woman, not just a brain." Many other bright women voiced the same sentiment, and many men expressed a corresponding aspiration—a desire to be more tender and compassionate. They were not saying that brains and warmth of feeling are incompatible. Rather, they were saying that a highly intellectual person runs the risk of becoming a detached person.

teachers who want everyone to learn what they teach and the way they teach it.

History records many examples of students who did not do well at school but made great names for themselves. If bright underachievers are carving out destinies of their own, they may be wiser and more mature persons than the ones who doggedly get high marks in all their school subjects. But the situation is not so simple. Many underachievers, while failing or doing marginal work at school, are not finding success or satisfaction by other routes. In the Terman study it was found that gifted individuals who were least successful in their occupations as young adults included a large proportion of persons who had a history of underachievement in high school.

Many studies have been made of bright underachievers on the assumption that, because their IQs are high, the reason for their lower-than-expected school performance must be due to nonintellectual factors—their personal and social characteristics. In several studies it has been found that underachievers do show more signs of personal maladjustment than persons who do well at school, but the findings as a whole are conflicting and inconclusive (Raph and Tannenbaum, 1961).

There is some evidence that some bright underachievers receive less constructive discipline and less intellectual encouragement and support at home. In a review of studies in this area, Raph and Tannenbaum (1961) note that students with a record of successful academic achievement tend to come from the higher socioeconomic and educational backgrounds, and from homes where there has been an emphasis on cultural pursuits. However, some youngsters who are good achievers come from homes in the lower socioeconomic and educational brackets. A study by Kahl (1953) indicates that low-status youngsters are more serious about schoolwork and have higher aspirations when their families are interested in "getting ahead" than when their parents are satisfied with their low status. According to Goldberg (1962), it appears that "within a given socioeconomic stratum a family's attitude toward their occupational status has a greater influence on the achievement expectations of the sons than does actual class membership [p. 19]."

Several investigators have also found that many underachievers come from disrupted homes. One special circumstance that has been observed in some boy underachievers is a lack of identification with their fathers (Goldberg, 1959;[9] Gowan, 1955).

Findings regarding the home throw some light on the relationship between underachievement and a young person's family situation, but they

[9] There are far more underachievers among boys than among girls. This is in keeping with other findings, showing that boys far outnumber girls in language difficulties, reading difficulties, and "problem behavior" at school.

leave much unexplained. Many successful students come from what appear to be unfavorable home environments, and many unsuccessful ones have what appear to be desirable backgrounds.

In view of the varying findings, Raph and Tannenbaum (1961) state that good or poor personal adjustment or desirable or undesirable home conditions do not, per se, account for expected achievement or for underachievement at school. "Despite the voluminous work done in this area, we do not as yet have a clear profile of traits that distinguish under-achievers from their comparably able peers who live up to scholastic expectations [p. 19]."

Several recent studies add to the picture of underachievers but do not solve the question of what is an effect of underachievement and what might be the cause. Bright high school underachieving students appear to have less favorable views of themselves than achievers. DeLeon (1970) found that underachievers had significantly more adjustment problems than achievers, involving different types of problems, such as low self-esteem, and unsatisfactory family and peer relations. Norfleet (1968) found that bright, underachieving college women were more immature, less poised, less tolerant, and less well socialized than achievers. Underachievers did not function well in unstructured situations and were less aware than achievers of their own needs and those of others. Achievers seemed to have made more satisfactory adjustments in relation to the search for values, goals, and identity and apparently were more able to use their potentials.

Even when a relationship seems to exist between poor achievement and emotional stress we cannot take for granted, without further evidence, that the former is due to the latter.

When parents of students who do poorly at school do not seem to set high standards before them, the reason may not be that they are unconcerned, but that they have become weary or discouraged, or regard it as futile or unkind to keep hammering away at them, or the reason might be that they value other achievements more than academic achievement.

The lack of clear evidence as to why students with favorable IQs do not achieve up to expectations raises the question as to whether such students actually *are* underachieving. It is possible that the expectations placed on them by others are unrealistic, based on a misconception of the power of a high IQ, and of the varied abilities measured by the test on which an IQ is based.

There are many components or "factors"[10] of intelligence, and an IQ is usually derived from the composite score on a test that includes several subtests (such as vocabulary, ability to perceive relationships, information, and reasoning from given facts). A person may earn a high IQ and still be

[10] In a discussion of components of the intellect, one might note that, with about fifty intellectual factors already known, there appear to be at least fifty ways of being intelligent.

quite uneven in his abilities on these subtests. Performance on the sampling of intellectual tasks used to determine IQ does not necessarily indicate how well a person might (or should) do on other intellectual tasks.

In discussing this point, Goldberg (1962) notes, for example, that intelligence accounts for only a small portion of the individual differences students show in their ability to learn a foreign language. She questions whether bright youngsters who fail French or Spanish should automatically be regarded as underachievers. In spite of their high IQ they may simply lack the kind of intellectual ability involved in learning a foreign language. Goldberg similarly points out that intelligence test scores account for only a modest portion of individual differences in ability in mathematics.

These observations regarding the limitations of the IQ as a basis for foretelling what a student will do, or prescribing what one should be expected to do, in school subjects, do not negate the importance of intelligence test scores. They do emphasize the point, however, that there are intellectual qualities that the typical intelligence test does not measure. They also underline the point that unless we know more about an adolescent than is told by their mental test ratings we should hesitate to belabor them or their parents if achievement is below expectations.

The Training of the Gifted

Today's gifted adolescents are the persons who most likely will influence our destinies. Although they have a great amount of ingenuity in finding their place in life, even extremely bright persons need proper nurture to achieve their full potential.[11] Terman and Oden (1940) noted that having an IQ in excess of 140 or 150 did not seem to add much to the achievement of the persons whom they studied in early adult years. This does not mean that those with IQs many points above 150 did not have a greater potentiality for achievement. Rather, according to Terman and Oden, it is likely that we have not learned in our educational system to bring the highest gifts to fruition.

The education of the gifted places a heavy responsibility on the school (but the same should be said regarding the education of the average student or the education of the handicapped). Many expedients have been used to provide for the gifted. These have consisted primarily in manipulations in the academic area, such as rapid promotion, provision of special classes, and what has been known as an "enriched" academic program. Each

[11] For a discussion of some of the achievements of intellectually gifted children and some of the problems they face, see Terman et al. (1925); Terman and Oden (1940). For a discussion of plans and provisions for the education of talented youth, see Passow et al. (1955); Goldberg (1962); and Klausmeier et al. (1968).

of these expedients apparently has both merits and shortcomings. The policy of segregating the gifted in special classes has been used widely. However, the mere fact of placing bright students in separate groups does not necessarily produce a higher quality of achievement or personal development. The provisions that are made to challenge their abilities and to encourage them to use their unique talents apparently are more important than simply placing them in a separate group (Goldberg and Passow, 1961).

Even if the best program of training is provided, however, it may fall short if it emphasizes only academic knowledge and skill. Observations bearing on this point are made by Hollingworth (1942) in a study of young people with exceedingly high IQs (180 or more). These observations indicate that young persons do not become intellectually great by the sheer force of high IQs. They may be brilliant, but unless in time their brilliance is combined with other qualities of mind and heart they will not become wise. They may scintillate on a quiz program, but unless they become committed to a search for knowledge that has meaning for them, their knowledge is not likely to have much meaning for anyone else. To get the maximum personal satisfaction and social usefulness out of their gifts, bright adolescents need to gain a healthy respect for the unique abilities that set them apart from others as well as for the motives and feelings that make them akin to others. Simply to add to the amount they are expected to learn is no solution. In the management of their personal affairs, people can be just as foolish in five languages as in one (Kubie, 1954). A student who has read ten books in an "enriched" course can be just as blindly moved by grievances, guilt, fears, and self-reproach as an ordinary student who barely manages to learn what is in one book. Murphy (1945) underlined this thought when he noted that the towering genius of the great scientist often lapses into childish babbling as he turns to problems in which his personal desires give structure to his thought.

Pleasures of the mind

As indicated in another chapter, besides being potentially a powerful tool, the mind of the normal adolescent can also be a source of joy. Among the significant satisfactions in life are the "pleasures of the mind"—the excitement of curiosity, the thrill of discovery, the triumph of finding an answer to a puzzling question or mastering a challenging problem. As young children most adolescents eagerly sought these pleasures. They scarcely had learned to talk before they came forth with a barrage of questions: What? How? Why? Where? They also began to speculate, to venture forth with answers of their own ("Behold the Child among his new-born blisses. See at his feet some little plan or chart." [Wordsworth]). In a recent study Ross and

Balzer (1975) found that when children were provided with answers to their questions, they asked more questions and tended to retain the information for a longer period of time. One might assume that the effect would be more striking if children were provided with answers to their personal questions. As Berlyne (1970) has stated, when children are encouraged by their parents and teachers to raise questions, lasting effects may occur. However, as time goes on, many eager questioners are likely to become more and more silent. They lose their zest and begin to act as if their "whole vocation were endless imitation."

Adolescents who lack interest and whose thinking is not challenged by what they are taught at school are likely to have poor academic records—which is serious enough—but they are likely also to suffer from more profound limitations. A person who is constantly labeled as a failure, or who is constantly on the edge of failure, lives in a depressing emotional climate.

Even youngsters who manage not to fail may lack the sense of achievement that contributes to mental health. Almy (1962) points out that schools have failed in their mental health role when youngsters find no intellectual stimulation at school and are "without commitments, with little sense of personal challenge, beset by apathy [pp. 470–71]."

To realize the mental health potentials of the intellectual part of the school's program, according to Almy, it is essential not just to get a youngster to learn to repeat the correct answers for academic questions but to help him understand the meaning of those answers for him.

The role of heredity and environment

Differences in mental ability have variously been ascribed to hereditary or environmental factors or various gradations between the two. The evidence for the hereditary position comes mainly from two types of studies. One type of research focuses on the correlation between intellectual abilities of samples with varying degrees of blood relationship. For instance, the correlations between monozygotic twins and dizygotic twins (who, like siblings, are derived from separate ova) may be compared. Another kind of evidence is based on parent-child correlations.

According to evidence from some studies, the correlation between the intelligence of monozygotic twins, reared together or reared apart, is higher than the correlation usually found between fraternal twins reared together.

In a longitudinal study, McCall et al. (1973) present data on the resemblance in IQ between parents and their children. The parents in this study had served as subjects in a longitudinal study when they were children.

At present their children are participating in the study. McCall's data indicate that the correlation between the parents' and children's IQs was higher when the parents were assessed at age seventeen than when the parents were evaluated as children. For example, the median correlation between the mothers' seventeen-year-old Stanford–Binet scores and their children's (between 40 and 126 months) was .53, whereas the median correlation of the mothers' Stanford–Binet score and their children's IQ score when the mothers were the same age as the children was .29. Furthermore, the parent-child correlations were not significant when the child was very young, but the correlations increased with age.

Similarities Between Children and Their Adoptive and Biological Parents

One of the most impressive investigations in this area is a long-term study of adopted children by Skodak and Skeels (1949), begun with about three hundred children in the 1930s. In 1946 it was possible to locate one hundred of the children who, with their adoptive parents, were willing to cooperate in a final phase of the study. The investigators regard these one hundred as representative of the original three hundred.

If the environment has an appreciable influence on IQ, one would expect to find evidence of this in adopted children. Adoptive homes are usually chosen with great care. Careful selection is possible because the number of couples desiring to adopt children has usually greatly exceeded the supply. The chances are that voluntary adoptive parents will try to provide as favorable an environment as possible. In addition adoption agents usually try to "fit the child to the home"—they try, for example, to place a child whose background suggests that he might be "college material" with adoptive parents who have a college background. Such "selective placement," if based on sound evidence, would have the effect of producing more similarity between adopted children and their adoptive parents than could be expected by chance.

On the average the adopted children in the Skodak and Skeels (1949) study consistently maintained a higher intellectual level than would have been predicted from the intellectual, educational or socioeconomic level of the true parents. This indicates that a favorable environment promotes intellectual growth.[12] However, the Skodak and Skeels study also shows that there is no uniform relationship between the foster home environment and children's mental test scores. There was practically a zero correlation

[12] By contrast, children who are kept in institutions that provide a bare minimum of care are not likely to rise above their predicted level; if anything, they are likely to show an impairment in their language development and mental test scores (Skeels et al., 1938).

between the mental test scores of the children and the educational level of the adoptive fathers and mothers. On various tests administered from about the two-year level to an average thirteen-and-a-half-year level, the correlations between the scores of the children and the educational level of the adoptive mothers ranged from .03 to .10; the corresponding correlations with adoptive fathers ranged from .00 to .06. On the other hand, when the adopted children had reached an average age of thirteen and a half years, the following correlations appeared when their performances were compared with their true parents from whom they were separated as infants:

1. Mental test scores of adopted children and *mental test scores* obtained by their true mothers: .38 and .42.
2. Mental test scores of adopted children and *educational status* of their true mothers: .31 and .32.[13]

Bayley (1970), in a reanalysis of the Skodak and Skeels data, as well as Honzik (1957), have also noted that there was little or no correlation between the IQs of the adopted children and their rearing parents. The correlation between the education of biological parents who were separated from the children at birth and the IQ of the children is quite similar to the parent-child correlations between children who are reared by their natural parents. The correlations in the literature reported between children's IQs (after the ages of two and one half to four) and the IQs of their natural parents as adults is generally found to be about .50 (Erlenmeyer-Kimling and Jarvik, 1963).

The findings that (1) there is a correlation between children's mental test scores and the education of their biologic parents from whom they were separated at birth and that (2) the correlation between foster children's intelligence scores and the scores of mothers from whom they were separated is substantial raise interesting questions.

There is no way that the educational status of an adopted child's true parents can directly influence the child's IQ. However, although the educational status a child's true parents attain may be influenced by environmental factors, such as family tradition and income, it is likely also to be influenced by their intelligence. To the extent that this is true, the resemblance between the intelligence of adopted children and their true parents' educational status indirectly reflects the influence of the genetic factors that produce a resemblance between the intelligence of adopted children and the intelligence of their true parents.

[13] The two coefficients are based on the children's scores on the 1916 and 1937 revisions of the Stanford–Binet Scale. Mental test scores were available for sixty-three of the mothers; information about educational status was available for ninety-two mothers.

Although there is a large accumulation of evidence to indicate that genetic factors have a substantial influence on a person's potential level of intellectual ability, there is also evidence that the environment makes a difference, especially from studies of children who have been transferred from a definitely substandard setting to a more stimulating one.[14]

Intelligence and Socioeconomic Status

Social class has been found to be related to mental ability. Correlations between family socioeconomic variables and mental test scores of children and adolescents have been reported by Bayley (1970). Correlations representing the first year of life were inconsistent and, on the whole, rather low. From about ages five to eighteen the correlations were consistently positive. At the adolescent level, the mental test scores of boys showed a higher correlation with fathers' occupation than with any other socioeconomic variable. Girls' test scores showed the highest correlation with mothers' and fathers' education (Bayley, 1970). A positive relationship between fathers' education and their offsprings' scores on intelligence tests has been confirmed by Dielman et al. (1974).

While family socioeconomic status has been found to be positively related to children's intellectual achievement, global environmental variables such as social class do not provide information about the more specific aspects of the environment. Within a particular social-class level there are differences in parental aspirations that may be related to the child's academic performance (Kahl, 1953). Several investigators, including Peisach et al. (1975) have called attention to the need to delineate the impact of specific environmental features in studying the relationship between the environment and the adolescent's performance. In the Peisach et al. study it was suggested that several dimensions, such as parental and child's aspirations and expectations, family interaction, social class, and maturity, may differentially affect language and cognitive functioning. It is advisable therefore to use a set of differentiated measures rather than a single global measure of social class in studying the relationship between environment and the adolescent's performance. Hansen (1975) found that home environmental variables such as emphasis on school achievement, freedom to engage in verbal expression, and parental involvement with the child were significantly related to the youngster's IQ.

---

[14] For an extensive review of studies in this area, see Fuller and Thompson (1960). See, also, for example, Bowlby (1952).

The Effects of Being Reared in
Substandard Institutions

Studies of children reared in extremely impoverished environments such as substandard orphanages have shown deleterious effects of mental and emotional deprivations on the individual's cognitive development (Bowlby, 1952; Spitz, 1945). In a pioneer study Skeels et al. (1938) found that the youngsters who were institutionalized were retarded in intellectual, motor, and social maturity. A small group of these children was given an enriched program and showed striking gains.

Available evidence indicates that an improvement in mental functioning is far more likely to appear when youngsters who have been deprived of intellectual nurture are placed in a stimulating environment (Skeels et al., 1938), than when youngsters in a moderately good environment are shifted to a setting that provides richer opportunities (Pritchard et al., 1940).

Schooling and Intelligence

A long-term study of an older group of adolescents deals with the effects of continued schooling on intelligence (Lorge, 1945). In this study 131 boys were tested between 1921 and 1922, at the age of fourteen, and again twenty years later, in 1941, at the age of thirty-four. In the meantime some of these people had dropped out of school at the end of the eighth grade, some had dropped out during high school years, some had completed high school, and some had completed one or more years in college. When classified according to similar IQs at the age of fourteen, most of the groups that had continued their formal education longer had higher average scores at the age of thirty-four.

The kind of ability measured by intelligence tests was affected by schooling. More schooling led to a gain. We have no precise way of determining whether such gains mean a general increase in intellectual power or just an increase in ability to perform the specific tasks demanded by an intelligence test. Lorge (1945) points out that intelligence tests are, to a large extent, built on tasks that are emphasized at school. They deal with information, reading, vocabulary, arithmetic, reasoning, computation, and the like. "Insofar as the tests favor the kinds of things taught in school, they will tend to favor people who have had the greater extent of schooling." This is quite an advantage, for whatever might be the nature of the gain, "it can be interpreted as meaning better ability in dealing with the intellectual environment [p. 490]."

However, in this study it was apparent that there are large differences in intelligence that cannot be attributed to schooling. Although persons with more schooling had higher average intelligence scores at the age of thirty-four than similar persons who had had little or no schooling after the age of fourteen, there still was a high degree of correspondence between the scores earned at fourteen and those earned at thirty-four, whether or not the persons had continued their schooling. A high-scoring boy who leaves school at fourteen is more likely in his thirties to have a higher score than a low-scoring boy who continues in school for several years. Although schooling is likely to raise the general level to some degree, it is not likely to raise a below-average rating to a far-above-average rating; much less is it likely to change the least able into the most able.

Intelligence as Related to the Emotional Climate of the Home

In some studies there is evidence that intellectual development is likely to vary with the emotional climate of the home. In a longitudinal study of children twenty-one months to eighteen years, Honzik (1967b) (as cited by Bayley, 1970) found that a close mother-son relationship was associated with higher IQs in sons. The father's friendliness to his daughter and parental harmony were positively related to the daughters' IQs. Findings by Honzik (1967) also indicate that boys and girls who obtain higher IQ scores are more likely to have parents who express concern about their achievement.

Intelligence as Related to Birth Order and Family Size

In several studies there is evidence that family size and birth order are related to intellectual development. As far back as 1874, Galton, in his study of men of science, noted that a large number of the eminent British men studied were only, or first-born, sons. Campbell (1971) reports similar findings. A positive relationship between birth order and intellectual aptitude is also maintained among those who are not among the most intellectually gifted. In a study of over 350,000 nineteen-year-old men born in the Netherlands, Belmont and Marolla (1973) reported that intellectual performance on the Raven Progressive Matrices (a nonverbal IQ test) declines somewhat with increased family size and increased birth order. With control on family size, first-borns did better than second-borns, and second-borns did better than third-borns, and so on. However, with large gaps in spacing between children, this pattern can be arrested or even reversed (Zajonc and Markus, 1975). Data obtained by Campbell (1971) suggest that first-borns are more likely to be successful in the occupational world and to be overrepresented among college students.

Race and IQ

Several investigators (Dredger and Miller, 1968; Jensen, 1968) have reported that the mean IQ scores of black children fall below the mean scores of white children. The lower scores obtained by black children on standardized tests have been assigned to either nature, nurture, or a combination of both (Eysenck, 1971; Gage, 1972; Jensen, 1969). Numerous situational variables such as motivation, language difficulties, physical factors, and rapport with the interviewer—alone or in combination—may impede performance on standardized tests. Other environmental and personality factors that may be related to the performance differences between blacks and whites may include teachers' differential expectations for blacks and whites (Rubovits and Maehr, 1973), and a tendency of white youngsters to take greater personal responsibility for making a good record (Friend and Neale, 1972; Garrett and Willoughby, 1972).

Intelligence tests' scores reflect multiple variables, both environmental and genetic. The relative importance of genetic and environmental determinants of intelligence as measured by intelligence tests of blacks and whites has become extremely controversial. Some people have concluded from this finding that blacks are genetically inferior to whites in certain intellectual capacities. A leading exponent of this view is Arthur Jensen. Having assembled a large number of research studies, Jensen (1968, 1969, 1972, 1973) concluded that whites are better at abstract thinking, whereas blacks are better at associative learning.

Many scientists, as well as many persons with no background in science, have disagreed with Jensen's position. Moore (1969), among others, makes certain criticisms of Jensen's studies. To begin with, real genetic differences between blacks and whites are difficult to determine. There has been such a mixing of the gene pools of both blacks and whites that a truly "pure" white or black is becoming less common, and race is hard to define on a genetic basis. Race is primarily an arbitrary social grouping based mainly on skin color, but even here, there are dark-skinned whites and light-skinned blacks who do not fit neatly into either category. Other workers prefer to attribute differential test scores to such environmental variables as:

1. Biased IQ tests. Questions and a vocabulary that are typical of a particular segment of the population are used, administered, and scored by people primarily from that same segment (white, college-educated, middle- or upper-middle-class, most with PhDs).

2. Environmental deprivation during the critical period for intellectual development. This period is regarded by some as occurring during the first four years of life (Bloom, 1964). Deprivation in the mother-child relationship or deprivation of specific stimuli necessary for optimal intellectual growth may be included here.

3. Conditions associated with low socioeconomic status. Socioeconomic conditions may involve deprivation leading to disturbances of fetal growth, poor prenatal as well as postnatal nutrition, and lack of wholesome stimulation in early childhood.

Dietary deficiencies during pregnancy, including an inadequate intake of proteins and vitamins, may have an adverse effect on the unborn child. Pica (eating unsuitable substances, such as dirt or paint), common among ghetto children, may result in lead poisoning from the ingestion of chips of lead-containing paint and affect intelligence. Poverty, crowded living conditions, maternal fatigue and anxiety, and lack of time or energy to provide the infant and young child with appropriate physical stimulation also may be disadvantageous. Lack of verbal stimulation in infancy and of a conventionally "correct" model of language usage in early childhood can similarly limit the intellectual nurture a disadvantaged child receives (Bayley, 1970).

There is evidence indicating that blacks and white in America differ in mean IQ scores by about fifteen points. But twin and sibling studies have indicated that differences apparently produced by environment may in individual cases run as high as twenty points.

It should also be noted that even though a trait's variation may be largely caused by genetic factors, the environment may still have an influence on the trait. Height is an example of a trait largely influenced by a genetic factor that may also be significantly influenced by environmental conditions (that is, the effect of diet and of childhood disease).

Two or more decades ago, when blacks migrated from the South to the North, the intelligence ratings of their children, on the average, rose in proportion to the duration of their stay in the North (Lee, 1951). Whether this would be found at the present time is uncertain in view of the amount of deterioration in ghetto areas during recent years.

It is possible that black children, instead of lacking abstract thinking ability, develop it at a later age than the children in Jensen's research.

It should be noted that both blacks and whites show a bell-shaped curve for the distribution of intelligence. Therefore, even if the reported statistical differences between blacks and whites are valid, a large number of blacks would still be smarter than a number of whites. Individual differences among blacks and whites far outweigh the average differences between blacks and whites as groups. An average white child is definitely inferior in IQ to a bright black child. What is needed is an educational opportunity for both blacks and whites to achieve the optimal intellectual growth possible for each individual.

Herrnstein (1973) has stated that higher IQ is related to upward social mobility: smarter people marry other smarter people, leading to the formation of a class of smart, successful people. He also states that the smarter upper classes' success is genetically founded, as people arrive at a natural hierarchy of ability abetted by great social mobility. But such great social mobility may not be possible for many in our culture today. Jencks (1972) believes that educational success reflects family background.

There are many factors that go into class and ethnic differences in IQ test performance, including personality and motivational differences and the expectations of others. It obviously is important to provide opportunity for all, and not to use test scores as a reason for limiting opportunity, especially in view of the unknown areas of genetics on the one hand, and the limitations of psychological testing on the other.

In conclusion it is clear that both hereditary and environmental factors play a role in determining intelligence. It is the interaction between heredity and environment in each specific case that determines the final result. Heredity alone, the genetic potential of a high IQ, requires an appropriately stimulating environment. Similarly, an enriched environment is of no use if the child lacks the innate capacity to make use of it. One further point should be added: in some instances children with apparently high intellectual endowments seem to show almost uncanny ways of using their potential intellectual abilities, but there are also persons with relatively low scores on intelligence tests who, on their own initiative, acquire exceptional cleverness and skills in many areas.

Intellectual ability and self-evaluation

By the time youngsters in our society reach adolescent age, they have been reminded on countless occasions of the tremendous value of mental ability. Through the school years their mental abilities are continually put to the test. Over and over again they are given grades or ratings—by their teachers, by their peers, and by themselves.

In the usual school a young person uses and tests his or her intellectual powers in a highly competitive situation in which the main test of his or her worth is the ability to master impersonal academic information. Many curious things happen when young people test and assess the properties of their minds in this competitive way. We might expect that those who are average or below, the "also-rans" in the academic marathon, would have a low opinion of their own worth, whereas those who lead the pack would glow with pride. In a quasi-longitudinal study, Kifer (1975) did find that successful academic achievement was likely to be accompanied by positive personality characteristics, whereas failure was a concomitant of lower levels of self-regard.

But while several studies have shown a positive relationship between self-esteem and achievement, others have shown a relatively low relationship (Badgett et al., 1971; Sharma, 1971). Although the evidence is not as conclusive as might be wished, it appears that many people who are exceptionally able feel inferior.

One apparent reason for this (although not the only reason) is that these people do not measure themselves against the average but compare themselves with their most able peers. Such a comparison is likely to be unfavorable, for not all can reach the peak. An extremely bright person who feels inferior is in a sense (to borrow a thought from William James) like a pugilist who has lost a bout for the world championship and feels he is not good, even though he can outfight every person on the globe—save one.

References

Albert, R. S. Cognitive development and parental loss among the gifted, the exceptionally gifted and the creative. *Psychological Reports*, 1971, **29**, 19–26.

Almy, M. Intellectual mastery and mental health. *Teachers College Record*, 1962, **63**(6), 468–478.

Backman, M. E. Patterns of mental abilities: Ethnic, socioeconomic, and sex differences. *American Educational Research Journal*, 1972, **9**, 1–12.

Badgett, J. L., Hope, L. H., & Kerley, S. A. The relationship between self-concept and academic aptitude of entering male college freshmen. *Psychology*, 1971, **8**, 43–47.

Bayley, N. Consistency and variability in the growth of intelligence from birth to eighteen years. *Journal of Genetic Psychology*, 1949, **75**, 165–196.

Bayley, N. Developmental problems of the mentally retarded child. In I. Philips (Ed.), *Prevention and treatment of mental retardation. Part II.* New York: Basic Books, 1966.

Bayley, N. Behavioral correlates of mental growth: Birth to 36 years. *American Psychologist*, 1968, **1**, 1–17.a.

Bayley, N. Cognition in aging. In K. W. Schaie (Ed.), *Theory and methods of research on aging*. Morgantown: West Virginia University Library, 1968.b.

Bayley, N. Development of mental abilities. In P. H. Mussen (Ed.), *Carmichael's manual of child psychology* (Vol. 1). New York: Wiley, 1970.

Bayley, N., & Oden, M. H. The maintenance of intellectual ability in gifted adults. *Journal of Gerontology*, 1955, **10**, 71–107.

Belmont, L., & Marolla, F. Birth order, family size and intelligence. *Science,* 1973, **182**, 1096–1101.

Berlyne, D. E. Children's reasoning and thinking. In P. H. Mussen (Ed.), *Carmichael's manual of child psychology* (Vol. 1). New York: Wiley, 1970.

Bloom, B. S. *Stability and change in human characteristics.* New York: Wiley, 1964.

Bond, H. M. Wasted talent. In E. Ginzberg (Ed.), *The nation's children, development and education* (Vol. 2). New York: Columbia U.P., 1960.

Bowlby, J. Maternal care and mental health. Geneva: *World Health Organization Monograph Series,* 1952 (2).

Bradley, R. C., & Earp, E. Children with original and novel ideas—the creative. In R. C. Bradley (Ed.), *The education of exceptional children.* Wolfe City, Texas: The University Press, 1970.

Campbell, D. Admission policies: Side effects and their implications. *American Psychologist,* 1971, **26**, 636–647.

Chambers, J., & Dusseault, B. Characteristics of college-age gifted. *Proceedings of the Annual Convention of the American Psychological Association,* 1972, **7**, 527–528. (Summary.)

De Leon, C. S. The relationship between personal-social problems and under-achievement in high school. *St. Louis University Research Journal,* 1970, **1**, 601–620.

Dielman, T. E., Barton, K., & Cattell, R. B. Adolescent personality and intelligence scores as related to family demography. *Journal of Genetic Psychology,* 1974, **124**, 151–154.

Dredger, R. M., & Miller, K. S. Comparative psychological studies of Negroes and whites in the United States: 1959–1965. *Psychological Bulletin Monograph Supplement,* 1968, **70**(3, Part 2).

Drews, E. M. A four-year study of 150 gifted adolescents. A report presented to the American Psychological Association, December, 1957 (mimeographed).

Drews, E. M. A critical evaluation of approaches to the identification of gifted students. In A. E. Traxler (Ed.), *Measurement and research in today's school.* Washington, D.C.: American Council on Education, 1961.

Droege, R. C. Sex differences in aptitude maturation during high school. *Journal of Counseling Psychology,* 1967, **14**, 407–411.

Eichorn, D. Asynchronizations in adolescent development. In S. E. Dragastin & G. H. Elder, Jr. (Eds.), *Adolescence in the life cycle: Psychological change and social context.* New York: Halstead Press, 1975.

Erlenmeyer-Kimling, L., & Jarvik, L. F. Genetics and intelligence. *Science,* 1963, **142**, 1477–1479.

Eysenck, H. *The IQ argument.* New York: Library Press, 1971.

Feldhusen, J. The right kind of programming for the gifted. In E. P. Willenburg (Chairman). *Special education: Strategies for educational progress.* Paper presented at the meeting of the Council for Exceptional Children, Toronto, Canada, April, 1966.

Flanagan, J. C., Dailey, J. T., Shaycroft, M. F., Gorham, W. A., Orr, D. B., Goldberg, I., & Neyman, C. A., Jr. *Counselor's technical manual for interpreting test scores.* (*Project Talent*). Palo Alto, Calif., American Institute for Research, 1961.

Freeman, F. A., & Flory, C. D. Growth in intellectual ability as measured by repeated tests. *Monographs of the Society for Research in Child Development,* 1937, **2**(2).

Friend, R. M., & Neale, J. M. Children's perceptions of success and failure: An attributional analysis of the effects of race and social class. *Developmental Psychology,* 1972, **7**, 124–128.

Fuller, J. L., & Thompson, W. R. *Behavior genetics.* New York: Wiley, 1960.

Gage, N. L. IQ hereditability, race differences, and educational research. *Phi Delta Kappan,* 1972, **53**, 308–312.

Garrett, A. M., & Willoughby, R. H. Personal orientations and reactions to success and failure in urban black children. *Developmental Psychology,* 1972, **7**, 92.

Gilbert, H. H. High-school students' opinions on reasons for failure in high-school subjects. *Journal of Educational Research,* 1931, **23**, 46–49.

Goldberg, M. A three year experimental program at De Witt Clinton High School to help bright underachievers. *High Points,* Board of Education of the City of New York, January, 1959, pp. 5-35.

Goldberg, M. *Research on the gifted.* Mimeographed report, Horace Mann-Lincoln Institute of School Experimentation, Teachers College, Columbia University, March, 1962.

Goldberg, M., Gotkin, L. G., & Tannenbaum, A. J. *Cultural, social and personal factors influencing talent fruition.* Mimeographed report, Horace Mann-Lincoln Institute of School Experimentation, Teachers College, Columbia University, 1959.

Goldberg, M., & Passow, H. A. The effects of ability grouping (First Draft), Talented Youth Project, *Interim Reports.* New York: Horace Mann-Lincoln Institute of School Experimentation, Teachers College, Columbia University, 1961.

Goodenough, F. L., & Maurer, M. M. *The mental growth of children from two to fourteen.* Minneapolis: University of Minnesota Press, 1942.

Gowan, J. C. The underachieving gifted child, a problem for everyone. *Journal of Exceptional Children,* 1955, **21**, 247–249.

Groth, M. J. Differences in parental environment needed for degree of achievement for gifted men and women. *Gifted Child Quarterly,* 1971, **15**, 256–261.

Hansen, R. A. Consistency and stability of home environmental measures related to IQ. *Child Development,* 1975, **46**, 470–480.

Herrnstein, R. J. *IQ in the meritocracy.* Boston: Little, Brown, 1973.

Hindley, C. B. The Griffiths scale of infant development: Scores and predictions from 3 to 18 months. *Journal of Child Psychology and Psychiatry,* 1960, **1**, 99–112.

Hollingworth, L. S. What we know about the early selection and training of leaders. *Teachers College Record,* 1939, **40**, 575–592.

Hollingworth, L. S. *Children above 180 IQ: Origin and development.* New York: World, 1942.

Honzik, M. P. Environmental correlates of mental growth: Predictions from the family setting at 21 months. *Child Development,* 1967, **38**, 337–364.

Honzik, M. P. Developmental studies of parent-child resemblance in intelligence. *Child Development,* 1957, **28**, 215–228.

Honzik, M. P., Macfarlane, J. W., & Allen, L. The stability of mental test performance between two and eighteen years. *Journal of Experimental Education,* 1948, **4**, 309–324.

Isaacs, A. F. Biblical research IV: Perspectives on the problems of the gifted and possible solutions as revealed in the Pentateuch. *Gifted Child Quarterly,* 1971, **14**, 175–194.

Jacobs, J. C. Teacher attitude toward gifted children. *Gifted Child Quarterly,* 1972, **16**, 23–26.

Jarvik, L. F. Thoughts on the psychobiology of aging. *American Psychologist,* 1975, **30**, 576–583.

Jencks, C. *Inequality.* New York: Basic Books, 1972.

Jensen, A. R. Social class, race and genetics: Implications for education. *American Educational Research Journal,* 1968, **5**, 1–42.

Jensen, A. R. How much can we boost IQ and scholastic achievement? *Harvard Educational Review,* 1969, **39**, 1–123.

Jensen, A. R. *Genetics and education.* New York: Harper, 1972.

Jensen, A. R. *Educability and group differences.* New York: Harper, 1973.

Jersild, A. T. *In search of self.* New York: Bureau of Publications, Teachers College, Columbia University, 1952.

Jersild, A. T., Lazar, E., & Brodkin, A. *The meaning of psychotherapy in the teacher's life and work.* New York: Bureau of Publications, Teachers College, Columbia University, 1962.

Jones, H. E., & Conrad, H. S. The growth and decline of intelligence: A study of homogeneous group between the ages of ten and sixty. *Genetic Psychology Monographs,* 1933, **13**(3).

Kahl, J. A. Educational and occupational aspirations of "common man" boys. *Harvard Educational Review,* 1953, **23**, 186–203.

Kifer, E. Relationships between academic achievement and personality characteristics: A quasi-longitudinal study. *American Educational Research Journal,* 1975, **12**, 191–210.

Klausmeier, H. J., Goodwin, W., & Ronda, T. Effects of accelerating bright, older elementary pupils—a second follow-up. *Journal of Educational Psychology,* 1968, **59**, 53–58.

Kubie, L. S. The forgotten man of education. *The Goddard Bulletin,* 1954, **19**(2).

Lee, E. S. Negro intelligence and selective migration: A Philadelphia test of the Klineberg hypothesis. *American Sociological Review,* 1951, **16**, 227–233.

Lorge, I. Schooling makes a difference. *Teachers College Record,* 1945, **46**, 483–492.

Maccoby, E. E., & Jacklin, C. N. *The psychology of sex differences.* Stanford, Calif.: Stanford U.P., 1974.

McCall, R. B., Appelbaum, M. I., & Hogarty, P. S. Developmental changes in mental performance. *Monographs of the Society for Research in Child Development,* 1973, **38**(3, Serial No. 150).

Moore, D. R. How much can we boost IQ and scholastic achievement? A discussion. *Harvard Educational Review,* 1969, **39**, 273–356.

Murphy, G. The freeing of intelligence. *Psychological Bulletin,* 1945, **42**, 1–19.

Norfleet, M. A. Personality characteristics of achieving and underachieving high ability senior women. *Personnel and Guidance Journal,* 1968, **46**, 976–980.

Osborne, R. T., & Gregory, A. J. The heritability of visualization, perceptual speed and spatial orientation. *Perceptual Motor Skills,* 1966, **23**, 379–390.

Owens, W. A., Jr. Age and mental abilities: A longitudinal study. *Genetic Psychology Monographs,* 1953, **48**, 3–54.

Owens, W. A., Jr. Age and mental abilities: A second adult follow-up. *Journal of Educational Psychology,* 1966, **57**, 311–325.

Passow, A. H., Goldberg, M., Tannenbaum, A. J., & French, W. *Planning for talented youth.* New York: Bureau of Publications, Teachers College, Columbia University, 1955.

Peisach, E., Whiteman, M., Brook, J. S., & Deutsch, M. Interrelationships among children's environmental variables as related to age, sex, race and socioeconomic status. *Genetic Psychology Monographs,* 1975, **92**, 3–17.

Pritchard, M. C., Horan, K. M., & Hollingworth, L. M. The course of mental development in slow learners under an "experience curriculum." National Society for the Study of Education. *Intelligence: Its nature and nurture* (Thirty-ninth Yearbook, Part 2). Bloomington, Ill.: Public School Publishing Company, 1940.

Raph (Beasley), J., & Tannenbaum, A. Underachievement: Review of the literature. Talented Youth Project, Horace Mann-Lincoln Institute of School Experimentation, Teachers College, Columbia University, 1961. (Revised, unpublished).

Ross, H. S., & Balzer, R. H. Determinants and consequences of children's questions. *Child Development,* 1975, **46**, 536–539.

Routh, D. K., & Tweney, R. D. Effects of paradigmatic response training on children's word associations. *Journal of Experimental Child Psychology,* 1972, **14**, 398–407.

Rubovits, P. C., & Maehr, M. L. Pygmalion black and white. *Journal of Personality and Social Psychology,* 1973, **25**, 210–218.

Schaie, K. W., & Labouvie-Vief, G. Generational versus ontogenetic components of change in adult cognitive behavior: A fourteen-year cross-sequential study. *Developmental Psychology,* 1974, **10**, 305–320.

Sears, P. S., & Barbee, A. H. *Career and life satisfactions among Terman's gifted women.* Paper presented at the Lewis M. Terman Memorial on Intellectual Talent, Johns Hopkins University, November 6, 1975.

Sharma, S. Self-acceptance and academic achievement: A review of research. *Indian Educational Review,* 1971, **6**, 118–125.

Skeels, H. M., Updegraff, R., Wellman, B. L., & Williams, H. M. A study of environmental stimulation: An orphanage preschool project. *University of Iowa Studies in Child Welfare,* 1938, **1**, 56.

Skodak, M., & Skeels, H. M. A final follow-up of one hundred adopted children. *Journal of Genetic Psychology,* 1949, **75**, 85–125.

Smith, M. W. Alfred Binet's remarkable questions: A cross-national and cross-temporal analysis of the cultural biases built into the Stanford–Binet Intelligence Scale and other Binet tests. *Genetic Psychology Monographs,* 1974, **89**, 307–334.

Smith, R. B. The development of an inventory for the measurement of inferiority feelings at the High School level. *Archives of Psychology,* 1932, **22**, 144.

Sontag, L. W., Baker, C. T., & Nelson, V. L. Mental growth and personality development: A longitudinal study. *Monographs of the Society for Research in Child Development,* 1958, **23**(2, Whole No. 68).

Spitz, R. A. Hospitalism: An inquiry into the genesis of psychiatric conditions in early childhood. *Psychoanalytic Study of the Child,* 1945, **1**, 53–74; 113–117.

Stolz, H. R., & Stolz, L. M. *Somatic development of adolescent boys: A study of the growth of boys during the second day of life.* New York: Macmillan, 1951.

Svensson, A. *Relative achievement: School performance in relation to intelligence, sex and home environment.* Stockholm: Almquist and Wiksell, 1971.

Tanner, J. M. Physical growth. In P. H. Mussen (Ed.), *Carmichael's manual of child psychology* (3rd ed.). New York: Wiley, 1970.

Terman, L. M., et al. *Mental and physical traits of a thousand gifted children, Genetic studies of genius* (Vol. 1). Stanford, Calif.: Stanford U.P., 1925.

Terman, L. M., et al. *The gifted child grows up: Twenty-five years' follow-up of a superior group. Genetic studies of genius* (Vol. 4). Stanford, Calif.: Stanford U.P., 1947.

Terman, L. M., & Oden, M. Status of the California gifted group at the end of sixteen years. National Society for the Study of Education. *Intelligence: Its nature and nurture* (Thirty-ninth Yearbook, Part 1). Bloomington, Ill.: Public School Publishing Company, 1940.

Terman, L. M., & Oden, M. *The gifted group at mid-life: Thirty-five years' follow-up of the superior child. Genetic studies of genius* (Vol. 5). Stanford, Calif.: Stanford U.P., 1959.

Thorndike, R. L. The prediction of intelligence at college entrance from earlier test. *Journal of Educational Psychology,* 1947, **38**, 129–148.

Thorndike, R. L. Growth of intelligence during adolescence. *Journal of Genetic Psychology,* 1948, **72**, 11–15.

Thorndike, R. L. Mr. Binet's test 70 years later. *Educational Researcher,* 1975, **5**, 1–6.

Thorndike, R. L., & Hagen, E. *Measurement and evaluation in psychology and education* (2nd ed.). New York: Wiley, 1961.

Thorndike, R. L., & Hagen, E. *Measurement and evaluation in psychology and education* (4th ed.). New York: Wiley, 1977.

Thurstone, L. L. *Multiple factor analysis: A development and expansion of the "vectors of mind."* Chicago: U. of Chicago P., 1947.

Wechsler, D. *The measurement of adult intelligence* (3rd ed.). Baltimore: Williams & Wilkins, 1944.

Zajonc, R. B., & Markus, G. B. Birth order and intellectual development. *Psychological Review,* 1975, **82**, 74–88.

8

fantasies, daydreams, and dreams

The imaginative life of the typical adolescent is rich and colorful, but others are not often allowed to get a glimpse of it.

Adolescents are veterans in the world of fantasy. They have gone through many phases in the development of their ability to imagine. In childhood they learned to deal with the images of things in place of the things themselves. They learned, in imagination, to go places and do things and enter into experiences without actually having to be there. Some adolescents

204

even went through childhood periods when it was hard for them to tell the difference between the fancied and the real. Some had imaginary companions so vivid and so similar to the substance of their own inner lives that they were hardly aware of the make-believe quality. Many also found thrills and adventure in daydreams of a "continued story" sort during their preschool and early elementary school years.

As they move toward the adolescent years, children lose some of the capacity they once had for becoming absorbed in imaginings so vivid as to seem almost real. As a child grows in understanding and awareness, the realities of life and of one's own experience intrude on one's make-believe. It becomes hard for most young persons, as they reach adolescence, to lose themselves completely in the vicarious kind of living that fancy can supply. Yet, in adolescence, as earlier, the typical young person has a rich fantasy life that continues to serve many of the functions imagination served in earlier years. These include both a kind of daring venture and a kind of retreat, sometimes a constructive means of dealing with life's problems, sometimes a means of evading them.

The functions of imagination

Through imagination, adolescents, like younger children, can leap over the barriers of time and space. They can transcend the limits of their

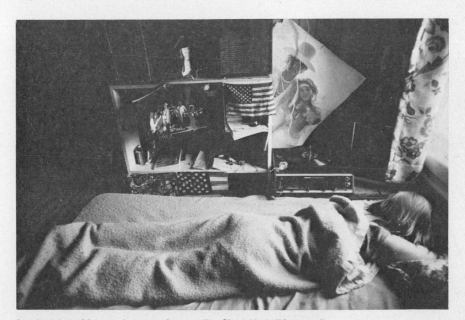

One function of fantasy is escape from reality. [Burk Uzzle/Magnum.]

own powers and vastly extend their reach. They can be great singers or actors, soldiers or statesmen. They can live in splendor even though their actual circumstances are drab and find companions who respect and admire them even though in everyday life they feel unaccepted. In daydreams the boy can woo and win the most wonderful girl, and the girl can love and be loved by the ideal boy.

When we thus speak in opposites, contrasting the fantasy of what might be and the reality of what is, we are dealing with a common form of imagining, but only one form. Although daydreams offer a means of escape from unpleasantness, the adolescent's imagination is not just a means of fleeing from a real to an unreal world. It serves many functions that are important in connection with the adolescent's aspirations and plans. Through imagination adolescents are coping with issues in life and struggling with unresolved problems from the past. They are striving to meet demands that press on them from within and from without and are giving structure to their hopes for the future.

The functions of fantasy can be categorized: it can (1) offer solace in difficult times; (2) act as a reminder of unfulfilled ambitions; (3) help to provide a thoughtful view of the future; (4) help one solve problems; and (5) allow the discharge of emotions that cannot be acted on in reality.

Fantasy as a Form of Solace

Even when adolescents' daydreams seem to be an unrealistic kind of wish-fulfillment and escape, these dreams are not completely idle. They help to make the adverse conditions of life tolerable. It is possible that life would be unbearable if one were unable, at times, in fancy, to find relief from the confines of the present. There are times when adolescents can make life livable through fantasy when actual circumstances are nearly intolerable. In bleak moments they are often able in their imagination to picture a better day. Those whose lot is harshest can sometimes find it is possible to enjoy a refuge through imagination.

Fantasy as a Reminder of Unrealized Aspirations

While an adolescent's fantasies may bring a kind of comfort, they also, in some instances, may serve to underscore discontent without relieving it. This happens, for example, when adolescents have daydreams of pleasure or glory or success far beyond anything they could realistically achieve. Then they feel miserable or angry with others or themselves because of the vast differences between drab reality and their glorious dreams.

Fantasy does not create desire, but it may, by giving a kind of imaginary substance to desire, leave a person with a deeper feeling that something is amiss. For example, a young person who longs to be recognized and accepted may desire to be a singer. If he or she imagines a future as a member of the school glee club, this imagining is tied to a desire and a plan within the reach of any youngster who has a moderately good voice. But if, regardless of whether they have a good voice, they leap in their fantasies to seeing themselves as operatic stars, they move far from reality. They may become so absorbed in this image of themselves that they do not even try out for the glee club.

It is likely that large numbers of adolescents (and probably also adults) now and then take flight into such a world, but on the whole they stay in touch with the realities. The more their compelling ideals, as embellished by their fancies, are removed from anything they can ever possibly be or achieve, the less likely they are to find something rewarding in the good things of life that do lie within reach. Fantasies may take the place of reality, but fantasies leave them empty-handed. And where such a discrepancy between the real and the ideal exists, there is likely to be some sort of disorder in the emotional life.

Fantasy as a Form of Thinking

One of the useful functions of the imagination is to help young persons see their exertions of the moment in a larger perspective. It enables them to take a panoramic view of life, to fit the present into a context linked with the past and extending into the future. If they are making some progress but also are having difficulty in their struggle for independence, they can imagine the day when they can earn their own keep, make their own decisions, and enjoy a kind of freedom their present life does not afford. Similarly, when they are working on assignments in school that, taken by themselves, are boring and meaningless, their labor becomes lighter when, in their imagination, they can see their present work fitting into an ambition that they might at some time realize.

One function imagination plays in the lives of some young people is to give them an opportunity for a kind of role playing. In their imaginations boys or girls can picture themselves in the role of a doctor, a mechanic, a farmer, a teacher, a nurse, a singer, or a social worker. The young person is likely to add a little more drama and color to these roles than they actually possess. Yet, the process of acting out this or that role in fantasy has a serious purpose. It is a kind of thinking.

Fantasy as an Aid to Problem Solving

Young people's imagination is helpful not only through what it anticipates for the future; it is helpful also in facing the problems of the present. This is underscored by the fact that not all daydreams are pleasant. A painful quality exists when, for example, fantasies give play to presentiments and fears. Through imagination they can "try out" the worst that might happen. When they give play to their resentments in their imagining, the experience is not a very pleasant one, although through fancies concerning what they might do to protect themselves from those who abuse them, or what they might do to avenge themselves on those who have done them wrong, they are struggling with a real problem. The ones who have meekly submitted to injustices may in fancy see themselves asserting their rights and through this dream get a better glimpse of what these rights are and the means they might use to fight for them.

Moreover, an imaginative activity that goes one step beyond fantasy into an actual acting out of something in an imaginary setting—such as occurs in role playing—may lead people to a deeper insight, and a better solution to some of their problems.

The Release of Emotion in Daydreams

Through daydreams adolescents can experience emotions and concerns about which they do not freely speak or even deliberately think.[1] In reverie hostile impulses may appear that in ordered thought they would thrust out as bad and utterly forbidden. They may, for example, picture a disliked teacher as being involved in an accident—perhaps a fatal accident. In so doing they are, in a sense, in their fancies, killing off their teacher. Similarly, in their fancies, they may give play to sexual desires they would not ordinarily deliberately plan. Hostile impulses and other desires that are expressed have something real about them, even when clothed in make-believe. It is because of this that the adolescent, like the adult, can often discover more concerning what they "really are like" by catching themselves in the middle of a daydream than by going through the process (usually futile) of making a list of their "good" and "bad" qualities.

---

[1] The relationship between imagination and feeling was emphasized in an early study by Libby (1908) and has been the subject of a study by Sanford et al. (1943). Symonds (1949) has given an excellent review of historic developments in the use of projective techniques through which the adolescent can express fantasies. Bellack (1975) has also reviewed the literature on several projective techniques.

The experimental study of fantasy

The study of fantasy and daydreams was primarily based on anecdotal reports until quite recently. Hume (1912) believed that fantasies that were derived from external experiences were more meaningful and were comparable to thoughts. According to Freud (1963, originally published in 1916), fantasies are the conscious derivatives of unconscious wishes, including sexual wishes, thereby allowing some inner gratification. According to this drive-discharge theory, fantasies first arise in early childhood when the child experiences the frustration of the immediate fulfillment of his or her wishes. Fantasy offers substitute gratification while the child is awaiting the real thing; and then, as the child matures, fantasy is used to replace real gratifications that are undesirable or impossible to achieve. Indeed, children's thinking probably begins with the formation of images.

In recent years there has been a renewed interest in the experimental study of fantasies; as Singer (1974) and Holt (1964) have noted, material that was previously ostracized by many workers is now on the verge of contributing to new and exciting advances in research. The study of subjective experiences has been avoided by some psychologists, but it is increasingly being considered a valid subject for study. Some investigators, through exploring the subjective dimension, have contributed to an understanding of the concept of the self, as described in Chapter 2. Fantasy has been studied by such workers as Schilder (1935), who was interested in the functional value of fantasies in personality development.

A number of studies of fantasies and daydreams have been conducted in recent years by Singer (1974). His work reveals some interesting findings: when one reclines, one's fantasy production increases; the largest amount of daydreaming appears to occur in most people while they are preparing to go to sleep; complex fantasies and thought chains occur that are often not connected with the reality of a person's immediate situation; and information from the external world may be incorporated simultaneously with daydreams (parallel processing), but switching back and forth between strictly internal material and external material also occurs (sequential processing). Singer (1974) has noted that daydreams appear to involve decreased alertness and attentiveness with reference to the external world. Singer believes some people are more likely to daydream than others, and that this then leads to an increase in "mental possibilities," or the ways in which one uses one's mental abilities. Singer (1974) found that 96 per cent of Americans have daily daydreams—which he believes is an important human ability as it prepares people to be aware of, and deal with, their inner mental functioning and accurately to tell fantasy from reality. The daydream themes he found centered around sexual fantasies, fantasies of success or failure, and escape fantasies.

Adolescent fantasy

Daydreaming was regarded at one time as a special characteristic of adolescence; now it is known to begin in early childhood and last through old age. However, Singer and McCraven (1961), using a questionnaire, found that adolescents reported a higher frequency of daydreams than persons in other age groups.

Themes appearing in the daydreams of older adolescents and adults are shown in Table 8.1, based on a study reported by Shaffer and Shoben (1956) that included a group of college undergraduates (64 men and 131 women) with a median age of twenty-one years and a group of graduate students (83 men and 112 women) with an average age of twenty-eight years. The entries under the "Ever?" heading presumably include many responses pertaining to earlier years, but there are some substantial differences between the percentages recorded in the "Ever?" and "Recently?" columns. As can be seen, there is a high degree of resemblance between the older and the younger groups, and many themes are frequently named—such as performing mental feats and being successful in a vocation. In both groups a large proportion reported past and present daydreams with a sexual theme. A large proportion also reported daydreams in which there was an element of worry.

The Nature of Adolescent Fantasy

At the age of about twelve or thirteen there may occur an inhibition of outspoken fantasy play of various kinds brought about by social pressure, the increasing importance of the adult world and adult ways of looking at things, and the psychophysiological changes of puberty. Although younger children often openly engage in make-believe play, there is a gradual internalization of such play, which frees the individual from the danger of exposure and possible embarrassment. The individual adolescent's cognitive style and interests influence the degree and type of internalization. Fantasy content is also a product of the adolescent's special skills and abilities and of his or her role differentiation. A daydream or fantasy may then reflect the adolescent's ideas and feelings about the future as well as remnants from the play of childhood.

Normal adolescents seem to distinguish quite readily between fantasy and reality. There are also certain types of daydreams that seem to have

Table 8.1. The occurrence of types of daydreams among two groups of students

Percentage of students reporting each type

| | Ever? | | | | Recently? | | | |
| | Undergraduate | | Graduate | | Undergraduate | | Graduate | |
	M	W	M	W	M	W	M	W
1. Physical feat	91	60	96	58	30	3	13	2
2. Physical attractiveness	89	95	94	96	34	63	17	56
3. Mental feat	88	92	89	90	48	42	47	61
4. Vocational success	100	98	99	93	81	69	78	64
5. Money or possessions	100	97	94	95	69	66	51	52
6. Display	78	76	90	83	22	16	19	19
7. Saving	89	63	90	66	14	5	14	8
8. Grandeur	67	48	63	39	11	7	6	0
9. Homage	81	72	81	66	16	13	24	18
10. Sexual	97	96	96	89	74	73	63	71
11. Death or destruction	39	44	60	46	9	9	10	9
12. Martyr	70	79	64	62	9	15	10	12
13. Worry	92	89	87	91	45	56	49	50
14. Other types	63	53	52	51	30	20	24	23
15. Repeated daydreams	89	93	83	87	48	51	36	47
Median number of types	13	12	13	11	5	5	4	5

Source: From *The psychology of adjustment* by L. F. Shaffer and E. J. Shoben, Jr., Boston: Houghton Mifflin Co., 1956. Reprinted by permission.

less of a wish-gratifying meaning: "negative" daydreams show the doubts and fears characteristic of adolescent turmoil and can be seen in fantasies about ethical or moral issues, as well as in disturbing daydreams about one's physical or mental make-up or abilities.

According to Singer (1974) daydreaming reaches a peak at fourteen to seventeen but then declines during the first months of college or work because of the realistic pressures of the working world or college studies. The adolescent's ability or inability to use fantasy as a source of inner gratification may also influence a person's need for, and introduction to, early sexual behavior; if a person cannot achieve gratification through fantasy, there will be more of a drive to participate directly in sexual activities. The ability to fantasize, then, is also connected with the ability to delay immediate gratification, which has played an important role in the rise of civilization. The more cognitive skills adolescents have, the more fantasy and daydreams they are likely to engage in. Part of the turmoil of adolescence may stem from the necessity of abandoning unrealistic fantasies over a short time, as the adolescent tests all sorts of ideas against reality.

Adolescent fantasy, then, is seen to have several characteristics: The fantasy play of childhood continues into early adolescence; one's future possibilities as an adult are incorporated into the fantasy life; emotional dimensions and cognitive abilities expand and points of interest are more fully explored and incorporated into fantasy; there is, for a while, an increase in time devoted to daydreams; and the adolescent interacts with a wider variety of people than does the child and is able to devote more time to daydreaming than the adult.

Projective techniques

The term *projective techniques* covers a number of methods that have been used to stimulate a flow of thought and fancy that may reveal something about a person's inner life he or she might not divulge if directly questioned. These methods take advantage of the fact that the experiences a person has had will determine in part what he or she projects or reads into what is heard or seen—for example, when listening to music or when looking at a picture. Similarly, one might see a distant cloud as the fleece of a lamb, or as a cold snowbank, or as the beard of an aged man. Again, in looking at a farm scene, one person may think of long, hard hours of toil, another of fertility, and yet another of the joy of tilling the soil. In making up a story about a certain subject one person may give the tale a happy ending while another has it end in misfortune.

The theory underlying the use of projective techniques is that when people respond they are revealing something about themselves and in so doing may reveal aspects of their feelings and their character that even they had not clearly recognized (Singer, 1969).

An early contributor to projective methods was Rorschach, who devised the famous "ink blots" comprising the Rorschach Test (1942). This test consists of a set of cards, each one of which contains a large ink blot. The blots vary in contour and include some that are in black and white and others in several colors. The person to whom the test is given is asked to tell what each blot might be or what he or she sees in it. There are standard directions for giving the test, and elaborate criteria have been worked out for interpreting the results.[2]

Ames et al. (1958) found that during adolescence Rorschach responses change significantly from one year to the next, indicating the inner changes the adolescent is undergoing.

Pictures have also been widely used as projective techniques in studies of adolescents as well as of older and younger persons. One of the pioneers in the use of pictures as a projective technique was Murray (1938), who developed what is known as the Thematic Apperception Test (TAT).[3]

The Contents of Adolescent Projections

Symonds (1949) conducted a study of adolescent images and projections using an adaptation of the TAT, and in 1961 Symonds and Jensen published a follow-up study of the adolescents first studied in 1949. Symonds used forty-two pictures that an artist had prepared according to Symonds's specifications. One showed a boy carrying a suitcase: he might be seen as one who is running away, or going on a journey, or seeking a job. Another showed two boys, one well dressed and one less well dressed, who apparently had had an unfortunate experience, sitting together and looking worried and disconsolate. One picture showed a kneeling woman looking intently through a keyhole. In another picture a girl was shown walking upstairs, with shadows suggesting nighttime, a clock showing the time at about three-thirty, and a shadowy figure standing at the head of the stairs.

Symonds (1949) obtained responses to his forty-two pictures from twenty boys and twenty girls at the junior and senior high school levels. The opening statement of the directions given to those who took the test read: "This is a test of creative imagination. I want to find how much imagination you have. Here are some pictures which I am going to show you one by one and I want you to make up a story on each picture." The directions then

[2] For a discussion of the Rorschach Test, see, for example, Rorschach (1937) and Mischel (1976).

[3] Other projective procedures include play techniques; role playing, in what is sometimes called a psychodrama; and drawing and painting, including the drawing of a human figure.

proceeded to give more specific instructions to the respondent and indicated some of the questions he or she should seek to answer.

In treating his results, Symonds made a distinction between what he called psychological and environmental themes, arbitrarily defined as follows: what you do to another person is psychological; what another person does to you is environmental. Tables 8.2 and 8.3 show the frequency with which various themes occurred in the young people's responses when these were classified into categories under the two headings.

Erotic themes appeared in stories told by thirty-six of the forty young people (late in the 1940s), but there were few instances when these were openly expressed as sex. Twenty-four mentioned marriage; twenty mentioned boy-girl situations and relationships; thirteen referred to friendship; and eight spoke directly about love and falling in love. The theme of love was expressed in episodes relating to dating, auto rides, marrying, and living happily thereafter. The stories about love usually dealt with social relationships rather than physical contact.

Table 8.2. "Psychological" themes occurring in the responses given by forty adolescents to forty-two pictures in the Symonds picture-story test

	By cases			By occurrences		
Themes	Total	B	G	Total	B	G
Aggression,	40	20	20	1,562	988	574
Eroticism	36	17	19	459	286	173
Negative emotion; depression	29	15	14	349	187	162
Anxiety	28	14	14	310	130	180
Altruism	28	14	14	401	198	203
Success; ambition	25	11	14	268	156	112
Repentance; reform	24	14	10	305	217	88
Positive emotion	22	10	12	193	78	115
Excitement	18	12	6	312	247	65
Escape	16	11	5	136	107	29
Thinking; decision	16	9	7	248	118	130
Morality; goodness	15	8	7	112	58	54
Jealousy	13	5	8	52	23	29
Concealment	10	5	5	119	55	64
Wrong; badness	10	7	3	81	60	21
Guilt; conscience	10	3	7	58	19	39
Yearning; wanting	7	3	4	54	19	35
Fatigue	6	2	4	31	17	14
Craziness	5	3	2	33	24	9
Waiting	5	1	4	25	3	22
Dreams; daydreams	4	2	2	15	8	7
Miscellaneous				376	142	234
Total				5,499	3,140	2,359

Source: From *Adolescent fantasy* by P. M. Symonds, New York, Columbia University Press, 1949. Reprinted by permission.

Table 8.3. "Environmental" themes occurring in the responses given by forty adolescents to forty-two pictures in the Symonds picture-story test

Categories	By cases			By occurrences		
	Total	B	G	Total	B	G
Family relationships	40	20	20	1,595	766	829
Economic	38	20	18	632	370	262
Punishment	33	18	15	614	484	130
Separation; rejection	32	18	14	397	185	212
Accidents; illness; injury	28	14	14	297	189	108
School	28	15	13	251	122	129
Social; gangs	21	9	12	130	70	60
Place of residence	17	8	9	98	56	42
Appearance	13	3	10	75	15	60
Strangeness; unusualness	12	8	4	125	85	40
Discussion; advice	10	7	3	54	33	23
Age	10	5	5	46	23	23
Gossip	8	5	3	55	31	24
Entertainment	7	3	4	41	23	18
Work	7	3	4	39	15	24
Night	4	2	2	25	12	13
Food; eating	4	3	1	22	16	6
Mail; writing	4	2	2	14	7	7
Miscellaneous				294	211	83
Total				4,804	2,713	2,091

Source: From *Adolescent fantasy* by P. M. Symonds, New York, Columbia University Press. 1949. Reprinted by permission.

Every adolescent boy and girl studied by Symonds told at least three stories in which there were themes of aggression ranging from mild criticism and rebuke to robbery and murder. Even the boys and girls who gave the appearance of being mild and gentle in real life told stories filled with destructive violence. Symonds observed that a boy would sometimes gasp with surprise when a story he had told was repeated to him; he would act as though he had expressed violence without fully recognizing its nature at the time, as though he were now annoyed and anxious about it.

The way adolescents end a story in which they have given play to their imagination is of special significance, according to Symonds. Many of the adolescents in his study consistently gave happy endings to their stories. Only a few permitted endings to be tragic or fatal. However, when individuals characteristically find a happy ending (as in fairy tales where "they lived happily ever after"), we cannot assume that they are more hopeful or that the ventures in their lives usually take a happier turn than is true for those who do not always describe happy endings. The happy ending may even denote a feeling of guilt. Symonds points out, for example, that there are adolescents who permit themselves to create an aggressive story (in a fantasy, for example, about a boy in a speeding car who knocks down a woman) but do not permit themselves to end the story on a harmful and destructive note. Some adolescents allow themselves aggressive fantasies and then make some kind of amends at the end so that no drastic damage is done.

An interesting finding in this study was that although adolescents expressed guilt when they had given play to their aggressive fantasies, they did not, in general, express guilt when they had gone into the theme of love. This may be due to the fact that in themes of love the young people did not let their fantasies go as far as they did in expressing themes of aggression.[4]

In this study of adolescent fantasy, there were some differences between boys and girls. Boys were more direct and, in a sense, more primitive in expressing their passions than girls. Boys, for example, more often gave stories with themes of violence, death, crime, and murder. The girls also voiced aggression, but they tended to show it by disobedience, resistance, rebellion, and coercion, rather than through violent means. One somewhat unexpected finding was that boys more frequently than girls brought in themes of love or falling in love. Girls, on the other hand, more often brought in themes pertaining to friends and children.

When older and younger adolescents were compared, it appeared that the younger people seemed to be freer in expressing hostility without feeling guilty. The older individuals in the study tended more often than the younger ones to show disappointment and to voice concern about the future. The older ones seemed also to show greater seriousness by bringing in themes of *wondering, thinking,* and *musing.*

The fantasies pertaining to school in Symonds's study are especially interesting, and they are in keeping with other findings, cited elsewhere in this book, concerning the meaning, and frequently the apparent meaninglessness, of school in the life of the adolescent. In their projections adolescents did not regard school as a particularly happy place. Punishment and the threat of failure hung over many of these adolescent storytellers when they spoke about school. The adolescents seldom expressed affection for their teachers but pictured them more often as stern, threatening, and avenging.[5]

Twenty-eight of the forty adolescents in Symonds's investigation took part in a follow-up study from 1953 to 1954, thirteen years after the

[4] It is interesting to observe that adolescents in the Symonds study let themselves go more freely in projecting passions leading to violence than in projecting passions leading to making love.

[5] It is possible that the students who happened to take part in this study tended to be more melancholy in their view of school than the typical high school student—although there is no good reason to think so for, in selecting persons for the study, an effort was made to obtain volunteers who were typical (neither predominantly bright nor dull) and not considered to be "problem" children.

original inquiry (Symonds and Jensen, 1961). These twenty-eight persons, in 1953, ranged from twenty-five to thirty-one years in age.

A substantial number of the stories told by these persons in 1953 and 1954 were, in general, quite similar to those they had told thirteen years earlier, but there were some notable changes. There was a *decrease* in themes dealing with violent aggression or punishment for aggression.[6] There was an *increase* in themes dealing with depression and guilt.

As adolescents, these people had had many hopeful fantasies, but thirteen years later there were many expressions of disappointment, discouragement, and dejection. This shift had been foreshadowed in the 1940 study, for at that time the older adolescents emphasized discouragement and disappointment more than the younger ones. Symonds and Jensen (1961) regard the increase in depressive themes as signifying two tendencies: disillusionment about adolescent hopes and a shift from an outgoing form of aggression (fantasies of violence and crime) to aggression turned inward in the form of self-recrimination, and feelings of inferiority, discouragement, and hopelessness.

As noted earlier, according to Symonds's interpretation, many of the persons in this study confirmed, in their actual conduct as adults, the fantasy themes they had expressed as adolescents, especially in the area of later vocational choices. In some instances the resemblance between adult conduct and earlier fantasies was striking. Six girls, in adolescence, had expressed fantasies that depicted strong hostility toward mother figures. Three of these later married against their mothers' wishes and in spite of "vehement protest." A boy who had expressed hostility toward father figures in adolescence directed his hostility against bosses in later real life; he had had ten different jobs since leaving school, and he left most of them following a quarrel or disagreement with the boss. Symonds and Jensen (1961) describe several other similarities between early fantasies and later conduct. However, many fantasies were not borne out, and the evidence is not firm enough to show how well and in which instances an account of adolescent fantasies will foreshadow what will happen in later life.

In a review of the literature on imaginative behavior, Klinger (1969) points out that themes concerning future vocations and higher education, athletics, achievement, romance, and sex appear in all studies of adolescent fantasies. Although some of the adolescent themes may be found at younger ages, the fantasies of adolescents have been found to contain material that is far more complex.

There are several more recent studies that attempt to assess adolescent fantasy life using modified projective techniques. Bamber (1973) used

[6] In 1940, fifteen of the persons, as compared with six in 1953, told stories about criminal death. The total number of stories dealing with crimes against persons or property, or criminal death, fell from ninety-seven in 1940 to thirty-one in 1953.

three techniques and compared fourteen- to fifteen-year-olds with twenty-three-year-olds. He found that adolescents viewed adolescence and adult life more positively than childhood, whereas adults viewed both childhood and adult life more positively than adolescence. Singer (1969), as part of a study of seventy-three "normal" adolescent boys reported by Offer (1969), discusses outcomes of tests administered to these boys: the Rorschach, seven cards included in the Apperception Test (TAT), and the vocabulary subtest of the Wechsler Adult Intelligence Scale (WAIS). The first two are standard projective tests. The WAIS is a standard test used to measure the intelligence, but test results of parts of the WAIS can be interpreted to yield information about personality variables as well. The vocabulary subtest correlates well with total score on the WAIS and, hence, gives a quick assessment of general intelligence. Examples of the cards chosen from the TAT include a boy looking at a violin on a table, a boy leaning against a couch with a gun near him, and a young woman leaning on a man's shoulder. There was much homogeneity in the TAT responses, with several main themes. Mothers were depicted as comforting, understanding, and warm. Ambivalence toward leaving the mother's care was expressed. The boys were not depicted as being masculine, like their fathers, but as expecting to be so in the future. There was little involvement among sixteen-year-olds in the sexual side of dating, perhaps reflecting their ambivalence toward leaving mother. Independence was valued, but a longing for childhood and a fear of separation from parents also appeared. The boys tended to judge themselves. They admired their fathers but showed what was interpreted as an unconscious wish for more closeness to father. Parental authority was generally adhered to in the stories. There was a good deal of open competition with siblings, and the boys seemed to express a feeling that they would not win in this competition. They appeared to attempt to deal with conflicts openly and showed trust in adults.

Rorschach responses in this study, as interpreted by Singer (1969), revealed some social and emotional constriction, with stereotyped thinking and a relative lack of emotional awareness. There was a great deal of defensiveness, with limited interests, but with the ability to plan rationally for the future. There was a large range of responses in response to each Rorschach variable, suggesting that boys display much diversity in coping with problems. The responses tended to reveal a good sense of humor, along with some self-criticism. The boys' responses were deemed to reveal anxiety about being different from peers, although differences were also seen to be valued. The boys' responses were interpreted as showing them able to master frightening situations.

The vocabulary subtest scores revealed that the boys showed average intelligence, but the contributions of intelligence scores to personality variables was unclear.

Some Rorschach responses judged to be "abnormal" were given by the (presumably) normal boys in this study, indicating that a wide range of coping mechanisms may be called on to meet the stresses of adolescence and that one must not be too quick to deem an adolescent abnormal if behavior and thinking are shown that in an adult would probably indicate abnormality.

In a study of fantasy in a group of freshmen and sophomore high school students in a small town, Zucker and Fillmore (1969) used questionnaires about book or movie preference as projective indicators of fantasy. They found that the responses were strongly sex related. The boys' first preferences were books or movies dealing with adventure or war, and the second preferences dealt with sports. Girls' first preferences were for themes of suffering and hardship and second for themes of teenage life and romance.

A study of written TAT responses by a group of college students was undertaken by Murstein (1972). There were differences between the sexes in this study, too. Women appeared to tell somewhat more positive stories than men, with more positive endings. Women also told more stories involving one person helping another and saw things in a more conventional way than did men.

Dreams

There have been two outstanding contributions to the study of dreams, one theoretical, the other emerging from laboratory studies. The first, going back to 1900, rests on Freud's clinical work on the interpretation of dreams. The reception of Freud's contribution has ranged from wholehearted (and sometimes overliteral) acceptance to outspoken or mute rejection. But its impact has been tremendous. The second major contribution is more recent and deals with the physiologic processes associated with dreams.

The Psychological Nature of Dreams

Put most simply, dreams are mental activities of a certain type that occur during sleep. Although men have speculated about the meaning of dreams for centuries, it was not until Freud published his monumental work, *The Interpretation of Dreams*, in 1900, that a systematic and integrated theory about dreams was put forward. This work has influenced almost all succeeding investigations about dreams in one way or another and has served as the anvil on which others have sought to hammer out their own ideas concerning dreams.

According to Freud (1955, originally published in 1900), dreams are derived from private mental material that is unacceptable to the dreamer's conscious mind. Such unacceptable material usually consists of sexual and aggressive impulses that go against the person's conscience or the demands of reality and, hence, are repressed (forgotten) during the day. However, because there is not a sharp difference, according to Freud, between unconscious mental activity during the day and at night during dreaming, such material is retained and expressed in dreams where it may not be recognized as such because it is presented in a distorted fashion.

According to Freudian theory, dreams include both a manifest and a latent (hidden or disguised) content. Even though the barriers against the recognition of forbidden thoughts and impulses are, presumably, less rigid during sleep than during waking hours, it appears that even in dreams there are certain inhibitions against the outright display of forbidden material. In Freudian terms, what might be called a psychic censor is at work. As we will note later in this chapter, laboratory studies and surveys of dream narratives confirm Freud's theory that sexual and aggressive impulses have a prominent role in dreams. It is interesting to note, however, that sex (which is associated with the creation of life) appears to be more severely censored in dreams than aggressiveness (which frequently is associated with destructiveness).

The Physiological Correlates of Mental Activity During Dreams

Modern conceptions of the functions and origins of dreams and their relationship to sleep took form in the 1950s through the pioneering work of Dement and Kleitman (1957a, 1957b); Dement (1960); and Kleitman (1960); and their colleagues. Recent works reviewing the dream research field include Dement (1974); Petre-Quadens and Schlag (1974); and Woods and Greenhouse (1974).

In a study of infants (Aserinsky and Kleitman, 1953) it was noted that eye movements occurred periodically during sleep. Later, in work with older persons, it was discovered that rapid eye movements (REMs), along with distinctive brain-wave patterns as measured by an electroencephalograph (EEG) machine, usually (in about 80 per cent of the instances) signified that a dream was in progress. The dreaming was verified by immediately awakening the sleeping individual. A laboratory device has been designed to record REMs. REM patterns, associated with the distinctive EEG patterns, occur at intervals during sleep, occupying 20 to 25 per cent of the time a young adult is asleep. REM periods were thought to alternate with periods of sleep that did not include dreaming or manifest the distinctive brain wave pattern. However, recent research (see, for example, Vogel, 1975) has indicated that dreamlike states probably also occur in the non-REM (NREM) periods of sleep (when no rapid eye movements occur).

Because people tend to forget their dreams rapidly on being awakened, investigators who do laboratory research on dreams have found it expedient to ask their subjects, upon awakening them, to describe the most recent parts of their dream and then to recall as much as they can about the rest of the dream (Roffwarg et al., 1962). In this way at least part of the dream is likely to be described in detail.

Other signs of body changes were noted during REM sleep (such as increased pulse, blood pressure, and respiratory rates and occasional body movements), indicating that major happenings were occurring in the nervous system during periods of dreaming. As shown by Foulkes (1962) and other workers, in non-REM (NREM) periods people may report dreamlike states (less organized and emotionally distorted than actual dreams), memories of real events, and thoughts similar to the realistic thinking that occurs during the day. The relationship of this dreamlike activity to dreaming was investigated further by Foulkes and Vogel (1965), who reported dream occurrences outside of REM periods. This NREM activity, although it resembles daytime thinking, may be carried over into dreams much as the "day residue"—that is, memories and events of the day which occur quite often in dreams. NREM and REM dream reports of the same night have been found to be related in content (Rechtschaffen et al., 1963). NREM period thinking may differ from daytime thought in its lack of direction and its inclusion of secondary "unimportant" thoughts or images that ordinarily would be suppressed and ignored during directed daytime thinking (Rechtschaffen et al., 1963).

NREM mental activity is both visual and hallucinatory and is like dreams in these respects. Dreaming has been reported to occur at the onset of sleep, before REM periods commence (Foulkes and Vogel, 1965), and also may occur even during relaxed periods of wakefulness (Vogel, 1975).[7]

A night's sleep encompasses from four to six cycles, each lasting approximately from sixty to ninety minutes. These cycles are recorded by the EEG and represent changes in brain-wave patterns. Each cycle comprises four stages, and REMs occur first during the first stage of the second sleep cycle. Subsequently, they recur during the first stage of all following cycles. The REM stage of sleep is characterized by EEG recordings different from each of the NREM stages of sleep. Typically, REM stages increase in length throughout sleep concurrent with longer dreams; NREM stages and periods of sleep without dreams decrease, although there is a good deal of variation from person to person in the duration and number of sleep cycles.

[7] There are many findings regarding sleep patterns; the recurrence of EEG and REM cycles that are not distinctly tied to adolescence will not be detailed in this chapter.

Each cycle after the first consists of a REM and three NREM stages. The NREM stages are distinguished by different EEG recordings, representing different brain-wave activities during each stage. There appears to be a waking cycle of oral activity corresponding to the REM cycle during sleep (Friedman and Fisher, 1967).

Reports from subjects indicated that mental activity during the onset of sleep was dreamlike—that is, visual and hallucinatory, with plots and activity, but without much emotion (Foulkes and Vogel, 1965). There was a high incidence of such mental activity during sleep onset (Vogel et al., 1972). These findings also appeared to show that dreams were not limited to REM sleep. REM and sleep onset reports of the same subjects were similar (Foulkes et al., 1966). It should be noted, however, that when people are deprived of REM time and then allowed to sleep as much as they will, a "rebound" effect is seen and there is more than the usual amount of REM time. There have been other studies of REM deprivation and of other aspects of REM sleep periods that are not distinctly relevant to adolescence and will not be reviewed here.

In a recent review of work dealing with REM deprivation in animals and humans, Vogel (1975) points out that REM deprivation (through artificial interference with sleep) is not the same as dream deprivation, as was previously believed. In humans REM deprivation probably does not lead to the development of mental disturbances, as was once believed (Vogel and Traub, 1968).

Adolescent Sleep and Dream Patterns

The sleep and dream patterns of adolescents (aged fourteen to eighteen years) and younger children have been compared with adult patterns in a study by Roffwarg et al. (1962). As we have noted, in young adults the "dream time per cent" (fraction of total sleep during which periods of rapid eye movements occur) usually ranges between 20 and 25, with an average of about 22. The average dream time per cent shown by a small sampling of adolescents was 18.5, with a range from 14 to 25 on individual nights. It appears that the adolescent dreams during a somewhat smaller percentage of his sleeping time than adults. Adolescents seem to dream about as much as children in an age range from five to thirteen years (who also showed an average dream time per cent of 18.5). The investigators state that their "expectation that there would be an increase in the per cent of dreaming at puberty along with the general upsurge in sexual drive at the same time was not borne out [Roffwarg et al., 1962, p. 10]."

This study also noted that although they retained some characteristics found in younger children, adolescents' sleep-dream patterns in many ways resembled those of young adults. Other investigators noted that during the later parts of a night's sleep, periods of rapid eye movements last longer in adolescents than in younger age groups and closely resemble the duration of corresponding periods at the young adult level. However, younger adolescents sometimes differed from adults in the earlier part of the night's sleep. Younger adolescents frequently "miss" the first REM period. In preadolescent children the first period of rapid eye movements commonly shown by adults is also usually delayed. This finding may arise from the fact that children and young adolescents are physically more active than adults and require a larger period of heavy sleep to take the edge off their body fatigue before they enter a "light sleep" cycle when dreaming is most likely to occur.

Dreams as an Aid to Knowledge About the Adolescent Personality

Dreams potentially offer a rich source of information about adolescents in general. Often, however, it is very difficult, and it may seem impossible, to decipher the cryptic messages they tell.[8] At the present time, dream interpretation is more an art than an exact science, and judging from writings on the subject, even "experts" are often baffled by their own dreams and the dreams of others. There are, however, some rudimentary principles that might help a student of adolescence, or adolescents themselves, in making a start toward understanding the meaning of dreams.

One principle is that although dreams are often very complex there are some aspects that frequently can be observed in simple form. These include the mood or emotional tone of the dream; the underlying theme or themes; the "problem" with which the dream deals; the "solution" the dream offers or fails to achieve; the elements of conflict the dream contains; and the thread of continuity that runs through several dreams during a single night or through dreams that recur over a longer period.

Another feature that often stands out clearly is the general drift or direction of movement in a series of dreams. A series of recurring dreams about missing the bus, for example, may "move" in the direction of more and more difficulty in getting there on time, or more and more instances of making it—at first barely and then with ease—followed by no more dreams about catching a bus. Similarly, a series of dreams about animals may start

[8] Perhaps more could be done to tap this source of self-knowledge than commonly is thought. This opinion is based on the view that the general tendency to ignore dreams, or to treat them as capricious hallucinations, does not spring solely from the fact that dreams are hard to understand, but from a general tendency in the culture to ignore the subjective dimensions of life.

with dreams about menacing creatures that become more menacing with time, or that, as the series continues, are mastered. Dreams that include automobiles may begin with some in which the dreamer is a passenger in a car, careening at a dizzy pace, and end with the dreamer in the driver's seat, in complete control of the vehicle. We can suspect that a person has a conflict about asserting him- or herself if, in one dream after another, he or she plays a passive, inadequate role or repeatedly dreams of persons who are hostile.

Another principle is that a person may be able to find meanings in dreams if he tries not to be deceived by characteristics that make dreams seem bizarre and full of nonsense.

Dreams Contrasted with Waking Feelings and Thoughts

There are many deceptive characteristics of dreams. If these are viewed casually, they are likely to obscure the meaning of a dream; if examined more carefully, they may be revealing.

THE APPEARANCE OF OPPOSITES

Dreams sometimes contain just the opposite of what seems to be happening in reality: the timid adolescent boy dreams that he fights the town bully. In such dreams the action seems farfetched; yet, if viewed from the standpoint of an adolescent's own striving, such dreams are not so far-fetched. In his fancies the timid boy may have had an angry impulse to thrash the bully.

EXAGGERATION

Dreams often seem to exaggerate the "point." Fighting, destruction, dismemberment, and terror frequently are more violent than anything that occurs in the dreamer's waking moments. Dreams sometimes are brazen. An adolescent girl who, in actual life, is just a little daring in her choice of a low-cut party dress may, in her dreams, appear in a very daring costume, or perhaps with no dress at all. Such exaggeration makes dreams seem unreal. Yet, it might be possible to detect in the dream a hard core of truth.

ILLOGICAL FEATURES

The dream, instead of following the logical sequence of ordered thought, is often completely (or so it seems) illogical. Events that seem out of place and actions that are incongruous are brought together. Events in real life that were separated by many years are thrown together, as when a new acquaintance is seen in a setting that is from one's past. However, when a dreamer, in waking moments, examines these incongruities, he or she may find that they have an underlying thread of meaning.

DISPLACEMENT

The phenomenon known as displacement often occurs in dreams. The young person who has had a quarrel with his or her mother may dream that he or she is fighting with an aunt; dreamers who are questioning the authority of their fathers may dream about arguing with a teacher or a preacher. Such displacement in dreams may obscure the meaning of the dream; yet, similar displacements of feeling often occur also in waking life.

CONDENSATION

Another phenomenon that occurs in dreams is condensation, where a little detail in the dream may embrace a broad meaning. Condensation would be occurring, for example, if a young person who is in the habit of dawdling and leaving tasks unfinished were to have a dream in which he should be fully clothed but neglected to put on one of his socks. The symbol of the missing sock may stand for a weakness that perhaps worries him and appears in many ways in his everyday life.

The Language of Dreams

Many images that appear in dreams may not be the ones the dreamer would prefer to use in his waking thoughts. The visual image of an open or closed door, for example, may symbolize meanings that could be more readily understood if they appeared in words that could be heard or read. The language of a dream is often a picture language.

Sometimes dream imagery may appear as almost a literal kind of symbolism. For example, a boy who was angry at being rebuffed by a girl with the nickname of "Chick" dreamed that he ran over a chicken while driving a garden tractor.

The "language" of the dream may take the form of signs that are like metaphors or other figures of speech. We use many metaphors in everyday speech. We say, for example, that we have the *key* to the problem; let us keep an *open mind*; I am in *deep water*; let us not *close the door* to new ideas; *quick as a flash*; he is *up to his neck* in trouble; *catch it on the wing*; I am *in the dark*; he is *playing with fire*. We also have various metaphoric expressions for states of feeling, such as: I feel *trapped, empty, stuck, lost, caught in a jam, torn between* two desires. The metaphors of the door (which may be open, closed, or stuck), of an empty space, of being lost, and of being in the dark are common in dreams.

In commenting on the use of metaphors, Hadfield (1954) points out that the metaphors in ordinary speech as well as in dreams may be mixed, and he cites a fragment from a speech by a member of parliament to illustrate this point: "I smell a rat, I see it floating in the air, but mark my words, I will nip it in the bud."

Dream Symbolism

The "language of the dream" is, as we have pointed out, often a wordless language, just as a musical symphony or a painting is wordless. There have been many theories concerning the interpretation of dream symbolism. Freud and his followers have especially emphasized sexual and aggressive symbols in dreams. Actually, dreams are so complex, and the play of imagery in the dreams so varied and so personal, we cannot assume that a certain symbol (such as a snake or a ship) always has a certain fixed meaning. The same symbol may mean different things in the dreams of different persons or even in the dreams of the same person and, according to some views on the subject, the same symbol may have several meanings even within a single dream.

Even if it were established that certain dream contents have a fixed and universally symbolic meaning the problem of untangling the dream would remain. Each dream is a personal document, uniquely interwoven with the dreamer's life. For this reason dreams must be examined in the context of the dreamer's experience. Someone else's interpretation of one's dream material has no significance whatsoever unless one can grasp a personal meaning, can fit the pieces together in a way that clicks and makes sense in one's mind.

The Content of Adolescent Dreams

Several studies (including Foulkes, 1967, and Kramer et al., 1969) have investigated the content of adolescent dreams. According to Foulkes et al. (1967, 1969), who studied REM dream reports of young children, preadolescent boys, and young adolescent boys (one group was normal and the other group was emotionally disturbed), dream content reflected the preoccupations of waking life in all three groups. The boys who had not yet reached puberty focused more on members of their family and pets than the adolescents in this study. However, the adolescent boys dreamed of family characters more often than young adults. The adolescent boys' dreams as well as the preadolescents' often centered around other boys. In contrast to the adolescent boys whose dreams more often included school settings, the younger boys' dreams more often included play settings. Adolescents' dreams of relations with others often showed more hostility than those of younger boys. With increased age there was an accompanying increase in dreams that included typical adolescent concerns such as future occupational plans and marriage, as well as present concerns with athletics and with male–female relationships. In general the dreams were often of a more or less realistic nature, although the dreams of emotionally disturbed adolescents were of a more bizarre quality than those of normal adolescents.

Judging from other accounts as well, there is a large degree of resemblance between the content of themes of adolescent, preadolescent, and postadolescent dreams.[9]

In a study in 1933 in which four hundred children were asked about their dreams (Jersild et al.), the content was found to include such "pleasant" topics as adventures, achieving wanted goals, games, sports, relationships with friends and relatives, and getting presents. "Unpleasant" dreams included such topics as violence, being lost, falling, and being chased by monsters or ghosts. Unpleasant dreams were noted more often than pleasant dreams and aggressive dreams more often than dreams of friendship. The absence of sexual content may be related to the date of the study; in 1933 most adults, much less children, didn't talk openly about their sexual thoughts or feelings.

Preadolescents (aged eleven to twelve years) reported considerably more dreams involving prestige, achievement, and independence than did younger subjects. It seems likely that such dreams would increase in frequency during the adolescent years.

Adolescent Sexuality and Dreams

Sexual excitation during REM sleep is often clearly evident. Many adolescent boys occasionally have dreams that end in nocturnal emissions. These seem to occur most frequently in late adolescence and diminish in the twenties. In some sex dreams there is an obvious sexual contact or physical approach. But in others there is little or no manifest sexual content in the main part of the dream; the ejaculation at the end of a so-called wet dream often seems to come as a nonsequitur—if the dream is viewed solely from the viewpoint of its manifest content. Such dreams may illustrate how a person's conscience stands so vigilantly on guard against forbidden impulses and acts that even during sleep, when inhibitions are likely to be more relaxed than in waking moments, one cannot permit oneself openly to dream one's desires but pursues them in a disguised way.

The sexual content of dreams of young men was studied by Fisher et al. (1965) at the Mount Sinai Hospital in New York City in connection with their discovery that erections of the penis occur both in dreams that manifestly have an erotic connotation and in dreams that appear to be quite without any sexual content. The presence of erections was noted by using a plastic tube around the penis. The tube was attached to instruments that recorded any change in penile size. Erections were reported in association with 95 per cent of REM periods, so that an erection is present during 20 to

[9] The dream content in childhood and young adulthood has been studied more systematically than the content in adolescence.

25 per cent of a young man's sleep. When subjects were awakened during a state of erection, they reported dream content including aggressive and sexual activity (but not intercourse) as well as dreams that appeared to be symbolic of sexual activity. As cyclical erections occur during dreams throughout life, Fisher believes that dreaming is closely connected with great sexual excitation.

Cohen (1973) investigated differences in the dream content of college men and women. Men and "masculine" women were more often found to have dreams dealing with aggression. If a person's sex-role orientation (masculine or feminine attitudes or interests) was contrary to the stereotype (discussed in Chapter 2), his or her dreams were more likely to be unpleasant than if the sex-role orientation corresponded with the stereotype. The author concluded that sex-role orientation, rather than biologic gender, was fundamental in affecting dream content.

According to Swanson and Foulkes (1968), women reporting an increase in sexual feelings during menstruation often had more hostile dreams concurrently. This study suggests that affect arousal may have an effect on dream content.

PREDOMINANCE OF AGGRESSIVENESS OVER FRIENDLINESS IN DREAMS

As noted elsewhere in this chapter, there is a close association between dreaming and sexual arousal (at least in males, as indicated by the fact that REM sleep is usually accompanied by an erection), and there also often is an undercurrent of aggressiveness or hostility in dreams. In dreams involving aggression the dreamer may be the victim (someone else in the dream strikes, chases, or threatens to harm the dreamer) or the aggressor. This does not mean, of course, that there is a monopoly of sex and aggressiveness in dreams. The manifest content of dreams, as narrated by the dreamer, ranges far and wide into happenings and experiences connected with everyday life. Moreover, the emotional tone of dreams similarly covers a wide range—from joy to sorrow, from pride to self-reproach, from apprehension to a feeling of triumph over fear. It is interesting to note, however, that in large collections of dream reports, happenings involving aggression far outnumber friendly interchanges.

This was apparent in the study by Jersild et al. (1933) of groups of children that included some youngsters of adolescent age and a number of preadolescents. It also appeared, quite dramatically, in studies by Hall (1962) and Hall and Domhoff (1962a, 1962b). In a collection of over 3,000 dream narratives obtained from persons ranging in age from two to eighty years, there were 1,490 that included acts of aggression, as compared with 711 acts of friendliness. Aggression exceeded friendliness at all age levels, and in the dreams of both boys and girls. Moreover, the friendly acts tended to be rather mild, such as exchanging greetings or doing a small favor. By contrast, the aggressive acts tended to be considerably more imposing, including stealing or destroying and ranging from physical attack to murder.[10]

Aggressiveness appears frequently in adolescent fantasies that have been evoked by projective techniques. To what extent aggressiveness, as compared with other emotional themes, appears in adolescents' spontaneous daydreams has not yet been established by systematic research. It is likely that most adolescents, perhaps all, have had daydreams colored by anger or schemes for taking revenge or "putting someone in his place." But, except, perhaps, in delinquents with a strong streak of vindictiveness, it seems likely that a large proportion of daydreams involve pleasant, rather than baleful, imagery.

In their discussion of the finding that the content in dreams consists of "a lot of hate, a little love" Hall and Domhoff (1962b) question whether an abundance of aggressiveness in dreams at night might reduce the impulse to be aggressive during the day, but they indicate that we do not have the necessary scientific evidence to answer this question.

Exploration Through Free Association

The common practice when individuals seek to explore their dreams with professional help is to draw on their own "free associations"—snatches of feeling and thought that come to their minds, fragments of old memories, ideas and recollections that, on the surface, may seem to have no logical relationship at all with one another or with the content of the dream.

The process of free association is very different from an exercise in logic. It is a kind of search, with no previous fixed notion of where the search will end and no previous idea of what may be found. It is far more akin to the divergent than the convergent forms of thinking described in Chapter 6. But it is, if anything, even more *divergent* than the thinking there described—for in free association thinkers are not even *trying* to think, in the usual sense of that term. They do not have an anticipated answer. They do not give an orderly structure to their ideas. Instead of directing their thoughts, they follow the vagaries of their minds. This might be called the cogitation of a lazy mind were it not for one thing: the person who undertakes it is seeking; he or she makes a plunge into the unknown.

[10] The findings here reported were made available by way of three prepublication mimeographed reports generously sent to the senior author by Dr. Calvin S. Hall.

Dreams as a Stimulus for Self-discovery

In Chapter 7 we cited authorities who maintain that schools place too much emphasis on conventional thought patterns and too little on original, imaginative, and unconventional forays of thought. In the opinion of the writers dreams might provide the starting point for an even more venture-some endeavor—a kind of thinking that is not only divergent and creative, but self-revealing, in the sense that it leads a person to a clearer view of divisive and conflicting elements in his or her existence. In the opinion of the writers dreams can provide a challenge to self-revealing thinking. In dreams conflicting, scattered, disorganized, and chaotic fragments of life are combined within one drama. On surface appearance the dream is even more fragmented and confused than the experiences of life from which it springs. But it offers a means of self-discovery when examined through a process of free association. This kind of thinking may be in the power of practically everyone. In their daily lives adolescents do a great deal of thinking of this sort, but usually without an effort to examine it. Often the chain of free association is broken when a young person's thought brings up unpleasant recollections or leads him or her into forbidden or suppressed desires. The process often stops at the very point where a bit of self-discovery might be achieved.

The process of free association is a kind of thinking that can be cultivated. A person who is undergoing therapy practices this kind of thinking when he or she comes again and again to the brink of self-revelation and retreats, and then through other routes comes to the same brink again and again, until finally he or she takes the plunge. This kind of thinking through free association may also be cultivated by persons working by themselves.

Practically nothing has been done in schools to encourage thinking by free association and to discover what it might produce. It would be a revolutionary thing in education to introduce this kind of thinking by way of a study of dreams. It would require a radical departure from the usual academic undertakings, a revision of teacher-training programs, a great amount of courage, and a great deal of exploring and experimentation. But the day might yet come when inquiry into the inner world of dreams and fantasies will be regarded as a respectable endeavor, perhaps more signifi-cant than much of what is now included in the course of study.

References

Ames, L. B., Metraux, R. W., & Walker, R. N. *Adolescent Rorschach responses.* New York: Paul B. Hoeber, 1958.

Aserinsky, E., & Kleitman, N. Regularly occurring periods of eye motility, and concomitant phenomena, during sleep. *Science*, 1953, **118**, 273–274.

Bamber, J. H. Adolescent marginality: A further study. *Genetic Psychology Monographs*, 1973, **88**, 3–21.

Bellack, L. *The TAT, CAT, and SAT in clinical use.* New York: Grune, 1975.

Cohen, D. B. Sex role orientation and dream recall. *Journal of Abnormal Psychology*, 1973, **82**, 246–252.

Dement, W. The effect of dream deprivation. *Science*, 1960, **131**(3415), 1705–1707.

Dement, W., & Kleitman, N. Cyclic variations in EEG during sleep and their relation to eye movements, body motility, and dreaming. *Electroencephalography and Clinical Neurophysiology*, 1957, **9**, 673–690.a.

Dement, W., & Kleitman, N. The relation of eye movements during sleep to dream activity: An objective method for the study of dreaming. *Journal of Experimental Psychology*, 1957, **53**, 399–346.b.

Dement, W. C. *Some must watch while some must sleep.* San Francisco: Freeman, 1974.

Fisher, C., Gross, J., & Zuch, J. Cycle of penile erection synchronous with dreaming (REM) sleep. *Archives of General Psychiatry*, 1965, **12**, 29–45.

Foulkes, W. D. Dream reports from different stages of sleep. *Journal of Abnormal and Social Psychology*, 1962, **65**, 14–25.

Foulkes, D. Dreams of the male child: Four case studies. *Journal of Child Psychology and Psychiatry*, 1967, **8**, 81–98.

Foulkes, D., Larsen, J. D., Swanson, E. M., & Rardin, M. Two studies of childhood dreaming. *American Journal of Orthopsychiatry*, 1969, **39**, 627–643.

Foulkes, D., Pivik, T., Steadman, H. E., Spear, P. S., & Symonds, J. D. Dreams of the male child: An EEG study. *Journal of Abnormal Psychology*, 1967, **72**, 457–467.

Foulkes, D., Spear, P. S., & Symonds, J. D. Individual differences in mental activity at sleep onset. *Journal of Abnormal Psychology*, 1966, **71**, 280–286.

Foulkes, D., & Vogel, G. W. Mental activity at sleep onset. *Journal of Abnormal Psychology*, 1965, **70**, 231–243.

Freud, S. *The interpretation of dreams.* 1900 (Standard ed., Vols. 4–5). London: Hogarth, 1955.

Freud, S. *Introductory lectures on psycho-analysis.* 1916–1917 (Standard ed., Vols. 15–16). London: Hogarth, 1963.

Friedman, S., & Fisher, C. On the presence of a rhythmic, diurnal, oral, instinctual drive cycle in man: A preliminary report. *Journal of the American Psychoanalytic Association*, 1967, **15**, 317–343.

Hadfield, J. A. *Dreams and nightmares.* London: Penguin Books, 1954.

Hall, C. S. *Friends and enemies in dreams.* Preprint. Coral Gables, Fla.: Institute of Dream Research, 1962.

Hall, C. S., & Domhoff, B. *Aggression in dreams.* Preprint. Coral Gables, Fla.: Institute of Dream Research, 1962.a.

Hall, C. S., & Domhoff, B. *Friendliness in dreams.* Preprint. Coral Gables, Fla.: Institute of Dream Research, 1962b.

Holt, R. R. Imagery: The return of the ostracized. *American Psychologist*, 1964, **19**, 254–264.

Hume, D. *An enquiry concerning human understanding.* Chicago: Open Court, 1912.

Jersild, A. T., Markey, F. V., & Jersild, C. L. Children's fears, dreams, wishes, daydreams, likes and dislikes, pleasant and unpleasant memories. *Child Development Monographs, 12.* New York: Teachers College, Columbia University, 1933.

Kleitman, N. Patterns of dreaming. *Scientific American Reprints.* San Francisco: Freeman, 1960.

Klinger, E. Development of imaginative behavior: Implications of play for a theory of fantasy. *Psychological Bulletin,* 1969, **72**, 277–298.

Kramer, M., Baldridge, B. J., Whitman, R. M., Ornstein, P. H., & Smith, P. C. An exploration of the manifest dream in schizophrenic and depressed patients. *Diseases of the Nervous System,* 1969, **30**, 126–130.

Libby, W. The imagination of adolescents. *American Journal of Psychology,* 1908, **19**, 249–252.

Mischel, W. *Introduction to personality* (2nd ed.). New York: Holt, 1976.

Murray, H. A., Barrett, W. G., & Homburger, E., *Explorations in personality.* New York: Wiley, 1938.

Murstein, B. I. Normative written TAT responses for a college sample. *Journal of Personality Assessment,* 1972, **36**, 109–147.

Offer, D. *The psychological world of the teen-ager: A study of normal adolescent boys.* New York: Basic Books, 1969.

Petre-Quadens, O., & Schlag, J. D. (Eds.). *Basic sleep mechanisms.* New York: Academic, 1974.

Rechtschaffen, A., Vogel, G., & Shaikun, G. Interrelatedness of mental activity during sleep. *Archives of General Psychiatry,* 1963, **9**, 536–547.

Roffwarg, H. P., Dement, W. C., & Fisher, C. *Observations on the sleep-dream pattern in neonates, infants, children and adults.* Unpublished report of investigation supported by Research Grant MY-3267 to Drs. Fisher and Dement from the National Institutes of Mental Health, Bethesda, Md., 1962.

Rorschach, H. *Psychodiagnostik, Methodik und Ergebnisse eines wahrehmungsdiagnostischen Experiments* (3rd ed.). Berlin: Huber, 1937.

Rorschach, H. *Psychodiagnostics, a diagnostic test based on perception* (P. Lemkau and B. Kronenberg, trans.). New York: Grune, 1942.

Sanford, R. N., Adkins, M. M., Miller, R. B., & Cobb, E. A. Physique, personality and scholarship. *Monographs of the Society for Research in Child Development,* 1943, **8**(1).

Schilder, P. The image and appearance of the human body: Studies in the constructive energies of the psyche. *Psyche Monographs,* **4**. London: Kegan Paul, Trench, Trubner, 1935.

Shaffer, L. F., & Shoben, E. J., Jr. *The psychology of adjustment.* Boston: Houghton, 1956.

Singer, P. R. Psychological testing: Thematic apperception test, Rorschach test, and WAIS vocabulary scale. In D. Offer (Ed.), *The psychological world of the teen-ager: A study of normal adolescent boys.* New York: Basic Books, 1969.

Singer, J. L. *Imagery and daydream methods in psychotherapy and behavior modification.* New York: Adacemic, 1974.

Singer, J. L., & McCraven, V. G. Some characteristics of adult daydreaming. *Journal of Psychology*, 1961, **51**, 151–164.

Swanson, E. M., & Foulkes, D. Dream content and the menstrual cycle. *Journal of Nervous and Mental Disease*, 1967, **145**, 358–363.

Symonds, P. M. *Adolescent fantasy*. New York: Columbia U.P., 1949.

Symonds, P. M., & Jensen, A. R. *From adolescent to adult*. New York: Columbia U.P., 1961.

Vogel, G. W. A review of REM sleep deprivation. *Archives of General Psychiatry*, 1975, **32**, 749–761.

Vogel, G. W., Barrowclough, B., & Giesler, D. D. Limited discriminability of REM and sleep onset reports and its psychiatric implications. *Archives of General Psychiatry*, 1972, **26**, 449–455.

Vogel, G. W., & Traub, A. C. REM deprivation: I. The effect on schizophrenic patients. *Archives of General Psychiatry*, 1968, **18**, 287–300.

Woods, R. L., & Greenhouse, H. B. (Eds.). *The new world of dreams*. New York: Macmillan, 1974.

Zucker, A., & Fillmore, K. M. Masculinity-femininity in fantasy preferences: An indirect approach. *Journal of Projective Techniques*, 1969, **33**, 424–432.

part four

EMOTIONAL DEVELOPMENT

9

emotions; love, joy

This chapter will deal first with certain general characteristics of emotion and then move on to a discussion of love and joy. The next two chapters will deal further with emotion, including fear, anger, and anxiety. The material that immediately follows in this chapter may be familiar to some readers, but we believe it is an appropriate introduction to the sections and chapters that follow.

The role of emotion

It is in the realm of emotion, the affective dimension of experience, that adolescents are most poignantly aware of their existence as separate selves, distinct from all other creatures. When adolescents report what they most admire or deplore about themselves, as reported in a study by Jersild (1952), they mention emotional characteristics more often than other attributes, such as their physical endowments or intellectual abilities.

Psychological attributes of emotion

Emotion comprises the *affective*, as distinguished from cognitive, volitional, or motivational, aspects of experience, although the three last named processes play an important role in the arousal of an emotional experience and how it will be resolved.

When fully aware of what is involved in an emotional episode, a person usually (at the moment or as an afterthought) can identify three ingredients: *perception* of the circumstance that aroused the emotion, such as the menacing approach of a snarling dog; *feeling*, perhaps of being afraid; and *impulse*, such as an impulse to flee or to use a means of self-defense.

Many physiological phenomena may occur, some noticeable, such as a rapid heartbeat, and some not directly discernible.

Oftentimes the psychological and physical responses in an emotional state are not clearly defined in a person's awareness: the feelings may be blurred, the person may not clearly recognize what aroused him, and there may be no decisive impulse to flee, as in fear, or to strike back in anger. Adolescents sometimes, for example, are gloomy without being able to clearly describe how they feel, why they are depressed, and what to do about it.

In the process of development, emotions are aroused by external conditions, as in the example of fear, or by internal conditions, such as physical discomforts that are not easy to explain, or by temptations that make a person feel uneasy or guilty.

The neurological aspects of emotion

The areas of the nervous system involved in emotion include the "higher" centers, the regions of the cerebral cortex, that function in perception, reasoning, concept formation, imagination, and the other mental activities discussed in earlier chapters. The areas also include parts of the brain stem known as the hypothalamus and the limbic lobe (MacLean,

1973; Osler, 1968), as well as the more primitive autonomic division of the nervous system that regulates involuntary functions, such as the activity of the endocrine glands. Among these glands are the adrenals, which, as described in the classic studies by Cannon (1929), in times of intense excitement, pour secretions into the blood stream, mobilizing energies for fight or flight in an animal's struggle for existence. The fact that in an intense emotional state there is activation not only of the "newer" higher brain centers, but also of the phylogenetically older parts of the nervous system that a person is not able consciously and deliberately to control has important consequences.

Emotion as related to needs, drives, and motives

Emotion may be aroused by anything that gratifies or furthers a person's needs or desires, or anything that frustrates a person's drives. As children grow older and enter adolescence there is a complicated interplay between their emotions, their motives, and their hopes and plans for the future.[1] The needs and motives associated with emotion are as varied and numerous as all the processes involved in the business of living.

In infancy such needs obviously include those associated with hunger and thirst and bodily comfort. Many studies suggest, however, that the needs of infants extend beyond the gratification of body appetites or relief from body distress. The extent to which an infant's wants are satisfied, or left unheeded, may have a significant impact on a person's life in adolescence and later years. Studies by Harlow (1958) of infant monkeys have yielded findings that appear also to apply to human infants. Human infants need contact with a person who cares for them, usually the mother. Without a mother and lacking contact with a mother, infant monkeys will cling to a makeshift substitute "mother," such as one made of cloth. It seems that "contact comfort" is important for the well-being of infants even before they are mature enough, through their own initiative and actions, to seek out and establish contact with another creature or thing. As will be noted in this chapter, infants deprived of contacts with fellow creatures are unlikely, at adolescence, to establish normal relationships with peers or normal mating and mothering activities when they have reached the capacity to produce offspring.

As children move from infancy through childhood and into adolescence, there is both an expansion and contraction of conditions that arouse emotion. Many childhood fears are laid by as noises that once frightened

[1] Cofer (1972) discusses the interplay of motives and emotion.

them become familiar, and persons or things that once were strange similarly become familiar and are taken in stride. If their development follows a normal course, children also become immune to conditions that once aroused anger, such as a slight delay in feeding when they are hungry.

As children grow older and their capabilities expand, they derive pleasure from using their abilities, but such pleasures quite often also recede as youngsters move toward or into adolescence. Infants who are just beginning to walk are likely to plunge into this activity, often with shouts of glee, even though they stumble and fall. Young children also gain pleasure from making an intellectual discovery that seems to satisfy their curiosity. They appear to experience what might be called pleasures of the mind. Many years ago the senior author spoke of such self-impelled activity and pleasure as illustrating the developmental principle of endogenous motivation expressing itself in the spontaneous use of growing abilities. In a somewhat similar vein, Maslow (1968) speaks of self-actualization as a basic human motive. And, on a wider scale, Lecky (1945) and many other authors have spoken of self-enhancement and a need to protect and sustain a cherished view of oneself as important motives. (As we will note in Chapters 10 and 11, anything that threatens to disturb a person's view of him- or herself is likely to produce an emotional reaction, such as anger, anxiety, or depression.)

For some adolescents many of the motivations that gave emotional zest to life at an earlier age lose their strength. Some who eagerly walked, at the age of one or thereabouts, choose to walk only if they have to. Some do not use or seem to enjoy other motor activities, even though they now are stronger and speedier than they were at a less mature stage of growth. The behavior of such persons seems to suggest, as mentioned earlier, that an important mark of maturity is a strong inclination to rest. But, then again, there are many adolescents who seem to enjoy their increased mobility and strength.

In the intellectual sphere many adolescents seem also to have lost the joy they once derived from satisfying their curiosity and from learning something new. Fortunately, however, their zest for learning is likely only to be dormant, and with good fortune, the joy in acquiring new knowledge can be revived.

There are, of course, many other motives that can produce emotion in adolescence (Group for the Advancement of Psychiatry, 1968). The desire to be accepted by peers is one such motive. The drive for independence is another. And, of course, sexual drives, manifested in various ways since infancy, have an added urgency with the onset of puberty. Motives are also imbedded in an adolescent's plans for the future, and anything that promises to further such plans or threatens to defeat them is likely to produce an emotional response.

The same condition can result in varied emotional responses, depending on the person's wishes and expectations (Lewin, 1951). Persistent lack of response, or lack of motivation, may lead to feelings of guilt, shame, dissatisfaction, and self-derogation. For example, if an adolescent boy wishes to impress a girl who admires athletic prowess, he will be happy if he is selected for a varsity team. If, on the other hand, he wants to impress a girl who admires intellectual ability and downgrades athletic ability, his making the team may not fill him with the same feeling of joy—it might even depress him for a while. Or, if one values social position, one might admire someone just elected class president, but if one is rebelling against society's values, such an election would have quite a different meaning.

The interplay between emotion and cognition

The conceptual development that occurs as persons approach and enter the adolescent stage of growth, as described in Chapter 6, vastly enlarges the potential ramifications of emotion in their lives. If, for example, they happen to join with elders who have a pessimistic view of life, they may have apprehensive forebodings of future disaster. If they have a more optimistic view they can relish the thought of happy days to come. They may become angrily impatient when what they conceive as social injustice is not corrected or enthusiastic in sharing ideals for improving the conditions of life.

The interplay between emotion and cognition, including perception and reasoning, is complicated by the fact that it usually is easier to revive and examine a cognitive process than to reinstate a feeling that occurred in the past. In the example used earlier in this chapter, one can revive the picture of the approach of a snarling dog, but one cannot restore the feeling of fear (unless the experience was lastingly traumatic). One can reexamine the steps in one's thinking in dealing with a problem and even verify the solution. But if the thinking process solves a problem that was emotionally disturbing, it is difficult to resurrect the feelings connected with the problem.

Cognitive processes—including memory, reasoning, and learning— can usually be evaluated in terms of external, objective criteria or factual data; green elephants do not exist, whereas green grass does. Emotional reactions are not so verifiable; they may be noted as being of a particular intensity or particularly suitable for a certain occasion, but they cannot be measured in terms of external fact. Similarly, if feelings are experienced consciously they must be felt as real; one cannot experience an abstract feeling as one may think about abstract ideas.

It is more difficult for a person to change a deeply ingrained feeling, such as fear of failure, than to change a thought, such as the notion that one did poorly on a test when one later discovers he or she earned a grade of A.

Concealment of emotion

Most adolescents have been under pressure, since early childhood, to conceal their feelings. They are told not to cry. They learn not to show fear, to avoid being looked on as "chickens" or "fraidy-cats." They learn that a show of anger, instead of gaining a sympathetic inquiry, is more likely to evoke retaliation and thus add fuel to their rage.

Emotions are frightening to many people, probably because they fear losing control of their emotions. This may be one of the major reasons children are taught to overcontrol their expressions of feeling, leading to subsequent problems in sharing with others, in enjoying relating to other people, and in feeling comfortable with oneself. Feelings of alienation, emptiness, and depression are the result of this emotional constriction, and they account for a large part of the emotional disability and its effects seen in our society. Although people are eager to learn new ideas and encourage intellectual learning, learning about feelings and being aware of one's feelings remains taboo for too many people.

The Suppression and Repression of Emotion

Concealment of emotions may be done knowingly or unknowingly. If it is done knowingly, when, for example, a person feels anger but thinks it prudent not to show it, it is called suppression. If it is done unknowingly, it is called repression, as when a person who is affronted acts in a conciliatory way but has no conscious feeling of anger. One might believe instead that one's *real* experience is a desire to please the one who has abused him or her. One finds excuses for the provocation and blames oneself and feels guilty instead of realistically ascribing one's wrath to the persons who anger one. When an affront that naturally would produce anger is thus shoved aside, as though it did not exist, but still leaves a mark that the person is not aware of, we say it is repressed. It is down but not out. When the anger that has been banished thoroughly from awareness still rankles, but in ways undetected by the angry person, it resides in what psychoanalysts call the unconscious. A person who knowingly conceals feelings is suppressing something; a person who unwittingly conceals feelings is repressing something.

Developmental and Cultural Aspects of Concealing Emotion

The influences that lead adolescents to disguise, suppress, or repress emotion reside both within adolescents themselves and in the culture.

Changes that occur in the natural course of development lead to many changes in emotional response. The growing child becomes increasingly able to cope with many conditions that once were disturbing. With increased ability the child can take in stride many things that once produced anger or fear. As language ability develops, there is less need to strike out in anger or to cry. Also, as one grows older one is better able to view things in a larger perspective, to bide one's time, to make allowances. As a child's emotions become more differentiated with increasing age, so do the factors that encourage hiding one's emotions become stronger with age.

Most adolescents have had the experience of loving, as well as being loved, but many of them have learned to conceal even this worthy emotion. Quite apart from their own tendency to become less demonstrative in showing their feelings, youngsters are under pressure from others in childhood and adolescence to control their open expression of affection. It is "babyish" for an older child, especially a boy, to caress others or to seek a caress. A boy is likely to be jeered if he tenderly avows that he loves a playmate or a teacher. There are strong taboos against affection both on the playground and in the classroom.

The prohibitions against a display of affection are also strengthened, as youngsters grow older, by fears about the intermingling of tenderness and sex. Many youngsters who gladly accepted a little hug or pat from their teachers in nursery school would be flabbergasted if a high school teacher hugged them (and the teacher probably would be embarrassed if observed in the act). Because of such taboos, many persons recoil more from tenderness than from anger.

When tenderness is taboo it is, as we have noted, due in part to the fact that sex is taboo; and sex is taboo, in part, because society, of necessity, must impose some sexual restraints. But what often seems to happen is that tenderness becomes a forbidden emotion while sexual impulses survive. Such a dearth of tenderness occurs when sex is more closely linked in the adolescent's mind with the ideas of aggression and exploitation than with the sentiment of love.

During childhood most adolescents, and especially boys, were told not to cry; and so adolescents, and notably adolescent boys, seldom cry even though the conditions of their lives are such that they might weep if they felt free to show their feelings. From early childhood adolescents have had fears, but they have been told not to show them. Pressures on males not to show weakness result in a tendency in males to be more defensive than females and less likely to reveal weakness (Sarason et al., 1964).

Much of the blunting of emotion in children takes place because adults in their own upbringing were taught to conceal and fear their emotions. One consequence is that adults often are disturbed and become anxious when children cry or are frightened or show anger. They may basically be kindhearted people but feel threatened by another's show of feeling. They hurriedly tell a child not to cry or not to be afraid or angry without giving the child a chance to express, and themselves a chance to discover, why he or she is upset. In so doing they cut themselves off from the child and curb the child's right to have feelings. At adolescence, with the upsurge of the emotional and physical changes of puberty, concealment of feelings becomes more difficult to maintain. This accounts in part for the sudden changes of emotion so characteristic of the adolescent. Emotions heretofore concealed may suddenly explode, although most of the adolescent's feelings remain hidden. There may be a wide discrepancy between the adolescent's outer behavior and his or her inner emotional reactions and fantasies. In their emotional reactions adolescents may appear, at times, to be quite irrational, or show a kind of edginess or irritability or depression that, as perceived by another person, is unexplainable.

The weighty influence of peers on adolescent behavior extends into spoken and unspoken codes pertaining to the expression of emotion.

It is generally considered unmanly for male team members to cry after having lost an important game; however, if the team leader or star athlete becomes overwhelmed in such a circumstance and cries, the other team members may then feel free to also vent their feelings. In some groups boys, and even girls, are permitted to show anger openly with fists or hairpulling. Also, in some groups boys are encouraged to display fearlessness by taking risks, such as in reckless driving.

Affection and love

An important feature of the adolescent's emotional life is his or her capacity to feel affection for others and to receive affection from others. The ability to accept affection is as essential as the ability to feel and to give it. As a young person reaches emotional maturity, the distinction between giving and receiving becomes harder to make, and the two are often merged.[2]

[2] Aspects of affection are also treated in other sections, including those dealing with parent-child relationships, relationships between friends and between members of the opposite sex, and compassion as a component of emotional maturity.

The Beginnings of Affection

The importance of affection has been brought home to the adolescent from the time of early infancy (Lewis, 1972). The adolescent begins life as one who is helpless. Affectionate behavior from others is closely linked to his or her physical survival, and affectionate behavior from others is an important factor in his or her psychological well-being. Also, in early childhood the individual goes out to others with affectionate pats and caresses.

One theory concerning the origin of love is as follows: The primary needs of children are those connected with their animal wants—food, drink, and protection against the elements. It is satisfying for children to have these needs gratified, and this influences their feelings toward those who gratify them; they are a part of the total situation in which gratification occurs. Feelings arising from gratification become associated with certain persons and conditions. Children eventually love their mothers because the children originally liked the food, warmth, and comfort their mothers provided.

Another theory concerning the origin of love is that it is not just a by-product of the gratification of animal wants but an inherent and primary element of human nature. According to this view, it is as "natural" to love and to seek love as it is to eat.

In discussing contrasting views, Sorokin and Hanson (1953) summarize evidence supporting the idea that there is an "enormous power for creative love, friendship, and nonviolent and nonaggressive conduct in human affairs and in social life [p. 99]."

Children apparently can develop the capacity for friendliness and affection even though they receive far less attention than the average youngster, but it probably is impossible for them to develop this capacity with *no* friendly contacts. (Even children in a crowded, understaffed institution have human contacts, which must seem friendly and gratifying to them, when they are fed, bathed, and clothed by attendants who are hurried but not unkind.)

Evidence that children seek and need affection and will go to great lengths to establish bonds of affection appears in a study by Freud and Dann (1951). These investigators describe a small group of refugee children who were bereft of their parents; they were rootless, homeless, and moved hither and yon in infancy. Lacking any stable parent substitutes from whom they could receive affection and on whom they could confer their affection, these children acquired strong attachments to one another. They used each other as their "real love objects." When finally placed in a settled refuge they were, at first, antagonistic to adults but intensely loyal to one another.

In the latest information available to the present writers, a report kindly forwarded to the senior author by Goldberger (1968), these children are described as young adults. The total picture of these individuals' adjustments to life—including adoption, employment, and marriage—seemed, at the time of this report, to be as favorable as one might expect from any children, chosen at random, who had been followed from childhood into adult years.

Among the best-known current discussions of the origins of love are Harlow's (1958, 1962), which have been referred to briefly, based on a study of monkeys, some reared by their own mothers and others by mechanical substitute mothers. Harlow's findings with monkeys, if generalized into the human domain, indicate that positive emotional responses are first established in the mother-child relationship and later can be generalized to extend to other people.[3] Many of Harlow's monkeys were studied from infancy through adolescence and after they had reached sexual maturity.

In one experiment four baby monkeys received their milk from the artificial breasts of wire mothers and four received milk from cloth mothers, but all had access to both a wire and a cloth mother. The infants fed by wire mothers, as well as those fed by cloth mothers, spent far more time with the cloth mother. They would rush to her when frightened, use her as a secure base from which to venture out to explore the surroundings, cling to her and seek comfort through contact with her. According to Harlow (1958), the "contact comfort [p. 676]" a baby can derive from a mother is more important than the mother's milk in the development of affectional responses.

The artificially reared monkeys seemed to thrive as babies, but as they passed through adolescence and reached maturity a different story emerged (Harlow, 1962). They failed, or had difficulty, in developing normal social relationships, normal affectional relationships, and normal sex behavior with other monkeys. Males and females did not mate as monkeys normally do. Many fought viciously with each other, and even those who attempted sex behavior did so in an infantile and "unreproductive" way.

Eventually, after much effort had been made to help the monkeys to overcome their lack of sexual responsiveness, a few of the artificially reared monkeys became mothers. But Harlow reports that this success in imparting "the priceless gift of motherhood" to these monkeys was a "Pyrrhic victory," for the mothers who had never known a real mother of their own were "helpless, hopeless, heartless mothers devoid or almost devoid of any maternal feelings."

Harlow's earlier studies, indicating that monkeys need the lively give and take between themselves and other monkeys when they are young in

[3] There is a fascinating similarity between human and monkey babies in their response to mothering. As they grow older, they normally show strong affectional ties. Harlow (1962) believes that his data regarding social and affectional development in monkeys "have almost total generality to man [p. 5]."

order to develop their social, affectional, and sexual potentialities, have substantially been confirmed in later studies by Harlow and his associates and by other investigators.

Deprivation of Love and Affection

Human babies have not been reared experimentally by wire or cloth mothers, but many are reared with a minimum of "mothering." Among these are institution-reared foundlings, orphans, and children from broken homes. Findings in studies of such children have varied greatly. Some investigators report that babies separated from their mothers are likely to suffer from severe impairment, such as emotional shock, apathy, lack of ability to become emotionally attached to other human beings, and general developmental retardation (see, for example, Rutter, 1972; Spitz, 1951). Children reared in an institution with a lack of mothering may show restriction in the intellectual as well as in the emotional sphere, lacking spontaneity, freedom to form emotional ties with others, and freedom to think, as manifested by an inability to assume what Goldstein and Sheerer (1941) have called the abstract attitude (tending to think concretely rather than conceptually).

Being reared in an institution does not, in itself, necessarily produce emotional disaster or other drastic impairments (see, for example, a review by Casler, 1961; Dennis, 1960; Rheingold and Bayley, 1959). In this context Rheingold and Bayley (1959) note that children reared in institutions that provide less mothering than youngsters commonly receive at home differ greatly in their all-round development and in their emotional responsiveness, just as home-reared children do.

Other studies dealing with the effects of parental "warmth"—acceptance or rejection, cruelty, or harshness—are reviewed in other chapters, notably those that discuss the self (Chapter 2) and parent-child relationships (Chapter 12). Similarly, the subject of adolescent love, falling in love, and courtship activities will be discussed in a later section (Chapter 14).

The Effects of Love

Evidence from personal testimony and from a number of studies dealing with the practical effects of a loving attitude in social relationships has been reviewed by Sorokin and Hanson (1953). They cite illustrations and findings in support of the position that love and kindness can stop aggression and enmity; that love begets love and hate begets hate; that love is an important factor in human vitality and longevity; that there is in love a therapeutic force, a power to cure (here they cite, among other matters, the importance of a friendly and accepting attitude on the part of a therapist); that love is linked to the mainspring of life and that without the manifestation of biological love-energy in the care parents give their children, man would die out; that love has a creative power in social movements; and that love constitutes the supreme and vital form of human relationships.

Where there is love there is freedom—freedom to venture far out, to take the chance of making a mistake without a paralyzing fear of punishment and freedom to feel the sweep of other emotions. There also is freedom to think new and creative thoughts.

Joy

The joys of adolescence have received less attention from research workers than anger, fear, and other forms of "problem behavior" that involve distress rather than pleasure. Yet, in writings on adolescence one can discover a great deal of joy if one reads between the lines.

One source of joy is sheer physical pleasure. [Leonard Freed/Magnum.]

Each advance in an individual's growth adds to the possibilities of life and opens the way for new or richer satisfactions. When things go well we can assume that adolescents often experience joy, as when they are warmly accepted as companions; when they fall in love and their love is reciprocated; when they are successful in ventures that are important to them, in and out of school; when hopes they have held are realized; when they are respected for their maturity and appreciated as people who not only can carry added responsibilities but also can be granted new privileges; and when these qualities are especially noticed and appreciated by others.

Some of the joys that adolescents have themselves described as being outstanding in their lives are listed in Table 9.1. The material in this table was drawn from accounts young people wrote when asked to describe one of the happiest days of their lives. The information would be more meaningful if it had been possible to explore a little more deeply into why the happenings were regarded as having been especially pleasing.

The table includes younger children as well as adolescents in order to show certain age trends. It can be noted that as children grow older they give less attention to holidays, birthdays, and the like and that the people in the middle and late teens mention self-improvement and benefits befalling others more than younger children do. Boys mention sports and going to places of amusement more than girls, and girls mention companionship and social relationships more than boys.

In a study of college students, Lunneborg and Rosenwood (1972) asked students what made them happy. A number of the college men and women mentioned achievement imagery in response to this question; for instance, "success" and "a rewarding career" were frequently mentioned as bringing happiness. Other sources of happiness mentioned by the students included finding one's identity and developing self-awareness.

Pleasure from Mastery and Achievement

We have noted that young children obtain pleasure from trying out their growing abilities. Karl Bühler several generations ago referred to this as "function pleasure." In elaborating on this idea, White (1959) reports that a person is impelled toward competence.

Several investigators (see, for example, Harter, 1974, 1975) have reported that children of school age are motivated to solve problems for the gratification inherent in arriving at a correct solution. Harter (1975) has postulated that, with an increase in age what White has called effectance motivation becomes increasingly important compared to other motives, such as the need for approval. Among young adolescents the desire to solve intellectually challenging problems for intrinsic gratification was found to be

Table 9.1. Frequency of responses in various categories when children described "one of the happiest days of my life." The values represent the percentage of children giving one or more responses in each category.

No.	Grades 1–3 ages 6–9 Boys 363	Girls 331	Grades 4–6 ages 9–12 Boys 309	Girls 343	Grades 7–9 ages 12–15 Boys 282	Girls 290	Grades 10–12 ages 15–18 Boys 159	Girls 171
Receiving or having or otherwise enjoying material things, gifts, toys, money, living quarters	8.7	8.1	10.4	7.2	10.1	4.5	5.6	3.1
Holidays, festive occasions, birthdays, Christmas, etc.	39.1	40.5	32.4	38.9	6.3	10.1	0.6	6.5
Sports, games, hiking, hunting, bicycling, etc.	10.2	6.4	9.1	5.5	12.4	5.8	13.0	7.3
Going to miscellaneous places of recreation, going to camps, traveling, going to resorts, to parks	9.6	9.0	10.1	11.4	9.7	13.9	30.2	6.9
Self-improvement, success in school, educational opportunity, evidence of vocational competence, getting a job	2.4	2.3	2.9	1.9	4.8	4.1	13.6	15.9
Happenings connected with school, including last day, end of school, going to a certain school	3.6	3.4	5.4	4.3	14.0	11.1	7.0	5.4
Relationship with persons (explicitly described), companionship, being with certain friend, return home of relatives, etc.	7.7	15.9	8.0	15.8	10.5	22.0	8.7	19.9
Residing in, moving to, a certain city or community	1.3	1.0	0.8	2.9	0.9	2.9	1.4	5.0
Benefits befalling others, or mankind in general, including end of war	0.6	0.8	3.2	2.8	2.2	2.6	7.9	9.7

Source: From *Children's interests* by A. T. Jersild and R. J. Tasch, Bureau of Publications, Teachers College, Columbia University, 1949. Reprinted by permission. The table omits several categories—hobbies, movies, radio programs, art activities, and so forth—mentioned by only small percentages of children.

of considerable importance, particularly among adolescents who are not motivated by the need for praise and approval. In contrast, among adolescents who are greatly motivated by the need for adult approval, the data suggested that they were less motivated to solve difficult problems for the sake of problem solving.

Boredom

The condition of boredom that prevails when there is an absence of joy or zest has not received much attention in research studies, except indirectly and by inference, even though it is an affliction that often is widespread among adolescents. We may assume boredom, ranging from mild to acute discomfort, when students lack interest in their work at school, hang around with nothing to do, or get into scrapes in order to stir up excitement. Boredom in the form of a kind of uneasy restlessness seems often to occur among young people who are relatively unpopular with others (see, for example, Laughlin, 1954). It has been found in studies of delinquents that delinquents, as compared with nondelinquents, are under considerable pressure to be "on the go" and are in need of distractions (see, for example, Healy and Bronner, 1936).

Adolescents who are bored a great deal of the time are probably also individuals who often are anxious or resentful. Their boredom may be due in part to the barrenness of their environments; it may also occur because they do not have the freedom to throw themselves into interests of their own choosing, or because they feel ill at ease when left to themselves—as though they were unable to enjoy or even to endure their own company in solitude. The relationship of boredom, an absence of pleasure, to feelings of anger and sometimes depression is borne out by clinical experience. Adolescents may take risks and elicit punishment out of a sense of boredom, in reality giving play to hidden anger. Some delinquents probably commit antisocial acts for this reason.

References

Cannon, W. B. *Bodily changes in pain, hunger, fear and rage* (2nd ed.). Englewood Cliffs, N.J.: Appleton, 1929.

Casler, L. Maternal deprivation: A critical review of the literature. *Monographs of the Society for Research in Child Development*, 1961, **26** (2, Serial No. 80).

Cofer, C. N. *Motivation and emotion.* Glenview, Ill.: Scott, Foresman, 1972.

Dennis, W. Causes of retardation among institutional children: Iran. *Journal of Genetic Psychology*, 1960, **96**, 47–59.

Freud, A., & Dann, S. An experiment in group upbringing. *The psychoanalytic study of the child* (Vol. 6). New York: International Universities Press, 1951.

Goldberger, A. Personal communication, 1968.

Goldstein, K., & Scheerer, M. Abstract and concrete behavior: An experimental study with special tests. *Psychological Monographs*, 1941, **53**(2).

Group for the Advancement of Psychiatry. *Normal adolescence.* New York: Scribner, 1968.

Harlow, H. F. The nature of love. *American Psychologist*, 1958, **13**, 673–685.

Harlow, H. F. The heterosexual affectional system in monkeys. *American Psychologist*, 1962, **17**, 1–9.

Harter, S. Pleasure derived by children from cognitive challenge and mastery. *Child Development*, 1974, **45**, 661–669.

Harter, S. Mastery motivation and need for approval in older children and their relationships to social desirability response tendencies. *Developmental Psychology*, 1975, **11**, 186–196.

Healy, W., & Bronner, A. F. *New light on delinquency and its treatment.* New Haven, Conn.: Yale, 1936.

Jersild, A. T. *When teachers face themselves.* New York: Bureau of Publications, Teachers College, Columbia University, 1952.

Jersild, A. T., & Tasch, R. J. *Children's interests.* New York: Bureau of Publications, Teachers College, Columbia University, 1949.

Laughlin, F. *The peer status of sixth and seventh grade children.* New York: Bureau of Publications, Teachers College, Columbia University, 1954.

Lecky, P. *Self-consistency: A theory of personality.* New York: Island Press, 1945.

Lewin, K. Formalization and progress in psychology. In D. Cartwright (Ed.), *Field theory in social science: Selected theoretical papers.* New York: Harper, 1951.

Lewis, M. State as an infant-environment interaction: An analysis of mother-infant interaction as a function of sex. *Merrill-Palmer Quarterly*, 1972, **18**, 95–121.

Lunneborg, P. W., & Rosenwood, L. M. Need affiliation and achievement: Declining sex differences. *Psychological Reports*, 1972, **72**, 795–798.

MacLean, P. D. *A triune concept of the brain and behavior.* Toronto: University of Toronto Press, 1973.

Maslow, A. H. *Toward a psychology of being* (2nd ed.). New York: Van Nostrand, 1968.

Osler, G. Personal communication, October 18, 1968.

Rheingold, H. L., & Bayley, N. The later effects of an experimental modification of mothering. *Child Development*, 1959, **30**, 363–372.

Rutter, M. Maternal deprivation reconsidered. *Journal of Psychosomatic Research*, 1972, **16**, 241–250.

Sarason, S. B., Hill, D. T., & Zimbardo, P. G. A longitudinal study of the relation of test anxiety to performance on intelligence and achievement tests. *Monographs of the Society for Research in Child Development*, 1964, **29**(7, Serial No. 98).

Sorokin, P. A., & Hanson, R. C. The power of creative love. In A. Montagu (Ed.), *The meaning of love.* New York: Julian Press, 1953.

Spitz, R. A. The psychogenic diseases in infancy: An attempt at their etiologic classification. *The psychoanalytic study of the child* (Vol. 6). New York: International Universities Press, 1951.

White, R. W. Motivation reconsidered: The concept of competence. *Psychological Review*, 1959, **66**, 297–333.

10
anger, aggression, and fear

Adolescents, like younger and older persons, are often angry and often afraid. Fear and anger are both aroused by conditions that threaten or seem to threaten the adolescents' well-being—their physical safety, comfort and welfare, plans and desires, pride, or anything that they value and wish to protect. When threatened by conditions they feel able and willing to oppose, they respond with anger. When they are overwhelmed, or do not trust their strength, adolescents become frightened and retreat. Anger and fear are

254

interrelated in complicated ways with each other and with other emotions. Adolescents may be angry but afraid to show it. They may be angry about being afraid. Fear may appear in the guise of anger, and anger may be imbedded in other feelings, such as depression and self-pity.

Anger

It is through their anger that adolescents most sharply assert their demands and interests. But they have gone through a long series of experiences that determine how their anger will be provoked and how it will be expressed or suppressed. The basic conditions that arouse anger remain much the same throughout life, but there are changes with age in the particular circumstances that provoke it. Many obstructions that made children lose their temper have little effect on adolescents. Some threats that aroused fear when they were smaller arouse anger now that they are older. But their anger continues to be evoked by the thwarting of their actions or intentions and by any assault on their self-esteem.

When we try to understand anger in adolescents it is easier to identify what it is that makes them angry than to tell *why* it makes them angry. To inquire into the why, it usually is necessary to study an adolescent over a period of time.

When young persons' tempers flare often and easily we may suspect that they are overly sensitive, that they tend to feel abused because of events in their past, or that their self-regard is shaky.

But if adolescents display what seems to be the opposite trait, showing no anger when most persons would be angry, we can also suspect that something is wrong. They may be afraid of showing anger to others. They may even be afraid of the meaning their own anger has for themselves. They may have surrendered the right to demand from others the kind of respect and consideration human beings have a right to demand. But if they seem to have surrendered this right it is likely that even when they appear outwardly calm and serene they are angry within.

Conditions That Arouse Anger

During adolescence anger is most often provoked by persons rather than things. There are many unavoidable frictions in the give and take of everyday life. There also are thwartings and restraints imbedded in the culture. These are transmitted by individuals, frequently by parents.

Both students and nonstudents who responded to a check list (Evans and Stangeland, 1971) reported that a large number of specific situations

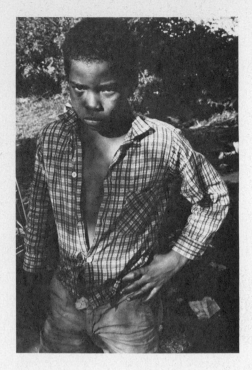

The basic conditions that arouse anger remain much the same throughout life. [Burke Uzzle/Magnum.]

produced anger. Among them were minor and major chance annoyances; people who were inconsiderate, self-opinionated, or destructive (for example, people being cruel to children); and criticisms (for instance, being teased about one's faults). Restrictions of various sorts were also checked with high frequency.

At the college level Rice (1975) found that anger was aroused by what female students regarded as unfair treatment or favoritism shown by parents to the adolescents' siblings. Many adolescents are annoyed not only by specific parental practices, but also by parental traits and habits (Stott, 1940a).

As children grow older, and as their relations with persons outside the home become increasingly important to them, there is an increase in the frequency of annoyances pertaining to persons other than their relatives (just as nonrelatives play an increasing role in their everyday joys and satisfactions). Older adolescents, for example, more frequently than younger persons, mention nonrelatives in what they dislike outside of school (Jersild and Tasch, 1949).

In the Rice study (1975), the following situations were found to make the adolescents angry: hypocritical, insincere, inconsiderate, intolerant, and dishonest people; being teased or criticized; someone being unfair to them;

things not going right; and not doing well in school. Anger also appears when adolescents are in situations that reflect injustices.

Grievances connected with school are reported more frequently by adolescents than by younger children. In the study by Jersild and Tasch (1949) there was an increase in the early teens, and an even larger increase in the late teens, in the proportion of individuals who mentioned persons when describing what they *disliked most* at school. The percentages of persons rose from 5.5 in the primary grades to 29 per cent in the senior high school. A large proportion of responses concerning what was disliked most included an element of resentment. Anastasi et al. (1948) found that students who kept diary records of their emotional experiences reported that schoolwork constituted 12.7 per cent of all anger situations.

Conditions That Increase Susceptibility to Anger

Adolescents, in common with others, are likely to become angry more readily if they are hungry or tired (Gates, 1926; Young, 1937). Stratton (1929) found that adults who have a history of illness during childhood tend to be somewhat more subject to anger than persons who had no history of serious illness.

To understand the meaning of adolescents' anger in their relationships with people, it is important to consider not only what people are doing to them, but also what others expect or demand of them. Teasing, which frequently arouses anger in the adolescent, illustrates this point. One youngster teases out of spite, another in a spirit of fun. One youngster who is teased may be amused, another may become very angry. The teasing that arouses anger may be of a malicious sort that would anger anyone, or it may be of a playful sort that would rile only a thin-skinned and insecure person.

When adolescents are thwarted or provoked by other persons, such provocations are most likely to be anger arousing if the other persons are provoking intentionally or if they are *perceived* as provoking intentionally. When individuals perceive another as being deliberately offensive they view themselves not only as justified in anger, but also as justified in retaliating or seeking revenge.[1]

Anger and Injured Pride

Adolescents are likely to resent any kind of assault on their pride and self-regard. Any experience of failure may produce shame, but there are two

---

[1] This cognitive aspect of anger provocation, and other elements involved in anger, have been discussed by Feshbach (1970) and Kaplan and Goodrich (1957).

conditions involving shame that are especially wrath producing. One condition is linked to demands placed on adolescents by others, the other is tied to demands adolescents make on themselves.

Shame containing an element of resentment is especially likely to occur if adolescents again and again are thrust into situations where they fail. Some adolescents face such conditions day after day, at home or at school. Failure has a bitter taste. It has been called psychic poison. Failure is no less bitter to adolescents just because, as seen by someone else, it was their fault that they failed. Indeed, the failure that youngsters blame in whole or in part on themselves is probably the most bitter of all. Moreover, failure does not lose its sting just because it is repeated again and again. When we consider how frequently, in the lives of many adolescents, the experience of failure at school is repeated, without any good coming from it or any growth ensuing from it, it is easier to understand why it is that some young people lash out irrationally in acts of vandalism and other forms of violence or go about sullenly as though consumed with hate.

Direct Expressions of Anger and Hostility

Young children go through a phase when they may feel quite free to show their rage openly and violently by thrashing out, making angry outcries, kicking, pushing, and biting. Adolescents, in contrast to elementary school children, move from physical to verbal aggression. In response to verbal threats, insults, or physical violence, adolescents are more likely to use verbal rather than physical attacks. This does not, however, mean that physical violence disappears. In a study of 7,000 junior and senior high school students, DeCecco and Richards (1974) noted that in 19 per cent of the incidents reported involving conflict, violence was mentioned as the means used to resolve conflict. Verbal aggression, discussion, avoidance, and fantasy were used in the remaining incidents to cope with conflict. These investigators reported that more peer violence was mentioned in senior than in junior high school. There was more adult use of force at the high school level as compared with the junior high school level. Furthermore, the students felt that they were victims of adult violence far more often (four or five times) than they were provocateurs.

CRYING

Crying and ranting are other methods of directly displaying anger. During the first year of life boys appear to cry as often, and for similar lengths of time, as girls (Bell and Ainsworth, 1972; Clarke-Stewart, 1973). Although crying decreases with age, girls continue to be given the privilege of crying much more freely than boys. This difference in freedom to cry may account in part (although only in part) for the fact that boys far more often show their resentments in aggressive ways.

In the management of anger, adolescent males often face a dilemma, especially if they are being annoyed by females. When exasperated to the point of rage, a male is not supposed to weep, nor is it manly for him to hit a female, even if she happens to deserve a clout or two.

Furthermore, males in our society are placed in a double bind: they are expected not to be sissies, yet they fear loss of peer or parental approval if they display angry retaliation (Lewis et al., 1971).

VERBAL AGGRESSION

Most adolescents have acquired many ways of making a verbal "attack," such as name calling, belittling, and sarcastic remarks. One method of verbal attack is to call attention to the undesirable qualities of someone else. Other methods include gossip, tattling, and slander.

Teasing. Teasing is a common device for expressing hostility. It can be developed into such a fine art that the blame for a quarrel is placed not on the teaser, but on the one who is teased when at last he or she loses his or her temper and strikes back.

Swearing. Swearing is another obvious way of giving vent to anger. Some boys do not begin to swear in earnest until they reach adolescence, even though swearing is a rather childish activity. Youngsters who have scruples against profanity often build a vocabulary of "polite" swear words. Due to social taboos against swearing by women, girls often weep in situations where boys use profanity.

Concealed, Delayed, or Circuitous Expressions of Anger

The training adolescents have received in curbing the impulse to show anger is one of the most impressive features of their education. One result is that many adolescents have learned a great variety of devious ways of venting anger and hostility. But often their success in curbing their anger is deceptive, and often it is gained at a high price. Evidence that they have not really succeeded in smothering their rage appears when they blow their tops over some trivial annoyance. It touches off anger that has been smoldering for a long time.

"STORED-UP" ANGER

Some who tolerate annoyance without becoming angry at the moment feel anger later in a delayed reaction (which is healthier than not feeling it at all). Young people may be unjustly criticized at school, for example, but it may not be until that evening, or the next day, that their anger hits them. Their anger comes too late for them to do anything directly about it, and so they may seethe within themselves and take it out on themselves, perhaps losing their appetite for supper and getting a bellyache in the bargain.

A tendency toward a delayed feeling of anger—not feeling its sharp edge at the moment of provocation, but then being riled by it later—appears frequently among adults (Jersild et al., 1962), and we may assume it occurs often among adolescents also. Such anger appears when a person who has been offended without striking back thinks up a "snappy comeback" an hour or a day (or even some years!) after the event.

ANGER IN FANTASIES

Anger frequently shows itself in fantasies and daydreams. Angry individuals have images of revenge, of someone else coming to grief, and of scenes of personal triumph that put the offending individuals in their proper place. Fantasies expressing aggression were frequently noted by Bellack (1975) in his study of adolescent fantasy.

Aggressive fantasies are often so violent and lurid that the adolescent would be mortified if they could be projected on a screen for others to see. They sometimes envision acts of revenge so stark that the adolescent would recoil from the thought of acting them out. This happens, for example, when young people let their minds wander into the possibility of an accident befalling someone they resent.

The label *death wish* has been given to fantasies in which someone is imagined to have died or is imagined to be in a situation that might cause death. Studies of adolescent fantasies, particularly by means of projective techniques, indicate that such imaginings are quite common. Often when such imaginings occur, they are checked before the final fantasied blow falls. Moreover, adolescents—or people at any age who have such fantasies—are likely, if they have second thoughts, to avow to themselves that they did not really mean to kill. If they describe such imaginings to others, they are likely to maintain that they are just idle and meaningless flights of fancy. In a sense they are meaningless, for, fortunately, few such fantasies are enacted. They represent impulses that seldom are carried over into a deliberate plan or scheme to do harm. But the fact that the impulses are there, even if in an embryonic form, is significant. It can be extremely self-revealing if individuals allow themselves to examine their fantasies.

According to some who have made a study of fantasies, it is also possible that these imaginings serve a purpose. This has been summed up in the quip: "A death wish a day keeps the doctor away." They may serve as an escape valve in allowing a limited discharge of anger.

Fantasy may serve the purpose of decreasing the individual's desire to attack. Some maintain that the adolescent may calm down following daydreaming "because his thoughts are otherwise occupied and he ceases to brood about the insult he has suffered [Berkowitz, 1973, p. 106]." Others speculate that there is some evidence of catharsis as a result of fantasy (Pytkowicz et al., 1967).

DISPLACED ANGER

When adolescents do not feel free to express their anger directly against their offenders, they will, like adults, frequently direct their anger at someone or something else. They may, for example, smash objects when angered by a person whom they do not want to attack. (In some areas a great amount of such displaced anger is manifested by broken bottles, smashed windows, and other results of destructiveness.) Or, they may direct their anger against animals, as when they hurt the family cat, or cruelly crush ants or bugs underfoot. They may turn their anger against other persons, as when they hit a boy after being angered by a girl.

The following example illustrates the concept of displacement. Barbara, a seventeen-year-old girl, was looking forward to going out on a date with one of the boys in her class. At the last minute, Charles called off the date because he said he was ill. Barbara suppressed her anger and pretended that she was not disappointed.

Later Barbara was reading a book and her sister asked her what time it was. Barbara flew into a rage when she was interrupted and the two sisters started to quarrel. The original anger and aggression were displaced onto Barbara's sister. Adolescents may turn their anger, induced at home, against school, or turn school-induced anger against those in their homes (DeCecco and Richards, 1974).[2]

One way of giving vent to hostile impulses in a disguised way is to ally oneself with causes, to join militant groups, or to take violent sides in political disputes. Through championing various causes, adolescents may give play to their hurt feelings, their need for vindication, or their impulse to take revenge, although none of these motives is apparent to them or perhaps to those who observe their behavior. This obviously does not mean that

[2] Because of displaced anger, adolescents may behave quite differently at home than at school. They may be very aggressive in one setting and seem quite serene in the other. As a consequence, parents and teachers do not see them in the same light. When this happens, parents and teachers have difficulty in understanding each other's views concerning youngsters' behavior and demeanor.

championing a cause is necessarily a sign of displaced anger. But one thing that makes the championing of a cause so convenient an expression of hostility for both adolescents and adults is that in the guise of promoting a certain idea or principle, a person can make harsh comments about others without being guilty of an obvious personal attack. Displaced hostility may also take the form of prejudice. Other expressions include antisocial acts, rebelliousness at school, and sexual promiscuity of a sort that hurts others or oneself.

PROJECTED HOSTILITY

One way of dealing with anger and hostility is to externalize it, to impute it to others. When individuals do this they convince themselves that it is others who are angry, bitter, and unfair and that their own anger, if they are aware of it, is righteous indignation and a necessary defense against others who are at fault. It is usually less uncomfortable, for example, when one is in a bad mood, linked to some conditions within oneself, if one can attribute the difficulty to someone or something else. In so doing, adolescents, in a sense, locate their anger outside themselves. High school students who are not easy to get along with may, for example, discuss their problems in getting along with others and the bitterness these problems arouse, as though the problems were entirely due to others. When individuals thus externalize their anger they disown responsibility for it.

Under some conditions it is a merciful thing that individuals can, by this means, escape from some of the bitterness of their own rage. When they are angry there is a need to attach blame somewhere, and if they cannot blame someone or something else, the only one left to blame is themselves. There are young people whose lives at times are so filled with bitterness that it would be almost intolerable for them to face this bitterness as something located entirely within themselves. So the ability to externalize anger serves in a way to protect individuals from facing realities within themselves that might involve them in overwhelming feelings of guilt and self-reproach.

The feeling of being abused.   Externalized anger is frequently manifested in grievances. Often adolescents seem to be full of grievances, speaking and acting as though they were an especially abused group. The grievances and the feeling of being abused may show, for example, in a chronic complaint against their background, their school, their community, certain persons in the neighborhood, or those belonging to particular racial or religious groups. All adolescents often have been, and are, to some extent abused by others and by the limitations within their own circumstances of life. Many of their complaints and grievances are therefore justified. We are not now, however, speaking of grievances of this sort. Instead, we are speaking of grievances through which adolescents find a whipping boy for their own resentments.

It is important to remember, however, that once adolescents have a grievance, whether it is based on realistic grounds or not, their grievance will influence what they see and hear. So a grievance can nourish itself. If adolescents have a grievance, their perceptions will be affected. They may see a smile as a smile of contempt, even though the smiling person is actually friendly. They may perceive an assignment at school as another evidence of unfairness, when actually it is not so intended.

When individuals have a grievance, they may be selective not only in what they perceive, but also in what they remember. They may remember when they were punished, forgetting the times they were treated with kindness. They may remember an act of unfairness that happened long ago, forgetting the many occasions on which they have been treated in a fair and even a very favorable way. It is because of this fact of selective retention that what individuals recall, when they tell the story of their childhood or of happenings that occurred only a month or a year ago, may reveal more about their current attitudes toward themselves and others than about past events.

In dealing with an adolescent who carries a grievance it is very difficult for an adult to see beyond it and to perceive, in a sympathetic way, the total operation in which the adolescent is involved. From the adolescents' own points of view, a long-standing grievance is completely justified. Adolescents with grievances are likely to arouse resentment in others. Everyone has a natural tendency to become annoyed and defensive in dealing with someone who complains chronically and apparently unreasonably.

Parents, teachers, and fellow students are likely to argue with the ones who have grievances. They cannot be blamed for this, but the simple fact is that argument will not help those who feel abused to see the light. They are more likely to be helped if they can, at an odd moment, get a glimpse of themselves. This sometimes happens when individuals with grievances have sounded off so violently in a discussion that even they can hear an echo of their anger. Such a glimpse of self is more likely to occur in a situation in which they are accepted and do not quickly have an opportunity to reinforce their grievance by arguing with someone who is quick to argue with them.

A person with a grievance can also sometimes get what almost amounts to a revelation by hearing a playback of a recording made while he or she was voicing his or her grievances. There is no guarantee that insight will result from this device, but it is an example of one way in which a person may see or hear himself or herself from a little distance and get a glimmering of attitudes that ordinarily are so acutely felt and so vigorously defended that it is impossible to look at them objectively.

Anger Directed Against Self

There is a close interweaving of anger directed against adolescents by others, anger directed by adolescents against others, and anger directed by adolescents against themselves. Their tendency to be angry will be influenced strongly by their attitudes toward themselves, but these attitudes in turn will be influenced by the attitudes others have shown toward them. They are likely, for example, to be "angry with themselves" if they fail to live up to their expectations, but these expectations have been influenced by what others once expected of them.

Much of the exasperation one sees in the behavior of adolescents arises from a lack of tolerance for their own limitations. They may become angry, for example, if they expect to find an answer to a problem and then find no answer.

Their demands on others are likely to have much in common with the demands they make on themselves. If they are intolerant of their own stupidity, they are likely to be intolerant of stupidity in others. But if they are intolerant of their own stupidity, or what they regard as stupidity, this is an attitude they have acquired. So we have a triangular situation: they tend to visit on others what they think was visited on them and what they now also visit on themselves. This may not invariably hold true, but it provides an important key to understanding adolescents. If we see them from one side of this triangle, we can make a pretty good guess about the other two sides.

Anger directed at self may take many forms. It may appear in a tendency to be severely self-critical, far beyond what is reasonable or helpful. We may suspect self-directed hostility when adolescents again and again blame themselves for a mistake long after the event is over but do nothing in the meantime to remedy the mistake or to avoid repeating it. One adolescent, for example, who seemed to have a large amount of anger directed against himself, was given a chance as a freshman to take the leading part in a high school play; he hesitated so long that the part was given to someone else. He then became so involved in blaming himself for having missed this opportunity that he missed other opportunities to take part in subsequent plays.

A self-critical attitude may be so strong that adolescents will not even try to make the team or the honor roll or be accepted by the group they admire. They operate on the grounds that they do not really deserve to participate and perhaps, unwittingly, because they would be bitter in their self-accusation if they should try and fail. This is a sign of depression.

Sometimes when adolescents direct their anger against themselves they do so because they have learned that it is safer to blame themselves than to blame others. Anger directed against the self may also occur because they have learned, through being the butt of constant criticism and complaint, to adopt the view that if anything goes wrong it is their fault.

Another way, according to some authorities, in which hostility directed against the self may be expressed is in psychosomatic illness. The theory here is that some allergies, unaccountable headaches, and other aches and digestive upsets have a psychological origin, a feature of which is unresolved hostility. The physical pain presumably is preferable to the pain of self-hate experienced as such.

Yet another sign that is probably often an expression of anger turned inward is a tendency again and again to get into various self-punishing scrapes and difficulties, including accidents. According to this view it is not entirely "accidental" when certain individuals repeatedly do things that get them into trouble, such as openly defying a friendly teacher when there is nothing to be gained by defiance, or when they continually get injured by banging into things or stumbling on the stairs.

Adolescents' Reports of How They Coped with Anger

In a study by Husni-Palacios and Scheur (1972), less than 4 per cent of adolescents indicated that their feelings of anger were directed at the cause of the frustration. Approximately one third of the students felt that it was preferable to express their anger in a passive manner, suffering it quietly. They tended to withdraw, experience depression, and cry or sulk when aroused by anger. Although one third of the students reported that they expressed their anger at the environment through verbal (shouting and swearing) or physical means, they usually did not express their anger at the source of the frustration. They displaced it onto others. The mechanisms used to cope with anger by many of the high school students were inadequate and seemed likely to lead to future difficulties.

The Right to Be Angry

We have noted in many parts of this discussion that it is difficult for adolescents to face the meaning of their anger. They are not dealing with anger in a forthright and constructive way when they recognize their tendency to become angry but feel guilt about this tendency. Adolescents may be completely justified in feeling remorseful about a particular outburst of anger; their anger might have been out of proportion to the occasion, or it might have inflicted more hurt on another than they intended, or it might have been regrettable in other ways. But when they deplore their tendency to become angry—their susceptibility to feel anger—they are deploring an essential element in their natures. They are repudiating an emotion that is unavoidable and inescapable in the normal course of life. They are, in effect, denying their right to be human beings.

In a study by Jersild (1952), 18 per cent of a group of 1,600 junior and senior high school students singled out their temper or tendency to become angry when writing compositions on the theme, "What I Dislike About Myself." At the college level (200 students) the percentage was 19.5. If these persons had been asked specifically about their anger it is probable that a far larger number would have deplored it. On the other hand, only about 3 per cent mentioned anger in describing what they liked about themselves, and in practically all instances this represented approval of their ability to control their anger rather than their freedom to feel or display it.

Repudiation of the right to be angry goes far beyond simply deploring anger of which people are aware; it occurs also when people disavow anger, project it on others, are so threatened by it that they suppress it before they have felt its full surge, or feel and express hostility without recognizing it for what it is (by way, for example, of snobbery and malicious gossip).

To grant oneself the right to be angry is quite different from blindly giving way to anger by punishing others or oneself and then condoning such conduct. The right to be angry does not mean a right to strike out in rage against everyone and everything. It does not mean that the angry one should be permitted to indulge in unrestrained violence. The right to be angry does mean, however, that individuals do not always have to blunt their anger before it has a chance to develop, or punish themselves through feelings of guilt because they have had angry impulses.

The more realistically young persons can accept their anger, the more likely it is that they will use anger in ways that are healthy and constructive and in ways that, in the long run, may add to their own well-being and the welfare of others.

When adolescents are able thus to accept anger to some degree as something inherent in the human struggle, they will be better able to perceive how other persons' hurts and strivings are revealed through anger. And if they can now and then look objectively at their own anger it may give them a revelation about themselves.

It is unfortunate that the process by which such a revelation might take place is so often blocked at home and at school. It is, of course, necessary to block adolescents when their anger becomes so violent that it is damaging to others and to themselves. But it is helpful when adolescents' elders try to hear them out when they are angry, thus availing themselves of the adolescents' anger as a way of understanding them and indirectly as a way of helping them to understand themselves.

Aggression

Aggression may be defined as more or less violent physical or verbal behavior directed against a person or object (Moore and Fine, 1968). Aggressive feelings—the wish to express anger in violent behavior—may exist without being acted on. Another definition of aggression is of "action carried out in a forceful way [Hinsie and Campbell, 1960, p. 21]." Aggression and aggressive impulses have been studied by many investigators.

Freud and his followers have viewed aggression as an innate drive, subject to modulation and control by the *ego* and *superego*. Lorenz (1966), well known for his study of animals, also regards aggression as an innate drive.

This paradigm of an innate amount of aggressive drive has been challenged by several workers, who believe that aggression is a conditioned response to some stimulus, either some frustrating situation or observing another person act aggressively and modeling similar behavior.

The work of Dollard and Miller (1950) deserves special attention. These investigators state that aggression is a basic drive that must be expressed in some way. They stress the importance of learning in the way one deals with aggressive impulses, not unlike the psychoanalysts, who maintain that culture channels instinct. Dollard and Miller (1950) originated the frustration-aggression hypothesis, which states that frustration inevitably leads to aggression. These authors later modified their theory to be more in line with that of the social learning theorists. Bandura (1973) and Berkowitz (1973) dispute the original frustration-aggression hypothesis, and note that many other factors, including modeling and individual differences, enter into the relationship between frustration and aggression, since aggression may be inhibited by learned factors.

In a study by Eron et al. (1963), aggression in school children was found to be positively related to punishment for aggression at home, especially maternal punishment of boys.

The form an aggressive act takes does seem to be mediated by cultural factors. Even if the aggressive impulse stems from innate psychobiological forces, culture appears to channel such an impulse into certain pathways specific for each culture.

Aggressive rebellion in some boys may take the form of delinquent behavior (Offer, 1969), such as car theft or shoplifting. In girls, self-destructive sexuality is a more common expression of adolescent rebellion. In Offer's study, 25 per cent of the adolescent boys interviewed stated that they had taken part in one or more delinquent acts. Aggressive impulses in many other adolescent boys were channeled into competitive games or sports. Most of the overt expression of aggressive impulses was aimed at siblings. Such a direct expression of aggression in deed or fantasy was rare in adolescence compared to childhood. A tendency toward aggressive activity has been found to remain quite stable from adolescence to adult life and is more stable in men than in women (Kagan and Moss, 1962).

Sex Differences in Aggression

Within our own culture, as well as in a variety of others, males appear to be more overtly aggressive than females (Whiting and Pope, 1973). The results of numerous modeling studies attest to this widely documented finding. In the typical modeling study, the individual is exposed to an aggressive model. Following this exposure the male tends to be openly more aggressive than the female. For example, college men, after seeing a model give a supposed electric shock to another individual, shocked their victims for a longer period of time than college women (Larsen et al., 1972). Another approach used in the study of aggression involves observing individuals in their natural settings. This technique was employed by Whiting and Pope (1973) in their cross-cultural analysis of sex differences in children. Their results suggest that boys are more verbally aggressive and engage in more rough-and-tumble play than girls. When attacked by their peers, boys tend to react with counteraggression more frequently than girls. Males of varying ages also report more aggression than girls (Brissett and Nowicki, 1973; Ferguson and Maccoby, 1966). Even in their daydreams males give evidence of being more aggressive. Male college students reported a higher frequency of overtly aggressive and hostile dreams than females in a study by Wagman (1967).

Not only is aggression more apparent in a male than a female, but adolescents themselves appear to feel that aggression in a male is more socially desirable than in a female. Urberg and Labouvie-Vief (1976) asked adolescents to check the adjectives that described their idea of an ideal male and female. Aggression in this study referred to those behaviors that attack or hurt others. Both males and females judged aggression and dominance to be male traits and to be more desirable in males than in females.

What factors account for sex differences in aggression? Certainly differential learning on the part of males and females plays a role, although the processes are not completely known at the present time (Bandura, 1973). Having summarized the research in this area, Maccoby and Jacklin (1974) believe that sex differences in aggression may have a biological foundation. They give the following reasons in support of their views: "(1) Males are more aggressive than females in all human societies for which evidence is available. (2) The sex differences are found early in life, at a time when there is no evidence that differential socialization pressures have been brought to bear by adults to 'shape' aggression differently in the two sexes. (3) Similar sex differences are found in man and subhuman primates. (4) Aggression is related to levels of male sex hormones and can be changed by experimental administrations of these hormones [pp. 242-43]."[3]

Television and Aggression

Adolescents, like persons of other ages, have at their disposal a vast amount of ready-made, substitute aggression. They can revel in violence by way of television, movies, and reading matter. In many movies and television shows, there is an orgy of killing.

Obviously, we cannot assume that individuals who watch killing on the screen would like to be killers themselves. Yet we can say that when viewers seek out a program in which people are killed wantonly and in cold blood, or under a thin pretext of preserving law and order, they are at least passive participants in the carnage. Even though, on the conscious level, it would be morally repugnant to them to commit homicide, they would not be passive participants in scenes of violence unless these in some way appealed to impulses that are latent within them.

A great deal of attention has been centered on the effect television may have on the development of aggression in the individual. There are those who maintain that violence portrayed in the media has no effect, and neither heightens nor decreases aggression. To date, as noted by Berkowitz (1973), most of the evidence suggests that observing aggression on the screen does not have a cathartic effect that leads to decreased aggression.

Eron et al. (1974) studied youngsters in the third grade and then ten years later. Aggression in the third-grade boys was positively related to their preference for viewing violence on television. Of greater interest is the fact that early viewing of violent television—that is, in grade three, seemed to be associated with a greater likelihood of aggressiveness in adolescence. It should be noted that these findings only pertain to boys. These investigators contend that their findings are in accord with Bandura's (1973) thesis: namely, children will imitate the behavior of any significant model even if it appears on television. Furthermore, aggression may occur even when the individuals watching television are not angry or emotionally aroused (Murray, 1973). Liebert and Baron (1972) sought to find out if nationally known TV programs would increase the likelihood of youngsters engaging in aggressive acts aimed to hurt their peers. Children exposed to aggressive films in comparison to those who viewed neutral programs were more willing to engage in interpersonal aggressive acts and aggressive play. It should be

[3] Reviews of this area can be found in Money and Ehrhardt (1972).

noted that quite often the underlying situation might be that children disposed to be aggressive choose to view films portraying aggression.

According to Mischel (1976), the potential effect of viewing aggressive models may be increased when the "models are shown reaping great rewards for their violence [p. 388]." Although, as noted, there are studies showing negative effects from exposure to televised violence, research in this area is controversial at the present time.

Fear

Adolescents, in common with younger children and adults, experience fright at times. Some of them experience fear only on occasions when they happen to run into danger. Some have recurring fears that are touched off again and again by happenings in their daily lives, by dreams, or by their own trends of thought. Some experience states of dread lasting days or even weeks at a time. Some struggle with fears that arise out of the problems of life. No one who throws himself or herself into the possibilities of life can live without fear. The only way to evade fear is to surrender to fear, as happens when individuals are so afraid that they do not reach for what the present or an uncertain future might bring.

In this section we will consider some of the fears of adolescence as they can be observed or as they have been described under the name of fear or other terms. In Chapter 11 we will deal with the topic of anxiety. In some ways anxiety is related to fear, but it comprises more than we usually mean when we speak of the fears of everyday life.

Some Common "Fears"

At the time they are about to enter their teens, many children report fears of one or more of the following categories: animals; painful situations; danger or threat of bodily accidents and injuries; dreams; ridicule; failure; "bad" people, such as robbers and kidnappers; dangers associated with the dark or being alone in the dark; imaginary creatures such as ghosts; and characters met in stories, movies, radio programs, and the like (Jersild and Holmes, 1935). Youngsters in their teens report fewer fears of domestic animals than preadolescent children and more fears of physical harm (other than through attacks by animals; Winkler, 1949).

Several investigators (Bernstein and Allen, 1969; Braun and Reynolds, 1969; Landy and Gaupp, 1971) have studied fears among college students. In all three studies fear inventories were used. Some of the fears mentioned were fear over rejection, interpersonal relationships, noise, medical-surgical intervention, illness or injury to loved ones, automobile accidents, live organisms such as small creeping animals, death, physical assault, and achievement.

In a study of adolescent boys, over half reported worries related to achievement (Institute for Social Research, 1960). Included in this area were such concerns as passing their courses and graduating from high school, doing well in school, making the team, and selecting a suitable vocation. Another fear, particularly among women, is fear of success. Research in this area will be discussed in Chapter 18. Relationships with and acceptance by others, including both males and females, figured prominently in worries in the Institute for Social Research study. Concern with pressures of a realistic nature, such as obtaining money for dates, and actual or anticipated family problems were also mentioned. Lastly, personal problems such as guilt feelings were reported.

A more recent study of both male and female high school students in Indiana reveals that many of the fears and worries of this age group have not changed (Husni-Palacios and Scheur, 1972). Almost half of the students in this group reported that they worried about feelings of inadequacy, failure, not living up to expectations, and lack of self-confidence. Many of their worries were focused on their ability to cope with future problems and conflicts. Approximately 9 per cent of the sample expressed concern about war, peace, pollution, and a variety of environmental conditions. One-third of the students indicated that they were worried about many things and felt overwhelmed by their lack of ability to cope with life, with the problems confronting them, and with the problems that lay ahead.

Among the worries reported by sophomore, junior, and senior college girls in a study by Rice (1975) were not doing well in school, parental problems, not getting a good job, social relationships with others, not having enough money, future happiness, marriage, and sex.

In many (perhaps all) of these "worries" there is an element of emotional conflict: a desire for getting more sleep, for example, apparently clashed with motives that kept the person from going to bed or from falling asleep. In worrying over "being overweight" there may be a conflict between a craving for food (or perhaps a compulsion to eat) and a desire for a trim figure. In other words, more may be involved than a fear of this or that danger in the external environment. Many of these "fears" are symptoms of complicated personal problems.

As indicated by these reported fears, many young people of high school and college age are apprehensive about their personal limitations, their ability to look good in the eyes of others, and their ability to measure up to their own standards or to the standards by which others judge them. In a study of fears recorded in diaries by college girls, Anastasi et al. (1948) found that the largest number of fears centered on schoolwork (40.2 per cent). The second largest number (30.8 per cent) related to inferiority and loss of prestige. An interesting finding in this study was that schoolwork was reported as producing fear decidedly more often than anger (40.2 per cent of the fear-arousing situations as compared with 12.7 per cent of the anger-arousing situations). A deeper examination of many of the fears listed would probably reveal that they contain an undercurrent of anger. Fear is a painful emotion, and when the cause of it is attributed to persons, those persons are likely not only to be feared, but also resented.

In a study that included data from older adolescents and young adults of college age (Jersild and Holmes, 1935), many persons reported that they were still troubled by fears carried over from childhood years. The 303 persons who took part in the study gave written descriptions of over a thousand "fears" they recalled from childhood, and, of these, 349 were described as still persisting. This does not necessarily mean that about a third of the fears of childhood carry over into late adolescence and young adulthood. These students probably had forgotten many of their childhood fears; and it is possible that many apprehensions of childhood were replaced by other similar fears (such as fear of not doing well in one's job as a "replacement" for fear of failing at school).

The most frequently reported childhood fear was of animals, and about half of these fears were described as persisting in late adolescence or early adulthood. Another frequently mentioned childhood fear was of accidents and injuries, and over a third of these were described as persisting. Two fifths of the fears pertaining to personal failure, inadequacy, or ridicule that were described as arising during childhood were identified as persisting. Other fears carried over from childhood into late adolescence with less frequency; however, still in considerable number were fears associated with dangers in the dark and robbers and other criminal characters.

The Expression and Concealment of Fear

Adolescents are adept at disguising their fears, and their expression of fear may take many forms. The form that is easiest to detect is an outright show of fright, as revealed by running, clutching, calling for help, trembling, or obvious efforts to avoid or escape. There are moments in the lives of everyone when a situation is so frightening that fear is openly shown.

But fear may be concealed behind a manner of bravado, suggesting just the opposite of fear. Clinically, this is called a counterphobic reaction. Frightened individuals may also show anger, which serves as a means of protest or counterattack designed to blunt the experience of fear or to protect against having to face a frightening situation. A simple form of this appears when individuals are afraid of going to the dentist and snarl with anger when they are reminded that they should go.

Fear may also appear in the guise of extreme mildness and conformity. Extremely "good" adolescents may be frightened people who use their goodness as a means of protecting themselves from fear of punishment, disapproval, or rejection.

"Irrational" Fears

As in earlier childhood, a large proportion of the fears reported in adolescence are irrational in the sense that they are out of proportion to the dangers that actually exist. Many bright young people fear that they will do poorly on examinations even though they have always done well and have no real reason to think that they will not continue to do well. Such irrational fears, although centered on an external danger, probably are symptoms of inner conflict, which we will examine in the next chapter.

References

Anastasi, A., Cohen, N., & Spatz, D. A study of fear and anger in college students through the controlled diary method. *Journal of Genetic Psychology*, 1948, **73**, 243–249.

Bandura, A. *Aggression: A social learning analysis.* Englewood Cliffs, N.J.: Prentice-Hall, 1973.

Bell, S. M., & Ainsworth, M. D. Infant crying and maternal responsiveness. *Child Development*, 1972, **43**, 1171–1190.

Bellack, L. *The thematic apperception test, the children's apperception test and the senior apperception technique in clinical use* (3rd ed.). New York: Grune, 1975.

Berkowitz, L. Control of aggression. In B. M. Caldwell and H. Ricciuti (Eds.), *Review of child development research* (Vol. 3). Chicago: U. of Chicago, 1973.

Bernstein, D. A., & Allen, G. J. Fear survey schedule (II): Normative data and factor analyses based on a large college sample. *Behavior Research and Therapy*, 1969, **7**, 403–407.

Braun, P. R., & Reynolds, D. J. A factor analysis of a 100 item fear survey inventory. *Behavior Research and Therapy*, 1969, **7**, 399–402.

Brissett, M., & Nowicki, S., Jr. Internal versus external control of reinforcement and reaction to frustration. *Journal of Personality and Social Psychology*, 1973, **25**, 35–44.

Clarke-Stewart, K. Interactions between mothers and their young children: Characteristics and consequences. *Monographs of the Society for Research in Child Development*, 1973, **38** (6–7, Serial No. 153).

De Cecco, J. P., & Richards, A. K. *Growing pains: Uses of school conflict.* New York: Aberdeen Press, 1974.

Dollard, J., & Miller, N. E. *Personality and psychotherapy: An analysis in terms of learning, thinking, and culture.* New York: McGraw-Hill, 1950.

Eron, L. D., Huesmann, L. R., Lefkowitz, M. M., & Walder, L. O. How learning conditions in early childhood—including mass media—relate to aggression in late adolescence. *American Journal of Orthopsychiatry,* 1974, **44**, 412–423.

Eron, L. D., Walder, L. O., Toifo, R., & Lefkowitz, M. M. Social class, parental punishment for aggression, and child aggression. *Child Development,* 1963, **34**, 849–867.

Evans, D. R., & Stangeland, M. Development of the reaction inventory to measure anger. *Psychological Reports,* 1971, **29**, 412–414.

Ferguson, L. R., & Maccoby, E. E. Interpersonal correlates of differential abilities. *Child Development,* 1966, **37**, 549–571.

Feshbach, S. Aggression. In P. H. Mussen (Ed.), *Carmichael's manual of child psychology* (Vol. 2). New York: Wiley, 1970.

Gates, G. S. An observational study of anger, *Journal of Experimental Psychology,* 1926, **9**, 325, 336.

Hinsie, L. E., & Campbell, R. J. *Psychiatric dictionary* (3rd ed.). New York: Oxford U.P., 1960.

Husni-Palacios, M., & Scheur, P. The high school student: A personality profile. *Proceedings of the 80th Annual Convention of the American Psychological Association,* 1972, **7**, 565–566.

Institute for Social Research. A study of boys becoming adolescents. Ann Arbor: Survey Research Center, University of Michigan, 1960.

Jersild, A. T., & Holmes, F. B. *Children's fears.* New York: Bureau of Publications, Teachers College, Columbia University, 1935.

Jersild, A. T., & Tasch, R. J. *Children's interests.* New York: Bureau of Publications, Teachers College, Columbia University, 1949.

Jersild, A. T., et al. *In search of self.* New York: Bureau of Publications, Teachers College, Columbia University, 1952.

Jersild, A. T., Lazar, E., & Brodkin, A. *The meaning of psychotherapy in the teacher's life and work.* New York: Bureau of Publications, Teachers College, Columbia University, 1962.

Kagan, J., & Moss, H. A. *Birth to maturity: A study in psychological development.* New York: Wiley, 1962.

Kaplan, D. M., & Goodrich, W. A formulation for interpersonal anger. *American Journal of Orthopsychiatry,* 1957, **27**, 387–395.

Landy, F. J., & Gaupp, L. A. A factor analysis of the fear survey schedule III. *Behavior Research and Therapy,* 1971, **9**, 89–93.

Larsen, K. S., Coleman, D., Forbes, J., & Johnson, R. Is the subject's personality or the experimental situation a better prediction of a subject's willingness to administer shock to a victim? *Journal of Personality and Social Psychology,* 1972, **22**, 287–295.

Lewis, W. C., Wolman, R. N., & King, M. The development of the language of emotions. *American Journal of Psychiatry,* 1971, **127**, 1491–1497.

Liebert, R. M., & Baron, R. A. Some immediate effects of televised violence on children's behavior. *Developmental Psychology,* 1972, **6**, 469–475.

Lorenz, K. *On aggression.* New York: Harcourt, Brace and World, 1966.

Maccoby, E. E., & Jacklin, C. N. *The psychology of sex differences.* Stanford, Calif.: Stanford U.P., 1974.

Mischel, W. *Introduction to personality* (2nd ed.). New York: Holt, 1976.

Money, J., & Ehrhardt, A. *Man and woman, boy and girl.* Baltimore: Johns Hopkins, 1972.

Moore, B. E., & Fine, B. D. *A glossary of psychoanalytic terms and concepts.* New York: American Psychoanalytic Association, 1968.

Murray, J. P. Television and violence: Implications of the Surgeon General's research program. *American Psychologist,* 1973, **28**, 472–478.

Offer, D. *The psychological world of the teen-ager: A study of normal adolescent boys.* New York: Basic Books, 1969.

Pytkowicz, A. R., Wagner, N. N., & Sarason, I. G. An experimental study of the reduction of hostility through fantasy. *Journal of Personality and Social Psychology,* 1967, **5**, 295–303.

Rice, F. P. *The adolescent: Development relationships and culture.* Boston: Allyn, 1975.

Stott, L. H. Adolescents' dislikes regarding parental behavior and their significance. *Journal of Genetic Psychology,* 1940, **57**, 393–414.a.

Stott, L. H. Home punishment of adolescents. *Journal of Genetic Psychology,* 1940, **57**, 415-428.b.

Stratton, G. M. Emotion and the incidence of disease: The influence of the number of the diseases and of the age at which they occur. *Psychological Review,* 1929, **36**, 242–253.

Urberg, K. A., & Labouvie-Vief, G. Conceptualizations of sex roles: A life span developmental approach. *Developmental Psychology,* 1976, **12**, 15–23.

Wagman, M. Sex differences in types of daydreams. *Journal of Personality and Social Psychology,* 1967, **7**, 329–332.

Winkler, J. B. Age trends and sex differences in the wishes, identifications, activities, and fears of children. *Child Development,* 1949, **20**, 191–200.

Whiting, B., & Pope, C. A cross-cultural analysis of sex differences in the behavior of children aged three to eleven. *Journal of Social Psychology,* 1973, **91**, 171–188.

Young, P. T. Laughing and weeping, cheerfulness and depression: A study of moods among college students. *Journal of Social Psychology,* 1937, **8**, 311–384.

11
anxiety

To understand adolescents—or persons at any stage of life—it is essential to come to grips with the concept of anxiety, for it provides a key to much that is baffling in an adolescent's conduct.

Anxiety has many facets that cannot be encompassed in any simple definition. We will, however, begin with a very general statement and then add to it as the chapter proceeds.

Anxiety prevails when individuals are at odds with themselves. It can also be defined in very general terms as a persisting or recurring distressful psychological state arising from an inner conflict. The distress may be experienced as a feeling of vague uneasiness or foreboding, of being on edge, or as any of a variety of other feelings—fear, anger, restlessness, irritability, depression, or other diffuse and nameless ones.

The underlying conflict springs from a clash between incompatible impulses, desires, or values. Such a conflict prevails when a person is angry but is afraid of giving offense. It also exists when a person is eager to be popular but has strong scruples against doing what is necessary to become popular.

Anxiety can exist as a conscious state when the anxious persons are aware of the nature of their conflict and the ways in which the conflict affects their feelings and their conduct. But it has elements beyond the reach of awareness when anxious persons do not recognize what is troubling them, or realize why they feel as they do, and are unaware of ways in which their behavior is influenced by their anxiety. When persons who are afraid of disapproval go out of their way to please people and then resent the fact that they have allowed others to take advantage of them, their anxiety is on a conscious level as long as they are aware of what is happening. But the anxiety has what might be called unconscious elements if these people see themselves as ones who are very generous rather than as ones who are afraid to give offense—if they do not recognize that it is they who invite others to take advantage of them.

The labels *normal* and *neurotic* are used by some authors in discussing anxiety. Broadly speaking, a person beyond the stage of early childhood has normal anxiety (also referred to as objective, uncomplicated, realistic anxiety) when he consciously recognizes the nature of his conflict, is aware of the feelings connected with it, and seeks to resolve it, as best he can, in a thoughtful, constructive way. By contrast, a person is said to have neurotic anxiety if he is not aware of the underlying conflict, does not recognize why he feels as he does, and uses "unconscious defense mechanisms" or "pseudosolutions" to deal with the conflict.

A further characteristic of anxiety is that it precipitates strategies or defenses for coping with the distress and inner conflict.

Examples of adolescent anxiety

Conflicting impulses appear in the following example of an adolescent boy who felt anxious about expressing his opinions. He was in a school where everyone was encouraged to "speak his mind." But he was unable to speak out, even when he disagreed with something others had said. He wanted to disagree openly but had strong inhibitions against opposing someone else. So during periods of "free" public discussion he was silently engaged in an inner battle that left him in a "nervous" and sullen mood after the discussion.

As a child and preadolescent he had been taught not to be pushy or outspoken in any way that might offend others, and he was chastised for not heeding this lesson. For example, once he was severely scolded by his father for frankly telling some adult neighbors that they had taken unfair advantage in a business deal. His father privately agreed with him and felt incensed about the deal but was mortified by the boy's having expressed this opinion outside the family circle. Thus, the idea of speaking out frankly in public became associated in the boy's mind with disapproval and with the idea that taking issue with another person's opinions would be construed as a personal attack and would produce retaliation.

This adolescent boy was aware of the conflict between his desire to speak out and his fear of doing so, and to that extent his anxiety was on the conscious level. He did not, however, recognize the irrational nature of his inhibition against speaking out. His inhibitions were a carry-over from an earlier situation in which being outspoken actually was reproved by others. In his present situation, where being outspoken was encouraged, he was unwittingly acting out an old fear.

The anxiety here would have been further removed from conscious awareness if the boy had managed to repress his awareness of his fear of speaking out. Such repression would occur, for example, if he no longer experienced his inhibition against speaking out as a weakness but regarded it as a virtue, an evidence that he had the good sense and strength of character to keep his mouth shut when all around him were babbling.

Our next example is that of a girl in her late teens. She was attracted to a certain boy and had fantasies about some day marrying him, but these fantasies threw her into a conflict. He belonged to another religious faith, and she realized that her parents and the family tradition she had absorbed were opposed to such a union. Therefore, she was both drawn to the boy and driven to reject him, and this was reflected in her actions. At times she tried her best to charm him. But at other times she said and did things to make him feel inferior and miserable—such as reminding him that he had little money, or disparaging his friends. She finally "resolved" her conflict by telling him, in a painful scene, that they would have to stop seeing one another because of the difference in their faiths. He accepted this verdict and did not try to see her again. But her conflict was not actually resolved. Despite feelings of guilt and shame, she continued for a time to try to get in touch with him.

This sketch and the others reported here illustrate elements of what have been referred to as normal anxiety as well as characteristics of neurotic anxiety.

In this anxiety situation the girl was conscious of a realistic cause for concern: she was aware that marriage with the boy would wound her parents and that a marriage between persons with different religious backgrounds may not turn out well. On the other hand, there were aspects of the total anxiety situation that she did not understand: why, for example, in spite of her strong religious views, she was attracted to a boy belonging to another faith. She did not recognize that the attraction was, in effect, a rebellion against her parents.

When she attacked the boy's pride in order to make him feel inferior she was using tactics that some writers about anxiety have called unconscious defense mechanisms. The attacks served two "purposes" that she did not recognize at the time. First, they were a form of revenge: although she was fond of the boy she also resented him, for her attachment to him caused her much anguish. Second, by hurting his feelings she was inviting him to become so offended that he would have nothing more to do with her. If he left the scene, she would no longer have a tangible reminder of the conflict that centered around him.

The details of our next example are drawn from extensive interviews with a postadolescent young man who had strong sexual urges and strong inhibitions against them. On the conscious level he had a conflict between his sexual desires and his conscience, a conflict that is quite common in adolescent boys and girls.

Following an episode of relatively mild sex play with a girl, he suffered acute anxiety. Because he had strong moral scruples about sex, he felt anguish and remorse about what he had done. Yet, he still had the desires that had led him to yield to temptation, and these were a continuing threat to his moral scruples.

To cope with this conflict he developed defenses against it. These were to a large degree unconscious—in the sense that at that time he did not perceive the relationship between these defenses and his conflict about sex. His main defense was to use his ambitions for success as a means of protecting himself. He resolved to work hard and to save his money to pay for his schooling. This resolve meant that he could not have dates because, as he saw it, he could not afford them. Having no dates meant that he was, to that extent, protected from the danger of intimacy with any girl.

In his struggle with anxiety this adolescent did many contradictory things, as anxious people often do. He could not help being attracted by girls, but in his fantasies he preferred girls whom he regarded as "out of reach" because of their wealth and popularity. When such girls were friendly toward him, indicating that perhaps they were not out of reach, he retreated. At the same time he built up a dream girl in his fantasies, a girl so glorious that no one could be the living model. This dream girl helped to protect him from becoming infatuated with a real girl.

Although he pictured himself as having too humble a station in life to be attractive to girls who attracted him, he also pictured himself as one who would get girls to "fall" for him. He bolstered this with the further thought that he did not want to break a girl's heart. So, as he saw it, he must be careful not to show an interest in any girl who might fall in love with him.

The record of this adolescent shows other aspects of anxiety. There was a dichotomy between his public and private behavior. In the eyes of others he was sexually "pure," and he was admired for his success in schoolwork. (This is what is known as a secondary gain from defenses against anxiety.) But in his fantasies he was far from pure. Furthermore, although a feeling of guilt was the *leitmotif* underlying much of his behavior, he was also, perversely, self-righteous. For a time he took a strong stand against social dancing; according to his "reasoning" it was too erotic. Yet, dancing would have been an innocent activity compared with his own erotic fantasies.

Thoughts and images and temptations as well as overt behavior may cause anxiety. Thoughts of engaging in sexual acts or masturbation may cause anxiety even though the adolescent does not actually have sexual relations. Hostile feelings and other forbidden impulses may also cause anxiety.

Anxiety-producing stresses in adolescence

It is generally agreed that unresolved childhood problems play an important role in the anxieties that prevail in adolescence and later periods of life. It is also probable that individuals will continue to use the maneuvers for coping with conflicts that they used as young children. However, each period of life brings issues that are new in the sense that persons face possibilities and responsibilities that differ from those they have faced before, or must make choices they have not been required to make at an earlier time; and these issues may precipitate anxiety or aggravate an earlier tendency to be anxious. Adolescents who exhibit many symptoms of anxiety are more likely to regard new situations as threatening than those who are less anxious.

Everything that adolescents recognize about themselves for the first time, every venture that they accept or decline, and every decision they make, may threaten earlier ideas, perceptions, and attitudes they have acquired regarding themselves.

In planning their careers and surrendering some of their earlier fantasies about the future, adolescents face issues that previously were not pressing. Many young people are seriously confronted for the first time with facts about themselves and their backgrounds (the social status of their family, their religion, their ethnic origins, and their prospective earning power) that may produce serious conflicts.

Young persons who struggle with the problem of whether to continue their schooling face a conflict that usually does not come to a head until the teenage years.

As noted in Chapters 3 and 4, the course of physical growth itself has many emotional repercussions in adolescence, such as the stresses connected with early or later maturing, adolescent obesity, and concern about development of the genitals and secondary sex characteristics. In the sphere of sex, they have urges and face temptations, choices, and hazards that are more critical than their earlier experiences with sex. In their interpersonal relations they face problems of independence-dependence, conformity-nonconformity, and self-assertion-self-negation.

Theories of anxiety

Most of the theories that help to illuminate anxiety at the adolescent level emphasize factors that affect a person's well-being from the time of infancy and early childhood. Freud's theories have influenced those who fully accept his views as well as some writers who have adopted important elements of Freudian theory while also taking positions that deviate from Freud.

An adequate exposition of the developmental background of anxiety would require a book-length treatise, which is not feasible here. For reviews of theories of anxiety the reader is referred to May (1950) and Hoch and Zubin (1950). Jersild has given condensed accounts in previous books (see, for example, Jersild, 1955 and 1960).

Anxiety and Self-determination

As we have noted, an adolescent faces numerous choices and must make many decisions. The process of choosing sometimes involves little more than an objective calculation of the advantage or disadvantage of one alternative compared with another. But often the adolescents' choices involve something more profound, for they are, in effect, "choosing themselves"—making decisions about what they are, who they are, and what they might become.

The interplay between anxiety and the self, notably "choosing oneself" was discussed over a century ago by Kierkegaard, a Danish philosopher who anticipated many ideas that have been incorporated into psychoanalysis and psychology.[1]

According to Kierkegaard, a unique attribute of human beings is their *awareness of possibility*. This awareness of possibility includes, and is intimately interrelated with, *awareness of freedom*: freedom to seize what is possible or to reject or evade it, freedom to choose one alternative rather than another. According to this view, without freedom there would be no inner conflict, but where there is freedom—awareness of possibility—anxiety is inevitable. The freedom of which he speaks is the freedom everyone knows as a personal experience when he perceives the possibilities that lie before him and is convinced that he can make a choice and is free to change his mind. As noted in Chapter 1, from a scientific and philosophical point of view, the idea of freedom may be a form of self-deception. Certainly the concept of freedom is controversial. But some degree of freedom, from the point of view of a person's own experience, is a psychological reality. Even if a person adopts a philosophy of determinism and regards everything that happens as a link in an impersonal, unbreakable chain of cause and effect, he cannot escape from the idea that he has the ability to choose and is to some degree responsible for his choices. It is within the boundaries of this freedom that human beings weigh alternatives, debate with themselves, feel guilt, and, according to Kierkegaard, "will" to be themselves by seizing or evading possibilities for realizing their potentialities. In so doing, according to this view, they have a hand in creating what they are and what they might become. They can venture or play it safe. They can assert themselves or drift with the crowd. Without choice there would be no conflict, without conflict there would be no anxiety.

Kierkegaard vividly describes anxiety as a painful experience and describes how a person can learn from it or try, in vain, to escape from it. Encounters with anxiety, according to him, offer opportunities to acquire greater self-awareness, greater strength within oneself, larger vistas of freedom or possibility, a more realistic interpretation of life, more inward "certitude," and increased power to deal with anxiety. On the other hand, individuals may try to evade the challenge of "possibility" and their freedom to make commitments by attributing events to fate, or by trying to shut themselves off, adopting rigid beliefs, resorting to superstition, or taking refuge in conformity or in academic abstractions.

Throughout his writings, Kierkegaard describes many of the symptoms of self-negating efforts to deal with anxiety that are prominently discussed today. In his own language he speaks of what we currently call the

---

[1] References to anxiety and man's predicament in facing the choices that lie before him appear in many writings by Kierkegaard that have been translated into English by Lowrie, including *Either/Or* (1949), *Stages on Life's Way* (1940), and, notably, *Sickness Unto Death* (1941) and *The Concept of Dread* (1944).

organization man, the person who seeks safety and security in conformity, in outer-directedness. He also often speaks of what we currently refer to as the man in the ivory tower—the person who amasses knowledge and spins abstract theories that are purely academic, with little or no personal meaning.[2]

Freud's Theory of Anxiety

Freud's view of the roots of anxiety is a part of his vast structure of psychoanalytic theory. He emphasizes inborn drives, particularly a sexual drive (libido) and an aggressive drive. These drives, constituting the *id*, in his account, are unconscious, but some of the desires and impulses emanating from them eventually reach the level of consciousness. The id operates on the "pleasure principle" with insistence on immediate gratification. Also, as noted earlier in Chapter 2, included in the psychic structure are the *ego* and *superego*. The ego is described as having an *executive* function, operating on a "reality principle," regulating through manifold processes the often-conflicting demands of the id and the outside world. The superego, representing what is commonly known as the conscience, also helps to regulate relations between the id, ego, and societal demands; conflicts around the superego is responsible for feelings of guilt. The instinctual, unconscious drives of the id are described as constituting a "primary process" type of thinking, as contrasted with "secondary process" thinking, which consists of the conscious and logical thoughts of the ego.

One of the many functions of the ego is to regulate mechanisms of defense, which, if successful, help to ward off feelings of anxiety. Some such mechanisms will be discussed later in this chapter.

An important feature of Freud's system is the theory of infantile sexuality. The child's sexual (libidinal) impulses lead, among other things, to an Oedipal (or Electra) conflict at about age four to six when a child, according to Freudian theory, wishes to have the parent of the opposite sex as a sexual partner and wants to get rid of the parent of the same sex.

In his accounts of anxiety, Freud draws special attention to two factors: first, the young child's helplessness and dependence on the love and care of his or her parents and, second, the unresolved conflict between a child's desire for instinctual gratification and the conditions that prevent such gratification.

The young child's helplessness, according to Freud, produces a need for love that the child is destined never to renounce. It makes the child

[2] In one passage, Kierkegaard (1944) speaks of a speculative philosopher who found a new proof for the immortality of the soul, "then came into mortal danger and could not produce his proof because he had not his notebooks with him [p. 124]."

vulnerable to *separation anxiety*. Such anxiety may occur if the child finds him- or herself in a situation of being left alone—apparently abandoned—being left with a stranger instead of the mother or being in the dark (and thus separated from the visible presence of the mother). These situations produce anxiety when in effect they mean to the child the loss of the loved person.

Anxiety as a Reaction to a Harsh Environment

According to Horney (1937), anxiety in general results not so much from fear of our impulses as from fear of our repressed impulses. She agrees with Freud's view that anxiety may result from any impulse that, if expressed, would incur danger. Sexual impulses may fall in this category, but the extent to which such impulses may be dangerous depends on attitudes toward sexuality that may vary in different cultures and also over a period of time in any particular culture. She regards repressed hostile impulses as a more important source of anxiety. Anxiety may occur when a child (or an older person) is driven to build defenses against a harsh environment—an environment that is unreliable, menacing, and unjust, but that a person does not have the power to change, that does not permit a direct counterattack, and that undermines a person's ability to place trust in him- or herself. Such an environment threatens a person's individuality and interferes with a person's ability to realize his or her potentialities. It generates hostility, but it is dangerous for a child to express hostility against those on whom the child's life and everyday care depend. According to Horney's account, someone in this predicament is driven to adopt other solutions or strategies. But these solutions, in turn, may involve a person in further difficulties, as we will note as this chapter proceeds.

Anxiety and Interpersonal Relationships in Adolescence

We have described anxiety as resulting from an inner conflict. A conflict of this sort, which resides within the person, is sometimes referred to as *intrapsychic*—within the psyche of an individual. But the conflicts that underlie anxiety arise in a social context; they are both intrapsychic and interpersonal.

The fact that anxiety is influenced by interpersonal relationships is indicated in a study by Templer et al. (1971). They found a positive relationship between adolescents' anxiety concerning death and their parents' anxiety concerning death.

The influence of interpersonal relationships on the development of the self and on anxiety has been emphasized forcefully in the writings of Sullivan (1947, 1948, 1953). In Sullivan's account (1953), anxiety in adolescence, and the consequences of such anxiety in the young person's personality development, have a history extending back to infancy. According to Sullivan, the mother or "mothering person" communicates her anxiety to her infant child through a process of empathy—defined by Sullivan as emotional contagion and communion—before the youngster is consciously aware of what is going on. She also induces anxiety through gross or very subtle acts or signs of disapproval. According to Sullivan, the self comes into being through a child's endeavor to cope with anxiety-inducing disapproval and to preserve the feelings of security, self-approval, and self-esteem that come with approval.

According to Sullivan, young persons have gone through a vast number of experiences that influence what he calls their self-system—what is incorporated within it and what is excluded from it by selective inattention, dissociation, and other means. The self-system young people already have established includes attitudes toward self and toward others that influence their reactions to people and events during adolescence. But, in the process of maturation during preadolescent and adolescent years, two developments occur that can add a deeper dimension to the young person's interpersonal relationships and can also result in new occasions for insecurity and anxiety.

One of these developments, according to Sullivan, is a need for (and, all being well, a capacity for) interpersonal *intimacy*. The other is what Sullivan (1953) calls "maturation of the lust dynamism [p. 279]." "Lust is the felt aspect of the genital drive [1953, p. 295]." This corresponds to the libidinal drive in Freud's theory. The need for intimacy normally first appears in preadolescence, according to Sullivan. The young person who, as an infant, had an inherent need for tenderness from the mothering person now is able to bestow it and share it and has a need to do so. Intimacy, in Sullivan's account, means emotional closeness with another—*collaboration*, love. Intimacy involves mutuality, "an intimate exchange with a fellow being [1953, p. 246]." "It is a matter of *we* [1953, p. 55]." The need for intimacy is at first best fulfilled, according to Sullivan, through relationships with a member of the same sex—a chum.

Young people may face "disasters" in connection with the need for, and fulfillment of the need for, intimacy, if the timing of their development is out of step with that of other persons with whom they might establish an intimate relationship. In discussing this Sullivan calls attention to the well-known fact that young people differ markedly in their rate of maturation. This may cause disturbances in young people's interpersonal relationships if, due to a slower rate of development, they have no need for intimacy when most of the other persons of their age have this need.[3]

With the development of a "need for lustful satisfaction, which is connected with genital activity in pursuit of the orgasm [1953, p. 264]," there is (all going well) a growing interest in achieving intimacy with a member of the opposite sex. In connection with this development there are several circumstances that may lead to a disturbance in interpersonal relationships—with consequent anxiety.

One source of difficulty is that "our culture provides us with singular handicaps for lustful activity . . . , lust promptly collides with a whole variety of powerful dynamisms in the personality [1953, p. 266]." Disapproval by others of children's early sexual interest in their genitals and their impulses to play with them leads them to regard their genitals as bad. Children are thus, in effect, taught to repudiate a part of themselves. The genitals are not incorporated into what they regard as an approved and worthy self. Consequently, at adolescence sexual desires may clash with the self-system. To accept their sexuality they must, in effect, revise their self-system. They must incorporate into it, as worthy and approved, a part of their person that they previously regarded as unworthy and unapproved.

At times sexual impulses have been reported to contribute to a great deal of anxiety during adolescence. Intense impulses that at other periods are unnoticed emerge, and adolescents may feel overwhelmed and afraid they may act out sexual behavior that is in conflict with internalized standards or conscience.

Yet, according to Sullivan, conflicts in connection with sex do not arise simply from a clash between the adolescent's desires and his conscience. There may be an equally serious, or perhaps more serious, "collision" between the adolescent's intimacy needs and his sexual needs. In discussing ways of dealing with this conflict, Sullivan notes the widespread tendency among boys to distinguish between "good girls" and "bad girls." The good girls are for friendship and for a future state of marriage; they are the ones who "can satisfy a person's loneliness and spare him anxiety [1953, p. 269]," whereas bad girls are persons who can satisfy his lust. But this does not solve the conflict. According to Sullivan, the adolescent boy cannot consort with bad girls without loss of the self-approval and self-respect that are his security against becoming anxious. Girls may have corresponding feelings about themselves in their relationships with boys.

[3] One form of failure in achieving intimate interpersonal relations is seen in the condition of loneliness. Loneliness, according to Sullivan, is a phenomenon encountered only in preadolescence and thereafter. "Loneliness in itself is more terrible than anxiety [1953, p. 262]," and as a driving force it may compel people to seek companionship even though they are intensely anxious about relating to others.

Anxiety Due to Conflict Between Competitive Strivings and Need for Group Membership

The need for peer approval has an important influence during adolescence. One consequence of the anxiety accompanying this need is that adolescents may accept without reservation the ideals of the leader or the adolescent group (Freud, 1958). On the other hand, adolescents have the need to achieve success through independent competitive means. As pointed out by May (1950), individuals' needs to become both independent and autonomous, and at the same time contributing and accepted members of their social group, may lead to conflict.

Anxiety Arising from Repressed Guilt

Underlying practically all the decisions and commitments made in adolescence are ethical or moral issues: what is right or wrong and better or worse, from the adolescent's point of view or from the point of view of other

Competitive strivings may result in anxiety. [Abigail Heyman/Magnum.]

persons. Individuals are likely to be anxious when their conscience, or superego, is overly severe, harsh, and punitive, driving them to repress wholesome promptings of their natures and to strive for a perfection that is beyond human reach. Such individuals are assailed by guilt that goes beyond the limits of healthy remorse. But individuals can also become anxious if they go to the other extreme by repressing feelings of guilt that cannot go unheeded if they are to satisfy the needs and follow the teachings that impel them to be accepted members of society. Mowrer (1950, 1953) states that the conflicts that cause anxiety involve moral or ethical issues (a point mentioned also by other authors). He maintains that anxiety arises from unconscious, repressed, and repudiated guilt.

Here is another thread in the complicated skein of anxiety in adolescence and in other periods of life: persons can become anxious if their morals demand more of them than any human being can attain, or if they try to sidestep moral responsibilities that no person, as a member of the human race, can successfully disavow.

Evidences of anxiety in adolescence

For many adolescents temporary periods of anxiety may occur that are then followed by the development of more effective patterns of behavior. Some adolescents, however, may experience some disorganization of the personality that may interfere with their further development (Group for the Advancement of Psychiatry, 1968).

It would not be possible to make an exact estimate or measurement of the prevalence of anxiety in adolescents without making a prolonged study "in depth" of each individual in a large, representative group. One difficulty is that anxiety that involves repression and unrecognized defenses is usually not perceived for what it is. However, findings that have emerged from studies of what has been called manifest anxiety indicate that the typical young person is aware of, and will report, many personal problems that probably should be regarded as symptoms of what some writers refer to as neurotic anxiety. In a study of about 2,000 students, Taylor (1953) applied a test of manifest anxiety containing fifty items. The number of symptoms a person could report ranged from zero to fifty. The average score was about fifteen.

When persons of high school and college age are studied by means of projective tests such as the Rorschach and TAT (referred to in Chapter 8), the typical person gives responses that, according to the interpretation schemes devised for these tests, represent symptoms of conflict and a more or less disturbed state of mind (see, for example, Frank et al., 1953).

In a psychiatric interview in a study of normal adolescent boys, Offer (1969) asked the boys to describe their feelings and experiences with anxiety. Then they were asked how common, long, and uncomfortable their feelings with anxiety were. Most of the boys reported feelings of anxiety and indicated that they occurred frequently in a variety of situations. From such evidence as is available it can be assumed that anxiety may be widespread among adolescents.

In trying to perceive and assess symptoms of anxiety one must remember that they are as numerous as the frailties, perversities, and inconsistencies of human behavior. Symptoms of anxiety often crop out in behavior that seems sullen and ornery, that is annoying to others, or in behavior that seems queer. Many of the symptoms have been touched on in earlier sections, but it is useful to review these symptoms and to note others that have not previously been mentioned.

We may suspect that adolescents are anxious if they respond in a way that is out of proportion to the occasion, or *overreact*: by being greatly upset by little things; bitterly angry at something that seems trivial; plagued with guilt beyond the limits of genuine remorse; worried or fearful out of proportion to any overhanging threat; or afraid of dangers that actually do not exist, continuing to be afraid in spite of reminders from their own experiences that there is nothing to fear.

We may also suspect that adolescents are anxious if they *underreact*: if they shrink from any show of anger when anger is justified or are apathetic and unmoved in situations where normally persons would feel joy or apprehension or grief. Adolescents are probably suffering from anxiety if they have unaccountable moods, such as being depressed, or have sudden outbursts of crying for no apparent reason, or feel "out of sorts" and edgy without knowing why.

Anxiety probably prevails if adolescents are driven by compulsions. There are many of these, among them an unrelenting compulsion to compete or an unaccountable urge to repeat acts that previously brought them into trouble and that, from a rational point of view, they know will get them into trouble again. Adolescents have compulsions that probably signify anxiety when they are in a fever of activity—when they have an urge to rush hither and yon, are unable to sit still or to relax—as though they are unable to bear the thoughts that spring up in an unoccupied moment.

Adolescents are probably suffering from anxiety also if they act distinctly out of character—if they have mild and friendly ways but now and then do things that are unnecessarily cruel. It is also likely that adolescents are anxious if they are exceedingly rigid in their attitudes, are self-righteous, markedly smug, prudish, or dogmatic. Adolescents are also probably in the grip of anxiety if they impose impossible standards on themselves, if they expect more of themselves than anyone could possibly demand of them, and then deplore themselves for not living up to these standards.

We can assume that practically all adolescents of adequate intelligence who are backward in their studies are also anxious to some degree. It is likely that they have been made to feel that it is their own fault if they do not do well. So they may feel guilty, as though one part of them were blaming another part of them about not living up to the expectations placed on them by others. Or they may feel guilty and also feel a strong resentment toward those teachers who fail them but yet be in conflict about this resentment.

At the adolescent level there are already those who seem to be anxious to the point of despair. We may suspect that a state of despair or near despair exists in adolescent delinquents who do desperate things, as though bent on destroying themselves.

On a milder scale, anxiety probably prevails when adolescents complain bitterly about their parents and find serious fault with them much of the time. It is not easy to feel anger at a parent without also having a guilty notion that one should be a dutiful and loyal child. Anxiety probably prevails among young persons who have turned against their background, their upbringing, the social group in which they were reared, or the religious or racial group into which they were born. When adolescents turn against their home and the environment and traditions in which they were reared, they are turning against something that is part of themselves. Unless they resolve this conflict in some way, they will probably be anxious to some degree.

In emphasizing the prevalence of anxiety in this way we are not trying to paint a gloomy picture of human existence. As noted by Offer (1969), the anxiety experienced by adolescents is rarely crippling in nature. Oftentimes it serves as a prelude to good performance.

Defenses against anxiety as a source of further anxiety

Since anxiety is a painful state it will induce measures to bring relief. One way of trying to relieve the pain is to face it—to learn from it, to move through it, to come up against it as one who pushes forward against an adverse wind. But this is not an easy thing to do at any stage of life, and it is especially difficult for a child. As a consequence, the anxious person may seek to sidestep anxiety by many means.

The defenses persons adopt to blunt or evade conflicts that underlie their anxiety involve them in new conflicts. Accounts of the struggle with anxiety that are especially revealing have been offered by Anna Freud (1958) and Horney (1939, 1945, 1946, 1950).

Strategies in Dealing With Anxiety as Described by Horney

Karen Horney describes strategies for dealing with anxiety that probably all can perceive in themselves or others at some time. These strategies at first may be quite rational and normal, used by individuals as a means of protecting themselves, but they may become so strongly entrenched within the personality that they persist, compulsively, even when the difficulty that gave rise to them no longer prevails. According to Horney, a further condition of anxiety arises when these strategies are threatened, as happens when they conflict with reality or with one another.

MOVING AGAINST OTHERS

One strategy individuals may develop in trying to survive in a threatening environment is to move against others, not in open warfare but by means of becoming competitive; seeking to surpass others in sports or in schoolwork or in business or in romantic conquests or in any area of life.

MOVING AWAY FROM OTHERS

Another strategy, according to Horney, is to move away from others: to withdraw, to remain aloof and detached. We see this strategy when we see adolescents who have no spontaneity, when the ecstasies of life seem not to stir them and sorrows leave them unmoved. Detached persons may go through the motions of being interested in others, but their feelings are not suited to their actions and their thoughts. They remain emotionally removed. Bookishness may be a form of detachment when it is not something freely chosen but a means of keeping aloof from the flesh and blood of human existence. Detached adolescents may go through the motions of making friends without actually moving emotionally close to anyone or allowing anyone to come close to them. Such detachment may take the form of asceticism, intellectualization, or isolation.

MOVING WITH OTHERS

A third strategy, according to Horney, is moving with others: a policy of compliance, conformity, and self-effacement. The compliant ones move with the tide. They yield. They try to placate and appease. At the adolescent level the compliant ones may be the "good" ones who are ready to let others direct what they should do or learn or think; they even may be ready to let others use them as doormats. Compliant, appeasing adolescents may be the ones who always clean up after a party while the others are at play, or the ones who always put a coin in the parking meter while other fellow passengers saunter off.

Horney does not regard any of these forms of conduct per se as a mark of anxiety. There are times when a person spontaneously or deliberately competes, or complies, or holds himself or herself aloof, and the same person may use one or the other of these strategies at different times and in different situations. But these forms of conduct are pseudosolutions, or neurotic, when a person is driven blindly to employ them as defenses.

To the extent that individuals live according to such pseudosolutions they are playing an assumed role. They do not reflect what they would be and do if they were free to use their resources and to draw on them in an unfettered manner.

Freudian Theory of Defenses Against Anxiety

According to Freud and psychoanalytic theory, feelings of anxiety serve to warn the ego, or self, of impending danger, usually in the form of a repressed impulse. The ego then uses specific defense mechanisms to ward off forbidden and dangerous impulses.

Such defense mechanisms operate at all times in all people, ranging from normal people to hospitalized psychotic patients. People with different personality structures use varying defense mechanisms. Although defense mechanisms were first elaborated on by psychoanalysts such as Anna Freud (1958), they are acknowledged by many psychologists who are not committed to psychoanalytic theory.

The following section briefly describes several defense mechanisms and gives examples of the ways they work.

REPRESSION

The basic defense mechanism, according to psychoanalytic theory, is repression, which serves to keep disturbing thoughts or feelings out of conscious awareness. Forgetting may be an example of repression, especially when we forget something or are unable to remember something highly charged with emotion. The other defense mechanisms to be described here often serve to produce or reinforce the repression. Persons who unwittingly use the "strategies" described by Horney in the preceding pages are struggling to prevent repressed material from entering into conscious awareness.

Projection. This defense, of which the person is unaware, consists of attributing unacceptable or forbidden impulses to persons, objects, or conditions outside the self. For example, someone who has difficulty dealing with unacceptable angry impulses may attribute them to another person, who is then perceived as being angry.

Denial.   Another defense mechanism is denial. The ego simply does not recognize unacceptable aspects of reality as true and substitutes a fantasy to help get rid of the dangerous aspect of reality. For example, if an adolescent suffers a major loss or blow to his or her self-esteem, he or she may just not admit the fact of the loss to be true.

Displacement.   This mechanism refers to the transfer of feelings that are unacceptable if directed toward one person onto another substitute person. For example, if a son has repressed feelings of hatred for his father, he may be consciously aware of anger toward policemen or other male authority figures but not aware of being angry at his father.

Rationalization.   This mechanism consists of substituting a false, but seemingly plausible, explanation for the presence of unacceptable thoughts or feelings. For example, someone who has failed an examination might attribute the failure to the unfairness of the questions rather than to any lack of intelligence or of understanding of the material.

Reaction formation.   This mechanism comprises the substitution of an acceptable feeling or idea for its opposite unacceptable feeling or idea. For example, a mother who harbors unconscious resentment of her children may become oversolicitous and overprotective of them, remaining unaware of her resentment.

Undoing.   An act that stands for an unacceptable impulse is undone or reversed. Compulsive expiation after a symbolic aggressive act would be an example of this mechanism—for example, compulsive repetitious hand-washing.

Turning Against the Self.   This mechanism refers to a redirection of an unacceptable impulse from its original object to the self and is seen particularly in depression and masochism. Depression, for example, may be seen as more acceptable than anger toward an important person.

Intellectualization.   Unacceptable impulses are controlled by being submerged in intellectual activities. It is seen when adolescents become excessively interested in philosophical questions or adopt an ascetic viewpoint. Intellectualism is sometimes referred to as a flight into an ivory tower.

Regression.   A reversion may occur to earlier successful modes of functioning to avoid or to try to deal with emotional conflicts.

Sublimation.   Unacceptable impulses are unwittingly changed to personally and socially acceptable goals. This mechanism is regarded as one of the more mature mechanisms and may be seen operating in conflict-free activities that contribute to personality integration. A wish to smear or be dirty, for example, may be changed into the desire to create beautiful paintings. However, simplistic interpretations of sublimation should be avoided as this mental process is usually quite complex in its working.

It should be noted that according to psychoanalytic theory usually several defense mechanisms work simultaneously to help keep unacceptable thoughts and feelings from conscious awareness.

Sex differences in manifest anxiety

Scales have been designed to measure both "general" (General Anxiety Scale for Children, GASC) and more specific symptoms (Test Anxiety Scale for Children, TASC). In tests of anxiety, using both a cross-sectional and a longitudinal approach, Nesselroade and Baltes (1974) found that female adolescents tended to be more anxious than males. In a 1974 summary of the literature in this area, Maccoby and Jacklin (1974) also concluded that girls and women get higher scores on the general anxiety scales. It may be that girls obtain higher scores because they are more likely to admit to feelings of anxiety than boys. For instance, males are more likely to respond in the negative when asked, "Do you sometimes dream about things you don't like to talk about?" Furthermore, Maccoby and Jacklin (1974) suggest that the tendency of girls to get higher scores on anxiety scales is due to the fact that some of the items are related to special fears of girls or specific circumstances they have been told to avoid. On the other hand, there are few "items in the scale that relate to the boy's special fear of appearing cowardly in the eyes of his age-mate, his fear of public humiliation or failure, etc. [Maccoby and Jacklin, 1974, p. 188]."

In general we do not have at the present time a clear picture of sex differences in anxiety, if they do exist. While some observational studies suggest that there are no sex differences, teachers' ratings and reports by youngsters suggest that girls may be more inclined to be subject to anxiety. Results based on scales such as the Taylor Manifest Anxiety Scale are not conclusive.

One of the limitations of measuring anxiety by means of scales is that it is difficult to produce scales with a high degree of validity or to distinguish between readily recognized symptoms and underlying states of conflict.

Anxiety and performance

Several investigators have studied the relationship between measurements of anxiety and performance (for a review see Gaudry and Spielberger, 1971). From a number of studies it appears performance is high when anxiety (as measured by tests) is at a moderate level. At either extreme, low or high anxiety, performance is poor. It has been surmised that individuals whose scores are at the low end of the anxiety continuum may lack motivation. At the high end of the continuum the individual is regarded as perhaps overwhelmed by anxiety. However, the relationship between anxiety and performance depends on many interacting factors in both the individual and the situation.

The amount of anxiety adolescents experience when trying to learn something is influenced by the complexity and difficulty of the material they are expected to master. O'Neil et al. (1969) measured the anxiety of college students who were then required to learn difficult material in one experimental situation and easy material in another situation. As shown in Figure 11.1 the students gave evidence of the greatest anxiety when they were working on the difficult task; the next highest level of anxiety appeared prior to the study, and the lowest amount of anxiety occurred during an easy task.

Some adolescents are at a great disadvantage when they have to learn complex material. Apparently, high levels of anxiety interfere with their

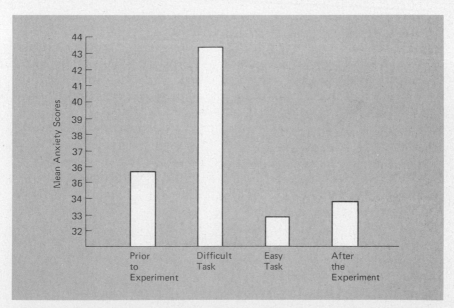

Figure 11.1.   State anxiety and learning. [Adapted from "Effects of state anxiety and task difficulty on computer-assisted learning" by H. F. O'Neil, Jr., C. D. Spielberger, and D. N. Hansen, *Journal of Educational Psychology*, 1969, *60*, 343–350.]

ability to concentrate. Moreover, according to Ganzer (1968), the performance of students who score high on a test of anxiety drops sharply when other individuals observe them learning a task; students low in anxiety do not appear to be affected by the presence of others.

From various studies by Spielberger (1962) it appears that the effect of anxiety on learning depends on the adolescent's level of ability. His findings suggest that students of average ability who scored high on an anxiety scale more often had lower college grades and more often left college as a result of academic failure. However, it appeared that students who scored high on a scholastic aptitude test, and also showed a high anxiety level, were able to achieve at a high level in college in spite of anxiety. Indeed, their anxiety may have stimulated them to increased effort in their intellectual work. (See Figure 11.2.)

Extreme stresses and anxiety

Individuals subjected to life-threatening danger often experience extreme anxiety reactions that may persist even when the danger is over. According to Chodoff (1963), individuals who had been in Nazi concentration camps and had managed to survive often experienced extreme anxiety when confronted with stress in later years. In general not only is anxiety difficult to extinguish, but factors other than those of the original situation,

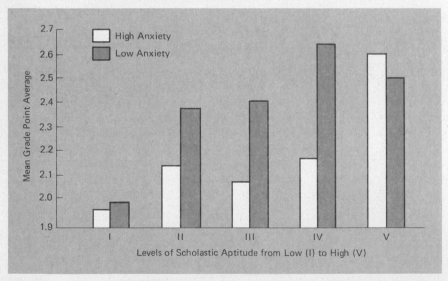

Figure 11.2.   Effects of anxiety on academic achievement. [Adapted from "The effects of manifest anxiety on the academic achievement of college students" by C. D. Spielberger, *Mental Hygiene*, 1962, *46*, 420–426.]

which are not anxiety producing in themselves, may evoke anxiety. For example, after an adolescent girl had been attacked by a man, her fear and anxiety generalized to all men. Under these conditions she was entirely unaware of the source of her anxiety when in the presence of men.

Although potentially traumatic events may lead to anxiety, this does not necessarily mean anxiety is bound to occur. Reactions to extreme stress seem to suggest that some children and adolescents are indeed resilient in dealing with extremely adverse conditions. This appeared in a study dealing with fourth- through eighth-grade elementary school children living in different settlements in Israel during the Arab-Israeli war of 1967 (Ziv et al., 1974). One group had been exposed to frequent shellings from across the border, and the other group had not been exposed to shellings. In many respects the shelled group was similar to the nonshelled group. Although there were some differences between the groups, the youngsters in the shelled settlement seemed able to cope with stress. These youngsters in comparison to the nonshelled group showed more covert aggression and appeared to value the personality trait of courage. In a response to a sentence-completion item inquiring into their preferred dreams they mentioned peace, victory in war, and cessation of bombings.

Adolescents' reactions to stress have been shown to be affected to varying degrees by the extent to which the adolescents believe they have control over their future lives (Houston, 1972).

Manifest anxiety and uncertainty

Anxiety may arise in individuals because they are uncertain of others' reactions to them, uncertain of what is expected of them, or not sure of what to expect in a certain situation. In a study of adolescent high school girls, Kaczkowski and Owen (1972) asked the girls to write a description of the last time they were anxious. An analysis of their written descriptions of anxiety revealed that over 90 per cent of the girls mentioned that they felt anxious because they lacked knowledge of what was expected of them.

That adolescents may experience anxiety because they are uncertain of the evaluations of others was brought out in a study by Naditch and Morrissey (1976). Cuban refugees in Florida were asked whether they felt they knew how satisfied their parents and peers were with their behavior on dates. Those adolescents who reported they were uncertain of the evaluations of significant others in terms of their dating behavior were more likely to experience anxiety and depression.

References

Chodoff, P. Late effects of concentration camp syndrome. *Archives of General Psychiatry*, 1963, **8**, 323–333.

Frank, L. K., Harrison, R., Hellersberg, E., Machover, K., & Steiner, M. Personality development in adolescent girls. *Monographs of the Society for Research in Child Development*, 1953, **16**(53).

Freud, A. Adolescence. *The psychoanalytic study of the child*, 1958, **13**, 255–278.

Ganzer, V. J. Effects of audience presence and test anxiety in learning and retention in a serial learning situation. *Journal of Personality and Social Psychology*, 1968, **8**, 194–199.

Gaudry, E., & Spielberger, C. D. *Anxiety and educational achievement*. New York: Wiley, 1971.

Group for the Advancement of Psychiatry. *Normal adolescence*. New York: Scribner, 1968.

Hoch, P., & Zubin, J. (Eds.). *Anxiety*. New York: Grune, 1950.

Horney, K. *The neurotic personality of our time*. New York: Norton, 1937.

Horney, K. *New ways in psychoanalysis*. New York: Norton, 1939.

Horney, K. *Our inner conflicts*. New York: Norton, 1945.

Horney, K. *Growth through love and sex*. New York: Auxiliary Council to the Association for the Advancement of Psychoanalysis, 1946.

Horney, K. *Neurosis and human growth*. New York: Norton, 1950.

Houston, B. K. Control over stress, locus of control, and response to stress. *Journal of Personality and Social Psychology*, 1972, **21**, 249–255.

Jersild, A. T. *When teachers face themselves*. New York: Bureau of Publications, Teachers College, Columbia University, 1955.

Jersild, A. T. *Child psychology* (5th ed.). Englewood Cliffs, N.J.: Prentice-Hall, 1960.

Kaczkowski, H., & Owen, K. Anxiety and anger in adolescent girls. *Psychological Reports*, 1972, **31**, 281–282.

Kierkegaard, S. *Stages on life's way*. (W. Lowrie, trans.). Princeton, N.J.: Princeton University Press, 1940.

Kierkegaard, S. *Sickness unto death*. (W. Lowrie, trans.). Princeton, N.J.: Princeton University Press, 1941.

Kierkegaard, S. *The concept of dread*. (W. Lowrie, trans.). Princeton, N.J.: Princeton University Press, 1944.

Kierkegaard, S. *Either/Or*. (W. Lowrie, trans.). Princeton, N.J.: Princeton University Press, 1949.

Maccoby, E. E., & Jacklin, C. N. *The psychology of sex differences*. Stanford, Calif.: Stanford U.P., 1974.

May, R. *The meaning of anxiety*. New York: Ronald, 1950.

Mowrer, O. H. Pain, punishment, guilt, and anxiety. In P. H. Hoch & J. Zubin (Eds.), *Anxiety*. New York: Grune, 1950.

Mowrer, O. H. Some philosophical problems in mental disorder and its treatment. *Harvard Educational Review*, 1953, **23**, 117–127.

Naditch, M. P., & Morrissey, R. F. Role stress, personality, and psychopathology in a group of immigrant adolescents. *Journal of Abnormal Psychology*, 1976, **85**, 113–118.

Nesselroade, J. R., & Baltes, P. B. Adolescent personality development and historical change: 1970–1972. *Monographs of the Society for Research in Child Development*, 1974, **39** (1, Serial No. 154).

Offer, D. *The psychological world of the teen-ager: A study of normal adolescent boys.* New York: Basic Books, 1969.

O'Neil, H. F., Jr., Spielberger, C. D., & Hansen, D. N. Effects of state anxiety and task difficulty on computer-assisted learning. *Journal of Educational Psychology*, 1969, **60**, 343–350.

Powell, M. G. Comparison of self-ratings, peer ratings, and expert ratings on personality adjustment. *Educational and Psychological Measurement*, 1948, **8**, 225–234.

Rogers, C. R. A study of the mental health problems in three representative elementary schools. A study of health and physical education in Columbus public schools. *Monographs of the Bureau of Educational Research, 25.* Columbus: Ohio State University Press, 1942.

Spielberger, C. D. The effects of manifest anxiety on the academic achievement of college students. *Mental Hygiene*, 1962, **46**, 420–426.

Spivack, S. A study of a method of appraising self-acceptance and self-rejection. *Journal of Genetic Psychology*, 1956, **88**, 183–202.

Srole, L., Langner, T. S., Michael, S. T., Opler, M. K., & Rennie, T. A. C. *Mental health in the metropolis: The Midtown Manhattan study* (Vol. 1). New York: McGraw-Hill, 1962.

Stein, D. G., & Rosen, J. J. *Motivation and emotion.* New York: Macmillan, 1974.

Sullivan, H. S. *Conceptions of modern psychiatry.* Washington, D.C.: William Alanson White Foundation, 1947.

Sullivan, H. S. *The meaning of anxiety in psychiatry and in life.* New York: William Alanson White Institute of Psychiatry, 1948.

Sullivan, H. S. *The interpersonal theory of psychiatry.* New York: Norton, 1953.

Symonds, P. M., & Sherman, M. Personality survey of a junior high school. In W. T. Donahue (Ed.), *The measurement of student adjustment and achievement.* Ann Arbor: University of Michigan Press, 1949.

Taylor, J. A. A personality scale of manifest anxiety. *Journal of Abnormal and Social Psychology*, 1953, **48**, 285–290.

Templer, D. I., Ruff, C. F., & Franks, C. M. Death anxiety. Age, sex and parental resemblance in diverse populations. *Developmental Psychology*, 1971, **4**, 108.

Weiss, J. M. Psychological factors in stress and disease. *Scientific American*, 1972, **226**, 104–113.

Ziv, A., Kruglanski, A. W., & Shulman, S. Children's psychological reactions to war-time stress. *Journal of Personality and Social Psychology*, 1974, **30**, 24–30.

part five

THE ADOLESCENT'S SOCIAL WORLD

12
parents, home, and family

Adolescents' relationships with their parents may be viewed as a three-act drama. In the first act young adolescents continue, as in earlier childhood, to need their parents; they are dependent on them and are profoundly influenced by them. The adolescents begin, however, to become more keenly aware than they were before of their parents as persons. Increasingly they are absorbed in the larger world outside the home. They begin, in a psychological sense, to leave their home to move into this larger world in which they eventually must reside as self-directing adults.

303

The second act of the drama might be called "The Struggle for Emancipation." To achieve stature as adults the adolescents must outgrow their childhood dependency on their parents. They must renounce major allegiance to their parents and be able, under normal circumstances, to shift their allegiance to prospective mates. Eventually, most of them must be prepared to assume the role of parents. Although the struggle for emancipation sometimes is a relatively quiet campaign in which adolescents steadily assume more and more responsibility for themselves, often the campaign is turbulent, full of conflict and laden with anxiety both for the adolescents and for their parents.

In the third act, if all has gone well, the struggle subsides, as the young persons take their place among adult peers. But the drama has not ended, for the influence of their parents extends into adult life. Many persons who, in their teens, rebelled against their parents' ideas and attitudes adopt these same ideas and attitudes as their own when they enter their twenties (Bath and Lewis, 1962); and many persons keep assessing and reassessing the view they have of their parents and their feelings about their parents several decades after adolescence is over (Jersild et al., 1962). Some retain undercurrents of bitterness toward their parents; some acquire a deeper feeling of tenderness; some, when they have children of their own, for the first time fully appreciate or recognize what their parents meant to them.

Interactions between parents and children

Within recent years there has been a growing tendency to view parent-child relationships as an interactive system instead of only examining the effect of parental behavior on the child. For example, whereas delinquency in adolescents was viewed by some as the result of parental rejection, some investigators are now considering the possibility that a rebellious and antisocial delinquent may result in rejecting parents.

The interactionist approach to the development of the individual has been emphasized by Thomas and Chess (1972), who express the view that development is "a constantly evolving process of interaction between the child and the environment from the first days of life onward (and even prenatally) [p. 332]." In addition to examining specific aspects of the environment, they consider it essential to take note of differences between individuals in their responses to the environment. According to Thomas and Chess (1972), the "basic issue determining normal development appeared to be the existence of a consonance or 'goodness of fit' between the child with his individual characteristics and the demands and expectations of the intra- and extrafamilial environments [p. 336]."

To appreciate the nature of the interaction between parents and adolescents it is necessary to recognize, as emphasized here, that the parent-adolescent relationship extends back to the time when the adolescent was born. It is essential, also, to recognize that, in the typical family situation, parents are not all-powerful persons who can control a child's destiny, for better or for worse. It is true that harsh, abnormal, and abusive parents can have traumatic effects on children, especially at the infancy level. But in the usual family, there are limits to what parents can or cannot do. These limits are determined to an important degree not only by the qualities of the parents, but also by temperamental qualities of their children, often manifested from the time of birth. The influence of the social environment, especially the young person's peers, also obviously is an important factor.

On the basis of her classic studies of young children, Shirley (1941) concludes that each child has a tough core of temperamental qualities that prevents him or her ever from becoming a complete puppet in the hands of others. Many other research workers, including the famed Arnold Gesell, also have emphasized the concept that each child, from an early age, displays an individuality of his or her own that cannot be attributed to any ascertainable influence in the environment, including the environment as structured by parents. This concept was emphasized in the fascinating studies by Blatz and Millichamp (1937) of the Dionne quintuplets, who received a tremendous amount of press coverage in the 1930s. These five sisters were so much alike that casual observers could not tell them apart. Yet each had distinctive characteristics that, in turn, influenced the way others responded to her. These investigators draw the arresting conclusion that the environmental characteristics most influential in molding an individual are those resulting from that individual's response to his social environment. This does not, of course, rule out the fact that a person's development is influenced to an important degree by environmental factors that are not of his or her own making.

Currently, the studies by Thomas and Chess and their associates are outstanding in demonstrating that a person's temperamental qualities play an important role in his or her interactions with others in the environment. In earlier works, infants were classified in terms of nine objectively defined ways of responding, designated primary reaction patterns (Thomas, 1966; Thomas et al., 1963). Although these were formulated on the basis of behavior exhibited by infants, we list them here, in abbreviated form, because of their obvious potential significance in influencing the interaction between parents and children prior to, and (to some extent) during adolescence:

1. Activity level, including diurnal proportion of active and inactive periods; mobility in connection with everyday routines.
2. Rhythmicity, including predictability and rhythmicity or unpredictability in relation to the sleep-wake cycle, hunger, appetite, and elimination.
3. Approach or withdrawal in response to a new stimulus, such as a new food.
4. Adaptability (to new or altered situations).
5. Intensity of reaction.
6. Threshold of responsiveness—intensity level of stimulation necessary to evoke a discernable response.
7. Quality of mood.
8. Distractability.
9. Attention span and persistence.

On the basis of these categories one might construct a hypothetical child who is easy to live with and to rear, or one who is not. In the interaction between parents and the child it would require a great deal of ingenuity, patience, and forebearance for parents to keep their cool and function effectively as "good" parents if, for example, their child was hyperactive, was unpredictable, was prone to respond to a new food as though it were poison, had difficulty in adapting to each new situation, responded to all situations with a high level of intensity, had a short attention span, and was markedly inclined to be unpleasantly moody. If, on the other hand, a child, on all counts, leaned to the opposite extreme, parents might respond by taking him or her for granted and fail to pay attention to his or her needs.

But a child with a presumably difficult pattern of behavior is not necessarily headed for trouble, and the developmental history of the child who presumably should be easy to rear is not necessarily going to be serene. A study by Friedman (1965) showed how an exceptionally patient and resourceful mother was able to spare her potentially "difficult" child from becoming a "problem" child, whereas another child, who predictably would be "easy" to rear, had a less able and serene mother and ran into difficulties. We will return again to findings at the adolescent level by Thomas and Chess (1972) in Chapter 20.

Most of the research dealing with parent-adolescent relationships, as discussed in the remainder of this chapter, has dealt with statistical correlations or comparisons between child-rearing variables and measures of adolescent behavior.

The assumption underlying many quantitative studies has been that parental behavior is likely to be antecedent to the adolescents' behavior rather than a consequence of the adolescents' behavior. Indeed this is often the case. However, sometimes the adolescents' behavior may be the antecedent of parental behavior. Several recent studies have shown that children do indeed affect the behavior of their parents (Harper, 1971; Hoffman, 1975; Osofsky, 1971; Yarrow et al., 1971). Only long-term inquiry into the process of interaction between the child and his environment will allow one to infer causal relationships.

Methodological issues involved in the study of parent-child interaction

A major limitation in some of the research in the area of parent-child relations is the questionable nature of the data. Many studies depend on interviews with the adolescent and parent. Reports by parents and their offspring may be distorted to varying degrees because of their inability to recall past events, their initial perceptions, their ability to verbalize, and their need to defend or justify their attitudes or behavior. The interviewer's skill may also affect the content of the material presented. Those studies that depend on ratings made by observers may also be subject to some distortions. A case in point is a study by Zegiob et al. (1975) suggesting that mothers are more and more positive in their verbalizations when they are aware that they are being observed. For these reasons, Martin (1975) notes that a direct approach using behavioral measures should be used if possible. However, Martin also notes some of the limitations of a direct approach: "the unknown effects of the presence of the observer, the representativeness of the sample of interaction observed, and the coding of the flow of interaction into unity for analysis [p. 470]." A second limitation of research in this area is that the context of the situation is often not taken into consideration. For instance, a mother may respond differently depending on whether her husband is present or absent.

Objective and subjective aspects of relationships with parents

Unfortunately, many studies dealing with objective dimensions of parent-child relationships and behavior do not adequately take account of the subjective dimension: the intentions and attitudes underlying a parent's overt behavior and the way in which the adolescent perceives and judges a parent's motives and behavior. An adolescent's perception may be unrealistic from every standpoint except his own—but to the young person this perception is *real*. The young person's perceptions may, at the time, play a more important role than the parent's actual behavior. An adolescent may, for example, perceive the parent as angry—and resent the anger—while actually the parent is not angry but worried and anxious.

Once a young person has formed a certain perception of his or her parents (viewing them, for example, as unfair or showing favoritism toward a brother or sister), the person usually is able to find further evidence to support this view. Even the best parents are likely to be, or to seem, unfair at times, or to praise one of their children when another would also welcome a word of praise. When this happens, a young person's attitudes, whether based on a realistic perception of his or her parents or not, tend to become self-perpetuating. They remain unexamined until, for example, many years later, a child of his or her own, in a surprising emotional outburst, claims to be treated unfairly.

Later in this chapter we will note that many young persons in later years revise the perception they had of their parents when they were adolescents. Sometimes this revision results in an assessment that is just the opposite of their earlier views.

The importance of family relationships

The importance of family relationships is emphasized when adolescents tell about their early lives. The role of the family also is emphasized to a marked degree when adults view their own adolescence in retrospect. Several times, while teaching graduate courses on the psychology of adolescence, the senior author has asked students to write an account of conditions and events that, in their judgment, were most helpful or most trying and burdensome during their adolescent years. These accounts have regularly mentioned the home and relationships with parents more than any other single factor. A tally of one sampling showed that over 90 per cent referred to home life, naming such matters as family accord or discord, problems relating to discipline, authority, grievances against parents, help received from parents in time of stress, etc. Rosen (1955) asked adolescents to name persons whose opinions were of great importance to them. Ninety per cent of the adolescents named one or both parents as people whose opinions mattered a great deal to them, and it is striking that in most cases the parents were named *first*. Many adolescents have singled out their parents as their adult ideals (Douvan and Adelson, 1966); and they have indicated that parental disapproval would be difficult to bear, even harder than disapproval by a best friend or favorite teacher (Epperson, 1964).

As might be expected, adolescents are likely to acquire the beliefs, values, attitudes, and behavior of their families. Family socialization experiences both present and past may either enhance or hinder the individual's ability to cope with the developmental tasks of adolescence. However, adolescents may, for a time, prefer values and beliefs that differ from those of their parents and then later adopt parental values and beliefs as their own.

As might be expected, adolescents are likely to acquire the beliefs, values, behavior, and interests of their families. [Burt Glinn/Magnum.]

The role of parental affection in an adolescent's upbringing

The experience of being loved, and of loving, is one of the essentials of healthy human growth. The affection parents and their offspring have for one another is seldom (probably never) unmixed with other emotions. But a strong foundation of parental love during childhood gives youngsters an invaluable resource as they embark on an adolescent career; and continued assurance of the parents' love is an invaluable asset during adolescent years.

Adolescents who are loved for their own sakes do not constantly have to calculate how to procure or retain the good will of the parents. They can put their trust in their parents' goodwill, even when they are at odds with them and sorely try their patience. Young persons who can count on their parents' love have greater freedom to venture, to explore, to be themselves, to find themselves, to test their powers, and to cultivate their own judgments in making choices and in weighing one possibility against another in planning the future. They have leeway to make mistakes, such as those who tread new ground are bound to make, without having to fear the mistakes will be fatal. Such people are also likely to be more immune to shattering guilt than the ones who are unloved.

Adolescents who are realistically confident of their parents' love are spared many burdens. In a clash of wills with their parents, they can directly fight for their rights, as they see them, without also having to fight a rear-guard action of grievance or revenge.

Limitations in the Power of Parental Love

Although parental love accomplishes much for an adolescent, it obviously cannot accomplish everything. Parental love does not protect the young person against disappointments and errors of judgment. It cannot cure any inherited weaknesses that the adolescent might have. It cannot defend against the malice of persons with whom the adolescent deals outside the home or eliminate prejudice. It cannot guarantee good conditions at school. Loving parents cannot spare the young person from temptations. They cannot control the accelerator when the child drives a car. Their moral example may help, but it alone cannot keep the child from falling in with deviant companions. They obviously cannot rid life of all the conditions that might lead a young person into folly, grief, or disaster.

The Unloved or "Rejected" Adolescent

The lot of adolescents who are unloved or rejected by their parents is a hard one. Unless they can find substitute parents or crumbs of affection outside the home they must face life's uncertainties and hurts without help from others, and they must reach for what life might offer with no one to guide or encourage them.

Most of the studies dealing with the role of lack of affection on the fortunes or misfortunes of adolescents are of an ad hoc variety. Studies have been made, for example, of adolescents who are emotionally disturbed, or delinquent, or who are failing at school, to discover conditions in their upbringing that might account for their misfortune. A number of clinical studies do indeed suggest many fruitful hypotheses for further investigation; however, many of the studies have a number of methodological shortcomings, and generalizing from their findings would be questionable.

One difficulty in obtaining an adequate measure of affection, or—as it is also referred to—wholehearted *acceptance* and its opposite, *rejection*, is that these conditions cannot be assessed simply by noting overt behavior. It is possible to observe whether an unfeeling parent cruelly beats his child, openly neglects, scares, derides, and humiliates him. But such stark cruelty and rejection are not typical. The usual family muddles along with less harshness than this. Judging by many surveys, it is not just the exceptional home, but also the usual home, that produces persons with serious problems. Emotionally rejecting, unspoken attitudes are much harder to evaluate than actual physical abuse or neglect.

Anna Freud (1955), in a warning against loose usage of the concept of rejection, notes that no matter how devoted a mother might be, she cannot meet all the boundless demands made by a child. She is speaking here about young children, but the same principle no doubt also applies to adolescents and their parents.

The influence of peers

Although parents obviously play an important role in the development of adolescents, it should also be noted that, in the United States, several investigators of youth subcultures have emphasized that peers may have a greater influence than parents in many areas (Coleman, 1961; Munns, 1972). Munns (1972) had a group of male adolescents rate themselves, their peers, their mothers, and their fathers on the Allport-Vernon Lindzey Study of Values Scale, a scale designed to measure the values persons embrace in economic, aesthetic, social, political, theoretic, and religious areas. The male adolescents in this group reported values that were more similar to those of their peers than those of their parents. In another study Brittain (1969) found that urban adolescents were more in accord with their peers than with their parents in matters of dress and dating. Thus, the peer culture may decrease the influence of the parents in many areas. However, it should also be noted that adolescents' relationships with their peers are affected by their past and present relationships with their parents. For example, when adolescents have parents with strong traditional values, they apparently are better able to resist the potential negative aspects of the peer group (Coles, 1975). Also, adolescents may select peer groups that are similar to their parents and that reinforce parental values.

Increased awareness of family characteristics and circumstances

To a greater extent than in their earlier years, preadolescents and adolescents become aware of, and sensitive to, conditions in the home and characteristics of the family that might affect their own pride and prestige: the physical appearance of their parents and siblings; the condition of the furniture; the habits and manners of their parents and brothers and sisters;

and the social and economic status of the family. Some adolescents show a strong reformist spirit, especially if they are ambitious and eager to have their family (and themselves) look well in the eyes of others: father should not laugh so loudly at his own jokes; mother should be more tidy; sister Mary should improve her mind instead of reading movie magazines.

The impulse to reform, although it is not displayed by all adolescents, may be so strong for a time that youngsters are hard to live with. This is especially so if the youngsters' criticisms touch on matters concerning which the parents or other members of the family already feel inferior or defensive. This impulse to reform, sometimes extending to asceticism, may also be a reaction to the adolescents' awareness of unacceptable feelings or thoughts in themselves; it helps them to rid themselves of these thoughts or feelings by reforming those on whom the thoughts or feelings may be projected.

Views regarding the roles of father and mother

Several investigators have reported that youngsters and adolescents perceive their mothers as being more nurturant—more actively concerned about their offspring's development and well-being—than their fathers (Dahlem, 1970; Kagan and Lemkin, 1960). Both male and female adolescents reported that their mothers exert more influence than their fathers, reflecting perhaps the greater role of the mother in the child-rearing process (Stinnett et al., 1974). On the other hand, findings reported by Stinnett et al. (1974) indicate that females, as compared with males, more often report receiving praise and affection from their fathers. One wonders if this is related to the fact that it is more socially acceptable for a father to express affection to a daughter than to a son.[1]

Additional findings suggest that parents react differently to sons and daughters (Rothbart and Maccoby, 1966). Although it does appear that youngsters perceive their mothers to be more affectionate than their fathers (Dahlem, 1970; Kagan and Lemkin, 1960; Stinnett et al., 1974), there is the suggestion that the opposite-sex parent is viewed as more lenient than the same-sex parent. In a study by Lambert et al. (1971), it was reported that fathers more often took the point of view of and were more permissive with girls than with boys, whereas mothers more often took the side of and were more permissive with boys than girls. To quote Martin (1975), "Oedipus and Electra are alive and doing reasonably well in the family picture. Of course, a less psychoanalytic explanation in terms of parents conforming to

[1] It may be that father-daughter affectional bonds are closer than father-son bonds from very early in childhood.

culturally prescribed role-expectations about their relationships with their sons and daughters might apply equally well [p. 525]."

LaVoie and Looft (1973) attempted to explore some of the linkages between parental characteristics and resistance to temptation by males. The adolescents were left alone in a room for a half hour and their handling of prohibited objects (deviation behavior) was recorded. In this study it appeared that maternal warmth and dominance were found to be positively related to the sons' resisting temptation but no such relationship was found with reference to fathers' characteristics. It was also found that maternal, but not paternal, communicativeness was positively related to their sons' ability to resist temptation. There is the suggestion in these data that mothers play a more important role than fathers in the acquisition of self-control by adolescent boys. The authors speculate that since the father is absent during most of the day, the adolescent must attend for the most part to the wishes of the mother. The father's role may be restricted, according to these authors, to one of inculcation through instruction or as a role model in some, but not all, situations. Moreover, the mother may discuss the implications of the adolescent's transgressions with her son more often than the father does. Of course, in some families the adolescent is also absent during most of the day.

An inability of fathers to assert themselves and a low level of communicativeness in mothers have also been found to be related to lack of control and deviant behavior in preadolescents and adolescents (Alkire, 1972; LaVoie, 1973). According to Hetherington and McIntyre (1975), mothers play a more significant role than fathers in their sons' acquisition of self-control. The greater involvement of the mother with her son and her greater communicativeness may play a role here (LaVoie, 1973; LaVoie and Looft, 1973).

Parental acts that annoy adolescents

Within the family circle many details of life are a potential source of annoyance to adolescents—and to parents. A large proportion of adolescent complaints against parents arise in connection with the young person's desire for independence and the wish to act and look grown–up.

In a study of conflicts between adolescents and their mothers, Block (1937) obtained responses from over five hundred junior and senior high school boys and girls to a list of fifty complaints. Among the complaints checked by the largest percentages (over 60 per cent of the adolescent boys and girls) were the following:

- Pesters me about my table manners
- Pesters me about my manners and habits

- Holds my sister or brother up to me as a model
- Scolds if my school marks are not as high as other people's
- Objects to my going automobile riding at night with boys
- Insists that I tell her what I spent my money for
- Won't let me use the car
- Insists that I eat foods that I dislike but that are good for me

The harassed parent

Even when the family situation is as good as human affairs permit, parents of adolescents face problems for which they have no good solution.

Changes in customs and manners and in economic conditions from one generation to the next mean that adolescents are likely to demand privileges and rights their parents did not demand in their youth. But this difference between the generations accounts for only a small portion of the problems that beset parents.

When parents worry, for example, about hazards connected with adolescents and the automobile, accident statistics indicate that such worry is to a large degree well founded. More than that, grounds for worry come right to their own and neighboring homes. A father whose son had just completed the teen years reported that every teenage boy within his own and his son's acquaintance had had a mishap with automobiles, ranging from arrests for speeding and reckless driving to minor or serious smashups and collisions. In the area of sex, statistics regarding illegitimate births and the high incidence of marital difficulties among those who marry in their teens all proclaim that parents have reasonable grounds for concern. Similarly, the high percentage of adolescents who use legal and illegal drugs give realistic cause for parental concern. When parents of adolescents worry, they may not be "Nervous Nellies" flying in the teeth of reality—they often worry about hazards that actually exist.

Yet, if parents could view the situation dispassionately, they often might realize that the adolescent who seems to be rejecting them by not following their advice and warnings actually may be struggling to grow up. The young person probably is not being unfeeling or cruel just for the sake of hurting the parents. If they could view the matter objectively, parents might even welcome seeming acts of rejection as a sign of healthy growth. But it is difficult for parents to be that objective, especially when they have tried for years, and are still trying, to give their child as much devotion as they can.

Many parents have a feeling of failure when their adolescent children are critical of them, get into scrapes, flounder, or seem to be bewildered, confused, or emotionally distressed.

Parental Feelings of Guilt

Any real or imagined "failure" in the upbringing of adolescents, or any mishap that befalls the adolescent, is likely also to stir up feelings of guilt in parents, especially if they have high standards for themselves and their offspring. Such guilt feelings are nurtured by much of what they read and hear about the responsibilities and shortcomings of parents. These feelings of guilt are reinforced by feelings of helplessness when parents face dilemmas that are almost impossible to resolve. When parents of adolescents let down their hair they can list many such dilemmas.[2] For instance, parents are told they should prevent late parties, early dating, early marriage, speeding, drinking, and sexual misconduct.

In rearing their adolescent children, parents not only face confused and frequently smug and guilt-provoking advice from experts, but they also frequently feel that they stand alone, with little or no moral support from anyone else.

In the opinion of the present writers, the lot of parents and adolescents would be much easier if all who pass judgment on them or make pronouncements about them would acknowledge and respect the multiplicity of factors that determine human behavior.

Reactivation of Parent's Unresolved Problems

A parent's anxiety about the problems that confront his or her adolescent son or daughter is intensified if these problems touch on unresolved problems of his or her own (Anthony, 1975). Probably every parent, to some degree, is vulnerable on this score. Adolescents face issues in the area of sex; so do a great many seemingly "well-adjusted" parents. Adolescents must make decisions with regard to the work they will do in adult life; many parents feel regret about, or dissatisfaction with, the occupational choices they made. It is important for an ambitious adolescent to prepare himself or herself to get ahead; in the parent population, there are vast numbers of persons who are vigorously competing and endlessly trying to get ahead. Adolescents of marriageable age must make choices as to the person they wish to marry; judging from divorce statistics and studies of marital discord, a large proportion of parents apparently have second thoughts as to whether they made the right choice.

[2] The senior author vividly recalls the roar of agreement voiced by a group of parents—all college graduates—when one parent exclaimed: "Nothing you do is right. You're damned if you do and damned if you don't."

Parents as confidants

Some parents succeed better than others in becoming the confidants of their children. In a study by Graves et al. (1974), a number of college men reported that when they were growing up their mothers listened to them when they returned from school. Boys and girls often find that they can confide more readily in their mothers than in their fathers, according to a study by LaVoie and Looft (1973). Perhaps this is related to the father's traditional role as family disciplinarian.

Children who feel free to confide in their parents, according to this study, showed better adjustment than those who do not confide—when adjustment is determined by such criteria as social compliance, emotional stability, desirable character traits, and obedience in the classroom. These findings suggest that the confider also tends to be a conformer. Moreover, there was also some evidence, but not conclusive evidence, that children who in school are rebels or unruly somewhat more often come from homes in which there was not a confiding relationship between the parent and the child.

Although it is valuable for an adolescent to have someone with whom to share his or her perplexities, it cannot always be assumed that people who confide the most about intimate matters will face the hurdles of adolescent development most successfully. The person who is confiding may be one who is depending to an undue degree on the parents and is prolonging his or her dependency on them.

Communication Difficulties

Parents of adolescents, in a study by Wakefield (1970), were able to predict the responses of their offspring to a problem check list in some areas, such as employment, better than in other areas, such as social relations. No evidence, however, is given by Wakefield's data to suggest that the adolescents' liking for their parents is related to their parents' awareness of their offsprings' specific problems, although it seems plausible that a relationship should exist.

In many situations it would be good if youngsters and parents alike could openly express their feelings to one another. But often it is difficult for them to do this. One reason is that an open avowal of feeling—a youngster's feeling, for example, that his parents are unfair—is likely to sound like an accusation. Children may fear losing their parents' love if they express their true feelings openly. A more important reason is that the feelings parents and their offspring have about one another often are mixed and unclear.

Several illustrations of this appeared in a study by Jersild et al. (1962) referred to earlier in this chapter. One woman felt as a child and as an adolescent that her mother basically disapproved of her. Disapproval usually causes resentment, but as a child and adolescent this person did not recognize resentment (which, later, as a young adult, she was able to detect). Instead, she felt unworthy and guilty, and she strove endlessly to win her mother's approval. Even if she had been able to tell about her guilt, her mother might not have been able to understand. The mother might have felt a wave of guilt herself, or perhaps annoyance. In such a situation it would be hard for either the daughter or the mother to talk freely and to get to the heart of the matter, although, in spite of this, after a painful scene or two, it is likely that the mother and daughter might be able to communicate more freely and establish a closer relationship.

In an experimental situation, LaVoie and Looft (1973) reported that the most frequent criticism of parental discipline expressed by adolescent boys occurred when the family imposed punishment without allowing the adolescent to present his view of the behavior in question.

THE VALUE OF AN "OUTSIDER'S" VIEW

When youngsters reach adolescence they and their parents have been swimming in the same emotional stream for so long that it is difficult for them to examine the stream. To ask them to do so is almost like asking a fish to get out of the water and examine the eddies and currents in its native pool. For this reason it is often more valuable for adolescents, and their parents as well, to confide in an outsider than to try to confide in one another.

The outsider may be a psychiatrist, psychologist, teacher, or counselor who has a gift for helping others. The outsider is not personally responsible; he or she is less likely to be threatened or to feel accused or guilty. He or she, if gifted with some understanding and properly trained, can help clarify confused feelings and bring them out into the open. An outsider may be far more able to help someone else than to help his or her own kin—much as doctors, it is said, can trust their hands to be steadier and can be more confident in their judgment when operating on a member of someone else's family.

Parental satisfactions

Although adolescence is a time that tries the souls of even the most doughty parents, it also brings great satisfactions when things go moderately well. Parents see a new creature unfolding before their eyes; yet this new creation retains fond and familiar traits of an earlier day. In the physical sphere alone it is fascinating to watch a child grow.

It is even more rewarding, although sometimes baffling, to take part in the drama that goes on when the young person more and more insistently claims the rights and privileges of a young adult and shows that his or her claims are justified. In spite of all the misgivings they have about what their adolescent offspring does when alone in the family car, parents in due time can sit back comfortably and let their (properly licensed) son or daughter do the driving. Parents, although concerned about dress, grooming, and achievements, can also get a thrill from an adolescent's becoming appearance and successes and may even turn to him or her for advice. It is gratifying when a son or daughter or both urge mother and father to take it easy and go on a vacation, or when the children tell their parents not to worry about clearing the snow from the driveway because they will do it. It is even more intensely gratifying when adolescents take decisions into their own hands and, in spite of parental misgivings, do a good job of it.

The process through which parents adapt themselves to the fact that their children are "grown up" is beset by many trials, but one must look far to find anything more heartwarming than the end product when all turns out well.

Varieties of parental attitudes and practices in child rearing

Various labels have been used to designate what seem to be the characteristic or predominant attitudes or patterns of behavior displayed by parents in rearing their children. We have already made reference to parental acceptance and rejection. In the old days, parents were often described as *strict* or *lenient.* In recent decades other terms have been used, such as *permissive, restrictive, democratic, dictatorial, authoritarian,* and *authoritative.*

These descriptive terms are convenient for research purposes. However, they usually designate a more-or-less, rather than an all-or-none, state of affairs. They may also conceal more than they reveal. One father described as strict may be a cold, self-righteous despot; another may be a firm disciplinarian, devoted to his children, who reproves or punishes more in sorrow than in anger. One parent may be quite consistently strict; another may be strict in some ways and not in others—for example, forbidding bad language but not forbidding his children to tease the neighbor's dog or younger children.

Partly by reason of varying connotations, varying contexts, and differences in the way children, even within the same family, respond to their parents, it seldom (if ever) is found that a certain type of parent invariably produces a certain type of offspring. Rather, qualifying modifiers must be used, such as "It is *more likely* that," or "It occurs *more often* that" children eventually will adopt as their own or internalize rules of conduct if their parents firmly, but democratically, give reasons for the rules they want to apply and, in a spirit of give and take, listen to, and make allowance for, their children's reasons in the matter, than if the parents apply rules in an arbitrary fashion.

According to studies by Baumrind (1966, 1968, 1975), *permissive* mothers use reasoning and provide the adolescent with explanations for family rules but place few limits on the actual behavior of the adolescent. In presenting herself as a resource person for her child, the mother takes great care to avoid the use of power-assertive control. Moreover, few demands are made on the child to assume responsibility for household chores. The *authoritarian* parent, as described by Baumrind (1968), uses power-assertive techniques of control (for instance, physical punishment and deprivation of privileges). An attempt is made to mold the behavior of the offspring to conform to a fixed standard of conduct. In contrast, the *authoritative* parent in Baumrind's account seeks to provide the child with reasons for the required behavior. In enforcing these demands the parent uses a firm, consistent, and rational approach. Although authoritative parents, in this account, regard obedience to adult requirements as necessary, they still value independence in their offspring. Authoritative parents, in addition to providing the child with the rationale behind their rules and regulations, expect and reward verbal give and take. While recognizing their own self-interest, the mother or father is also aware of the unique qualities and interests of the child. In short, the authoritative parent uses both reason and power in socializing the child.

The findings of Baumrind's studies suggest that the *patterns* of parental characteristics are reflected in their offsprings' characteristics. In two studies of young children, Baumrind (1967, 1971) reported that children of permissive or authoritative parents tended to be more responsible, and achievement-oriented than children of authoritarian parents.

Having reviewed the literature in the areas of normal, as well as abnormal, development, the present writers believe that the evidence presently available lends support to Baumrind's position that "Authoritative control can achieve responsible conformity with group standards without loss of individual autonomy or self-assertiveness [1975, p. 141]." It is essential to note Baumrind's distinction between authoritative (firm, but not overly restrictive, control) and authoritarian (restrictive) control. Restrictive discipline may result in irresponsible, passive, and submissive behavior. Baumrind (1966) further speculates that controls of an authoritarian nature, and permissive noncontrol "may both shield the child from the opportunity to engage in vigorous interaction with people [p. 904]."

In a study of children somewhat older than those in Baumrind's investigation, and including young adults, Allaman et al. (1972) suggest that harsh parental practices are likely to be associated with lack of independence and individuality in the offspring. Several investigators have found that excessive parental use of power-assertive discipline (physical punishment and deprivation of privileges) is often associated with aggression in delinquent males (Bandura and Walters, 1959; Hetherington et al., 1971) as well as in delinquent adolescent females (Hetherington et al., 1971). Martin (1975) has suggested that aggression by the adolescent toward the parent may result in further aggression expressed by the parent. On the other hand, parents of delinquents have also been found to be lax and inconsistent (Glueck and Glueck, 1950; McCord et al., 1959).

With the emergence of the period of formal operational thinking, adolescents have the capacity to begin to critically evaluate parental directives and to become aware of alternatives. Parents are then placed in the position of having to defend their points of view on rational grounds. With this in view, Baumrind (1975) expresses the opinion that although parents do not have to relinquish their authoritative role, they will find that the use of power in adolescence is ineffectual. "She [mother] makes limited use of power to settle parent-child divergences, and then primarily to guard her personal interests or to break a stalemate when the adolescent's objection is based, not on principle, but on pique [p. 143]." At this time during their lives, adolescents need someone to listen to as well as argue with. "The authoritative parent can state and defend her own thesis vigorously, and yet not limit the freedom of the adolescent to express and argue for his antithesis [p. 143]."

In a study of Swedish adolescents, Pikas (1961) reported that rational authority (authority in which rational concern for the welfare of the child is expressed) was accepted by adolescents, whereas inhibiting authority (authority based on the need to exploit) was rejected by the adolescents.

In a study of seventh- through twelfth-graders from unbroken homes, Elder (1963) examined levels of parental power based on adolescent ratings of parental behavior and the adolescents' wish to model their behavior after their parents as well as to maintain relationships with peers approved of by their parents. Three types of parental power structures were identified: autocratic, democratic, and permissive. The parents described as permissive allowed their adolescents to have more influence than the parents themselves had in decision making, whereas the parents described as democratic made the final decisions even though the adolescents were encouraged to participate in the discussions of relevant issues. On the other hand, the parents labeled as autocratic did not permit their adolescents to present their viewpoints regarding their own behavior or to participate in regulating their own behavior. Acceptance of parental behavior as a model for their own behavior was found to be higher among offspring of parents described as democratic than among either permissive or authoritarian parents. Moreover, the findings suggest that there is a greater likelihood that adolescents will view their parents' behavior as a model as well as form relationships with peers approved by the parents when the parents are perceived by the adolescents as frequently explaining their rules and presenting the rationale for their behavior. As might be predicted, there was a greater tendency for boys to model their behavior after their fathers and girls to model their behavior after their mothers, regardless of parental child-rearing techniques or frequency of explanation.

Several investigators (Aronfreed, 1968; Cheyne, 1971) have reported that when the rules are clearly explained and the consequences of the behavior are mentioned, there is less deviation from the rules.

Outgrowing childhood dependency on parents

Adolescents and young adults are in the process of achieving independence in a practical way when they strike off on their own, establish their own living quarters, begin their careers, and earn their own keep.

Outgrowing psychological dependency is more complex. The roots of psychological dependency run deep. Often they have hidden or unconscious elements. Adults may be financially self-supporting (and even support their parents) and yet be subservient to their parents in childish ways. Such dependency may prevail even when they go out of their way to defy their parents. They probably would not need to be defiant if they were not still struggling, perhaps blindly, against parental domination. This particular type of defensiveness is called reaction formation.

It should be noted that emancipation from one's parents is not the same as repudiation of them (although, in the struggle to take command of their own affairs, many young people go through a phase of repudiating their parents). Individuals who are thoroughly emancipated can feel affection for their parents, cherish worthy ideals they have been taught, and heed the commandment "Honor thy father and thy mother." The essential element in emancipation is the freedom, desire, and ability to take responsibility for one's thoughts, feelings, moral judgments, and practical decisions. Emancipated individuals may seek advice from their parents, but they will not allow their parents to dictate their decisions. They respect their parents' moral values, but they measure what is right and wrong by their own convictions and not simply in terms of what they think their parents will approve or disapprove.

When adolescents strive to achieve independence and emancipation from their parents, they are gradually but drastically reversing a pattern of behavior they showed in their infancy. Infants cling to their parents, they desire to have them close at hand, and during a stage of infancy, babies cry when their mothers leave them alone. At a later stage, they protest when parents go for an outing, leaving the youngsters in the care of others. One of the most common and most severe fears of young children is fear of separation from parents. But in adolescence, the children who once were afraid their parents might abandon *them,* now, in effect, set out to abandon their parents, although with some hesitation and occasional retreats into increased dependence.

Steps Toward Independence

When conditions are favorable, youngsters can make important strides toward independence during preadolescent years, such as getting part-time jobs through their own initiative; taking complete responsibility for spending or saving the money they earn; pursuing interests and hobbies of their own even though these are quite different from the interests of their parents; or deciding to go to summer camp (if their parents can afford it) even though they anticipate spells of homesickness. A decrease with age in dependency was noted in a study of ten- to twelve-year-olds (Golightly et al., 1970), but the process of relinquishing dependent behavior usually continues throughout several ensuing years. Gold and Douvan (1969) found a shift toward greater autonomy with increasing age during the teens in areas such as dating and employment on the part of adolescent girls. These findings were replicated with a different sample of both male and female adolescents. Although a shift toward greater autonomy occurred in all areas, the shift in dating was the largest. (See Table 12.1.)

On a more subtle level, preadolescent and adolescent youngsters are moving toward independence when they are free to raise questions about their parents without regarding such questioning as disloyal, or feeling guilty about it.

Gradually, changes occur during adolescence in what has been called emotional autonomy—that is, greater independence from the family. Gold and Douvan (1969) believe that emotional autonomy is more difficult to achieve than behavioral autonomy (such as holding jobs and having money). Changes with age in several aspects of emotional autonomy appear in Table 12.2.

While some growth toward greater independence occurs in many of the areas listed in Table 12.2, over all the differences between the younger

Table 12.1. Indices of behavioral autonomy for girls at eleven and eighteen and for boys and girls aged fourteen to sixteen

Item	Change in girls from 11–18		Girls 14–16 (N = 822) (in %)	Boys 14–16 (N = 1045) (in %)
	(N = 206) from (in %)	(N = 148) to (in %)		
1. S dates or goes steady	4	94	72	59
2. S has a job outside home	34	60	56	47
3. S has some independent funds	63	84	74	
4. S spends most of free time with				
a. friends	22	46	32	
b. family	68	44	56	

Note: The data for boys are incomplete because some questions asked in the study of girls were not included in the boys' study.
Source: From *Adolescent development: Readings in research and theory* by M. Gold and E. Douvan. Boston, Allyn and Bacon, 1969, p. 132. Reprinted by permission.

and older adolescents are not outstanding. Even at the age of eighteen, the girls were found to be quite family-oriented and compliant. A large proportion of the oldest adolescents selected adult ideals from within the family. In response to a projective questionnaire, these same adolescents indicated that they would give up a job and come home at the request of their parents if necessary.

Although the findings are not consistent, research generally suggests that there is greater dependency in females than in males and that girls may receive more encouragement than boys to be emotionally dependent. Furthermore, adults may be more tolerant of the expression of dependency in females (Hartup, 1965; Kagan and Moss, 1960).

Theoretical Models of Parental Behavior and Their Relation to Adolescent Independence

What are the ways in which different aspects of parental behavior might affect the adolescent's striving for emotional growth? Some areas that have been investigated in some depth are those of parental discipline and control and parental warmth and affection.[3]

[3] Attempts have been made to account for the manner in which different aspects of parental behavior are related to each other. One method of analyzing the relations between various parent behaviors in an attempt to simplify the understanding of relations is called factor analysis (Becker, 1964).

Table 12.2. Indices of emotional autonomy for girls at eleven and eighteen and for boys and girls aged fourteen to sixteen

Item	Change in girls from 11–18		Girls 14–16 (N = 822) (in %)	Boys 14–16 (N = 1045) (in %)
	(N = 206) from (in %)	(N = 148) to (in %)		
1. S thinks friendship can be as close as family relationship	53	71	61	42
2. S disagrees with parents about:				
a. Ideas	12	46	34	
b. More than one issue out of six	54	59	56	
3. S would take advice of friends on more than one issue out of six				29
4. S chooses adult ideal				
a. outside the family	22	48	38	36
b. within the family	66	52	55	45
5. Projective: Response to request from lonely mother to give up good job and return to hometown				
a. reject request	8	26	18	
b. comply, conditionally comply	78	59	66	
6. Projective: Response to parental restriction				
a. accept, reassure parents	51	38	36	
7. Projective: Response to conflict between parent-peer pressure				
a. parent oriented	78	61	63	
8. S chooses as confidante				
a. friend	5	33	26	
b. one, both parents	67	36	45	
9. Part in rule making				
a. S has some part	45	64	58	
10. Attitude toward parental rules				
a. Right, good, fair	47	56	56	

Note: The data for boys are incomplete because some questions asked in the study of girls were not included in the boys' study.

Source: From *Adolescent development: Readings in research and theory* by M. Gold and E. Douvan, Boston, Allyn and Bacon, 1969, p. 134. Reprinted by permission.

THEORETICAL MODEL OF PARENTAL BEHAVIOR

As shown in Figure 12.1, instead of considering a variety of aspects of parental behavior, one might think of two dimensions of behavior: Love versus Hostility and Control versus Autonomy.

Examination of Figure 12.1 indicates that a cooperative mother can be conceived of as loving and autonomy granting, whereas a possessive

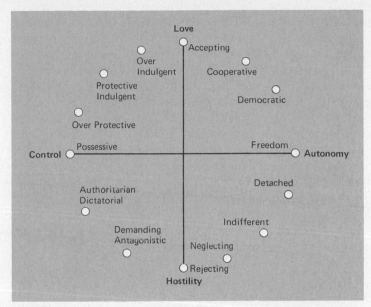

Figure 12.1. Maternal behavior. [From "A circumplex model for maternal behavior" by E. S. Schaefer, *Journal of Abnormal Social Psychology*, 1959, 59, 226–235. Copyright 1959 by the American Psychological Association. Reprinted by permission.]

mother may be regarded as loving and controlling. Schaefer (1959, 1961), using factor analytic techniques, developed the model presented in Figure 12.1 to describe parents with varying approaches to child-rearing. Parental behavior could then be viewed in terms of different combinations of two-dimensional concepts. The warm end of the warmth-versus-hostility dimension has been defined in a number of ways: as "accepting, affectionate, approving, understanding, child-centered, frequent use of explanations, positive response to dependency behavior, high use of reasons in discipline, high use of praise in discipline, low use of physical punishment, and (for mothers) low criticism of husband. The hostility end of the dimension would be defined by the opposite characteristics [Becker, 1964, p. 174]."

PARENTAL CHARACTERISTICS AND ATTITUDES AS RELATED TO DEVELOPMENT OF ADOLESCENT INDEPENDENCE

In general, adolescents who have warm, supportive parents are in better positions to accept responsibility for their actions and in general feel better about themselves. The nonaccepting parents tend to be extremely critical of their offspring, do not enjoy being with the adolescent, and have difficulty viewing things from the adolescent's point of view. McCord et al. (1962) found a higher percentage of rejecting parents among highly dependent boys than among moderately (within the normal range) dependent boys. Adolescents growing up in an environment characterized by hostility are more likely than other adolescents to develop difficulties in achieving independence as well as in other areas, including cognitive functioning, peer relations, and deviant behavior (Baumrind, 1975; Hetherington et al., 1971; Weiner, 1970).

In contrast to the restrictive parent, the permissive parent has difficulty setting limits for the adolescent in a firm and consistent manner and may indeed give in to nearly all his or her demands, reasonable or not. According to Trautner (1972), there is a decrease with age in the tendency of adolescents to respond to parental wishes in order to avoid punishment rather than in order to obtain parental love.

In a cross-cultural survey of high school students in America and Denmark, Kandel and Lesser (1972) examined the degree of independence apparently displayed by adolescents in these countries and the extent to which the family promoted the growth of independence in their adolescent children.

According to the findings, Danish parents are more democratic than American parents in dealing with adolescents. Not only does it appear that Danish parents enter into more extensive communication with their adolescents, but also that the Danish adolescents feel less inhibited in discussing their personal problems with their parents. But in both countries the data indicate that large numbers of adolescents maintain close relationships with their parents—feel close to their parents—and express the wish to be like them in many or most ways.

The data also suggest that adolescents in the United States conform to parental rules when specific rules exist, whereas in Denmark the greatest amount of conformity exists in the absence of rules. These findings suggest that Danish adolescents, to a greater extent than Americans, have internalized parental rules and regulations at an early age, whereas a number of American adolescents appear to need external constraints if they are to refrain from engaging in disapproved of behavior.

It may also be, as Kandel and Lesser propose, that the different socialization patterns manifested by these individuals during adolescence merely reflect differing antecedent socialization experiences. Kandel and Lesser (1969) suggest that the American parent perhaps may not adequately limit the behavior of the child early in life, whereas the Danish parent seems to exercise great control in childhood, resulting in greater self-direction in adolescence. Further research is needed into the question of cultural differences in the establishment of controls.

Table 12.3 presents data relating to family patterns and adolescents' reported feelings of independence. Examination of Table 12.3 indicates that adolescents whose parents are described as using a democratic approach, in

Table 12.3. Feelings of independence by joint parental authority pattern and country

% Adolescents	United States Joint Parental Authority			Denmark Joint Parental Authority		
	Authoritarian (in %)	Democratic (in %)	Permissive (in %)	Authoritarian (in %)	Democratic (in %)	Permissive (in %)
Who feel both parents give them enough freedom	58	82	68	60	88	78
Total N	(239)	(164)	(76)	(83)	(345)	(120)
Who feel parents should treat them more like adults	63	44	64	46	21	39
Total N	(201)	(133)	(63)	(59)	(276)	(105)

Note: Chi-square differences within countries significant at .001.

Source: From "Parent-adolescent relationships and adolescent independence in the United States and Denmark," by D. Kandel and G. S. Lesser, *Journal of Marriage and the Family*, 1969, 31, 348–358. Copyright 1969 by National Council on Family Relations. Reprinted by permission.

which the adolescents and parents participate together in the decision-making process, are more likely to feel independent than adolescents of permissive and authoritarian parents. The high rate of adolescents with permissive parents who report they are not being treated as adults may be related, according to the investigators, to the child's interpreting parental permissiveness as a sign of parental disinterest (Kandel and Lesser, 1969).

On the basis of a review of the literature on parent-child relations and independence among youngsters of various ages, Martin (1975) concluded that "the most convincing evidence at this time indicates that independent behavior is associated with a pattern of parent-child interaction in which the parent demands age-appropriate behavior, enforces rules firmly and consistently; encourages, listens to, and is occasionally influenced by communications from the child; and provides a generous measure of affection and approval [p. 508]."

Continuation of Dependence Beyond the Teens

The struggle for self-determination is still going on in the lives of many young people after they have finished high school and have gone on to college or a job.

Lloyd (1952) indicates, on the basis of a study of about 1,000 students belonging to five colleges in a southern state, that a large number had failed to attain emotional emancipation from their parents. In comparing college students who identified with their parents' religious denomination with those who did not, Dodrill (1974) reported that the latter showed greater tendencies to independent thinking.

How far a person of college age has gone toward achieving emancipation will depend, of course, on how strictly we define *emancipation.* The criteria of being a free and self-determining person could be made so stringent that hardly any adult at any age could be regarded as having become emancipated from his or her parents. At any rate, according to the criteria used in the findings cited here, many young adults are not completely emancipated.

ACQUIRING REALISTIC IMAGES OF PARENTS

As already noted, over the years youngsters build conceptions of their parents, their standards, and their expectations. These conceptions are realistic to the extent that the children see their parents as they are. But the image is distorted if the children misperceive parents because of the children's own needs and limited understanding. The children may perceive them as more perfect than they ever could be, as holding higher standards for them than they do, or as being more disapproving than they actually are.

Young people have taken a long stride toward independence when they are able to acquire an increasingly realistic perception of their parents.

As indicated in Chapter 2, there is an intricate relationship between a person's image of his or her parents and his or her self-image and between attitudes toward parents and attitudes toward self. As a consequence, anything that leads a person to examine, or to change, one dimension of this relationship is likely to lead to examination and change in the other.

CHANGING THE MODEL

In striving to achieve emancipation, some youngsters for a time renounce their parents as models and choose entirely new models. It is as though these adolescents were leaving mom and dad to run away with someone else. This, on the surface, seems like gross unfaithfulness. But it is part of the drama of growing up.

Many adolescents go through a process of re-evaluation of their parents as well as other adults. But their new cognitive abilities may sometimes lead them to judge their parents and other adults rather harshly (Scarlett, 1975). Illustrative of this is Anne Frank's illuminating comment in the *Diary of Anne Frank*: "Why do grownups quarrel so easily, so much, and over the most idiotic things: . . . I'm simply amazed again and again over their awful manners and especially . . . stupidity [Scarlett, 1975, p. 73]."

CHANGING THE PRIMARY OBJECTS OF LOVE

The parents, from whom young people must seek to become independent, were also (in most instances) the first objects of the adolescent's love. To realize their potentialities as adults, young people must change the primary objects of their love and attention—from parents to prospective mates, and ultimately, if they marry, to the spouse. Later, their love must also embrace their children.

Difficulties Parents Face in "Letting Go"

Adolescent emancipation is not simply an issue facing the son or daughter; it is also frequently a problem for parents. Some parents find it difficult to let go of a child. Ever since the youngster was an infant they have had him or her in their care. The habit of watching over the child is strong. It is especially hard for parents to let go of an offspring in adolescence if they have not gotten into the habit of gradually allowing the youngster to have more and more freedom and self-determination.

There are other circumstances that may make it hard for a parent to let a child "grow up." A mother who has given her all for her children may become anxious at the prospect of being without a mission in life. This may lead to the "empty nest" syndrome, a depressive syndrome seen in some mothers whose children have left home. Parents who have lived their lives through their children—by proxy, so to speak—seeking through them to achieve pleasures they have never enjoyed or ambitions they never realized may be very troubled when their offspring want to go on their own way.

A parent who has leaned on his or her children for emotional support, using them as though they were as much *his* or *her* parents as he or she theirs, may feel insecure and abandoned at the thought that the offspring are now moving on into other relationships. Again, parents who have not been realistic in facing the fact that they are getting older may feel threatened by the reminders of age that come when their own children are becoming adults and want to enjoy the privileges of adults.

METHODS OF MAINTAINING
PARENTAL DOMINATION

There are many ways parents who are unwilling to let an adolescent son or daughter grow up can try to keep a hold on the young person. One way is to be very forbidding, denying adolescents the right to meet persons of the opposite sex, or the right to venture out on their own, or the right to go out and earn money. Another way is to appeal to the gratitude and loyalty of the offspring, making the child feel guilty: I have done so much for you, now you must stay near me and do things for me. Still another method is to belittle, to try to undermine, the young person's confidence in his or her ability to do for himself or herself. Yet another technique is to overwhelm youngsters with gifts and with help, doing everything for them and thereby implying (although perhaps not consciously) that they really cannot do much for themselves.

Mothers' assessments of the behavior of their offspring

Some differences between the problems mothers attribute to boys as compared with girls were found in a study by Tuddenham et al. (1974). The items showing generally small, but consistent, sex differences between characterizations of boys and girls appear in Table 12.4. As shown in the table, boys were characterized as being vigorous, restless, and competitive more often than girls. Girls, on the other hand, were more often depicted as being neat, fussy, noncompetitive, and sensitive.

Furthermore, boys were described more often than girls as manifesting antisocial behavior. "They lie more often, take things, break things, and bully others. They show off, but they hide feelings and ward off affection [Tuddenham et al., 1974, p. 962]." In contrast, girls are viewed as more dependable and mature. However, tension may be expressed more often by girls in fearfulness or nailbiting.

The postadolescent reassessment of parents

While achieving independence, many adolescents have a less favorable image of their parents than they had before; however, in the end, if all goes well, they see them more kindly as well as more realistically. In many instances this does not occur until some years beyond the adolescent period. Mark Twain is reported to have said that when he was a boy of fourteen his father was so stupid he could scarcely stand to have the old man around, but by the time he got to be twenty-one Twain was astonished at how much his father had learned in the last seven years.

In a study by Jersild et al. (1962), previously mentioned, it was noted that a large proportion of older persons claimed that they had changed or modified the perceptions that they had earlier had of their parents. A girl who idealized her father, regarding him as a far more worthy creature than her mother, later became convinced that her mother actually was a more heroic character. She remembered, belatedly, that it was through her mother's efforts that the family remained financially solvent, and that it was

Table 12.4. Mothers' reports of behavior of ten-year-olds: items showing consistent sex differences in four ethnic groups

	Items More Characteristic of Boys	Per cent Difference on			Items More Characteristic of Girls	Per cent Difference on	
No.	Item	"True" (Boys > Girls)	"Not true" (Girls > Boys)	No.	Item	"True" (Girls > Boys)	"Not true" (Boys > Girls)
96.	Likes to tease others	13.1	16.1	100.	Fussy about clothes	17.5	16.3
21.	Hates to sit still, restless	11.3	13.5	40.	Tries to keep things neat	13.5	13.8
12.	Hungry all of the time	10.6	10.6	99.	Hates to get dirty	11.3	14.2
23.	Likes vigorous exercise—athletics	11.8	7.9	22.	Likes quiet activities—reading or watching TV	10.1	10.6
77.	Has temper explosions—hits, kicks, or throws things	9.1	11.3	45.	Takes good care of smaller children	13.6	5.0
10.	Still wets the bed occasionally	9.0	9.2	80.	Doesn't mind losing in a game	8.3	10.3
75.	Flares up over nothing—gets mad easily	8.6	11.3	88.	Acts older than he/she is	10.4	7.0
57.	Is a "daredevil"; wants to do things that are dangerous	8.5	10.2	53.	Feelings get hurt easily	8.4	7.3
81.	Has to be the "winner"; hates to lose in any game	7.3	9.4	89.	Gives in to other children	7.4	4.8
37.	Messes up the house a lot	6.5	8.2	49.	Dislikes being left home when parents go out	6.7	7.2
51.	Hates to ask for help	6.0	6.6				

Note. Listed items show a consistent sex difference in all ethnic groups, a sex difference significant at the .01 level for ethnic groups combined, and an absolute difference of at least 5% in six or more of the eight possible sub-group comparisons, i.e., four ethnic groups on "true" response and four ethnic groups on "not true" response.
Source: From "Mothers' reports of behavior of ten-year-olds: relationships with sex, ethnicity and mother's education" by R. D. Tuddenham, J. Brooks, and L. Milkovich, *Developmental Psychology,* 1974, **10,** 959–995. Copyright 1974 by the American Psychological Association. Reprinted by permission.

the mother who was the more devoted parent, insisting, for example, on wearing the same winter coat year after year so that more of the family budget could be devoted to the other members of the family. A man who as a youth thought that his choice of a vocation deeply disappointed his father, some years later was surprised and relieved to discover that his father regarded the choice very favorably and for years had felt proud of his son. A son who, as an adolescent, viewed his father as a forbidding and unloving person, later changed his view. It was his father, he remembered, who had assumed the major responsibility of being the family disciplinarian. As in a revelation, he then also remembered that when he was a child it was his father, never his mother, who kissed him and his siblings goodnight.

Socioeconomic status and child rearing

Several studies have shown that middle-class parents as compared with parents of low socioeconomic status exhibit more warmth to their children, whereas parents of low socioeconomic status are more likely to use power-assertive techniques of discipline such as deprivation of privileges and physical punishment (Bronfenbrenner, 1958; Minton et al., 1971; Radin, 1972). Moreover, as Martin (1975) points out, recent studies show that middle-class mothers tend to verbalize more to their children when they are young. It is understandable that a parent of low socioeconomic status, perhaps harassed by worries about money, poor housing, and the like, might be more peremptory in dealing with children.

The abused child or adolescent

Extreme forms of parental abuse occurring at any given point during childhood or adolescence may have lasting and tragic effects.

Child abuse may be considered a pattern of disturbed parent-child relationship, rather than defined as a particular type of named psychiatric disorder. In 1972 there were 19 million children in the United States below the age of eighteen; out of that group there could be anticipated approximately 600,000 cases of child abuse reported to the authorities. This probably represents only a part of the total number of active cases (Saad, 1975). It is unclear what percentage of abused children are adolescents, but most abused children are quite young, as younger children are more vulnerable and unable to protect themselves and generate more psychological conflicts within the parents. According to Steele (1975), a small number (about 10 per cent) of abusive parents do show evidence of serious psychiatric disturbance, which often must be treated before the pattern of child abuse becomes accessible to change. Many authorities believe the percentage of seriously disturbed parents to be much higher. Although child abuse is seen at all socioeconomic levels and in all ethnic groups, environmental deprivation and stress certainly play a role in many cases of child abuse. Gregg and Elmer (1969) found that abusive parents came from lower socioeconomic backgrounds more often than nonabusive parents and were less able to provide proper health care for their children.

Many people, of course, face crises without becoming abusive in dealing with their children. In some people with poor impulse control, feelings of aggression and anger can be displaced from other situations or people onto children, with an acting out of the aggressive impulses (Bennie and Sclare, 1969). In such cases it is often appropriate to remove the child from the parents' care, at least for a short time. In almost all cases of abuse, it is found that the parents were themselves abused when they were children, and they have carried on this behavior through identification with their abusive parents. Because of the early origins of abusive behavior, treatment tends to be difficult and lengthy, although some workers have experimented with short-term treatment techniques.

Abuse and neglect may be either physical, emotional, or both (Fontana, 1971). Abusive parents find it extremely difficult to give love to their children (lack of mothering ability) and are often involved with the children in a battle for control. Discipline is difficult for such parents to achieve, and physical coercion and fear of physical punishment are frequently used as disciplinary measures. Of course, there are many nonabusive parents who also use such means of discipline. Abused children (and their parents) have difficulty trusting people and getting close to others and tend to have feelings of low self-esteem. Severe, repeated criticism is common in such families, and severe physical punishment results in the injuries seen commonly in child-abuse cases. Excessive demands are often made on the child, and when these are not satisfied abusive techniques are resorted to in an attempt at changing the child's behavior. There is also in American culture the idea that "punishment builds character," which is probably untrue but gives sanction to some of the feelings and rationalizations of abusive parents.

In addition to the traits noted here, abusive parents tend to be immature and dependent, looking to external authority as a guide, rather than having the inner strength to think for themselves. Or rebellion against society may occur, but with the same immaturity and dependence present beneath the surface. It is hard for such people to enjoy themselves or their relations with their children, and they often have a minimal amount of social life. One goal of treatment of such parents is to try to help them find some gratification in life and to overcome their difficulty in relating to other people.

That there is now greater concern with this problem than ever before is indicated by the fact that it is mandatory to report cases of child abuse in every state (Fontana, 1971). Another specific area of concern is that of subtle, unnoticed brain damage resulting from physical abuse, which may also lessen the child's ability to mature in a healthy fashion. Many abused children will probably, as already implied, become child abusers when they are parents, and this generational transmission of patterns of abuse is a main facet of the problem. There may also be a causal connection between child abuse and later juvenile delinquency (Button, 1973).

The changing role of the family

Since the 1900s family life in our society has changed dramatically. Extended families (including grandparents, uncles, aunts, and cousins) were far more common in the past than today, and nuclear families (children and their parents) more often had relatives who lived in the neighborhood. This often resulted, during earlier decades, in adolescents having greater exposure to a larger number of individuals of varying ages (Demos, 1970). Not only were adolescents exposed to a variety of relatives of varying ages, but they were familiar with most adults in the neighborhood in which they lived. Bronfenbrenner (1970) points out the advantages and disadvantages of this situation: "If you walked on the railroad trestle, the phone would ring at your house, and your parents would know what you had done before you got back home. People on the street would tell you to button your jacket and ask why you were not in church last Sunday. Sometimes you liked it and sometimes you didn't—but at least people *cared* [p. 96]."

Most present-day adolescents are living in an environment that differs from this. As a result of urbanization, the extended family has been reduced to a nuclear one with one or two adults, and most neighborhoods no longer serve the functions they did in the past. As a consequence, adolescents have been restricted, to a large extent, from having contact with a wide variety of adults.

Among the factors that have led to the relative isolation of adolescents from adults are occupational mobility, consolidated school districts, the disappearance to some extent of a close-knit neighborhood, and different patterns of social life in groups that differ in age. Coles (as cited in Woodward and Malamud, 1975) has pointed out that the stresses that plague lower-class family life are also prevalent among middle-class suburban families: "Fathers are moved around by corporations, mothers and kids cannot strike deep roots, conversations with grandparents are confined to three minutes at the reduced, Sunday-night rate [p. 53]."

Within the family itself changes have also occurred. According to Bronfenbrenner (1970), adolescents spend less time with their parents than they did years ago. Frequently, the adolescent leaves home early in the morning and does not return home until dinner time. Mothers are frequently not home because of social obligations or because they are engaged in part- or full-time work. Indeed, Condry et al. (as cited by Bronfenbrenner, 1970) reported that sixth-graders spent only two to three hours a day with their parents on the weekend. On the basis of research by Stinnett et al. (1974), this situation seems to be magnified for male, as compared with female, high school students. As far as the mother is concerned, many of the activities she engages in with her daughter are activities in which she would be involved under any circumstances; her daughter's participation does not require any extra effort on her part.

In a reinterpretation of data derived from a survey of child-rearing practices over a twenty-five-year period, Bronfenbrenner (1970) now believes that the data suggest not only a trend toward permissiveness, but also "the same facts could be viewed as reflecting a progressive decrease, especially in recent decades, in the amount of contact between American parents and their children [p. 98]."

Family life in this country over the years has changed from the model of dominant husband and submissive wife to more egalitarian families. As far back as 1964, Bowerman and Elder (1964), in a study of 20,000 white adolescents in grades seven to twelve, found that almost 50 per cent of the adolescents reported that their parents' relationship was characterized by egalitarianism. Paternal dominance was reported by 34 per cent and maternal dominance by 20 per cent of the adolescents. From this it appears that an egalitarian relationship between mothers and fathers is the most frequent type of American family in a white sample. One might further speculate that this is even more predominant today than ten years ago.

Some mention of the communal family should be made. As part of life in some communes, children are treated as any other member, whether it be participating in discussion or smoking marijuana, and an effort is made to allow the children to grow naturally, autonomously, and freely (Berger et al., 1972). What the consequences are for the individual of being exposed to this type of early socialization experience for later development are not presently known.

Maternal Employment

Within the past thirty years the number of employed married women with children has increased dramatically. Concern has been expressed with regard to the effects of maternal employment on the child. The effect of maternal employment on the child is dependent on several factors, such as the mother's attitude and that of her family, her ethnic and socioeconomic status, the quality of maternal surrogates, the nature as well as amount of her employment, and the age and sex of her children. Because adolescents are learning, or have learned, what might be regarded as appropriate sex-role behavior by observing and identifying with their parents and modeling their behavior after their parents, one might expect that maternal employment would affect the adolescents' conceptions of the role played by the female. In some cases it appears that a girl's self-concept and behavior are affected by whether her mother is employed. Data in a study by Hartley (1961) suggest that daughters of working mothers view women as more active in the world outside their home than daughters of nonworking mothers.

Several investigators have reported that maternal employment has an effect on the division of labor between the male and female. Spouses of employed women participate to a greater extent in the running of the house as well as in the care of the children. In families where both parents are employed, the division of household tasks has been found to be more egalitarian, and this trend appears to be increasing (Hall and Schroeder, 1970). In a study of adolescents' views of maternal employment, King et al. (1968) reported that ninth-graders whose mothers were employed tended to see maternal employment as less of a threat to the marital relationship than those whose mothers were not employed. Adolescents also tended to be more accepting of maternal employment when their fathers actively participated in household chores. As might be expected, young as well as older adolescent girls whose mothers work report that they too wish to and expect to work when they are mothers (Almquist and Angrist, 1971).

Maternal employment has also been found to be associated in females with less traditional conceptions of sex-role behavior and a higher evaluation of competence. College-student daughters of employed women more often report that they resemble their mothers and more often report that they wish to be like them (Baruch, 1972 as cited by Hoffman, 1974).

Inconsistent findings have emerged from studies comparing the academic achievement of children of working and nonworking mothers.

Despite inconclusive findings with respect to the reactions of boys to maternal employment, it does seem that adolescent sons of working mothers more often express disapproval of their fathers than sons of nonworking mothers (Douvan, 1963; Hoffman, 1974). One might speculate that some adolescent boys from lower socioeconomic homes may interpret employment by their mothers as an indication that their fathers have failed. Adolescents from the lower social classes, whose mothers are employed, less often name their father as the man they admired than adolescents whose mothers were not working (Propper, 1972).

According to Baruch (1972), the probability that children of working mothers will have a positive attitude toward maternal employment is increased when the mother has successfully integrated her role as mother and worker.

At the present time, more research is needed to assess the effects of maternal employment. In a review of the literature on the effects of maternal employment on the child, Hoffman (1974) concludes that findings concerning the mother's emotional state suggest that the mother who obtains satisfaction from her work, who has arrangements that do not place an undue strain on her dual role, and who does not feel so guilty that she tries to overcompensate is likely to do quite well and, under certain conditions, better than does the nonworking mother.

One-Parent Families

Whereas a nuclear family normally consists of a mother, father, and children living together, single-parent families include an on-going (nuclear) family comprising one parent and one or more dependent children.[4] There is some evidence that the largest percentage of one-parent families occurs among the black urban poor. According to estimates of Rainwater (1966), almost two thirds of poor urban black youngsters will not have had both parents living continuously with them throughout their first eighteen years. As common observation suggests, the overwhelming majority of one-parent families are headed by a female; however, there has been an increase in male-headed households in the past few years. This recent trend is related to the fact that in divorce proceedings fathers have increasingly asked for and been awarded the custody of their children, whereas mothers now, more than was true years ago, are rejecting custody of their children.

One cannot overestimate the difficulties the lone parent faces in having sole responsibility in dealing with both the small and pervasive problems of adolescents. The breakup of an association that once was regarded as stable may involve suffering and a feeling of abandonment that has long-lasting effects for the parent as well as the adolescent. A major portion, or the entire responsibility, for the social, emotional and moral rearing of the adolescent is then carried by the remaining parent. Not surprisingly, the adolescent may suffer from the loss of a parent or may have divided loyalties when the parents part. Because of the reactions of other adults and peers they may feel ashamed or bitter (Report of the Committee on One-Parent Families, 1974).

[4] For a review of children in fatherless families see Herzog and Sudia (1973) and Hetherington and Deur (1971).

Father or mother absence cannot be considered apart from such variables as the number, sex, and age of the siblings, the timing of the absence, the availability of surrogates, the personality correlates and behavior of the parents, and the sociocultural milieu (Marsella et al., 1974).

Moreover, it is important to take account of the cause of separation—that is, whether it is due to death, divorce, or abandonment—as well as of variations in family functioning, as they may have different effects on the child. According to Hetherington and McIntyre (1975), most studies of the effects of paternal absence have paid little attention to these factors. Despite the weaknesses of many of these studies, we will present a few of the relevant ones.

Males from father-absent homes are more likely than those in normal two-parent homes to be deprived of adequate knowledge of masculine behavior of which one aspect is the role of the husband-father. Motivation to marry among males from homes without fathers has also been found to be less (Broderick, 1965) than among males with fathers. In a study of the effects of father absence on personality development in adolescent daughters, Hetherington (1972) reported a few deviations from stereotyped sex-role behavior, as assessed by traditional measures, and in relations with peers of the same sex. Girls who had been deprived of a father due either to divorce or death reported that they felt more tension and anxiety when they were with males. Daughters of divorced parents exhibited more attention-seeking behavior in relations with members of the opposite sex and exhibited earlier heterosexual behavior than daughters from intact homes. Hetherington (1972) proposes that an adolescent female deprived of the opportunity to interact with a warm, supportive, and appreciative father is less likely than one who is not thus deprived to acquire the necessary interpersonal skills and competence that are necessary for establishing relationships with males.

Seventh-grade boys from homes without fathers, in a study by Hoffman (1971), scored lower on measures of moral judgment and values, guilt, and conformity with rules than boys from father-present homes. As many parents are aware, it may be particularly important for parents to be sensitive to the special needs of their adolescents during periods when fathers are absent.

Although a two-parent family is not confronted with the particular strains and stresses of a one-parent family, it does not necessarily follow that an adolescent in a two-parent family is presented with a better child-rearing situation. A child in a one-parent family may, for example, be better off than a child whose parents stay together in an atmosphere of discord and open hostility.

References

Alkire, A. A. Enactment of social power and role behavior in families of disturbed and nondisturbed preadolescents. *Developmental Psychology,* 1972, **7**, 270–276.

Allaman, J. D., Joyce, C. S., & Crandall, V. C. The antecedents of social desirability response tendencies of children and young adults. *Child Development,* 1972, **43**, 1135–1160.

Almquist, E. M., & Angrist, S. S. Role model influences on college women's career aspirations. *Merrill-Palmer Quarterly,* 1971, **17**, 263–279.

Anthony, E. J. The reaction of adults to adolescents and their behavior. In J. J. Conger (Ed.), *Contemporary issues in adolescent development.* New York: Harper, 1975.

Aronfreed, J. *Conduct and conscience.* New York: Academic, 1968.

Bandura, A., & Walters, R. H. *Adolescent aggression.* New York: Ronald, 1959.

Baruch, G. K. Maternal influences upon college women's attitudes toward women and work. *Developmental Psychology,* 1972, **6**, 32–37.a.

Bath, J. A., & Lewis, E. C. Attitudes of young female adults toward some areas of parent-adolescent conflict. *Journal of Genetic Psychology,* 1962, **100**, 241–253.

Baumrind, D. Effects of authoritative parental control on child behavior. *Child Development,* 1966, **37**, 887–907.

Baumrind, D. Child care practices anteceding three patterns of preschool behavior. *Genetic Psychology Monographs,* 1967, **75**, 43–83.

Baumrind, D. Authoritarian versus authoritative parental control. *Adolescence,* 1968, **3**, 255–272.

Baumrind, D. Current patterns of parental authority. *Developmental Psychology Monograph,* 1971, **4** (1, Pt. 2).

Baumrind, D. Early socialization and adolescent competence. In S. Dragastin & G. H. Elder, Jr. (Eds.), *Adolescence in the life cycle: Psychological change and social content.* New York: Wiley, 1975.

Baumrind, D., & Black, A. E. Socialization practices associated with dimensions of competence in preschool boys and girls. *Child Development,* 1967, **38**, 291–327.

Becker, W. C. Consequences of parental discipline. In M. L. Hoffman & L. W. Hoffman (Eds.), *Review of child development research* (Vol. 1). New York: Russell Sage Foundation, 1964.

Bennie, E. H., & Sclare, A. B. The battered child syndrome. *American Journal of Psychiatry,* 1969, **125**, 975–979.

Berger, B., Hackett, B., & Millar, R. M. The communal family. *The Family Coordinator,* 1972, **21**, 419–427.

Blatz, W. E., & Millichamp, D. A. The mental growth of the Dionne quintuplets. In W. C. Blatz, D. A. Millichamp, & M. W. Charles (Eds.), *Collected studies of the Dionne quintuplets.* University of Toronto Studies, Child Development Series, No. 12. Toronto, Canada: University of Toronto Press, 1937.

Block, V. L. Conflicts of adolescents with their mothers. *Journal of Abnormal and Social Psychology,* 1937, **32**, 193–206.

Bowerman, C. E., & Elder, G. H. Variations in adolescent perception of family power structure. *American Sociological Review,* 1964, **29**, 551–567.

Brittain, C. V. A comparison of rural and urban adolescents with respect to peer vs. parent compliance. *Adolescence,* 1969, **4**, 59–68.

Broderick, C. B. Social heterosexual development among urban negroes and whites. *Journal of Marriage and the Family,* 1965, **27**, 200–203.

Bronfenbrenner, U. Socialization and social class through time and space. In E. E. Maccoby, T. M. Newcomb, & E. L. Hartley (Eds.), *Readings in social psychology.* New York: Holt, 1958.

Bronfenbrenner, U. *Two worlds of childhood: U.S. and USSR.* New York: Russell Sage Foundation, 1970.

Button, A. Some antecedents of felonious and delinquent behavior. *Journal of Clinical Child Psychology,* 1973, **2**, 35–37.

Cheyne, J. A. Some parameters of punishment affecting resistance to deviation and generalization of a prohibition. *Child Development,* 1971, **42**, 1249–1261.

Coleman, J. S. *The adolescent society.* New York: Free Press, 1961.

Coles, R. In K. L. Woodward, & P. Malamud. The parent gap. *Newsweek,* September 22, 1975, pp. 48–56.

Dahlem, N. W. Young Americans' reported perceptions of their parents. *Journal of Psychology,* 1970, **74**, 187-194.

Demos, J. *A little commonwealth: Family life in Plymouth colony.* New York: Oxford U.P., 1970.

Dodrill, C. B. Personality characteristics of students not identifying with their parents' denominations at entrance into a Christian college. *Journal of Psychology and Theology,* 1974, **2**, 216–222.

Douvan, E. Employment and the adolescent. In F. I. Nye & L. W. Hoffman (Eds.), *The employed mother in America.* Chicago: Rand McNally, 1963.

Douvan, E., & Adelson, J. *The adolescent experience.* New York: Wiley, 1966.

Elder, G. H., Jr. Parental power legitimation and its effect on the adolescent. *Sociometry,* 1963, **26**, 50–65.

Epperson, D. C. A reassessment of indices of parental influence in "the adolescent society." *American Sociological Review,* 1964, **29**, 93–96.

Fontana, V. J. Which parents abuse children? *Medical Insight,* 1971, **3**, 16–21.

Freud, A. Safeguarding the emotional health of our children—An inquiry into the concept of the rejecting mother. *Child Welfare,* 1955, **34**, 1–4.

Friedman, P. The relationship between primary reaction patterns in early infancy and behavior in early childhood. Unpublished doctoral dissertation, Teachers College, Columbia University, 1965.

Glueck, S., & Glueck, E. T. *Unraveling juvenile delinquency.* Cambridge, Mass.: Harvard U.P., 1950.

Gold, M., & Douvan, E. *Adolescent development: Readings in research and theory.* Boston: Allyn, 1969.

Golightly, C., Nelson, D., & Johnson, J. Children's dependency scales. *Developmental Psychology,* 1970, **3**, 114–118.

Graves, D., Walters, J., & Stinnett, N. Relationship between perceptions of family life and attitudes concerning father-son interaction. *Journal of Genetic Psychology,* 1974, **124**, 303–310.

Gregg, G., & Elmer, E. Infant injuries: Accident or abuse? *Pediatrics,* 1969, **44**, 434–439.

Hall, F. T., & Schroeder, M. P. Time spent on household tasks. *Journal of Home Economics,* 1970, **62**, 23–29.

Harper, L. V. The young as a source of stimuli controlling caretaker behavior. *Developmental Psychology,* 1971, **4**, 73–88.

Hartley, R. E. What aspects of child behavior should be studied in relation to maternal employment? In A. E. Siegel (Ed.), *Research issues related to the effects of maternal employment on children.* University Park, Pa.: Social Science Research Center, 1961.

Hartup, W. W. Dependence and independence. *The Sixty-second Yearbook of the National Society for the Study of Education,* 1965, **52**, Part 1, 333–363.

Herzog, E., & Sudia, C. E. Children in fatherless families. In B. M. Caldwell & H. Ricciuti (Eds.), *Review of child development research* (Vol. 3). Chicago: U. of Chicago, 1973.

Hetherington, E. M. Effects of father absence on personality development in adolescent daughters. *Developmental Psychology,* 1972, **7**, 313–326.

Hetherington, E. M., & Deur, J. L. The effects of father absence on child development. *Young Children,* 1971, **26**, 233–248.

Hetherington, E. M., & McIntyre, C. W. Developmental psychology. *Annual Review of Psychology,* 1975, **26**, 97–136.

Hetherington, E. M., Stouwie, R. J., & Ridberg, E. H. Patterns of family interaction and child-rearing attitudes related to three dimensions of juvenile delinquency. *Journal of Abnormal Psychology,* 1971, **78**, 160–176.

Hoffman, L. W. Effects of maternal employment on the child: A review of the research. *Developmental Psychology,* 1974, **10**, 204–228.

Hoffman, M. L. Father absence and conscience development. *Developmental Psychology,* 1971, **4**, 400–406.

Hoffman, M. L. Moral internalization, parental power, and the nature of parent-child interaction. *Developmental Psychology,* 1975, **11**, 228–239.

Jersild, A. T., Lazar, E., & Brodkin, A. *The meaning of psychotherapy in the teacher's life and work.* New York: Bureau of Publications, Teachers College, Columbia University, 1962.

Kagan, J., & Lemkin, J. The child's differential perception of parental attributes. *Journal of Abnormal and Social Psychology,* 1960, **61**, 440–447.

Kagan, J., & Moss, H. A. The stability of passive and dependent behavior from childhood through adulthood. *Child Development,* 1960, **31**, 577–591.

Kandel, D., & Lesser, G. S. Parent-adolescent relationships and adolescent independence in the United States and Denmark. *Journal of Marriage and the Family,* 1969, **31**, 348–358.

Kandel, D. B., & Lesser, G. S. *Youth in two worlds.* San Francisco, Calif.: Jossey-Bass, 1972.

King, K., McIntyre, J., & Axelson, L. J. Adolescents' views of maternal employment as a threat to the marital relationship. *Journal of Marriage and the Family,* 1968, **30**, 633–637.

Lambert, W. E., Yackley, A., & Hein, R. N. Child training values of English-Canadian and French-Canadian parents. *Canadian Journal of Behavioral Science*, 1971, **3**, 217–236.

LaVoie, J. C. Punishment and adolescent self-control. *Developmental Psychology*, 1973, **8**, 16–24.

LaVoie, J. C., & Looft, W. R. Parental antecedents of resistance to temptation behavior in adolescent males. *Merrill Palmer Quarterly*, 1973, **19**, 107–116.

Lloyd, R. C. Parent-youth conflicts of college students. *Sociology and Social Research*, 1952, **36**, 227–230.

Marsella, A. J., Dubanoski, R. A., & Mohs, K. The effects of father presence and absence upon maternal attitudes. *Journal of Genetic Psychology*, 1974, **125**, 257–263.

Martin, B. Parent-child relations. In F. D. Horowitz (Ed.), *Review of child development research* (Vol. 4). Chicago: U. of Chicago, 1975.

McCord, W., McCord, J., & Verden, P. Familial and behavioral correlates of dependency in male children. *Child Development*, 1962, **33**, 313–326.

McCord, W., McCord, J., & Zola, I. K. *Origins of crime.* New York: Columbia U.P., 1959.

Minton, C., Kagan, J., & Levine, J. A. Maternal control and obedience in the two-year-old. *Child Development*, 1971, **42**, 1873–1894.

Munns, M., Jr. The values of adolescents compared with parents and peers. *Adolescence*, 1972, **7**, 519–524.

Osofsky, J. D. Children's influences upon parental behavior: An attempt to define the relationship with the use of laboratory tasks. *Genetic Psychology Monographs*, 1971, **83**, 147–169.

Pikas, A. Children's attitudes toward rational versus inhibiting parental authority. *Journal of Abnormal and Social Psychology*, 1961, **62**, 315–321.

Propper, A. M. The relationship of maternal employment to adolescent roles, activities, and parental relationships. *Journal of Marriage and the Family*, 1972, **34**, 417–421.

Radin, N. Father-child interaction and the intellectual functioning of four-year-old boys. *Developmental Psychology*, 1972, **6**, 353–361.

Rainwater, L. Crucible of identity: The Negro lower-class family. *Daedalus*, 1966, **95**, 172–216.

Report of the Committee on One-Parent Families (Vol. 1). London: Department of Health and Social Security, 1974.

Rosen, B. C. The reference group approach to the parental factor in attitude and behavior formation. *Social Forces*, 1955, **34**, 137–144.

Rothbart, M. K., & Maccoby, E. E. Parents' differential reactions to sons and daughters. *Journal of Personality and Social Psychology*, 1966, **4**, 237–243.

Saad, Z., & Nagi, I. Child abuse and neglect programs. *Children Today*, May–June, 1975, **4**, 13–17.

Scarlett, G. Adolescent thinking and the diary of Anne Frank. In J. J. Conger (Ed.), *Contemporary issues in adolescent development*. New York: Harper, 1975.

Schaefer, E. S. A circumplex model for maternal behavior. *Journal of Abnormal and Social Psychology*, 1959, **59**, 226–235.

Schaefer, E. S. Converging conceptual models for maternal behavior and for child behavior. In J. C. Glidewell (Ed.), *Parental attitudes and child behavior.* Springfield, Ill.: Thomas, 1961.

Shirley, M. M. Impact of mother's personality on the young child. *Smith College Studies in Social Work,* 1941, **12**, 15–64.

Steele, B. F. *Working with abusive parents from a psychiatric point of view.* U.S. Department of Health, Education, and Welfare, 1975.

Stinnett, N., Farris, J. A., & Walters, J. Parent-child relationships of male and female high school students. *Journal of Genetic Psychology,* 1974, **125**, 99–106.

Thomas, A. *Progress report: Primary reactions in childhood.* Unpublished manuscript, New York University Medical School, 1966.

Thomas, A., & Chess, S. Development in middle childhood. *Seminars in Psychiatry,* 1972, **4**, 331–341.

Thomas, A., Chess, S., Birch, H. G., Hertzig, M. E., & Korn, S. *Behavioral individuality in early childhood.* New York: New York U.P., 1963.

Trautner, H. M. Relationships between parental child-rearing practices and parental orientation in 10–12 year old girls. *Zeitschrift,* 1972, **4**, 165–182. (Abstract)

Tuddenham, R. D., Brooks, J., & Milkovich, L. Mothers' reports of behavior of ten-year-olds: Relationships with sex, ethnicity, and mother's education. *Developmental Psychology,* 1974, **10**, 959–995.

Wakefield, W. M. Awareness, affection and perceived similarity in the parent-child relationship. *Journal of Genetic Psychology,* 1970, **117**, 91–97.

Weiner, I. B. *Psychological disturbance in adolescence.* New York: Wiley, 1970.

Woodward, K. L., & Malamud, P. The parent gap. *Newsweek,* September 22, 1975, pp. 48–56.

Yarrow, M. R., Waxler, C. Z., & Scott, P. M. Child effects on adult behavior. *Developmental Psychology,* 1971, **5**, 300–311.

Zegiob, L. E., Arnold, S., & Forehand, R. An examination of observer effects in parent-child interactions. *Child Development,* 1975, **46**, 509–512.

13

adolescents and their peers

Adolescents' relations with their peers become increasingly important as they advance from infancy toward the late adolescent years. During the period of puberty to young adulthood, dealings with peers become even more significant. When they leave adolescence and become young adults, all other adults are their peers, at least in a legal sense. They must find their place in a society that includes not only their own age group but adults who, although older, are on a par with them as voters, citizens, parents, job holders, and in many other ways.

344

Adolescents' relations with their peers are important in connection with all aspects of their development, as we have noted in earlier sections of this book. In this chapter and the next we will focus more specifically on these relationships.

In many respects adolescents have a society of their own, overlapping with, and yet distinct from, the larger society in which they live. There is a great amount of "ganging up" among them. Some belong to an organized gang, with a name, rigid rules, and clearly defined power structure; but such adolescents constitute only a small minority. In the more typical situation, adolescents operate as a loosely organized, but powerful, confederation. Through this, adolescents exert an influence on each other and pressure on their parents.

Adolescents in concert with each other help to determine what "goes." They influence the moral climate, help to decide the proper way to dress, and develop their own lingo and rules of etiquette (President's Science Advisory Commission Panel on Youth, 1973).

Adolescents as preceptors

Much of the education adolescents provide for one another comes through an opportunity to test their views and theories. Such a test enables the young person to "think out loud" and to observe how others react. In their conversations, adolescents often advance extravagant ideas. In the guise of expressing what seems to be an impersonal theory, they have an opportunity to express ideas that have important personal meanings—ideas about themselves, parents, teachers, persons in authority, personal problems, attitudes about sex, ideas concerning relationships with the opposite sex, ideas about schooling, about joining the military service, and a host of other issues.

In order to express their attitudes and views, they have to formulate them so that others can understand and respond, and this is an incentive to formulating them as clearly as they can in their own minds. In adolescence, as in earlier childhood, a person's thinking is sharpened and clarified by the need to formulate his private thoughts in language and logic that *others* can understand. Others are not likely to get the drift of their thoughts if they themselves have not formulated them clearly in ways they understand.

Escape from loneliness

Adolescence is not only a time of intense sociability but, for many, a time of loneliness. Adolescents live in solitary isolation when they cannot share their concerns with others and when the only close companions they can find are those who dwell within their own imagination. There are many conditions in adolescence—and adult life[1]—that cut persons off from one another. We have discussed some of these in earlier chapters dealing with the ways in which young persons and adults conceal their feelings and thoughts from one another.

Loneliness occurs not only in those who physically are alone. It can occur in its most acute form when a person is in the midst of a crowd, joining in the banter and enforced sociability. Some adolescents feel their loneliness most vividly when they are at a party or dance. A boy and a girl can dance together for hours in what seems to be close contact, but unless there is some feeling of intimacy, each may feel as lonely as ever.

In adolescence, as in later periods of life, individuals try to build barricades against loneliness. They become joiners. They sing the sorority's or fraternity's songs. They clasp their hands together and cheer for the team or for the "cause." But the formal wrappings of "togetherness" do not fulfill the deeper need that underlies a person's loneliness. One of the great rewards of a close friendship in adolescence is that it helps the young person to escape from the pangs of loneliness.

Relative impact of parents compared with peers on adolescent behavior

Some authors, in discussing the relative influence of parents and peers, maintain that there are profound differences between the present generation of adolescents and their parents and other adults. Exponents of this position include Mead (1970) and Friedenberg (1969; 1969a). According to Mead (1970) adolescents are exposed to many experiences and influences that differ from those that prevailed when their parents were adolescents. To the extent that this is true, parents can no longer tell their offspring, "I was once a youth like you" because the parents were not like their offspring. Friedenberg (1969) has speculated that young people aren't rebelling against their parents, they're abandoning them. It has been argued that irreconcilable differences between the generations have resulted in present-day adolescents turning toward their peers for leadership and guidance in major areas of their life.

A study that made a comparison of parental and adolescent attitudes toward contemporary issues related to drugs, sex, war, and religion was made by Orloff and Weinstock (1975). The differences between adolescents

[1] Almost all adults who were interviewed informally in a study (Jersild, 1955) spoke of being lonely to a small or large degree. In response to a more formal written inventory, about half of a group of 229 respondents reported one or more conditions of loneliness as representing a "problem" in their lives.

and their parents are interpreted as supporting the view that there is a "generation gap." (Actually, the idea that a younger generation is less responsible and lacking in proper respect for the views of older people goes back to the time of Plato.)

However, findings in other studies support the view that the generation gap between today's adolescents and their parents has been exaggerated (Campbell, 1969). For the most part, according to Campbell, parental expectations and adolescent values are similar, and when conflict occurs between adolescents and their parents it is frequently associated with matters that are of minor significance, compared with more pervasive and basic values. As was noted in Chapter 12, several investigators have reported that a large proportion of adolescents report that they have satisfactory relationships with their parents.

In a study of female adolescents who gave peer-conforming as opposed to parent-conforming responses to dilemmas of a hypothetical nature, Brittain (1963) reported that the former group had lower status among peers. This is not in keeping with the idea of a generation gap. Students who had excellent relationships with their parents were found by Stone (1960) to be active in high school organizations. One could assume on the basis of Stone's findings that peer-group status and harmonious and close parent-adolescent relationships are quite compatible. Other investigators have also reported congruity between parents' values, aspirations, attitudes, and expectations and those of their offspring in a variety of areas (Bengston, 1970; Brook et al., 1974; Lukoff and Brook, 1976). In some aspects of decision making, parents may actually serve as more important guides than peers. For example, parents had a greater influence on their children's future educational goals than their best school friends (Kandel and Lesser, 1969).

Still another position intermediate between the two extremes just presented may involve, according to Bengston (1970), selective areas of continuity and difference in the attitudes and ideas of the older and younger generation. For instance, adolescents and their parents may be similar in some areas, such as their basic values, and hold differing views in other areas, such as what is considered appropriate dress. Whether the adolescent is affected by parental, as opposed to peer, pressure may depend on the content of the particular situation. As Bengtson (1970) suggests, it is necessary to delineate specifically those areas in which similarities and differences might be expected to occur and the nature and extent of these similarities and differences.

What can be said of the adolescents' view of the concept of a generation gap? In a study by Lerner (1975), adolescents and their parents were instructed to rate the degree of their own agreement with each item of a Contemporary Topics Questionnaire (CTQ), dealing with topics such as war, racism, drugs, sex, and clothing. Adolescents were asked to indicate what their parents' ratings might be, and parents were asked to indicate what they thought their offspring's ratings might be. The items in the scale and ratings given by parents and their offspring are shown in Table 13.1. The authors state that a generation gap might be assumed if one "group's attitudes centered around one point of the attitude scale and the other group's attitudes centered around a significantly different point on the scale [a "significant difference" was designated as two scale points] [p. 118]." For example, in response to item 31 ("Premarital sexual activities are and always should be considered immoral"), the mean self-rating by adolescents was 6.1, indicating moderate disagreement; the mean rating ascribed by adolescents to their parents on this item was 3.4, representing an approximate midpoint between "slightly agree" and "neutral." Parents gave this item a mean rating of 3.7, about halfway between "slightly agree" and "neutral." In surmising how their adolescent offspring would respond to this item, parents gave a mean rating of 4.6, slightly above halfway between "neutral" and "slightly disagree." In other words, there was more similarity between the parents' ratings of their own stand on this issue and what they thought their adolescent offspring might be than between the stand taken by the adolescents and what they thought might be the stand taken by their parents. A gap apparently existed in the minds of the adolescents, but not, according to the criterion used in the study, in the minds of the parents.

In connection with some items in Table 13.1, it seems that adolescents regarded their parents as more austere or forbidding, or less tolerant, than they actually were, as judged by the parents' self-ratings.

With few exceptions, Table 13.1 does not show serious attitudinal disagreements between adolescents and their parents in their views on contemporary issues, although parents and adolescents perceived some gaps between the generations. Adolescents tended to overestimate the differences between themselves and their parents, whereas parents tended to underestimate the differences. The investigators caution the reader against going too far in generalizing their findings. Differences between parents and adolescents may be affected by the socioeconomic and educational backgrounds of the individuals who are studied.

An extensive analysis of noncollege and college-age youths conducted by CBS News (Yankelovich, 1969) revealed that 72 per cent of the former group and 66 per cent of the latter group felt that there was an overemphasis of the concept of a generation gap in our society.

Peer culture

Peer groups can be viewed as a bridge between childhood and adulthood. Approximately 80 per cent of urban adolescents are involved in

Table 13.1. The 36 CTQ items and mean responses for the two generational groups. Members of each group were asked to (1) rate themselves (on an attitude scale of 1–7) and to (2) estimate how members of the other group would rate themselves on the same issue

CTQ Item	Mean adolescent ratings		Mean parent ratings	
	Self	Parents	Self	Children
1. My conscience would bother me if I killed a man in war.	2.5	3.1	3.2	2.1
2. Premarital intercourse is acceptable for men but not for women.	5.7	4.7	5.9	5.0
3. In respect to youth, shoplifting is of greater moral concern than is premarital sex.	3.7	4.8	4.4	3.5
4. Racial equality deserves more attention in America than does curtailing obscenity.	1.6	3.7	2.9	2.3
5. Laws dealing with drugs, such as marijuana, are in dire need of revision.	2.0	4.1	2.8	2.2
6. A home setting for healthy adolescent development is best described as having consistent restrictions.	3.3	2.4	2.1	2.3
7. All war is immoral.	3.8	4.4	3.6	2.2
8. Authority of the police must be increased rather than decreased.	4.4	2.5	2.0	3.3
9. Marijuana should be legalized.	3.3	6.2	5.7	3.7
10. A person's appearance is his own concern, and others should tolerate whatever that person wears.	2.2	5.5	4.1	2.0
11. Disappointment or concern would overshadow approval if a close friend admitted smoking marijuana.	5.0	2.0	2.2	3.4
12. Universities should not oppose radical groups but should provide them with the protection that others have.	3.0	5.4	4.8	3.0
13. All organizations should be afforded equal and adequate police protection, if necessary, at meetings.	2.5	3.3	3.0	2.1
14. Political power of the United States military establishment is reaching a dangerous level.	2.6	3.7	3.8	2.6
15. As a parent, I would be concerned if my child of 18 years attended a lecture given by an advocate of the use of LSD.	4.2	2.3	2.9	3.7
16. Suspension from high school for smoking should be enforced, rather than allowing this behavior to exist.	5.5	2.9	4.1	5.5
17. Need for strict law enforcement by the police has been justified and generated by the action of troublemakers.	4.1	2.0	1.6	3.4

Note: 1 = "strongly agree," 2 = "moderately agree," 3 = "slightly agree," 4 = "neutral," 5 = "slightly disagree," 6 = "moderately disagree," and 7 = "strongly disagree."

Table 13.1. (Continued)

CTQ Item	Mean adolescent ratings		Mean parent ratings	
	Self	Parents	Self	Children
18. Birth-control devices and information should be made available to all who desire them.	1.5	3.8	1.9	1.7
19. Black people have many just grievances, but they expect too much too soon.	4.4	2.2	2.8	3.6
20. A woman's place is in the home.	5.0	3.6	4.7	4.8
21. A school's dress code is a reasonable demand that students should abide by.	5.1	2.2	1.9	4.1
22. In civil disorders, the police do their job as well as can be expected.	4.5	2.5	3.1	3.8
23. The Church is playing an active role in shaping people's moral character.	5.5	3.4	3.5	4.4
24. Black revolutionaries are harmful to the advancement of their race.	4.1	2.1	2.1	2.8
25. Anti-abortion laws are absurd; the woman, and not the government, should have control over her reproductive functions.	2.0	3.9	2.6	2.4
26. Premarital sexual activities have no place in our present society.	6.3	3.2	4.0	4.7
27. Sex education in the public schools is immoral.	6.7	5.6	6.2	6.3
28. It is moral to flee to Canada to escape the draft.	3.0	5.2	5.5	3.9
29. Revision of America's legal system could help bridge the "generation gap."	3.2	3.9	3.7	2.9
30. I would not hesitate to experiment with marijuana.	3.4	6.6	6.5	4.7
31. Premarital sexual activities are and always should be considered immoral.	6.1	3.4	3.7	4.6
32. LSD is a dangerous drug that requires strict, prohibitive law enforcement.	2.8	1.5	1.3	1.9
33. Those who use drugs are usually careless about their personal appearance.	5.3	2.2	2.6	3.6
34. Laws dealing with drug conviction are too harsh.	2.7	5.0	4.7	3.3
35. The "New Left" (society's radical element) has no valid reasons for its positions.	5.4	3.0	3.9	4.4
36. A home setting for healthy adolescent development should be highly permissive.	4.6	5.1	6.1	5.5

Note: 1 = "strongly agree," 2 = "moderately agree," 3 = "slightly agree," 4 = "neutral," 5 = "slightly disagree," 6 = "moderately disagree," and 7 = "strongly disagree."

Source: From "Showdown at generation gap: Attitudes of adolescents and their parents toward contemporary issues" by R. Lerner. In H. D. Thornburg (Ed.), *Contemporary Adolescence: Readings* (2nd ed.). Copyright © 1971, 1975 by Wadsworth Publishing Company, Inc. Reprinted by permisssion of the publisher, Brooks/Cole Publishing Company, Monterey, California.

Peer groups can be viewed as a bridge between childhood and adulthood. [Alex Webb/Magnum.]

some form of group behavior, according to Dunphy (1963). Several authors (Bronfenbrenner, 1970; Coleman, 1961; and Reisman, 1950) have described what appears to be an increase in the influence of the adolescent peer group as compared with the influence of adults in recent years. Although their views have been questioned by various critics (Elder, 1975), their research has highlighted a number of developments in American society. For example, Bronfenbrenner (1970) has provided evidence that a trend toward age segregation during the past several decades has had the result that adolescents may become intensely involved in groups lacking adult supervision.

What is the nature of the peer culture? The President's Science Advisory Commission (1973) has described several elements or characteristics: Looking inward is one element that has been said to characterize the youth culture. Adolescents have increasingly looked to their peers rather than to adults for information. For instance, the underground press operated by young people grew to a national weekly circulation of over two million readers (Swift, as cited by Starr, 1974). Throughout the 1960s, much of the music adolescents were exposed to was dominated by youth itself (President's Science Advisory Commission, 1973). In the fashion industry much of the clothing adolescents bought was produced by young people (Starr, 1974).

Another element that is believed to characterize the youth culture is "the psychic attachment of youth to others their own age [President's Science Advisory Commission, 1973, p. 115]." A number of youths have expressed dissatisfaction with the status quo (Braungart, 1974) and instead are displaying a pattern of intimacy and openness among closely knit groups of friends. The peer group apparently is increasingly fulfilling the adolescent's need for closeness. A press toward autonomy and concern for the underdog also characterizes a number of today's adolescents. Concern for the underdog has been expressed at times as an increase in concern for many minority groups. Concern for, and mutual acceptance of, females by males has apparently also increased. Data obtained from a statewide sample of Illinois teen-agers (Berger et al., 1972) indicated that almost three quarters of these adolescents felt that women should speak their minds instead of just being agreeable.

Groupings that are homogeneous in age may have a beneficial as well as a harmful influence, since the peer group provides an environment in which the adolescents may or may not affirm their values. The adolescents' need for psychological security as they move out of the family circle is often supplied by the peer group (Campbell, 1969). The peer group may assist adolescents in evaluating themselves from varying perspectives. Involvement with the peer group may also enable the adolescents to become acquainted with and learn to relate to individuals of diverse backgrounds, preparing them for the demands of an industrial society. During this period the adolescents have their eye on the future more than was true earlier (Braungart, 1974; Piaget, 1967), and the peer group may help the adolescent to defer needs for immediate gratification in the process of working toward a goal that cannot be reached until some time in the future. In the meantime, involvement in contemporary peer concerns may allow the adolescent to feel that the present need not be meaningless. Peers also play an important part in the adolescent's development of skills and interests.

Three peer groups have been singled out by Thornburg (1975): high school youths, noncollege youths, and college youths. Although there is considerable overlap among these groups, there are some interesting differences. High school students appear to place greater emphasis on resolving the developmental tasks of adolescence. Social life and athletics are of great importance to these students, as noted in the studies by Coleman (1961) and Friesen (1968). Noncollege youth in the age group of seventeen to twenty-three have been found to be more traditional, conforming to conventional interests and standards, than college youth (Yankelovich, 1969). The discrepancy between parents' values and the values of their offspring appears to be greater among college youth than among noncollege youth. Several investigators (Keniston, 1971; Reich, 1970) have reported that the value system of the college peer group is changing. Although the evidence is still scanty, there may be a change in the direction of values that challenge established authority to a greater extent than was true in the past. In college youth groups there has been some evidence of increased closeness with peers and a movement away from some traditional values of achievement and success.

The fact that reliance on peers varies depending on the issue under consideration and is not identical in different countries has been highlighted by Kandel and Lesser (1972).

As shown in Table 13.2, Danish and American male and female adolescents rely on friends for advice and guidance in some areas and parents in other areas. Danish, in contrast to American, adolescents report that they are more likely to depend on friends than parents in a number of areas, such as advice relating to morals and values.

It is likely that situational factors can have an effect on the influence of the peer group on the adolescent, as indicated in a study by Devereaux et al. (1974) of six hundred Israeli eleven- and twelve-year-olds. These subjects were selected from twenty-nine kibbutzim and from classrooms located in the city of Tel Aviv. They were asked to describe the "socializing" behaviors of their peers. A salient aspect of life in a kibbutz is that the children live in special houses with peers of similar ages under the supervision of a *metapelet* (child-care agent) rather than with their parents, as is customary in the United States. This system was designed to promote the sharing of equal responsibilities for the home and family by the husband and wife. A kibbutz child and adolescent spends the largest proportion of the day with age mates—eating, sleeping, attending classes, working, and participating in recreational activities. A few hours in the evening are spent in close contact with the adolescent's parents. Under these conditions one would expect that the kibbutz peer group would exert a powerful force in the socialization of the adolescent. The data in this study reveal that the kibbutz peer group, compared with urban nonkibbutz age mates, plays a greater role in disciplining and controlling the behavior of its members. Deviant behavior is controlled in part by members of the peer group by the use of power-assertive techniques, such as threatening violence, or social isolation, or acting cold and unfriendly. On the other hand, the kibbutz peer group, which emphasizes a cooperative, egalitarian ideology—differing in this way from an urban peer group—was found to be similar to its urban counterpart in the ways in which the youngsters give support to one another.

Friendships and relationships with peers

The most important peer relationships are those that exist between close friends. The factors that draw two adolescents together into a close

Table 13.2. Person whom adolescent would rely upon for advice and guidance

Person relied upon

Type of problem	Friends (in %)	Mother (in %)	Father (in %)	Siblings (in %)	Teacher (in %)	Guidance Counselor (in %)	Other (in %)	Total N
School grades								
U.S.	3	15	5	2	43	31	1	(1,057)
Denmark	6	25	19	3	42		5	(955)
Career plans								
U.S.	4	23	17	3	3	46	4	(1,053)
Denmark	4	23	53	2	8		10	(947)
College								
U.S.	3	15	15	2	10	52	3	(994)
Denmark	8	18	28	2	38		6	(846)
Personal problems with parents								
U.S.	25	20	7	16	2	6	24	(1,042)
Denmark	28	26	9	30	3		4	(912)
Personal problems not involving parents								
U.S.	33	32	10	10	2	3	10	(1,032)
Denmark	49	26	7	13	2		3	(923)
Morals and values								
U.S.	17	39	12	6	3	2	21	(1,008)
Denmark	49	22	12	9	5		3	(911)
Dating								
U.S.	35	36	13	11		1	4	(1,027)
Denmark	47	33	7	9			4	(926)
What clothing to buy								
U.S.	30	51	6	9			4	(1,018)
Denmark	20	61	6	8			5	(936)
Choice of friends								
U.S.	30	40	10	10	1	1	8	(972)
Denmark	31	27	11	25			6	(861)
What books to read								
U.S.	27	10	4	5	48	3	3	(999)
Denmark	52	7	15	10	14		2	(904)

Note: All differences between United States and Denmark for each problem significant at .001 level (chi-square test).
Source: From Youth in two worlds by D. B. Kandel and G. S. Lesser, San Francisco, Jossey-Bass, 1972, p. 119. Reprinted by permission.

companionship are complex and not well understood. From ordinary observation one can note, however, that in some companionships the relationship is that of leader and follower. Some companionships appear to have an ulterior purpose, as when one youngster ingratiates himself or herself with a popular member of the group as a means of gaining prestige and the other youngster "uses" him or her as though he or she were a convenient, unpaid servant.

The most meaningful companionships, however, are those in which two young people share each other's company as equals, feel at home with each other, and feel free to confide their innermost thoughts and feelings to each other. In such a relationship there is trust, there is no need to pretend, and there is no need to be on guard against betrayal of shared secrets. Adolescents who have a relationship of this kind can reprove each other without condemning each other.

A friendship of this kind is likely to occur between two persons who are more alike than dissimilar in some of the more obvious characteristics, such as intelligence and socioeconomic status. But there are subtleties underlying the affinity that these measures do not reveal. Two friends may differ in ways that one might expect would keep them apart. For example, one of them may have much stronger moral scruples than the other.

When adolescents find a "real" friend they possess something very precious. They are not only tasting the joys of companionship, but are also discovering themselves. To the extent that they are able, they bring out, for open display, doubts, resentments, and concerns of many kinds. In the process they may gain a deeper assurance of their own worth. They may discover feelings they hardly knew they, or others, possessed—and be able to express them in a way they ordinarily would not allow.[2] Such sharing plays an important part in the adolescents' lives when parent-adolescent ties of dependence are becoming looser and conflicts between generations may occur (Wieder and Zimmerman, 1974). (They may also expose themselves to the sorrow of parting, but the sorrow of parting from a friend is likely to be outweighed by the value of having had a friend.)

One characteristic of a close companionship is its effortlessness. There is no need for the usual formal and superficial social amenities. Even when the companions have been separated for weeks they can easily slip back into their old relationship as though they had seen each other just an hour before.

[2] In a companionship between two boys in their late teens, reported to one of the authors, a time arrived when one had to move to a distant place. The boys were roommates. In the middle of the night before the leave-taking, one of the boys awoke and heard his companion crying. Without revealing that he was awake he also began quietly to cry. These boys were robust, masculine characters who would never allow themselves to cry in public.

Another characteristic is that close companions can tolerate silence. They may chatter at a great rate one moment and then go through long periods when neither says anything. This is in contrast to the behavior of persons who are "friends," but only in a formal sense. This contrast is more apparent among older adolescents and adults than among younger persons. In a typical gathering of two or twenty older persons, who superficially are friends, silence produces uneasiness—if it ever occurs. The atmosphere is pierced with remarks by one person and then another chimes in. Often, in such a gathering of friends, there is a grim undercurrent of competitiveness.

But there are other marks that also differ from the usual behavior among persons who are friends, in a formal way. One of the most conspicuous marks is an outspokenness such as would have provoked a duel among nonfriends in the days when knighthood was in flower. This appears more often among boys than girls. One can almost measure the depth of the companionship between boys by the epithets they now and then goodhumoredly hurl at one another.

According to Douvan and Adelson (1966), friendships during the adolescent period are likely to be intense and help to promote emotional support and security during a time when the adolescent is attempting to become less dependent on his or her parents. These investigators have described three patterns of friendship relations, which vary with age, among girls. According to their account, during the early stage of adolescence, at ages eleven, twelve, and thirteen, friendship is centered on activity—whatever the youngsters are doing together. A friend who is agreeable and does not interfere with the ongoing activity is considered to be quite desirable. In general, friendships during this period are more superficial than at later stages. During the second stage, when girls are fourteen, fifteen, and sixteen, according to these investigators, friendships may be more intense and intimate. "The mere sharing of activity diminishes, to be replaced by a relation that is mutual, interactive, emotionally interdependent; the personality of the other and the other's response to the self become the central themes of the friendship [p. 283]." What adolescents desire in a friend is someone with whom they can share their concerns, who understands them and is sensitive to their needs. As compared with younger and older girls, adolescents of this age relate that they desire a friend who will be loyal and trustworthy. At this age, girls frequently date boys and seem to need their like-sexed friends to guide and comfort them in these new relationships.

Following this, there comes a stage of friendship described by Adelson and Douvan (1975) as occurring among girls of seventeen and eighteen that is characterized by calmness. At this time, the adolescent has acquired many of the social skills necessary to establish and maintain a relationship. She has probably succeeded in establishing her personal identity to some extent. More likely than not, her understanding of friendship is fairly complex. In this late adolescent period girls emphasize the desire to have a friend with whom they can share confidences, as did the girls in early adolescence. However, there appears to be a difference in that now they are more sensitive to the personality and unique characteristics of their friends. In addition to being able to tolerate differences in their friends, older adolescents are likely to place some value on the uniqueness of their friends.

In a review of the literature on sex differences in friendship patterns, Maccoby and Jacklin (1974) concluded that friendship patterns among girls may be more intimate than among boys, probably because the number of friends is smaller in the former group.. The evidence, however, does not clearly demonstrate that girls reveal themselves to their friends to a greater degree than boys. Several investigators (see Jourard and Friedman, 1970) have reported no sex differences in self-disclosure in late adolescence.

In addition to being more dependent on their friends for activities—for example, participating in sports—boys tend to be more sociable in terms of the number of friends with whom they interact, whereas girls in larger groups more often than boys establish small subgroups. Female adolescents, as compared with males, do not appear to be more interested in and better able to establish interpersonal relationships "unless one regards girls' *intense* (that is, "best friend") relationships as revealing more of this capacity than the more dispersed social relations of boys [Maccoby and Jacklin, 1974, p. 211]."Although there are some qualitative differences in social relations between the sexes, Maccoby and Jacklin (1974) concluded that, in general, members of both sexes appear to be highly sociable.

With increased age there are, of course, changes in the interaction between males and females. At early ages elementary school boys and girls seem to prefer to interact with members of their own sex. By the fifth grade, girls prefer boys more than boys prefer girls. The situation may change in grades six and seven, with both males and females becoming more positively oriented to one another, even though the boys seem to change at a more rapid rate. After this period, heterosexual interests continue to develop and become more meaningful with increased age.

Interpersonal Attraction

PROPINQUITY AND INTERPERSONAL ATTRACTION

As might be expected, individuals who are geographically close to one another are more likely to choose one another as friends than individuals who are more physically remote. After students have been seated next to one another in class for a length of time, they more often report that they are attracted more to their neighbors than to non-neighbors (Byrne, 1961).

SOCIOCULTURAL FACTORS AND INTERPERSONAL ATTRACTION

Adolescents tend to choose friends similar to themselves in economic status (Bonney, 1946; Byrne et al., 1966), religious and ethnic affiliation, and race (Goodnow and Taguiri, 1952; Loomis, 1943).

As noted elsewhere, parents may directly influence an adolescent's selection of friends or indirectly affect choices when adolescents have internalized parental values. "All boundary-maintaining systems, such as social class, religion, community, race, and morality, have the effect of reducing the range of choices available to the adolescent, which in effect means that those adolescents more likely to be chosen as friends and associates are precisely those reared in homes substantially similar to the subject's home [Campbell, 1969, p. 843]."

OTHER FACTORS INFLUENCING INTERPERSONAL ATTRACTION

Other factors that, to varying degrees, have been found to influence interpersonal attraction include: similarity in abilities, attitudes, and opinions (Festinger, 1954); in personality attributes (Duck and Spencer, 1972); in occupational and educational aspirations (Haller and Butterworth, 1960); and in behavior that confirms a person's self-concept (Secord and Backman, 1964).

Social Acceptance, Rejection, and Isolation

There is a wide range in the extent to which the individual adolescents are regarded as acceptable members of their peer group. At one extreme, an adolescent may be very popular—highly regarded by all and disapproved of by none. At the other extreme, an adolescent may be unpopular—disapproved of or ignored by everyone.

One of the systematic ways of getting information about the extent to which an adolescent is accepted or ignored or rejected is the *sociometric* method (Jennings, 1947; Moreno, 1954). For example, each person writes the names of individuals desirable as seatmates or as close friends or as guests at a home party. Each person may be asked to name those he or she definitely does *not* care to have as companions. A procedure used by some investigators (Izard, 1960) requires the subject to make a limited number of choices, such as most and least preferred member of the group. Another procedure is to provide each member with a list of all other members of his group and ask him to rate each one on a scale ranging from a high degree of acceptance to complete rejection. To be authentic, the sociometric procedure must be administered by an unbiased person who is able to get the cooperation of those who respond.

When choices have been made, it is possible to raise many interesting questions, such as: Who is chosen most or least often? Who chooses whom? To what extent do various persons choose those who also choose them, or choose those who do not choose them? Are the choices heavily centered on a few popular members of the group, or are they widely distributed? Is there evidence that there are several little cliques or social islands within the group?[3]

Information obtained by means of the sociometric technique can be shown graphically in a *sociogram*. A simple illustration of data derived from a sociometric approach is shown in Figure 13.1A, and the corresponding sociogram in Figure 13.1B shows choices (but not rejections).

Lines going in one direction only → indicate a choice that is not reciprocated; if A chooses B and B chooses A, the lines are shown as going in both directions ↔. The oblong figure shows Fred as not having been chosen by anyone.

Another procedure that yields interesting results is a "Guess Who" test. This contains brief sketches of personal traits—such as, this is a person who always is fair; this is a person who always has to have the last word—and the members of the group are asked to write in the names of persons in the group whom, in their view, such descriptions fit.

Name and Number	Sex	Age	Chooses	Chosen by	Rejects	Rejected by	Mutual choices
1. Adam	M	16	2, 3	3, 4	10		3
2. Jonathan	M	15	6, 9	1, 9	4, 10		9
3. James	M	16	1, 4, 5	1, 5	8	9	1, 5
4. Justin	M	16	1, 5, 8	3, 8	10	2	8
5. Jeffrey L.	M	15	3, 8	3, 4			3
6. Paul	M	17	7, 9	2	10		
7. Ian	M	16	9	6	10		
8. Alex	M	16	4	4, 5, 9		3	4
9. Jeffrey S.	M	16	2, 8	2, 6, 7	3		2
10. Fred	M	16				1, 2, 4, 6, 7	

Figure 13.1A.

[3] Studies using sociometric methods appear widely in the literature on adolescence. Many such studies are published in the journal, *Sociometry*.

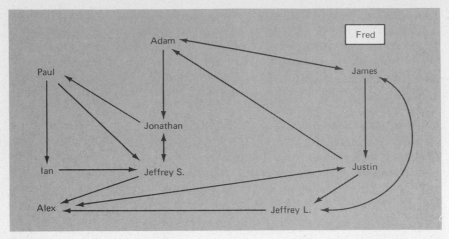

Figure 13.1B.

Characteristics of Adolescents Who Are Well Liked

Research studies have listed many characteristics of adolescents who are regarded as most acceptable and least acceptable by members of their group. Such lists are a little misleading, of course, because it is usually a person in his or her totality rather than just a certain one of his or her traits that attracts or repels others. However, it is worth noting some of these traits. In his review of the literature on peer interaction and social organization, Hartup (1970) concludes that there is a remarkable consistency concerning the variables associated with popularity.

One psychological characteristic frequently named in a person who is liked is that he or she likes others.[4] Another frequently mentioned characteristic is a certain kind of freedom and spontaneity and willingness to enter into things, which may be described in terms such as "active in games," "you can have fun with him or her," "willing to take a chance," "initiates games and activities." Other qualities frequently mentioned are liveliness, cheerfulness, and gaiety (described in such terms as "enjoys a joke," "is cheerful and happy"). Fairness and good sportsmanship; being "natural" and free of pretense; ("not conceited," "enjoys a joke on himself"); and tidiness and cleanliness are also sometimes mentioned, as are qualities such as "seems to come from a good home."

Scattered data regarding adolescents show that those named far more frequently than the average in sociometric tests tend to be persons who have

[4] For studies bearing on this subject, see Ryan and Davie (1958), and Duck and Spencer (1972).

qualities that bring people together in constructive ways; who conform to the mores of the peer group; who are considered advanced in moral judgment by their peers; and who can initiate and plan. Quite clearly, the data do not imply that the popular individual is overly conforming; the popular person, however, does make compromises in order to achieve the most efficient working of the group (Moore, 1967).

Several investigators have found that there is a positive relationship between social acceptance and intelligence (Sells and Roff, 1967, as cited by Hartup, 1970) and between social acceptance and academic achievement (Muma, 1965). But, intelligence and academic achievement do not influence social acceptance as much as some other characteristics.

A small, but consistent, number of studies suggest that social acceptance is associated with physical appearance. The relationship between popularity and physical attractiveness and motor skills is discussed in earlier chapters.

Characteristics of Students in "The Leading Crowd"

In many (and perhaps nearly all) groups of adolescents, particularly in a high school community, there is a cluster, or aggregate, of young persons who can be called the leading crowd—persons who collectively rank above the average in prestige and social influence. The "crowd" may be closely or loosely knit, and among members of the crowd there may be varying degrees of friendliness, competitiveness, and even, at times, rivalries that border on hostility. In a large aggregation of adolescents, there may be ethnic and socioeconomic subgroups that have overlapping memberships or are completely distinct from each other.

As shown in Figure 13.2, Canadian high school students selected friendliness, good looks, money, and athletic ability as leading to membership in the leading crowd. The fact that academic excellence is least mentioned is striking (Friesen, 1968), and is consistent with findings, derived from another approach, mentioned in Chapter 5.

Figure 13.3 presents data on items considered by high school students as being important for popularity (Friesen, 1968).

We might note the tendency for high school students to select "being an athletic star," and "being in the leading crowd," as being most instrumental in achieving popularity. It seems from Figure 13.3 that "high grades, honor roll" are relatively unimportant in terms of popularity among adolescents, but it is also possible that there are many who secretly envy the most able students.

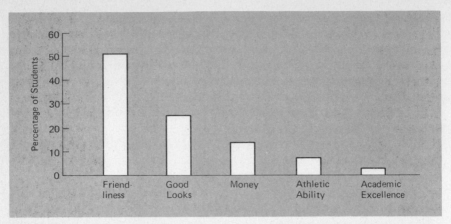

Figure 13.2. Major characteristics considered necessary for membership in leading crowd. [Adapted from "Academic-athletic-popularity syndrome in the Canadian high school society" by D. Friesen, *Adolescence*, 1968, *3*, 39–52.]

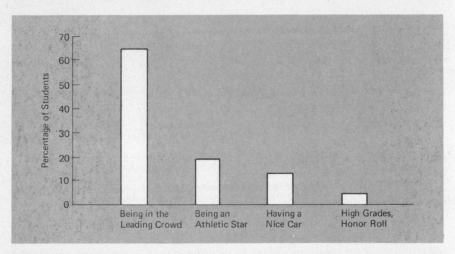

Figure 13.3. Items considered most important for popularity. [Adapted from "Adolescence-athletic-popularity syndrome in the Canadian high school society" by D. Friesen, *Adolescence*, 1968, *3*, 39–52.]

Characteristics of Students Who Receive Low Ratings Or Are Rejected by Their Peers

It has been observed (Jennings, 1947) that young people who are not frequently chosen and who are either isolated or rejected show many forms of behavior that have the effect of drawing people apart rather than bringing them together.

The general trend of the findings concerning adolescents who have a low level of acceptance by the group or who are ignored or rejected by members of the group is that they often, in the privacy of their own lives, are rather moody, troubled, and distressed. It has been observed, for example, that those with low social acceptance often seem to show symptoms of insecurity; many of them seem to be troubled by problems in their home environment and to be absorbed by difficulties in their own lives to such an extent that they lack the freedom to enter into lively give and take with others.

Consistency in Social Acceptance from One Age Level to Later Age Levels

The characteristics adolescents admire or dislike in one another were investigated by Tryon (1939) in a study in which responses were obtained from a large group at an average age of twelve years and again at the age of about fifteen. The findings showed certain differences between the evaluations made by boys and girls and also changes in values between the ages of twelve and fifteen, notably among girls. At twelve years, the girls described as most acceptable the kind of person who was rather quiet, gracious, conforming, and inclined to be nonaggressive. At fifteen years, on the other hand, the girls expressed less admiration for sedate and demure behavior and considerably more admiration for liveliness, ability to entertain, a tendency to be active, and the qualities of being a good sport and attractive to boys. Boys were more consistent in their evaluations from twelve to fifteen years. At the earlier age they expressed most admiration for boys who were skillful, daring, and leaders in games. At fifteen years, prestige for the boys still appeared in large measure to be determined by skill, aggressiveness, and fearlessness. In only one pair of traits was there a marked reversal on the part of boys in this group. At twelve years, being unkempt in appearance tended to be regarded more as a positive than as a negative quality, but at fifteen years this characteristic was disapproved of. What with present-day tastes in dress, the same findings might not emerge if the study were repeated.

In this group of young people, the traits that made boys attractive to girls also tended to rate high as traits giving a boy prestige within his own sex group. On the other hand, there was not so much overlapping between qualities that made a girl attractive to the opposite sex and admired by her own sex. Tryon makes the point that more demands are placed on girls than on boys for flexibility and for the capacity to readjust their values. However, Tryon also suggests that the fact that most of the girls, during the period of the study, had passed through the pubescent period, whereas probably less than half of the boys had done so, also had made a difference.

There is likely to be a great similarity from year to year in the extent to which a person is accepted by his or her peers (Hartup, 1970) during the preadolescent years. Consistency in peer acceptance has often been measured by giving individuals sociometric tests on two or more occasions.

As early as the age of two and a half, there is evidence that sociability is related to friendship and involvement with peers at a later age of at least seven (Waldrop and Halverson, 1975). At the elementary school level it has been noted that in some groups social acceptance scores remain almost as constant from year to year as the scores the children earn on tests of intelligence and academic achievement (Bonney, 1943a and 1943b). In a study by Laughlin (1954) children rated one another while in the sixth grade and again when they had moved on to the seventh grade in a junior high school. There was a marked tendency for youngsters to maintain their popularity ratings even after they had moved to the upper school, where there was a good deal of mixing of populations that had come from various elementary schools.

Repeated sociometric ratings were obtained in a longitudinal study over a period of three years by Sells and Roff (1967, as cited by Hartup, 1970). The social acceptance scores showed a fairly high degree of stability. (Test-retest correlation with an interval of one year was approximately .50. With an interval of three years, the coefficient was .40.) In retests of high school students' choices of leisure-time companions, Wertheimer (1957) found correlations ranging from .55 to .71, when comparisons were made over periods ranging from eight to twenty months. It is possible, however, that as a result of the shifts in group membership that occur when adolescents leave high school and go to college, there may also be a shift in the ratings they receive at the college level. The data on this question, however, are limited.

Acceptance and Social Adjustment

Youngsters who have qualities that make them acceptable to their peers obviously have many advantages. They are likely to be more secure both in their individual lives at school and in their social relationships outside of school than those who are rejected by others. In a study of over 2,000 adolescents, Feinberg (1953) found that young persons who were accepted by others had, on the whole, a more favorable view of themselves than the rejected ones, and that they had better relationships with their parents and teachers.

One of the issues raised is whether peer-group acceptance is related to feelings of self-esteem. Those youngsters who have qualities that make them acceptable to their peers should, theoretically, have advantages conducive to self-esteem. In a review of research in this area, however, Hartup (1970) concludes that the studies do not consistently confirm a relationship between self-esteem and peer acceptance. It is possible that some young people are uneasy about the foundations of their popularity.

Popularity with peers has been found to be associated with a number of indices of mental health. In a long-term follow-up study, Cowan et al. (1973) reported that unpopular children more often than popular ones were found in a communitywide psychiatric register. Social isolation has also been found to be related to high suicide rates (Stengel, 1972) and to delinquent behavior (Roff et al., 1972).

Discrepancies Between Personal and Social Adjustment

Although the adolescent who is highly accepted by his peers is a social success, we cannot take for granted that good social adjustment, as indicated by high popularity ratings, means good personal adjustment. Neither can we assume that a low degree of acceptance by peers is a sign that an adolescent is personally maladjusted. To judge the meaning of high or low acceptance by peers it is essential to consider the standards and values the peers are applying. As we have noted elsewhere, adolescents place a higher value on athletic ability than on intellectual ability. Yet, in adult life, an individual is likely to find that good brains are a more important personal and social asset than athletic ability.

To assess the meaning of high acceptance by peers it is also necessary to consider the price a person pays for it (see, for example, Wittenberg and Berg, 1952). Young persons who take extra pains to win popularity may be ones who lack confidence in themselves. They may be ones whose assurance of their own worth is so weak that they must endlessly strive to prove, by way of hard-won popularity, that they are worthy persons. Among those who win a high degree of social acceptance on a sociometric test, there are some who are "seriously disturbed" (Northway and Wigdor, 1947).

The fact that high acceptance by peers does not in itself reflect or produce a kind of mellow friendliness and friendly attitude toward others is shown in a study by Foshay (1951). He noted that children with high peer acceptance sometimes were quite inconsiderate of children with low peer acceptance or of other children with high acceptance.

Adult Judgments of Adolescents and Their Behavior

If an adolescent has qualities that make him or her well liked by peers, he or she probably will also impress adults as a likeable person, but there are many exceptions to this (see, for example, Gronlund, 1953). Adult appraisals of adolescents may be influenced as much or more by stereotyped ideas about adolescents and their own unrecognized needs as by what the adolescents are actually doing (Anthony, 1975). It is often difficult for adults to detect and appreciate the characteristics that influence the extent to which an adolescent is accepted or rejected by his or her peers. An adult is likely to misjudge an adolescent's standing with his or her peers if the adult sees the adolescent entirely from the viewpoint of adult goals and standards. Adults who judge adolescents mainly in terms of the respect and deference they show toward their elders may be using a standard that has little meaning when adolescents judge each other. According to Hurlock (1974), favoritism by teachers is shown at times toward students who achieve in the academic area as they are usually cooperative in the classroom setting and partly because it is ego satisfying to teachers to have students who have done well.

In one study in an institution (Fauquier and Gilchrist, 1942), it was found that teachers and house parents, when asked to judge who were the leaders among boys, identified less than 50 per cent of those the boys themselves named as leaders. In another area, the difficulty teachers have in understanding adolescents was brought out by a puzzled teacher who "likened the experience of his contact with adolescents to a ride on the big dipper, 'sometimes you are down, but you never know for certain when the next swing was coming' [Anthony, 1975, p. 113]."

Bonney (1947) found that high school teachers were more successful in identifying students who were well accepted by other students than in identifying those who were poorly accepted. In this study it was also found that teachers tended to overrate students who were outstanding in class and courteous in dealing with their teachers but lacked skill in interpersonal relations with their peers.

Competition

An important feature of adolescents' relationships with other persons is the way they compete and the needs in their lives they try to fill by competition. In the youth culture, competition may occur under a veneer of noncompetitive fun and good fellowship. Competitiveness may serve a cluster of motivations (Maccoby and Jacklin, 1974). An adolescent may, for example, be mainly interested in achieving the highest score ever attained on the college entrance board tests; in this case performance is measured against an abstract standard. Another student may be attempting to score higher than fellow students on a particular test. Still another adolescent may just be interested in achieving at a level congruent with his or her potential, without feeling that it is necessary to surpass someone else.

The typical adolescent has had a great amount of experience as a competitor. Most adolescents began during the preschool period to compare themselves with others—at the age of four or thereabouts—keeping an eye on what others were doing and trying to outdo them or at least do as well. According to Hurlock (1974), young children become aware that their parents prefer that they excel academically, or in athletics, as well as be part of the leading crowd. At a later time, they also discover that the social group rewards those who come out on top.

Much of children's growing perception of themselves comes about through comparing themselves with others. Their developing conceptions of who they are, what they are, and what they can do depend in part on opportunities to observe what others do and what others are. One way of testing one's strength and ability is to vie with others. Competition serves a healthy and important *developmental* purpose when children and adolescents try out their growing powers in spontaneous competition with others. Some competition of this sort is inevitable, and as long as it is an aid to realistic self-discovery it is healthy. Competition is also healthy when it is undertaken in a spirit of fun and when it adds to a person's zest for life. In the broader sense, competition may involve varying degrees of cooperation. In some team sports, competition between the teams and cooperation within the team prevail.

It is also good for youngsters to compete if that is necessary in order to safeguard their own self-interest in a realistic and equitable way. It is a sign of good health if youngsters see to it that they get their chance even if it means that they have to vie with someone else to get it, vigorously strive to get their proper share of things to work with, and actively seek, in dealings with adults, to get the attention that is their due.

What can be said concerning the intensity of competition and the identity of the opponent? As noted elsewhere in this book, many females in the past have been reluctant to win in competition with males, out of fear that to do so would seem unfeminine, and some males feel threatened by competition with females who might surpass them.

Adult Models of Competition

Competition is not only a developmental phenomenon but also a pervasive *cultural* condition in the adolescent's world. The American adolescent (in common with adolescents in many areas of the world) is surrounded by an adult society saturated with competition. People compete for attention, for possessions, for power, and for prestige. They compete in the sphere of love and sex.

Most adolescents emulate the competitiveness that prevails in the adult world. For example, a class discussion at school is often a competitive marathon (as discussions frequently are at the adult level). In almost every group, some adolescents are especially adept and aggressive in this kind of competition. They watch their timing and then plunge in to have their say when a previous speaker has barely closed his mouth. In the meantime, other members of the class, equally competitive but less adept, silently make speeches to themselves.

Observation of adults indicates that men are more likely to be involved in open competition with their contemporaries than females, in terms of jobs and position, although the pattern apparently is changing.

Unhealthy Aspects of Competition

While competition can be healthy and constructive, it can also be employed in unhealthy ways. Competitiveness is unhealthy when it is not employed as a form of venturesome self-discovery but represents a compulsive need to outdo others. It may be a symptom of low self-esteem that drives people endlessly to "prove" their worth by surpassing others. Individuals are victims of self-defeating competitiveness when their need to surpass others is so strong that they are unable wholeheartedly to enjoy any activity or experience for its own sake. Competitive individuals are also defeating themselves when, in struggling to be viewed as a success, they antagonize the very persons whose good opinion they are trying to win (we noted some aspects of this in the discussion of anxiety in Chapter 11). The most serious self-defeating aspect of competitiveness is that individuals who must incessantly prove their worth by surpassing others can never really succeed. They may win many battles, but they wage a losing war. The acclaim they might win from others can never serve as a substitute for confidence in themselves.

There are many other contrasts between healthy and unhealthy competition. Individuals who are the masters of their competitiveness use it discriminately. Whether they compete for the fun of it (in a friendly game of bridge) or for an ulterior purpose (such as competing with others in an examination to qualify for a promotion), they choose where and how and when they will compete. They also choose not to compete when there is no reason to do so, and they do not enter contests that are outside their field of competence. Compulsive competitors, on the other hand, are often indiscriminate. They plunge in, even when they have nothing to gain—other than to gratify a need to get attention. They may try to impress people whose opinions really do not matter. It is difficult for them to listen to a conversation without horning in. They are constantly making a mental comparison between themselves and others.

Competition is unhealthy, too, when it is a symptom of an underlying streak of hostility, offering an opportunity to gloat over others. Such hostility is compounded by deceit when the competitors pretend they are competing in sportsmanlike fashion while looking for opportunities to violate the rules of the game. Competitiveness with underlying hostility is frequently carried on by persons who, when competing by proxy as spectators, cheer when a member of the opposing team is hurt or jeer when an opponent by proxy comes to grief.

One of the mildest, but most common, forms of callous competition is manifested by persons who are inveterate bores in conversation. If someone has a toothache they cannot give themselves time to sympathize with the sufferer; instead, they are quick to recall a humdinger of an ache they once had; or they break in to announce that their teeth have always been perfect or that they have the best (or the poorest) dentist in six counties. If the talk is of travel, they insist on reporting regretfully that they have not traveled, or on describing the travels they have made. If the other person has had an accident, they quickly recount accidents they have been in or speak of their prudence in avoiding accidents.

Adolescents may have burdensome competitive tendencies even though they do not seem to be competitive. Their competitiveness may be so strong that they dare not take the chance of losing, carefully avoiding open competition for a grade or a place on a team or for a date. It may be so desperately important for them to make a good showing that they will not risk the chance of making a poor showing.

When individuals are driven by competition, even moments of great triumph have a melancholy flavor. If the motives that won for them were ulterior and devious they may dimly perceive that their triumph is a symptom of weakness and not a sign of strength.

Conformity

Several accounts of adolescent socialization have suggested that conformity to peer pressure increases between the ages of seven to twelve or thirteen and then gradually decreases. The percentages of males who conformed to peer influence at various ages in one study are shown in Figure 13.4.

As shown in Figure 13.4, conformity to the group rose in middle childhood and then declined after age twelve-thirteen.

Conformity and competition have much in common, for both the one who conforms and the one who competes judge their conduct according to the pace and standards set by others.

The pressure to conform exercises a powerful influence on the behavior of young persons at the high school and college levels (Coleman,

Figure 13.4. Percentages of conformity as a function of age level (*n* = 36 per age level). [Adapted from "Conformity development as a function of self-blame" by P. R. Costanzo, *Journal of Personality and Social Psychology*, 1970, *14*, 366–374.]

1961; Friesen, 1968). A desire to conform is closely linked with a desire to be accepted and liked. In polls of teenage attitudes and opinions conducted during a period of seventeen years, Remmers and Radler (1957) note that American teen-agers show substantial class differences but those of low income and high income are similar in their desire for popularity and their conformist attitude and similar in that their highest concern is to be liked. According to Remmers and Radler this is the most striking and consistent fact that has emerged from polls through a period of seventeen years.

In their urge to conform, many teen-agers do things they claim they actually disapprove of, such as using illegal drugs. Remmers and Radler (1957) say that the whole matter is summed up in the comment of a teenage girl who said it is hard for a teen-ager to say, "I don't care to" when all the rest of the gang say "Ah, come on."

Conforming behavior may extend through the entire community of adolescents—as when teen-agers conform to the conduct of the crowd they are running around with or act according to the standards of a certain gang. A youngster who does things generally viewed as bad in order to be regarded as a good guy by members of the gang is a conformist according to the mores of that group, even though, in the eyes of others, he is a nonconformist. Remmers and Radler (1957) state that probably one of the most important factors leading to delinquency is a need to be accepted by the gang.

Conformity is not, of course, limited to adolescence—it pervades adult society as well. Complete nonconformity would, of course, mean chaos.

Only about one fourth of the young persons who took part in the survey by Remmers and Radler (1957) claimed that they often disagreed with the prevailing opinion in the group to which they belonged. We might expect that there would be more nonconformists than this if schools were succeeding in getting students to think for themselves.

Social leisure-time interests and activities

Most of the adolescents' leisure-time interests and occupations are shared with others. They are undertaken not only for their own sake but as a basis for companionship. Even homework is often done jointly with someone else, or is the subject of long telephone conversations.

Among the most common leisure-time activities teen-agers frequently share with others are hanging around with friends; going to the movies; attending church services; playing or watching games; participating in sports; attending club meetings; and going to parties or discotheques (Lukoff and Brook, 1976). Reading is usually a solitary occupation. However, many young people do not seem to pursue this very passionately. In a survey by Gallup and Hill (1961), one third of high school and college students said they had not read a book in the four months preceding the time the survey was made. This presumably refers to leisure-time reading, for more persons than this must have done some required reading at school. Hobbies also are sometimes solitary undertakings, but a hobbyist frequently joins a club, or at least now and then exhibits his hobby to others.

Before television sets were available in a majority of homes, a large proportion of youngsters visited friends who had a set. Even now that TV sets are common, persons usually prefer to watch with a companion. According to a study conducted by Lukoff and Brook (1976), 57 per cent of boys and girls of high school age reported that they watched at least three hours of TV a day and 24 per cent reported watching at least two hours of television a day. This represents one of the most universal and time-consuming adolescent leisure-time activities. Many youngsters will sit alone for long periods of time at the TV set, but often this seems to be from lack of opportunity to do something else or lack of an available companion. Scott (1953) found that 85 per cent of a group of children reported that they watched television an average of over two hours a day, but a smaller proportion (59 per cent) named television as their first choice as a leisure-time activity.

"Youthese"

The significance of language and its consequences for behavior has been stressed by Kluckhohn (1954), who notes that the vocabularies of different languages both reflect and perpetuate habitual and distinctive ways of categorizing experience or modes of thought. In addition to this, he says that the way people behave toward one another is, in part, a function of what they call each other. Each generation of adolescents has a special lingo, a favored set of expressions with which they spice their conversation. Based on observations of peer groups as well as intensive interviews of adolescents, Schwartz and Merten (1967) contend that the adolescents' perceptions of their social world are incorporated in a distinctive argot. At times adults have difficulty understanding that argot (Schwartz and Merten, 1967). In a discussion of this "tribal tongue," Gallup and Hill (1961) note that often it is imaginative and sometimes obscene. It changes frequently and is quickly out of date; and older adolescents abandon expressions when younger ones take them up. In the past or currently, this dialect of youth has included expressions such as groovy (attractive person); grade chaser, brownie, brain, out of it (bright person); wheels, hog, cubes, junk heap (cars); coffin nail, cancer stick, smoke, twig, sticks (cigarettes); rat patrol, fuzz, gun gang, smokey (police and the law); busted (to be arrested); the hold, doomsday, brain stretchers, dull (school, teachers, and exams) (Grinder, 1973). Some expressions seem to be more durable than others, especially when taken over by adults. Many expressions are vivid but, according to Gallup and Hill (1961), are difficult to translate precisely. The terms listed here may already be out of date.

Adolescents and Automobiles

Driving a car serves many motives and purposes. It greatly increases the young person's range of action. The neighboring town, and even the neighboring state, is just next door. Driving a car gives the beginner one of the most impressive and thrilling experiences of being grown up enough to do what adults do. A car is also a form of self-display. A boy can use it not only to visit his girlfriend, but also to impress her and others. Cars also provide a place for love-making. They are a source of endless conversation and activity when hot rodders get together.

According to some claims, the car has a deep significance in connection with an adolescent's strivings and conflicts. For a boy, the power he has under his control may bolster his feelings of masculinity and potency. For a girl, driving a car may be an important symbol of independence. It has also been suggested that the automobile serves as a sexual symbol and as a means of facing sexual conflicts or vicariously satisfying sexual desires. When a car does all this, in addition to serving as a means of transportation, the advertisers are almost guilty of understatement in claiming that a certain auto is an "all-purpose" car. It is no wonder that young people are so eager for a car and so many actually have one.

In a study by Elder (1972), 40 per cent of high school seniors reported that they owned their own car. A number also noted that although they did not own their own car they did have access to a car.

Speeding in a car is often prompted by a desire to impress others or to share a thrill with others (although these are not the only motives). According to one study of middle-class thirteen- to fourteen-year-old boys and fifteen- to nineteen-year-old boys, approximately 6½ per cent of the younger boys and 31 per cent of the older boys reported having participated in drag races along highways with friends (Vaz, 1969). Largely as a consequence of speeding, a large proportion of youth has been in auto accidents. The proportion of accidents among drivers is much higher among boys than girls.[5] However, the fact that girls have fewer accidents than boys while driving a car themselves does not spare the girls from a high accident rate while riding in automobiles as passengers.[6]

During the teens, speeding often seems to afflict youngsters as a contagious disease. Some boys seem to be proud of getting a ticket for speeding, even though they thereby risk the loss of their driver's license—and many do have their licenses suspended or revoked. Furthermore, over a quarter of thirteen- to fourteen-year-old boys and almost two thirds of fifteen- to nineteen-year-old boys reported having driven a car without a driver's license in a study of middle-class boys by Vaz (1969).

One sign that a youngster has grown in "social maturity" (much to the relief of his parents) is that he no longer drives at a furious teenage pace. Some persons never seem to achieve this maturity, for a large proportion of adults are speeders. The dangers of driving were brought out by the President's Commission on Law Enforcement (1969), which reported that of the 49,000 people who lost their lives in automobile accidents in 1965, more than half of the deaths resulted from accidents involving either negligent manslaughter or driving while intoxicated. Evidence to show that many adolescents do slow down as they enter and move through their twenties is that the accident rates decline (and automobile insurance rates, for boys, are sharply reduced).

Youth movements

Youth movements begin in the reactions of young men and women to the historic, social, political, cultural, and psychological trends and issues in

[5] In the poll mentioned here, 29 per cent of male high school seniors and 12 per cent of female seniors, as drivers, had one or more accidents; among upperclassmen in college, the corresponding percentages were 51 and 25; and among working youths, 52 and 21 percent.

[6] The percentage of boys and girls who had been in accidents as passengers was about the same for boys and girls among high school seniors (38 and 35 per cent) and among college upper-class boys and girls (43 and 41 per cent).

a particular society at a particular time. Conflicts of interest between groups and contradictions in the social structure are particularly likely to generate youth movements. When young people want something they cannot have in a given social structure, movements may arise as a protest, or as an effort to try to satisfy their wishes (Liebert, 1971).

The reasons adolescents are often in the vanguard of radical movements are unclear, but perhaps they stem in part from the adolescent's search for moral principles (Piaget, 1965) and for identity. An adolescent's acquaintance with politics begins in childhood but receives a big boost with the establishment of formal operational thinking at age eleven or twelve. Adolescents become able to conceptualize abstract ideologies, which are given emotional drive for expression by the massive psychophysiological changes that occur at puberty. According to several investigators (Braungart, 1971; Keniston, 1971; Kohlberg, 1970), the politics of the most politically active adolescents often reflect the social, familial, intellectual, and political values learned from parents at an earlier age. But, in their effort to achieve independence or to protest against the reign of the older generation, many adolescents for a time espouse political views that differ from those of their parents.

The wave of political activism that swept the country, and indeed the world, during the 1960s has been described as an outcome of many influences.[7] The baby boom following World War II provided a larger than usual number of adolescents in one generational group. The percentage of adolescents attending college shot up in the 1960s (Douglas, 1970), and in some institutions a college-aged subculture developed with its own ideologies and life-styles. The increase in the number of adolescents in the population in the 1960s is now tapering off, and demographic studies have predicted an even greater decline in the percentage of adolescents in the 1980s (Moynihan, 1973). According to Braungart (1975), only a small percentage (less than 5 per cent) of college students are political activists, and it may be that with changes in the values of adolescents this percentage will drop in future years.

College-centered movements that appeared in the 1960s represented concerns about civil rights, the Vietnam war, amnesty, women's liberation, homosexual (gay) rights, black power, free speech, and ecology. Some of the persons involved in these movements formed subgroups, such as Students for a Democratic Society (SDS) and Weathermen, which grew out of the anti-Vietnam war movement and led to the formation of a "New Left." These groups often tended to be international in scope; for example, a

[7] In view of the fact that the activism here discussed seemed to arise quite suddenly, and then, in its overt manifestations at least, appeared rather soon to subside, some of what has been said about it is, understandably, less conclusive than one could wish.

youth group in Stockholm might be as likely to demonstrate for civil rights and against the Vietman war as a group in Los Angeles.

The causes of the appearance of so many protesting groups in the 1960s, as opposed to the dearth of protests in the "silent 1950s," are manifold and must be sought in the interplay of historical, economic, psychological, political, and social trends. Sometimes a charismatic leader may play a role in propelling people into activism. President Kennedy, with his call to "ask not what your country can do for you, but what you can do for your country," probably inspired many with his plea for idealistic self-sacrifice. Civil rights became a primary cause early in the 1960s, whereas the antiwar movement predominated later in the decade. It should be noted that there have been wars and charismatic leaders in the past, and these doubtless will recur, each time inspiring a variety of reactions. So it is and has been for all social, political, and historical movements, which tend to repeat themselves. Given the proper concatenation of events, college protest groups will probably once again become active, as they were in the 1930s and 1960s.

To trace in detail the specific causes of each of the various protest movements that occurred in the recent past is beyond the scope of this chapter, but it is appropriate to offer a brief overview of the complexity of a subject about which many books and articles have been written. It seems clear that arguments attributing youth movements to a single cause, such as economic recession, should be viewed with skepticism. Although it is true that the adolescent unemployment rate increased in the 1960s (Moynihan, 1973), this does not serve by itself to explain the growth or the diversity of protest movements of that decade. Some who have examined the matter point to more specific intergenerational conflicts and suggest that in some groups there was a more total rejection of adult values than has occurred before (Friedenberg, 1969, 1969a; Reich, 1970).

Attempts to explain the behavior and moods of youth in the 1960s range from speculation to factual observations. In the latter category, for example, there is evidence of what seems to be a trend away from intellectualism (Yankelovich, 1969). College Board scores and the reading abilities of students going to college are lower than they once were. More students have appeared to be interested in participating in political activities in the early 1970s than in the late 1960s. Some groups have shown a decrease in religious beliefs (Hastings and Hoge, 1970). A leftward swing in political beliefs in the 1960s seems to have been followed by a more conservative stance in some areas. According to Astin (1976), of the American Council on Education, a majority of students support the conservative view today. There has been a greater acceptance of the view that women should play a more significant role in the occupational world—but this seems to reflect a changing attitude in the population at large.

The characteristics of student activists have been studied by several investigators (Keniston, 1971; Kerpelman, 1972; Liebert, 1971; Starr, 1974; Whittaker and Watts, 1971). Some findings from these studies follow, although it should again be noted that findings and theories dealing with relatively recent complex social phenomena must be viewed as tentative.

Demographically, most protests—and, hence, most student activists—began at the prestigious schools in the country: primarily private liberal arts colleges and universities and large state universities, such as Swarthmore, Columbia, Yale, and the University of California at Berkeley, and then spread to other colleges and some high schools (Foster and Long, 1970).

Studies of personality and demographic characteristics have not revealed that left-wing student activists differed from college students in general in age, sex, and college level (Braungart, 1975; Smith et al., 1970). They did tend to come from middle- and upper-middle-class families in which the parents had college degrees and often postgraduate education. Many of them had prestigious, high-status occupations.

Gradually, as the decade progressed, parental socioeconomic status became less significant in distinguishing activists from nonactivists (Kasschau et al., 1974). Activists often came from cities and their suburbs (the proportion of people living in the cities has tripled in the last 100 years) and from the coasts, rather than from the middle of the country (Braungart, 1971; Keniston, 1971). Parents of left-wing activists tended to be politically liberal and involved, passing these views on to their children (see, for example, Troll et al., 1969). Few activists came from radical or very conservative homes. Jewish persons and those with liberal or nonpracticing Protestant backgrounds were most commonly found in activist groups, with a smaller representation of persons with a Catholic and conservative, religious Protestant background. The activists themselves tended to be nonreligious (see, for example, Smith et al., 1970). Quakers and Unitarians were more numerous than Baptists and Presbyterians.

Many investigators have suggested that the political and religious views of student activists represented values learned in the home (Haan et al., 1968; Keniston, 1971; Kohlberg, 1970). These values were said to include humanitarianism, social interest, idealism, and self-expression (Starr, 1974). College appeared to play a catalytic role in students' willingness to protest. Students with a white-collar parental background were more disposed to protest than students with a blue-collar background. Blue-collar youth who did not attend college were more inclined to protest in behalf of right-wing causes, but college students in the blue-collar group who did protest were more likely than their noncollege counterparts to espouse left-wing causes (Kasschau et al., 1974).

Most activists had parents who espoused liberal and egalitarian socialization methods; few authoritarian or overpermissive parents were represented in the activist groups, according to several well-known investigators (Haan et al., 1968; Keniston, 1971). This is in contrast to the finding of others that parents of activists were overpermissive. Some investigators reported a low incidence of psychological problems in activists, but others expressed the view that many, particularly the leaders of activist groups, showed more psychopathology than the college student population in general (for example, see Coles, 1967). Many activists did show more intellectual interests than the general student population, often achieving high grades and high scores on intelligence tests. Activists tended to be involved in nonpolitical extracurricular activities, off campus as well as on campus, in addition to their political interests.

Behavior common to protesting youths, including "hippies" and "flower children" (the "counterculture"), was often seen among activists, such as nonconformity in the areas of dress, drug use, and sex.

Student activists tended to major in the humanities, social sciences, and theoretical areas of biological and physical sciences, rather than in applied fields such as engineering, geology, or business. Their later postgraduate interests also were in the areas of social service and humanistic endeavor, rather than in business, medicine, or law.

Three groups of ex-students were included in a follow-up study by Fendrich (1974): former civil rights activists protesting from 1960 to 1963, ex-students active in student government at that time, and ex-students who were not active in any kind of politics. Would student activists move into the mainstream of society (according to a maturation hypothesis) or would they maintain their separateness and sense of alienation as a generational unit? According to Fendrich (1974), persons who were activists as students were likely, after completing their schooling, to continue to be politically active. Former activists had neither entered the mainstream, nor had they dropped out (the disillusionment hypothesis). They tended to be involved in educational and service industries (college teachers and social workers and writers, especially) and participated in voluntary political activities designed to lead to economic and political changes. Whether later activists would follow this model was unclear. Political involvement of activists continued to be marked, with 71 per cent having participated in a demonstration since college. It is possible that there is no distinct cause and effect between student activism and later political attitudes, but that both spring from continuing underlying factors.

Theoretical Explanations of
Student Activism

Several theories have been offered to explain student activism. Theories have included the psychoanalytic concept of oedipal rebellion (Bettelheim, 1963; Feuer, 1969), socialization and family values (Flacks, 1971; Keniston, 1971), moral growth (Block et al., 1968), and political status (Braungart, 1971). The idea of conflict between generations has been widely discussed, especially the "generational unit" model originated by Mannheim (1952). This model finds youth movements leading to social changes occurring within generational units, which are defined as groups of members of the same generation who have been exposed to the same sociohistorical forces and have developed a common identity (Braungart, 1974). Another generational unit might have experienced the same sociohistorical forces but developed a different identity. A different theory has been the structural-functional model espoused by Parsons (1963). According to this theory the various groups, forces, and institutions in society, when effective, function as an integrated whole; if there is failure of integration the consequence is disaffection, rebellion, and alienation.

An example of this is seen in the protests against the Vietnam war; prior to the United States involvement in Vietnam, there was, on the whole, a smooth interplay between college students, colleges and universities, and various branches of government. When the United States became increasingly involved in the Vietnam conflict, integration between these groups broke down for several reasons as societal groups opposed one another. The result was a sharp increase in the number of youths who were rebellious and felt alienated from society as a whole. According to Eisenstadt (1963), another proponent of this theory, youth movements represent the rebellion of youth against adult rules and status, in a context in which youths perceive themselves as being discriminated against within the structural differentiation of society. They feel alienated; they seek to be the equals of adults in all spheres of life, a status adult society has denied them.

Age differences are important in both of these theories. The theories differ in conjectures regarding the effects of such age differences on the individual and the groups to which he or she belongs. According to Mannheim (1952), when youths join political groups (different generational units) of either conservative or liberal bent, such groups are reacting to the same historic events in different ways. The members of a group differ from members of another group in their particular inner psychological structure and perception of events. Functionalists referred to earlier (Parsons and Eisenstadt) suggest the existence of an already highly organized and stable society with its parts working together as one integrated whole; generational unit theory, in contrast, emphasizes the evolution of society to better-integrated, smoother-working, and higher forms of social structure. The latter theory further posits that youths are in better touch than their elders with the current issues that particularly affect their generation. Generational unit theory can account for the coexistence of conservative and radical youth movements in the same age group. But it is more difficult for functionalist theory to explain such divergence because it views each generation as a complete whole.

Political typologies have been formulated by some investigators to try to further examine student political activists. For example, Block et al. (1968) advance the view that there are six student types: apathetic, alienated, individualist, activist, constructivist, and antisocial. Although in the past there have been proposed student typologies, such typologies have not focused on political beliefs as the one presented here did, but on personality types or types of problem-solving techniques.

It may be said in conclusion that views regarding the origins of activist youth movements remain somewhat speculative. There is a dispute over whether there is generational conflict (the generation gap) and regarding how such conflict expresses itself in ideology and political activism. Although there is some agreement concerning certain characteristics of activists, it does not appear that there is a firm and generally accepted theory that fully embraces the complexity of the interplay of social, historical, economic, cultural, and psychological factors that underlie student activism.

References

Adelson, J., & Douvan, E. Adolescent friendships. In J. J. Conger (Ed.), *Contemporary issues in adolescent development.* New York: Harper, 1975.

Anthony, E. J. The reactions of adults to adolescents and their behavior. In J. J. Conger (Ed.), *Contemporary issues in adolescent development.* New York: Harper, 1975.

Astin, A. W. Freshman dreams. *Newsweek,* January 26, 1976, p. 60.

Baird, L. L. Who protests: A study of student activists. In J. Foster & D. Long (Eds.), *Protest! Student activism in America.* New York: Morrow, 1970.

Bengtson, V. L. The generation gap: A review and typology of social-psychological perspectives. *Youth and Society,* 1970, **2**, 7–32.

Berger, A. S., Gagnon, J. H., & Simon, W. *Gender role expectations among adolescents.* Paper presented at the American Sociological Association, New Orleans, August, 1972.

Bettelheim, B. The problem of generations. In E. Erikson (Ed.), *Youth: Change and challenge.* New York: Basic Books, 1963.

Block, J., Haan, N., & Smith, M. B. Activism and apathy in contemporary adolescents. In J. F. Adams (Ed.), *Understanding adolescence.* Boston: Allyn, 1968.

Bonney, M. E. The constancy of sociometric scores and their relationship to teacher judgments of social success and to personality ratings. *Sociometry*, 1943, **6**, 409–424.a.

Bonney, M. E. The relative stability of social, intellectual and academic status in grades II to IV, and the interrelationships between these various forms of growth. *Journal of Educational Psychology*, 1943, **34**, 88–102.b.

Bonney, M. E. A sociometric study of the relationship of some factors to mutual friendships on the elementary, secondary and college levels. *Sociometry*, 1946, **9**, 21–47.

Bonney, M. E. Sociometric study of agreement between teacher judgments and student choices; in regard to the number of friends possessed by high school students. *Sociometry*, 1947, **10**, 133–146.

Braungart, R. G. Family status, socialization and student politics: A multivariate analysis. *American Journal of Sociology*, 1971, **77**, 108–130.

Braungart, R. G. The sociology of generations and student politics: A comparison of the functionalist and generational unit modes. *Journal of Social Issues*, 1974, **30**, 31–54.

Braungart, R. G. Youth and social movements. In S. E. Dragastin & G. H. Elder, Jr. (Eds.), *Adolescence in the life cycle: Psychological change and social context.* New York: Wiley, 1975.

Brittain, C. V. Adolescent choice and parent-peer cross pressures. *American Sociological Review*, 1963, **38**, 385–391.

Bronfenbrenner, U. *Two worlds of childhood: U.S. and USSR.* New York: Russell Sage Foundation, 1970.

Brook, J. S., Whiteman, M., Peisach, E., & Deutsch, M. Aspiration levels of and for children: Age, sex, race and socioeconomic correlates. *Journal of Genetic Psychology*, 1974, **124**, 3–16.

Byrne, D. The influence of propinquity and opportunities for interaction on classroom relationships. *Human Relations*, 1961, **14**, 63–69.

Byrne, D., Clore, G. L., Jr., & Worchel, P. Effect of economic similarity–dissimilarity on interpersonal attraction. *Journal of Personality and Social Psychology*, 1966, **4**, 220–224.

Campbell, E. Q. Adolescent socialization. In D. A. Goslin (Ed.), *Handbook of socialization theory and research.* Chicago: Rand McNally, 1969.

Coleman, J. S. Athletics in high school. *Annals of the American Academy of Political and Social Science*, 1961, **338**, 33–43.

Coleman, J. S. *The adolescent society.* New York: Free Press, 1961.

Coles, R. Psychiatric observations on students demonstrating for peace. *American Journal of Orthopsychiatry*, 1967, **37**, 107–111.

Costanzo, P. R. Conformity development as a function of self-blame. *Journal of Personality and Social Psychology*, 1970, **14**, 336–374.

Cowan, E. L., Pederson, A., Babigian, H., Izzo, L. D., & Trost, M. A. Long-term follow-up of early detected vulnerable children. *Journal of Consulting and Clinical Psychology*, 1973, **41**, 438–446.

Devereaux, E. C., Shouval, R., Bronfenbrenner, U., Rodgers, R. R., Kav-Venaki, S., Kiely, E., & Karson, E. Socialization practices of parents, teachers, and peers in Israel: The kibbutz versus the city. *Child Development*, 1974, **45**, 269–281.

Douglas, J. D. *Youth in turmoil*. Washington, D.C.: U.S. Government Printing Office, 1970.

Douvan, E., & Adelson, J. *The adolescent experience*. New York: Wiley, 1966.

Duck, S. W., & Spencer, C. Personal constructs and friendship formations. *Journal of Personality and Social Psychology*, 1972, **23**, 40–45.

Dunphy, D. C. The social structure of urban adolescent peer groups. *Sociometry*, 1963, **26**, 230–246.

Eisenstadt, S. N. Archetypal patterns of youth. In E. H. Erikson (Ed.), *Youth: Change and challenge*. New York: Basic Books, 1963.

Elder, G. H., Jr. The social context of youth groups. *International Social Science Journal*, 1972, **24**, 283.

Elder, G. H., Jr. Adolescence in the life cycle: An introduction. In S. E. Dragastin and G. H. Elder, Jr. (Eds.), *Adolescence in the life cycle: Psychological change and social context*. New York: Wiley, 1975.

Erikson, E. H. *Identity: Youth and crisis*. New York: Norton, 1968.

Fauquier, W., & Gilchrist, J. Some aspects of leadership in an institution. *Child Development*, 1942, **13**, 55–64.

Feinberg, M. R. Relation of background experience to social acceptance. *Journal of Abnormal and Social Psychology*, 1953, **48**, 206–214.

Fendrich, J. M. Activists ten years later: A test of generational unit continuity. *Journal of Social Issues*, 1974, **30**, 95–118.

Festinger, L. A theory of comparison processes. *Human Relations*, 1954, **7**, 117–140.

Feuer, L. S. *The conflict of generations*. New York: Basic Books, 1969.

Flacks, R. *Youth and social change*. Chicago: Markham, 1971.

Foshay, A. W. The teacher and children's social attitudes. *Teachers College Record*, 1951, **52**, 287–296.

Foster, J., & Long, D. (Eds.). *Protest! Student activism in America*. New York: Morrow, 1970.

Friedenberg, E. Current patterns of generational conflict. *Journal of Social Issues*, 1969, **25**, 21–38.

Friedenberg, E. Z. The generation gap. *Annals of the American Academy of Political and Social Science*, 1969a, **382**, 32–42.

Friesen, D. Academic-athletic-popularity syndrome in the Canadian high school society (1967). *Adolescence*, 1968, **3**, 39–52.

Gallup, G., & Hill, E. Youth: The cool generation. *Saturday Evening Post*, December 22–30, 1961, pp. 63–80.

Goodnow, R. E., & Taguiri, R. Religious ethnocentrism and its recognition among adolescent boys. *Journal of Abnormal and Social Psychology*, 1952, **47**, 316–320.

Grinder, R. E. *Adolescence*. New York: Wiley, 1973.

Gronlund, N. E. Relationships between the sociometric status of pupils' and teachers' preferences for or against having them in class. *Sociometry*, 1953, **16**, 142–150.

Haan, N., Smith, M. B., & Block, J. Moral reasoning of young adults: Political-social behavior, family background, and personality correlates. *Journal of Personality and Social Psychology*, 1968, **10**, 183–201.

Haller, A. O., & Butterworth, C. E. Peer influences and levels of occupational and educational aspirations. *Social Forces*, 1960, **38**, 289–295.

Hartup, W. W. Peer interaction and social organization. In P. H. Mussen (Ed.), *Carmichael's manual of child psychology* (Vol. 2). New York: Wiley, 1970.

Hastings, P. K., & Hoge, D. R. Religious change among college students over two decades. *Social Forces*, 1970, **49**, 16–28.

Hurlock, E. B. *Personality development*. New York: McGraw-Hill, 1974.

Izard, C. E. Personality similarity and friendship. *Journal of Abnormal and Social Psychology*, 1960, **61**, 47–51.

Jennings, H. H. Leadership and sociometric choice. *Sociometry*, 1947, **10**, 32–49.

Jersild, A. T. *When teachers face themselves*. New York: Bureau of Publications, Teachers College, Columbia University, 1955.

Jourard, S. M., & Friedman, R. Experimenter-subject "distance" and self-disclosure. *Journal of Personality and Social Psychology*, 1970, **15**, 278–382.

Kandel, D. B., & Lesser, G. S. Parental and peer influences on educational plans of adolescents. *American Sociological Review*, 1969, **34**, 212–223.

Kandel, D. B., & Lesser, G. S. *Youth in two worlds*. San Francisco: Jossey-Bass, 1972.

Kasschau, P. L., Ransford, H. E., & Bengtson, V. L. Generational consciousness and youth movement participation: Contrasts in blue collar and white collar youth. *Journal of Social Issues*, 1974, **30**, 69–94.

Keniston, K. A second look at the uncommitted. *Social Policy*, 1971, **2**, 6–19.

Keniston, K. *Youth and dissent*. New York: Harcourt, 1971.

Kerpelman, L. C. *Activists and nonactivists: A psychological study of American college students*. New York: Behavioral Publications, 1972.

Kluckhohn, C. Culture and behavior. In G. Lindsey (Ed.), *Handbook of social psychology* (Vol. 20). Reading, Mass.: Addison-Wesley, 1954.

Kohlberg, L. Moral development and the education of adolescents. In E. D. Evans (Ed.), *Adolescent readings in behavior and development*. New York: Holt, 1970.

Laughlin, F. *The peer status of sixth and seventh grade children*. New York: Bureau of Publications, Teachers College, Columbia University, 1954.

Lerner, R. M. Showdown at generation gap: Attitudes of adolescents and their parents toward contemporary issues. In H. D. Thornburg (Ed.), *Contemporary adolescence: Readings* (2nd ed.). Monterey, Calif.: Brooks/Cole, 1975.

Liebert, R. *Radical and militant youth*. New York: Praeger, 1971.

Lindzey, G., & Byrne, D. Measurement of social choice and interpersonal attractiveness. In G. Lindzey & E. Aronson (Eds.), *The handbook of social psychology* (Vol. 2). Reading, Mass.: Addison-Wesley, 1968.

Loomis, C. P. Ethnic cleavages in the southwest as reflected in two high schools. *Sociometry*, 1943, **6**, 7–26.

Lukoff, I. F., & Brook, J. S. *Activities Index*. Unpublished data, 1976.

Maccoby, E. E., & Jacklin, C. N. *The psychology of sex differences*. Stanford, Calif.: Stanford U.P., 1974.

Moreno, J. L. Old and new trends in sociometry: Turning points in small group research. *International Social Science Bulletin*, 1954, **17**, 179–193.

Moynihan, D. "Peace"—Some thoughts on the 1960s and 1970s. *The Public Interest*, Summer 1973, **32**, 3–12.

Muma, J. R. Peer evaluation and academic performance. *Personnel Guidance Journal*, 1965, **44**, 405–409.

Northway, M. L., & Wigdor, B. T. Rorschach patterns related to the sociometric status of school children. *Sociometry*, 1947, **10**, 186–199.

Orloff, H., & Weinstock, A. A comparison of parent and adolescent attitude factor structures. *Adolescence*, 1975, **10**, 201–205.

Parsons, T. Youth in the context of American society. In E. H. Erikson (Ed.), *Youth: Change and challenge*. New York: Basic Books, 1963.

Piaget, J. *The moral judgment of the child*. New York: Free Press, 1965.

Piaget, J. *Six psychological studies*. New York: Random, 1967.

President's Commission on Law Enforcement. In D. R. Cressey & D. A. Ward (Eds.), *Delinquency, crime and social process*. New York: Harper, 1969.

President's Science Advisory Commission Panel on Youth. *Youth: Transition to adulthood*. Washington, D.C.: Office of Science and Technology, 1973.

Reich, C. A. *The greening of America*. New York: Random, 1970.

Reisman, D. (with N. Glazer & R. Denney). *The lonely crowd*. New Haven, Conn.: Yale, 1950.

Remmers, H. H., & Radler, D. H. *The American teenager*. Washington, D.C.: Bobbs, 1957.

Roff, M., Sells, B., & Golden, M. M. *Social adjustment and personality development in children*. Minneapolis: University of Minnesota Press, 1972.

Ryan, F. R., & Davie, J. S. Social acceptance, academic achievement, and aptitude among high school students. *Journal of Educational Research*, 1958, **52**, 101–106.

Schwartz, G., & Merten, D. The language of adolescence: An anthropological approach to the youth culture. *American Journal of Sociology*, 1967, **72**, 453–468.

Scott, L. F. A study of children's TV interests. *California Journal of Educational Research*, 1953, **4**, 162–164.

Secord, P. F., & Backman, C. W. Interpersonal congruency, perceived similarity, and friendship. *Sociometry*, 1964, **27**, 115–127.

Smith, M. B., Haan, N., & Block, J. Social-psychological aspects of student activism. *Youth and Society*, 1970, **1**(3), 261–288.

Starr, J. The peace and love generation: Changing attitudes towards sex and violence among college youth. *Journal of Social Issues*, 1974, **30**, 73–106.

Stengel, E. *Suicide and attempted suicide*. Middlesex, England: Penguin, 1972.

Stone, C. L. Some family characteristics of socially active and inactive teenagers. *Coordinator*, 1960, **8**, 53–57.

Thornburg, H. D. Socialization and values. In H. D. Thornburg (Ed.), *Contemporary adolescent readings* (2nd ed.). Monterey, Calif.: Brooks/Cole, 1975.

Troll, L., Neugarten, B. L., & Kraines, R. J. Similarities in values and other personality characteristics in college students and their parents. *Merrill-Palmer Quarterly*, 1969, **15**, 323–336.

Tryon, C. M. Evaluation of adolescent personality by adolescents. *Monographs of the Society for Research in Child Development*, 1939, **4**(4).

Vaz, E. W. Juvenile delinquency in the middle-class youth culture. In D. R. Cressey & D. A. Ward (Eds.), *Delinquency, crime and social process*. New York: Harper, 1969.

Waldrop, M. F., & Halverson, C. F., Jr. Intensive and extensive peer behavior: Longitudinal and cross-sectional analysis. *Child Development*, 1975, **46**, 19–26.

Wertheimer, R. R. Consistency of sociometric status position in male and female high school students. *Journal of Educational Psychology*, 1957, **48**, 385–390.

Whittaker, D., & Watts, W. A. Personality characteristics associated with activism and disaffiliation in today's college-age youth. *Journal of Counseling Psychology*, 1971, **18**, 200–206.

Wieder, D. L., & Zimmerman, D. H. Generational experience and the development of freak culture. *Journal of Social Issues*, 1974, **30**, 137–161.

Wittenberg, R. M., & Berg, J. The stranger in the group. *American Journal of Orthopsychiatry*, 1952, **22**, 89–97.

Yankelovich, D. *Generations apart*. New York: Columbia Broadcasting System, 1969.

14

dating, courtship, and early marriage

Dating

Dating provides one of the most thrilling pastimes in adolescence and some of the most outstanding memories of adolescence in later years of life. In our society, dating has provided adolescents with the opportunity to improve their interpersonal and social skills and to try out roles that characterize the marital relation without having to commit themselves to the responsibility of

385

marriage (McDaniel, 1969). In the words of Hill and Aldous (1969) dating "is playful interaction rather than 'playing for keeps' [p. 909]."

In addition to providing friendship, affection, and at times love, dating may be the means by which adolescents prove or maintain status in our society (Skipper and Nass, 1966). Dating also prepares the way for eventual mate selection. Cooperation with peers of the opposite sex is enhanced to some extent as a result of dating. At the same time, some adolescents have also used dating as a means of sexual experimentation (Rice, 1975).

Although dating has proven to be quite beneficial in orienting the adolescent toward marriage and helping him or her to develop more intimate relationships with the opposite sex, some adolescents have been hurt or even exploited by their dating partner. Then, too, some dates are "so superficial and circumscribed that couples never transcend the 'patter' of their respective 'lives' [Hill and Aldous, 1969, p. 910]."

As is to be expected, many youngsters embark on their first "real date" with some apprehension and shyness (Christensen, 1952), but usually this wears off in time.[1] Some also begin dating in order to conform to group expectations, rather than from an impelling personal desire (Crist, 1953), but more adolescents date because they want to than because they think they ought to.

Dating includes a vast range of activities beyond formal arrangements for "calling" or "going out" to the movies or a party or dance. Some youngsters "date" by means of long private telephone conversations long before they start to "go together" in public. Often, by prior understanding or an unspoken arrangement, boys and girls meet or seemingly "just happen" to meet in the halls or library at school, on the street, at a soda fountain, a community fair, a school dance, or elsewhere. Such meetings, whether by prearrangement or chance, usually do not require that the youngsters must request permission from their parents to have a date. Neither do they commonly require that the boy is obligated to call for the girl at her home or take her home or spend money to entertain her. Through rendezvous of this sort many young persons actually are dating even though they are not going together or dating in the usual meaning of the term.

Adolescents are more likely than their mothers to stress the importance of going out on dates. In a study of Danish and American high school students and their mothers, Kandel and Lesser (1972) reported that many more American and Danish adolescents, in contrast to their mothers, consider dating to be of high importance.

A large proportion of adolescents, particularly girls, would like to start dating before their parents want them to do so. In a study published in

[1] For a description of a dating adjustment scale for college students, see Herold (1973).

1924, Smith found that girls reported they were first interested in going out with boys at some time in the age range from ten to eighteen years; the median age was fourteen years. However, it was not until the typical girl reached sixteen that she received permission from her parents to go out with boys. In a more recent survey conducted by Bell and Chaskes (1970), it was noted that the average coed began to date at 13.2 years. According to several studies, by age seventeen, nearly all adolescents have begun to date (see, for example, Dickinson, 1975).

Adolescents from families of high socioeconomic status are more likely to date early than adolescents from homes low on the socioeconomic scale (Lowrie, 1961). In a study of the dating behavior of high school students, Dickinson (1975) reported that black and white adolescents were quite similar in the age when they first started dating and in frequency of dating, as shown in Table 14.1.

Frequency of Dating

Sociocultural, personality, and attitudinal factors are related to frequency of dating. There is considerable variation in dating patterns among high school students (Cameron and Kenkel, 1960). As might be expected, older students tend to date more frequently than younger students. Students who date more often at older ages tended to date at earlier ages than students who do not date as frequently (Lowrie, 1961). Sex differences in frequency of dating occur among high school students; girls tend to date more often than boys (Lowrie, 1956).

Dickinson (1975) studied the dating behavior of black and white sophomore, junior, and senior high school students in 1964 and 1974 and found that the dating frequency was quite similar in blacks and whites, before and after the school system was desegregated. (See Table 14.1.)

Among the other factors that have been reported to be related to frequency of dating and desire to date a particular individual are physical

Table 14.1. Frequency distribution (in percentages) of dates by year and race

Frequency of dates	Whites		Blacks	
	1964	1974	1964	1974
Less than once a month	23	17	23	13
Less than once a week but at least once a month	10	24	12	31
At least once a week	67	59	65	56
(N)	(216)	(270)	(88)	(128)

Source: From "Dating behavior of black and white adolescents before and after desegregation" by G. E. Dickinson, *Journal of Marriage and the Family,* 1975, **37**, 602–608. Copyright 1975 by National Council on Family Relations. Reprinted by permission.

attractiveness (Byrne et al., 1970; Walster et al., 1966), personality characteristics, and family rules (Vockell and Asher, 1972). In a study based on a sample of data from Project TALENT, Vockell and Asher (1972) found that high school students with high levels of both academic potential and achievement tended to date less often than their contemporaries at lower levels. Moreover, some students who dated more often participated less in extracurricular activities. Based on their results, Vockell and Asher (1972) proposed that "many students do not find the rewards they need in school, and so they are forced to make a choice between school activities and their own social activities [p. 382]."

Dating Behavior

Some adolescents (and some postadolescents) have one date after another that involve no more than companionable talk and going to a place of entertainment, to the beach, or the like; but such behavior is exceptional. Eventually (or immediately) the daters begin to woo and court one another.

The most frequent types of activities engaged in by white and black high school students are presented in Table 14.2.

As shown in Table 14.2, black dating behavior was found to be more similar to white dating behavior in 1974 than in 1964 (Dickinson, 1975).

A variety of factors influence what occurs between adolescents on a date. Most dates involve some physical contact ranging from holding hands and kissing or hugging to actually having intercourse. It appears that most dates eventually involve necking or petting. Petting appears to have increased considerably among the young in recent years, according to a study by Miller and Simon (1974). They report that for fourteen- and fifteen-year-olds, light petting is normative. Approximately half of their sample engaged in it. In a national study of adolescents ranging in age

Table 14.2.   Most frequent activity on date by year and race in percentages

Activity	Whites		Blacks	
	1964	1974	1964	1974
Parties	9	17	33	11
Dancing	4	0	42	27
Movies	64	49	17	27
Driving around	21	25	8	33
Bowling	2	9	0	2
(N)	(204)	(221)	(83)	(104)
	$\chi^2 = 29.008$, $p < .001$, $df = 4$		$\chi^2 = 28.093$, $p < .001$, $df = 4$	

Source: From "Dating behavior of black and white students before and after desegregation" by G. E. Dickinson, Journal of Marriage and the Family, 1975, 37, 602–608. Copyright 1975 by National Council on Family Relations. Reprinted by permission.

between thirteen and nineteen, approximately half reported having had sexual intercourse (Sorenson, 1973). Those adolescents who had not had premarital intercourse had engaged in a variety of other activities including necking and petting. A small minority had none of these experiences.

As might be expected, younger adolescents are more conservative in their sexual attitudes and behavior than older ones (Sorenson, 1973). Although girls are still more conservative than boys in their sexual attitudes, it appears that the sex differences are narrowing with time (Conger, 1975; Sorenson, 1973). For instance, in the study by Robinson et al. in 1972, the percentage of college males who engaged in heavy petting in 1965 and 1970 was 71 and 79.3, respectively; however, the corresponding percentages for females in 1965 and 1970 were 34.3 and 59.7. Thus, there was a 25.4 per cent increase among the females but only an 8 per cent increase among the males. In several studies (Yankelovich, 1969), college youths, and particularly those who are more liberal in their political orientation, appear to be more permissive sexually.

Going Steady

One custom that is considerably more frequent among adolescents now than some years ago is going steady. Going steady may for some adolescents be almost as serious as being engaged, whereas for others it means little more than a temporary understanding that the boy or girl will not date anyone else as long as the period of going steady lasts. The consequences of going steady vary with different individuals. Some critics have inveighed against going steady on the ground that it may isolate the adolescent from his or her peers and thus restrict the range of social contacts.

The percentage of black and white sophomore, junior, and senior high school adolescents who report going or having gone steady at two different points in time is presented in Table 14.3.

Table 14.3.   Frequency distribution (in percentages) for the response to the question: "Are you now or have you ever gone steady?" by year and race

Go steady	Whites		Blacks	
	1964	1974	1964	1974
Yes	62	80	54	68
No	38	20	46	32
(N)	(249)	(282)	(105)	(139)

Note: White adolescents reported going or having gone steady significantly more often than black adolescents in both 1964 and 1974. Both whites and blacks are "going steady" significantly more often today than in 1964.
Source: From "Dating behavior of black and white adolescents before and after desegregation" by G. E. Dickinson, Journal of Marriage and the Family, 1975, 37, 602–608. Copyright 1975 by National Council on Family Relations. Reprinted by permission.

Table 14.3 indicates that the percentage of white students who reported having gone steady over the last decade increased from 62 to 80 per cent. The percentage of blacks who reported going steady also increased.

Some parents in the United States try to enforce rules against going steady. What is the effect of these rules on the adolescents' behavior? According to Kandel and Lesser (1972), in this country, "the proportion of adolescents showing the behavior favored by parents is *highest* when the parents have a *specific* rule about it [p. 79]." For instance, 70 per cent of adolescents do *not* go steady when their families have rules against going steady, in contrast to 59 per cent when they have no rule. In contrast, according to the same study in Denmark, the percentage of adolescents who go steady is greater when the parents do not have specific rules against going steady. Based on these and other parent-adolescent findings, these investigators maintain that adolescent socialization processes in the United States and Denmark differ. In the United States parents must enforce specific rules with respect to dating as well as other behavior if they want their offspring to do what is expected of them. The Danish adolescents seem to be more likely to have internalized parental wishes, are more self-regulating, and seem to act in an approved manner without parental constraints.

Engagement

In the most common meaning of the word, an "engaged" couple is one that has made a commitment and achieved a relationship that approaches the status of marriage. An important part of the engagement relationship is, of course, the ability to share attitudes and personal experiences of a very intimate nature. Engaged individuals also have an incentive and are better able than persons who have made no commitment to evaluate the compatibility of their family backgrounds. It is well known that, during the engagement period, many individuals prepare themselves for their future roles as husband or wife, re-evaluate their previous relationships and commitments, and prepare for the wedding and honeymoon. If for some reason the relationship ceases to be satisfying, it seems evident that the individuals should feel free to discontinue it.

Differences in Attitudes of Boys and Girls Regarding Dating and Popularity

On a number of visits to high school classes in which students were discussing boy-girl relationships, the senior author noted that more girls than boys spoke up in favor of the practice of going steady and seemed to feel more deeply about it. The reasons girls gave for wanting to go steady seemed to indicate a desire for "security." There are many indications that dating, going steady, and other forms of boy-girl relationships have a deeper personal meaning for girls than for boys.

From many studies and discussions it appears that girls view dating, going steady, courtship, and prospective marriage in a more purposeful and mature way than boys. They give relatively more emphasis than boys to the prospect of having a happy home and family, whereas boys give relatively more emphasis to sex relationships (see, for example, Lantagne, 1958). On the other hand, girls apparently depend more heavily than boys on their popularity with the opposite sex as a means of bolstering their own self-regard. The importance girls attach to being popular with men appears in a study by Jameson (1941). He found that unhappy states of mind due to an inability to be popular with men was reported by a large proportion of college girls and by a larger proportion of girls who were juniors (66.4 per cent) than by members of the same class when they were freshmen (29.5 per cent). It is not unlikely that the self-esteem of present-day girls is not as dependent on popularity with boys as was true in 1941.

In a discussion of the conflicts relating to sex that girls encounter in college, Binger (1961) speaks of the dilemmas girls face due to their need to be approved by men. If they are stand-offish on a date boys may not try to see them again, but if they take the first step in accepting the boy's advances the boy will take over, unless he himself is very timid. Binger speaks of the relationship between the sexes at the college age as being in an experimental phase, motivated partly by idealism, partly by a spirit of rebellion against parents or others in authority, partly by a desire young people have to find out about themselves, partly by loneliness, partly by a new conventionality and a wish not to miss anything, "but above all, for the girls, by the feeling of approbation which the steady attention of one boy gives them [p. 43]."

Binger emphasizes the need for giving young people an opportunity to express their perplexities, to cultivate their gift for understanding themselves and others, and to find some ethical and aesthetic pattern for their lives. According to Binger (1961), many students "are distressed by the formless chaos that surrounds them [p. 44]." A cautionary note is needed about this work: it is possible that in the years between the early 1960s and the late 1970s females have become more self-assured.

Courtship Ideals

In a study of college students, physical attractiveness was found to be related to popularity (Black, 1974) but, in naming the qualities they regard as most desirable in a prospective mate, adolescents usually emphasize character traits more than intelligence or physical appearance.[2] Good looks receive a higher rating by boys as desirable in a girl than by girls as something desirable in a boy. Girls give more emphasis than boys to such traits as considerateness, dependability, ambition, and similarity of backgrounds. Boys give relatively more emphasis than girls to youthfulness, attractiveness, and popularity.

Love between the sexes, falling in love, and being in love

During adolescence most young persons in our culture become ripe for the experience of "falling in love." Many of them, before reaching adolescence, show romantic attachments to persons of the opposite sex. At the elementary school age and even before, many youngsters are tenderly devoted to a boy- or girlfriend and go through acts of courtship, such as bearing gifts or walking together to and from school. About two fifths of the men and women who took part in a study by Hamilton (1929) reported that they had had their first "love affairs" between the ages of six and eleven. Such attachments may have a deep emotional intensity, but they are not likely to have the erotic intensity of ventures in love that occur during adolescence and later years.

In our language we have a large array of terms to describe the amorous endeavors of adolescence and preadolescence. Some of these terms have a condescending touch, as when we speak of "calf love" or "puppy love." Actually, such labels do not do justice to the young person. His or her passion, as far as he or she is concerned, is real, even though it may be short-lived and even though it may strike others as a bit awkward. Another term is *infatuation*, which suggests feelings that are at fever heat but not likely to last. Somewhat in the same class is the "crush," which suggests a violent romantic attachment that may or may not last.

More honored in everyday usage is the state of falling in love or being in love. The experience of being in love seems to differ so much in different persons that it would be difficult to present a typical picture of what the experience involves. Even the same person will have different experiences as he or she falls in love now with one person and then with another. In general, in our society, love is considered a highly desirable basis for marriage and courtship.

---

[2] For instance, Stroebe et al. (1971) reported that physical attractiveness has a greater effect on dating than on marrying.

During adolescence most young people become ripe for the experience of falling in love. [Burt Glinn/Magnum.]

Adolescent Love

The adolescents' needs for affiliation, love, and affection are alluded to in a study by Lunneborg and Rosenwood (1972). These investigators reported that when college students are asked, "What makes you happy?" they often mention themes related to the need for affiliation.

The most dramatic instances of adolescent love occur when adolescents fall in love with a person of the opposite sex and are convinced their love is "true." Some authors have questioned how true an adolescent's true love actually is. According to Dion and Dion (1973), who studied college students, a relationship exists between perception of internal versus external control of one's life events and romantic love. People who felt primarily influenced by external events beyond their control were more likely to experience romantic love in an idealistic way. Adolescents are also at times swept with other loving sentiments—for their parents, their home, the family cat or dog (and, in an earlier day, they felt tenderly about their favorite horse). Rubin (1970) has made an effort to study romantic love objectively, using techniques of quantification.

Although our information about the sway of love in the life of adolescents is limited, such glimmerings as we have indicate that to love and to be loved are supremely important in their lives (Rosner, 1972). We see this when a delinquent will suffer in loyal devotion to his gang (Elliott and Voss, 1974). We see a striving for love when young people feel and express an impulse for doing idealistic things. Their idealism may be visionary and a mixture of many motives. But the germ of love is there when a young person feels an impulse to give of himself or herself and not just to take.

THE SUBSTANCE OF ADOLESCENT LOVE

Adolescent love is more than a biological condition, and, as Piaget and Inhelder (1961) have maintained, an adolescent in love, as distinguished from a child in love, usually complicates his feelings by constructing a romance or by invoking social or even literary ideals. As emphasized by Scarlett (1975), adolescent love may be considered a desire for relationships with significant others who are not part of the adolescent's family but who will demonstrate understanding and acceptance of the adolescent as an equal. Scarlett (1975) further points out that Anne, in "The Diary of Anne Frank," considers the diary to be a friend when she writes: "I hope I shall be able to confide in you completely, as I have never been able to do in anyone before, and I hope that you will be a great support and comfort to me [p. 78]."

Frequency of Love

In the usual course of events it seems rarely to happen that two adolescents meet and then love each other (and no one else before or after) with equal intensity and go on to live happily ever after. Matters do not usually progress with such comfort, equality, speed, and finality.

The average young person falls in love not once, but several times, during early and late adolescent years. In a study of 153 women aged fifteen to thirty-five years, judged to be normal, 109 of whom were single and 44 married, Landis et al. (1940) found that over a third reported having been in love three to five times, and almost half said they had had six or more love affairs. These reports do not reveal how intense, absorbing, or prolonged each episode was. But they do suggest that it is unlikely that the first love will be lasting.

Although the evidence indicates that the average girl (there is not a comparable amount of evidence concerning boys) is likely to be intensely attracted by several males before the end of the teens, it appears also that the information she gives regarding her love life will be influenced by the phrasing of the questions asked.

Broderick (1966) conducted a large-scale study of 1,000 adolescents ranging in age from ten to seventeen. Among the ten- to eleven-year-olds, Broderick noted that a large proportion of males and females reported having fallen in love within the preceding year. Although the cumulative number of adolescents who had reported being in love for the first time changed from year to year, the cumulative number did not increase with age. One possible interpretation of these findings as proposed by Broderick (1966) is that the earlier loves were no longer considered love as new relationships were formed. Approximately half of the twelve- to thirteen-year-olds stated that they had been in love within the past two years. At the ages of fourteen to fifteen, more boys than girls reported having been in love two or more times. Among the sixteen- to seventeen-year-olds, about two-thirds of the adolescents reported that they had been in love for some time during the previous year.

Emotional Elements of "Being in Love"

To be in love or to fall in love may have strikingly different meanings in the lives of different persons—and different meanings also at different times within the life of one person, as already indicated. To be in love also has different meanings in different cultures (Goode, 1970; 1974). There are differences in the intensity of feeling, in the depth of involvement, and in the strength and tenacity of purpose. It is conceivable that one person who is often in love has a great capacity for loving, whereas another might fall in love often because he or she has relatively little capacity for becoming deeply attached to any one person. Again, one person might run from one love affair to another as though desperately seeking to stifle a doubt or resolve a difficulty in his own life, whereas another person, with more inner poise and self-assurance, might not love so hectically or so often.

The experience of being in love is a compound of many impulses and many emotions. It may include heights of ecstasy and depths of pain. To varying degrees, varying with the circumstances, it can involve a play of all the human emotions, ranging from overwhelming tenderness to bitter anger and from joy to oppressive fears and deep sorrow. Every resource in man's emotional make-up is brought into play when two persons on a high tide of feeling are carried into a relationship that, when consummated, leads to emotional intimacy, mating, and the begetting and rearing of children in an atmosphere of love.

Although the mature person who is in love will have an open or hidden desire for sexual contact with the one he loves, the erotic element varies greatly in different love relationships. A boy may be attracted to a girl, or a girl to a boy, seek to be near each other, speak admiring words, and desire to gaze on each other and share tender confessions without having any clear sexual intention. In the Hamilton (1929) study grounds were found for believing that the first experience of amorous attachment in a child is not necessarily combined with sex. In a review of literature dealing with this topic, Grant (1948) cites the translated work of Moll, Buhler (1931), and several other investigators who indicate that there can be amorous attraction between children without any obvious erotic desire.

In contrast to these observations there is the view that love consists primarily of a refinement of the sexual impulse. One version of this is the view that a person in love is one in whom sexual desire is inhibited, so that instead of appearing directly, in its physical form, it is expressed through tenderness and other sentiments. Another version is that the person in love actually is suffering from sexual frustration, which expresses itself through an idealization of the loved object and endows the loved one with great glamour and desirability.

In commenting on this issue, Grant (1948) notes that emotional aspects of sexual behavior have been persistently neglected in scientific psychological studies. Accordingly, although it is easy to cite opinions, it is difficult to come to any precise conclusion.

At any rate, the person who is in love has many experiences and impulses that cannot be explained by sexual desire alone. The very fact that love is centered on this person rather than on another indicates that many complex factors other than sex are involved. If sex were the only consideration, practically anyone of the opposite sex, with the usual biological equipment, would do. But love does not work that way among persons who are in love or who are seeking someone to love.

One conspicuous quality in the behavior of the person who is in love is that he or she desires, almost desperately, to be with the loved person rather than with any other member of the opposite sex. The lovers seek one another's company as something of supreme value.

The one who loves has feelings of tenderness, an impulse to cherish, comfort, and protect, and a desire to do things that will bring joy to the other person. In these sentiments there is a large amount of other-centeredness. They are what distinguish what is known as true love from an infatuation consisting primarily of physical appetite. These sentiments give the state of being in love an aspect of unselfishness. The gratification that comes through the exercise of tenderness comes through the medium of having taken thought of someone else. It involves a disposition to give emotionally rather than simply to take.

The expression of these tender sentiments takes many forms, ranging from bounties involving considerable sacrifice to thoughtful little acts or gifts. The value of these expressions does not depend on the magnitude of what is done or given but in the feelings they convey. Frequently, they are most eloquent if offered with seeming inadvertence or if they compress within a small token a large amount of meaning. The girl maneuvers in various ways, for example, to make things easier for the boy who does not have much spending money. The boy has perhaps overheard or observed that the girl is fond of a certain flower or that she has lost her umbrella, and, then, when he brings a flower or an umbrella as a gift, it becomes a special expression of thoughtfulness.

Unless the sentiments of the persons who are in love are mixed with a desire to inflict hurt or a need to overcome feelings of inadequacy, the one who happens to be brighter, or more handsome, or wealthier, or of more prominent family background, or socially more popular will not play up such matters in a manner that might, by unspoken comparison, belittle the other person.

Many other currents of feeling may come into play when an adolescent is in love. There will be a vast amount of joy when love is reciprocated. It is overwhelmingly gratifying to feel warmly accepted by the one who counts most. In discussing this phase of the experience of love, Wenkart (1949) states that the adolescent's desire to have someone acknowledge, accept, and appreciate his uniqueness as a separate self prepares the way for his first love. When an adolescent finds one of the opposite sex who thus accepts him, he is confronted with an inner wealth he never knew he had and this feeling may mean that the first love experience is like a revelation.

Unfortunately, persons who are in love may be so overwhelmed by their feelings that they become blind to faults or conditions that in time might create unhappiness. The person who is in love may overlook bad habits, weaknesses of character, and symptoms of emotional immaturity that to a disinterested onlooker do not bode well for the future. Similarly overlooked may be differences in background, age, economic status, ideals, religious affiliation, and other social and cultural conditions that, in time, may require very difficult and perhaps insurmountable practical and psychological adjustments.

Healthy and Unhealthy Aspects of Being in Love

Loving and remaining in love are two of life's greatest fulfillments. But being in love may have roots in attitudes that are not particularly healthy. The difference between what might be regarded as healthy and unhealthy love is not easy to define, but by being arbitrary it is possible, at least in broad outline, to note some distinguishing features.

An unhealthy condition prevails when the love a person professes is not a spontaneous giving and sharing of affection. For example, there is an unhealthy element if a person with deep-seated attitudes of inferiority seeks blindly to combat his or her lack of self-regard by going through the motions of being in love and of getting someone to fall in love with him or her. Such a person is using the one he or she "loves" as a means of dealing with his or her own maladjustment. If being in love and being loved would free one from one's affliction, it probably would be a good thing. But there is no guarantee that such a cure will occur.

There is an unhealthy attitude if a person with a long-standing grievance wittingly or unwittingly uses one love affair after another as a means of making conquests that inflict hurt on other persons.

An unhealthy element also exists if a person who is dependent to a childish degree uses the maneuver of being in love and having others fall in love with him or her in order to continue dependency and to avoid the struggle of growing up, or, on the other hand, seeks to dominate another as his or her parents perhaps once dominated him or her. Similarly, there is an unhealthy element if a male goes from one love affair to another, driven by a continuing doubt concerning his manliness, and if a woman does the same because she is driven by doubts about her ability to fulfill a feminine role.

In these examples it is not assumed that a love relationship must be completely pure and untouched by any human frailty in order to be called healthy. Such perfection is beyond human possibility. But we do assume that there is something unhealthy afoot when a person seeks, through the glamour and excitement of being in love, a kind of relief from problems that will have to be resolved before the ability to love wholeheartedly is achieved.

Although the data are still scanty, Driscoll et al. (1972) have suggested that parental opposition may lead to romantic love. For both married and unmarried couples, the greater the pressure of parental interference, the greater the intensity of romantic love may become.

We might ask, "What are some of the characteristics of healthy love between the sexes?" Several authors have expressed views on this subject. Macmurray (1937) mentions, for example, the kind of love in which there is *mutual self-discovery*. Horney (1946) speaks of friendship at its best as being the essence of love. Love, according to Horney, affords an opportunity for sharing—sharing responsibility, joy, and important undertakings—and it requires emotional sincerity. According to Horney, love also involves accepting the loved one as he or she is, which is not possible unless one can accept oneself. This acceptance is not achieved simply by being blind to the other person's shortcomings, nor by unwillingness to look at weaknesses that might be remedied. Where there is such acceptance, the people who love are better able to see the loved ones as they really are, without having to endow the loved one with a glamour he or she does not possess or to delude themselves into seeing in this loved person an ideal of perfection they have never been able to realize within themselves.

In a discussion of love in healthy people, Maslow (1953) mentions qualities he regards as characteristic of the love of persons who are actualizing themselves. The discussion does not center on young adolescents, and it deals with a degree of self-acceptance that is probably beyond the reach of many, yet it is instructive in describing a kind of maturity some persons probably become capable of achieving in late adolescence.

In addition to noting features commonly regarded as associated with loving, such as tenderness, a desire for nearness, feelings of generosity, a desire to share secrets, and the like, Maslow names other features that, in some ways, are more rugged and profound. According to him, persons who love one another in a healthy way can allow themselves to be honest; they can let their hair down; they can drop their defenses; and they do not continually have to conceal or impress or pretend. They can accept variations in their moods and in the intensity of their feelings. And they can allow themselves considerable freedom in the roles they play without being bound by stereotyped notions of what a supposedly manly man or womanly woman should be and do. They can be active or passive in love-making, take aggressive or unaggressive roles, and accept the role of being the weaker or the stronger. Maslow mentions, among other characteristics, that those who love in a healthy way accept one another's individuality. They tend to be less concerned with appearances or with obvious economic or educational shortcomings than with attributes belonging to the character and the inner life.

Maslow states that in observing several relatively healthy young college men and women he noted that the more mature they become, the less attracted they are by such characteristics as handsome, good looking, good dancer, nice breasts, physically strong, tall, and good necker and the more they speak of compatibility, goodness, decency, companionship, and considerateness. Maslow expresses the belief that the tendency to give greater weight to character than to physical appearance is probably characteristic of increasing *health* rather than increasing *age*.

Adolescence and marriage

During the past few decades, the age of first marriage has declined. Glick and Landau (1950) cited census data indicating that the estimated median age of first marriage for men at the time of the 1890 census was 26.1 years; it dropped to 24.3 years in 1940. By 1970 the median age at first marriage declined considerably to 23.2 years for males. For women the corresponding figure was 22 years in 1890; 21.6 years in 1940, and 20.8 years in 1970. Since 1970, there has been a slight increase in the age at first marriage (Rice, 1975).

Many adolescents marry soon after high school, and many marry while they are still in high school. Marriages among young people who are still in college are far more common than some generations ago. At the high school age, marriages by girls far outnumber marriages by boys (Parke and Glick, 1967).

When adolescents marry they are expected to accept each other for better or for worse. They probably hope to live happily ever afterward. Many marriages are permanent, and many report they are happy in their marriages. But some are not happy.

As reported by Landis and Landis (1968), the divorce rate is the highest when both partners are under the age of twenty. The divorce rate varies considerably in different sections of the country. Udry (1971) (as cited in Rice, 1975) found that race and age at first marriage are also related to male divorce rates. Among black males who marry between the ages of fourteen and twenty-one, over 40 per cent end up in divorce, whereas approximately one quarter of the marriages terminate among white males of this age.

Apart from divorces, there are many incompatible persons who are separated. And among those who are living together there are many who do not regard their marriages as being particularly happy (De Lissovoy, 1973). As might be expected, marriage, like all other human institutions, has its tensions, and the married relationship, like any human relationship, has its stresses and strains.

Marital Choice

Much of the work on marital relationships suggests that individuals tend to marry persons who are similar to them (known as the practice of *homogamy*) in a number of social characteristics. Married pairs are likely to be similar in terms of age, parental education, socioeconomic status, and values (Lewis, 1975).

Several investigations indicate that parents and peers serve to promote homogamy. According to Coombs (1962) parents directly or indirectly use their influence to ensure that the adolescents will select mates who will be similar to them in a number of important areas. Friends also play a role in marital choice. For instance, the friends of an adolescent may let him or her know verbally or nonverbally whether they approve or disapprove of the adolescent's marital choice.

Characteristics of Those Who Marry Early

A first point to note in examining the literature on early marriages is that "the greater the heterosexual involvement at an early age, the more likely early marriage will occur [Bartz and Nye, 1970, p. 262]." This theoretical proposition is based on several pieces of evidence.

Girls who married before completing high school were compared with a control group of girls who remained unmarried in high school in a study by Burchinal (1959). These girls (sixty in each group) had been students in eleven high schools in nine Iowa communities. Members of the married group were matched as closely as possible with those in the control group with respect to school attended, grade in school, urban or rural residence, age, level of father's occupation, parents' educational level, religious affiliation, and so on.

Data concerning whether the married girls were pregnant prior to marriage were obtainable in the case of fifty-eight girls. Of these, twenty-three, or about 40 per cent, were premaritally pregnant. Other studies (Inselberg, 1961) also confirm a high rate of premarital pregnancy among early marriages. However, Inselberg (1961) notes that because the rate of premarital pregnancy is higher among girls who marry early, it cannot be assumed that these girls engaged in more premarital intercourse than girls who were not premaritally pregnant.

A second piece of evidence for the relationship between greater heterosexual involvement and early age at marriage comes from studies of early dating. As noted in an earlier context, the ones who married earlier dated at an earlier average age, had their first "steady" at an earlier average age, had a larger number of steadies, and said they had been in love with a larger number of steadies (Bartz and Nye, 1970). Data derived from 32,000 individuals who were part of a follow-up study on Project TALENT indicate that adolescents from lower socioeconomic groups tend to marry at an earlier age than those of higher socioeconomic status (Bayer, 1968). One might speculate that those adolescents who are involved in extended education postpone marriage until they have completed their education.

Several other reasons for early marriage have been suggested. In the words of Bartz and Nye (1970): "The more optimistic a girl's expectations and attitudes toward marriage, the more likely early marriage will occur [p. 261]." (For research on the marriage role expectations of black adolescents, see Rooks and King, 1973.)

Among the reasons that have been advanced to explain early marriage are poor social adjustment, dissatisfaction with home life, a broken home, rebellion against parents, a need for affection that was not gratified at home, loneliness, unfair discipline, and improper exercise of authority by the father or mother. However, Burchinal's study (1959) did not support the view that strained parent-adolescent relationships play a significant role in influencing girls to marry before they have completed high school. Almost half of the girls reported that although their parents had been against their marriage, and tried to talk them out of it, or wanted them to wait, most of their parents had accepted the marriage once it was consummated. Burchinal points out that if a strained parent-adolescent relationship actually did exist prior to marriage, such relationships apparently, from the girls' points of view, improved rapidly soon after they were married.

As measured by a personality test, similarities between the married and unmarried girls were more conspicuous than differences. Moreover, almost an equal number of girls came from homes in which both parents were living together (80 per cent of the married and 82.2 per cent of the unmarried). Burchinal points out that if the theory of strained parent-adolescent relationships is correct, it would require more rigorous methods of investigation than the tests he applied.

High School Policies Regarding Student Marriages

In a study that included a number of high schools in Illinois, Cavan and Beling (1958) observed that many high schools did not have a policy for dealing with married students, and when policies did exist they varied greatly from school to school. A large number of students who marry while in high school drop out of school after marriage, with the number being higher among girls than boys (De Lissovoy and Hitchcock, 1965; Ivins, 1960). Although the percentage of married adolescents who remain in school is small, these people represent a very large aggregate of young persons if projected in terms of the total youth population. Therefore, the school policies regarding marriages among students assume great importance. In a study of 759 public high schools by Brown (1972), the formal (written) and informal (verbal) policies regarding married students were examined. It is striking that only one third of the schools allowed married students to attend school without any restrictions. (See Table 14.4.)

Usually high school marriages are frowned on, but some principals have reported that married students were more serious and a good influence on the student body.

In a group of eighty-four schools, there were about one third in which students who marry were made to leave school even though the law did not require it (Cavan and Beling, 1958). Only a small number of schools viewed teenage marriages as presenting a situation in which the school had the responsibility to help the student make a success both of marriage and schooling. Cavan and Beling (1958) describe one school in which the dean of

Table 14.4. Types of verbal and written policies in effect on married students in 475 participating school districts

Content of policy	Respond-ing schools	%
1. Married students are allowed to attend regular day school with no restrictions imposed solely because of their married status.	160	33.6
2. Married students are allowed to attend regular day school but are not allowed to participate in cocurricular activities.	398	83.8
3. Married students are allowed part-time attendance in the regular day school. Each case is considered by the board of education.	8	1.7
4. Married students must make application to the board of education through an authorized member of the administration to remain in the regular day school.	6	1.3
5. Each case will be judged on its own merits.	36	7.6
6. A special committee is appointed and makes a recommendation to the board. If the student is allowed to remain in the day school, there are no restrictions based solely upon his married status placed upon him.	4	0.8
7. Pregnancy brings immediate expulsion.	36	7.6
8. If both students are enrolled, one must withdraw, the choice being theirs.	3	0.6
9. Married students must make application through an authorized member of the administration. If the student is allowed to remain in the regular day school, his cocurricular activities are subject to regulation by either the board or by the administrative staff.	50	10.6
10. All married students are suspended from school for a prescribed period of time immediately after marriage.	7	1.5
11. Failure to report marriage immediately after marriage shall constitute justification for immediate suspension.	16	3.4

Source: "Married students in public high schools: A Texas study" by B. B. Brown, *Family Coordinator,* 1972, **21,** 321–324. Copyright 1972 by National Council on Family Relations. Reprinted by permission.

girls tried to help the students. If a girl in the school became pregnant, she was encouraged to remain in school during the first few months of her pregnancy and then allowed to continue her studies at home.

A special effort was made to help girls who were thinking of getting married as a means of resolving a personal problem (such as difficulty at home or a desire to escape loneliness) to find ways of resolving that problem rather than, in a sense, escaping from it by taking refuge in marriage. This effort also involved an endeavor to bring parents into the situation.

In view of the great load of responsibilities high schools already carry, it is likely that many will resist the idea that one function of the high school should be to dissuade young people from marrying or to help those students who do marry to make a go of it while continuing their education. Yet, as Hill and Aldous (1969) have noted, preparation for normal marriage and parenthood should be available for all and not be restricted to those who are precociously married or become premaritally pregnant.

Marriages at the high school level often involve a poignant human situation. Such marriages cannot be brushed aside as though they meant little more than foolish behavior on the part of a few willful persons. The decision to marry or the necessity for marriage because of pregnancy springs from the total social context in which young people live. To that extent they represent a social responsibility, and in many communities there probably is no institution that can deal with this problem more effectively than thoughtful and humane members of a high school faculty.

Actually, if high schools provided students with help in understanding themselves and in dealing with their personal problems—as many persons think high schools should—they would probably provide some counsel for those who are seeking through marriage to escape from their personal problems. In other words, the schools would not be taking on a new responsibility for dealing with young people in the process of meeting their responsibility for the emotional welfare of the total student body.[3]

Living as mates without the formality of marriage

It's a matter of common knowledge (or, at least, belief) that in recent years an increasing number of young people have been living together as husband and wife without being legally married. Rice (1975) has presented some of the literature relating to alternative styles of marriage.

Some other adolescents prefer to live in communes. Those who elect to live in communes generally reject traditional middle-class values. In their study of rural hippie communes, Berger and Hackett (1974) found that some, but by no means all, communes can sustain the sense of kinship and close personal relations that many adolescents and adults fail to get from religion, their community, their occupation, or the nuclear family. But these studies have not specified the immediate and future consequences for the adolescents of choosing a nontraditional living arrangement. There is a need for longitudinal studies that focus on the effects these alternative life styles will have as the people become older.

References

Bartz, K. W., & Nye, F. I. Early marriage: A propositional formulation. *Journal of Marriage and the Family*, 1970, **32**, 258–268.

[3] From a humanitarian point of view, it should be remembered that helping young people who are planning a marriage that might end in failure does not simply mean helping them only; it means helping thousands of babies who each year are the innocent victims of teenage divorce.

Bayer, A. E. Early dating and early marriage. *Journal of Marriage and the Family*, 1968, **30**, 628–637.

Bell, R. R., & Chaskes, J. B. Premarital sexual experience among coeds, 1958 and 1968. *Journal of Marriage and the Family*, 1970, **32**, 81–84.

Berger, B. M., & Hackett, B. M. On the decline of age grading in rural hippie communes. *Journal of Social Issues*, 1974, **30**, 163–183.

Binger, C. The pressures on college girls today. *Atlantic Monthly*, 1961, **207**(2), 40–44.

Black, H. K. Physical attractiveness and similarity of attitude in interpersonal attraction. *Psychological Reports*, 1974, **35**, 403–406.

Broderick, C. B. Socio-sexual development in a suburban community. *The Journal of Sex Research*, 1966, **2**, 1–24.

Brown, B. B. Married students in public high schools: A Texas study. *Family Coordinator*, 1972, **21**(3), 321–324.

Buhler, C. Zum Probleme der sexuellen Entwicklung. *Z. Kinderheilkunst*, 1931, **51**, 612–642.

Burchinal, L. G. Does early dating lead to school-age marriages? *Iowa Farm Science*, 1959, **13**(8), 11–12.

Byrne, D., Ervin, C. R., & Lamberth, J. Continuity between the experimental study of attraction and real-life computer dating. *Journal of Personality and Social Psychology*, 1970, **16**, 157–165.

Cameron, W. J., & Kenkel, W. F. High school dating: A study in variation. *Marriage and Family Living*, 1960, **22**, 74–76.

Cavan, R. S., & Beling, G., A study of high school marriages. *Marriage and Family Living*, 1958, **20**, 293–295.

Christensen, H. T. Dating behavior as evaluated by high-school students. *American Journal of Sociology*, 1952, **57**, 580–586.

Conger, J. J. Sexual attitudes and behavior of contemporary adolescents. In J. J. Conger (Ed.), *Contemporary issues in adolescent development*. New York: Harper, 1975.

Coombs, R. H. Reinforcement of values in the parental home as a factor in mate selection. *Marriage and Family Living*, 1962, **24**, 155–157.

Crist, J. R. High school dating as a behavior system. *Marriage and Family Living*, 1953, **15**, 23–28.

De Lissovoy, V. High school marriages: A longitudinal study. *Journal of Marriage and the Family*, 1973, **35**, 245–255.

De Lissovoy, V., & Hitchcock, M. E. High school marriages in Pennsylvania. *Journal of Marriage and the Family*, 1965, **27**, 263–270.

Dickinson, G. E. Dating behavior of black and white adolescents before and after desegregation. *Journal of Marriage and the Family*, 1975, **37**, 602–608.

Dion, K. L., & Dion, K. K. Correlates of romantic love. *Journal of Consulting and Clinical Psychology*, 1973, **41**, 51–56.

Driscoll, R., Davis, K. E., & Lipetz, M. E. Parental interference and romantic love: The Romeo and Juliet effect. *Journal of Personality and Social Psychology*, 1972, **24**, 1–10.

Elliott, D. S., & Voss, H. L. *Delinquency and dropout*. Lexington, Mass.: Heath, 1974.

Glick, P. C., & Landau, E. Age as a factor in marriage. *American Sociological Review*, 1950, **15**, 517–529.

Goode, W. J. The theoretical importance of love. In R. L. Coser (Ed.), *The family: Its structures and functions.* New York: St. Martin's, 1974.

Goode, W. J. *World revolution and family patterns.* New York: Free Press, 1970.

Grant, V. W. A major problem of human sexuality. *Journal of Social Psychology*, 1948, **28**, 79–101.

Hamilton, G. V. *A research in marriage.* New York: A. and C. Boni, 1929.

Herold, E. S. A dating adjustment scale for college students. *Adolescence*, 1973, **29**, 51–60.

Hill, R., & Aldous, J. Socialization for marriage and parenthood. In D. Goslin (Ed.), *Handbook of socialization theory and research.* Chicago: Rand McNally, 1969.

Horney, K. *Growth through love and sex.* New York: Auxiliary Council to the Association for the Advancement of Psychoanalysis, 1946.

Inselberg, R. Social and psychological factors associated with high school marriages. *Journal of Home Economics*, 1961, **59**, 766–772.

Ivins, W. Student marriages in New Mexico secondary schools: Practices and policies. *Marriage and Family Living*, 1960, **22**, 71–74.

Jameson, S. H. Adjustment problems of university girls arising from the urge for recognition and new experience. *Journal of Social Psychology*, 1941, **144**, 129–144.

Kandel, D. B., & Lesser, G. S. *Youth in two worlds.* San Francisco, Calif.: Jossey-Bass, 1972.

Landis, J. T., & Landis, M. G. *Building a successful marriage* (5th ed.). Englewood Cliffs, N.J.: Prentice-Hall, 1968.

Landis, C., Landis, A. T., & Bolles, M. M., et al. *Sex in development.* New York: Paul B. Hoeber, 1940.

Lantagne, J. E. Interests of 4,000 high school pupils in problems of marriage and parenthood. *Research Quarterly of the American Association for Health, Physical Education and Recreation*, 1958, **28**, 407–416.

Lewis, R. A. Social influences on marital choice. In S. E. Dragastin & G. H. Elder Jr. (Eds.), *Adolescence in the life cycle: Psychological change and social context.* New York: Wiley, 1975.

Lowrie, S. H. Factors involved in the frequency of dating. *Marriage and Family Living*, 1956, **18**, 46–51.

Lowrie, S. H. Early and late dating: Some conditions associated with them. *Marriage and Family Living*, 1961, **23**, 284–291.

Lunneborg, P. W., & Rosenwood, L. M. Need affiliation and achievement: Declining sex differences. *Psychological Reports*, 1972, **31**, 795–798.

Macmurray, J. *Reason and emotion.* Englewood Cliffs, N.J.: Appleton, 1937.

Maslow, A. H. Love in healthy people. In A. Montagu (Ed.), *The meaning of love.* New York: Julian Press, 1953.

McDaniel, C. O. Dating roles and reasons for dating. *Journal of Marriage and the Family*, 1969, **31**, 97–107.

Miller, P. Y., & Simon, W. Adolescent sexual behavior: Content and change. *Social Problems*, 1974, **22**, 58–76.

Parke, R., Jr., & Glick, P. C. Prospective changes in marriage and the family. *Journal of Marriage and the Family*, 1967, **29**, 249–256.

Piaget, J., & Inhelder, B. *The growth of logical thinking from childhood to adolescence.* New York: Basic Books, 1961.

Rice, F. P. *The adolescent: Development, relationships and culture.* Boston: Allyn, 1975.

Rooks, E., & King, K. A study of the marriage role expectation of black adolescents. *Adolescence*, 1973, **8**, 317–324.

Robinson, I. E., King, K. & Balswick, J. O. The premarital sexual revolution among college females. *Family Coordinator*, 1972, **21**, 189–194.

Rosner, H. Of music, magic, and mystery: Studies in adolescent synthesis. *Journal of the American Psychoanalytic Association*, 1972, **20**, 395–416.

Rubin, Z. Measurement of romantic love. *Journal of Personality and Social Psychology*, 1970, **16**, 265–273.

Scarlett, G. Adolescent thinking and the diary of Anne Frank. In J. J. Conger (Ed.), *Contemporary issues in adolescent development.* New York: Harper, 1975.

Skipper, J. K., Jr., & Nass, G. Dating behavior: A framework for analysis and an illustration. *Journal of Marriage and the Family*, 1966, **28**, 412–420.

Smith, G. F. Certain aspects of the sex life of the adolescent girl. *Journal of Applied Psychology*, 1924, **8**, 347–349.

Sorenson, R. C. *Adolescent sexuality in contemporary America: Personal values and sexual behavior ages 13–19.* New York: World, 1973.

Stroebe, W., Insko, C. A., Thompson, V. D., & Layton, B. D. Effects of physical attractiveness, attitude similarity, and sex on various aspects of interpersonal attraction. *Journal of Personality and Social Psychology*, 1971, **18**, 79–91.

Vockell, E. L., & Asher, J. W. Dating frequency among high school seniors. *Psychological Reports*, 1972, **31**, 381–382.

Walster, E., Aronson, V., Abrahams, D., & Rottmann, L. Importance of physical attractiveness in dating behavior. *Journal of Personality and Social Psychology*, 1966, **4**, 508–516.

Wenkart, A. *Healthy and neurotic love.* New York: The Auxiliary Council to the Association for the Advancement of Psychoanalysis, 1949.

Yankelovich, D. *Generations apart.* New York: Columbia Broadcasting System, 1969.

15

the delinquent adolescent

Almost all adolescent boys, and a large proportion of adolescent girls, have at some time committed offenses that, by strict legal interpretation, are delinquent acts. However, only a small proportion of delinquent acts are officially recorded (Pepinsky, 1976). Records kept by social work agencies in a large city revealed that almost one third of the children who were committing acts for which they could be charged as delinquent were entirely unknown to the police (Kvaraceus, 1954). There is some evidence from

408

other countries to support these findings. For example, a large number of English school boys, in a study by Gibson (1967), reported having committed delinquent acts and managed to escape being caught. Indeed, the true incidence of any type of deviance is virtually unknown at the present time (Gibbs and Erickson, 1975).

Moreover, when young persons commit offenses that actually receive attention, the police may or may not take action that will result in a court record. If the young person comes from a "good" middle-class home, parents, teachers, clergymen, and others are likely to intercede for him. A lower-class youngster from a broken home is less likely to be protected in this way. In this regard, Gibbs and Erickson (1975) have pointed out that individual acts are rarely evaluated without attention paid to the social identity of the individual (for example, male or female, younger or older), situational conditions (for example, time and place), and the person or object at whom the deviant behavior was directed.

In the narrowest legal sense, a "delinquent" is a young person (usually eighteen years or younger) who has committed an offense that, if committed by an adult, would be punishable by law. But more is needed before an adolescent officially is a delinquent. He or she must be caught or apprehended; have an accuser—the one who has been offended, or the police or some other person or persons; and he or she must appear and be convicted by the court (Tutt, 1974). Behaviorally, adolescents can be considered delinquent if they act in a way that is discordant with the norms of society (Thornburg, 1975).

Sex and ethnic differences in delinquency

Only a small proportion of adolescents belong to "the delinquent" group, as officially defined. However, even though the group is small proportionately, it is distressingly large in actual numbers. Many accounts of juvenile delinquency are based on the *Uniform Crime Reports* of the FBI and records prepared by metropolitan law enforcement agencies. The accuracy of the data depends on the record-keeping procedures used and definitions or policies regarding juvenile delinquents. At times, data have apparently been deliberately distorted for political reasons (Pepinsky, 1976). A partial solution to this problem, used in many studies, involves asking the adolescents to report their own delinquent behavior. Self-reported delinquent behavior is also, of course, subject to understatement. In a study of comparable and representative samples of thirteen- through sixteen-year-old adolescents, Gold and Reimer (1975) used self-reports to obtain a twofold measure of delinquency in 1967 and 1972: (1) *total frequency score*, which is the sum of those incidents considered to be chargeable rather than insignificant; and (2) *total seriousness index*, which is each act reported by an individual weighted in terms of its seriousness and then summed for a total seriousness score.

The particular types of delinquent behavior items included running away from home, stealing, committing assault, joining in gang fights, as well as other items. The validity of measures of self-reported delinquency has been discussed elsewhere by Gold (1970). A major finding of the Gold and Reimer study was that the style rather than the amount of delinquency had changed between 1967 and 1972. The boys scored higher on larceny, threatened assault, trespassing, illegal entry, and gang fighting in 1967 than in 1972. However, illicit use of drugs was far higher in 1972 than in 1967. The girls reported less larceny, property destruction, and illegal entry in 1972 than in 1967. Although the overall delinquent behavior of females is rising, males still exceed females in the number and seriousness of the illegal acts they commit (Golenpaul, 1976; Simon, 1976).

The fact that sex differences in delinquent activities appear to be lessening is based on official statistics as well as self-report studies. As recently as 1970 the *Juvenile Court Statistics* recorded approximately a three-to-one ratio of male to female delinquency cases disposed of by the juvenile courts. However, based on self-reported delinquency data, Kratcoski and Kratcoski (1975) found that the ratio of male to female adolescent delinquent acts was closer than the official reports. Based on official reports, it appears that the number of girl delinquency cases disposed of by juvenile courts is rising. The number was more than double in 1970, compared to 1963. In a study of eleventh- and twelfth-grade adolescents, these same investigators (1975) reported that adolescent males more often than females engage in aggressive acts such as breaking into buildings, fist fights, and destroying property. In other areas that reflect adolescent culture orientation, such as drinking and drug use, there are few, if any, sex differences (Brook et al., 1975). The absence of sex differences in some areas of delinquency suggests that any empirical investigation of delinquency in future studies must pay as much attention to females as has been accorded to males in past research.

A comparison of the delinquent behavior of white and black adolescent males and females indicates that little change occurred between 1967 and 1972 for either the blacks or whites in total frequency and total seriousness of delinquency (Gold and Reimer, 1975). According to Davis (1976), crime among blacks occurs most often within the black community and is directed at blacks.

Age Differences

With increased age there is an increase in the percentage of adolescents who could be classified as juvenile delinquents (Tutt, 1974). However, the number of adolescents who use illegal drugs rises steadily with age during adolescence (Brook et al., 1975). It may be that the increase in delinquency rates merely reflects an increase in drug use. Whether or not the use of illicit drugs is included, crime appears to be most prevalent in large cities and lowest in rural communities (Gold and Reimer, 1975).

Characteristics of delinquents

The fact that many young persons violate the law without being discovered, or, if discovered, without being prosecuted, means that statistics regarding the actual incidence of delinquent conduct are incomplete (Brooks and Doob, 1975). This means that findings regarding the characteristics of delinquents, or the "causes" of delinquency, are based mainly on a limited sampling of persons who commit delinquent acts. In those cases where self-reports are used there is also likely to be under-reporting. Even so, it is instructive to examine what these findings reveal.

As compared with "normal," or nondelinquent, children (or as compared with siblings in the same family who do not become delinquent), the delinquents, as a group, make an unfavorable showing on almost every measure that has been applied.[1]

It has been noted that youngsters who engaged in one form of delinquency did not necessarily engage in other forms of delinquency. One of the most widely documented findings in the delinquency literature is that having friends who are delinquent is closely associated with one's own tendency to engage in delinquent acts.

As a group, delinquents compared with nondelinquents have lower average intelligence (Glueck and Glueck, 1974). Delinquency has also been found to be associated with poorer school performance. In a study by Senna et al. (1974) the delinquency measure consisted of several dimensions: physical aggression, crimes against property, shaking down others for money, reckless driving, and using hard drugs. These investigators reported there was some tendency for low school performance to be associated with various forms of delinquency; however, the relationship between low academic performance and delinquency, although significant, was not high.

In a study of a sample of thirteen- to sixteen-year-old boys and girls, Gold and Mann (1972) obtained data concerning school grades and self-reports of delinquency. On the basis of their findings, they propose the following theory regarding a causal sequence in delinquency: scholastic failure, which leads to lowered self-esteem, which leads to an increased

---

[1] For studies of the characteristics of delinquents, see Glueck and Glueck (1950, 1968, 1974), Healy and Bronner (1936), and Hirschi and Rudisill (1976).

probability of delinquency as a defense of self-esteem. Although this model applied to a number of boys, it was not found to be applicable to female adolescents. Lower levels of achievement motivation have also been found in delinquent as compared with nondelinquent boys (Tutt, 1974).

According to the Gluecks (1974), more delinquents than nondelinquents have a record of difficulty in early childhood (such as difficulty in toilet training, severe illnesses, or accidents). As children, more of them were impulsive, lacking in self-control, and extremely restless. More of them have a history of being adventurous, extroverted, and stubborn (Ahlstrom and Havighurst, 1971; Glueck and Glueck, 1974). Many of them also are more suggestible than nondelinquents. These traits facilitate the impulsive, self-centered action that is so characteristic of delinquents.

Delinquent girls tend to be more external in their orientation (viewing their future as controlled by luck, fate, or other external forces) than nondelinquent girls (Duke and Fenhagen, 1975). In contrast the nondelinquent girls are more internal in their orientation (viewing themselves as having some control over their fortunes) than delinquent girls. Several investigators have reported that delinquency and cheating in experimental conditions could be predicted to some extent from low levels of moral judgment (Kohlberg, 1963). Adolescents who engage in delinquent acts often perceive themselves as having less chance for success in the world than those who are not involved in deviance. Gang membership in particular is associated with some reduction of occupational goal levels. Such a view is consistent with the finding that delinquent boys are less successful educationally then nondelinquents (Glueck and Glueck, 1974).

In the sphere of activities that come close to delinquent conduct, delinquents far surpass nondelinquents in the number who have a record of stealing rides or truck hopping, keeping late hours, smoking at an early age, sneaking into theaters, running away from home, and gambling. They have much more frequently sought places outside the home for play and recreation (such as street corners and distant neighborhoods). They have more often sought their companions among gangs and delinquents (as noted earlier) and persons older than themselves.

Although these and other group differences characterizing delinquents are impressive, they tell very little about the individual delinquent or how he or she came to be a delinquent. Practically every description of delinquents as a group (with the exception of the fact that they are known to have committed delinquents acts) has a *but* connected with it. Delinquents are below average in intelligence, but many have good minds and the majority of young persons below average in intelligence do not officially become delinquent. Most delinquents have a history of difficulties in early childhood, but many do not; and many children who have a difficult childhood do not become delinquent. Even in traits that show conspicuous differences, such as aggressiveness and impulsiveness, delinquents and nondelinquents as groups are more alike than unlike.

Another limitation in most of the general information about delinquents is that this information has been obtained *after* the youngsters are in trouble. As we have noted in an earlier chapter, information about the earlier life history of individuals who are presently in trouble is likely to be colored. The young people themselves, their parents, teachers, and others are likely to single out happenings that seem to explain, excuse, or confirm the fact that they were heading for trouble; similar happenings in an inquiry into the history of nondelinquents may be unnoticed or explained away.

A history that is reconstructed in retrospect by a few interviews or a questionnaire usually cannot adequately reveal the experiences in the past that had a critical or crucial bearing on an individual's present condition. Similarly, an inventory of the delinquents' earlier unfavorable characteristics does not reveal which of these, if any, had an important influence on their delinquent tendencies. Neither does such information reveal how this or that personality or character trait came into being. For example, from later case histories, which record that some delinquents have a more violent temper than their nondelinquent neighbors or siblings, we cannot tell whether from the time of birth they had a predisposition toward reacting violently or whether they began life as serene children and then were goaded into violence by a harsh environment. Furthermore, we cannot retrace the steps through which this particular disposition had an increasingly important role in the youngsters' lives as they grew older, feeding itself, so to speak, when the children's anger provoked anger in others and their response reinforced and aggravated their tendency to retaliate.

To get authentic information about the genesis of delinquent behavior and how it differs from the genesis of nondelinquent behavior it would be necessary to study a group of children longitudinally and intensively from the time of birth (with as much information as possible about their parents' genetic background, personality traits, attitudes, and values) and then, at a later time, when some have become delinquent and others have not, to examine the earlier developmental history for clues that might explain or predict what later transpired. The examination of the record of earlier development (up to the time of the first court appearance) should preferably be made by one who does not know who the delinquents and nondelinquents are. If the researchers know in advance who is a delinquent and who is not, they can easily apply the wisdom of hindsight to find all sorts of reasons to "explain" why one child became a serious and persistent lawbreaker, while another became, on the whole, a law-abiding person.

Parent-adolescent relations

Some investigators have found that adolescents from broken homes are more likely to be juvenile delinquents than adolescents from intact homes, whereas others have reported that the probability of being a juvenile delinquent is no greater among those coming from a home where the parents are separated or divorced than among those coming from a home where the parents are living together (Wilkinson, 1974). On the basis of a review of the literature in this area, Wilkinson (1974) concluded that further research must be done before conclusions can be made concerning the significance of the broken family as a factor in delinquency etiology.

Studies of adolescents are often made in the interpersonal context of the family, which, according to Jacobs (1975), is necessary if we are to understand more fully the etiology, development, and maintenance of behavior that departs from normality. The classic work on parental factors as related to juvenile delinquency was done some time ago by Glueck and Glueck et al. (1950). In comparing delinquents with nondelinquents, Glueck and Glueck reported a much higher percentage of criminalism among the immediate family members (grandparents, parents, and siblings) of delinquents than among nondelinquents. Drunkenness was also found more often among family members of delinquents. These findings with respect to juvenile delinquents emerged in all other groups of offenders examined by the Gluecks. These same investigators summarized their findings with respect to physical and mental status of family members of delinquents as compared with nondelinquents as follows: "On the whole, then, the *forebears of the delinquents were more heavily burdened with physical and mental pathology than those of the control group of nondelinquents* [Glueck and Glueck, 1974, p. 56]."

A number of studies have compared the parental models of hyperaggressive adolescents with those of nonaggressive adolescents. McCord et al. (1959) reported that sons of criminals with cruel and neglecting fathers more often became criminals themselves, as compared with boys whose fathers were cruel and neglecting but were not involved in crime. That violence can breed violence is shown in a longitudinal study that examined child abuse cases over three generations (Silver et al., 1969). In this study it was found that the offspring of assaultive parents are likely to use abusive behavior at some future date. Bandura and Walters (1959) studied adolescent aggression in a population of middle-class boys from intact homes. Adolescents who showed antisocial aggression, as compared with those who were neither aggressive nor passive, more often had parents who provided a model and reinforcement for combative attitudes and behavior. In contrast, parents of nonaggressive boys did not support the use of physical aggression as a means of settling conflicts; however, they did encourage their sons to be firm. Of course, parents are not necessarily the prime transmitter of aggression; peers in particular and extrafamilial adults may serve as models for the adolescent.

Contemporary explanations of juvenile delinquency have also tended to emphasize the friction between the culture of foreign-born parents and that of their native-born offspring. A comparison of migrant adolescents (adolescents born outside the United States), first-generation native-born adolescents (adolescents born in this country to immigrant parents), and second-generation natives revealed a higher proportion of delinquency among the first-generation adolescents than among the migrants or second-generation natives (Glueck and Glueck, 1974). Similarly, Lukoff and Brook (1974) reported a higher proportion of contact with heroin users among first-generation natives than among either migrants or second-generation natives. These findings are of interest because they suggest that when a degree of continuity exists between parental and adolescent values and beliefs, the probability that deviant behavior will occur is reduced.

Two other parental factors have been viewed as having a significant impact on the developing individual: the nature of the affectional interaction between the parents and their offspring and the type of parental discipline (Becker, 1964; Hoffman, 1970; Tutt, 1974). A larger proportion of parents of delinquents have reported that one or both parents used disciplinary practices that were erratic, extremely lax, or unreasonably rigid. In a comparison of delinquents and nondelinquents, Glueck and Glueck (1974) reported that the family life of delinquents was characterized by parental indifference or hostility and that the offspring were less attached to their parents.

Whereas earlier studies of parental characteristics as related to juvenile delinquency have tended to treat all delinquents as though they were a homogeneous group, Hetherington et al. (1971) point out that a recent study suggests that there are several dimensions of delinquency: (1) the unsocialized, psychopathic dimension that is correlated with lack of socialization and regard for others; (2) the neurotic, disturbed dimension that is related to social withdrawal and depression; and (3) the socialized, subcultural dimension that involves the acceptance of the social norms of a group that can be characterized as delinquent. In their study of juvenile delinquency, Hetherington et al. (1971) found differences in parental child-rearing attitudes between the parents of adolescents classified as nondelinquent, neurotic delinquent, psychopathic delinquent, and social delinquent. For instance, the parents of the nondelinquent were less hostile, had more expectations for their offspring that were of a positive nature, and were less neurotically involved than parents of delinquents. They also generated more warmth than parents of neurotic or psychopathic delinquents.

Theories of the causes of delinquency

Several theories with varying degrees of plausibility have been proposed in an attempt to explain the causes of delinquency.[2] Prior to the turn of the century many criminologists believed that the cause of crime rested in the biology of the individual. At a later time the cause was located in the psychology of the offender, and most recently it has been located in the sociocultural aspects of the individual's environment. According to Hirschi and Rudisill (1976), some present-day investigators are now more interested in the characteristics of those who are in a position to judge or label the delinquent than in the study of delinquents themselves. Because investigators from a variety of fields, including the biologic and social sciences, have studied delinquency, it should not come as a surprise that the list of causes of delinquency is quite varied.

Working within a psychological-biological and to some extent a sociocultural framework, Glueck and Glueck (1974) explored the relationship between maturation and delinquency. In their follow-up study of delinquents, the Gluecks (1968) found that by the time their delinquents reached the ages of twenty-six to thirty-one, a substantial number could no longer be described as delinquents or criminals.

In a review of the literature on the causes of crime and delinquency, Hirschi and Rudisill (1976) note that much of the research between 1915 and today is characterized by a multiple factor approach. "This approach allows research to incorporate variables from theories both dead and alive: family relations, school performance, social class, and even body type and intelligence [p. 18]." Much research has shifted from concern about individual differences to an emphasis on responses by normal individuals to normal (or abnormal) situations.

One of the major theories of delinquency, *differential association,* has been espoused by Sutherland (see Sutherland and Cressey, 1960). Sutherland has proposed that individuals learn delinquent behavior from others within intimate small groups. They learn to value delinquent acts through the influence of a delinquent subculture to which they are exposed. The main emphasis in this theory is on a subculture that is conducive to delinquency rather than on individual characteristics.

Another approach to delinquency proposed by Merton (1961) emphasizes that individuals vary in their opportunity to achieve success by

[2] For readers seeking a lengthier exposition of the main theories as well as a critical evaluation of them, see Hirschi and Rudisill, 1976; Nettler, 1974.

legitimate means in a culture characterized by what has been called the Protestant ethic: success, hard work, and so on. According to Merton (1961), because many individuals from lower socioeconomic groups are unable to achieve success through legal means, they may be more likely to engage in delinquent acts as a way of attaining it. For some adolescents, it is maintained, illegitimate means are the only options available. Several sociologists who have been influenced by Merton view the subculture of these adolescents as existing in the form of the gang. Three types of subcultures have been described by Cloward and Ohlin (1960): *criminal, conflict,* and *retreatist.* The criminal subculture exists in working-class areas where adolescent delinquency can become part of adult organized crime. The conflict subculture exists in disorganized areas where the emphasis is on winning by coercion the opportunities that are perceived as lacking. The retreatist culture is said to emerge from what is conceived to be a "double" failure: the adolescents do not have opportunities for criminal activities, they are unable to gain status in conflict groups, and they, therefore, are likely to retreat into drugs. In the view of Cloward and Ohlin (1960) gangs, underachievement in school, inadequate work performance, and inadequately cohesive ties with the home are all conditions predominantly associated with lower socioeconomic status.

The delinquent adolescent may drift in and out of delinquent acts. [Danny Lyon/Magnum.]

Another theory of delinquency has been set forth by Matza (1964). In contrast to the theorists already mentioned, he emphasizes the similarities between delinquent and nondelinquent adolescents. He points out that adolescent delinquents are very much aware of the deviant nature of their acts and tend to feel guilty about them. For this reason, a variety of rationalizations evolve within the subculture, designed to make delinquency more acceptable to its members. Sykes and Matza (1957) refer to this as using techniques of neutralization: for instance, the justification given for aggression is that it is necessary for self-defense. A second major point made by Matza is that adolescents are not involved in full-time conflict with traditional middle-class society. The delinquent adolescent tends to drift only occasionally into delinquent acts. Lastly, Matza contends that delinquency is an act that is given up with considerable ease.

According to Matza (1964), delinquency is due in part to the fact that adolescents are in a transitional stage between childhood and adulthood, are concerned about their identity, and need to be accepted by their peers. In his view adolescents conform to what they perceive to be the peer group's norms because they feel that they would lose their status in the peer group if they did not conform.

Environmental, genetic, and existential factors

Delinquent conduct is obviously influenced by the environment and is a response to it. An adolescent would not become a thief if the environment did not provide something for him to steal and strong enticements to do so. However, the explanation as to why one adolescent steals and another does not is less obvious. Environmental pressures and social disapproval vary in different segments of society; but even in subcultures where attitudes toward misconduct are rather tolerant, youngsters differ in the seriousness of the crimes they commit, and many avoid a delinquent career. Moreover, many youngsters who do not live in a delinquency subculture become delinquent.

The question as to what predisposes one person, and not another, to juvenile crime is least clear when we consider youngsters who go bad even though they have what seems to be a favorable environment.

At present most authors place their emphasis on environmental causes of delinquency, with little or no mention of heredity (Hood and Sparks, 1970). This contrasts with some earlier speculations to the effect that criminal tendencies are inherited—the criminal springs from "bad seed." Actually, no delinquent has a gene—or set of genes—that produced in him a motive to steal a TV or a car.

But an adequate approach to understanding the problem of delinquency (or any other human condition) requires an appreciation of the fact that human beings are not just putty in the hands of the environment. The infant, the child, and the older youngster are not just oysters drifting with the tides in Chesapeake Bay. Their way of life is shaped by their interaction with the environment.

Gang Delinquency as a Cultural Phenomenon

Miller (1958, 1969)[3] has offered an impressive account of cultural forces that are at work in a lower-class community that is described as a generating milieu of gang delinquency. According to Miller, the gang delinquency of adolescent street-corner groups in lower-class communities differs from the delinquent subculture that has arisen in areas where there is a conflict between middle-class and lower-class cultures and where the lower-class members deliberately violate middle-class norms. The gang-delinquency culture he speaks of is in a lower-class community with a "long-established, distinctively patterned tradition with an integrity of its own [p. 5]." According to him, the traditions, attitudes, and values of this culture are "designed to support and maintain the basic features of the lower-class way of life [p. 19]."

In the lower-class culture Miller describes, one focal concern is about "trouble" as related to law-abiding or non-law-abiding behavior. In certain situations getting into trouble is a recognized source of prestige.

In this culture, according to Miller (1958), there is also an emphasis on toughness. "The model for the 'tough guy'—hard, fearless, undemonstrative, skilled in physical combat—is represented by the movie gangster of the thirties, the 'private eye' and the movie cowboy [p. 12]."

Another quality that is emphasized is smartness—the ability to outsmart, outthink, and outfox others and to avoid being outwitted, "taken," or duped.

Yet another feature of this culture is the search for excitement, a thrill, through such means as alcohol, gambling, and playing the numbers.

According to Miller (1958), another focal concern is with *fate*—fortune, or luck. Many lower-class individuals feel that their lives are subject to a set of forces over which they have relatively little control. This is sometimes associated with the view that it is futile to work toward a goal—if

[3] Miller (1958) is speaking of what he calls the "hard-core" lower-class group, which, in his estimate, comprises about 15 per cent of the population or "about twenty-five million." According to Miller, systematic research would probably reveal "at least four to six major subtypes of lower-class cultures [p. 6]."

luck is with you, things come your way; if luck is against you, it doesn't pay to try.

In this culture, as described by Miller, there is a discrepancy between overt and covert attitudes toward autonomy and authority. While expressing resentment against external authority, many lower-class people do not desire to be autonomous. Some even seek environments in which they are subject to a great amount of external control—such as the armed forces or correctional institutions.

Persons in this culture, as described by Miller (1958), have a great desire to "belong." Some also attach great importance to status, mainly the status of seeming to be an adult. The status sought is not that of a responsible adult but what can be found through external symbols, such as having a car, ready cash, and freedom to drink and smoke. Action designed to gain status is more concerned with status itself than with questions as to whether it is achieved by legal or illegal or moral or immoral means.

Miller (1958) points out that there are large variations in the ways in which individuals respond to these standards. The ones who adopt them do not seek to better their lot but to perpetuate it; they do not seek to be free but to be governed by external authority; and they do not seek to attain self-direction, freedom of action, or responsibility for themselves.

Miller does not say what coerces or impels some individuals to get into and stay in such a society while others find something quite different. But from his account, it is easy to see that a person who has once moved into it, or has been born into it, would have difficulty in getting out.

Several other investigators have written about the extent of crime among street gang members (see, for example, Cohen, 1969a, b). Recently, Friedman et al. (1975) presented some interesting data relating to characteristics of juvenile street gang members. The subjects of their study were boys between the ages of fifteen and eighteen, some of whom had official court and police records, and all of whom came from poor and disadvantaged families. Their data suggest that the most powerful predictors of gang membership were the adolescents' reports of having engaged in acts of violence and reporting the advantages of belonging to a gang. It was also found that adolescents who openly rebelled against one or both of their parents, such as by physical or verbal attacks, were more likely to become members of gangs than other youngsters. Several other factors differentiated gang members from nongang members. Gang members had been arrested more often for nonviolent crimes and showed more truancy and more alcohol abuse. Although gang and nongang members differed in many ways, it is interesting to note that they also were similar in many ways.

Social Disabilities and Gang Behavior

According to Short (1966), adolescents who are members of gangs appear to be at a disadvantage in terms of a number of basic interpersonal skills. He has further noted that gangs tend to be loosely structured and are limited in their capacity for concerted action. "With few exceptions, they do not minister effectively, if at all, to the adolescents' growing needs with respect to education, vocational training, or motivation, to preparation for family life, or participation in other aspects of community life [p. 455]." Moreover, members have difficulty in presenting themselves in an employment situation and in their relations with authority inside the school setting. Indeed, they are often at a complete loss in terms of personal interactions if they are removed from the arena with which they are familiar.

In comparing delinquent boys with nondelinquent boys, Bandura and Walters (1959) found that the former were less "warm" than the latter in terms of their interaction with their peers. Short and Strodtbeck (1965) further reported that gang boys tend to evaluate nongang boys more highly than fellow members of their gang.

During adolescence, independence-dependence conflicts tend to be accentuated and adolescents have difficulty displaying their dependency needs. It seems that this difficulty is magnified in gang boys, if Short (1966) is correct, as any show of dependence may be interpreted as a sign of weakness. Gang members are expected to be tough and exploitive rather than tender and affectionate with girls.

Delinquency as a Personal Problem

In contrast to the delinquency that is generated by a given subculture, much delinquency is an outgrowth of individual predicaments that might arise in any culture. Delinquency may be a form of problem-solving behavior, a symptom of emotional maladjustment, or a response to cumulative frustrations.

DELINQUENCY AS A FORM OF PROBLEM SOLVING

Seen from the delinquent's point of view, delinquent acts may be a means of meeting a need or solving a problem. The need may range from a momentary desire—such as a desire to take an apple from a fruit stand—through a need to fit in with his group, to a persisting, irresistible urge to act out hostile impulses. The underlying motive may be to gain favor in the eyes of a gang, to show off, or to take revenge. The means of expressing the underlying motive may be quite incidental: it may be through stealing or vandalism or a physical attack on another person or sexual misconduct or placing a nail-studded board on a highway. Similar delinquent acts may spring from different motives, and similar motives may lead to differing forms of delinquent behavior. For this reason, it usually is less significant to ask what a delinquent did than to inquire why he did it.

About one quarter of normal adolescent boys studied by Offer (1971) had participated in delinquent acts such as stealing or vandalism and serious physical fights. Although many of these acts were performed in an attempt to deal with personal problems, it is important to note that the vast majority of adolescents ceased committing these acts after a few trials. Many of these boys learned to channel their aggressive impulses into sports, studying, work, or sexual activities. This suggests that an important step in efforts to prevent delinquency is not necessarily an effort to eliminate personal problems, but to help adolescents to cope with their personal problems in a socially acceptable manner.

DELINQUENCY AND EMOTIONAL MALADJUSTMENT

Many delinquents are emotionally disturbed or have personality disorders (Glueck and Glueck, 1974) that would make life a burden to them and to others even if they did not violate the law. According to Redl and Wineman (1951), small amounts of frustration can disturb the equilibrium of the delinquent. In some cases even the mildest fears or anxieties can lead to a breakdown in the controls of the delinquent. These investigators, who have dealt with severely disturbed youngsters, have remarked that some delinquents have difficulty in perceiving cause-and-effect relationships. Thus, when they engage in delinquent acts they may not be aware of the consequences of the act. The inability to distinguish between cause and effect can be illustrated by a situation that was seen by one of the present writers several years ago. A young man attempted to kidnap a five-year-old boy. The mother was able to recover the child. The young man's response on being caught kidnapping was to be indignant at the mother for not staying closer to her son and thereby tempting him. On the other hand, according to Kessler (1966), some delinquents may experience feelings of guilt following their deviant behavior, with chronic depression or attacks of anxiety. Some delinquents who are emotionally disturbed may be regarded as "healthier" than some other emotionally disturbed children. They are, so to speak, doing something about their distress (even though it brings distress to others). They are openly expressing their aggressive impulses (Grinker, 1971). In this respect they have more of a vital spark; they are more venturesome than disturbed youngsters who are entirely withdrawn and eventually are classed as mentally ill. Many delinquents seem to work out their problems sufficiently well to settle down as law-abiding citizens in later years.

Many youngsters who are emotionally disturbed are not delinquent, and youngsters can be delinquent without being emotionally disturbed (Kessler, 1966). Miller (as cited in Kvaraceus and Miller, 1959), states that the middle-class offender is more likely to be an emotionally disturbed person than the lower-class offender. Many young people in lower-class groups commit acts that are delinquent from a legal point of view (such as truancy and theft), but that are not condemned by the lower-class group to which they belong. When the social group tolerates or condones delinquent actions, the young person has less reason for feeling anxious or guilty than when these actions are condemned. In a middle-class group, where the standards are more rigorous and where a youngster faces severe disapproval for acts that may not be condemned in a lower-class group, misconduct represents a more severe defiance of the social norm and, therefore, is more likely to involve emotional turmoil.

Public response to delinquents

During the 1960s public distress about crime and drug abuse resulted in an increased demand for law and order. For instance, 44 per cent of the American public reported in 1966 that the criminal justice system was overly lenient. By 1970, according to Erskine and Siegel (1975), 64 per cent of the American public felt this way. In 1973, 75 per cent of the American public reported that the courts were too lenient with alleged offenders. Erskine and Siegel (1975) further speculate that present-day public concern about the crime rate has lost some meaning because of the turmoil caused in the early 1970s by misconduct by high government officials.

Delinquent acts inflict innumerable hardships upon those against whom they are directed—anger, fear, grief, loss of property, and loss of life. When individuals meet such hardship *directly*—as when juveniles have entered their homes and stolen their things—they feel outraged, angry, and they also have an uneasy feeling, a feeling that their home has been violated and is not a safe place. If they did not feel angry they would be less than human. Similarly, a driver whose fenders have been wrinkled by a speeding juvenile is bound to feel anger mixed with fear. It is difficult also for a teacher not to feel annoyed, or even helplessly angry, when a delinquent pupil obviously hates the school and the teacher, even if the teacher is just a convenient target for resentments aroused by other persons and conditions.

There is little in delinquent conduct, especially when it is aggressive, that appeals to sentiments of kindness and sympathy—unless the aggrieved person can look beyond the delinquents' manifest ill will and sense their hidden hurts, anxiety, and desperation. However, it seems that attitudes toward delinquents are sometimes more severe among those who have not been victims of delinquent acts than among those who have. In the population at large, including parents, teachers, and jurists, there are many persons who want delinquents to be treated harshly, whereas others who have actually suffered from acts of delinquents feel compassion for them.

According to Kvaraceus (1958), there is considerable evidence that the public, and even some professional workers, are less interested in attacking the problem of delinquency than in attacking the delinquents themselves. Prescriptions for dealing with delinquency often seem to be designed more for revenge than for prevention or reform.

Moreover, the press and public opinion, when not attacking the delinquent, sometimes turn their spite against the parents and even against professional workers who are hired to help the offender. Kvaraceus (1958) calls attention to "a rash of antiparent legislation enacted in many states" and "get tough with parents' attitudes visible in most communities." A punitive attitude toward the delinquent as a person, as distinguished from an effort to combat delinquency as a problem, appears also in "periodic waves of criticism leveled against 'soft' courts, 'muddle-headed psychiatrists,' and 'egg-headed researchers' [p. 5]" who undertake to study and work with the nonconforming child.

Exploitation of delinquents and delinquency

Delinquents are often exploited by adults. The kind of exploitation that is most obvious, and that arouses the greatest public indignation, occurs when vicious adults use teen-agers for criminal purposes, such as prostitution and other forms of traffic in sex, for the sale of drugs, or as accomplices in burglary, pickpocketing, shoplifting, and other forms of theft. However, it is not just criminals who exploit delinquents and delinquency. The exploiters may be respectable members of society who use delinquents to satisfy "psychic needs" (Kvaraceus and Miller, 1959).

Delinquents as Scapegoats

The practice of finding a scapegoat is a common one in our society and apparently in most others. The scapegoat is frequently an institutionalized target of repressed hostility. According to Miller (as cited in Kvaraceus and Miller, 1959) the delinquent "serves today to syphon off much of the aggression inevitable in any complex society such as our own [p. 16]." In the past, ethnic and racial groups have served as scapegoats, and they still serve this purpose (as may be noted with examples of prejudice). However, according to Miller, it is no longer fashionable in certain groups to display hostility toward ethnic and religious groups. As these "traditional and established hostility targets have lost their utility" many people, according to Miller, have sought other, more "respectable," scapegoat groups. Delinquents provide one such group. According to Miller, one can hate them with gratifying vengeance.

Commercial Exploitation of Delinquents

Delinquents often are "best sellers" in popular fiction and the main attraction in movies. They are often depicted as heartless, conscienceless, and monstrous characters. Their lurid pictures on covers help to sell paperbacks. Thus portrayed, they have great sales value as a means by which the viewer or reader can find a vicarious outlet for aggressive impulses and sexual desires. Delinquents who are so portrayed enable the viewer or reader to be a voyeur without risk of being caught, to participate in all kinds of sordid adventures without staining their clothes or besmirching their public morals.

Miller states that the portrayal of the delinquent in the mass media is frequently an inaccurate and exaggerated fabrication. It is often as superficial and phoney as the portrayal of criminals in the old "crime doesn't pay" radio programs. But even though it is manufactured as commercial entertainment, this fabrication may also have sinister effects. According to Kvaraceus and Miller (1959), the "distorted picture begins to actualize itself" when youngsters begin to act out what they have seen. When parents, teachers, and other adults accept and perpetuate the fictional image of "the delinquent," they "actually help to bring into being the very situation which they so sanctimoniously condemn [p. 29]."

Temporary and persisting law-violating behavior

Many persons who were delinquent in their early teens go from bad to worse, whereas many others, as we have noted, cease their criminal behavior in their late teens and twenties. This appears in a follow-up study by Glueck and Glueck (1940), of 1,000 boy delinquents who had been brought into the Boston Juvenile Court at an average age of thirteen and a half years. When 846 of these had reached an average age of twenty-nine,[4] records of the intervening years showed that as the years had gone by, there had been a steady decrease in the number who continued to be offenders. Almost 40 per cent had ceased to be criminals.

Moreover, among those who continued to commit crimes there was a drop in serious offenses. During the period between the time of the first contact with the delinquents included in the study and the follow-up fifteen years later, the proportion of serious offenders—among those who still were committing crimes—dropped from 75.6 to 47.8 per cent. There also was a marked decrease in arrests for property crimes (stealing). Although there was an increase in crimes against persons (assault and battery), crimes of this sort constituted a small proportion of causes for arrest (6.9 per cent) in the older group.

One of the sharpest increases occurred in arrests for drunkenness (none at all in the earlier years and 43 per cent of all arrests in the third five-year period of the follow-up study). This high incidence of arrests for drunkenness indicates that many persons who, when young, directed aggressive acts against others, commit self-destructive acts when they are older (an alcoholic often inflicts dangers and hardships on others, but he invariably also inflicts damage on himself).

From the evidence in this follow-up study and in other research, Glueck and Glueck (1940) advance the theory that "the physical and mental changes that comprise the natural process of maturation offer the chief explanation of this improvement in conduct with the passing of the years [p. 264]." In the same context, they note that through the process of maturation—"the development and integration of a person's physical and mental powers"—a person who has reached adulthood has more capacity for "self-control, foresight, and planfulness"; he or she is better able to postpone immediate desires for later ones and to profit by experience. They note also that with the passage of time, "the human being loses some of his energy and aggressiveness; he tends to slow down and become less venturesome [p. 269]."[5]

The Gluecks point out that there are marked individual differences in the pattern and rate of maturation. They found that, in later years,

[4] In the meantime, some had died and it was not possible to get complete information about some of the others.

[5] This theory—that changes occur in the human organism in the process of maturation that are not due to learning or conditioning alone—is in keeping with findings from many studies of children (several studies on this subject, including some of his own research, have been reviewed by Jersild, 1960). However, while naming maturation as an important factor in accounting for less rambunctious and impulsive behavior in young adults, the Gluecks (1940) also point out that there is need for more systematic study to examine in detail what is involved in the process of maturation through the teens and into early adult years.

delinquents, or former delinquents, resemble each other more in their conduct when compared in terms of the number of years that have elapsed since the onset of their delinquency than when compared according to chronologic age. (For example, persons who became delinquent at twelve and persons whose delinquency began at age fifteen are more alike five years later, at the respective ages of seventeen and twenty, than when the conduct of the latter group at age seventeen is compared with the conduct of the former group at age seventeen.) They found a "marked resemblance" in conduct "at a point equidistant from the time of onset of delinquency" among youngsters living in different communities and subjected to many and varied kinds and qualities of correctional treatment. This suggests that "delinquent tendencies, at least in young persons, are inclined to run a course that is not too readily modifiable by present methods of treatment [Glueck and Glueck, 1940, p. 265]."

In this study the authors also found that the delinquents who had reformed after fifteen years "were endowed with a better heredity and enjoyed a more wholesome early environment [p. 265]" than those who continued to commit crimes. The process of maturation was "apparently facilitated by the better equipment of certain offenders and retarded or blocked by the poorer resources of others [p. 265]."

Although it is encouraging to find that many young offenders mend their ways as they grow older, it is disturbing to note that over half of them continue to commit crimes or to run afoul of the law.

Hostility toward those who desire to help

One of the severest obstacles in efforts to help delinquents is their hostility. Most of them have felt the lash of punishment, disapproval, and rejection. Even when not physically punished, they sense the anger directed against them. The fact that their own conduct has provoked anger in others does not lessen their anger.

Moreover, juvenile delinquents (as well as nondelinquents) often face an unequal struggle with hostile adults. This happens, for example, when spiteful policemen are out to get juveniles who may or may not be offenders. Jersild has records of many instances in which adolescents who drive a car within the speed limit have, on suspicion, been stopped by police, who then take off, leaving the car's contents strewn about.

Whatever their role in provoking the hostility of others might be, juvenile delinquents are likely to encounter many situations where they feel helpless rage. It is often directed against persons who are eager to help the delinquent. This means that teachers, social workers, and others who try to befriend a delinquent frequently get nothing but a sullen response. One of the most demanding aspects of working with delinquents is to appreciate the hurt and tragedy that often lie hidden beneath the sullen mask.

Concern about the problem of delinquency obviously extends beyond the plight of delinquents themselves. It should include concern about those who bear the brunt of delinquency. In almost every community today there are persons who have been the victims or live in fear of becoming the victims of juvenile crime, with a growing number of elderly people among them.

References

Ahlstrom, W. M., & Havighurst, R. J. *400 loses.* San Francisco: Jossey-Bass, 1971.

Bandura, A., & Walters, R. H. *Adolescent aggression.* New York: Ronald, 1959.

Becker, W. C. Consequences of different kinds of parental discipline. In M. L. Hoffman & L. W. Hoffman (Eds.), *Review of child development research* (Vol. 1). New York: Russell Sage Foundation, 1964.

Brook, J., Lukoff, I., Whiteman, M., & Gordon, A. S. Teen-age drug use in an urban ghetto: Preliminary findings. Unpublished manuscript, Columbia University, 1975.

Brooks, W. N., & Doob, A. N. Justice and jury. *Journal of Social Issues,* 1975, **31**, 171–182.

Cloward, R. A., & Ohlin, L. E. *Delinquency and opportunity.* New York: Free Press, 1960.

Cohen, B. The delinquency of gangs and spontaneous groups. In T. Sellin & M. Wolfgang (Eds.), *Delinquency: Selected studies.* New York: Wiley, 1969a.

Cohen, B. Internecine conflict: The offenders. In T. Sellin & M. Wolfgang (Eds.), *Delinquency: Selected studies.* New York: Wiley, 1969b.

Davis, J. A. Blacks, crime and American culture. *Annals of the American Academy of Political and Social Science Crime and Justice: 1776–1976,* 1976, **423**, 89–98.

Duke, M. P., & Fenhagen, E. Self-parental alienation and locus of control in delinquent girls. *Journal of Genetic Psychology,* 1975, **127**, 103–107.

Erskine, H., & Siegel, R. L. Civil liberties and the American public. *Journal of Social Issues,* 1975, **31**, 13–29.

Friedman, C. J., Mann, F., & Friedman, A. S. A profile of juvenile street gang members. *Adolescence,* 1975, **10**, 563–607.

Gibbs, J. P., & Erickson, M. L. Major developments in the sociological study of deviance. *Annual Review of Sociology,* 1975, 21–42.

Gibson, H. B. Self-reported delinquency among school boys and their attitude to the police. *British Journal of Social and Clinical Psychology,* 1967, **6**, 168–173.

Glueck, E. Identification of potential delinquents at 2–3 years of age. *International Journal of Social Psychiatry,* 1966, **12**, 5–16.

Glueck, S., & Glueck, E. *Juvenile delinquents grown up.* New York: The Commonwealth Fund, 1940.

Glueck, S., & Glueck, E. *Unraveling juvenile delinquency.* New York: The Commonwealth Fund, 1950.

Glueck, S., & Glueck, E. *Physique and delinquency.* New York: Harper, 1962.

Glueck, S., & Glueck, E. *Delinquents and nondelinquents in perspective.* Cambridge, Mass.: Harvard U.P., 1968.

Glueck, S., & Glueck, E. *Of delinquency and crime.* Springfield, Ill.: Thomas, 1974.

Gold, M. *Delinquent behavior in an American city.* Belmont, Calif.: Brooks/Cole, 1970.

Gold, M., & Mann, D. Delinquency as defense. *American Journal of Orthopsychiatry,* 1972, **42**, 463–479.

Gold, M., & Reimer, D. J. Changing patterns of delinquent behavior among Americans 13 through 16 years old: 1967–1972. *Crime and Delinquency Literature,* 1975, **7**, 483–517.

Golenpaul, A. *Information please almanac atlas and yearbook* (13th ed.). New York: Gollenpaul Associates, 1976.

Grinker, R. R. What is the cause of violence? In J. Fawcett (Ed.), *Dynamics of violence.* Chicago: American Medical Association, 1971.

Healy, W., & Bronner, A. F. *New light on delinquency and its treatment.* New Haven, Conn.: Yale, 1936.

Hetherington, E. M., Stouwie, R. J., & Ridberg, E. H. Patterns of family interaction and child-rearing attitudes related to three dimensions of juvenile delinquency. *Journal of Abnormal Psychology,* 1971, **78**, 160–176.

Hirschi, T., & Rudisill, D. The great American search: Causes of crime 1876–1976. *Annals of the American Academy of Political and Social Science: Crime and Justice: 1776–1976,* 1976, **423**, 14–22.

Hoffman, M. L. Moral development. In P. H. Mussen (Ed.), *Manual of child psychology* (Vol. 2). New York: Wiley, 1970.

Hood, R., & Sparks, R. *Key issues in criminology.* New York: McGraw-Hill, 1970.

Jacobs, T. Family interaction in disturbed and normal families: A methodological and substantive review. *Psychological Bulletin,* 1975, **82**, 33–65.

Jersild, A. T. *Child psychology* (5th ed.). Englewood Cliffs, N.J.: Prentice-Hall, 1960.

Kessler, J. *Psychopathology of childhood.* Englewood Cliffs, N.J.: Prentice-Hall, 1966.

Kohlberg, L. Moral development and identification. In H. Stevenson (Ed.), *Child psychology: 62nd yearbook of the national society for the study of education.* Chicago: U. of Chicago, 1963.

Kratcoski, P. C., & Kratcoski, J. E. Changing patterns in the delinquent activities of boys and girls: A self-reported delinquency analysis. *Adolescence,* 1975, **10**, 83–91.

Kvaraceus, W. C. *The community and the delinquent.* New York: World, 1954.

Kvaraceus, W. C. *Juvenile delinquency.* Washington, D.C.: Department of Classroom Teachers, American Educational Research Association of the National Education Association, 1958.

Kvaraceus, W. C., & Miller, W. B. *Delinquent behavior.* Washington, D.C.: National Education Association, 1959.

Lukoff, I. F., & Brook, J. S. A socio-cultural exploration of heroin use. In C. Winick (Ed.), *Sociological aspects of drug dependence.* Cleveland: CRC Press, 1974.

Matza, D. *Delinquency and drift.* New York: Wiley and Sons, 1964.

Matza, D., & Sykes, G. M. Juvenile delinquency and subterranean values. *American Sociological Review,* 1961, **26**, 712–719.

McCord, W., McCord, J., & Zola, I. K. *Origins of crime: A new evaluation of the Cambridge-Somerville youth study.* New York: Columbia U.P., 1959.

Merton, R. K. *Social theory and social structure.* New York: Free Press, 1961.

Miller, W. B. Lower class culture as a generating milieu of gang delinquency. *Journal of Social Issues,* 1958, **14**, 5–19.

Miller, W. B. White gangs. *Transaction,* 1969, **6**, 11–26.

Nettler, G. *Explaining crime.* New York: McGraw-Hill, 1974.

Offer, D. Coping with aggression among normal adolescent boys. In J. Fawcett (Ed.), *Dynamics of violence,* Chicago: American Medical Association, 1971.

Pepinsky, H. E. The growth of crime in the United States. *Annals of the American Academy of Political and Social Science: Crime and Justice in America: 1776–1976,* 1976, **423**, 23–30.

Redl, F., & Wineman, D. *Children who hate.* New York: Free Press, 1951.

Senna, J., Rathus, S. A., & Siegal, L. Delinquent behavior and academic investment among suburban youth. *Adolescence,* 1974, **9**, 481–494.

Short, J. F., Jr. Juvenile delinquency: The sociocultural context. In L. M. Hoffman & M. L. Hoffman (Eds.), *Review of child development research* (Vol. 1). New York: Russell Sage Foundation, 1966, pp. 423–468.

Short, J. F., & Strodtbeck, F. L. *Group process and gang delinquency.* Chicago: U. of Chicago, 1965.

Silver, L. B., Dublin, C. C., & Lourie, R. S. Does violence breed violence? Contributions from a study of the child abuse syndrome. *American Journal of Psychiatry,* 1969, **126**, 404–407.

Simon, R. J. American women and crime. *Annals of the American Academy of Political and Social Science Crime and Justice in America: 1776–1976,* 1976, **423**, 31–46.

Sutherland, E. H., & Cressey, D. R. *Principles of criminology.* Chicago: Lippincott, 1960.

Sykes, G. M., & Matza, D. Techniques of neutralization: A theory of delinquency. *American Sociological Review,* 1957, **22**, 664–670.

Thornburg, H. D. (Ed.). *Contemporary adolescence: Readings* (2nd ed.). Monterey, Calif.: Brooks/Cole, 1975.

Tutt, N. *Care or custody.* New York: Agathon Press, 1974.

Wilkinson, K. The broken family and juvenile delinquency: Scientific explanation or ideology? *Social Problems,* 1974, **21**, 726–739.

16

drugs and youth[1]

In recent years there has been increasing public concern about the licit and illicit use of drugs by adolescents. Persons at all levels of society have reacted to this problem with emotions ranging from worry and apprehension to

[1] The findings and observations on which this chapter is based have been assembled by Dr. Judith S. Brook, who is doing research on the use of drugs by adolescents, and Dr. David W. Brook, who is a member of the Committee on Alcoholism and Drug Abuse of the New York District Branch of the American Psychiatric Association.

horror and outrage. There is good reason to be alarmed by drug abuse, especially when it involves addiction to "hard" drugs—not only because of the dangers confronting the victims of such addiction, but also because addicts can become a menace to the community.

Although many concerns about the drug problem are realistic, some are not supported by research findings. A widely held belief, according to Josephson (1974), is that one who uses certain drugs, such as marijuana, is doomed to become a heroin addict. Actually, although many heroin addicts have used other drugs, the majority of marijuana users do not proceed to heroin use.

Another widely held assumption is that drug use leads to crime, prompted by the need for money to support an expensive habit. Some drug users need several hundred dollars a week to cover the cost. Repeatedly, news items report that male users have committed robbery to obtain the funds they need. Female drug users are frequently reported as engaging in prostitution (although it is recognized that prostitution is not limited to females or to drug users). Hard-drug use is often associated with crime, but delinquent and criminal behavior may have begun prior to, rather than as a consequence of, the use of drugs. However, once a drug habit has been established, there may be an increased pressure to commit crime.

It has also been assumed (according to Josephson, 1974) that drug abuse in advanced technological societies may have sprung, in part, from "overmedication" due to massive advertising and excessive drug prescriptions by physicians. It is probable that there are persons who overuse or misuse psychotherapeutic drugs, but recent research suggests that this aspect of the problem has been exaggerated (Mellinger et al., 1974).

It should be noted that although everyone involved in research or treatment regards hard-drug abuse as an extremely serious problem, some of the literature dealing with the effects of certain drugs is controversial. Available research studies vary in the exactness of the methods that have been used and in underlying theoretical assumptions. There is no strong consensus on the definition of drug abuse. Furthermore, in formal research, or in evaluating one's own personal observations or impressions, it is important to distinguish between a confirmed addict (a habitual user) and an individual who has tried a particular drug out of curiosity (once or on a few occasions) and has then discontinued use.[2] If information is obtained by questioning to elicit "self-reports," the information so obtained may be questionable because it appears that many adolescents have a tendency to

[2] A distinction among experimental, social, situational, intensive, and compulsive use of drugs has been made by the National Commission on Marijuana and Drug Use (1973). The Final Report of the Commission of Inquiry into the Non-Medical Use of Drugs—Le Dain Report (1973) differentiates among experimental, occasional, and regular use of drugs.

underreport or to overreport their drug usage. Validation of self-reports has met with little success, with the exception of matching reports of heroin use with urinalysis. To gain as much authenticity as possible, a study of drug usage should use a longitudinal approach rather than rely on retrospective reports.

This chapter will discuss the physiological and psychological effects of deviant drug use as well as sociocultural and personality factors associated with the use of drugs. The discussion will deal first with the drugs most widely used by adolescents—alcohol and marijuana—and then proceed to deal more briefly with amphetamines, LSD, heroin, and multiple-drug use.

Alcohol

Throughout history one of the most widely used psychoactive drugs has been alcohol. The aggregate individual and social costs resulting from excessive use of alcohol are far greater than those accruing from other psychoactive drugs (McGlothlin, 1975). Although some have praised alcohol as the "nectar of the gods," others have viewed alcohol as "second only to war" as a problem with which civilization must cope.

Alcohol and tobacco are frequently used by adolescents. [Charles Gatewood/Magnum.]

At the present time, many authorities regard excessive drinking as a serious problem at the adolescent level. Chafetz, who is Director of the National Institute of Alcohol Abuse and Alcoholism, believes that unless adolescents are helped to adopt a more responsible attitude with respect to alcohol, the situation may become catastrophic (National Institute of Alcohol Abuse and Alcoholism, 1975). Brunswick (1969), of the Columbia University School of Public Health, has reported that adolescents themselves consider the consumption of alcohol as one of their major health problems.

Incidence

With the recent publicity given to alcohol use among adolescents, it probably does not come as a surprise that alcohol (a *legal* drug) is used by a greater number of adolescents than any of the illegal drugs (Kandel et al., 1976). In a national survey conducted in 1974 by the National Institute of Alcohol Abuse and Alcoholism (1975), preliminary results indicated that 94 per cent of the boys and 87 per cent of the girls in high school have had at least some experience with alcohol. While the vast majority of adolescents in these student surveys do not drink regularly, or are light to moderate drinkers, it has been estimated that roughly 3 to 6 per cent of adolescents are problem drinkers. According to Chafetz, approximately 1.3 million adolescents, twelve to seventeen years of age, are problem drinkers, and 750,000 have been identified as hard-core alcoholics (Cohen, 1975).

An illustration of the incidence of problems that have resulted from the increase in excessive drinking follows: the number of adolescents under eighteen who have been arrested for offences attributed to alcohol (that is, driving while intoxicated) increased nationally by 135 per cent between 1960 and 1973 (Kelley, 1974).

At the high school level, Kandel et al. (1976) found an increase with age in the use of hard liquor. They also found that boys reported heavier use of alcohol than girls.

Psychological and Physiological Effects

Alcohol has a depressing effect on the activity of the central nervous system. As is true in connection with other psychoactive drugs, there are wide individual differences in response to a given amount of alcohol. One individual may become lethargic after a drink or two, whereas another individual may for a time become more animated. Moreover, a dose that initially seems to be stimulating may later have a sedative effect.

In social settings many adolescents use alcohol as a means of lessening inhibitions and to obtain a feeling of well-being and camaraderie. Other adolescents may use alcohol to relieve tension and anxiety. Bouts of heavy drinking by individuals with certain psychiatric or neurological problems may be accompanied by aggression or violence (Final Report of the Commission of Inquiry into the Non-Medical Use of Drugs, 1973). Because alcohol use may result in a general lessening of inhibitions, one might expect that alcohol would have a specific aphrodisiac (sex-drive stimulating) effect. However, alcohol rarely enhances sexual activity (Gay and Sheppard, 1973). As the old saying goes, alcohol enhances the desire but lessens the ability; very large doses lessen both desire and ability.

According to the Final Report of the Commission of Inquiry (1973), small amounts of alcohol may result in improved performance under certain circumstances, but performance on tasks requiring selective attention, psychomotor coordination, and abstract thinking is often impaired by moderate amounts of alcohol (Forney and Harger, 1965). Heavy alcohol use resulting in drunkenness is usually accompanied by one or more of the following symptoms: disorientation, slurred speech, impairment in vision, and poor muscular control. At very high doses it has been noted that unconsciousness can occur, as well as failure in respiration and circulation—which, in extreme cases, may result in death (Forney and Harger, 1965). Several psychiatric and neurologic disorders have been found to be correlated with chronic heavy use of alcohol. Irreversible damage of the peripheral nervous system, brain damage, and psychiatric problems have been observed in adults who are chronic heavy users of alcohol. Delirium tremens, which may be life-threatening, may result from the abrupt cessation of alcohol intake after a bout of heavy drinking in an alcoholic. Although there are limited empirical data available, concern has been expressed regarding the effects that heavy alcohol consumption might have on the maturational process in adolescents (Final Report of the Commission of Inquiry, 1973—from this point on, this reference will be referred to as the Le Dain Report).

Social and Cultural Factors Associated with Use of Alcohol

In an extensive review of the literature on drinking prior to college, Maddox (1970) concludes that an overwhelming majority of adolescents have their first drinking experiences at home in the presence of their parents or other relatives. This is not surprising in view of the fact that in many communities it would be almost impossible to find a home where alcoholic beverages, ranging from beer to wine or hard liquors, are not available. A number of clinical studies of adolescent problem drinkers, as well as studies of adult alcoholics, have found that one or both of the parents of these adolescents were heavy drinkers (MacKay, 1961; McCord et al., 1960). College students who were high users of alcohol more often tended to have parents who were high users of alcohol than low users of alcohol, according to a study by Gusfield (1970). But questions remain as to why many adolescents are abstainers or light drinkers even though their parents are drinkers and why adolescents take to drink even though there is little or no drinking in their homes.

Another aspect of the adolescent drinking problem that needs to be explored is the extent to which it might be associated with a tendency of young people to demand privileges that in times past were reserved for a later age. In the preceding chapter we noted, for example, that in recent decades young adolescents have demanded the right to have dates at an earlier age than once was regarded as appropriate. We noted also that questions have been raised as to whether some adolescents might be more precocious in their desires than in their ability to assume responsibility. An answer to such questions will not solve the problem of drinking, but it might help to convince older persons that they cannot, as much as in the past, count on youngsters to be content with soda pop while older folk imbibe stronger stuff.

A number of studies have examined the role of peer-group support in the adolescent's use of alcohol. In a longitudinal study of junior and senior high school students, Jessor et al. (1972) found that students who were abstainers and changed to the status of drinkers the following year perceived significantly more social support for drinking from peers than students who were abstainers and remained abstainers.

In studies of college-student peer groups, both Gusfield (1970) and Rogers (1970) reported that members of fraternities are more likely to drink than nonfraternity college students.

Several studies have inquired into the relationship between religious affiliation and adolescents' use of alcohol; the findings have not been consistent, but there is general agreement that persons who have a strong commitment to an organized religion are less likely to become problem drinkers (Maddox, 1970).

Personality Correlates of Adolescent Alcohol Use

Among the personality traits that variously have been found to be more common to young people who are problem drinkers than to those who do not have this problem are anxiety, depression, impulsivity, and aggressivity (Williams, 1966). Clinical observations of depression among adolescents have been reported by MacKay (1961), who notes symptoms ranging from loss of appetite, insomnia, restlessness, loss of self-esteem, anger, and bizarre appetite, to feelings of hopelessness and suicide attempts.

In a longitudinal study it was reported that adolescents who were abstainers and then shifted to a drinking status one year later had lower expectations of attaining conventional goals, such as academic achievement, and valued independence more and had greater tolerance of deviance than abstainers who remained abstainers from one year to the next (Jessor et al., 1972; Jessor and Jessor, 1975). Alcohol use was found to be associated with less conservative views concerning sex, religion, and morality in a study by Groves (1974). Measures of sociability and social participation in peer activities and campus life also were found to be positively associated with alcohol use. These life-style variables do not fully account for variation in alcohol use because there are many unsociable, conservative students who drink and many sociable ones who don't.

Motivations for Adolescent Drinking Behavior

The use of alcohol is a dynamic process that is related to many factors. Some possible reasons for initial experimentation with alcohol are one or more of the following: curiosity; a desire on the part of boys to appear more masculine or daring; peer influence or support; identification with older siblings or parents; or the need to appear grown-up (Maddox, 1970; Zucker, 1968). Other motives for excessive drinking are far more complex than those mentioned and are not completely understood at the present time. Popular notions of the effects of alcohol suggest that alcohol provides relief from anxiety and depression. Williams (1966) provides some evidence that this may indeed be the case when problem drinkers are slightly to moderately intoxicated, but not when they are extremely intoxicated. Nevertheless, the adolescent may use alcohol in an attempt to achieve relief from persistent personal problems or conflict situations. According to the National Commission on Marihuana and Drug Abuse (1973) motivation to continue compulsive use "stems primarily from the need to elicit a sense of security, comfort or relief related to the person's initial reasons for regularly using the drug; that is, it is primarily psychologically motivated and reinforced [p. 97]."

Marijuana

Marijuana and hashish are derived from *Cannabis sativa*, a herbaceous plant found throughout the tropical and temperate parts of the world.

Marijuana consists of a mixture of crushed cannabis leaves, flowers, and small twigs. In the United States marijuana is often referred to as grass or pot.

It should be noted that the whole issue of the pros and cons of marijuana usage and its legalization has become involved with politics. Certain interested scientists have taken a strong view one way or the other; those who believe marijuana is harmless or beneficial want its use more or less completely legalized, and those who believe it is very dangerous want the current penalties for its use kept or increased.

Studies of student marijuana use have dealt with a number of issues, as is indicated subsequently.

Incidence of Marijuana Use

Although it is true that marijuana is smoked by adults, its use is primarily concentrated among the young. Indeed, it is during this period of the life cycle when experimentation and eventual use of marijuana makes its first appearance.

Recent evidence from New York State (Kandel et al., 1976) indicates that approximately one third of adolescents have used at least one illegal drug. Marijuana (29 per cent) was found to be the most frequently used illegal drug in this study (Kandel et al., 1976). The percentage of individuals who have used marijuana increases to age twenty-five and then begins to decline (National Commission on Marihuana and Drug Abuse, 1973). Averaging data from numerous surveys of drug use, the National Commission concluded that among young people marijuana use appears to be leveling off. Nevertheless, others think that marijuana use is increasing among high school students (Hicks, 1975). Among college students the use of marijuana appears to have increased sharply from 5 per cent in 1967 to 51 per cent in 1971 (Gallup Opinion Index, 1972). In a study of marijuana use in a large metropolitan university, Martino and Truss (1973) reported that about three fourths of the students interviewed had tried marijuana. Data obtained from medical and law students at a large university revealed high rates of marijuana use, 73 and 68 per cent, respectively (Slaby et al., 1972). The fourth annual report of *Marijuana and Health* (1974) continues to support previous statements indicating that marijuana use by college and university students is increasing. It is extremely difficult to make predictions concerning the leveling off or increased use of marijuana in the future, as a particular drug may be in fashion one year and not in another. Furthermore, it is important to note that data from numerous studies (see, for example, Kandel et al., 1976) indicate that continued regular use of marijuana is less common than experimental use of marijuana. Among the nation's three million high school seniors it was estimated that 6 per cent used marijuana on a daily basis between 1974 and 1975 (Hicks, 1975).

Physical and Psychomotor Effects of Marijuana

Although marijuana has been regarded by some, including the legislators responsible for laws concerning its use, as a narcotic drug, it is non-narcotic and not physiologically addicting (National Commission on Marihuana and Drug Abuse, 1973). The usual "social" dose of marijuana is from 2 to 18 mg of tetrahydrocannabinol (THC—the active substance in the drug). Many variables are important in determining the actual dosage, as well as the potency of the particular batch of marijuana that is being used. Short-term physical effects include blood pressure changes, slight loss of muscular strength, an increased pulse rate, and an increased appetite shortly after use. There is no solid evidence of chromosomal damage, although this is a controversial area (Grinspoon, 1971; National Commission on Marihuana and Drug Abuse, 1973).

Some findings show that both marijuana and tobacco can result in altered cell division and growth in cells grown in tissue culture (Leuchtenberger et al., 1973). It is, of course, difficult to go from these findings to the effects of marijuana smoking on the in vivo lung and on other organ systems.

Some impairment of cognitive and psychomotor abilities has been noted with higher dosage levels, most clearly in connection with unfamiliar or complicated tasks (see, for example, National Commission on Marihuana and Drug Abuse, 1973). The impairment on simple intellectual and psychomotor tests after smoking marijuana occurs most often with inexperienced subjects, although experienced subjects most often report getting "high" (Weil et al., 1968). Perhaps this difference is caused by an increased sensitivity to the drug with prolonged use. Spontaneity of speech may be impaired (Weil and Zinberg, 1969). Depending on the dosage, impairment of driving performance may follow the use of marijuana, similar to the driving impairment noted after the use of alcohol.

Psychological Effects of Marijuana

Subjective effects of marijuana vary widely, from difficulty in remembering things to anxiety or pleasure. Short-term memory impairment has been confirmed by some investigators (see, for example, Casswell and Marks, 1973). It has been suggested that such impairment of memory may be connected with a speeding up of psychic processes thought by some to be seen in intoxication with marijuana (Tinklenberg, 1972). Because thinking may occur more rapidly, some investigators believe that the usual associative processes seen in ordinary thinking may not occur, and that parts of thoughts may be skipped, including aspects of memory. These effects appear to be related to the dosage, to the subject's expectations, to the subject's personality traits, and to the social milieu.

Marijuana available in the United States is usually weak and acts to give a mild high. However, if the active components of the drug are isolated and given in a concentrated form, effects similar to those of the hallucinogenic drugs, such as LSD, may occur. Low doses of marijuana subjectively can produce mood changes (a high) and relaxation. Moderate doses can produce perceptual changes—visual changes such as brighter, more vivid perception of colors; auditory changes such as more acute perception of sound; and changes in the perception of time. High doses, as noted, also may produce illusions, delusions and hallucinations, especially concerning the body image (Nowlis, 1969). People may feel that their bodies are distorted in shape and that their organs are in the wrong places or are functioning improperly.

Under favorable conditions in a stable person with a low dosage, initial subjective changes occur ten to thirty minutes after smoking marijuana (Coles et al., 1970). Initial anxiety soon disappears, and calmness and a sense of warmth and lightness develop. Other effects reported in the literature include a disconnectedness of ideas (Coles et al., 1970), and a flight of ideas that the person has difficulty in remembering later. Aggressive feelings may be diminished, as may sexual feelings, although some report an increased ability to enjoy sex.

Dangers of Marijuana

Although there may have been an unwarranted punitive overreaction to marijuana use, such as placing persons under arrest and treating them as criminals if a small amount of the drug was found in their possession, some investigators believe the dangers from chronic or heavy dosage in adolescence can be very severe and alarming.

A danger of chronic marijuana use in some is the occurrence of habituation, or psychological dependence—not characterized by physical withdrawal symptoms as is the case with narcotics, but causing psychic withdrawal symptoms, such as anxiety and sleeplessness, especially following chronic high dosage. Other symptoms of withdrawal are restlessness, loss of appetite, sweating, and hyperactivity. This syndrome is of sudden onset, six to eight hours following the last use, and the acute effects are over in forty-eight hours (Jones, 1974). It is not clear whether this occurs following withdrawal from chronic low dosage. Probably only about 5 per cent of users smoke enough to become habituated, but habituation (psychic and emotional dependence) can be associated with loss of interest, apathy, neglect of personal hygiene, and difficulty in concentration (Wikler, 1970). Drug use probably also impairs one's ability to cope realistically with the demands and frustrations of daily life, an important task of the adolescent period in preparation for adult life. Most marijuana users do not go on to use narcotics (Coles et al., 1970; National Commission on Marihuana and Drug Abuse, 1973); it is unclear what role marijuana use plays in the small percentage who do later use narcotics. Perhaps the multiple-drug use of these people is determined more by preexisting personality factors than by the use of marijuana per se.

Another danger is that of an acute psychotic reaction following marijuana use. Although some authorities believe that such a reaction is rare, many clinicians see this kind of reaction more often than is the general impression. Probably psychotic reactions occur in previously predisposed people, usually of borderline adjustment, in whom the psychological effects of marijuana serve as a precipitating factor. It is also possible that in some people, for unknown reasons, marijuana produces a toxic psychosis through its actual physical effects on the brain. In the clinical experience of one of the present authors, a young man with a borderline personality was seen who suffered a bizarre reaction following one episode of infrequent marijuana use: a perceptual alteration occurred that caused him to lose all sensation of touch over the surface of his body for forty-eight hours. After that time his sense of touch rapidly returned to normal. It is known that marijuana can have varied, if unclear, effects on sensory functions. In the experience of many clinicians, quite a few of the psychotic reactions to marijuana are of a bizarre nature. It may be that such psychotic reactions are also influenced by the subject's immediate state of mind (that is, being anxious or frightened) and by the social milieu (that is, being alone, with friends, or with someone who is not fully trusted).

Some adverse reactions may be attributable to certain substances commonly added to marijuana in order to stretch the amount, such as strychnine, opium, rhubarb, or talcum powder.

There are no findings to indicate a clear-cut link between marijuana use and psychopathology. Clinical reports, such as presented here, are numerous, and although uncontrolled, must be considered (Chopra and Smith, 1974). Hochman and Brill (1973), in a study of college students, found no significant differences between users and nonusers in academic performance or motivation and found no evidence that preexisting psychopathology, as such, is a significant determinant of marijuana use, including chronic use.

Sociocultural Correlates of Adolescent
Marijuana Use

Various social subgroups differ in the level of their marijuana use. Adolescents in the West, followed by those in the Northeast, have used marijuana more than those located in other parts of the country. Youngsters of higher socioeconomic status report more marijuana usage than those of lower status (Josephson, 1974; Josephson et al., 1972; Suchman, 1968). However, findings by Brook et al. (1975) suggest that family income is relatively unimportant in accounting for adolescents' use of marijuana, especially when other characteristics in the total picture are taken into account.

Research on the association between ethnicity and marijuana use is scarce. While Johnston (1973) reported that the proportion of persons reporting marijuana use among blacks was higher than among whites, other investigators have found whites report slightly more marijuana usage than blacks (Bloom et al., 1974). In some studies other variables that have been found to be related to marijuana use were not included in the analysis of ethnicity and marijuana usage. Thus, different ethnic patterns may be reflecting other factors.

AGE, SEX, AND MARIJUANA USE

With increased age there is an increase in the use of marijuana among high school students (Brook et al., 1975). Several studies have reported that marijuana use is higher among males than among females (see, for example, Smart and Fejer, 1972). However, with the exception of findings reported by Josephson (1974), there appears to be a trend toward a decline in these differences (Brook et al., 1975; Kandel et al., 1976). Brook et al. (1975) have speculated that the recent trend toward sexual equality among adolescents and the increased acceptance of similar standards for males and females has already had a significant impact on the drug scene in some locales, such as ghetto areas in New York City.

PARENT AND PEER INFLUENCES ON
ADOLESCENT USE OF MARIJUANA

In an exhaustive study of high school students' drug use, Kandel (1973) obtained data pertaining to adolescents' use of drugs as well as independent data from their best friends. Having a close friend who used marijuana was found to be an important concomitant of the adolescent's use of marijuana.

In a study of high school students from a ghetto community (Brook et al., 1975), it was found that the degree of an adolescent's involvement with drug-using friends is closely related to the adolescent's own drug use.

Table 16.1. Perceived number of friends who use marijuana and adolescents' marijuana usage

Number of friends using marijuana

Self drug use	None		Only a few		Some		Most	
	N	%	N	%	N	%	N	%
Nonusers	174	100	79	84	40	69	33	43
Users	0	0	15	16	18	31	44	57
	174	100	94	100	58	100	77	100

Note: p < .001.

Source: Adapted from "Teen-age drug use in an urban ghetto" by J. Brook, I. F. Lukoff, M. Whiteman, and A. S. Gordon. Report submitted to the National Institute of Law Enforcement and Criminal Justice, 1975, p. 47.

As shown in Table 16.1, 100 per cent of adolescents whose friends do not use drugs report they themselves do not use marijuana. Of those who perceive *most* of their friends as using marijuana, nearly four times as many use marijuana as compared with adolescents who report only a few of their friends use the drug.

It appears that the presence of illicit drug users in one's environment provides opportunities for learning attitudes and rationalizations supportive of illicit drug use. Unfortunately, to the authors' knowledge, there is virtually no evidence at present that would enable one to know whether potential or actual users initially select peers who are users because of their own use or whether it is the peer group that has a significant impact on the nonuser. Only longitudinal studies will be able to provide information regarding this question.

There are still a number of youths who are nonusers even though they are acquainted with varying numbers of peers who use marijuana. It is possible that contact with marijuana users has little effect on youths who are neither committed to peers nor dependent on them for social approval. Moreover, adolescents with certain family backgrounds or personality characteristics may be less responsive to peer pressure than some of their peers.

The recent literature indicates that the variations in drug use are associated with differing family structures and conditions. Adolescents whose family members use drugs are more likely to use drugs than adolescents whose families do not use drugs (Brook et al., 1975).

Table 16.2 indicates that the highest incidence of illicit drug use is among adolescents who reported that *both* their family and friends used illicit drugs.

The number of illicit drug users in this group was considerably higher than among adolescents who reported peer but no family use of drugs. These findings are consistent with those of Kandel (1974), whose work is unique in that she obtained independent best friends' and parental reports. Thus, *both*

**Table 16.2.   Perceived family and peer marijuana use and the
adolescent's use of marijuana**

	Peer marijuana use	
	None	Used
Family marijuana use	Adolescents who used marijuana (in %)	(in %)
Never used	0	21
Used	0	62

Note: N = 403. Only six adolescents reported family but no peer use.
Source: Adapted from "Teen-age drug use in an urban ghetto" by J. Brook, I. F. Lukoff, M. Whiteman, and A. S. Gordon. Report submitted to the National Institute of Law Enforcement and Criminal Justice, 1975, p. 49.

parents' and peers' use of drugs apparently influences the adolescents' use of drugs.

Many other aspects of family life have been found to be related to differential involvement with marijuana. In a large survey of suburban teen-agers ranging in age from twelve to eighteen, Tec (1970) reported that availability and quality of parental models for behavior, parental recognition of their adolescents' achievements, and perceptions of the family as warm and supportive were negatively related to marijuana use.

Personality Correlates of Marijuana Users

In an inquiry into variations in marijuana use, Jessor et al. (1973) made a combined cross-sectional and a longitudinal study of junior and senior high school and college students. High school nonusers reported higher expectations with regard to academic achievement, less tolerance of deviance (deviation from conventional standards), and more positive attitudes toward religion than users. Nonusers value achievement more and independence less than users. In response to questions designed to probe how they perceived their environment, nonusers, as compared with users, reported greater parent-peer compatibility; they claimed parents had a greater impact than peers on their own beliefs and perceived their peers as less inclined to sanction drug use. Other problem-prone types of behavior, such as excessive alcohol consumption, appeared more often in the data obtained from users. The findings at the junior high school level corresponded for the most part with those reported here.

In their longitudinal study of high school students, these investigators were able to demonstrate that many personality, environmental, and behavioral variables were predictive of later use of marijuana. However, the longitudinal data of the college study did not support the results obtained with the high school sample, perhaps, as Jessor et al. (1973) suggest, because of the high rates (70 per cent) of marijuana use at the college level. "Under such circumstances of widespread use and availability, the prediction of onset may depend more on factors such as the crowd one happens to find oneself in or the vicissitudes of a particular relationship than on the systematic pattern specified in problem behavior theory [Jessor et al., 1973, p. 14]."

A number of other investigators asked whether there is a pattern of personality traits common to many marijuana users. There appears to be some agreement that nonusers compared with users of marijuana are more conservative, more religious, and less likely to major in the social sciences or humanities (Hogan et al., 1970). In his summary of personality studies of psychoactive drug users among students, Goldstein (1971) noted that college nonusers score higher on the average than users on scales designed to measure feelings of self-satisfaction and lower on scales designed to assess flexibility.

In a study of college-student drug users, Groves (1974) included in a questionnaire a number of life-style dimensions that have been shown to be associated with marijuana use in past studies. A statistical analysis yielded six dimensions that were then related to the students' use of drugs. The most significant predictor of marijuana use was the dimension characterized as countercultural. The common theme measured in this dimension was an espousal of alternatives to the Protestant ethic. Groves (1974) points out that the more countercultural tend not so much to think in terms of future rewards for present work but rather in terms of personal and moral values. Broadly conceived, the counterculture rejects the major legal and social institutions in our society. Invoking the concept of the "hang-loose ethic," Suchman (1968) emphasized that marijuana use can be viewed as a sign of dissent from conventional society with its accompanying Protestant ethic. A tendency toward being countercultural and a dissenter would seem to some extent to be necessary if one sets out to use illegal drugs. However, it is hard to believe that such factors are decisive when as many as 70 per cent of the members of a certain group use marijuana (as noted in a study reviewed on an earlier page).

Other illicit drugs

Amphetamines and Amphetamine-like Drugs

Amphetamines and amphetamine-related drugs such as Benzedrine, Methedrine, and Dexedrine are synthetic amines that activate the central nervous system and usually evoke the stimulation of emotions accompanied by increased responses of the autonomic nervous system. Terms used to refer to these substances by illicit drug users include speed, bennies, uppers, pep or diet pills, jolly beans, and eye openers. Amphetamines have frequently been employed by physicians as a means of diet control—a practice now frowned on by most physicians—and illegally by students cramming for exams, athletes attempting to increase their performances, and by other adolescents wishing general stimulation or "fun" (that is, a high).

As with barbiturates, amphetamines are usually administered orally but can be sniffed or injected. It is a widely held belief that many adolescent speed freaks generally inject the drugs. For the most part, the speed trip has not received widespread acceptance by the so-called hip community. In addition to other effects, use of speed may lead to feelings of persecution, hostility, and aggression. Because of the possible harmful psychological and physical effects of the drugs, several individuals familiar with adolescent users have expressed opposition to the use of amphetamines.

The psychological and physiological effects of the drugs are dependent on the dose, method of administration, and the social context within which the drug use occurs. Moderate doses of amphetamines may increase blood pressure, heart rate, and respiration rate, dilate the pupils, and depress the appetite; the effects generally last for four hours or so. Increased wakefulness and alertness, decreased feelings of fatigue, and increased performance on simple tasks may accompany their use (Le Dain Report, 1973). With a moderate dose of amphetamines, some individuals may experience inability to concentrate, anxiety, lack of ability to sleep, nausea, dizziness, and other adverse symptoms. High doses of amphetamines can result in delirium, hallucinations, delusions, psychosis, untoward aggression, and other severe symptoms. Several investigators (see, for example, Kramer, 1972) have reviewed the effects of high-dose use of amphetamines. Severity of withdrawal symptoms varies, but they are usually accompanied by intense fatigue and sometimes excessive hunger or depressed feelings. Chronic use of speed may also lead to extreme weight loss, diseases of the liver and cardiovascular system, psychiatric problems, and in some cases cerebral hemorrhage (stroke). Among adolescent drug users, one may hear the slogan that "Speed kills."

Some individuals report that high doses of amphetamines or LSD prolong sexual activity and some report they take the drug for the euphoria it produces or because it makes them feel more confident (Cox and Smart, 1972; Gay and Sheppard, 1973).

There appears to be substantial agreement that the illegal use of amphetamines is related to use by peers and a wish for a euphoric experience (Le Dain Report, 1973; Levine et al., 1972). At the same time, depression has been frequently mentioned as a precipitating cause of amphetamine use. One of the present authors has observed from his clinical experience with amphetamine users that many are usually chronically depressed, and the drug affords the user some relief from feelings of low self-esteem, anxiety, and feelings of emptiness that result from the individual's inability to cope with his or her personal problems.

Although the vast majority of adolescents do not use amphetamines, it is still significant that the proportion at the junior high school level, senior high school level, and college level who have taken stimulants at least once number approximately, 9, 19, and 24 per cent, respectively (National Commission on Marihuana and Drug Abuse, 1973). Among high school and college students its use may be increasing, but as with some of the other drugs, a number of adolescents discontinue using amphetamines after some experimentation. Moreover, the percentage of those who use heavy doses is small compared with those who use small or moderate amounts.

The actual amount of amphetamines produced legally in this country has been overwhelming. In 1971 firms in the United States produced enough amphetamines to make eight billion pills and capsules (Ellinwood, Jr., 1974). This presents serious problems to the individual and society at large, because the psychological and physical effects can be severe and tolerance (the need to increase the dosage to recreate the effects) develops quickly.

Barbiturates

Barbiturates include drugs that are derived from barbituric acid. These drugs depress the central nervous system. Because barbiturates are often prescribed medically, few adolescents have to resort to illegal means in order to obtain barbiturates if they can obtain them from parents and other adults. Slang terms used to refer to barbiturates are downers, sleeping pills, barbs, goof balls, reds, and blues.

The consensus concerning the psychological effects of low doses of barbiturates appears to be that the effects are similar to those produced by alcohol, including, for a time, a relaxed feeling, a sense of well-being, and some decrease in alertness and attention. Paradoxically, the same dosage may in some persons produce sociability and joviality: "There may be decreased inhibition of certain drives and depending on the individual, one might feel more amorous, aggressive, creative, playful or hungry [Le Dain Report, 1973, p. 417]."[3] At higher doses, emotional lability, depression, slurred speech, and difficulty in walking may be observed. During heavy

[3] See also Blum et al., 1972.

intoxication, delirium, symptoms of paranoia, and untoward aggressiveness may accompany its use. According to the Le Dain Report (1973), heavy doses of barbiturates may lead to a syndrome characterized by reduced motivation and drive. However, validation of this phenomenon is not presently available. A number of deaths from barbiturate poisoning have been reported in the literature; however, it is not at all certain how often this occurs. Barbiturate addiction and withdrawal as a cause of death made the headlines in 1975 in the case of twin brothers, gynecologists, who, according to newspaper accounts, apparently manifested some severe personality disorders prior to their deaths.

According to Cohen (as cited in the Le Dain Report, 1973, pp. 354–355), the abuse of barbiturates may lead to flaws in personality development, even without the manifestation of physical problems resulting from such abuse. Evasion of the vicissitudes of daily life with drugs during maturation may hinder emotional growth and the development of problem-solving attitudes. This impairment of emotional development is perhaps the most tragic aspect of adolescent drug abuse.

LSD (Lysergic Acid Di-Ethyl Amide)

LSD is a semisynthetic derivative of lysergic acid, which acts on the central nervous system, even though the mechanisms by which this takes place are not known at present. Hofmann (as cited in the Le Dain Report, 1973) describes his experience after taking an extremely small dose of LSD, which he expected would be harmless.

> After forty minutes I noted the following symptoms in my laboratory journal: slight giddiness, restlessness, difficulty in concentration, visual disturbances, laughing. And later: I lost all count of time. I noticed with dismay that my environment was undergoing progressive changes. My visual field wavered and everything appeared deformed as in a faulty mirror. Space and time became more and more disorganized and I was overcome by a fear that I was going out of my mind. The worst part of it being that I was clearly aware of my condition. My power of observation was unimpaired .... Occasionally I felt as if I were out of my body. I thought I had died. My ego seemed suspended somwhere in space, from where I saw my dead body lying on the sofa .... It was particularly striking how acoustic perceptions, such as the noise of water gushing from a tap or the spoken word, were transformed into optical illusions [*Note*: this is known as synesthesia]. I then fell asleep and awakened the next morning somewhat tired but feeling perfectly well.[4]

[4] National Commission on Marihuana and Drug Abuse (Le Dain Report), 1973, pp. 354–355.

Hallucinogens in the United States were popularized as a result of Aldous Huxley's portrayal of his mescaline experiences in a book entitled *The Doors of Perception* (1954). Two professors of psychology at Harvard, Timothy Leary and Richard Alpert, brought LSD to the attention of adolescents in the 1960s. Their slogan was "Turn on, tune in, and drop out" of established institutions. Their book, *The Psychedelic Experience* (Leary et al., 1964) was the bible of the psychedelic drug movement.

Based on several national and state survey results, McGlothlin (1974) estimates that the percentage of adolescents who have used hallucinogens one or more times in grades seven through eight and nine through twelve are 2 and 8 per cent, respectively. Approximately 18 per cent of college students have tried hallucinogens. Because tolerance to LSD occurs rapidly, the daily use of hallucinogens occurs rarely. After taking LSD the individual must wait four to six days before he or she can again experience its full effects (McGlothlin, 1974). Approximately one quarter of the college students who have used hallucinogenic drugs report using them once or more per month, but high school students report more frequent use, with about one quarter of those who have experimented with the drug reporting usage of one or more times per week (McGlothlin, 1974). In a ten-year follow-up study of experimental medical LSD use, McGlothlin and Arnold (1971) reported that a number of LSD users either discontinued their use of the drug or decreased the frequency of their use. Several factors have been cited for lack of long-term chronic use of hallucinogens: lack of physical dependence of the type seen in other drugs such as opiates and barbiturates; rapid build-up of tolerance; lack of predictable effects—mood alteration may vary on different occasions with the same individual; and lack of a feeling of uniqueness of the experience with continued use (McGlothlin, 1974).

More males than females have reported using LSD, and the sex difference is greater among frequent users (Gallup Opinion Index, 1972). Although use of hallucinogenic drugs originated in the 1960s among upper- and middle-class white youngsters (and is still greater among the middle and upper classes), use has spread to the lower socioeconomic groups and minority groups (Braucht et al., 1973).

Because users of hallucinogens also frequently use marijuana, many of the correlates of marijuana use tend to be also applicable to users of hallucinogenic drugs. Nonusers tend to be more conventional in their beliefs, attitudes, values, and behavior than users of hallucinogens. Nonusers more often than users live at home, have established more harmonious relationships with their parents, and have greater success in school and in the world of work. Nonusers participate more in organizations, athletics, have sexual relations at a later age, and are less likely to be political activists.

The psychological effects of LSD vary depending on the amount of the drug taken, the personality of the individual, his or her past psychological history and future expectations, the motivating factors for the use of LSD, as well as the particular setting in which the drug is taken. It appears that LSD may variously have no demonstrable effect on performance on intelligence tests, or tests of memory and learning, or may temporarily impair or (rarely) improve performance (see, for example, Cohen, 1968).

Gross impairment of judgment, changes in visual perception (that is, colors appear more vivid), and changes in visual imagery may accompany an LSD experience (Cohen, 1968). "Visions of luminescent colors, flashes of light, gemlike objects, intricate geometric and kaleidoscopic patterns, landscapes, and architectural forms are commonly reported [Le Dain Report, 1973, p. 367]." Many LSD users have reported changes in their body image; for instance, the individual may perceive that parts of his or her body are detached. Several investigators (see, for example, Cohen, 1967) have reported that LSD users may experience dreamlike, floating sensations. Time perception may be altered so that minutes seem like hours.

When changes in visual perception and other sensory changes occur, according to Hoffer and Osmond (1967), the individual is generally aware that these alterations can be attributed to the effects of the drug. A widely held (but unsupported) belief among LSD users is that the drug enhances their ability to solve abstract problems and enhances their ability to think creatively. Contrary to myth, LSD does not appear to have an aphrodisiac or sex-drive-stimulating effect (Gay and Sheppard, 1973).

Many of the conclusions regarding adverse psychological reactions to LSD are based on faulty methodology, but certain recurring and consistent patterns are worth noting. An LSD bad trip, ranging from an unpleasant experience to extreme terror and panic reactions, has been observed. Although the frequency of suicide is not known, accidental deaths have been described: "For example, a few individuals have jumped from buildings or trees apparently under the delusion that they could fly or were indestructible [Le Dain Report, 1973, p. 372]." Some LSD experiences have been accompanied by prolonged psychotic episodes; however, in a number of cases, prior psychopathology has existed. Nevertheless, there appear to be adverse psychological consequences of LSD use in individuals without obvious prior psychopathology (Le Dain Report, 1973).

LSD may produce chills, headaches, and nausea as well as an increase in the activation of the brain (as measured by the EEG), resulting in increased alertness and decreased appetite. Some clinical material contains reports of LSD-related tremors and, in a few cases, even convulsions.

The literature on LSD-related chromosome damage is as extensive as it is controversial at present. Both sides have brought forth evidence to support their respective positions. This literature has been reviewed in particular by the Le Dain Report (1973).

To the extent that adolescents are vulnerable to peer conformity and pressure, one might speculate that with the addition of hallucinogenic drugs, their susceptibility to the beliefs and values of others would be increased whether or not these peer values are concordant with their own. But in speculating about the future use of hallucinogens, McGlothlin (1974) points out that the decline of the psychedelic movement "will reduce the group identification and other attractions of hallucinogen use and eventually will result in a decline in their use [p. 298]."

Heroin

One of the most dangerous illicit drugs is heroin, derived from morphine, which comes from the opium poppy plant (*Papaver somniferum*). In the United States, heroin is generally the drug of choice among opiate narcotic users.[5] Terms frequently used to refer to heroin include H, junk, smack, and horse. Heroin is generally administered by illicit drug users by subcutaneous (skin popping) or intravenous (mainlining) injections.

The effects of heroin vary among different individuals and situations and are said to be dose-related. Chronic regular use of heroin is accompanied by psychological dependence (an intense craving to continue the use of heroin) and physical dependence (a physiologic state of adaptation to heroin that results in withdrawal symptoms such as tremors, delirium, and cramps when the drug is discontinued). It is possible for occasional users of the drug to remain nonaddicted. The high of heroin is often accompanied by nausea, and at times drowsiness, inability to concentrate, and apathy.

According to the Le Dain Report (1973), it appears that feelings of euphoria, or well-being, may accompany the regular use of the drug in some users as a part of the high produced by the drug.

Perhaps the seriousness of habitual use of heroin can best be presented by a summary description of the "classic" severe heroin withdrawal syndrome presented in the Le Dain Report (1973), supplemented by one of the present writers' observations of addicts in withdrawal:

> Some hours following his last "fix," the addict shows increasing restlessness and irritability, to the point where at the end of seven to eight hours the addict paces the room and begs pleadingly for another fix. He complains of chills and shivers piteously, cuddling in a fetal position on the bed under a

[5] Methadone has been used as a means of controlling opiate narcotic dependence; however, it has been adopted in the recent past by illicit users of drugs, and illegal methadone is itself now a major source of addiction.

blanket to ward off the chills. During these chills he shows goose bumps, explaining why being without drugs is known as cold turkey. The addict may beat at the walls and mutter to himself. He may lapse into a rather lengthy deep sleep (the "yen sleep"), but restlessness persists when the addict awakens. Painful abdominal cramps are frequent (often spreading to other parts of the body), and nausea, vomiting, and watery diarrhea occur. Diaphoresis (profuse sweating) occurs, and muscular fasciculations (twitchings) occur particularly disturbingly in the legs. The addict continues to plead for a fix and may literally climb the walls in agony. If given a fix, the symptoms disappear shortly and the addict feels strong and well.

Many medical complications may occur as a consequence of street-heroin use. Among some heroin users hepatitis, tetanus, infectious endocarditis, lung abnormalities, scarred veins, and muscle tissue changes have been observed (Le Dain Report, 1973). Several investigators (see, for example, Cherubin, 1968; Sapiro, 1968) have also reported a greater frequency of tuberculosis, pneumonia, and venereal disease among illicit heroin users than in the general population. In higher doses unconsciousness may result. According to the Le Dain Report (1973), the "primary toxic overdose symptoms are coma, shock, and, ultimately, respiratory arrest and death [p. 309]."

Although the figures vary considerably, it has been estimated that over 1 per cent of the heroin population dies yearly from violent causes—such as suicide—infectious diseases, or as a direct result of the drug—such as an overdose (Le Dain Report, 1973).

One property of heroin is the relief from pain the individual experiences. Some users have reported feelings of euphoria, contentment, inability to concentrate, apathy, and lethargy. The heroin user is generally introduced to the drug by a friend. As use of the drug increases, one tends gradually to isolate oneself from nonusing friends, increasing one's involvement with the illicit drug subculture. As time goes on he or she devotes a considerable portion of the day to activities related to drugs. According to Chambers (1974), the committed user can function in some areas—for example, stay in school—but the level of personal and social functioning declines markedly in most areas. In their study of narcotic addicts, Nurco and Lerner (1974) indicate that the life style of the addict revolves around feeding his or her habit. They make this point succinctly when they state that "regular meals, family life, jobs, etc. hardly exist, so all-absorbing is the use of and search for drugs [p. 268]."

The second report of the National Commission on Marihuana and Drug Abuse (1973) estimated that .6 per cent of youth (twelve to seventeen) and 1.3 per cent of adults (eighteen and over) had tried heroin. Surveys of this type often do not include the street-addict population. As has previously been mentioned, most individuals who have tried heroin terminate its use after initial experimentation. Only a small proportion of students continue to use the drug and reach a state of dependency.

One of the most important studies in the area of narcotic drugs was conducted by Robins (1973) on enlisted army men who were stationed in Vietnam. In Vietnam pure heroin was readily available at low cost. On their return to the United States, a random sample of these men was interviewed. Forty-four per cent had used opiates in Vietnam and 20 per cent reported that they were addicted. After one year, they were reinterviewed and only 2 per cent reported that they were current users; the percentage of addiction was .7. This study demonstrates that drug-using behavior is strongly dependent on environmental conditions. Some of the factors mentioned for discontinued use were the high cost of heroin use in the United States; the low quality of the heroin, which required intravenous injections; family and peer sanctions; as well as a relief from the horrors of combat in an unpopular war (Robins, 1973). This study also demonstrates that many individuals are able to discontinue the drug after use. In a follow-up study of veterans three years after their return from Vietnam, Robins (1975) reported that the low rate of drug dependency persisted.

Heroin use by adolescents begins usually in their late teens. Only a small percentage of adolescents use heroin. The ethnic composition of adolescent heroin users is disproportionately nonwhite. According to Vaillant (1966), addicts suffer deprivation due to minority status. Male users outnumber female users; however, the sex differences are not as large for occasional users (Le Dain Report, 1973).

For the most part, chronic heroin users have performed poorly in school despite being average or above average in intelligence (Vaillant, 1970). Summarizing the research in this area, Braucht et al. (1973) concluded that many investigators concur "that addicts have some mental problems or a weak or disturbed personality [p. 98]"; nevertheless, there is little agreement concerning the specific dynamics of the personality disturbance.

Stages in adolescent drug use

Kandel (1975), based on data from two longitudinal studies of high school students, proposes several sequential stages of adolescent involvement with drugs: "Beer or wine or both; cigarettes or hard liquor; marijuana; and other illicit drugs [p. 912]." The first drug used by adolescents appears to be beer or wine, a legal drug. If adolescents then decide to use other drugs, they are likely to use cigarettes or hard liquor, also legal drugs. If adolescents who smoke or use hard liquor progress to other drugs, they are then likely to use marijuana, rather than the other illicit drugs such as cocaine or heroin. Rarely do adolescents proceed from nonuse of drugs or use of legal drugs to illicit drugs other than marijuana without having used marijuana. Some of the marijuana-using adolescents may then proceed to the use of other illicit drugs; but the majority of marijuana users do not go on to use other illicit drugs. To quote Kandel: "Although the data show a clear sequence in drug use, a particular drug does not invariably lead to other drugs higher up in the sequence. Many youths stop at a particular stage and do not progress further; many regress to lower drugs [Kandel, 1975, p. 914]."

Multiple-drug use

Within the past few years, much concern has been centered on the multiple-drug use or polydrug use of adolescents. Indeed, in a summary of studies related to multiple-drug use, the Le Dain Report (1973) stated that multiple-drug use is common in our society.

During the 1970s, methadone obtained illegally has frequently been used in conjunction with alcohol. Even with individuals on methadone maintenance, a large proportion drink excessively. This has resulted in a number of individuals who use both methadone and alcohol developing cirrhosis of the liver more rapidly than other alcoholics. Among younger alcoholics the tendency to use multiple drugs occurs more frequently than among older alcoholics (Kaufman, 1975). Some drug use among younger persons is of a "show-off" variety, declining when they are more sure of themselves.

Because two or more drugs taken simultaneously may produce a greater effect than would be expected by adding the individual effects of each drug (synergism) or may produce antagonistic effects (counteract the expected response to the drug), it would seem essential to provide adolescents with the information available, although more information is needed regarding the interactive effects of various drugs.

Some adults, even including members of the medical profession, are not aware that a particular drug (even if harmless and used in moderation) may be dangerous when combined with other drugs. For instance, there is some limited evidence which suggests that opiates taken in conjunction with alcohol can produce greater toxicity (including death) than would result from using either drug alone (Deichmann and Gerarde, 1969).

Concluding comments on the causes of drug use

As is the case with the legal drugs such as alcohol and tobacco, many talented professionals have attempted to investigate the motivations for use of the various illicit drugs. It is commonly assumed that drugs provide the adolescent with gratification in terms of relief from the distressing everyday realities and inner conflicts he or she must face, as well as gratification of a pleasurable euphoric nature. Although the majority of adolescents use drugs initially to satisfy needs of curiosity or experimentation, the many who continue use do so because the drugs fulfill psychological needs at some level (Balter, 1974). Because the adolescent's use of drugs is a complex process that interacts with a multitude of social forces, differences are great among theorists with respect to the adolescent's motivations for drug use. Even though we cannot provide the reader with an overall explanation nor delineate the causes in order of importance, we can present some of the underlying themes that have appeared in the literature.

Over the past few decades a number of drugs have become widely available to adolescents through both legal and illegal channels. At the same time, due to advanced technology, adolescents have been exposed to, and influenced to some extent by, the advertising media. While modern advertising focuses on the legal use of drugs such as sedatives, aspirin, and a variety of over-the-counter remedies, it does not foster or even suggest the general idea, even for the very young child and the elderly, that dependence on drugs to relieve both physical and psychological discomfort is not the most rational approach to living.

Although many professionals agree that adolescent use of drugs is related to personal dissatisfaction and a search for meaning, there is some lack of agreement as to the nature of this search. Perhaps, as suggested by the National Commission on Marihuana and Drug Abuse (1973), the adolescent's indifference and boredom would be relieved if the family, schools, and other institutions in society could assist the adolescent in assuming personal responsibility rather than attempt to relieve him or her of facing the difficulties in his or her life.

Another theme that appears in the literature is that a number of illicit users of drugs, in particular chronic drug users, do not accept themselves on many levels. One way of coping with lack of self-acceptance is for the adolescent to escape from this suffering into the "oblivion of intoxication" (Le Dain Report, 1973). "We could reduce the vulnerability to harmful drug use very greatly if we could remove the conditions that contribute to lack of self-acceptance [p. 24]."

Until recently, many schools, universities, and other institutions have not attempted to accommodate themselves to the changing demands of adolescents, associated, in part, with earlier physical maturation. This position is expressed most strikingly in the following statement:

> We have to realize that the eighteen-year-olds are now adults, and that by the time they are twenty-one they must be able to find places of *active*

responsibility. They must be made participants, but more, they must be made equals. We must make it a deliberate policy to open and to create posts of authority (in business and in public affairs) for young people.[6]

Although not anticipated originally, the extension of schooling has contributed toward segregating adolescents from the stabilizing influences of adult life (for example, supporting oneself) and increased the influence of peer groups. Most prominent in this milieu is the focus on the present and immediate, as reflected in the curriculum, rather than on the "past as perspective for the future [National Commission on Marihuana and Drug Abuse, 1973, p. 106]." These patterns of emphasis on present and immediate gratification have been singled out as most costly and are believed by the National Commission on Marihuana and Drug Abuse (1973) to bear on adolescent illicit drug use.

The notion of alienation also represents a major theme in the literature on adolescent drug use. As defined by Keniston (1960), the alienated syndrome refers to "an explicit rejection of what are seen as the dominant values of the surrounding society [p. 174]." A number of adolescents are believed to be alienated from the prevailing institutions and may thus turn to drugs in their search for meaning and relevance.

Some professionals believe that chronic drug users, because of more vulnerable personalities (compared to occasional drug users), are more prone to use drugs to cope with their inner conflicts and poor self-image. "We feel that any influence that strengthens the individual's acceptance of self is likely to play a prophylactic role in relation to drug use [Le Dain Report, 1973, p. 33]."

Societies undergoing rapid social change, such as exists in America today, are confronted with the segregation of adolescents from their parents and the ascendance of the peer group. We have referred to this in other sections of this book. Adolescents, therefore, have less impetus for acquiring "established patterns of cooperation and mutual concern [Bronfenbrenner, 1970, p. 117]."

It should be added, of course, that many parents, especially those over forty or fifty, are baffled, and even frightened, when they see that their offspring or the peers of their offspring resort to drugs—behavior that was alien and unknown in the parents' lives when they were teen-agers. For these reasons those working in the area of prevention and treatment of adolescent drug use must give priority to assisting the families of adolescents as well as the adolescents themselves in understanding the nature of drug use.

[6] Cited by the National Commission on Marihuana and Drug Abuse (Le Dain Report), 1973, p. 105).

References

Balter, M. B. Drug abuse: A conceptual analysis and overview of the current situation. In E. Josephson & E. E. Carroll (Eds.), *Drug use: Epidemiological and sociological approaches.* New York: Wiley, 1974.

Bloom, R., Hays, J. R., & Wenburn, G. M. Marijuana use in urban secondary schools: A three-year comparison. *International Journal of the Addictions,* 1974, **9**, 329–335.

Blum, R. H., et al. *The dream sellers: Perspectives on drug dealers.* San Francisco: Jossey-Bass, 1972.

Braucht, G. N., Brakarsh, D., Follingstad, D., & Berry, K. L. Deviant drug use in adolescence: A review of psychosocial correlates. *Psychological Bulletin,* 1973, **79**, 92–106.

Bronfenbrenner, U. *Two worlds of childhood: U.S. and USSR.* New York: Russell Sage Foundation, 1970.

Brook, J., Lukoff, I., Whiteman, M., & Gordon, A. *Teenage drug use in an urban ghetto: Preliminary findings.* Unpublished manuscript, Columbia University, 1975.

Brunswick, A. F. Health needs of adolescents: How the adolescent sees them. *American Journal of Public Health,* 1969, **59**, 1730–1745.

Casswell, S., & Marks, D. F. Cannabis and temporal disintegration in experienced and naive subjects. *Science,* 1973, **179**, 803–805.

Chambers, C. D. Speculations on a behavioral progression typology of pleasure-seeking drug use. In C. Winick (Ed.), *Sociological aspects of drug dependence.* Cleveland: CRC Press, 1974.

Cherubin, C. E. A review of the medical complications of narcotic addiction. *International Journal of the Addictions,* 1968, **3**, 163–175.

Chopra, G. S., & Smith, J. W. Psychotic reactions following cannabis use in East Indians. *Archives of General Psychiatry,* 1974, **30**, 24–27.

Cohen, S. *The beyond within: The LSD story* (2nd ed.). New York: Atheneum, 1967.

Cohen, S. A quarter century of research with LSD. In J. T. Ungerleider (Ed.), *The problem and prospects of LSD.* Springfield, Ill.: Thomas, 1968.

Cohen, S. Teenage drinking: The bottle babies. *Drug Abuse and Alcoholism Newsletter,* 1975, **4**, 7.

Coles, R., Brenner, J. H., & Meagher, D. *Drugs and youth: Medical, legal and psychiatric facts.* New York: Liveright, 1970.

Cox, C., & Smart, R. G. Social and psychological aspects of speed use: A study of types of speed users in Toronto. *International Journal of the Addictions,* 1972, **7**, 201–217.

Deichmann, W. B., & Gerarde, H. W. *Toxicology of drugs and chemicals.* New York: Academic, 1969.

Ellinwood, Jr., E. H. The epidemiology of stimulant abuse. In E. Josephson and E. E. Carroll (Eds.), *Drug use: Epidemiological and sociological approaches.* New York: Wiley, 1974.

Final report of the commission of inquiry into the non-medical use of drugs (Le Dain Report). Information Canada, Ottawa, 1973. (Catalogue No. H21-5370/2).

Forney, R. B., & Harger, R. N. The alcoholics. In J. R. Di Palma (Ed.), *Drill's pharmacology in medicine* (3rd ed.), New York: McGraw-Hill, 1965.

Gallup Opinion Index, No. 80. Princeton, N.J.: American Institute of Public Opinion, February, 1972.

Gay, G. R., & Sheppard, C. W. Sex-crazed dope fiends: Myth or reality? In E. Harms (Ed.), *Drugs and youth: The challenge of today.* Elmsford, N.Y.: Pergamon, 1973.

Goldstein, J. W. *Motivations for psychoactive drug use among students.* Pittsburgh, Pa.: Department of Psychology, Carnegie-Mellon University, 1971.

Grinspoon, L. *Marihuana reconsidered.* Cambridge, Mass.: Harvard U.P., 1971.

Groves, W. E. Patterns of college student drug use and life styles. In E. Josephson & E. E. Carroll (Eds.), *Drug use: Epidemiological and sociological approaches.* New York: Wiley, 1974.

Gusfield, J. The structural context of college drinking. In G. L. Maddox (Ed.), *The domesticated drug: Drinking among collegians.* New Haven, Conn.: College and University Press, 1970.

Hicks, N. Drug use called up among youths. *New York Times,* October 2, 1975, p. 22.

Hochman, J. S., & Brill, N. Q. Chronic marihuana use and psycho-social adaptation. *American Journal of Psychiatry,* 1973, **130**, 132–140.

Hoffer, A., & Osmond, H. *The hallucinogens.* New York: Academic, 1967.

Hogan, R., Mankin, D., Conway, J., & Fox, S. Personality correlates of under-graduate marijuana use. *Journal of Consulting and Clinical Psychology,* 1970, **35**, 58–63.

Huxley, A. *The doors of perception.* New York: Harper, 1954.

Jessor, R., Collins, M. I., & Jessor, S. L. On becoming a drinker: Social-psychological aspects of an adolescent transition. *Annals of the New York Academy of Sciences,* 1972, **197**, 199–213.

Jessor, R., & Jessor, S. L. Adolescent development and the onset of drinking: A longitudinal study. *Journal of Studies on Alcohol,* 1975, **36**, 25–51.

Jessor, R., Jessor, S. L., & Finney, J. A social psychology of marijuana use: Longitudinal studies of high school and college youth. *Journal of Personality and Social Psychology,* 1973, **26**, 1–15.

Johnston, L. *Drugs and American youth.* Ann Arbor, Mich.: Institute for Social Research, 1973.

Jones, R. T. Reported in *Marihuana and health, 1974.* Rockville, Md.: National Institute of Drug Abuse, 1974, p. 109.

Josephson, E. Trends in adolescent marijuana use. In E. Josephson & E. E. Carroll (Eds.), *Drug use: Epidemiological and sociological approaches.* New York: Wiley, 1974.

Josephson, E., Haberman, P., Zanes, A., & Elinson, J. Adolescent marijuana use: Report on a national survey. In S. Einstein & S. Allen (Eds.), *Student drug surveys.* Farmingdale, N.Y.: Baywood Publishing, 1972.

Kandel, D. Adolescent marijuana use: Role of parents and peers. *Science,* 1973, **181**, 1067–1070.

Kandel, D. Inter- and intragenerational influences on adolescent marijuana use. *Journal of Social Issues,* 1974, **30**, 107–135.

Kandel, D. Stages in adolescent involvement in drug use. *Science,* 1975, **190**, 912–914.

Kandel, D., Single, E., & Kessler, R. The epidemiology of drug use among New York State high school students: Distributions, trends and change in rates of use. *American Journal of Public Health,* 1976, **66**, 43–53.

Kaufman, E. Polydrug abuse: A new epidemic? *The Bulletin of the American Psychiatric Association,* **18**, 1975, 1.

Kelley, C. M. *Uniform crime reports for the United States—1973.* Washington, D.C.: U.S. Government Printing Office, 1974.

Keniston, K. *Youth and dissent: The rise of a new opposition.* New York: Harcourt, 1960.

Klonoff, H. Marijuana and driving in real-life situations. *Science,* 1974, **186**, 317.

Kramer, J. C. Some observations on and a review of the effects of high-dose use of amphetamines. In C. J. C. Zarafonetis (Ed.), *Drug abuse: Proceedings of the International Conference.* Philadelphia: Lea, 1972.

Leary, T., Metzner, R., & Alpert, R. *The psychedelic experience.* New Hyde Park, N.Y.: University Books, 1964.

Leuchtenberger, C., Leuchtenberger, R., & Ritter, U. Effects of marijuana and tobacco smoking on DNA and chromosomal complement in human lung explants. *Nature,* 1973, **242**, 403–404.

Levine, S. V., Lloyd, D. D., & Longdon, W. H. The speed user: Social and psychological factors in amphetamine abuse. *Canadian Psychiatric Association Journal,* 1972, **17**, 229–241.

Lukoff, I., & Brook, J. A sociocultural exploration of reported heroin use. In C. Winick (Ed.), *Sociological aspects of drug dependence.* Cleveland: CRC Press, 1974.

MacKay, J. Clinical observations on adolescent problem drinkers. *Quarterly Journal of Studies on Alcohol,* 1961, **22**, 124–134.

Maddox, G. L. Drinking prior to college. In G. L. Maddox (Ed.), *The domesticated drug: Drinking among collegians.* New Haven, Conn.: College and University Press, 1970.

Marijuana and health. Fourth Annual Report to Congress from the Secretary of Health, Education, and Welfare. Washington, D.C.: U.S. Government Printing Office, 1974.

Martino, E. R., & Truss, C. V. Drug use and attitudes toward social and legal aspects of marijuana in a large metropolitan university. *Journal of Counseling Psychology,* 1973, **20**, 120–126.

McCord, W., McCord, J., & Gudeman, J. *Origins of alcoholism.* Stanford, Calif.: Stanford U.P., 1960.

McGlothlin, W. H. The epidemiology of hallucinogenic drug use. In E. Josephson & E. E. Carroll (Eds.), *Drug use: Epidemiological and sociological approaches.* New York: Wiley, 1974.

McGlothlin, W. H. Drug use and abuse. *Annual Review of Psychology,* 1975, **26**, 45–64.

McGlothlin, W. H., & Arnold, D. O. LSD revisited: A ten-year follow-up of medical LSD use. *Archives of General Psychiatry,* 1971, **24**, 35–49.

Mellinger, G. D., Balter, M. B., Parry, H. J., Manheimer, D. I. & Cisin, I. H. An overview of psychotherapeutic drug use in the United States. In E. Josephson & E. E. Carroll (Eds.), *Drug use: Epidemiological and sociological approaches.* New York: Wiley, 1974.

National Commission on Marihuana and Drug Abuse. *Drug use in America: Problems in perspective* (Second Report of the Commission). Washington, D.C.: Superintendent of Documents, U.S. Government Printing Office, 1973.

National Institute of Alcohol Abuse and Alcoholism. Young people and alcohol. *Alcohol Health and Research World,* Experimental Issue, Summer, 1975, pp. 2–10.

Nowlis, H. H. *Drugs on the college campus.* New York: Anchor Books, 1969.

Nurco, D. N., & Lerner, M. Occupational skills and life-styles of narcotic addicts. In C. Winick (Ed.), *Sociological aspects of drug dependence.* Cleveland: CRC Press, 1974.

Robins, L. N. A follow-up of Vietnam drug users. *Special Action Office Monograph Series,* **A**, 1973, 1–23.

Robins, L. N. *Veterans' drug use three years after Vietnam.* Unpublished manuscript, 1975.

Rogers, E. Group influence on student drinking behavior. In G. L. Maddox (Ed.), *The domesticated drug: Drinking among collegians.* New Haven, Conn.: College and University Press, 1970.

Sapiro, J. D. The narcotic addict as a medical patient. *American Journal of Medicine,* 1968, **45**, 555–588.

Slaby, A., Lieb, J., & Schwartz, A. Comparative study of psychosocial correlates of drug use among medical and law students. *Journal of Medical Education,* 1972, **47**, 717–723.

Smart, R. G., & Fejer, D. Relationships between parental and adolescent drug use. In W. Keup (Ed.), *Drug abuse: Current concepts and research.* Springfield, Ill.: Thomas, 1972.

Suchman, E. A. The "hang-loose" ethic and the spirit of drug use. *Journal of Health and Social Behavior,* 1968, **9**, 146–155.

Tec, N. Family and differential involvement with marihuana: A study of suburban teenagers. *Journal of Marriage and the Family,* 1970, **32**, 656–664.

Tinklenberg, J. R., Kopell, B. S., Melges, F. T., & Hollister, L. E. Marihuana and alcohol. *Archives of General Psychiatry,* 1972, **27**, 812–815.

Vaillant, G. E. A 12-year follow-up of New York narcotic addicts: 3. Some social and psychological characteristics. *Archives of General Psychiatry,* 1966, **15**, 599–609.

Vaillant, G. E. The natural history of narcotic drug addiction. *Seminars in Psychiatry,* 1970, **2**, 486–498.

Weil, A. T., & Zinberg, N. E. Acute effects of marijuana on speech. *Nature,* 1969, **22**, 434–437.

Weil, A. T., Zinberg, N. E., & Nelson, J. M. Clinical and psychological effects of marijuana in man. *Science,* 1968, **162**, 1234-1242.

Wikler, A. Clinical and social aspects of marihuana intoxication. *Archives of General Psychiatry,* 1970, **23**, 320–325.

Williams, A. F. Social drinking, anxiety and depression. *Journal of Personality and Social Psychology*, 1966, **3**, 689–693.

Zucker, R. A. Sex-role identity patterns and drinking behavior among adolescents. *Quarterly Journal Studies on Alcohol*, 1968, **29**, 868–884.

part six

EDUCATION AND VOCATION

17

the adolescent at school

In this chapter we will first discuss the adolescent in high school and then give a brief account of college youth. This will be followed by a discussion of issues that are important from a personal and educational point of view at both the secondary and college levels.

465

Each adolescent is susceptible to being inspired, restored, or impaired by school. [Constantine Manos/Magnum.]

High school youth

The high school has—or might have—a powerful influence in shaping adolescents' concepts of what they are and what they might be. It impinges on most facets of young persons' lives in their transition from childhood to adulthood. It is a way station toward the larger world into which the young persons are moving. When youngsters succeed in high school, their future remains open. When they fail and leave school, it usually means that many doors to the future have been closed.

In many respects the high school is in a more strategic position than the home to influence the lives of adolescents. The school has more access to and can exercise more authority over the peer group. Also, high school teachers and counselors are freer than parents to view adolescents (other than their own children) objectively. Teachers are not as emotionally involved with adolescents as are their parents. If an adolescent confides an aspiration, or has a problem, or confesses a weakness, the high school teacher has less reason than the parent to feel personally responsible for his or her state of mind. This should, or could, enable high school teachers to counsel other parents' adolescents with more freedom than they possess in counseling their own adolescent son or daughter.

What adolescents bring to their high school experience will have an important influence on what they get from it. With the exception of those few whose lives have been blighted at an early age almost beyond repair, each adolescent student is still teachable and malleable. Each is still in a condition to be inspired, or restored, or impaired.

Nature of the High School

At the present time adolescents spend far more time in school than they did years ago. Due to the present structure of the high school, they are segregated with peers who are close to them in chronological age. At the same time, they are deprived of contact with adults for a large part of the day, with few exceptions. In general, schools have increased tremendously in size. Accompanying this change in size, teachers have increasingly specialized according to grade and subject matter. Furthermore, adolescents are separated from one another not only according to age, but also, to a great degree, according to social class and ethnic and racial backgrounds. For example, adolescents from a particular ethnic group tend to have friends who are similar to them in ethnic background. According to Coleman (as cited in the President's Science Advisory Commission, 1973), a consequence of this arrangement is that many adolescents are living in a world that has only threads of connection with adult society and in which a self-contained system of adolescent values, attitudes, and beliefs is emerging.

Today's adolescents are kept in school for an increasingly long period of time and are thereby deprived of assuming responsible positions in many areas. Work and education are frequently divorced from one another, although there have been some attempts to establish school-work programs.

FORMAL VERSUS INFORMAL SCHOOLS

As an alternative to the traditional school, a number of informal (open) schools based on the experiences of some British schools have been established in the United States. In contrast to the traditional school, informal schools supposedly emphasize individualized instruction, capitalize on intrinsic motivation, and promote cooperative learning. The teacher assumes the role of a resource person. In a recent study of schools varying along the formal-informal dimension in structure, Groobman et al. (1976) reported that the students in informal schools had more positive attitudes toward school and learning in general. However, there were no differences between the students in the formal and informal schools in terms of the students' academic skills or self-esteem. In the opinion of the present writers some students flourish in an informal school environment. Other students are unable to cope with the demands for self-reliance in the more informal setting. For these students, a more conventional atmosphere is most beneficial for their future development.

Self-image at Adolescence and the Schools

The developments that occur in young people during early and middle adolescence present educators with a serious challenge. Among the stresses faced by many adolescents is a need to change the image they have of themselves (Erikson, 1959; Blos, 1962; A. Freud, 1958). The physical and psychological changes that require a modification of the self-image were noted in an earlier chapter.

In a study by Simmons et al. (1973), data were obtained from students in grades three to twelve. The findings indicate that a disturbance of the self-image is more likely to occur in adolescence than in earlier years. The findings suggest that the early adolescent has become more self-conscious; less assured in his self-esteem and in his picture of himself; and inclined to believe that parents, teachers, and peers of the same sex view him less favorably than at an earlier time.

Disturbances in the self-image seemed to occur especially when adolescents were between their twelfth and thirteenth birthdays, so investigators wondered whether the adolescents' movement to junior high school contributed to an increase in such disturbances. As shown in Table 17.1, a larger percentage of the twelve-year-olds in junior high school than the twelve-year-olds in elementary school reported lower self-esteem and greater self-consciousness and instability of self-image.

Table 17.1.   Disturbance of the self-image by school context among twelve-year-old children

Self-image disturbance	Twelve-year-old children		
	In elementary school	In junior high school	Acccording to χ^2 analysis
% low self-esteem (global)	22% (167)	41% (59)	p <.01
% low self-esteem (specific)	28% (151)	46% (57)	.10 > p >.05
% high self-consciousness	27% (172)	43% (61)	p <.05
% high instability of self-image	30% (158)	53% (60)	p <.01

Note: The term *global* refers to individuals' general feelings toward themselves as assessed through a number of general questions.
Source: From "Disturbance in the self-image at adolescence" by R. G. Simmons, F. Rosenberg, and M. Rosenberg, *American Sociological Review*, 1973, **38**, 553–568. Reprinted by permission.

Moreover, examination of Table 17.2 indicates that these findings emerged from reports by blacks as well as whites, adolescents from different social class backgrounds, and adolescents with high as well as low grades in school.

Table 17.2. Disturbance of the self-image among twelve-year-olds in the sixth or seventh grade, by race, social class, and marks in school

Self-image disturbance	Race				Social class				Marks in school			
	Blacks		Whites		Middle class		Working class		A's and B's		C's and below	
	6th	7th	6th	7th	6th	7th	6th	7th	6th	7th	6th	7th
% low self-esteem (global)	18% (106)	33% (27)	30% (61)	47% (32)	14% (21)	44% (16)	21% (119)	36% (39)	20% (49)	37% (30)	23% (104)	42% (24)
% low self-esteem (specific)	33% (92)	46% (26)	19% (58)	45% (31)	48% (21)	41% (17)	26% (108)	44% (36)	17% (47)	39% (28)	29% (91)	50% (24)
% high self-consciousness	28% (109)	32% (28)	27% (62)	52% (33)	24% (21)	53% (17)	29% (122)	38% (40)	22% (50)	37% (30)	29% (106)	58% (26)
% high instability of the self-image	31% (104)	50% (28)	26% (53)	56% (32)	35% (20)	71% (17)	27% (112)	44% (39)	30% (47)	52% (29)	28% (96)	54% (26)

Source: From "Disturbance in the self-image at adolescence" by R. G. Simmons, F. Rosenberg, and M. Rosenberg, American Sociological Review, 1973, **38**, 553–568. Reprinted by permission.

In sum, the transition into junior high school appears to be stressful for many adolescents; age seems to make little difference within the same school class.

A number of definite changes in the social environment of adolescents take place as they enter junior high school. For instance, the school is generally larger and more impersonal; decisions regarding courses of studies must be made—whether to pursue an academic, commercial, or vocational course of study; and the student is confronted with many more teachers. It is interesting to note that Simmons et al. (1973) did not find a corresponding disturbance of the self-image occurring as the adolescents moved from junior to senior high school.

Attitudes Toward High School

During the 1960s and early 1970s many American high schools and colleges were confronted with student conflict, unrest, storm, and stress (Morgan and Wicas, 1972). Students complained about restrictions concerning proper attire and the length of their hair. They expressed opposition to the grading system, which they felt was unfair at times, and the curriculum, which they considered to be irrelevant or lacking in personal meaning. At the time of this writing the somewhat intense negative feelings that some students expressed seem to have quieted down on the campuses.

In spite of these dissatisfactions there are far more high school students who say they like school than say they do not like it. In a survey of tenth-grade boys, Bachman (1970) found that the majority had favorable attitudes toward school. (See Table 17.3.)

Nevertheless, a number of adolescents expressed negative attitudes toward high school. It appears that dissatisfaction and rebellious attitudes are more likely to be exhibited by a militant minority than by the student body as a whole.

As shown in Table 17.4, other sources were seen by some adolescents as providing greater opportunities than school for some of the adolescents.

In a poll taken in 1953, Remmers and Radler (1957) found that a "sense of discipline and responsibility" received the highest rating as the most important goal of a high school education (named by 38 per cent), and the second highest rating was given to "knowing how to get along with other people" (35 per cent). Sixty per cent of the high school students said they would like more help than they were getting in planning their education or in making a career choice.

In evaluating the academic program a large proportion of students, according to a Gallup poll (Gallup and Hill, 1961), said they wished the requirements were stiffer. Many said the courses are too easy. This should be

Table 17.3. Positive school attitudes

| Item content | Frequencies (in %) I feel this way: | | | |
	Very much	Pretty much	A little	Not at all
I feel satisfied with school because I learn more about things I want to know	37	41	17	4
Education has a high value because knowing a lot is important to me	56	32	9	2
I think this school is a real chance for me; it can make a real difference in my life	48	34	13	4
Even if I could get a very good job at present, I'd still choose to stay in school and get my education	60	25	10	5
I have put a great deal of myself into some things at school because they have special meaning or interest for me	32	42	21	3
I enjoy school because it gives me a chance to learn many interesting things	31	45	20	3
School gives me a chance to be with people my own age and do a lot of things that are fun	45	38	13	2
I think school is important, not only for the practical value, but because learning itself is very worthwhile	50	36	11	2
All people should have at least a high school education	69	22	5	2
I enjoy being in school because I feel I'm doing something that is really worthwhile	41	37	18	3
An education is a worthwhile thing in life, even if it doesn't help you get a job	45	34	14	6
I like school because I am improving my ability to think and solve problems	39	42	15	3
I believe an education will help me to be a mature adult	53	32	10	3
I like school because I am learning the things I will need to know to be a good citizen	36	41	18	4
School is satisfying to me because it gives me a sense of accomplishment	32	42	21	3

Source: From *Youth in transition, vol. II: The impact of family background and intelligence on tenth grade boys* by J. G. Bachman, Ann Arbor: Institute for Social Research, The University of Michigan, 1970, 107. Copyright 1970 Institute for Social Research of The University of Michigan. Reprinted by permission.

taken with a grain of salt, however. If the students did not feel they were getting enough intellectual nourishment at school there was nothing to prevent them from supplementing it with a little reading and study of their own. However, according to the same poll, young people spent relatively little time reading, and only a small proportion of their reading was of a serious nature.

When students say they want harder assignments it is likely that some of them actually would prefer to be required to learn more than they do. But it is also likely that some say this because of an uneasy conscience about what they are doing at school. In many instances, there is a lack of "closure" in

Table 17.4. Negative school attitudes

| | Frequencies (in %) I feel this way: | | | |
Item content	Very much (1)	Pretty much (2)	A little (3)	Not at all (4)
Instead of being in this school, I wish I were out working	6	9	32	52
School is very boring for me, and I'm not learning what I feel is important	8	14	37	40
If I could get the job I wanted, I'd quit school without hesitating	9	10	19	61
A real education comes from your own experience and not from the things you learn in school	11	21	44	22
I am in school in order to get a job; I don't need the education and training	9	11	28	51
I can satisfy my curiosity better by the things I learn outside of school than by the things I learn here at school	13	25	42	19
I feel I can learn more from a very good job than I can here at school	8	14	37	40
I feel the things I do at school waste my time more than the things I do outside of school	7	12	34	46

Source: From *Youth in transition, vol. II: The impact of family background and intelligence on tenth grade boys* by J. G. Bachman, Ann Arbor: Institute for Social Research, The University of Michigan, 1970, 108. Copyright 1970 Institute for Social Research of the University of Michigan. Reprinted by permission.

what they learn. This happens, for example, when students memorize their assignments in geometry but actually do not grasp the underlying principles. It happens also when students have learned the assignments in a course in French or Spanish but cannot use the language well enough to order a meal in a French restaurant or must rely on sign language when they make purchases in a Spanish grocery store. Moderately bright students cannot help but feel that they are dabblers when they learn enough to pass the examinations in a number of subjects but have no real mastery of any of them.

A majority of students in the study by Johnson (1958) said they liked high school better than elementary school, but the reasons they gave for liking high school did not touch primarily on the academic program. Many youngsters, for example, liked high school better because there were more activities, more privileges, and an opportunity to meet more friends. Relatively small percentages of pupils spoke of high school courses as being more interesting or as inspiring an interest in learning.

Several studies indicate that as young people advance into and through high school a large number show a decreased interest in the academic program.[1] In general there is a decrease in student morale with age (Kniveton, 1969; Yamamoto et al., 1969).

[1] For studies bearing on this, see Jersild and Tasch (1949), Jersild (1952), and Demos (1960).

In a study by Jersild and Tasch (1949), the evidence indicates that as youngsters move up through the grades many of them become less eager about things that definitely belong to school, are more inclined to complain, and are relatively more interested in recess periods, in social activities connected with school, and in games and sports than in schoolwork as such. (See Table 17.5.)

However, although there is this decline in interest in the academic program, a substantial proportion of students retain an interest in it. In grades one through six, 81.4 per cent of the pupils mentioned academic subjects, or information gained from academic subjects, as what they liked best in school. At the seventh- through twelfth-grade levels, 52.8 per cent mentioned items in this category. High school youth, more often than younger children, expressed a dislike of teachers, the school program, discipline, and rules and regulations. Almost 10 per cent of junior high school students (as compared with less than 1 per cent of those in the elementary grades) mentioned relief from school duties or the last day of school when describing the "happiest day" of their lives.

There are many reasons for a decline of interest in school during adolescence. For one thing, the adolescent has many interests the school cannot readily satisfy. Moreover, many young people are more critical as adolescents than they were when they were younger concerning circumstances in their lives, both in and out of school. Another reason may be that the high school demands more homework than did the earlier grades. In addition it reminds some young people of unpleasant realities of which they were not so pointedly reminded before, such as shortcomings accumulated in earlier grades, lacks in academic skills, and poor work habits. For these and many other reasons we might expect a larger number of older students to feel lukewarm about school.

Table 17.5. Percentage of students giving responses in selected categories when reporting what they liked best and disliked most at school

Grade	Like best I–VI	Dislike most I–VI	Like best VII–XII	Dislike most VII–XII
Age	6–12	6–12	12–18	12–18
Number of students	996	996	602	602
Games, sports, gym, recess, etc.	5.1	5.4	31.9	2.8
Academic subjects and information	81.4	42.7	52.8	46.2
Art	11.5	4.8	10.5	3.2
People	4.0	4.6	5.3	15.1
Students	1.0	4.1	4.0	7.0
Teachers	3.1	.2	.7	8.0
Others	0	.2	.7	.8

Source: Adapted from Children's Interests by A. T. Jersild and R. Tasch, New York, Teachers College, Columbia University, 1949. Reprinted by permission.

However, many of the students who express a dislike of what they have to learn at school mention serious topics when they tell what they *would* like to learn more about. In a study by Jersild and Tasch (1949), 27 per cent of the students mentioned matters under the general heading of self-improvement, self-understanding, and preparation for a job when asked what they would like to learn more about. In this investigation the social studies, including history, civics, and local and world affairs, were consistently mentioned as "liked least" more often than they were mentioned as "liked best." Yet, when the students named things they would like to learn more about, many of them mentioned topics in the area of social studies. From discussions with the students it appeared that social studies are often taught in an academic way with little personal meaning.

Teachers' and Pupils' Perceptions of Causes of Failure

Students and teachers differ considerably in their ideas about what causes high school students to fail. Such differences are shown in Table 17.6, from a study by Gilbert (1931) briefly referred to in an earlier chapter.

Teachers regarded lack of intellectual ability as the most important reason for failure in high school subjects, but students placed lack of such ability as among the least important reasons. The students gave greatest emphasis to lack of motivation rather than lack of ability. They gave laziness and dislike of the subject as two of the most important reasons for failure. Many of the other reasons listed in the table also indicate some lack of

Table 17.6. Rank order, from 1 (most important) to 9 (least important) of various reasons for students' failure in high school subjects as judged by 830 students and 50 teachers

	Boys	Girls	Boys and girls	Teachers
Lack of brains	9	8	8	1
Laziness	1	1	1	2
Dislike for subject	2	3	2	6
Dislike for teacher	8	7	8	9
Hard to study at home	4	4	4	3
Clubs and teams	5	9	9	8
Shows and parties	7	5	5	4
Dates	6	6	6	7
Sickness	3	2	3	5

Source: Adapted from "High-school students' opinions on reasons for failure in high-school subjects" by H. H. Gilbert, *Journal of Educational Research*, 1931, **23**, 46–49. Reprinted by permission. The original table gives separate findings for Freshmen, Sophomores, Juniors, and Seniors.

motivation, stressing the point that students are more interested in diversions outside the classroom than in some of the things that are taught at school.

It cannot be ascertained from Table 17.6 whether the teachers or the students were more nearly correct in the reasons they gave for failure. When the teachers ascribed difficulty in school to lack of ability more often than did the students, the teachers were perhaps in one way more realistic than the students. However, the table also suggests that the teachers were not as realistic as they might have been. They gave a rather low rating to "dislike for subject" as a reason for students' failure. Yet, teachers need only reflect on the courses they have taken, or if they are honest with themselves, perhaps courses they have given, to realize that some courses are uninspiring.

The fact that sickness was ranked high by the students as a reason for failure is interesting because sickness is a good excuse for staying home from school and for falling behind in the work at school. Undoubtedly sickness does make it difficult for some students to complete their assignments at school, but sickness can also be used as an excuse for not attending class (or for not studying at home) when the real reason is a lack of interest.

Qualities Adolescents Like and Dislike in Their Teachers

"Good" teachers have their own unique qualities. Moreover, the "goodness" of teachers does not depend on them alone; it depends also on the characteristics and motives of those they teach. Highly motivated students will, for example, warmly approve of a teacher who "knows his stuff and puts it across" even though, in an out-of-class situation, they might not like this teacher as a person.

Some of the characteristics students single out for special mention when they describe teachers whom they like best or dislike most are shown in Table 17.7. One fact stands out in this table—namely, that the students emphasize the teachers' qualities as human beings and the emotional qualities that they bring into their personal relationships with their students far more than their academic competence. Similar findings have emerged from other studies (see, for example, Feldman and Newcomb, 1969). The two categories that include mention of the teachers' kindness and friendliness as individuals and their tendency to be considerate and thoughtful of the learner when they act in the role of disciplinarian include considerably more responses than the category pertaining to the teachers' performances as instructors and as sources of information. Even in this latter category there were subcategories (not here reproduced) that deal with the human

Table 17.7. Relative frequency of mention of various characteristics in descriptions by students of teachers whom they "liked best" and "liked least or disliked most"

Teachers liked best

Grade level	IV–VI	VII–XII
Number of persons reporting	303	298
Number of characteristics named	370	604
	(in %)	*(in %)*
Human qualities as a person: kind, sympathetic, companionable, "she likes us," cheerful, etc.	22	28
Qualities as director of class and as disciplinarian: fair, impartial, has no pets, discipline strict but firm and fair, does not treat failure to learn as moral wrong, etc.	24	26
Performance as a teacher, teaching: makes things interesting, knows a lot, explains well, helps individuals with their lessons, permits students to express opinions	27	32
Participation in students' games, activities	6	3
Physical appearance, dress, grooming, voice	7	5
Other	14	6

Teachers disliked most

Number of persons reporting	99	265
Number of characteristics named	170	459
	(in %)	*(in %)*
Human qualities as a person: harsh, unkind, sarcastic, ridicules, "makes fun of you," sour, glum, cross, nervous, "queer," etc.	21	32
Qualities as director of class and disciplinarian: unfair, has pets, punishes too much, rigid, too strict, constant scold, treats failure to learn as moral wrong, preachy, etc.	43	35
Performance as teacher, teaching: dull, dry, poor at making assignments, doesn't know much, no help for individual pupils, too much homework, etc.	17	18
Participation in students' interests and activities	1	1
Physical appearance, grooming, voice, etc.	8	7
Other	10	7

Source: From "Characteristics of teachers who are 'liked best' and 'disliked most'" by A. T. Jersild, *Journal of Experimental Education* (1940), **9**, 139–151. Reprinted by permission.

side of teachers, such as their willingness to let students express their opinions and have a voice in the affairs of the class.

Evaluations of teachers have been found to be affected by a number of attributes that are related to the student. In a study of college freshmen, Kennedy (1975) found that students who received higher grades than they expected at the beginning of the course rated their teachers more favorably than those students whose grades were equal to what they expected or lower than they expected. A related study of prior teaching evaluations and ratings of teaching performance was conducted by Perry et al. (1974). Students in their study had information, from other students who had previously taken the course, about their instructors' effectiveness prior to their taking the course. As might be expected, the students' prior information affected their ratings of the overall excellence of their instructors.

Adolescent Educational and Occupational Aspirations, Expectations, and Achievement

Adolescents' educational and occupational aspirations and expectations have been found to be of importance in terms of their future achievement in school as well as in the world of work. Recognizing that this is the case, many researchers have attempted to examine the adolescent's aspirations and expectations and the factors related to them. By expectations we refer to what have been rated as realistic plans concerning the future; by aspiration we refer to that which adolescents wish, whether or not the wish is realistic. Most research studies have found that middle-class children and adolescents have higher expectations and aspirations than members of the lower social classes (Brook et al., 1974; Wylie and Hutchins, 1967). One might conjecture that several factors are operating. One possibility is that middle-class students are identifying with parents who have probably achieved a higher socioeconomic status than those parents of peers who represent a lower socioeconomic level. Socioeconomic standing may also affect the likelihood of being in a college preparatory curriculum and having college-oriented friends, which may affect academic performance and college plans (Alexander and Eckland, 1975b).

Traditionally, boys have had higher occupational and educational expectations and aspirations than girls (Karmel, 1975). This probably reflects the fact that traditionally males have been favored over females in most occupations. In recent years more opportunities have been opened for women, and anyone who desires greater equality between the sexes hopes and expects that favoritism for males will continue to decline in future years.

With respect to school achievement, adolescents with higher socioeconomic backgrounds are more likely to achieve at a higher level than adolescents from lower socioeconomic levels. The reasons for this are varied. Parents of higher socioeconomic status have a higher average level of intelligence, variously interpreted as due to environmental or genetic factors. Certainly it is likely that more opportunities for cognitive enrichment will be available in the homes of middle-class adolescents than in the homes of lower-class youngsters. As Coleman (as cited in the President's Science Advisory Commission, 1973) has pointed out, the schools most often attended by youngsters of the lower class are not as well equipped as those attended by youngsters of middle socioeconomic status. The values of the peer group and the family with respect to education may also play a role in producing these observed differences in achievement between adolescents from lower and middle socioeconomic backgrounds (Alexander and Eckland, 1975a).

Parental Educational and Occupational Aspirations and Expectations as Related to Adolescent Aspirations

Several investigators (Bronfenbrenner, 1958; Brook et al., 1974) have found that middle-class parents have higher aspirations for their adolescents than parents from low socioeconomic backgrounds. In accordance with this, adolescents with higher socioeconomic backgrounds more often report that their parents encouraged them to attend college (Wylie and Hutchins, 1967), and members of the middle class express more concern than those of the lower class with the importance and necessity of education (Cloward and Jones, 1963).

Parental aspirations have been found to be higher for sons than for daughters (Brook et al., 1974; Lukoff and Brook, 1976; Wylie and Hutchins, 1967). Economic factors may be relevant to this finding. Parents may have higher aspirations for their sons because they believe that the sons will eventually have to support a family. The girl may be valued more in terms of her spouse's occupation and in terms of her feminine role as a homemaker.

In a longitudinal study of tenth-grade boys, Bachman (1970) examined the impact of home background factors and intelligence on the adolescent's college plans and occupational aspirations. The findings regarding the differential impact of these factors on college plans are pictured in Figure 17.1.

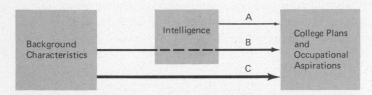

Figure 17.1. Impact of background and intelligence on college plans and occupational aspirations. *A* designates that intelligence is directly related to college plans. *B* refers to the fact that home background factors have an influence on intelligence which in turn is related to college plans and occupational aspirations. *C* indicates that family characteristics have a direct impact on college plans and educational aspirations as well as the indirect influence via intelligence noted under *B*. [From *Youth in transition, 2: The impact of family background and intelligence on tenth-grade boys* by J. G. Bachman. Ann Arbor: The Institute for Social Research, 1970. Copyright 1970 by The Institute for Social Research of the University of Michigan. Reprinted by permission.]

As shown in Figure 17.1, family background factors are positively related to intellectual functioning, which in turn has an effect on educational plans; some aspects of family background (apparently both hereditary and environmental) have a direct impact on college plans.

Socioeconomic level and family size have both been found to be associated with educational plans. The higher the social class level and the smaller the family, the more likely it is that the individual will have high educational expectations (Bachman, 1970; Brook et al., 1974). In a study of younger children, white children's aspirations tended to resemble parental aspirations at both lower and higher socioeconomic levels. The aspirations of black children also tended to resemble those of black parents of higher, but not of lower, socioeconomic status. In a study of an older adolescent sample, parents' aspirations and expectations for their children were highly related to their children's own expectations and aspirations (Lukoff and Brook, 1976).

Peer Influences on the Educational Plans of Adolescents

Peer groups also influence the plans and achievements of adolescents (Alexander and Eckland, 1975b; Coleman, 1961). High school students and their best friends were asked how much education they expected to complete in a study by Kandel and Lesser (1969). The educational aspirations of the adolescents were positively related to those of their best school friends. This investigation also explored the impact of friends as compared with the impact of mother on the educational expectations reported by adolescents. One finding was that when there is a discrepancy between the mother's educational plans and the plans of the adolescent's best school friend, the mother's influence is likely to prevail. Thus, 49 per cent of the adolescents reported that they planned to continue their education beyond high school when their mothers expected them to, even in cases where the adolescent's best school friend planned to discontinue schooling at the high school level. In contrast, 21 per cent of the adolescents planned to continue beyond high school when their best friend also expected to, even though the mother's expectations were low. In general the adolescent's plans were in agreement with those of both mother and friend. Kandel and Lesser (1969) conclude that "the present results suggest that it is misleading to speak of separate adolescent cultures or of general peer *versus* parental influences. The particular content area under discussion must be specified; for certain values or areas, peers may be more influential than parents; for other issues, the reverse may be true (cf. Brittain, 1963). On the issue of the adolescent's future life goals, parents have a stronger influence than peers [p. 222]."

Conflicting Motives and Changing Aspirations of Women

Studies by Horner (1970) have investigated what has been called the motive to avoid success. This may act as a barrier to achievement. When Horner speaks of motive to avoid success, she is referring to a tendency to experience higher levels of anxiety as a result of "anticipating the negative consequences of success." Achieving women, according to Horner, are most likely to experience the detrimental effects of a fear of success.

Margaret Mead (1968), the well-known anthropologist, pointed out that Americans consider both femininity and competitive achievement as quite desirable but mutually incompatible. Thus, some female adolescents feel that if they achieve in the educational or occupational sphere they will do so to the detriment of their femininity. Because most achievement situations are of a competitive nature, and competitiveness, according to stereotyped views, is a masculine quality, adolescent females who compete may regard themselves as masculine and may also be regarded by others as masculine. This dilemma may result in anxiety and may be reflected in a motive to avoid success.

In one of Horner's (1970) efforts, adolescent boys and girls were asked to write a story in response to the following cue: "At the end of first term finals Anne/John finds herself/himself at the top of her/his medical school class." Sixty-five per cent of the female stories, but only 10 per cent of the male stories, contained imagery connoting fear of success. Elements in the stories regarded as representing fear of success included statements about negative consequences anticipated as a result of achieving success; conflict about success, such as questioning one's femininity; the use of defense mechanisms, such as denial of achievements; and bizarre responses, such as the story in which Anne is "attacked and maimed for life" as a result of being successful. These results were obtained in a sampling of white persons. In samples of blacks the men expressed greater fear of success imagery than black women, 67 and 29 per cent, respectively, in one study.

In response to the verbal question, "Are you more likely to tell your boyfriend or the boys in your classes that you have gotten an A or a C?" virtually all of the females rated as low in fear of success said they would report having attained an A, but only 33 per cent of the females rated as high in fear of success said they would report an A. According to Horner (1970), a number of females, when presented with a conflict between their picture of themselves as being both feminine and as developing their skills and abilities, may resolve their conflict by adapting their behavior to their stereotype of sex-role behavior. One consequence of this is that females may disguise their talents, or in more extreme cases refrain from developing their abilities, in order to feel more feminine. Of course, this can result in a great loss to the individual as well as society.

Within the recent past, several studies have attempted to replicate Horner's study with varying results. Using procedures similar to Horner's and based on students at the same university, Hoffman (1974) reported that 65 per cent of the females and 79 per cent of the males told stories containing "motive-to-avoid-success" imagery, suggesting that a change had taken place between the time of the two studies. A study by Winchel et al. (1974) suggested that the proportion of females giving fear-of-success responses was higher in coed high schools (where male competition is present) than in non-coed high schools. These findings lend support to Horner's position that the motive to avoid success is greater in competitive situations. For this reason, some persons have argued against the prevailing trend toward coeducation. As a matter of fact, a report entitled *Opportunities for Women in Higher Education* by the Carnegie Commission on Higher Education (1973) indicates that a high proportion of successful women have attended non-coed colleges. The commission suggests that the experience of attending a women's college is partially responsible for their success. "In women's colleges, female students are not reluctant to participate actively in class discussion for fear of losing their feminine appeal in the eyes of male students. They have far greater opportunity to gain experience in leadership roles in campus organizations and activities than women in coeducational institutions, where the top leadership positions nearly always go to men [p. 73]."

The advantages women might gain from attending coed institutions must, however, be considered in the light of possible disadvantages. Such advantages include a greater opportunity to have interpersonal relationships with males and to get to know their own reactions to the presence of men.

In view of the conflicting data in this important area and the significance a motive of avoiding success may have in the total scheme of development, it is clear that further research is needed, with particular attention to factors involved in the arousal of this motive and the methods used in assessing or measuring it. A further discussion of the motive-to-avoid-success theory appears in Chapter 18, "Vocational Development."

Sex Difference, Achievement Motivation, and Self-concept

In a review of the literature concerning sex differences in achievement, Maccoby and Jacklin (1974) test the assumption that males are more oriented than females toward achievement for its own sake. They reject this assumption on the basis of the available literature. Furthermore, they note that females receive better grades throughout the school years, even though they do not get higher aptitude or achievement test scores. This suggests that females must have some combination of effort, interest, and better work habits than males. Another widely held assumption is that both sexes are motivated to achieve, but males are interested in the task itself, whereas females work for praise and the approval of others. However, available research does not support this assumption.

With respect to self-esteem, females manifest as much satisfaction with themselves as males until the college years. During the college years, men appear to have more confidence than women in their ability to control future events that affect them and to perform on several tasks assigned to them. *Internal control* has been found to be associated with achievement in males but not in females.

Youth in college

Most beginning college students are adolescents in the sense that they are still continuing the process of "ripening" and maturing. They are still growing in intellectual power. Many of them are still working on tasks that confronted them earlier in the adolescent period, such as "finding themselves" and striving for independence and self-direction.

Youth Enters College

Because the impact of college on adolescents is affected by what they are like prior to college and by the nature of the transition from high school to college, it makes sense to study adolescents in high school and then follow them through a college setting.[2] One such study was conducted by Goodman and Feldman (1975), who were interested in comparing the perceptions of adolescents of their ideal college, both before and after the students were at college. Additionally, they compared the expectations of adolescents of what college would be like, with their perception of it after having spent two years there. In general they found that the students' perceptions of their ideal college were at a much higher level than their later perception of the college they attended. The students further indicated that they expected more from their college than was actually provided. Adolescents had to learn to deal with the discrepancies between their expectations and reality. In commenting on what prospective students expect from college, Stern

[2] Studies of this nature have been conducted by Taube and Vreeland (1972) and Trent and Medsker (1968).

(1970) noted that "no mere college" is able to satisfy the students' expectations. "The student comes to realize this after he has been on campus for a short while, and the disillusion can nowhere be more acute than at the large universities where the discrepancy between student needs and institutional environment is the most extreme [p. 177]." Stanfiel and Watts (1970) suggest that "entering freshmen tend to expect the moon and usually find something more mundane [p. 134]."

The College Population

The present-day college enrollment, compared with some years ago, includes a larger percentage of the total young population, a larger proportion of persons aged twenty-five or over, a larger representation of students from lower socioeconomic levels and minority groups, a substantial number of married students, and a larger proportion of students earning part or all of their college expenses. Within recent years there has been a decrease in the enrollment among white male youths (Young, 1973).

The dropout rate has not changed greatly. In a compilation of dropout statistics, Havighurst et al. (1972) report that slightly under a third of the students complete one to three years of college. One quarter of the students in 1971 completed four years of college. The percentage of those completing college was highest among white males. Of those who graduate from college, a number are able to find work or enter graduate school, but since 1971 the number of dropouts who are not employed has increased considerably.

Outcomes of College

Due to the diversity among college students and large differences in the entrance requirements and scholastic standards of various colleges, it is difficult to generalize about "the college student" or about what is meant by a "college education." However, students and colleges do have many characteristics in common. Liberal arts colleges, for example, are designed to provide a "liberal" education. Liberal education has been variously defined, but most college faculty members would probably agree that it aims to provide intellectual nurturing and discipline, to promote knowledge and enlightenment, to encourage a disposition to take a thoughtful and sometimes critical view of things, to inquire into the logic and facts underlying an issue instead of resorting to emotional bias or intellectual preconceptions, and to cultivate an appreciation of the arts, the humanities, and all branches of learning.

When students go to college, a feast for the intellect is laid out before them. The library is a storehouse of the wisdom of the past. In the laboratory they can use equipment that has been wrought by the minds of great scientists and engineers. Members of the faculty are ready to bequeath to them the fruits of their scholarly labors. A college student can be, in large measure, an heir of all the ages. In addition college students have an opportunity to share their thinking with fellow students. And, with proper encouragement, they can not only enjoy what other scholars offer them, but they can also begin to make original scholarly contributions of their own.

What do the students derive from all this during their four years at college? The most obvious outcomes appear in the practical sphere when students use the four-year period to acquire information and skills that they can apply when they leave college. It seems that typical students place a high value on a college education but not mainly for intellectual reasons; available studies suggest that students place a higher value on the prestige of being a college graduate, on vocational opportunities that become available, and on friendships made there that will be of help one day.

In many of the studies that have been made of the outcomes of a college education, it is apparent that the investigators have assumed that the college should have an influence on a student's personal philosophy and outlook on life. This is perhaps an unrealistic assumption, for many colleges do not claim that it is their aim to influence any student's philosophy of life and make little or no systematic effort to do so. Moreover, judging by their own statements, it seems that many students who go to college are not consciously seeking to examine their personal values or to formulate a more mature philosophy. At this stage of development, they may select peers who are similar to them in terms of their beliefs and values, thereby reducing the likelihood of their changing in any one of these areas. Therefore, it probably should not be regarded as surprising if we find that many persons who have gone to college do not change their outlook on life to a great degree.

One of the most extensive studies of the impact of college has been reported by Jacob (1957), who used a variety of standardized tests designed to measure the values and opinions of several thousand college students in a number of institutions. According to Jacob's findings, some colleges seem to have a "peculiar potency" in providing an institutional atmosphere, a "climate of values" in which students are "decisively influenced." But, according to the tests Jacob applied, something less than this usually occurs.

Average students in a majority of colleges show some changes in thought and outlook, although not to what might be called a decisive degree, during their college years. Typical students, as they move from the freshman through the senior year, become more tolerant, more concerned about civil liberties, and better able to apply critical thinking in social science, which results in an increased tendency to reach judgments by reason.

The drift toward a greater tolerance and interest in civil liberties does not, however, in the typical student, seem to result in an active concern about social issues or a zeal for participation in civic affairs.

Jacob also found, according to the measures he used, that one trend in the thinking of students as they continued in college was toward uniformity: the seniors in his study were, on the average, more similar than freshmen in their values and beliefs. Many students moved toward the norm, giving up any extreme views that would set them apart from others.

The trend toward intellectual uniformity described by Jacob has also been observed by others. Sanford (1958) notes that in the peer culture in college the accent is on moderation and leveling. Students should be noncontroversial and, in making an ethical decision, consider what others think so that the decision very likely will conform to the morality that prevails in the culture as a whole.

However, the trend toward uniformity in dealing with controversial ideas and ethical issues (as indicated by professed abstract moral values in response to a paper-and-pencil test) does not necessarily mean that students in all colleges increasingly adopt similar formulas in dealing with personal issues in their own lives. In a long-term study of students in a women's college referred to in Chapter 1, Sanford (1957) noted that senior girls were, on the average, more self-critical and more uncertain of themselves than they were as freshmen. The seniors in this study, as described by Sanford showed greater breadth of consciousness, more self-insight, and more familiarity with their inner life. They had more capacity for discrimination and were more aware of their inner impulses. Sanford regards this increase in self-scrutiny as a sign of increased maturity and believes that the college had a considerable influence in bringing it about. He also notes that the average senior in his study was less complacent and more "upset" than she was in her freshman year. She had learned to question her earlier values but had not yet fully established a new and firm set of values of her own. Moreover, many of the seniors in this group were also troubled by the fact that the life that awaited some when they left college differed from their mode of life while in college.[3]

The changes that occurred in the college population Jacob studied seemed (with a few exceptions) to be unrelated to the particular course of study pursued by students in college and (with some exceptions) seemed to be relatively independent of the quality of instruction offered by individual

[3] It is not clear whether the college women in Sanford's study were an exceptional group, as compared with the majority of students in Jacob's population, or whether differences in the findings of the two studies were due to differences in the methods that were used and the kind of information the women were asked to give.

teachers. Values expressed by students who were most interested in the social sciences differed little from those of students majoring in engineering, business administration, natural science, and agriculture. The social science students ran with the pack in most of their expressed interests and values.

Feldman and Newcomb (1969) have reviewed the voluminous literature concerning the impact of college on students. In some respects their findings are similar to, and in others different from, those in Jacob's *Changing Values in College* (1957). They found that changes appeared between the freshman and senior years of college in a number of characteristics. Authoritarianism and prejudice seem to decrease, while sensitivity to aesthetic experiences and a liberal attitude toward public issues appear to increase during the four years of college. With considerably less uniformity, there is some increase in the intellectual domain: for instance, students are better able to think at an abstract level. Changes may also occur in the personal sphere, such as increased independence and self-confidence.

In spite of the limitations of data in evaluating net changes, it seems likely that seniors tend to be more aware of their emotions than freshmen and are freer to express their emotions in words or behavior.

College can also assist young people in achieving emancipation from the family, developing independence, and acquiring the necessary organizational skills, attitudes, and motivations for success in the occupational world. Numerous adolescents believe that college has enabled them to acquire greater knowledge, increased reading comprehension, increased skill in the use of language, and an increase in those cognitive skills that enable them to analyze and solve problems, make inferences, and to analyze material critically (Feldman and Newcomb, 1969).

As might be expected, the impact of the college depends on the nature of the college as well as the entering student's characteristics. Typically, at the "traditional" small, private college where there is more informality and an opportunity to acquire close personal relationships, there is the potential for significant institutionalwide impact. The greatest college impact is likely to occur among students who are exposed to an environment that differs from their previous environment but is not markedly different. If there is a high degree of divergence between a student's previous milieu and the social and intellectual influences encountered at college, a student may actively resist what the college offers (Feldman and Newcomb, 1969).

A study of Harvard students by Perry (1970) reported that students are likely to become aware of what is happening in their own development: "Those students whom we saw as 'progressing' made their own awareness of maturation clear, explicitly or implicitly, and conveyed a sense of satisfaction in it. Those whom we perceived as standing still, or stepping to one side, or reaching back, acknowledged that they were avoiding something or denying something or fighting something, and they regularly remarked on an uneasiness or dissatisfaction akin to shame. Some others referred to periods in which they felt they had 'moved too fast' and had become alarmingly confused. In short, the students experienced quite consciously an urge toward maturation, congruent with that progression of forms we were learning to see in their reports [p. 50]."

One favorable finding about college students indicates that they take a more humane and thoughtful view of human foibles than younger persons do. Although it is not clear from the evidence whether this is a result of growing older or of going to college, the evidence on this score, in a study by Porter (1959), is impressive. Porter compared a number of groups with regard to their attitudes toward a list of child-behavior problems. High school seniors, to a far greater degree than college seniors, advocated punishment as a means of dealing with a child who had problems (38.4 per cent of the responses at the senior high school level were punitive as compared with 10.7 per cent at the senior college level). On the other hand, college seniors more often advocated an effort to study the child to find the cause of the behavior (19.2 per cent of the college and 5.9 per cent of the high school seniors' responses included this recommendation). College seniors also relatively more often advocated such steps as talking to the problem child, giving praise and encouragement, and making an adjustment in the work assigned at school.

Academic, utilitarian, and personal aspects of secondary and higher education

According to DeCecco and Richards (1974), conflicts in school provide opportunities for a "creative resolution" of school problems and for further growth. These authors believe that school is an appropriate place for increasing self-understanding on the part of teachers, students, administrators, and parents. Conflict in schools can occur at several levels, and teachers have three options in dealing with students: teach the way they always have, allow the students complete freedom, or negotiate with the students to try to satisfy their needs.

According to DeCecco and Richards, participation in decision making is one of the ways individuals and groups might keep institutions responsive to their changing needs and interests and provide a democratic solution to school problems. Furthermore, they maintain that the school has a responsibility for helping students find effective ways of participating in the civic affairs of their communities and society.

In many studies that have been made of high school and college students, it appears that the instructors' aims and hoped-for outcomes of education differ from the students' aims and hoped-for outcomes. Instructors usually aim to promote intellectual competence and scholarly interests, but the students' main motives for going to high school and college seem to be to conform to what others do and to "get ahead," rather than to become absorbed in scholarship. Students name occupational advantage as a main reason for planning to go to college (Slocum, 1958), and this, presumably, is their main reason for taking courses in high school that will enable them to apply for entrance to college. After they enter college, students continue to name socioeconomic advantage as the main goal of a college education (Jervis and Congdon, 1958). Unfortunately, the occupational world is not prepared, as this is written, to cope with or to accommodate a large number of people who, according to conventional academic standards, are highly educated.

A marked discrepancy also often exists between the instructors' academic preoccupations and the student's personal concerns. In a study noted in Chapter 1, that included college and high school girls, Frank et al. (1953) drew a sharp contrast between the impersonal intellectual content of what the students were required to study and the highly charged emotional concerns that prevailed in their own lives. When thus beset by personal problems, the students must manage, as best they can, to live in two worlds: the academic world and the world of their own personal preoccupations.

Additional evidence of a difference between the preoccupations of instructors and students appears in statistics regarding high school and college dropouts. Although the figures vary from study to study, most would agree that a relatively large proportion of students drop out of high school. From a review of findings by Feldman and Newcomb (1969), it also appears that a large proportion of the students who enter college do not remain to graduate. Although among those who drop out there are many who are below average in ability as compared with the rest of the student body, many who are well below the average college student in intelligence remain to graduate. On the other hand, many with the highest levels of ability drop out. When students drop out, it usually is taken to mean that *they* have failed. At the college level, a great deal of attention has been given to the question: What can we learn about those who have failed in the past that will enable us in the future to reject similar persons when they apply for admission?

Less often is it assumed that perhaps in some way the school has failed. Much more attention has been given to the frequency of dropouts than to the question of what institutions might do to prevent failure and possibly to help remedy those shortcomings within the college and within the individual student that produce failure.

A relatively new approach is to view student withdrawal as a function of the "match" between the personality, abilities, and attitudes of the student and the pressures and rewards inherent in the college environment

(Williams, 1967). Withdrawal from college is more likely when there is a high degree of incongruence between the person and the school environment.

High Student Respect for Teachers

Although several studies indicate that there is a discrepancy between the goals of college students and what their instructors regard as most important, it is interesting to note that college students have a high respect for the integrity of their teachers. In a study by Reynolds (1958), students in twenty institutions were presented with this proposition:

> It has been said that ideals are nice if you can afford them, and that life consists of a series of compromises. Listed below are a number of fields of work. In which do you think you would have to "conform" the least and make the fewest concessions with your personal beliefs?

In response to this, college teaching topped the list (with an average rank of 1.8). College instructors were regarded as more true to their personal beliefs than doctors (medicine had an average rank of 4.5). And college teachers were almost in a world apart from persons in government service (with a rank of 10.1); and persons in labor organizations were next to the bottom in ranking on personal integrity (with an average rank of 11.8). The sharpest difference was between persons in college teaching and persons in politics. The highest rank of college teaching (1.8) contrasted with the lowest rank (12.5) of persons in politics. (This finding should, of course, be taken with some grains of salt, for it is safer for college teachers, once established in their jobs, with tenure, to be uncompromising in their ideas than it is for an elected official. However, it still is interesting to note that the teachers rated so high.)

The Problem of Personal Meaning

In the discussion of the aims of education there has been much controversy as to whether education should be concerned with the student's emotional welfare. Many have claimed that education designed to help students to use their minds effectively should center exclusively on cultivating intellectual competence and academic knowledge of an impersonal sort. According to this view, education should not be concerned with personal problems or what sometimes has been called personal adjustment. It should aim at mental excellence, not at mental health.

But such a view negates the idea that education should help students to use their minds effectively. One of the most profound ways in which individuals can employ their minds is to inquire into the properties of the mind and the conditions within themselves that influence their mental lives. Such an inquiry inevitably will touch on personal concerns and problems. According to this view, the idea that education should not be concerned with personal adjustment is unfortunate from a social point of view and untenable from an intellectual point of view.

There are reasons for believing that the lack of interest in an academic program shown by many students is not just due entirely to their own shortcomings, to poor teaching in earlier grades, to competing interests in the outside world, but that it is due in part to shortcomings inherent in the program itself. It is important that the students find something of *meaning* and *value* for themselves in what is being taught in order to be interested in what is being taught. One of the most frequent reasons given by college students for loss of interest in high school subjects was a failure to see the need for the subjects (Shuttleworth, 1938).

If students are compliant, ambitious, and fairly bright, they can manage to learn even the most meaningless things. But if students have little spunk or are not ambitious enough to learn something just because someone else thinks they ought to, the road is not so smooth. Where there is no personal involvement, it is hard to find anything meaningful. Moreover, this is not a problem facing students alone. Many teachers report that they can see little or no meaning in much of what they have to learn and in much of what they have to teach (Jersild, 1955).

The problem of personal meaning has two major facets. First, where there is meaning students are intellectually absorbed. Their minds are active in learning things that really count for them. Learning for them is a *living* thing rather than a mechanical exercise of memorizing something that someone else requires. What the students are learning helps them in satisfying ways to realize and appreciate their capacity for using their minds. Through their learning they are pressing forward into a widening world of knowledge and experience. They are on the way toward finding themselves, realizing their potential, exercising their curiosity, and getting a sense of achievement.

The other facet is that what is meaningful is not only a challenge to the intellect, but is also significant from the point of view of concerns and issues in the students' personal lives. They are able to relate what they learn to themselves. In the opinion of the present writers, education that is really meaningful will inevitably touch on personal issues and concerns, including emotional problems. In practically all chapters of this book there is a reference to these concerns and problems: those connected with vocational choice; the struggle for identity and for autonomy; concerns connected with sex—with the young person's need for relating himself or herself intimately to others; and the need for coming to grips with all the forces in the outer and the inner worlds that produce conflict, anxiety, loneliness, grief, and resentment.

Learning that has a personal meaning for students might help them to gain insight into the conditions in their private lives that affect their emotional welfare. It also is likely to increase their ability to accept the joys of living and learning and their ability to cope with life's adversities.

Education for Self-understanding

According to the views set forth here, one important aim in the education of adolescents is to help them to understand themselves. The idea that the pursuit of knowledge should embrace self-knowledge is an ancient one. It was expressed by Socrates over two thousand years ago when he repeated the admonition "Know thyself," which had been brought down to him from earlier times. Education currently, and for generations, requires young people to study almost every subject except the most important subject—the young people themselves. But although the idea of self-knowledge has, to a large extent, been ignored in practice, it is widely accepted, in theory, as representing one of the most important goals in education.

In one of a series of investigations by the senior writer (Jersild, 1955), eleven groups of teachers and graduate students in education, totalling a thousand persons, were asked to give their reactions to the idea that schools should promote self-understanding. Over 90 per cent responded that in their judgment the idea was promising and worthwhile. In the various groups, from one half to two thirds of the persons expressed the view that the promotion of knowledge of self is or might be the most significant aspect of education.

At the college level, both students and instructors in the study by Jervis and Congdon (1958) mentioned self-fulfillment and self-understanding as the second and third most important benefits that higher education might provide. Other authors have more recently similarly proposed that a major goal of education should be to promote the development of the adolescent as a person (Feldman, 1972; Sanford, 1968).

Resources for Promoting Knowledge of Self

Every subject and skill in the course of study potentially offers an opportunity for helping students to understand themselves. Many areas of scholarship are really meaningful *only* if the students can relate what they learn to themselves—can experience the implications of what they are studying in terms of what is happening in their own lives.

Previously established attitudes and preconceptions are likely to influence, to a greater or lesser degree, students' responses to practically every subject they take in college. This means that when instructors present ideas, they have an opportunity to ask students to examine them in the light of their own attitudes.

Conventional academic subjects offer access to self-understanding. In a course in literature, students read the works of great authors. The language of great works of literature is a universal language: it dwells on experiences that are timeless and common to all mankind. It makes articulate many things that the reader clearly or dimly can perceive as belonging to his or her own existence. Under the leadership of an instructor who has the freedom to explore, a discussion of a work of literature will move far into personal meanings. In such a discussion, Hamlet is not just a remote prince, nor Lady Macbeth a vicious queen set off in a literary frame. The characters come alive. What they say, think, feel, and do can strike a resonant chord in the reader's own existence. If, through exploring and perceiving their kinship with an author or his or her characters, or their aversions to them, students become aware of conditions in their own inner lives that they previously had not perceived, they have made an advance in understanding themselves.

A course in history, like a course in literature, provides an almost inexhaustible source of human "case material" that can be used for self-examination. The heroes and villains of history were impelled by overt and covert motives such as exist to some degree in all of us. With proper encouragement, this or that student may discover in him- or herself the attributes of Cleopatra or Nero or King Henry VIII or Napoleon or, perhaps, the attributes of all four. In exploring the personal meaning of history students may discover in themselves some of the malevolence of a Hitler and some of the benevolence of a Lincoln. They may find that one of the issues over which the Civil War was fought still prevails right within their classroom or within their prejudices.

Other subjects also provide rich opportunities for self-examination and self-discovery. Biology could offer such opportunities through inquiry, for example, into sex and genetics. Courses in physical education could touch on a large range of personal issues—among them are all the psychological meanings and problems connected with physical development that were discussed earlier in this book. The social studies offer opportunities for self-exploration too. It would be difficult to find a subject more *social* and, at the same time, more personal and worthy of study than dating and boy-girl relationships or the open and hidden delinquency that prevails in most communities.

In the judgment of the present writers, an effort to delve into the personal meanings of standard academic subjects enriches the scholarly content of the courses. Moreover, every issue that prevails within the inner lives of adolescents, every problem that besets them, is present at school. Each classroom is populated with aspirations, hopes, ambitions, and currents of loyalty and tenderness, fears, resentments, disappointments, and sorrows. If students are being taught how to use their minds effectively, it is proper to try to deal with these issues and problems.

As we have noted, attention to some of these personal concerns can be incorporated to an important degree into the teaching of standard subjects. However, it may not always be feasible to do so, due to the varying interests and abilities of the teachers of the regular subject matter courses. There could also be special courses for dealing with personal concerns, staffed by interested teachers who are especially qualified by training and temperament to offer such courses.[4]

This is a controversial subject. The senior writer has had the privilege of working in classrooms with a number of teachers in such special courses and, in so doing, has observed that there usually is some opposition to the courses within the faculty and in the community at large. Many educators do not regard courses of this kind as academically respectable. Some parents may object to having their youngsters discuss personal concerns (although, in the senior writer's experience, such parents have been a small minority). Some parents and students (and faculty members) object because such courses do not help students to pass college entrance requirements.[5]

Premises Underlying Education for Knowledge of Self

Before proceeding further it will be useful to review and supplement the premises and assumptions underlying the idea that education should promote knowledge of self.

---

[4] The idea that teaching should aim to promote self-discovery, whether in regular courses or in special courses, does not imply that such teaching can take the place of special services for disturbed youngsters. It should be recognized also that teachers differ greatly in their aptitude and training for dealing with personal concerns and that some are able to inspire a zeal for learning (and thus promote their students' self-realization) even though they are not interested in their students' emotional development and accompanying personal problems.

[5] For discussions and findings dealing with the promotion of self-understanding at the high school and college levels, the teaching of psychology to high school students, and problems connected with such teaching, see Jersild (1952, 1955); Helfant (1952); Jersild and Helfant (1963); Ojemann (1961); Kubie (1954a); Jersild et al. (1962); Feldman and Newcomb (1969).

1. A large proportion of persons move from childhood and adolescence into adulthood with a burden of unresolved personal problems. Many of these are linked with the inevitable adversities of human existence. But an education designed to help young people to use their minds effectively should aim to help students to take a thoughtful view of their personal concerns.

2. As already noted, strictly from a scholarly point of view, the full meaning and value of many academic subjects (such as literature, history, biology, health, and physical education) can be achieved only if students can relate what is taught to their personal experiences.

3. It is possible, in education, to offer adolescents something more meaningful to them, as persons, than the usual impersonal academic routine. This might make an important difference in their lives, even though the teacher who tries to provide such instruction does not offer, or pretend to provide, the more intensive kind of self-scrutiny that psychotherapists try to provide.

4. Self-examination is more profitable when a person is in the process of making crucial decisions than after such decisions have been made.

5. In a receptive educational setting, adolescents show more desire, and capacity, for self-inquiry than has been recognized in the kind of education they usually receive.

When adolescents have an opportunity to work with teachers who open the door to self-inquiry, many of them eagerly respond as though they were hungry for help. Others do, however, hold back, at least for a time, as though they were resisting or had no problems to share (for statements regarding responses of students see, for example, the earlier-mentioned study by Jersild, 1952). In a study dealing with this matter, Jersild (1952) has pointed out that as soon as teachers take even a little step in the direction of dealing with personal problems, it is likely that a great number of problems will be revealed.

Self-understanding in Relation to Helping Others Understand Themselves

Earlier we cited findings that indicated that a large proportion of teachers regard the promotion of self-understanding as an important goal in education. The persons who took part in a study by Jersild (1955) were also questioned about the kind of help they thought they would need to put this idea into practice. About half to over four fifths of persons in the eleven groups indicated a need for a kind of education that might help them to deal with emotional issues in their own lives (as distinguished from abstract and professional or academic issues).[6]

In voicing a need for this kind of preparation, these teachers underscored the idea that to help others to obtain self-knowledge it is essential for the teachers to seek to understand themselves. This idea was emphasized also in a study by Barker (1946). Barker's findings, based on a combination of methods—including interviews, ratings, and case studies—led her to conclude that a philosophy of life and knowledge enabling teachers to deal more competently with problems in their own lives are fundamental if teachers are to help students to face problems.

When teachers believe that self-knowledge is essential for understanding or helping their students, how do they go about achieving such knowledge? At the present time, the most systematic means of seeking self-understanding is to undergo psychoanalysis or intensive psychotherapy. (In recent years an increasing number of teachers have sought help through these channels.) However, there are other resources. Everything that transpires between teachers and their students might help the teachers to learn something about themselves, as well as something about the students.

If teachers have the desire to examine themselves in the light of their experiences with students, they will have an opportunity again and again to inquire into the meaning of their own likes and dislikes, their prejudices, their anxieties, their attitudes toward persons in authority, their attitudes toward sex, their tendency to expect too little or too much of themselves or of others, their need to dominate others or to placate them, and their desire to face or their need to evade reminders of their own hopes, disappointments, wishes, and fears. Teachers can learn something about themselves by seeing a motion picture of themselves and their students during a class period or by hearing a recording of their voices.

One important means through which teachers can acquire self-knowledge is by comparing their perceptions of students with the perceptions other teachers report. For example, they and others independently record what they hear, see, and feel while listening to a class discussion. Then their impressions are compared. Differences between what they and others noticed or did not notice, differences in the feelings that were aroused and the assumptions that were made, and the conclusions that were drawn provide a starting point for self-examination. Through a comparison of observations of this sort teachers may discover that they were projecting feelings of their own in ways they did not at the time suspect. What they

[6] Between one fifth and one half of the members of the various groups expressed a need for help such as might be obtained through group therapy. We cannot assume that all who expressed a favorable attitude to the idea of therapy would take steps to procure it, although in some communities the percentage of teachers who have sought and received professional psychological help is quite large.

perceive "objectively" may be, to a large degree, a revelation of their own subjective state and thus tell more about themselves than about those whom they observe.

Feelings might be aired in a revealing and growth-producing way if individuals could help one another to learn to be free to come out from behind the curtain that commonly conceals their emotions from others and from themselves.

The teacher's and student's efforts to grow in self-understanding are more likely to take place through many little glimpses than through dramatic flashes of illumination. Now and then some individuals face an insight so brilliant that it almost blinds them for the moment and continues, thereafter, to pour new light into their lives. But more often the light is more a flicker than a flame. Frequently, the ones who gain an insight do so almost as though an afterthought—a way of underlining a truth they had already accepted but had not clinched in their thoughts.

Knowledge of self is not something that is acquired once and for all, like mastery of the multiplication tables. Even those who are quite blind to themselves have a little of it and a capacity to acquire more. And one of the outstanding marks of those who have achieved the deepest knowledge of self is that they are still seeking. No one procedure alone will give the answer, because the search for selfhood, when genuine, is pursued through all channels of experience as long as a person lives.

Adolescents who drop out of school

Although many students who enter high school do not graduate, this still leaves a decidedly larger number of young persons who now graduate from high school than did so a few decades ago.

Even though some persons question whether we should expect a majority of young people to go to high school or to finish high school, the fact remains that a high school diploma is a valuable possession. Given two young persons with similar ability, the one who has a diploma has a better chance in life than the one who does not. The lack of a diploma bars many young people from opportunities that might otherwise be open to them. They are left out when announcements of job openings read, "Only high school graduates should apply."

Moreover, the advantage of a diploma does not consist simply in a better chance for employment. Adolescents who have a diploma will glean pride and personal satisfaction, even though they might have been marginal students who just managed to slip through. People who do not have a diploma are considered by many as personal failures.

Dropping out can be considered a symptom of problems that interfere with the adolescent's ability to function in a typical high school environment. Moreover, dropping out of high school can in some cases lead to changes in the adolescent's personality, aspirations, and present and future behaviors.

Family Background and Ability as Related to Remaining In or Dropping Out of School

In a recent longitudinal study of male adolescents, Bachman et al. (1971) examined not only the causes of dropping out, but also the consequences of dropping out of school. A national sample of tenth-grade high school students was studied yearly by Bachman (1970) for four years. As might be expected, he found that both family background and ability factors were associated with educational attainment.

Adolescent boys who were more likely to enter college, in contrast to those who were less likely to enter college, came from higher socioeconomic backgrounds, came from smaller families, and more often reported coming from intact homes. Several other investigators (Astin, 1964; Panos and Astin, 1968) have reported that adolescents from lower socioeconomic backgrounds are more likely to be dropouts than adolescents with higher socioeconomic backgrounds. At the college level, persons who continue their education are more likely to have parents who are democratic and supportive and who express greater expectations for their offspring's future education (Hackman and Dysinger, 1970).

In the study by Bachman et al. (1971), boys with lower scores on intelligence, vocabulary, and reading tests were, as one might expect, more likely to drop out of high school. At the college level, the individual's ability has also been found to be an important factor in determining educational performance and the probability of graduating from college (Sewell and Shah, 1967; Wegner and Sewell, 1970).

Earlier in this chapter we noted that adolescents' attitudes toward school reflect, to a significant degree, what might be called the intellectual climate of their home lives: parental aspirations and expectations, the socioeconomic level of the home (which, to a large extent, reflects the level of education attained by one or both parents), and the degree to which adolescents identify themselves with their parents and accept them as models. The intellectual climate may, obviously, exert either a positive or negative influence on a young person's determination to remain in school or to drop out. An adolescent's decision to drop out of school is, of course, more likely if a negative home influence is combined with a low level of intellectual ability. But even a combination of low ability and an unfavorable intellectual climate at home may not produce a dropout. Some young people tenaciously persevere in their efforts at school even though the odds are against them.

Educational Experiences

Experiences in school as well as attitudes toward school were found by Bachman et al. (1971) to be highly related to educational attainment. The slogan "Nothing succeeds like success" seems to pertain to future educational attainment. As might be expected, those boys who had experienced failure in school by being held back or by receiving consistently low grades were more likely to drop out than those boys who received high grades and did not have to repeat a grade. A lack of interest in school subjects and a rebellious attitude toward school also are likely to lead to dropping out.

Personality Dimensions and Dropping Out

An adolescent who perceives himself or herself as lacking in ability to do academic work is more likely to drop out of school than one who has a more favorable view of his or her competence.

One reason advanced by some adolescents for attending school is to learn about themselves and to further their self-development. Among those adolescents who reported high needs for self-development, the dropout rate from high school was found to be lower in the study by Bachman et al. (1971).

Being moved by "internal" controls, as distinct from having to be pushed by "external" controls, also is a factor determining an adolescent's resolve to continue his or her education. People with internal controls, and who remain in school, are confident that they can manage to cope with future events. They do not view their future successes as dependent on outside factors, luck, or chance. They also are likely to perform at a higher level of achievement in school.

Dropouts are more likely to have lower levels of self-esteem than adolescents who continue their educations and to be more subject to negative affective states, such as depression, than those who finish high school and go on to college (Bachman et al., 1971). Feelings of lack of worthiness and negative affective states may be antecedent, rather than consequent, factors in the lives of dropouts; however, dropping out may intensify already existing feelings of low self-esteem. Findings by Bachman et al. (1971) also indicate that being involved in deviant behavior, such as delinquency, is similarly likely to precede, rather than follow, dropping out.

One reason that has been advanced for encouraging adolescents to remain in school is that unemployment is greater among dropouts, and salaries and job satisfaction are likely to be lower.[7] The situation is, of course, more complicated than simply the formality of leaving school. The personality factors that impel a person to drop out of school may impair the likelihood of getting and holding a job.

Dropouts' Perceptions of Dropping Out

One of the most interesting aspects of the study of dropout students is their perceptions of the reasons they left school. Findings pertaining to this subject, by Bachman et al. (1971), indicate that in a group of 125 high school students who quit high school and did not subsequently return to earn a diploma, reasons given for dropping out were distributed as follows: family reasons (including the need to help the family financially), sixteen; personal reasons (including a feeling of being grown up, desire for freedom and leisure, getting married), twenty-four; work and financial reasons (including a need to earn money, being more interested in work than in school), sixteen; school reasons (including learning difficulties, poor grades, lack of interest in schoolwork, and the like), thirty-six; authority reasons (including trouble or not getting along with teachers and other school personnel, strictness or bossiness of authorities, being expelled), twenty-four; other reasons, three; missing data, six. As can be noted, reasons related to schoolwork and school authority outnumbered reasons in other categories.

Among the responses given by the males in this study were "I was mostly just discouraged because I wasn't passing"; "I was bored. I had the grades but was just bored. It was the teachers—didn't make it interesting enough"; "School in general. It didn't teach me how to cope with society once I got out of school doors."

When asked how they later felt about having dropped out of school, by far the preponderant first responses indicated they regretted having left. Among such responses were "I made a mistake" and "I've had trouble in getting a good job." Dropouts who expressed negative feelings (such as the foregoing) outnumbered those who expressed positive feelings (such as, "I think it was the best thing for me to do") more than four to one. As one male phrased it: "Without a high school diploma, it's like a car without tires. It's very important—I realize my mistake [Bachman et al., 1971, p. 159]."

[7] Several investigators (see, for example, Levin et al., 1971) have presented findings regarding the advantages of college graduation in terms of future positions in the occupational and educational world.

Long-Term Effects of Dropping Out

The fact that many of those who drop out of schools have problems of one sort or another does not mean that all dropouts are "problem" cases; nor does the fact that many who chose or were compelled to quit school have regrets mean that most dropouts are impetuous or foolish. Moreover, when one considers the turmoil, rowdyism, and even the threat of bodily harm that prevail in some schools, it is understandable that some students want to get out. Among those who say they do not regret leaving school there no doubt are quite a few who are better off than they were before. In addition Bachman et al. (1971) note that quitting school does not, in itself, make things worse for those who previously had shown low self-esteem, delinquent tendencies, or symptoms of poor mental health. To assess what might be the long-term effects of dropping out would require more long-term follow-up research than now is available.

What to Do About the Dropout Problem

There probably is no cure that will induce all potential dropouts to finish high school. But anything that makes schooling more challenging and meaningful is likely to reduce the dropout problem. The history of education is replete with proposals for reforms that might make schooling more appealing to all students, including those who might want to quit. It has variously been proposed that the educational program should be more democratic, more integrated, more attuned to the learner's "felt needs"; and that it should emphasize "learning by doing" and be founded on active pupil participation in choosing, planning, executing, and evaluating the underlying purpose of the curriculum.

From time to time there have been schools, or individual classrooms, in which students marched to a livelier tune and were more than commonly eager to learn, usually under the influence of inspired teachers. But, by and large, pedagogy in the conventional academic subjects has not changed much with the passing years. Yet, it remains true that there are students who welcome every opportunity to learn, others who obediently go through the prescribed academic exercises, and others—in recent years notably at the adolescent level—whose attitudes have ranged from apathy to angry rebellion.

In the meantime, in the last decades high school attendance has extended into wider areas. Young people in outlying and rural areas, who once would have regarded high school as something beyond reach, are bussed to school. School buildings are more imposing, and costly facilities, practically unknown in earlier generations, have been added. But the general level of achievement in conventional academic subjects has, if anything, declined. Large numbers of students, after twelve years of schooling, do not, for example, reach what once was found to be an eighth-grade level of achievement in reading, as measured by standardized tests.

It is quite likely that school achievement would increase, and the dropout rate decrease, if the high school program somehow could appeal more effectively to the learners' interests. The typical adolescent was once an eager learner. As an infant he or she was curious. Infants spontaneously try to further their intellectual development. They will, for example, avidly add new words to their vocabulary, once they have achieved their thrilling first word. They seem to delight in solving problems.

In early childhood, and even at the elementary school level, children feast on what earlier in this book we have referred to as pleasures of the mind. But interest in the intellectual fare provided by the school diminishes as youngsters move through the grades and, as adolescents, are ready to enter high school. As pupils move into adolescence there are many competing nonacademic interests. But the reason also seems to be that even those who have advocated that education should be personally meaningful and minister to the students' "felt needs" have usually taken an academically narrow and ivory-tower view of what might be meaningful in supplying an answer to the learners' needs.

A disparity between what learners are taught to be interested in and what might be an interesting and personally meaningful line of inquiry was brought out in an informal adjunct to a large-scale survey of the interests of elementary and high school pupils by Jersild and Tasch (1949). After having responded to questions about their interests (including "What would you like to learn more about at school?"), a number of youngsters were asked to tell about their fears. As might be expected from earlier studies, all of the young persons revealed that they were beset by fears, in many instances very troublesome fears. Findings reviewed elsewhere in this book show that young persons not only are subject to fears, but also struggle with other emotional problems. Yet, it did not occur to a single person in the limited study, or to any among the hundreds who took part in the larger survey, to mention fears or other emotional problems when asked what they would like to learn more about. Apparently it had not occurred to them, and was never suggested to them at school, that fears or other forms of emotional distress might be as proper and respectable subjects for inquiry, study, and discussion at school as literature, algebra, or French. Yet, the authors and many other teachers have found that once the door to a search for knowledge of self has been properly opened by a sympathetic and understanding person, many students are pathetically eager to delve into the nature and meaning of their personal problems. If potential dropouts were given an opportunity to air their grievances, to delve into their feelings of discouragement, it is likely that at least some of them would reconsider their ideas about leaving school.

Increased opportunities to concentrate on a course of study best suited to their abilities might also help potential dropouts to remain in school. Such opportunities would be more palatable if no stigma were attached to a program differing from the conventional college preparatory program. Actually many high schools give students an opportunity to choose an "academic" course or a more vocationally oriented line of study—stressing, for example, mechanics, practical aspects of the work of an electrician, and various other courses that once fell under the heading of home economics. The fact that there is a drift toward more participation by males in household chores and child care should, eventually, make it more acceptable for boys to study home economics, cooking, child growth and development, and various aspects of home making that once were delegated almost entirely to females. A program that emphasizes practical skills appeals to many young people who are not interested in conventional academic subjects. The fact that many students now concentrate on courses with a practical orientation may account, in part, for the finding, mentioned on an earlier page, that scores on tests of conventional academic skills are now lower, on the average, than they were some decades ago.

One provision that probably would help to reduce the problems of those who contemplate leaving school is to remove the either-or dilemma they face. Having once quit school, many dropouts do not return, even though they may have regrets. They seem to regard the decision as irreversible. Actually, if they leave school to take a job or to assert their independence (or rebellion), it should not be impossible for them to keep their affiliation with school alive on a part-time basis. Some students might even be advised to leave school with the understanding that the doors would remain open and they would be welcome to return at a later time. As noted in Chapter 15, many persons who are delinquent during adolescence become law-abiding citizens when they are older and more mature. Dropouts are often quite immature when they quit school. In some areas, age sixteen, corresponding to about the tenth grade, is the time when many leave school. In most instances, sixteen is too early an age for adolescents to make a decision that may permanently shape their style of life in the years to come.

References

Alexander, K. L., & Eckland, B. K. School experience and status attainment. In S. E. Dragastin & G. H. Elder, Jr. (Eds.), *Adolescence in the life cycle: Psychological change and social context.* Washington, D.C.: Hemisphere Publishing Corporation, 1975.a.

Alexander, K. L., & Eckland, B. K. Contextual effects in the high school attainment process. *American Sociological Review*, 1975, **40**, 402–416.b.

Astin, A. W., Personal and environmental factors associated with college dropouts among high aptitude students. *Journal of Educational Psychology*, 1964, **55**, 219–227.

Bachman, J. G. *Youth in transition: The impact of family background and intelligence on tenth-grade boys* (Vol. 2). Ann Arbor: University of Michigan Press, 1970.

Bachman, J. G., Green, S., & Wirtanen, I. D. *Youth in transition: Dropping out—problem or symptom?* (Vol. 3). Ann Arbor: University of Michigan Press, 1971.

Barker, M. E. *Personality adjustments of teachers related to efficiency in teaching.* New York: Bureau of Publications, Teachers College, Columbia University, 1946.

Blos, P. *On adolescence: A psychoanalytic interpretation.* New York: Free Press, 1962.

Brittain, C. V. Adolescent choices and parent-peer cross-pressures. *American Sociological Review*, 1963, **28**, 385–391.

Bronfenbrenner, U. Socialization and social class through time and space. In E. E. Maccoby, T. M. Newcomb, & E. L. Hartley (Eds.), *Readings in social psychology.* New York: Holt, 1958.

Brook, J. S., Whiteman, M., Peisach, E., & Deutsch, M. Aspiration levels of and for children: Age, sex, race and socioeconomic correlates. *Journal of Genetic Psychology*, 1974, **124**, 3–16.

Carnegie Commission on Higher Education. *Opportunities for women in higher education.* New York: McGraw-Hill, 1973.

Cloward, R. A., & Jones, J. Social class: Educational attitudes and participation. In A. H. Passow (Ed.), *Education in depressed areas.* New York: Teachers College, Columbia University, 1963.

Coleman, J. S. *The adolescent society.* New York: Free Press, 1961.

De Cecco, J. P., & Richards, A. K. *Growing pains: Uses of school conflict.* New York: Aberdeen Press, 1974.

Demos, G. D. Attitudes of student ethnic groups on issues related to education. *California Journal of Educational Research*, 1960, **11**, 204–206.

Erikson, E. H. Identity and the life cycle. *Psychological Issues*, 1959, **1**, 1–171.

Feldman, K. A. Some theoretical approaches to the study of change and stability of college students. *Review of Educational Research*, 1972, **42**, 1–26.

Feldman, K. A., & Newcomb, T. M. *The impact of college on students.* San Francisco: Jossey-Bass, 1969.

Frank, L. K., Harrison, R., Hellersberg, E., Machover, K., & Steiner, M. Personality development in adolescent girls. *Monographs of the Society for Research in Child Development*, 1953, **16**(53).

Freud, A. Adolescence. *Psychoanalytic Study of the Child*, 1958, **13**, 255–278.

Gallup, G., & Hill, E. Youth: The cool generation. *Saturday Evening Post*, December 22–30, 1961, pp. 63–80.

Gilbert, H. H. High school students' opinions on reasons for failure in high-school subjects. *Journal of Educational Research*, 1931, **23**, 46–49.

Goodman, N.; & Feldman, K. A. Expectations, ideals and reality: Youth enters college. In S. E. Dragastin & G. H. Elder, Jr. (Eds.), *Adolescence in the life cycle: Psychological change and social context.* Washington, D.C.: Hemisphere Publishing Corporation, 1975.

Groobman, D. E., Forward, J. R., & Peterson, C. Attitudes, self-esteem, and learning in formal and informal schools. *Journal of Educational Psychology*, 1976, **68**, 32–35.

Hackman, J. R., & Dysinger, W. S. Commitment to college as a factor in student attrition. *Sociology of Education*, 1970, **43**, 311–324.

Havighurst, R. J., Graham, R. A., & Eberly, D. American youth in the mid-seventies. *The Bulletin of the National Association of Secondary School Principals*, 1972, **56**, 1–13.

Helfant, K. The teaching of psychology in high schools: A review of the literature. *School Review*, 1952, **60**, 467–473.

Hoffman, L. W. Fear of success in males and females: 1965 and 1971. *Journal of Consulting and Clinical Psychology*, 1974, **42**, 353–358.

Horner, M. S. Femininity and successful achievement: A basic inconsistency. In J. Bardwick, E. M. Douvan, M. S. Horner, & D. Gutmann (Eds.), *Feminine personality and conflict.* Belmont, Calif.: Brooks/Cole, 1970.

Jacob, P. E. *Changing values in college: An exploratory study of the impact of college teaching.* New York: Harper, 1957.

Jersild, A. T. Characteristics of teachers who are "liked best" and "disliked most." *Journal of Experimental Education*, 1940, **9**(2), 139–151.

Jersild, A. T. *In search of self.* New York: Bureau of Publications, Teachers College, Columbia University, 1952.

Jersild, A. T. *When teachers face themselves.* New York: Bureau of Publications, Teachers College, Columbia University, 1955.

Jersild, A. T., & Helfant, K. *Education for self-understanding.* New York: Bureau of Publications, Teachers College, Columbia University, 1953.

Jersild, A. T., Lazar, E., & Brodkin, A. *The meaning of psychotherapy in the teacher's life and work.* New York: Bureau of Publications, Teachers College, Columbia University, 1962.

Jersild, A. T., & Tasch, R. J. *Children's interests.* New York: Bureau of Publications, Teachers College, Columbia University, 1949.

Jervis, F. M., & Congdon, R. G. Student and faculty perceptions of educational values. *American Psychologist*, 1958, **13**, 464–466.

Johnson, A. H. The responses of high school seniors to a set of structured situations concerning teaching as a career. *Journal of Experimental Education*, 1958, **26**, 263–314.

Kandel, D. B., & Lesser, G. S. Parental and peer influences on educational plans of adolescents. *American Sociological Review*, 1969, **34**, 213–223.

Karmel, B. Education and employment aspirations of students: A probabilistic approach. *Journal of Educational Psychology*, 1975, **67**, 57–63.

Kennedy, W. R. Grades expected and grades received—their relation to students' evaluations of faculty performance. *Journal of Educational Psychology*, 1975, **67**, 109–115.

Kniveton, B. G. An investigation of the attitudes of adolescents to aspects of their schooling. *British Journal of Educational Psychology*, 1969, **39**, 78–81.

Kubie, L. S. The forgotten man of education. *The Goddard Bulletin*, 1954, **19**(2).a.

Kubie, L. S. Some unresolved problems of the scientific career. *American Scientist*, 1954, **42**, 104–112.b.

Levin, H. M., Guthrie, J. W. Kleindorfer, G. B., & Stout, R. T. School achievement and post-school success: A review. *Review of Educational Research*, 1971, **41**, 1–16.

Lukoff, I. F., & Brook, J. S. Unpublished data, 1976.

Maccoby, E. E., & Jacklin, C. N. *The psychology of sex differences*. Stanford, Calif.: Stanford U.P., 1974.

Mead, M. *Male and female.*. New York: Dell, 1968.

Morgan, L. B., & Wicas, E. A. The short, unhappy life of student dissent. *Personnel and Guidance Journal*, 1972, **51**, 33–38.

Ojemann, R. H. Investigations on the effects of teaching and understanding behavior dynamics. In G. Caplan (Ed.), *Prevention of mental disorders in children*. New York: Basic Books, 1961.

Panos, R. J., & Astin, A. W. Attrition among college students. *American Educational Research Journal*, 1968, **5**, 57–72.

Perry, R. P., Niemi, R. R., & Jones, K. Effect of prior teaching evaluations and lecture presentation on ratings of teaching performance. *Journal of Educational Psychology*, 1974, **66**, 851–856.

Perry, W. G., Jr. *Forms of intellectual and ethical development in the college years: A scheme*. New York: Holt, 1970.

Porter, R. M. Student attitudes toward child behavior problems. *Journal of Educational Research*, 1959, **52**, 349–352.

President's Science Advisory Commission, Panel on Youth. *Youth: Transition to adulthood*. Washington, D.C.: Office of Science and Technology, 1973.

Remmers, H. H., & Radler, D. H. *The American teenager*. Washington, D.C.: Bobbs, 1957.

Reynolds, N. B. Job ranking on an ethics scale. *Educational Record*, 1958, **39**, 192–193.

Sanford, N. "The uncertain senior." *Journal of the National Association of Women Deans and Counselors*, 1957, **21**, 9–15.

Sanford, N. The professor looks at the student. In R. M. Cooper (Ed.), *The two ends of the log*. Minneapolis: University of Minnesota Press, 1958.

Sanford, N. Education for individual development. *American Journal of Orthopsychiatry*, 1968, **38**, 858–868.

Sewell, W. H., & Shah, V. P. Socioeconomic status, intelligence, and the attainment of higher education. *Sociology of Education*, 1967, **40**, 1–23.

Shuttleworth, F. K. The adolescent period. *Monographs of the Society for Research in Child Development*, 1938, **3**(3).

Simmons, R., Rosenberg, F., & Rosenberg, M. Disturbance in the self-image at adolescence. *American Sociological Review*, 1973, **38**, 553–568.

Slocum, W. L. Educational planning by high school seniors. *Journal of Educational Research*, 1958, **51**, 583–590.

Stanfiel, J. D., & Watts, F. P. Freshman expectations and perceptions of the Howard University environment. *Journal of Negro Education*, 1970, **39**, 132–138.

Stern, G. G. *People in context: Measuring person-environment congruence in education and industry.* New York: Wiley, 1970.

Taube, I., & Vreeland, R. The prediction of ego functioning in college. *Archives of General Psychiatry*, 1972, **27**, 224–229.

Trent, J. W., & Medsker, L. L. *Beyond high school: A psychological study of 10,000 high school graduates.* San Francisco: Jossey-Bass, 1968.

Wegner, E. L., & Sewell, W. H. Selection and context as factors affecting the probability of graduation from college. *American Journal of Sociology*, 1970, **75**, 665–679.

Williams, V., The college dropout: Qualities of his environment. *Personnel and Guidance Journal*, 1967, **45**, 878–882.

Winchel, R., Fenner, D., & Shaver, P. Impact of coeducation on "fear of success" imagery expressed by male and female high school students. *Journal of Educational Psychology*, 1974, **66**, 726–730.

Wylie, R., & Hutchins, E. Schoolwork ability estimates and aspirations as a function of socioeconomic level, race and sex. *Psychological Reports*, 1967, **21**, 781–808.

Yamamoto, K., Thomas, C., & Karns, E. A. School related attitudes in middle-school age subjects. *American Educational Research Journal*, 1969, **6**, 191–206.

Young, A. M. The high school class of 1972: More at work, fewer in college. *Monthly Labor Review*, 1973, **96**, 26–32.

18

vocational development

by Mary Sue Richardson[1]

What are you going to be when you grow up? What are you going to do when you are out of school? These questions, familiar to most young people throughout their school years, become more critical during adolescence as youths approach major life decisions with respect to further educational and occupational plans. In the context of adolescence as the stage of life in which

[1] Mary Sue Richardson, Ph.D., is an associate professor in the Department of Counselor Education, New York University, New York City.

507

Work that is interesting and that offers self-expression and fulfillment is preferred by youth of today. [Burk Uzzle/Magnum.]

individuals are expected to establish a sense of identity (Erikson, 1968), these questions and decisions related to work can be viewed as major concerns around which young people establish a view of themselves in relation to adult societal roles (Douvan and Adelson, 1966). Young people struggling to decide on their future occupations and careers are, in a sense, engaged in the process of defining themselves as adults in the world.

Decisions about work are not only central to one's awareness of emerging identity in adolescence, but also continue to have a significant impact in adulthood. The degree to which adults are able to adjust to and are satisfied with their work is related to their overall adjustment and satisfaction in life (Crites, 1969).[2] Moreover, occupation is a significant determinant of an individual's social status and exerts a major influence on our way of life, on our values, and on our attitudes (Caplow, 1954). The work we do enables us to meet important human needs for economic survival and provides an arena in which we can develop self-esteem and personal fulfillment.

Although some might question the continued existence of the work ethic in the United States, several studies suggest that this ethic has not disappeared but has undergone some important transformations. Based on

[2] Some references cited in this chapter pertain to specific research studies, some to reviews of literature in a certain area, and some to a combination of both.

an examination of trends in the attitudes of young people between the ages of sixteen and twenty-five, sampled yearly from 1967 to 1973, Yankelovich (1974) concluded that youth from all socioeconomic levels, both males and females, have rejected the notion that work in itself is an important and meaningful activity. In place of the value attached to steady and secure work, the trends indicate that increasing numbers of youth are interested in and committed to work that they find personally rewarding and that offers opportunities for self-expression and fulfillment. Although there is some dispute about the degree to which the current occupational structure is able to meet these expressed needs (Special Task Force, Health, Education, and Welfare, 1973; Warnath, 1975), it is clear that young people today seek work that is interesting and in which they will be able to use and develop their special talents.

Looking more closely at the transition from child, adolescent, and student to adult worker, it is apparent that the choice process in our society is complex. Although there are literally thousands of occupations from which to choose, most young people have direct contact with an extremely limited number of these occupations. The complexity of the process is further magnified by the increase in the length of time most young people remain in school, divorced from contact with productive societal roles and embedded in an adolescent youth culture (Coleman, 1974). Nevertheless, most adolescents and young adults eventually manage to make decisions about their future and to express and implement choices about their expected and preferred occupations. Vocational psychology is a field that has attempted to explore and understand this important aspect of development (Crites, 1969). As a developmental sequence, choice processes are the major concern up to and including adolescence and young adulthood. In later stages of life, attention shifts to the adjustment of adult workers to their choices. Although this simple dichotomy is not entirely accurate with respect to later stages of life, as will be indicated later in this chapter, the predominant emphasis in this chapter will be theory and research related to vocational choice processes during adolescence and young adulthood. The term *occupation* refers to a specific set of related jobs and positions in the occupational structure. A career, on the other hand, incorporates the idea that there is continuity in vocational development. In traditional terms the sequence of jobs or positions pursued by an individual over time is defined as that person's career.

Social system variables

Although psychologists in general typically focus on "person," or personality variables, in their efforts to explain human behavior, it is important to place this person-centered approach in the context of what is known about the influence of major social-system or "extrapersonal" variables (see, for example, Crites, 1969; Osipow, 1973). Vocational behavior is one sphere of human functioning in which it is particularly critical to take into account the complex interaction of social structure and human personality. Occupations comprise a significant component of the overall social structure in our society. As such, certain variables associated with this social structure exert a significant and systematic influence on the vocational behaviors of individuals in the society. Some understanding of the nature of this influence will provide a framework for learning about the psychological processes associated with career development. In the following section the effects of socioeconomic status and minority-group membership on vocational development will be examined.

Socioeconomic Status and the Family

Although there are numerous ways to classify occupations, socioeconomic status is frequently used to rank occupations and is viewed as an index of social class. The socioeconomic status of occupations generally refers to some combination of the level of education required for occupational entry, amount of income typically earned by individuals in the occupation, and the degree of prestige associated with that occupation. A classic study by Hollingshead (1949) of "Elmstown's Youth" demonstrated that the occupational aspirations of youth in Elmstown were closely tied to the social class of their families. Since that time, numerous studies have found similar relationships.

Caplow (1954) proposed that societies can be viewed on a continuum from those in which occupational choices are totally limited by family background to those in which merit or talent alone determines an individual's occupational level. A study by Empey (1956) suggests that American society falls somewhere in the middle of this continuum. He examined the socioeconomic level of the occupational aspirations of adolescent boys in terms of both the absolute level of their choices and in relation to their fathers' occupational level. He found that boys from higher socioeconomic levels aspired to higher-level occupations than did boys from less advantaged backgrounds, a finding similar to the Hollingshead research. However, when boys' aspirations were compared to fathers' occupational level, a greater relative distance between these measures existed for the lower-class than for the higher-class boys, indicating that although social class has a significant impact on occupational choice, the influence is exerted within the context of general upward mobility in American society.

Most of the research cited here is limited to the effects of socioeconomic status on boys' occupational aspirations. The results differ when socioeconomic status of parents is related to girls' choices. In a number of studies that have looked at this relationship, parental socioeconomic status was essentially unrelated to girls' choices (see, for example, Goodale and Hall, 1976).

How is it that socioeconomic status affects the aspirations and plans of young boys? Havighurst (1964) suggested that the critical intervening variables are the influence of parental values and attitudes, the peer group with which the young person associates, the types of adult role models available, and differential rewards for academic achievement among diverse social classes. A number of studies provide data to support the view that parental values and attitudes are significant determinants of the educational and occupational plans of children. For example, Goodale and Hall (1976) indicate that in the case of boys links exist between parental socioeconomic background, the kinds of encouragement and hopes parents express for their children, the children's plans, and the children's subsequent occupational choices.

Minority Status

Relatively little attention has been given to the effect of minority-group membership on vocational development. Most of the available research has concentrated on the vocational development of blacks, much of which has not separated the influence of race from socioeconomic background (Crites, 1969; Smith, 1975). Although several studies suggested that black adolescents have unrealistic occupational aspirations, research by Thomas (1976) indicates that when lower-class black students are compared to white students from the same social class, no differences exist in the level of occupational aspirations. Moreover, if actual choice rather than preference is considered, neither group appears to be particularly unrealistic.

However, when we turn to the kinds of occupations chosen, there do appear to be well-substantiated differences between black and white college students. Black students, in general, express more interest in college majors and occupations in the social sciences, education, business, and health fields when compared to nonblack students, a greater number of whom choose physical and biological sciences, and engineering (see, for example, Boyer, 1972). The extent to which these interest patterns of black students are affected by their perception of patterns of occupational discrimination is unknown.

That racial discrimination does have a serious negative impact on the vocational development of black adolescents from poverty backgrounds is supported by the research on the identity formation process in poor black and white adolescents. Hauser (1971) found that young black adolescents experienced a greater incidence of negative self-images and a more static kind of identity development than a comparable group of white adolescents. It appeared that these young people were more likely to feel defeated before they got started and did not evidence the kind of progressive growth in identity found in the white sample. The characteristics found among young blacks can be expected to impede seriously the processes of occupational choice and selection. In contrast, minority-group membership seems to have an opposite effect on blacks from advantaged backgrounds. Rosen (1959) found that whereas disadvantaged blacks retreated from competition, black adolescents from higher social-class backgrounds expressed high-level occupational choices.

Psychological perspectives on vocational choice

Psychological approaches to the study of vocational-choice behaviors can be roughly categorized into two major groups according to the way in which vocational choice is conceptualized (Beilin, 1955). The first, and earliest, approach conceives of choice as essentially an event that occurs at one point in time (this approach has also been called a trait-and-factor approach). The major emphasis of theory and research derived from this approach is to attempt to explain the kinds of choices made on the basis of selected psychological factors. The second, and more recent, approach views choice as a process that occurs over time. Basic to this view is the idea that vocational choice follows a developmental pattern in which there is greater emphasis on processes related to choice than on the actual choice itself. In this section theory and research corresponding to both approaches will be examined.

Vocational choice as an event

The development of differential psychology (that is, the study of the ways in which individuals systematically differ from one another on a variety of psychological measures) in the earlier part of this century provided the main impetus for studies of vocational choice as an event in time. As it became clear that people differ in ability, interest, and personality characteristics, it was also apparent that occupations differ in the characteristics required for successful and satisfied work performance. The basic assumption underlying the "choice-as-event" approach is that people attempt to match their personal characteristics with those required by occupations in making vocational decisions. Although early proponents in the field assumed that there was a perfect match between an individual and an occupation, evidence began to accumulate that within each occupation there was sufficient leeway to enable a variety of different kinds of people to be successful. In fact, Crites (1969) has suggested that with the single exception of general aptitude, occupations are more similar than different in the characteristics shared by the people employed in them. Nevertheless, a review of the literature indicates that ability, interests, and personality variables are related to the kinds of choices people make (Crites, 1969; Osipow, 1973).

ABILITY

Occupations can be ranked roughly according to level of intelligence or amount of education required for occupational entry. Several studies have shown that general intelligence is significantly related to level of choice (Stubbins, 1950), and to kind of occupation chosen (Perrone, 1964), with more intelligent students choosing higher-level and non-person-oriented fields like science and the less intelligent tending to choose social service and business fields, which require less extensive educational preparation.

INTERESTS

In discussions of interests it is important to distinguish between what can be called inventoried interests and expressed interests. A number of tests have been developed that measure persons' interests by examination of their patterns of likes and dislikes across a variety of activities. Tests such as the Strong Vocational Interest Blank, the Kuder Preference Record, and the Vocational Preference Inventory provide profiles of inventoried interests. Another more straightforward way to assess interests is simply to ask people in which field they are interested. Questions tapping tentative occupational choices and preferences can be referred to as expressed interests. Studies have demonstrated that significant relations exist between inventoried and expressed interests (Gottfredson and Holland, 1975), but that expressed interests are more predictive of actual occupational entry than are inventoried interests (Gade and Soliah, 1975).

PERSONALITY

Other studies on the correlates of occupational choice have attempted to discover personality factors differentiating people who choose diverse occupations, several of which are derived from psychoanalytic personality theory. Bordin et al. (1963) developed a theoretical framework for understanding personality differences in occupational choice based on the extent to which occupations differ in opportunities for impulse gratification, the defense mechanisms typically employed by members of an occupation, and the characteristic ways people in an occupation manage their anxiety.

Segal (1961), in a study that compared creative writing and accounting students, found support for his hypotheses that accountants would be characterized by conforming personality characteristics and defensive styles such as isolation and intellectualization. In contrast, creative writers were found to be rebellious individuals who typically utilized defense mechanisms of projection and denial. These personality characteristics were linked to differences in early childhood experiences.

Whereas a number of other studies of personality as related to occupational choice have postulated the importance of early childhood experiences, Roe (1956) is credited with the most extensive theoretical formulation. It attempts to explain subsequent occupational choice based on early patterns of child rearing. Roe distinguished among three different kinds of parental child-rearing practices and familial interpersonal relationships and postulated that these early interpersonal atmospheres would affect personality and differentially relate to later choice of person- versus nonperson-oriented occupations. Although her theory has generated considerable research over the past twenty years, empirical support for the theory is weak. Although this may be due in large part to methodological flaws in the research designs used, it is also true that it is difficult to establish strong relationships between early childhood experiences and adolescent or adult choices, in view of the number of years that elapse between these stages of life and the variety of intervening events that can occur (Luckey, 1974, reviews research relating familial variables to vocational development).

Finally, investigators have examined a wide variety of other personality variables in relation to occupational choice. These include values, needs, risk-taking tendencies, achievement motivation, personality styles, and cognitive styles.

Holland's Theory of Vocational Choice

Up to this point a number of variables related to vocational choice have been presented. Holland (1966, 1973) has elaborated a more comprehensive theoretical model that falls in the tradition of viewing vocational choice as an event in time. He has proposed that there are six basic personality types and six corresponding occupational environments. Each personality type encompasses a broad range of personality characteristics and preferred styles of behavior and activities. For example, the person who is a social type has a high level of verbal and interpersonal skills. He or she enjoys the company of others and tends to relate to others in a helpful and cooperative way. Such a person prefers to work in occupations that provide a high level of social interaction.[3] According to his theory, people of similar types tend to cluster in certain occupations, thereby affecting the nature of the occupational environment so that it is comfortable and rewarding to them.

Although the types were conceived originally as independent from one another, research based on the theory indicated that some types are more similar psychologically than others. In the latest formulation of the theory, Holland (1973) provides a model to indicate degree of similarity among types. Any one person can be characterized by a mixture of different types that are more or less compatible with one another.

Holland postulates that two mechanisms are involved in the process of occupational choice. First, persons choose occupational fields that they perceive as similar to their predominant type. Second, the choice of level within the field is based on the combined influence of actual intelligence and a person's own self-evaluation of his or her ability.

Holland's theory has generated a great deal of research and substantial support has been found for many of his theoretical propositions. It can be criticized, however, on a number of grounds. The theory provides little explanation of the development of types in the first place and does not account for ways in which change might occur over time. As such, it is a relatively static theory. For a more dynamic theory of choice, it is necessary to turn to developmental theories of choice.

Vocational choice as a process

Although for most young people it may appear that the actual choice of an occupation is the critical point in vocational development, it has become clear that the process of vocational development extends over time and that important developmental changes occur prior to and subsequent to choice. In fact, the choices that are made undergo systematic changes according to the individual's stage of development. The notion of developmental stages is a pivotal one in vocational developmental theories, as it is in a variety of other developmental theories (Freud, Erikson, and Piaget, for example). It implies that at a particular stage of development, there are specific developmental tasks to be accomplished. The degree to which

[3] The other five types in Holland's system are the investigative, realistic, conforming, artistic, and enterprising. For further elaboration of this system and a review of supporting research, see Holland (1973) and Osipow (1973).

persons accomplish these tasks will affect the quality of their adaptation at that stage, as well as at subsequent stages. The conceptualization of stages and related tasks in vocational theories is based on attempts to understand that aspect of development most relevant to a person's vocational and occupational life (Beilin, 1955; Jordaan, 1974a). In the following section of this chapter, theory and research dealing with two major developmental theories will be briefly presented.[4]

Ginzberg, Ginsburg, Axelrad, and Herma Theory

Ginzberg et al. (1951) proposed a theoretical model of vocational development that incorporates aspects of basic personality development within the context of an orderly sequence of vocational developmental stages. The developmental stages postulated by Ginzberg et al. (1951) are the *fantasy stage,* which ends approximately at the age of eleven; a *tentative stage,* between the ages of eleven and eighteen; and, subsequently, the *realistic stage,* from eighteen into the early twenties.

In the fantasy stage, the child's choices are essentially unrealistic. What is important in this stage is that a child should shift from an early play orientation to a work orientation. In their attempts to cope with the frustration of their dependency, children emulate adult role models in a variety of occupations, without regard for their own talents and interests and with little attention to reality considerations. It is in this stage that children are most likely to pretend to be presidents, cowboys, astronauts, and movie stars—adult occupations that attract them due to their power, prestige, and glamour.

During the tentative stage, adolescents gradually become aware of their own abilities, interests, and values and develop a more realistic view, both of themselves and of the world of work. Moreover, they become aware of the need to make an occupational choice as they become increasingly independent of their families.

Finally, the adolescent enters the realistic stage of development in which he or she is expected to explore the variety of occupational alternatives, to begin to crystallize a choice, and, finally, to specify it in terms of a particular field and a specialized occupation within that field.

According to Ginzberg et al. (1951), maturation of the critical ego processes underlies and accompanies this stage-specific progression. The

---

[4] See also Hershenson (1968) and Tiedeman and O'Hara (1963) for accounts of other developmental theories.

ego processes considered critical in vocational development are reality testing, ability to delay gratification, development of an appropriate time perspective, and the ability to make compromises. These processes, related to emotional stability, mature over time and affect the adequacy of the vocational developmental process. Those individuals who, for any number of reasons, show delay of or defective ego development are likely to have difficulty with the tasks associated with the developmental stages.

A number of research studies have found general support for the stages of development as outlined by Ginzberg et al. and for the sequence in which these stages occur (see, for example, Montesano and Geist, 1964). Davis et al. (1962) suggest that the timing of the stages may be more variable than Ginzberg and his associates originally proposed. Additionally, research by Gesell et al. (1956) on young people between the ages of ten and sixteen indicates a lack of continuity in the developmental choice processes, with some adolescents moving from early decision to no decision at a later point in time—a finding that contradicts the continuity suggested by Ginzberg's theory.

In addition to research on the stages of development in Ginzberg's theory, several studies have examined characteristics of the choice process relevant to the hypothesized ego development underlying vocational development. For example, Hollander (1967) found that students' occupational choices became more realistic with increasing age, a finding that supports the maturation of reality-testing ability. In a classic study by Small (1953), the degree to which the first and second occupational choices of two groups of adolescent boys, a well-adjusted and poorly adjusted group, were realistic was examined. He found that the first choice of the well-adjusted group was more realistic than their second choice, but that the opposite was true for the poorly adjusted group. If adjustment is viewed as an indicator of the general maturational level of ego development, this finding supports Ginzberg's theory that ego strength will be associated with more realistic choices. Interestingly, when he examined his data by age, he did not find that reality of choices increased over time.

In a recent statement, Ginzberg (1972) has modified some aspects of his theory. Originally, he had proposed that decisions are essentially irreversible and represent a compromise for the individual between his or her needs and aspirations and what is realistically available. Ginzberg now recognizes that vocational development occurs over the life span—rather than being restricted to childhood and adolescence—and that the decisions made then are not irreversible. People can change directions any number of times, and their decisions represent their attempts to look for the best possible fit between themselves and the world of work, a process he now labels as optimization rather than compromise.

Super's Self-concept Theory of Vocational Development

Super (1957; Super et al., 1963), is generally recognized as responsible for the most highly developed and sophisticated developmental theory related to occupational choice (Osipow, 1973). Similar to Ginzberg's, his theory comprises a dynamic aspect of personality development viewed in progression through a series of developmental stages. Whereas Ginzberg focuses on ego development, Super highlights the importance of the development of a person's self-concept—that is, the ways in which persons view themselves. As a result of childhood experiences, persons develop a view of themselves that they then test out in a variety of role-playing experiences as they progress through childhood and adolescence. As the self-concept becomes more highly differentiated, a specific aspect of that self-concept, the vocational self-concept, becomes critical in adolescent choice processes. The vocational self-concept can be defined as a person's view of himself or herself in relation to the world of work. In making occupational choices, people attempt to implement their self-concept—that is, to choose occupations that they perceive as congruent with their pictures of themselves.

Research in general has supported this aspect of the theory. Oppenheimer (1966) found that the occupational preference hierarchy of male college students was positively related to the degree of congruence between their self- and occupational concepts. The more similarity there was between their self-concept and occupational preference, the more likely they were to place that occupation high on their list of preferences. In a study of adult nurses, Brophy (1959) found that similarity of self- and occupational concepts was positively related to level of vocational satisfaction.

Additional research has indicated that persons are more likely to implement their self-concepts in their occupational choices if they also possess a high level of self-esteem (Korman, 1969).

The stages of development as outlined by Super are roughly similar to Ginzberg's, with the exception that Super's model covers the entire life span. Associated with each stage are specific developmental tasks. (See Jordan, 1974, for a description of stages and related developmental tasks.) In the *growth* stage, childhood and early adolescence, the critical tasks for the child are to develop a concept of him- or herself and an orientation to the world of work. In the *exploratory* stage, which begins in early adolescence and ends in early adulthood, the young person moves from tentative choices to an early trial period, in which he or she attempts to implement choices with, as yet, relatively little commitment to these choices. The critical tasks during this stage are to crystallize a choice, further specify it in terms of selected occupations, and begin to implement the choice. As the name of this stage implies, it is hypothesized that exploratory behavior (that is, exploration of self and exploration of occupations) facilitates accomplishment of these developmental tasks. During the *establishment* stage, early adulthood to middle age, the person begins to settle down, his or her choices become stabilized, and he or she works to advance in the chosen occupation. From middle age until retirement, the *maintenance* stage, individuals are primarily concerned with preserving the gains they have achieved and with preparing for retirement. The *decline* stage, following retirement, is associated with a general slowing down and disengagement from the world of work.

A longitudinal study of adolescent boys (Career Pattern Study) was initiated by Super and his associates to test out aspects of this theoretical model. At this point research reports are available up to and including age twenty-five.

VOCATIONAL MATURITY

A major focus in the research based on Super's theory has been the construct of vocational maturity. Vocational maturity is defined as how well a person is progressing along a vocational developmental path when compared with his or her peer group (Super, 1974). Vocational maturity is viewed essentially as a set of coping behaviors that are important in order to accomplish developmental tasks. As such, persons with a high level of vocational maturity at one stage of development theoretically are expected to cope more adequately with developmental tasks—and, consequently, be more successful at that stage and at subsequent stages.

According to Super's (1974) model, a model only partially based on empirical data, critical dimensions of vocational maturity in high school (the exploratory stage) are a sense of planfulness about one's life, exploration of the world of work, amount of information about self and occupation acquired, ability to make decisions, and a reality orientation.[5] Research on the exploratory and establishment stages provides data on the kinds of behaviors expected at these stages and gives some support to the construct of vocational maturity.

Exploratory stage. Although it appears that crystallization of choice does occur in adolescence (see, for example, Madaus and O'Hara, 1967), studies indicate that the processes of crystallization and specification are far from complete for many young people by the twelfth grade. Using stability of choice (for example, the extent to which choices do not change) as an index of choice crystallization,[6] Flanagan and Cooley (1966) found a high level of unstable choices in a sample of highly talented young people. Only 31.4 per

[5] See Gribbons and Lohnes (1968), and Super (1974) for other models of vocational maturity.
[6] See Crites (1969) for a discussion of methodological problems in procedures used to determine choice stability.

cent of the research participants in their longitudinal study expressed stable choices in the twelfth grade. Furthermore, results of two other longitudinal studies, the Career Pattern Study (Jordaan and Heyde, in press) and the Career Development Study (Gibbons and Lohnes, 1968), indicate that many seemingly stable choices at this stage are also unrealistic, a finding that casts doubt on the long-term stability of the choice. In both of these studies, however, some measures of vocational maturity were signicantly related to developmental progress.

Based on examination of the career development of adolescents through the high school period, Gribbons and Lohnes (1968) were able to categorize their research participants according to four different developmental paths. Some adolescents seemed to have selected their occupational goals at an early stage and to have persistently pursued these goals—a pattern labeled *constant maturity*. The *emerging-maturity* group included those who most closely resembled Super's model of progression from lack of choice to increasing crystallization and specification of choice. Other adolescents seemed to pursue a path of *degeneration*, in which early aspirations and achievements deteriorated over time. Finally, the fourth group, *constant immaturity*, included those who were persistent in their pursuit of extremely unrealistic and fantasylike occupational goals.

Establishment stage. Although complete data from longitudinal studies on the establishment stage are not yet available, the Career Pattern Study and the Career Development Study have followed research participants up to the age of twenty-five. At this stage, in which individuals theoretically should be settling down and establishing themselves in an occupation, the Career Pattern Study (Super et al., 1967) indicates that approximately half of the sample had been pursuing stable goals since leaving high school, and that, by age twenty-five, fully 80 per cent of the sample could be characterized as stabilized. A significant number of the participants in the study had spent some of their time between eighteen and twenty-five floundering in their career development—that is, changing career directions and moving from job to job, with little sense of goal directionality. Even at age twenty-five, some continued to flounder.

In contrast to the Career Pattern Study, Gribbons and Lohnes (1969) found that only one half to two thirds of their sample were well stabilized by age twenty-five, a finding that may be due in part to the fact that their study included girls, many of whom had quit working to pursue marriage and family goals between the ages of eighteen and twenty-five.

In both studies some measures of vocational maturity in high school were positively related to career progress at this later stage of development, a finding that provides partial support for the construct of vocational maturity. In particular, measures of exploratory behavior in adolescence seemed to be the best predictors of future development (Jordaan, 1974a).

SUMMARY

Research suggests that the concept of vocational maturity is promising as a means of assessing the developmental progress of young people. Clearly needed are models of vocational maturity for stages of development other than adolescence and further empirical support for existing models. Moreover, LoCascio (1974) and Richardson (1974) have suggested that alternate models of vocational maturity may need to be developed for women, minority groups, and individuals from lower social classes for whom developmental tasks and related coping behaviors may differ from those explicated in current models.

Based on what is now known about vocational maturity, it is clear that young people should not be expected to make final occupational choices in early or middle adolescence. In this age group it is more critical that they engage in a wide range of exploratory behaviors—testing out their knowledge of themselves and gaining knowledge of occupations—and activities, such as part-time jobs, volunteer efforts, and a variety of courses of study. One intriguing finding from the Career Development Study (Gribbons and Lohnes, 1969) was that individuals who changed directions in their choices during and after high school were more vocationally mature than individuals who did not change. One can speculate that in a complex and variable social order such as American society, it may be more important to be able to modify one's decisions in light of changes in self and changes in opportunities available, rather than to persistently pursue a choice crystallized early. Moreover, it indicates that not only is occupational choice a process that occurs over time, but also that the choice itself is likely to change over time.

Female career development

Most theory and research in vocational psychology have focused predominantly on men. Because much of what has been written about vocational development assumes that work occupies psychological centrality in people's lives, it is questionable whether available theories are applicable to and relevant for understanding the vocational development process in women (Osipow, 1973; Zytowski, 1969). Bailyn (1965) has remarked that whereas most men can assume that they will spend the majority of their adult years working in some occupation or job and that, consequently, important vocational decisions relate to the kind of work they will do, women have a more basic choice to make regarding the importance of work itself in their lives. In recent years a substantial body of research has developed that addresses itself to specific aspects of women's career development. Although the emphasis in much of this research has been on discriminatory practices against women in occupations, the focus in this section will be on the psychological factors related to female career development.[7]

Facts about Women, Work, and Changing Aspirations

The most thorough and up-to-date picture of women's employment is based on government statistics (U.S. Department of Labor, 1975). Since 1950 the number of women in the labor force has doubled, with women now representing 39 per cent of all employed people in the United States. This increase in labor force participation has been due primarily to the increase in the number of older married women who have returned to work following a period of time spent at home with families. More recently, there has been a sharp increase in the rate of participation of young married women with small children.

Despite the greater numbers of women working, both married and single, at all points in the life cycle, the majority continue to be employed in the relatively few, stereotypically feminine occupations—secretary, waitress, elementary school teacher, and registered nurse. More women are employed in clerical jobs than in any other category, and, at the professional level, most women are found in teaching occupations. Emerging trends suggest that this concentration is decreasing, as women begin to move into predominantly masculine fields, such as the skilled trades and the professions of law and medicine.

It is apparent from these statistics that women no longer spend the major part of their adult lives with home and family responsibilities, and that work and occupations constitute a significant component of their life cycle (Van Dusen and Sheldon, 1976). Nevertheless, issues related to women's traditional sex roles, marriage and family, and differences in the sex-role socialization process for men and women have a significant impact on female career development.

Similar to changes that have occurred in the actual work participation of women are changes in young women's aspirations for their future roles. Whereas early studies demonstrated that only a minority of young women expressed serious interest in and motivation for the work role, more recent research shows that most college women plan to work—to combine a career with marriage and family responsibilities (Wilson, 1975). The traditional

[7] See Astin et al. (1971), Matthews (1974), and Osipow (1975) for reviews of research related to female career development.

feminine fields, however, continue to be predominant in their occupational choices. It appears that this sex stereotyping of interests begins early (see, for example, Schlossberg and Goodman, 1972) and increases with age (see, for example, Astin and Myint, 1971). In an interesting study by Barnett (1975) of the occupational preferences of adolescent boys and girls between the ages of nine and seventeen, the higher-level prestige occupations were more likely to be preferred by boys and rejected by girls at all age levels, a further indication of sex differences in patterns of choice.

Early studies of female career development categorized young women into two major groups, homemaking-oriented women with little or no interest in careers and career-oriented women interested in and motivated to pursue a future occupation. Further subdivisions were made in the career-oriented group to distinguish between those planning to pursue traditionally feminine occupations and those interested in untraditional, masculine, sex-typed careers. Osipow (1975) has recommended a fourfold typology based on degree of work or career commitment and sex-role stereotyping of occupational choice to classify the major dimensions in female career development. For example, a young women can be highly committed to a traditionally feminine occupation, while another young woman, who expresses a preference for an untraditional, masculine field, may have a lower level of overall career commitment. The distinction between career commitment (also called work-role salience) and traditionality of choice is supported by research demonstrating that these two dimensions are uncorrelated (Richardson et al., 1976).

Identity Development and
Female Adolescence

In a major study of identity formation in adolescence, Douvan and Adelson (1966) discovered that occupational choice was the central issue around which boys' identity development coalesced, whereas for girls, issues related to being appropriately feminine were more important. Others have suggested that occupational achievement becomes salient only after women have accomplished critical developmental tasks associated with intimacy, establishing a stable marriage, and beginning a family (Baruch, 1967). In contrast to these views, Patterson (1973) has proposed that there are two critical identity issues for young women, one related to occupational choice and one related to traditional sex-role issues. Moreover, these two issues are potentially conflicting for many young women. Although young girls may be relatively free from sex-role pressures in childhood, these pressures are accentuated in adolescence when girls become more concerned about their attractiveness to the opposite sex and their future roles as wives and mothers (Bardwick and Douvan, 1971).

Evidence for the existence of conflict between these two identity issues can be found in research on achievement motivation in women and on female perception of male attitudes toward women. Using projective cues to tap achievement motivation patterns, Horner (1972) found that many young women were characterized by a "motive to avoid success" in which high-level achievement was viewed as incompatible with traditional female role expectations.[8] (This topic is also discussed in Chapter 17.) Other studies have found that women frequently perceive men to expect and prefer a lower level of achievement orientation in women than they themselves prefer (Steinmann et al., 1964) and that perception of supportive male attitudes is critical to the choice of high-level careers among women (Hawley, 1971). The importance of male attitudes toward women suggests a source of conflict for many women. One encouraging sign is that college men today view female careers and achievement in a more positive light than has been true in the past (Almquist, 1974). This finding must be viewed with caution in the light of Komarovsky's (1973) research on the attitudes of college men toward female achievement. Beneath superficial endorsement of liberal roles for women she found that many young men from a select eastern college were threatened and anxious in the presence of highly-motivated and potentially successful college women.

Further evidence on the conflict-prone nature of adolescent female career development is provided indirectly by research on the stability of career commitment in young women. In a longitudinal study of college women, Angrist (1972) found that career commitment was highly unstable, with significant numbers of women showing great variation in their motivation to pursue a career role over the college years. This finding supports the view that a variety of other factors impinge on and affect the vocational development of women in adolescence. Additional data on the instability of adolescent female career development are provided by research that has unsuccessfully attempted to predict career patterns of adult women from data avilable in the college years (see, for example, Wolfson, 1976). Postcollege factors were found to be the most potent predictors of female career patterns.

Personality Factors in Female Career Development

Research on personality factors that differentiate career-oriented and homemaking-oriented groups reflects the changing attitudes toward

---

[8] In response to critiques of the motive-to-avoid-success research (Zuckerman and Wheeler, 1975), Horner et al. (1973) have developed a neutral set of cues and an empirically derived scoring system.

women and work (Matthews, 1974). Whereas early studies showed career-oriented women to be deviant and the products of disturbed backgrounds, more recent research has presented career-motivated women in a more favorable light. It has been suggested that the early negative profiles of career-oriented women were affected by sex-role bias in researchers (Helson, 1972). More recent studies have found high-achieving women to be serious, committed, and autonomous individuals, and suggest that women who reject the world of work in favor of traditional roles are less well adjusted, with a limited degree of personal development (Winters and Sorenson, 1975, review research in this area).

Theoretical Views

Although at this point there is no comprehensive theory available adequate to deal with the complexities of female career development, a number of attempts have been made to explain the emergence of a high level of career commitment in women. From a sociological perspective, Almquist and Angrist (1970, 1971) examined whether a high level of career commitment in college women could be better explained as the product of an enriched background (enrichment hypothesis) or as an indication of a deviant and maladjusted developmental process (deviance hypothesis). Their results partially confirmed the enrichment hypothesis, in that career-committed college women were characterized by more diverse kinds of work experiences and were more likely to have been influenced by strong male and female role models than the less career-committed women. The two groups did not differ in their involvement in dating and social relationships.

Zytowski (1969) formulated a series of theoretical propositions about women's career development, one of which stated that motivational factors are critical in affecting career commitment and degree of work participation among women (see Hoffman, 1972, and Stein and Bailey, 1973, for a discussion and review of research on female achievement motivation). Kriger's (1972) research on adult women suggests that women's general career commitment and choice of occupation (level and field) are related to different, though closely associated developmental variables. Results of her study, based, in part, on a modification of Roe's (1956) theory concerning the importance of the interpersonal atmosphere of parents and children, demonstrated that the restrictiveness or permissiveness of parental child-rearing practices was related to level of career commitment and that the kind of occupation chosen was more a function of achievement motivation. Other research has demonstrated that emotionally distant relationships with parents, especially fathers, and identification with the father, facilitate development of achievement motivation and a high level of career commitment in women (Oliver, 1975).

Although the research cited here pinpoints the father as the more important parent influencing career-related motivation of young women, one must take into account the kinds of roles that parents play, particularly mothers. Mothers who work, and are perceived by their daughters as satisfied with their careers, frequently influencc daughters to adopt more liberal attitudes toward women's roles and to place greater emphasis on the role of work in their lives (see Hoffman, 1975, for a comprehensive review of the effect of mother's role on daughters).

Problems in vocational choice and career counseling

Many young people experience problems in their vocational development. Statistics kept by a number of university and college counseling centers indicate that vocational problems are the largest single category of presenting problems among students (Sharp and Marra, 1971). Several attempts have been made to develop classification and diagnostic systems to understand more fully the nature of these problems. Crites (1969) has developed a comprehensive classification scheme based on aptitudes and interests and has also described other classification and diagnostic systems. In his schema the adjustment problem category includes persons whose aptitudes and/or interests are incongruent with expressed occupational preferences. Another category focuses on problems of indecision in which young people may have difficulty expressing a choice due to too many interests, a generalized inability to choose, or a lack of interest in making any kind of choice at all. Problems of lack of realism refer to those people who consistently choose occupations above or below their ability level or who choose occupations in which they have minimal interest.

Although Crites's system encompasses the majority of problem types, it provides little help in understanding the reasons why people experience these different kinds of problems. Bordin and Kapplin (1973) have examined vocational problems from the perspective of the close connection between vocational choice and identity formation in adolescence. Their diagnostic schema, based on degree of personality disturbance, ranges from those individuals with the lowest level of disturbance who simply have difficulty putting together their knowledge of themselves and their knowledge of the occupational world, to seriously disturbed individuals whose vocational problems are merely symptomatic of underlying maladjustment. In between these two extremes are individuals whose vocational problems are related to problems in identity development and those young people more seriously disturbed or dissatisfied with themselves who attempt to change themselves by their vocational choices. It is important to note, however, that a number of studies have shown that seriously disturbed people can make satisfactory vocational adjustments (Nathanson, 1976; Rennie et al., 1950).

In examining the kinds of problems adolescents experience in their vocational development, one must keep in the mind the developmental stage at which the problems occur. A high school student who chooses unrealistic goals discrepant with abilities and interest or one who has problems in making any kind of preliminary vocational decision is, in fact, experiencing expected age- and stage-appropriate problems. The same type of problem experienced by a college senior would be less appropriate for that age and, consequently, would be regarded as a more serious problem. This developmental perspective does not negate, however, the view that, even in normal vocational development, individuals have difficulties that cause them more or less concern and distress. A certain amount of conflict is likely to occur as young people negotiate a difficult transition from student to worker roles and from adolescent to adult status. Research on identity status in adolescence indicates that the experience of conflict is necessary for successful achievement of identity (Marcia, 1975).

Career counseling and vocational guidance are specific professional fields in which counselors are trained to assist young people with the normal problems expected in their vocational development. Morrill and Forrest (1970) have presented four different types of career counseling models. In the first model the focus is on a specific educational or occupational decision facing a young person in which the counselor seeks to help the individual to make the best possible choice. Counselors operating within the framework of this model are likely to employ interest and aptitude tests and occupational-educational information. In the second model more attention is given to the actual decision-making process, recognizing that vocational development is a continuous series of choices in which it may be more important to help young people learn decision-making skills applicable thoughout life than to concentrate on any one particular decision.[9] The developmental process underlying occupational choice is emphasized in the third model. Counselors using this model will focus on factors likely to facilitate the process of vocational development and will, for example, help young people become familiar with resources useful for exploratory purposes and encourage a planning orientation to occupational and educational decisions (Jordaan, 1974b). In the fourth model the emphasis is on helping young people to develop the ability to have control over their future as they move through the series of decisions facing them and to achieve self-related

[9] Due to constraints of space it has not been possible to cover decision-making theories of vocational development. See Jepsen and Dilley (1974) for a review of theories in this area.

objectives in the process of choosing. (Crites, 1974, has proposed another, more historically based conceptualization of career counseling models.)

Although any of these counseling models may be appropriate for young women as well as young men, the special nature of female career development suggests that, in addition, special efforts are required to combat the effects of sex-role stereotypes. Young women are likely to profit from counseling programs that encourage them to explore nontraditional occupations for women, expose them to models of women successfully engaged in a variety of occupations and following diverse career patterns, help them to think through values and attitudes about the role of work in their adult lives, and consider ways and means to cope with role conflicts they may experience in their vocational development. (Matthews et al., 1972; McEwen, 1975; and Schlossberg, 1972, have discussed special issues in counseling women.)

Although, traditionally, efforts to assist young people with their career development have been confined to counselors and guidance personnel, the federal government has taken a major role in recent years to enable entire school systems to become more fully involved in this function. In this movement attempts have been made to implement a number of models that infuse the curriculum with career-relevant materials and engage teachers as well as a variety of support personnel in education for careers (Hoyt et al., 1972; Marland, 1974). Although the success of these federally funded programs in career education is yet to be determined, their very existence attests to the importance placed on career development in current social and educational policy.

New directions

A number of changes are taking place in the theory and research on vocational development that have implications for future understanding of adolescent vocational development. In the first place, models of development with the modal pattern of career choice at some point in adolescence followed by lifelong commitment to that career are somewhat outdated. Although significant numbers of people may still follow such a developmental pattern, many adults are making career changes in mid-life. Certainly, the number of women returning to work after their children are grown is a prime example of such a career change. Even among men, however, there is an increasing incidence of mid-life career change (Brim, 1976; Hiestand, 1971). This phenomenon is due, in part, to the fact of technological change, in which specific skills and certain occupational specialities may become obsolete, forcing those employed in such occupations to change directions. It also can be traced to the increase in longevity of both men and women.

Given a longer and healthier life span, individuals may change over time and find that an earlier occupational choice no longer satisfies them. Viewed from this perspective, specific choices made in adolescence may be less important than the ability to make good decisions. Flexibility and willingness to change may be as critical as the ability to commit oneself to a particular goal.

In addition, a life-span perspective on vocational development has made more apparent the fact that persons' occupations may be more or less central in their lives, depending on their life stage and the nature of their involvement in other life areas. Responding to this, Super (1975) has proposed a new definition of career, not restricted to occupational or work-related roles. He defines career as the "sequence of major positions occupied by persons throughout life; it includes work-related positions and roles as student, employee, and pensioner, together with coordinate avocational, familial, and civic roles [p. 18b]." [10] In the context of this definition, the field of vocational and career development would encompass the complex interaction of developmental processes related to occupational and educational roles as well as processes involved in choosing and implementing other major adult roles, such as spouse, parent, community, and leisure roles. As such, it would facilitate theory development more appropriate for certain groups in society (that is, lower socioeconomic groups and women) for whom occupational roles traditionally have been less central. Regardless of whether this expanded definition is accepted in the field, it is likely that more attention will be paid to the interplay of occupational choice processes in adolescence with related developmental processes. We need to know more about the ways in which work-related decisions in young people are affected by their investment of energy in and commitment to other life areas, such as establishing satisfactory intimate relationships and decisions about the importance of family life.

References

Almquist, E. M. Attitudes of college men toward working wives. *Vocational Guidance Quarterly,* 1974, **23**, 115–121.

Almquist, E., & Angrist, S. S. Career salience and atypicality of occupational choice among college women. *Journal of Marriage and the Family,* 1970, **32**, 242–249.

Almquist, E., & Angrist, S. S. Role model influences on college women's career aspirations. *Merrill-Palmer Quarterly,* 1971, **17**, 263–279.

---

[10] It is important to note that, at this point, controversy exists in the field over the appropriateness of this expanded definition.

Angrist, S. S. Variations in women's adult aspirations during college. *Journal of Marriage and the Family,* 1972, **34**, 465–468.

Astin, H. S., & Myint, T. Career development of young women during the post-high school years. *Journal of Counseling Psychology,* 1971, **18**, 369–383.

Astin, H. S., Suniewick, N., & Dweck, S. *Women: A bibliography on their education and careers.* Washington, D.C.: Human Service Press, 1971.

Bailyn, L. Notes on the role of choice in the psychology of professional women. In R. J. Lifton (Ed.), *The woman in America.* Boston: Houghton, 1965.

Bardwick, J. M., & Douvan, E. Ambivalence: The socialization of women. In V. Gornick & B. K. Moran (Eds.) *Women in Sexist Society.* New York: Basic Books, 1971.

Barnett, R. C. Sex differences and age trends in occupational preference and occupational prestige. *Journal of Counseling Psychology,* 1975, **22**, 35–38.

Baruch, R. The achievement motive in women: Implications for career development. *Journal of Personality and Social Psychology,* 1967, **5**, 260–267.

Beilin, H. The application of general developmental principles to the vocational area. *Journal of Counseling Psychology,* 1955, **2**, 53–57.

Bordin, E. S., & Kapplin, D. A. Motivational conflict and vocational development. *Journal of Counseling Psychology,* 1973, **20**, 154–161.

Bordin, E. S., Nachmann, B., & Segal, S. S. An articulated framework for vocational development. *Journal of Counseling Psychology,* 1963, **10**, 107–117.

Boyer, A. E. *The Black college freshman: Characteristics and recent trends.* American Council of Education Research Reports, Vol. 8, No. 1, Washington, D.C.: ACE, 1972.

Brim, O. G., Jr. Theories of the male mid-life crisis. *The Counseling Psychologist,* 1976, **6**, 2–9.

Brophy, A. L. Self, role, and satisfaction. *Genetic Psychology Monographs,* 1959, **54**, 263–308.

Caplow, T. *The sociology of work.* New York: McGraw-Hill, 1954.

Coleman, J. S. The transition from youth to adult. *New York University Educational Quarterly,* 1974, **V**, 2–5.

Crites, J. O. Career counseling: A review of major approaches. *The Counseling Psychologist,* 1974, **4**, 3–23.a.

Crites, J. O. Career development processes: A model of vocational maturity. In E. L. Herr (Ed.), *Vocational Guidance and human development.* Boston: Houghton, 1974.b.

Davis, D. A., Hogan, N., & Strauf, J. Occupational choice of twelve-year-olds. *Personnel and Guidance Journal,* 1962, **40**, 628–629.

Douvan, E., & Adelson, J. *The adolescent experience.* New York: Wiley, 1966.

Empey, L. T. Social class and occupational aspiration: A comparison of absolute and relative measurement. *American Sociological Review,* 1956, **21**, 703–709.

Erikson, E. *Identity, youth and crisis.* New York: Norton, 1968.

Flanagan, J. C., & Cooley, W. W. *Project Talent: One-year follow-up studies.* Pittsburgh: School of Education, University of Pittsburgh, 1966.

Gade, E. M., & Soliah, D. Vocational Preference Inventory high point codes versus expressed choices as predictors of college major and career entry. *Journal of Counseling Psychology,* 1975, **22**, 117–121.

Gesell, A., Ilg, F. L., & Ames, L. B. *Youth: The years from ten to sixteen.* New York: Harper, 1956.

Ginzberg, E. Toward a theory of occupational choice: A restatement. *Vocational Guidance Quarterly,* 1972, **20**, 169–176.

Ginzberg, E., Ginsburg, S. W., Axelrad, S., & Herma, J. L. *Occupational choice: An approach to a general theory.* New York: Columbia U.P., 1951.

Goodale, J. G., & Hall, D. T. Inheriting a career: The influence of sex, values, and parents. *Journal of Vocational Behavior,* 1976, **8**, 19–30.

Gottfredson, G. D., & Holland, J. L. Vocational choices of men and women: A comparison of predictors from the Self-Directed Search. *Journal of Counseling Psychology,* 1975, **22**, 28–34.

Gribbons, W. D., & Lohnes, P. R. *Career development from age 13 to age 25.* Washington, D.C.: U.S. Department of Health, Education, and Welfare, Office of Education, Bureau of Research, 1969.

Gribbons, W. D., & Lohnes, P. R. *Emerging careers.* New York: Teachers College, Columbia University, 1968.

Hauser, S. T. *Black and white identity formation studies in the psycho-social development of lower socioeconomic class adolescent boys.* New York: Wiley-Interscience, 1971.

Havighurst, R. J. Youth in exploration and man emergent. In Borow, H. (Ed.), *Man in a world at work.* Boston: Houghton, 1964.

Hawley, P. What women think men think: Does it affect their career choice? *Journal of Counseling Psychology,* 1971, **18**, 193–199.

Helson, R. The changing image of the career women. *Journal of Social Issues,* 1972, **28**, 33–46.

Hershenson, D. B. Life stage vocational development system. *Journal of Counseling Psychology,* 1968, **15**, 23–30.

Hiestand, D. *Changing careers after thirty-five.* New York: Columbia U.P., 1971.

Hoffman, L. W. Early childhood experiences and women's achievement motives. *Journal of Social Issues,* 1972, **28**, 129–155.

Hoffman, L. W. Effects on child. In L. W. Hoffman & F. I. Nye (Eds.), *Working Mothers.* San Francisco: Jossey-Bass, 1975.

Holland, J. L. *The psychology of vocational choice.* New York: Wiley, 1966.

Holland, J. L. *Making vocational choices: A theory of careers.* Englewood Cliffs, N.J.: Prentice-Hall, 1973.

Hollander, J. Development of a realistic vocational choice. *Journal of Counseling Psychology,* 1967, **14**, 314–318.

Hollingshead, A. B. *Elmtown's youth.* New York: Wiley, 1949.

Horner, M. S. Toward an understanding of achievement-related conflicts in women. *Journal of Social Issues,* 1972, **28**, 157–176.

Horner, M. S., Tresemer, D. W., Berens, A. E., & Watson, R. I., Jr. Scoring manual for an empirically derived scoring system for the motive to avoid success. Unpublished paper, Harvard University, 1973.

Hoyt, K., Evans, R., Mackin, E., & Mangum, G. *Career education: What it is and how to do it.* Salt Lake City: Olympus, 1972.

Jepsen, D. A., & Dilley, J. S. Vocational decision-making models: A review and comparative analysis. *Review of Educational Research,* 1974, **44**, 331–349.

Jordaan, J. P. Life stages as organizing modes of career development. In E. L. Herr (Ed.), *Vocational Guidance and human development.* Boston: Houghton, 1974.a.

Jordaan, J. P. The use of vocational maturity instruments in counseling. In D. E. Super (Ed.), *Measuring vocational maturity for counseling and evaluation.* Washington, D.C.: National Vocational Guidance Association, 1974.b.

Jordaan, J. P., & Heyde, M. B. *Vocational maturity during the high school years.* New York: Teachers College Press, in press.

Komarovsky, M. Cultural contradictions and sex roles: The masculine case. In J. Huber (Ed.), *Changing women in a changing society.* Chicago: U. of Chicago, 1973.

Korman, A. K. Self esteem as a moderator in vocational choice: Replications and extensions. *Journal of Applied Psychology,* 1969, **53**, 188–192.

Kriger, S. F. n *Ach* and perceived parental child-rearing attitudes career women and homemakers. *Journal of Vocational Behavior,* 1972, **2**, 419–432.

LoCascio, R. Delayed and impaired vocational development: A neglected aspect of vocational development theory. *Personnel and Guidance Journal,* 1964, **42**, 885–887.

LoCascio, R. The vocational maturity of diverse groups: Theory and measurement. In D. E. Super (Ed.), *Measuring vocational maturity for counseling and evaluation.* Washington, D.C.: National Vocational Guidance Association, 1974.

Luckey, E. B. The family: Perspectives on its role in development and choice. In E. L. Herr (Ed.), *Vocational guidance and human development.* Boston: Houghton, 1974.

McEwen, M. K. Counseling women: A review of the research. *Journal of College Student Personnel,* 1975, **16**, 382–388.

Madaus, G. F., & O'Hara, R. P. Vocational interest patterns of high school boys: A multivariate approach. *Journal of Counseling Psychology,* 1967, **14**, 106–112.

Marcia, J. E. Monograph on ego identity status. Untitled and unpublished manuscript, Burnaby, British Columbia: Simon Fraser University, 1975.

Marland, S. P. *Career education: A proposal for reform.* New York: McGraw-Hill, 1974.

Matthews, E. E. The vocational guidance of girls and women in the United States. In E. L. Herr (Ed.), *Vocational guidance and human development.* Boston: Houghton, 1974.

Matthews, E. E., Feingold, S. N., Berry, J., Weary, B., & Tyler, L. E. *Counseling girls and women over the life span.* Washington, D.C.: National Vocational Guidance Association, 1972.

Montesano, N., & Geist, H. Differences in occupational choice between ninth and twelfth grade boys. *Personnel and Guidance Journal,* 1964, **46**, 150–154.

Morrill, W. H., & Forrest, D. J. Dimensions of counseling for career development. *Personnel and Guidance Journal,* 1970, **49**, 299–305.

Nathanson, S. The relation between personality traits and work performance of emotionally disturbed adolescents. Unpublished doctoral dissertation, New York University, 1976.

Oliver, L. The relationship of parental attitudes and parent identification to career and homemaking orientation in college women. *Journal of Vocational Behavior*, 1975, **7**, 1–12.

Oppenheimer, E. A. The relationship between certain self-construct and occupational preferences. *Journal of Counseling Psychology*, 1966, **13**, 191–197.

Osipow, S. H. *Emerging woman: Career analysis and outlooks*. Columbus, Ohio: Merrill, 1975.

Osipow, S. *Theories of Career Development*. 2nd Ed. Englewood Cliffs, N.J.: Appleton, 1973.

Patterson, L. E. Girls' careers—expressions of identity. *Vocational Guidance Quarterly*, 1973, **21**, 269–275.

Perrone, P. A. Factors influencing high school seniors' occupational preferences. *Personnel and Guidance Journal*, 1964, **42**, 976–980.

Rennie, T. A. C., Burling, S. T., & Woodward, L. E. *Vocational rehabilitation of psychiatric patients*. Cambridge, Mass.: Harvard U.P., 1950.

Richardson, M. S. Vocational maturity in counseling girls and women. In D. E. Super (Ed.), *Measuring vocational maturity for counseling and evaluation*. Washington, D.C.: National Vocational Guidance Association, 1974.

Richardson, M. S., Kwalwasser, L., & Shelov, M. Vocational maturity and career orientation in college women. Paper presented at the Eastern Psychological Association Convention, New York, 1976.

Roe, A. *The psychology of occupations*. New York: Wiley, 1956.

Rosen, B. C. Race, ethnicity, and the achievement syndrome. *American Sociological Review*, 1959, **24**, 47–60.

Schlossberg, N. K. A framework for counseling women. *Personnel and Guidance Journal*, 1972, **51**, 137–146.

Schlossberg, W. K., & Goodman, J. A. Woman's place: Children's sex stereotyping of occupations. *Vocational Guidance Quarterly*, 1972, **20**, 266–270.

Segal, S. J. A psychoanalytic analysis of personality factors in vocational choice. *Journal of Counseling Psychology*, 1961, **8**, 202–210.

Sharp, W. H., & Marra, H. A. Factors related to classification of client problem, number of counseling sessions, and trends of client problems. *Journal of Counseling Psychology*, 1971, **18**, 117–122.

Small, L. Personality determinants of occupational choice. *Psychological Monographs*, 1953, **67**, No. 1 (Whole No. 351).

Smith, E. J. Profile of the black individual in vocational literature. *Journal of Vocational Behavior*, 1975, **6**, 41–59.

Special Task Force, Health, Education, and Welfare. *Work in America*. Cambridge, Mass.: MIT Press, 1973.

Stein, A. H., & Bailey, M. M. The socialization of achievement orientation in females. *Psychological Bulletin*, 1973, **80**, 345–366.

Steinmann, A., Levi, J., & Fox, D. J. Self-concept of college women compared with their concept of ideal woman and men's ideal woman. *Journal of Counseling Psychology*, 1964, **11**, 370–374.

Stubbins, J. The relationship between level of vocational aspiration and certain personal data: A study of some traits and influences bearing on the prestige level of vocational choice. *Genetic Psychology Monographs,* 1950, **41**, 327–408.

Super, D. E. *The psychology of careers.* New York: Harper, 1957.

Super, D. E. *Measuring vocational maturity for counseling and evaluation.* Washington, D.C.: National Vocational Guidance Association, 1974.

Super, D. E. Career education and meanings of work. Paper prepared for the Office of Career Education, Office of Education, U.S. Department of Health, Education, and Welfare, 1975.

Super, D. E., Kowalski, R. S., & Gotkin, E. H. *Floundering and trial after high school. Cooperative Research Project No. 1393.* New York: Bureau of Publications, Teachers College, Columbia University, 1967.

Super, D. E., Starishevsky, R., Matlin, N., & Jordaan, J. P. *Career development: Self-concept theory.* New York: College Entrance Examination Board, Research Monograph No. 1, 1963.

Thomas, M. J. Realism and socioeconomic status (SES) of occupational plans of low SES black and white male adolescents. *Journal of Counseling Psychology,* 1976, **23**, 46–49.

Tiedeman, D. V., & O'Hara, R. P. *Career development: Choice and adjustment.* Princeton, N.J.: College Entrance Examination Board, 1963.

U.S. Department of Labor, Employment Standards Administration, Women's Bureau. *1975 handbook on women workers.* Bulletin 297.

Van Dusen, R. A., & Sheldon, E. B. The changing status of American women: A life cycle perspective. *American Psychologist,* 1976, **31**, 106–116.

Warnath, C. F. Vocational theories: Direction to nowhere. *Personnel and Guidance Journal,* 1975, **53**, 422–429.

Wilson, K. Today's women students: New outlooks and new challenges. *Journal of College Student Personnel,* 1975, **16**, 376–381.

Winters, C. J., & Sorenson, J. Individual factors related to career orientation in women. In S. H. Osipow (Ed.), *Emerging woman: Career analysis and outlooks.* Columbus, Ohio: Merrill, 1975.

Wolfson, K. P. Career development patterns of college women. *Journal of Counseling Psychology,* 1976, **23**, 119–125.

Yankelovich, D. *The new morality: A profile of American youth in the 70's.* New York: McGraw-Hill, 1974.

Zuckerman, M., & Wheeler, L. To dispel fantasies about the fantasy-based measure of fear of success. *Psychological Bulletin,* 1975, **82**, 932–946.

Zytowski, D. G. Toward a theory of career development for women. *Personnel and Guidance Journal,* 1969, **47**, 660–664.

19

moral development and religion

As young persons approach and enter the adolescent years they become increasingly able to *generalize* and *conceptualize* moral rules and principles. Studies on the processes that underlie moral judgments have multiplied during the last decade. In this section an examination of thought processes underlying the moral concepts of individuals varying in age will be presented. This will be followed by a discussion of the development of values and political thought in adolescence. A second part of this chapter will deal with the role of religion in the lives of adolescents.

535

Cognitive-developmental approach
to morality

A leading exponent of the cognitive-developmental approach to moral judgment is Piaget (1932). Even though his work is most directly related to children, his views on moral judgment are pertinent to adolescents. According to Piaget, morality includes both the individual's respect for the rules governing society and ideas about justice, with a concern for reciprocity and equality.

In his studies of the development of moral judgment, Piaget (1932) makes several distinctions between less mature and more mature moral ideas. According to Piaget there is a transition from *heteronomous* to *autonomous* moral judgment—from a morality based on laws laid down by others, toward a morality based on the individual's own judgment and convictions.

There is also a shift from *moral realism* to *moral relativism*. The moral realist makes a literal interpretation. He follows the letter of the law. He judges the seriousness of an act by its practical consequences: the person who stumbles and breaks a dozen eggs is morally more at fault than the one who deliberately smashes one egg. The moral realist also judges seriousness by the severity of the punishment that follows: a youngster who is flogged for stealing an apple has committed a greater offense than one who is mildly scolded for cheating on a test.

The moral relativist, on the other hand, takes account of intentions as well as practical consequences: a youngster who deliberately spills a drop of ink on another's handkerchief is a more serious offender than one who accidentally spills a bottle of ink on another's clothes. The relativist also makes allowances: a hungry boy who steals a pie is morally less culpable than a well-fed boy who snitches a doughnut and throws it away.

Piaget stresses the overriding importance of peer interaction in making the transition from moral realism to moral relativism. The first process that takes place in peer interaction is the individual's greater relative equality and learning to share in decision making. Rules are no longer viewed as coming from above but are seen as products of agreement and cooperation. The second process in peer interaction involves learning to take the role of the other. This ability to see things from the perspective of another individual sensitizes the individual to the inner states that underlie other people's acts.

Although Piaget's work is based on children under the age of twelve, common observation suggests that there are some adolescents and adults who still operate at a premoral stage of development. Nevertheless, in studies of moral judgments of adolescents it has been found that the average young person of adolescent age (and even prior to adolescence) is likely to subscribe to ideas of right and wrong that come close to the ideas held by adults.

One of the issues that has received some airing in recent years concerns the relation between *moral judgment* as described by Piaget and others and *overt behavior*. On the basis of several studies, there does not appear to be a close relationship between moral judgment as measured by psychological tests and interviews and such behavior as lying or cheating. The work of Dreman (1976), however, gives some evidence pertaining to the relationship between understanding intentions or underlying motives and moral behavior. Israeli first-, fourth-, and seventh-grade boys were given moral judgment stories adapted from Piaget and then given an opportunity to engage in sharing behavior. Those individuals who were able to evaluate the moral judgment stories on the basis of intentionality (the motivations of others) more often engaged in sharing behavior.

The importance of the development of moral judgment has also been highlighted in research with adolescents by Kohlberg (1969).[1] Kohlberg, like Piaget, believes that the individual's moral judgment is linked with, but not identical with, the individual's level of cognitive development. In his work he delineated three levels of moral judgment: namely, preconventional, conventional, and postconventional. Within each level are two stages. The moral levels and their accompanying developmental stages appear in Table 19.1.

According to Kohlberg, the six stages of moral development follow a developmental progression that is associated with increasing cognitive maturation. He further hypothesizes that individuals coming from different cultural backgrounds will all progress through the sequence of stages in the order listed in Table 19.1. Nevertheless, learning may, of course, affect the rate at which individuals progress through the various stages. Individuals are classified according to the stage of their moral judgment on the basis of their responses to a number of moral dilemmas.

The following is an example of one of the hypothetical stories of moral conflict used by Kohlberg (without detailed questions) to elicit moral judgment:

> Situation III. Heinz Steals the Drug. In Europe a woman was near death from cancer. One drug might save her, a form of radium that a druggist in the same town had recently discovered. The druggist was charging $2,000, ten times what the drug cost him to make. The sick woman's husband, Heinz, went to everyone he knew to borrow the money, but he could only get together about half of what it cost. He told the druggist that his wife was

[1] For a survey of studies dealing with the existence of adulthood moral stages, see L. Kohlberg, "Continuities in Childhood and Adult Moral Development Revisited." In P. B. Baltes and K. W. Schaie (eds.), *Life-Span Developmental Psychology* (New York: Academic Press, 1973).

dying and asked him to sell it cheaper or let him pay later. But the druggist said, "No." The husband got desperate and broke into the man's store to steal the drug for his wife. Should the husband have done that? Why? [Kohlberg, 1969, p. 379]

Elliot, a high school student, responded: "I think one individual's set of moral values is as good as the next individual's. . . . I think you have a right to believe in what you believe in, but I don't think you have a right to enforce it on other people [Kohlberg and Gilligan, 1971, p. 1074]." In this example the high school student is in a transitional stage. He can use conventional moral thinking but does not have a clear comprehension of universal moral principles.

According to Kohlberg (1969), the adolescent's moral reasoning does not correspond to one stage exclusively. Less than half of the individual's judgments fit a particular stage, the rest being just below or above the most frequent stage. At the college level not one of the subjects employed moral reasoning that was exclusively rated at any single level of development (Fishkin et al., 1973).

Holstein (1976) attempted to test Kohlberg's hypothesis that changes in moral judgment are in accord with a sequence of six irreversible stages. She found that when individual stages are examined, a step-by-step

Table 19.1. Kohlberg's scheme of moral levels and developmental stages of moral judgment

Levels	Developmental stages
Preconventional	Stage 1: Orientation toward obedience and punishment: The effect of an action is evaluated in terms of its goodness or badness, depending on the consequences of the act.
	Stage 2: Egoistic orientation: Right actions depend primarily on satisfaction of the self's needs and, at times, the needs of others. Orientation to reciprocity: Reciprocity is a matter of you do something for me and I'll do something for you.
Conventional	Stage 3: Good-boy—good-girl orientation: Individuals are oriented to obtaining the approval of others and of assisting others. Behavior is judged by intention—"He means well."
	Stage 4: Orientation toward maintaining the social order for its own sake: There is respect for authority.
Postconventional	Stage 5: Social-contract orientation: Right actions are defined in terms of general rights. Aside from what is agreed on, personal values and opinions determine what is right or wrong. Conscience plays an important role but is not yet clearly based on well-thought-out reasonable principles that apply to all.
	Stage 6: Universal ethical principles: There is an orientation to universal principles of justice, equality of human rights, and respect for the dignity of human beings.

progression from specific stage to specific stage within a level does not emerge, but the direction of movement is sequential from the preconventional to the conventional level. Moreover, higher-stage adolescents were found sometimes to regress to earlier stages, which raises questions about the irreversibility of Kohlberg's stages.

Prior to arriving at firm conclusions regarding Kohlberg's developmental stages, more sophisticated research will have to be conducted. For instance, in a recent pilot study of adolescents living in a ghetto community, one of the present writers was told by a male adolescent that it was difficult for him to identify with the characters in the stories. This difficulty is likely to interfere with the consistency of the person's moral responses. Of particular importance in evaluating a cognitive approach to moral development is the fact that the relationship between the individual's moral judgment and actual behavior is not high (Mischel, 1976). Moral judgment appears to be more highly related to measures of ideology, beliefs, and attitudes than to measures of action. At times individuals who state that they adhere to high moral principles may in fact commit harmful acts. The philosopher Pascal once commented that evil is never done so thoroughly or so well as when it is done with a good conscience. There have been numerous occasions in recent history when abstract moral principles have been invoked to justify atrocities. "In the name of justice, of the common welfare, of universal ethics, and of God, millions of people have been killed and whole cultures destroyed.... Presidential assassinations, airplane hijackings, and massacres of Olympic athletes have been committed for allegedly selfless motives of highest morality and principle [Mischel, 1976, p. 465]."

Moral Reasoning from the Viewpoint of Others

Piaget and Kohlberg have both emphasized that social interaction is a necessary condition for children to progress from one stage to the next in terms of the level of their moral reasoning. Social interaction facilitates the ease with which the individual can view things from the perspective of others. Those individuals who are able to take the role of another individual score higher on tests of moral judgment. Based on the work of Piaget and Kohlberg, Yussen (1976) hypothesized that, with the increase in the individual's level of moral judgment that accompanies growth, there would be an increase in the individual's ability to see things from the perspective of others who occupy different roles in society. To test his hypothesis, Yussen gave ninth, tenth, twelfth-graders, and college sophomores and juniors a moral judgment questionnaire. The students were then asked to answer a series of moral dilemmas for themselves and then as if they were an average policeman and an average philosopher. Yussen reasoned that individuals would feel that the moral judgment of a policeman would differ from that of a philosopher. In contrast to a policeman, a philosopher would probably be seen as more principled and governed by moral thought and logic (Kohlberg's stages 5 and 6). The results show an increase with age in the student's own level of moral judgment. Older individuals more often chose principled moral issues to resolve moral dilemmas. Moreover, with increased age there was an increase in role differentiation (the moral outlook of philosophers was said to be different from that of the policeman). That is, older individuals selected more principled issues for philosophers than for policemen. Among the older individuals more principled issues were described as characteristic of philosophers than of themselves. This suggests that older adolescents are capable of having a thought perspective higher than their own.

Sex Differences in Moral Judgments

One of the questions raised by Kohlberg's work and subsequent work concerning it relates to the moral judgment of male and female adolescents. To what extent, one might ask, are males and females of comparable ages similar or different in terms of their stages of moral development?

Both Keasey (1972), with eleven-year-old adolescents, and Weisbroth (1970), with older subjects, reported no sex differences in Kohlberg's moral judgment stages. However, Saltzstein et al. (1972) reported that female adolescents, as contrasted with males, gave relatively more "good-boy–good-girl" (stage 3) responses and fewer stage 1 and 2 or stage 4 and 5 responses. Maccoby and Jacklin (1974) speculate that because stages 1 and 2 and 4 and 5 contain greater elements of aggression and power orientation, the smaller representation of females at this stage is understandable. Further evidence of sex differences or similarities in moral judgment is needed before conclusions can be drawn.

Moral Judgments as Related to Emotional Adjustment

Although intellectual understanding has an important role in the development and application of moral concepts, motives and emotions also are important. Youngsters who rate higher than average in emotional adjustment are likely to make more mature moral judgments than persons with similar intelligence who are emotionally disturbed (Shumsky, 1956). Those with superior emotional adjustment are better able to take account of intentions and circumstances in judging the moral seriousness of various acts. Those who are emotionally maladjusted tend to be more punitive than those with more favorable adjustment and tend also to base their moral judgments on a concept of absolute authority.

Moral character

In a study of thirty-four children from their tenth to their seventeenth year, Peck et al. (1960) classified moral character according to five "types."

One was the *amoral type*, representing the most infantile, impulsive, and irresponsible kind of character, without internalized moral principles and without regard for the consequences of behavior. Next in the scale was the *expedient type*: a person described as primarily self-centered, one who considers other people's welfare only to gain his own ends and behaves morally only so long as it suits his purpose: to get what he wants and to avoid disapproval. Third was the *conforming type*, whose main moral principle was to do what others do and what they say he *should do*. Such a person, as described by the investigators, in conforming to his group and seeking to avoid disapproval, follows literal rules specific for each occasion, instead of having generalized moral principles. Fourth was the *rational conscientious type*. This person is described as one who has his own internal standard of right and wrong by which he judges his acts, but he is rigid in applying his moral principles. He regards an act as good or bad because he defines it as such and not out of consideration for the good or ill effects his conduct might have on others.

The fifth type described by Peck et al. is the *rational altruistic type*. This type, according to the classification scheme used by the authors, represents the highest level of moral maturity. Persons at this level have a stable set of moral principles by which they are guided. They try realistically to appraise the results of a given act and assess it in terms of whether it serves others as well. They are rational in their assessment of their conduct in the light of their principles and altruistic in showing a concern about the welfare of others as well as themselves.

Each of the subjects in the study was assigned to a type group according to the predominant configuration of his character profile, even though none of the persons was a "pure" type.

At age sixteen there were youngsters representing each of these five types. Five of the thirty-four were classed as having an amoral type of character. Four seemed unmistakably to belong to the rational-altruist group; and an additional five were classed as being "near" to this type. The remaining youngsters were distributed among the other types, with the largest single group (eight in number) classed as belonging to the conforming type.

"Ethics are all very well, but there are times when an adolescent must use his better judgment."

Figure 19.1.

These investigators found that there was a marked tendency for children to show the same level of morality at ages thirteen and sixteen as they had shown at the age of ten.

As can be seen, only a minority of the persons in this study reached what the authors regarded as the most mature type of moral development. It appears from this study that morals that are established by the age of ten persist into later years. After the age of ten moral character apparently was relatively unaffected by experiences at school or children's relationships with peers and other persons outside the home.

The development of value systems in adolescents

Adolescence, according to some psychologists, is a time when some individuals searching for an identity become critical of their childhood and begin to question their value systems. Although some believe that the basic value system of contemporary adolescents differs greatly from that of other generations, there is little hard evidence to support this view.

In the search for identity, some individuals begin to question their value systems. [Danny Lyon/Magnum.]

Beech and Schoeppe (1974) administered the Rokeach Value Survey, an instrument designed to measure the importance of particular values, as judged by those who responded to the instrument, to adolescents in grades five, seven, nine, and eleven. The adolescents were asked to rank two types of values, terminal and instrumental, corresponding to ends and means.

Values such as *a world at peace, freedom, honest,* and *loving* received high ranks by both males and females at all grades. The value *honesty* depicts a quality of relationship adolescents desire with one another. Their desires for affectionate and tender relationships are expressed in the high importance they place on *loving.* Both of these values are necessary for developing mature social relationships with others, a primary task of adolescence. Contemporary adolescents' need for warm, intimate, and close friendships has also been documented by Yankelovich's survey (1969). The value placed on *freedom* attests to an egalitarian outlook.

Many of the values of contemporary adolescents, based on findings of the Beech and Shoeppe study, are traditional in nature and become more so with increased age. An increase with age is shown by members of both sexes in the values of *a sense of accomplishment, self-respect,* and *wisdom.* There was also an increase in age in values represented by being *ambitious, broadminded,* and *responsible.* These values suggest growing self-confidence through achievement. Moreover, with increased maturity, there is an increase in viewing achievement as important.

Values represented by terms such as *cheerful, helpful,* and *obedient* decreased in importance with age, suggesting a rejection of childhood roles and a move in the direction of being a more autonomous, self-controlling adolescent. However, taken as a whole, this study suggests that the rank order of importance of various values is relatively stable from one age to the next during adolescence.

The values of noncollege youth appear to be more traditionally oriented than those of their peers who attend college. According to the results of an extensive analysis conducted by CBS News (Yankelovich, 1969), noncollege youth subscribe to traditional values about the importance of hard work as well as traditional views with respect to issues such as premarital and extramarital sex and abortion. By contrast collegiate youth are more liberal with respect to these issues. Noncollegiate youth, and the parents of both collegiate and noncollegiate youth, were found to be similar in their acceptance of traditional values such as "Hard work will always pay off," "Belonging to some organized religion is important in a person's life," and "Competition encourages excellence." In general there was considerable correspondence between adolescents and their parents, particularly in the case of noncollege youth and their parents.

The development of political thought

The development of political thought in adolescence has been explored by Adelson (1975) and his colleagues in studies that deal with adolescents' conceptions and judgments regarding the fundamental operations of politics and society. What follows is a brief summary of some of their findings, based on interviews conducted with a thousand adolescents, eleven to eighteen years of age. An example of the kind of situations presented in these interviews follows: "The interviewee is asked to imagine that a thousand people leave their country to form a new society, and once settled, confront the myriad problems involved in establishing and maintaining a social and political order [p. 64]." This is followed by a number of semiprojective questions about such topics as the functions of government, crime and justice, and the interaction of the citizens and the state.

According to Adelson and his colleagues, changes in the way individuals think about society and government are linked to changes in their cognitive development. One interesting age trend that emerged in this survey is that younger adolescents have relatively more difficulty in managing abstract concepts. In contrast older adolescents are better able to deal with abstract terms such as equality and justice. The data in these studies also reveal that the young adolescents' view of the future is constricted, and their sense of history is limited. The young child views the law as permanent and unchangeable. In contrast the older adolescent is capable of taking human intentions into account and accepting the fact that laws can be changed.

Interviews with black and white adolescents aged twelve to eighteen provided data relating to the possibility of eliminating crime, poverty, and racial prejudice (see Figure 19.2). The adolescents reported that poverty could be eliminated more easily than crime or prejudice. In general, with increased age, the adolescents were less hopeful that any of these social problems could be eliminated. The prevailing mood of the adolescents was pessimism with respect to the possibility of deep political and social change.

The role of religion

Adolescents' religious backgrounds, and the teachings of their religions regarding the nature and destiny of man, potentially can play an important role in determining their conceptions of who and what they are and what they might aspire to be.

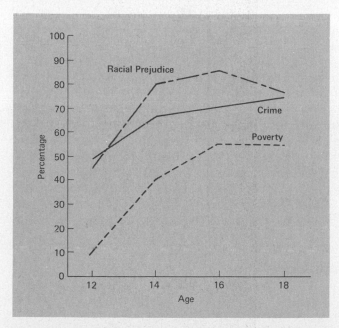

Figure 19.2. Pessimistic responses, by age, to the questions "Would it ever be possible to eliminate racial prejudice? Crime? Poverty?" [Adapted from "The development of ideology in adolescence" by J. Adelson. In G. H. Elder, Jr., and S. E. Dragastin (Eds.), *Adolescence in the life cycle: Psychological change and social context*. New York: Wiley, 1975.]

Religion, as we meet it in everyday life, consists of a system of professed beliefs, attitudes, and practices commonly centered on a place of worship. From the personal point of view of religious individuals, religion is that which is of ultimate concern. It is for many an answer to man's hunger for certainty, for assurance, for a faith to which they can cling, and for a sustaining hope.

From a social point of view, individuals seek through their religion to enter into meaningful relationships with others, reaching for a commitment they can share with others and seeking to join with others in common devotion to it. Although, as we will note later, religion frequently seems to be more a formal profession than a matter of deep personal concern, it still for many is the keystone to a philosophy of life. In a study published in 1948 Allport et al. found, for example, that 68 per cent of Harvard students and 82 per cent of Radcliffe students answered Yes to the question: Do you feel that you require some form of religious orientation or belief in order to achieve a fully mature philosophy of life? It would be informative to ask today's students the same question, because many investigators believe the importance of religion has declined over the past three decades.

Adolescence and religious expectations

In many religious denominations adolescence is regarded as an especially important period. Some religious groups have regarded adolescence as the time of "awakening," the time when a borrowed faith becomes a personal possession. In some religious groups it has been assumed that adolescence is a time when the young person is ripe for religious conversion or is ready to plunge into religion with more passionate certainty than he or she showed as a child. The rites of confirmation, bar mitzvah and bas mitzvah, and other forms of introduction into adult religious privileges, practices, and obligations, represent, for some persons, the most impressive acknowledgments of a young person's transition from childhood to responsible youthful adulthood.

Prevalence of religious beliefs and practices

The typical adolescent of high school and early college age is "religious," at least to the extent of assenting to a number of religious beliefs and taking part in religious observances. A large proportion of young people profess a religious faith and a belief in the necessity of religion in life.

The percentage of young people expressing belief in God has been found to vary in different populations, yet the percentage is often high. Unpublished data in a Gallup poll suggested that a large majority of adolescents expressed some kind of belief in God (Rice, 1975). However, the figures vary depending on the particular population that is being studied. For example, in an atypical population of students at Berkeley, only a small minority indicated that organized religion represented a significant commitment (Wuthnow and Glock, 1973).

An extensive analysis conducted by CBS News in 1969 (Yankelovich, 1969) revealed that 82 per cent of noncollegiate youth and 42 per cent of collegiate youth agreed with the following statement: "Belonging to some organized religion is important in a person's life." It is also of interest that 91 per cent of the noncollege youths' parents and 81 per cent of the college youths' parents agreed with this statement. These findings suggest that even though there is some skepticism among adolescents with respect to their religious beliefs, they still appear to profess traditional beliefs. Nevertheless, one must keep in mind that other investigators report that only a minority of students seem to have a strong religious commitment.

As regards church attendance, the results of a 1971 poll by Harris and Associates in a national sample of fifteen- to twenty-one-year-olds suggest that the percentage of high school and college students who attended church regularly was 58 and 43 per cent, respectively (*Change, Yes—Upheaval, No*, 1971). Parker (1971) notes that the present generation of adolescents has more commitment to basic ideals of morality than conformity to moral prescriptions. Religious forms of observance without commitment to active involvement do not appear to appeal to today's adolescents.

From an extensive overview of the literature by Moberg (1971), it is clear that college-age students are less likely to profess religious beliefs than high school-age students.

Religious beliefs and attitudes that are professed by persons at the college level tend to persist once they have left school. Nelson (1956), in 1950, applied several scales for the measurement of religious attitudes to about 900 persons who had responded as college students to the same scales in 1936. Eighty-six per cent of the persons showed either little or no shift in attitude or a shift toward more favorable attitudes; only 14 per cent shifted toward less favorable attitudes. As measured by these scales, the former college students were more religious, on the average, in 1950 than in 1936.

In several studies college women have described themselves as having stronger religious convictions and sentiments than men. However, Rohrbaugh and Jessor (1975) did not find sex differences in religiosity among college students. Several independent studies at the high school level have found that females are more religious and attend church more often than males (Rohrbaugh and Jessor, 1975; De Bord, 1969).

Polls of high school and college students and of the general population indicate that, for the vast majority of persons, an accepting attitude toward religion is a "must"—either as a matter of sincere conviction or of conformity. The percentages fall sharply when more specific questions are asked pertaining to the faith professed.

Within recent years a small minority of adolescents have been expressing interest in nontraditional forms of religion, such as Eastern religions, the search for mystical experiences, and involvement in activities such as the Jesus Movement, Sun Myung Moon's group, and the Divine Light Mission. Among freshmen in 1970 and seniors in 1971 at Berkeley, 3 and 8 per cent, respectively, reportedly identified with the Eastern religions (Wuthnow and Glock, 1973). Individuals in the Jesus People Movement profess to believe that one can overcome one's alienation and discover real meaning in life by establishing a personal relationship with Jesus Christ. They tend to emphasize subjectivism and at the same time appear to be suspicious of a rational approach. A number of adolescents in this movement had previously experimented with the youth counterculture, according to Balswick (1974). However, they became disillusioned with the permissiveness of hippie morality.

Influence of childhood experiences on religious attitudes in adolescence

The young person's total personality and upbringing until the time of reaching adolescence will have a significant bearing on religious orientation during adolescent and later years (Roberts, 1950).

To realize the meaning of love, as emphasized in religion, adolescents must draw on their own experiences with loving people. To realize what the concept of faith might mean, adolescents also must build upon the foundations of faith and trust that were established in their earlier development and upbringing. Many people have faith of some sort, whether formulated in religious terms or not. But it is difficult for adolescents to find meaning in the religious faith they are taught if religion has been presented to them only in the form of doctrines, creeds, and confessionals that they had to memorize, like the names of the states of the union. The same principle applies to other aspects of religion.

Most religions emphasize common devotion that binds people, giving individuals communion with something in which they are deeply involved and that also deeply involves them with others. To achieve such a state of devotion, young persons must draw on experiences of relatedness to others in their own lives.

Adolescents' church activities are influenced by parental participation in church activities. Stewart (1967) reported that adolescents attended church more often if their parents were frequent church attenders. Unpublished data by Lukoff and Brook (1976) suggested that maternal church attendance as reported by the mother is associated with adolescent church attendance only among females. Had these investigators obtained data on paternal church attendance, they might have found that the father who attended church more frequently was likely to have a son who attended church more often. Adolescents who adhere most strongly to traditional forms of religiosity reported that their parents were supportive and warm (Thomas and Weigert, 1972). Related to this, De Bord (1969) reported that when adolescents' denominational affiliations are similar to those of their mothers, they are more likely to attend church. Adolescent religiosity was also found to depend on parental religiosity.

According to Roberts (1950), individuals, as they move toward adolescence and adulthood, may show two types of reaction if they have been brought up in a situation in which there is a contrast between the religious precepts that are taught and the actual example of religious living that is shown them. They may cling desperately to a formal acceptance of ideals and religious convictions, or they may become cynical and reject religious beliefs.

Rosenberg (1975) studied the self-esteem of Catholic, Protestant, and Jewish junior high school and senior high school students living in religious environments that were either consonant with or discordant from their own religious backgrounds. Adolescents raised in mixed or similar religious neighborhoods had higher self-esteem than adolescents raised in neighborhoods where the religion of most others differed from the adolescents' own religious backgrounds. Although the differences between the groups were not large, particularly among the Protestants, the results were consistent.

If surveys were made of the attitudes young people have toward religious teachers and clergymen, the findings probably would parallel those obtained from similar studies of attitudes toward teachers in secular schools (such findings are reviewed in Chapter 17). The qualities of kindness, considerateness, and other "human" traits of the religious persons would probably be stressed more than their religious views, just as adolescents emphasize the human qualities of high school teachers more than their professional skills.

Developmental changes in expressed attitudes and beliefs

As adolescents move from the preteenage years toward their twenties, they normally will acquire a greater capacity for examining the meanings of beliefs and ideas that earlier they took for granted and accepted secondhand from their parents and teachers. In some cases they doubt what they passively accepted as children when they accepted religious teaching uncritically (Elkind, 1971).

As they move on in school, they will have an opportunity also to see their religious views in wider perspective. When they meet persons who differ from them in religion, they may find it necessary to look a little more closely at their own beliefs. If they take courses in science, literature, and philosophy, they will observe how human beings have striven to find and to phrase the truth and how various the answers are.

At the adolescent stage of development, Piaget, as well as others, recognizes that adolescents may be capable of envisioning ideal religions. They may compare their ideals with those of their family and society. "The adolescent is no longer content to live the interindividual relations offered by his immediate surroundings or to use his intelligence to solve the problems of the moment. Rather, he is motivated also to take his place in the adult social framework and with this aim he tends to participate in the ideas, ideals, and ideologies of a wider group through the medium of a number of verbal symbols to which he was indifferent as a child [Inhelder and Piaget, 1958, p. 341]." "For any true intellectual, adolescence is the metaphysical age par excellence, an age whose dangerous seduction is forgotten only with difficulty at the adult level [p. 341]."

General observation as well as research indicates that young people take a less literal view of things as they grow older (Adelson et al., 1969; Allport et al., 1948; Piaget, 1972).

One interesting finding in a study by Franzblau (1934) was that while still attending a religious school, older children tended to question teachings they had accepted at the age of twelve. Many of them rejected religious dogmas as they matured, even though they attended religious school faithfully. Neither did they seem to gain steadily in intellectual understanding of the meaning of religious teachings as they grew older and continued their education. In this study, as in studies dealing with children belonging to many religious denominations, it was found that there was no close relationship between knowledge of religious history or ceremonies, on the one hand, and growth of character, on the other.

A study by Kuhlen and Arnold (1944), dealing with changes in religious beliefs in the age range from twelve to eighteen, shows some shifts, but the similarities between twelve- and eighteen-year-olds are generally more pronounced than the differences.

During the college years the students' religious orientation seems to change in some respects, according to some investigators, but by no means according to all. In general, seniors as compared with freshmen, are less orthodox, more doubtful about the existence of "God," and more apt to think of a Supreme Being in abstract, impersonal terms. Having reviewed the literature in this area, Feldman and Newcomb (1969) point out that, although this trend is apparent, the changes are not always large, and in a number of studies the differences between freshmen and seniors are not statistically significant. Moreover, the amount and direction of change varies in different institutions (Parker, 1971). Furthermore, changes occur in both directions (Ferman, 1960). While some students say that religion has become less important, others note having experienced an increased concern for and attachment to religion. The direction of change also varies with the sample of students under investigation.

Although some young people, during the teens, go through a period of questioning some of their religious beliefs, some later return to them. Some persons, in their twenties or early thirties, when they become parents, take up religious practices that, for a time, they had neglected (see, for example, Bossard and Boll, 1943). Many others also, according to Pace (1941), expect to send their children to Sunday school even though they do not attend church themselves.

Emotional aspects of religious doubt

When one deals with religious doubt or, as some prefer, the religious crisis of adolescence, one inevitably must deal with a whole constellation of dimensions that constitute the total identity crisis of adolescents (Hoffman, 1970, 1971). As suggested by Rice (1975), adolescents confronted with their quest for religious identity ask, "Who am I? Why am I here? What is the purpose of life? What can I believe? What can I value? How should I live? [p. 309]."

From biographies and autobiographies we can see that religious experiences in adolescence may in some individuals be deeply charged with feeling, ranging from ecstatic joy to despair and despondency.

It is disquieting at any time of life to question what one has been taught by those one respects and loves. It is disturbing if one feels that one must reject what one has believed and taken for granted over a period of several years. To question one's religion, if it has played an important role, is equivalent to questioning an important foundation of one's approach to life. When young people question their religious beliefs, it is not just a doctrine or a theory that they are questioning. They are, in a sense, calling into question their own capacity for understanding as well as the relationship with those who have taught them and in whom they have placed their trust. The fact that doubt may be uncomfortable perhaps accounts in part for the fact that a large proportion of adolescents do not doubt very seriously.

One consequence of lack of serious inquiry into the meaning and implications of religious beliefs is that some beliefs are inconsistent with others. Allport et al. (1948) have noted such inconsistencies. For example, a large number of persons, while professing some type of belief in God, also maintained that religion should rule out supernatural elements.

Characteristics of adolescents who are religiously active

Lukoff and Brook (1976) compared personality, attitudinal, and behavior characteristics of adolescents who attended church more frequently with those who attended church less frequently. Their sample consisted of white, black, and West Indian adolescents thirteen to seventeen years of age.

Taken as a whole, the results of this study suggest that two processes, conformity-nonconformity and a process of using the behavior of others as a model for one's own behavior (modeling), may account for adolescent church attendance. Those who attend church less frequently are less likely to conform whether at the personality, attitudinal, or institutional level than those who attend church more frequently. At the personality level, the results suggest that those adolescents who are socially conforming are more likely to attend church. Those adolescents who perceive that the winning of rewards in life is dependent on their personal actions (internal control) are more likely to attend church than those adolescents who perceive rewards to be contingent on chance, fate, or others (external control).

Consequences of religion for the adolescent

Several investigators (Frazier, 1969; Lee and Clyde, 1974) note that religion may serve to prevent the adolescent from feeling alienated and may inhibit deviant behavior by censuring unconventional behavior. Adolescents who report greater church attendance and stronger religious beliefs appear to make more rigid moral judgments than their peers who are less religious. For instance, Wright and Cox (1967) reported that religious English adolescents were more likely to pass stricter judgment on a series of misbehaviors such as gambling, drunkenness, lying, or stealing than their less religious peers. However, religious beliefs have not been found to be related to moral behavior when the behavior has "payoff value" (Parker, 1971). Rohrbaugh and Jessor (1975) have suggested that religion results in adolescents becoming involved in a conventional atmosphere that serves to insulate them from engaging in problem behavior by providing them with or reinforcing their existing personal controls. Among high school students, those adolescents who reported more political activism, premarital sexual behavior, marijuana use, or general deviant behavior were less likely to be religious.

In a review of the literature on social activism, Braungart (1975) found that a much larger proportion of adolescent activists were nonreligious and secular in terms of their attitudes when compared with the general campus population.

Science, reason, and religion

Some adolescents have difficulty reconciling science and religion and believe there is an irreconcilable conflict between the two. Others never give the issue a second thought.

A conflict is likely to arise, especially among some thoughtful young people, as they move into late adolescence, if they have the view that they must choose religion or reason, or religion or science, but cannot choose both.

As adolescents mature and seek to fathom the meaning of life they will have many opportunities to observe that scientists who delve deeply into the secrets of nature may have something in common with theologians who try to interpret the meaning of life from a religious point of view. The closer scientists come to the boundary of the known, the more aware they become of the vastness and mystery of the unknown. They cannot help wondering what might be the meaning of what they know and what answers might ultimately emerge as men's minds penetrate farther and farther into space and more and more deeply into the essence of matter. When scientists thus begin to speculate about meanings, they may become involved in a search not unlike that of a religious person who raises questions about ultimate meaning.

References

Adelson, J. The development of ideology in adolescence. In S. E. Dragastin & G. H. Elder, Jr. (Eds.), *Adolescents in the life cycle: Psychological change and social context*. Washington, D.C.: Hemisphere Publishing Corporation, 1975.

Adelson, J., Green, B., & O'Neil, R. The growth of the idea of law in adolescence. *Developmental Psychology*, 1969, **1**, 327–332.

Allport, G. W., Gillespie, J. M., & Young, J. The religion of the postwar college student. *Journal of Psychology*, 1948, **25**, 3–33.

Balswick, J. The Jesus people movement: A generational interpretation. *Journal of Social Issues*, 1974, **30**, 23-42.

Beech, R. P., & Schoeppe, A. Development of value systems in adolescents. *Developmental Psychology*, 1974, **10**, 644–656.

Bossard, J. H. S., & Boll, E. S. *Family situations*. Philadelphia: U. of Pa., 1943.

Braungart, R. G. Youth and social movements. In S. E. Dragastin & G. H. Elder, Jr. (Eds.), *Adolescence in the life cycle: Psychological change and social context*. Washington, D.C.: Hemisphere Publishing Corporation, 1975.

Change, Yes—Upheaval, No. *Life*, 1971, **70**, 21–30.

De Bord, L. W. Adolescent religious participation: An examination of substructure and church attendance. *Adolescence*, 1969, **4**, 557–570.

Dreman, S. B. Sharing behavior in Israeli schoolchildren: Cognitive and social learning factors. *Child Development*, 1976, **47**, 186–194.

Elkind, D. The development of religious understanding in children and adolescents. In M. P. Strommen (Ed.), *Research on religious development*. New York: Hawthorne, 1971.

Feldman, K. A., & Newcomb, T. M. *The impact of college students*. San Francisco: Jossey-Bass, 1969.

Ferman, L. A. Religious change on a college campus. *Journal of College Student Personnel*, 1960, **1**, 2–12.

Fishkin, J., Keniston, K., & MacKinnon, C. Moral reasoning and political ideology. *Journal of Personality and Social Psychology*, 1973, **27**, 109–119.

Franzblau, A. N. *Religious belief and character among Jewish adolescents*. Contributions to Education, No. 634. New York: Bureau of Publications, Teachers College, Columbia University, 1934.

Frazier, E. *The Negro Church in America*. New York: Schocken Books, 1969.

Hoffman, M. L. Conscience, personality and socialization techniques. *Human Development*, 1970, **13**, 90–126.

Hoffman, M. L. Identification and conscience development. *Child Development*, 1971, **42,** 1071–1082.

Holstein, C. B. Irreversible, stepwise sequence in the development of moral judgment: A longitudinal study of males and females. *Child Development*, 1976, **47**, 51–61.

Inhelder, B., & Piaget, J. *The growth of logical thinking*. New York: Basic Books, 1958.

Keasey, C. B. The lack of sex differences in the moral judgments of preadolescents. *Journal of Social Psychology*, 1972, **86**, 157–158.

Kohlberg, L. Continuities in childhood and adult moral development revisited. In P. B. Baltes & K. W. Schaie (Eds.), *Life-span developmental psychology*. New York: Academic, 1973.

Kohlberg, L. Stage and sequence: The cognitive-developmental approach to socialization. In D. A. Goslin (Ed.), *Handbook of socialization theory and research*. Chicago: Rand McNally, 1969.

Kohlberg, L., & Gilligan, C. The adolescent as philosopher: The discovery of the self in a postconventional world. *Daedalus*, Fall, 1971, 1051–1086.

Kuhlen, R. G., & Arnold, M. Age differences in religious beliefs and problems during adolescence. *Journal of Genetic Psychology*, 1944, **65**, 291–300.

Lee, G., & Clyde, R. W. Religion, socioeconomic status, and anomie. *Journal for the Scientific Study of Religion*, 1974, **13**, 35–47.

Lukoff, I. F., & Brook, J. S. Unpublished data, 1976.

Maccoby, E. E., & Jacklin, C. N. *The psychology of sex differences*. Stanford, Calif.: Stanford U.P., 1974.

Mischel, W. *Introduction to personality* (2nd ed.). New York: Holt, 1976.

Moberg, D. Religious practices. In M. P. Strommen (Ed.), *Research on religious development*. New York: Hawthorne, 1971.

Nelson, E. Patterns of religious attitude shifts from college to fourteen years later. *Psychological Monographs*, 1956, **70** (17).

Pace, R. C. *They went to college*. Minneapolis: University of Minnesota Press, 1941.

Parker, C. A. Changes in religious beliefs of college students. In M. P. Strommen (Ed.), *Research on religious development*. New York: Hawthorne, 1971.

Peck, R. F., Havighurst, R. J., Cooper, R., Lilienthal, J., & Moore, D. *The psychology of character development*. New York: Wiley, 1960.

Piaget, J. *The moral judgment of the child*. New York: Harcourt, 1932.

Piaget, J. Intellectual evolution from adolescence to adulthood. *Human Development*, 1972, **15**, 1–12.

Rice, F. P. *The adolescent: Development, relationships and culture*. Boston: Allyn, 1975.

Roberts, D. E. *Psychotherapy and a Christian view of man*. New York: Scribner, 1950.

Rohrbaugh, J., & Jessor, R. Religiosity in youth: A personal control against deviant behavior. *Journal of Personality*, 1975, **43**, 136–155.

Rosenberg, M. The dissonant context and the adolescent self-concept. In S. E. Dragastin & G. H. Elder, Jr. (Eds.), *Adolescence in the life cycle: Psychological change and social context*. Washington, D.C.: Hemisphere Publishing Corporation, 1975.

Saltzstein, H. D., Diamond, R. M., & Belenky, M. Moral judgment level and conformity behavior. *Developmental Psychology*, 1972, **7**, 327–336.

Shumsky, A. *Emotional adjustment and moral reasoning in children*. Unpublished Doctor of Education dissertation, Teachers College, Columbia University, 1956.

Stewart, C. W. *Adolescent religion*. Nashville, Tenn.: Abingdon, 1967.

Thomas, D. L., & Weigert, A. J. Parental support, control and adolescent religiosity: An extension of previous research. *Journal for the Scientific Study of Religion*, 1972, **11**, 389–393.

Weisbroth, S. P. Moral judgment, sex, and parental identification in adults. *Developmental Psychology*, 1970, **2**, 396–402.

Wright, D., & Cox, E. A study of the relationship between moral judgment and religious belief in a sample of English adolescents. *Journal of Social Psychology*, 1967, **72**, 135–144.

Wuthnow, G., & Glock, C. Y. Religious loyalty, defection and experimentation among college youth. *Journal for the Scientific Study of Religion*, 1973, **12**, 157–180.

Yankelovich, D. *Generations apart.* New York: Columbia Broadcasting System, 1969.

Yussen, S. R. Moral reasoning from the perspective of others. *Child Development,* 1976, **47**, 551–555.

part seven

TOWARD THE FUTURE

20

personality development and self-fulfillment

This final chapter will summarize some of the main currents in the life of adolescents as they take their place in adult society, facing the future on a foundation built in the past. New material will, however, also be included in the chapter.

559

The meaning of personality

There are many definitions of personality, but it is generally agreed that personality eventually embodies the sum of an individual's traits and qualities and the manner in which these are integrated into one's total way of life. These traits and qualities include temperament and disposition; emotional tendencies; characteristic ways of thinking, feeling, and relating to others; strengths and weaknesses; and obvious and covert motivations. The "center" of personality, from an individual's own point of view, consists of all the ideas and attitudes embodied in an individual's awareness of his or her existence as a separate self, distinct from all others.

Theories of personality

There are also many theories regarding the dynamics of causal factors that govern the development of personality. Some of these theories seem to represent distinctly opposing views—such as the view that a person's traits are primarily native, or inborn, and determined by heredity, as distinct from the view that they are acquired in response to environmental influences and established primarily through a process of learning. It is usually not difficult to find support for opposing theories. There is impressive evidence, for example, that underlying genetic, biochemical factors may predispose a person to acquire certain types of personality disorders classed as mental illness. But mental health obviously is influenced by a wholesome or stressful environment, such as prevails when children are accepted wholeheartedly or are subjected to intolerable abuse.

Many of the varying theories of personal development differ not so much in representing opposing viewpoints as in the particular aspect or facet of development they emphasize. Earlier chapters in this book illustrate this point. Freud and Piaget, for example, are both renowned for the theories they have contributed. Freud stresses motivation and emotion; Piaget stresses cognition. Freud emphasizes the ways in which thinking may be used by a person to rationalize or avoid a direct confrontation with inner conflicts; Piaget emphasizes the developmental stages leading to rational, logical thought processes.

Psychoanalytic Theory

A comprehensive theory of personality has been offered by Freud and his followers. Freud's theories, as discussed in some detail in earlier chapters (notably Chapters 2, 8, and 11), stress inborn drives, notably a sexual drive (libido) and an aggressive drive. According to Freud's theory, as we have seen, there is a three-dimensional psychic structure, including the id, ego, and superego. The concept of the unconscious is also an important feature of Freudian theory. Noteworthy from a developmental point of view are Freud's concepts of infantile sexuality, a concept that has largely been confirmed by objective studies of young children; of Oedipal conflict at about ages four to six, when, according to Freud, the child wants to displace the parent of the same sex; of oral, anal, and phallic phases of libidinal development; of a latency stage, corresponding roughly to the elementary school years; and of the increased urgency of the sexual drive and the increased biological capacity for asserting that drive as children approach and enter the pubertal stage (genital phase).

Freudian theory also emphasizes defense mechanisms for dealing with inner conflict. These are described in Chapter 11, "Anxiety." Among many other aspects of Freudian theory are his emphasis on dreams (as providing a "royal road" to the unconscious) and on the insights that can be gained from free association, as distinguished from an orderly sequence of logical thinking. This is a sketchy account of Freudian theory; a full account would run into volumes.

Freud's theories have influenced the thinking of many who do not accept all of his views. Karen Horney, while acknowledging her great debt to Freud, emphasizes the point that conflicts that have a profound effect on personality development are not all rooted in early childhood but may arise at any stage of life. She also places emphasis on the role of the cultural environment, noting that societies differ in what is forbidden, or taboo (and, hence, a source of conflict), and that in a given culture there may be a change with time in what is forbidden. Horney's account of three major defenses against conflict as described in Chapter 11: moving against others (being competitive—seeking to surpass); moving away from others (with-drawing—remaining detached and aloof); and moving with others (being compliant and conforming) may be regarded as personality trends.

Carl Jung, who originally was associated with Freud and then developed psychoanalytic theories of his own, introduced two designations that are widely used in descriptions of personality: introversion and extroversion.

Adolph Adler, another one-time associate of Freud's, emphasized the mastery motive as prominent in personal development. He was responsible for the introduction of the label *inferiority complex* into popular descriptions of personality.

Social Learning Theory

According to social learning theory, personality traits are a consequence of learning, especially the type of learning that results from the individual's interaction with the social environment. Although social learning theorists differ in a number of ways, they all view personality as comprising habitual ways of reacting to circumstances that occur during the individual's development.

Some of the social learning theories emphasize the role of reinforcement in the individual's learning, especially in the type and pattern of reward or punishment that exists in the family and in society. For example, if the mother shows warmth and affection to her offspring when the child whines and clings to her, the chances increase that the child will show similar dependency on future occasions.

Some social learning theorists emphasize that an individual is not just a passive learner. "Men have long learning histories and long memories, and much of what has happened to them gets internalized and affects all their current responses and future expectations. A man interprets himself and his behavior—he evaluates, judges, and regulates his own performance. In addition to being rewarded and punished by the external environment, people learn to monitor and evaluate their own behavior and to reward and punish themselves, thus modifying their own behavior and influencing their environment [Mischel, 1976, p. 91]."

Theory of the Self as Related to Personality

Important contributions to the understanding of personality have been made by persons who have dealt with the concept of the self. Prominent among these are Carl Rogers (1963), Harry Stack Sullivan (1947, 1948, 1953), and P. Lecky (1945). Rogers holds that each individual has a great capacity for growth, self-realization, and self-understanding: for changing one's conception of self and one's attitudes, beliefs, and behavior. New experiences can be integrated into the self or denied. Maladjustment may occur if a person is unable to deny or avoid experiences that are inconsistent with an established self-concept. According to Rogers, maladjustment in the personality may also occur if there is a painful discrepancy between a person's real self, as he or she perceives it, and the ideal self that he or she aspires to attain. However, with added maturity, individuals may become increasingly aware of disparity between what they are and what they would like to be without necessarily becoming maladjusted (Katz et al., 1975). In common with Sullivan, whose ideas about the "self-system" are discussed in Chapter 11, Rogers maintains that healthy development requires acceptance and approval by others and a sturdy degree of self-acceptance.

The idea that the self is changeable and yet resists change is expressed in many writings about the self. According to Lecky (1945), a strong motive in all persons' lives is to maintain a consistent view of themselves. As indicated in an earlier chapter, the concept of the self occupies a central position in a theory of vocational development by Super et al. (1957). As noted in Chapter 18, Super has been recognized for being one of the leaders in applying developmental theory in a sophisticated way to occupational choice.

Erikson's Eight Stages of Man

As part of a life-span developmental approach, Erik Erikson has proposed a theory of development that views the individual from birth to death. In his view, development occurs in stages (as it does according to the views of Piaget and Freud); these stages are characterized by certain developmental tasks. Unless the individual succeeds in solving the problems at a particular stage, subsequent psychological development may suffer.

The eight stages of psychosocial development proposed by Erikson (1963) appear in Table 20.1. At each stage the individual must face new problems or psychosocial crises that may result in greater maturity or arrested development. At the stage of adolescence, individuals must cope

Table 20.1. Psychosocial stages of development

Erikson's psychosocial stages	Age	Body and psychosexual developmental stages	Personality accomplishment
Basic trust versus mistrust	0–1	Oral-sensory	Trust developed in other people
Autonomy versus shame, doubt	1–2	Muscular-anal	Feels mastery of physical functions and people around self
Initiative versus guilt	3–5	Locomotor-genital	Extra energy for doing things; sexual feelings toward parents
Industry versus inferiority	6–12	Latency	Learns skills in interaction with environment; especially in school
Identity versus role confusion	13–19	Puberty and adolescence	Requestioning of conflicts from past; expansion of social and sexual interests
Intimacy versus isolation	20–30	Young adult	Shares feelings with another
Generativity versus self-absorption	31–55	Adulthood	Concern with growing family and work productivity
Integrity versus despair	56 on	Maturity	Develops broad perspective of past life

Source: Adapted from *Childhood and society* by Erik Erikson, New York, Norton, 1963.

with the physiological changes that accompany puberty, the necessity of making choices about the opposite sex, and preparing for vocational plans. If adolescents cope with these demands, the result can be that they will view themselves as unique and integrated individuals. If all does not go well, the adolescent identity crisis can result in *identity diffusion*. Under these conditions, adolescents may feel that they do not have what is necessary to get started with real life and may view themselves both as confused about their roles and as being less than whole persons. According to Erikson, adolescents must form a revised conception of themselves that incorporates changes in the biological, psychological, and social spheres. At the next stage, early adulthood, if all goes well, individuals achieve the ability to commit themselves to others.

Older adolescents have a greater degree of ego identity than younger ones in Erikson's theory. Protinsky (1975) in a test of this hypothesis found that the older adolescents in his study appeared to be less confused, more secure and experienced, less anxious, and more integrated. Older adolescents were also more willing to wait for future gratification and were more certain of and comfortable with themselves. Moreover, they tended to regard work as a source of recognition. However, as noted in Chapters 1 and 17, there may be exceptions to this trend.

THE INFLUENCE OF PEERS IN PERSONAL DEVELOPMENT

In earlier chapters we have several times emphasized the influence of peers on adolescent attitudes and behavior. Involvement in peer groups, and the temporary stereotyping of behavior and ideals that takes place within the context of the peer groups, can provide adolescents with mutual support and knowledge about their attitudes, values, beliefs, and behavior. Within the peer groups, adolescents can more easily experiment with possible identities and test their self-conceptions against the views of their peers. In more intimate one-to-one relationships such as dating, adolescents are able to find whether they will be accepted if they behave in a particular manner. Deep emotional attachments and love relationships also provide adolescents with the chance to test their identities.

THE INFLUENCE OF CULTURAL FACTORS

In earlier sections we have noted that the personal development of adolescents is inevitably influenced by the values, controls, and pressures that prevail in the social milieu and culture in which they happen to be reared. A cross-cultural study by McClain (1975) deals with the role of cultural factors. Adolescents from Brussels, Munich, Knoxville, Tenn., France, and Málaga responded to a scale based on Erikson's psychosocial stages of development. A comparison of adolescent responses in different areas indicated that communities characterized by economic security provide conditions more favorable to the adolescent's development of a sense of well-being and self-esteem than communities with low standards of living.

Stability and change in personality development

Personality development manifests both continuity and change. There are many factors in development that should produce constancy in children's characteristics as they move from early childhood into adolescence and adulthood. Their genetic potentials were bequeathed to them when they were conceived. Furthermore, despite ups and downs in the fortunes of individual families, many important influences in the environment are more likely to remain stable than to change to a substantial degree. These include the family's socioeconomic status, the educational level of the parents (which might improve but not decline), parents' educational aspirations for their children, residence in a favorable or unfavorable neighborhood (which can mean favorable or harmful peer influences).

Varying Ramifications of Genetic Factors

There are some characteristics mainly determined by heredity that remain rather stable as time passes. Unless adversely affected by a poor diet or ill health, children's height at the age of three will show a high correlation with their mature height. But some hereditary physical characteristics, unforeseen prior to adolescence, may influence adolescents' self-esteem and the way they are esteemed by others. As noted in Chapters 3, 4, and 5, the course of personality development may be influenced by early or late onset of puberty, the shapeliness and attractiveness of a girl's body when her figure has changed from that of a girl to that of a young woman, and by variations in the genital development of boys.

The response to trends in adolescent physical development may range from increased pride to feelings of shame or inferiority, from a tendency to withdraw to a tendency to compensate through a show of bravado and cockiness.

Varying Ramifications of Social Sanctions

The attitudes of adults and peers may reinforce traits that were approved in preadolescent children or disparage traits that are regarded as more tolerable in children than in adolescents. Aggressiveness is generally regarded as more appropriate in boys than in girls, both before and during adolescence. Compliance and dependency are usually treated as more acceptable in girls than in boys.

Personality Repercussions of Increased Understanding of Social Status and Social Attitudes

In connection with their intellectual development and growth of understanding, youngsters who are approaching and entering adolescence may have a sharper perception of, and sensitivity to, the personal implications of social attitudes. With increased awareness, some adolescents of low socioeconomic status become less self-assured with regard to their acceptance by others who are more favorably situated.

An increased awareness of prejudices that discriminate against a person's religion, ethnic origins, or skin color may reduce that person's spontaneity and trust in the good will of others and, quite understandably, produce an undercurrent of bitterness and resentment.

Relatively Stable Characteristics

Evidence regarding the stability of personal characteristics is based on studies dealing with varying periods in the time span from infancy to adulthood. Many such strands of evidence are reported in preceding sections of this book.

As already noted in this chapter, there is, under normal circumstances, a high correlation between height at about age three and mature height. In the population as a whole, there is a high degree of constancy in mental ability, as measured by intelligence tests, from about age three or four to maturity. This does not rule out large fluctuations in individual scores.

Social acceptability, or popularity with peers, as measured by sociometric techniques, shows a high level of consistency from elementary school years at least into the junior high school level, although not as high as the consistency shown in scores on mental tests. Studies covering varying age spans indicate that self-acceptance, as measured by self-rating instruments, is more likely to show consistency than a significant change from year to year, but, as we have noted here, unforeseen changes in the course of development may be a threat to self-esteem.

Many youngsters who become delinquent adolescents show preado-lescent symptoms of delinquency. But further study is needed to determine how reliably delinquency might be predicted prior to adolescence.

In a study of behavior from infancy through adolescence, Schaefer and Bayley (1963) reported that children are consistent in dimensions of activity level and extroverted outgoingness.

A study by Kagan and Moss (1962) found consistency between childhood and early adulthood in ratings of achievement behavior, sex-typed activity, and spontaneity in both boys and girls. Although the correlations between these early and later behaviors were statistically significant, a number of individuals did not give evidence of stability. Among many females, but not males, dependency and passivity in childhood continued to be manifested at the adult level. Consistency through time of aggression in males was greater than in females. Kagan and Moss also found a high degree of consistency through time in competitiveness and in striving to achieve (mainly in the intellectual sphere).

A high degree of persistence in the ascendence-submission dimen-sion of behavior was found in a study by Stott (1957) of over a hundred youngsters, whose characteristics were first assessed at the nursery school level and then again after a period of about twelve years. Eighty-two per cent of the children showed no consistent direction of change.

Children who were studied intensively during their first two years in a classic investigation by Shirley (1933) were studied again at age seventeen by Neilon (1948). Judges were asked to match the unidentified two-year-old personality descriptions with descriptions of the same individuals at age seventeen. The judges were able to match the two descriptions far more accurately than could be expected by chance. But the sketches of some of the children were so dissimilar that judges either disagreed in their judgments or matched them incorrectly. (Mismatches might mean that the children had actually changed or they might mean that it is difficult, at best, to match a sketch at age two with a sketch at age seventeen. As noted in several earlier sections, children are likely to display their emotional tendencies less openly as they grow older. A child who overtly shows fear at two may conceal his tendency to be afraid at seventeen; an irascible two-year-old may, as a teen-ager, conceal his hot temper.)

As noted in the preceding chapter (Peck and Havighurst et al., 1960), individuals who were studied from age ten to seventeen in terms of their moral orientation, ranging from an amoral, impulsive, and irresponsible level of character formation to a high level of moral maturity, manifested a marked tendency to show the same level of moral maturity at ages thirteen and sixteen that they had showed at age ten.

Data in a study by Scarr (1969) suggest that heredity may play a significant role in determining whether an individual will be extroverted and show a tendency to be sociable or be introverted with a tendency to withdraw from social relationships.

As part of a series of investigations referred to earlier, Chess and Thomas (1975) made a longitudinal study of temperamental characteristics exhibited by children from infancy to adolescence. Whereas their study reveals continuity in some temperamental characteristics in some individuals, in others there may be a noteworthy change. Striking examples of both continuity and change appear in their report. A case description of one of their subjects gives an illustration of discontinuity. Nancy as a child was difficult temperamentally and provoked extremely negative responses from her parents, particularly her father, who was very critical of her behavior. "By age six years Nancy developed explosive anger outbursts, fear of the dark, thumb sucking and hair pulling and poor peer-group relationships [p. 6]." But in the course of her development her musical and dramatic talent became apparent. Her father began to view her explosive personality as a sign of being an artist rather than a "rotten kid." Both the father's and the mother's views of her changed. Now that "Nancy was permitted to adapt at her own pace, the positive aspects of her temperament came into evidence, and her self-image improved progressively [p. 7]." At adolescence she was considered to be bright and lively. She functioned well at school, had established good peer relations, and had an active social life. In this vignette we can clearly see how an individual's development can be affected by the interaction of environmental factors with what probably represent hitherto unexpressed innate characteristics.

Self-perpetuating Aspects of Personality Development

Many personal characteristics, when once established, tend to become firmly established as time goes on. This may be due to the effect a person's characteristics have on others, or to the way persons themselves rationalize or justify their characteristics, or to a combination of both of these factors.

Social Reinforcement of Personality Traits

In several earlier sections of this book it has been noted that a youngster's characteristics are nourished by the responses they evoke in others. For example, aggressive individuals are likely to arouse counter-aggression, and this adds fuel to their own aggressiveness. Similarly, youngsters who are socially outgoing are more likely than not to create a friendly atmosphere: they invite others to be friendly, and when they respond in kind they support their own friendly tendencies.

Reinforcement Through a Striving for Self-consistency

Youngsters' characteristics are often perpetuated through their own endeavors to maintain a consistent view of themselves. The concept of self-consistency has been explored more thoroughly in theoretical studies than in studies tracing the development of children from year to year. But this concept helps to account for much in adolescents that otherwise would be hard to fathom. We noted earlier in this chapter that the theory that individuals have strong motives to maintain a consistent view of themselves has been set forth by Lecky (1945). The same idea runs through many other writings dealing with the development of the self. In earlier chapters of this book there are many illustrations of the need persons have for building what seems to be a reasonable interpretation of themselves. Individuals try to construct what to them seems a logical and internally coherent accounting of their feelings and conduct even when in doing so they create difficulties for themselves.

In their striving for self-consistency, persons will perceive and interpret what happens to them in the light of their preconceptions. They will seek experiences that are in keeping with the conceptions they have of themselves. What they choose to hear and see will be influenced by their desire to maintain beliefs and attitudes they already have formed. Even their memory will abet them, in that they are more likely to remember happenings in their past that are in accord with a particular view they have of themselves. When their memories are not easy to manipulate, they are likely, in what they recall, to give greatest weight to those recollections that support ideas and attitudes concerning themselves they would like to maintain.

There is something that persists through time within each unique personality. When we deal with adolescents it is important to remember that their personal characteristics, habits, and attitudes have been a long time in the making. They are likely to be tenacious and not easily changed. It is especially important to bear this fact in mind when we deal with adolescents who are in trouble. If we do not, we are likely to demand too much of the adolescents, or to blame them or their parents, or to blame ourselves, when our efforts to help them seem to have little effect.

Capacity for Change

But there is a seeming paradox here. Even though there is a high degree of consistency in the adolescent's personality, and a considerable degree of resistance to change, the typical adolescent also has a capacity for flexibility and great potentiality for changing. Even an adolescent who is severely disturbed emotionally has a capacity for growth and self-repair. Indeed, Thomas and Chess (1975) reported that almost half of the adolescents who had been diagnosed as having behavioral disorders during the early years had recovered by adolescence and were functioning on a level comparable to that of adolescents who had not shown disorders in childhood.

Changes in the life situation may bring a change in the manifest aspects of an individual's personality. In a long-term study of a group of young persons, Anderson et al. (1959) found that some who were rated low in adjustment improved and achieved satisfactory adjustment when they were on their own and freed from home and school.

Moreover, some changes occur in the process of maturing. In an earlier chapter we noted that many persons who are delinquents in the teens become less aggressive and settle down as law-abiding citizens some years later.

Personality problems

All adolescents have "problems." They cannot live without encountering difficulties and predicaments that are linked with human existence. The adolescent who ventures must accept the risk as well as the promise that goes with each of his or her ventures. Adolescents who strive to realize their potentialities are bound to meet disappointments and frustrations. The more enterprising they are the more likely they are to face choices pertaining to the present and the future that involve conflict between contending motives within themselves. Such problems are part of the business of living. They are problems neither the "well-adjusted" nor the "maladjusted" can side-step. The only way to avoid them would be to retreat and withdraw from life; but to do that would be to create other problems, for unless the adolescent has been beaten down and discouraged to the point of apathy and despair, the urge to live and to do and to venture will be strong.

Adolescents may show signs of their turmoil in a number of ways such as rebelliousness, parental or peer conflict, anxiety, or mood swings. Whereas these phenomena may be signs of underlying psychopathology, they may also occur in adolescents who are coping effectively with their environment.

In addition to the problems that every creature must face as part of life, there are some problems that place an additional burden upon some adolescents. Such problems prevail when they are not simply laboring with concerns of the present, or struggling with uncertainties about the future, but are still fighting a rear-guard action with their past lives.

Irrational Hostility

Adolescents who stand out publicly as seriously disturbed comprise only a small number of those who struggle with unresolved personal problems. In Chapter 10 we noted, for example, the way in which attitudes of hostility make it necessary for some adolescents to refight old battles, as though those who had hurt them in the past had taken lodging in the persons they are dealing with in the present.

When adolescents attach old grievances to new persons and to new circumstances, they are not facing the tasks of life in a realistic way. They use their energy to fight fruitless battles. They may create an enemy where they might have found a friend. The result is that those who are punished most severely by the adolescents' unresolved attitudes of hostility are the adolescents themselves.

Anxiety

Another condition that has a prominent place among the personality problems of adolescents is anxiety (which was discussed at length in Chapter 11). Probably all adolescents are anxious to some degree. Anxiety may prevail as an inevitable, and even a constructive, response to the predicaments of human existence. But it may also be, and often is, a form of needless suffering and self-defeat.

It is impossible, on the basis of present evidence, to assess how widely self-defeating anxiety prevails in the total adolescent population, for often anxiety is hidden, both from the eyes of the anxious one and from others. It may even appear in the disguise of a virtue. An assessment of the more obvious signs of anxiety, known in the literature as *manifest anxiety*, indicates that the typical adolescent has many such signs.

Incidence of Problems Revealed by Ratings, Clinical Studies, and Reports by High School and College Students

At the risk of being repetitious we offer brief summaries of some of the surveys that have been made of personality difficulties in adolescence. Although there is much overlapping in the problems that have been reported, it is not possible to make a single cumulative count of various problem areas because of differences in the terminology and classification schemes used by the various authors. Although many of the statistics give a rather gloomy view of adolescents, it must be remembered that most of these young people manage to carry on in spite of their difficulties.

Two thousand high school students wrote essays on the subject of their personal problems in a study by Pope (1943). They mentioned about 7,000 problems. Many of the students expressed their problems in terms of difficulties presented by other persons and conditions in the external environment, without mentioning, and perhaps without recognizing, that some of the difficulty might reside within themselves. (Adults often show a similar tendency to externalize their problems, Gurin et al., 1960.) Almost half the students mentioned problems in their relationships with their teachers. Problems expressed as relating more directly to their own emotional adjustment, in such terms as feelings of "inferiority" or feelings of "superiority," were mentioned by 11 per cent.[1]

In a survey of the problems of over 5,000 high school youths, Elias (1949) found that 20 per cent or more of the young people named problems in each of the following categories (as phrased by Elias): Being able to talk to people; How to develop self-confidence; Daydream too much; Having a desirable personality; Losing my temper; Wanting people to like me; Concerned about the future; Choosing a vocation; What job best suited for; Don't know what I really want. Many students in this study, as in the study by Pope, named problems pertaining to school, such as being unable to concentrate, not studying enough, or being unable to express themselves well. The median student reported from fifteen to nineteen personal problems.

Many adolescents who responded to a questionnaire in a study by Albert and Beck (1975) gave answers that were symptomatic of moderate to severe depression. Some indicated they had thoughts of doing harm to themselves, but they were unable to carry them out. The types of problems mentioned by the students centered on interpersonal relations, school, home conflict, and the ability to establish their independence.

Problem areas mentioned by adolescents in response to essay questions in an investigation by Collins and Harper (1974) fell into the following categories: health and physical adjustment, religious and life values, and educational, social, personal, and family adjustment. Females in this study were especially concerned with interpersonal relations, whereas males expressed more concern with personal achievement and self-concerns. Although these students were Australian, many of the problems

[1] Among the investigations in this area are studies by Rogers (1942) and Ullman (1952). Other studies dealing with emotional problems in childhood and adolescence have been made by Havighurst and Taba (1949).

they mentioned are probably characteristic of adolescents in all industrial societies.

Findings reviewed in Chapter 18, based on statistics assembled by a number of universities and colleges, show that vocational problems constitute the largest single category presented by students to counseling centers. These problems may be aired by some students who are not severely disturbed; but, at the other extreme, they may be symptomatic of underlying maladjustment.

Schonberg (1974) studied students at Ohio State University and then compared his results with other previous investigations of students at the same school. The first such study was conducted in 1923. As compared with previous studies, Schonberg's students reported more worries. Worries concerning school, nervousness, helplessness, crowds, and stupidity increased between 1923 and 1970. Common worries in all decades concerned appearance, religion, marriage, and interpersonal relations.

A comparison of college students in 1958 and 1968 suggests that students in the late 1960s showed more signs of psychopathology (Schubert and Wagner, 1975). These students were given the MMPI, a personality assessment test. One reason for the change, as proposed by the authors, is that the subculture of the adolescent peer group in 1968 tended to glamorize the alienated personality.

Contrary to the findings of the two previously mentioned studies, Lustman (1972) concluded that there is nothing to suggest that there has been an increase in the incidence of transient symptoms and states associated with adolescent turmoil. His conclusions are based on his observations of students at Yale. It may be that the underlying conflicts are similar from one generation to the next, but the form they take varies with time.

One of the most extensive and exacting studies that has been made of the mental health situation in the adult population that adolescents will soon join is *The Midtown Manhattan Study* (Srole et al., 1962). According to the judgments of a team of psychiatrists, 18.5 per cent of the persons in the sample could be rated as mentally well. Over a third of the persons were rated as having mild symptoms from a psychiatric point of view, and another 21.9 per cent were classed as having moderate symptoms. Persons with marked and severe symptoms and those diagnosed as incapacitated were all regarded as having impaired mental health: the impaired group included 23.4 per cent, or almost a fourth of the sampling.[2]

In the study just cited, as in other studies (see, for example, Gurin et al., 1960), it was noted that only a small proportion of adults who suffer from psychological ailments seek, or are inclined to seek, psychological help. In

[2] Srole and his associates review findings in other large surveys, including a survey in Baltimore and an army study, and conclude that their findings are not exceptional.

this respect older adults do not differ much from young persons of high school or college age. It has not been customary for teachers and others in authority to encourage even distinctly troubled persons to heed the admonition "Know thyself" by seeking help. In the population at large there are millions of persons who would not hesitate for a moment to go to a dentist with a toothache, or to the doctor with a fractured arm, but who would not, when emotionally distressed, think of seeking professional help. One consequence of this attitude is that troubled adolescents, as they go about their task of growing up, may bear their emotional burdens in solitude. Most of them keep a lonely vigil with their troubles.

Although difficulties such as these place a burden on many adolescents' lives, the burden is not so severe that most of them are unable eventually to assume the responsibilities of adult life.

In a study of apparently normal adolescent boys, Offer (1969) concluded that most adolescents are fairly well adjusted. It is interesting to note that many popular, successful, and happy adults may have been unhappy and may have suffered from a number of problems as adolescents. Two independent long-term studies by Macfarlane (1963) and Chess and Thomas (1975) provide evidence in support of this conclusion. Macfarlane concluded that a large number of adults were leading far more productive lives than could have been expected on the basis of what was known about their adolescent personalities.

Reaching for maturity

Adolescence is a process of maturing, and, if all goes well, individuals will be more "mature" when they enter young adulthood than when they entered the adolescent phase of growth. However, the concept of maturity as related to adolescents should not be regarded as denoting a fixed state or an end point in the process of development. Maturity is a relative term, denoting the degree to which, at any juncture of their lives, individuals have discovered and are able to employ the resources that become available to them in the process of growth.

Emotional maturity is, in part, a biological product: it is linked with the physical maturation of the organism. Maturity is also a product of learning: it is only through training, discipline, and experience that the individual's psychological potential can be put to use. Maturity is, in addition, a cultural concept, for when we assess a person's maturity we do so, in large measure, in terms of standards and values of the culture in which he or she lives.

In assessing maturity in this or that sphere of life (cognitive, social, moral, and emotional), it is essential to take account of the level attained by the normal, or typical, person and also to consider the condition of exceptional persons (those who do not measure up to normal standards and those who exceed these standards). When adolescents are "immature" (for example, are more dependent than most persons of their own age or have "childish" moral standards), one question we face (among others) is how they came to be that way: is it because of inherent limitations, or because of unfortunate upbringing, or both? When an adolescent far exceeds normal standards, he provides a model of what a person with a superior endowment or with an optimum environment within a given culture, or a combination of these, can achieve. This model is a valuable one, for in defining the goals and desirable outcomes of adolescent development it is important to know not only what is *probable* under ordinary circumstances, but also what is *possible* under the best circumstances.

Intellectual Maturing

As noted in earlier chapters, when youngsters reach the age of ten or eleven, they begin to enter what Piaget has called the stage of *formal operations*. Adolescents in this stage begin to deal with generalizations, reason about possibilities, and are not limited to concrete objects and situations. Piaget described their ability to apply abstract principles when he noted that "thought takes wings." At the same time they have begun to master logical principles and can apply them to specific cases, at least in some areas. Thus, in response to the question: "If all unicorns have yellow feet and I have yellow feet, am I a unicorn?" most adolescents are able to answer no. Of great importance in the stage of formal operations is the fact that thinking becomes self-conscious: adolescents are able to take their thoughts as objects and think about them.

As was noted in Chapter 6, there are individual differences in the ages when adolescents enter the stage of formal operations. Some adolescents who are slow in developing may not reach the stage of formal operational thought until early adulthood. Other adolescents never reach this stage. Throughout adolescence and early adulthood, many individuals are increasingly able to apply formal operational thinking to more domains or activities. Piaget has referred to this phenomenon as *horizontal décalage* (Piaget, 1972). Associated with this, with increasing age during adolescence there is a preference for higher forms of thought and a rejection of lower forms of thought.

As noted in Chapter 7, another aspect of maturing in the intellectual sphere appears in an increase, with age, in the abilities that are measured by intelligence tests. This increase normally continues through the teens and probably into the twenties and beyond. In the college group, seniors are likely to earn higher average mental test scores than they earned as freshmen (Owens, 1953; Shuey, 1948).

During the teens and twenties and for many years thereafter, if all goes well, there also is likely to be a continuing increase in knowledge gained from experience, an increase in judgment, common sense, and what is known as horse sense. The fact that intelligence, as measured by current tests of mental ability, is not the monopoly of the young is nicely brought out in a study by Owens (1966). He compared the scores on arithmetic, reasoning, and verbal abilities of men in an adult follow-up study. Scores on the arithmetic test were highest at the age of nineteen, were lowest at age sixty-one, and in between these two points at age fifty. In contrast, scores on the reasoning test increased with age between nineteen and sixty-one. With respect to verbal ability, scores were highest at age fifty, followed by age sixty-one, and were lowest at age nineteen.

The capacity for creative thinking apparently continues to increase well beyond the twenties, as measured by the age at which persons who have gained distinction in science, literature, the arts, and other fields made their first contributions (Lehman, 1953). Because it takes time and opportunity to complete a creative task, it is possible that the underlying creative abilities reached their peak well in advance of the time when these persons first gained distinction. In some areas a few noteworthy creative persons made their first contribution before the age of twenty. But in practically all areas far more made their first noteworthy contribution in their twenties, thirties, forties, or beyond.

Physical Maturing

Although adolescents differ considerably in the timing of various physical developments, such as the growth spurt, the onset of the menarche in the female, and the ability to produce sperm in the male, most of them have reached the major developments leading to physical maturity by the time they reach the age of twenty. During this period, the girl increasingly looks more like a woman and the boy like a man.

Moral Maturing

According to available findings, moral standards, which first began to be established earlier in childhood, become fairly well-established during the period of adolescence. In contrast to younger children, adolescents' judgments are oriented more to abstract values and in some cases to their own standards of justice (Kohlberg, 1963). Although the evidence is still scanty, Kohlberg (1973) maintains that moral judgments continue to develop in late adolescence and early adulthood.

Ideally, from the point of view of a moral philosopher, growing individuals might be expected to move toward *moral autonomy*, with an internalized set of moral standards, convictions, and commitments. They would apply their moral principles in a rational way, with due regard for their social responsibilities. Also, ideally, morally mature young persons would be able, in passing judgment on others, to take account of the motives, intentions, and extenuating circumstances applying to others.

Actually, as we have noted in Chapter 19, many of the moral decisions made in late adolescence are based on conformity and expediency. There is no reason to believe, however, that in this respect adolescents differ from typical adults.

Maturing of Self-insight

There are some indications that many young persons, during the course of adolescence, acquire an increasing insight into themselves. But the evidence on this score is very fragmentary. We do not know what typical adolescents actually achieve by way of insight or what they potentially might achieve.

Here and there in earlier chapters we have noted that during the course of adolescence, or soon thereafter, many persons assume a more "mature" view of themselves. In the chapter on vocational development, it was pointed out that many young persons in the late teens are more realistic in their thinking about their vocational plans than they were at an earlier age. In Chapter 17 we noted that a study by Sanford (1957) indicated that seniors in a women's college were more inclined to examine their values and had more insight into themselves than they displayed as freshmen. These findings are consistent with more recent work with both males and females.

In Chapter 17 we also noted that students who took part in an investigation by Jervis and Congdon (1958) named growth in self-understanding as one of the most important objectives in college education; but the investigators report that self-understanding was the only objective the students felt was being inadequately met. Apparently these students regarded a gain in self-understanding as something that potentially *could* be achieved even though they were disappointed in what they actually did gain.

The study of adolescent boys by Offer (1969), cited earlier, suggests that adolescents show considerable maturity in evaluating their own strengths and weaknesses.

Steps toward emotional maturing

Much of what is said in this concluding statement discusses a kind of emotional maturity toward which adolescents are moving if they are realizing their possibilities.

Cultural Aspects of Emotional Maturity

From a cultural point of view adolescents are emotionally mature if they conform to the stereotype of maturity prevailing in the culture in which they live.

In one of the pioneer efforts to define emotional maturity as related to adolescence, Hollingworth (1928) notes that many of the tests of fitness for manhood and womanhood in ancient times were tests of the capacity to suffer. The assumption underlying them seems to have been that one who has fortitude and who can endure pain silently and without protest is a mature person. The mature lad in Sparta was one who could suffer intense pain without flinching or crying for help. But in another culture such a person might be regarded as having a childish notion of what it means to be mature.

In one cultural group a mature man has many wives and perhaps is looking for more, whereas in another cultural group it is a sign of immaturity when a man, once he has a mate, keeps chasing after others.

According to one set of standards, the person who is most rigorously competitive, and who is best able to sustain both the defeats and the triumphs of competition, is the most mature, whereas in another group it is not the one who is most competitive, but the one who is most cooperative, who is the most mature.

Psychological Meanings of Maturity

In naming what she regarded as mature behavior, Hollingworth (1928) stated that emotionally mature people are (1) *capable of gradations or degrees of emotional response*. They do not respond in an all-or-none fashion but are moderate and keep within bounds. They are also able (2) *to delay their responses*: they do not act impulsively as a young child would. They show their maturity also in (3) *their handling of self-pity*; they do not show unrestrained pity for themselves but feel no sorrier for themselves than others would feel for them.

Other early accounts of the meaning of emotional maturity have stressed the ability to bear tension, outgrowing of adolescent moodiness and sentimentality, and an indifference toward certain kinds of happenings that would arouse the emotions of a child or an adolescent but should not arouse an adult.

These accounts describe some aspects of self-control that, in our culture, we more or less take for granted as characteristics of a mature person. However, maturing emotionally does not mean simply controlling emotion or keeping a lid on feeling. Maturing emotionally also means an ability to use emotional resources to get satisfaction from enjoyable things; to love and to accept love; to experience anger when faced with frustrations that would arouse the temper of any reasonable person; to accept and to realize the meaning of the fear that arises when one faces frightening things, without needing to put on a false mask of courage; and to reach out and to seek what life might offer, even though to do so means to face both the possibility of gain and of loss and of enjoyment and grief.[3]

Capacity for Giving as Well as Taking

When all goes well, persons who are biologically able to beget children are also emotionally able to devote themselves to the care of children. There are, of course, young people who have the biological capacity for becoming fathers or mothers without possessing a psychological capacity for fatherly or motherly feelings. By contrast, a person may be capable of intense motherly or fatherly feeling even though he or she does not happen to have fathered or mothered a son or a daughter. Deutsch (1944–1945) has pointed out that a woman, for example, can be a *psychological mother* even though, being childless, she is not a *biological mother*.

The development of the capacity to give makes it possible for a father or mother to watch over a child in spite of fatigue and discomfort. It is this development that makes it possible for teachers to be *psychological* mothers or fathers and to devote themselves wholeheartedly to their students. It is a development that will help adolescents as they move into adulthood to be devoted to each other as husbands and wives in spite of the difficulties and frictions that occur in every marriage.

If this aspect of emotional development has not taken place during childhood, adolescence, and early adulthood, the job of being a parent or of assuming the role of a substitute parent (a role teachers and many others

[3] For other accounts of the meanings of maturity, see Allport (1961), Cole (1959), and Saul (1947).

occupy) will be a burden, and the task of having relations with people in the world at large will be filled with countless grievances and frustrations.

Increasing Realism in Appraising People

One aspect of emotional maturing is an increasing ability to see people as real persons, to perceive and appreciate the humanity of others, and not to expect the good person to be a perfect saint or the bad person to be an all-out sinner.

With allowance for many lapses, adolescents as they mature may be able to perceive, without becoming cynical, that even the teacher they like best is a human being who has weaknesses. They will realize that the pastor who urges his flock to be charitable also has uncharitable moments. They will recognize that school psychologists who help others to cope with their anxieties also have anxieties of their own.

Immature persons might respond to such signs of human frailty as something to blame, and they might take the line that, when others thus are less than perfect, they have a moral right to be a great deal less than perfect.

Reviewing Hopes and Aspirations

During the period of adolescence young people face the task of trying to bring their hopes into line with the realities of life. If all goes well, a process of selecting and discarding takes place, and although hopes run high in some youngsters, others are called on to make the kind of emotional adjustment that is required when plans that are visionary must be abandoned or reduced to a humbler scale. The process of trimming hopes and expectations is, of course, not limited to adolescence. For many persons it continues far into the years of adult life, and for some it begins much earlier in life.

Tolerance of Aloneness

As adolescents mature, many of them must be able to tolerate a feeling of being alone when they reach for independence, or what they regard as their independence. Some, in pursuing their own interests and working for goals they consider important, run the risk of being thought "strange," and strange people often are lonely people. For some, to be lonely is a condition that, although uncomfortable, is less painful, as they see it, than to follow the crowd on its own terms. Younger children, too, know

As adolescents mature, they must be able to tolerate solitude. [Burke Uzzle/Magnum.]

what it is to be lonely, but they have more freedom to seek comfort from others.

Increased Capacity for Compassion

Much of what has been said in this and earlier chapters suggests that compassion is the ultimate and most meaningful embodiment of emotional maturity. It is through compassion that persons achieve the highest peak and deepest reach in their search for self-fulfillment.[4]

Compassion means fellowship of feeling. It denotes a capability of entering the feelings involved in emotional experiences—joy or sorrow, anger or fear, pride or shame, hope or despair. To be compassionate persons must be able to enter into their own feelings, absorb them, and draw on them. Only to the extent that they have the freedom to experience the quality of their own feelings and to be at home with them can they respond with feeling to what someone else is experiencing.

To be compassionate, persons must be able to bear the brunt of an emotion, to feel its sharp edge, to taste its bitterness or sweetness, and then

[4] This section is built largely on some of the senior author's earlier efforts to develop a point of view regarding the meaning of emotional maturity (Jersild, 1955).

tolerate it, sustain it, and harbor it long enough to accept its meaning and to enter into a fellowship of feeling with the one who is moved by the emotion.

To be compassionate means to partake in passion, to participate in feeling rather than view it as a spectator might. Compassion has a greater sweep than anger, love, or fear, for it incorporates these emotions in a larger context of feeling.

To be compassionate is not simply to be sympathetic, tender, or thin-skinned. To be compassionate, individuals must also be able to be tough. Thin-skinned persons turn anxiously away when confronted with the pain, sorrow, or anxiety of another. Or they hastily tell the other, "Don't cry," "Keep a stiff upper lip," "Don't take it so hard"—not because this will help the other person, but because the other's tears are threatening to them and because they cannot endure seeing someone else tremble with fear or give way to anger.

But compassion is not all toughness. Compassionate persons respond to joy as well as to anger or fear. Moreover, they have a certain delicacy of response that enables them, at least sometimes and with some persons, to detect feeling even though it is not violently expressed.

A central and essential feature of compassion can perhaps best be expressed by the idea of *acceptance*. Compassionate individuals accept the fact of emotion in themselves and others without having an immediate and overruling impulse to defend, to attack, to excuse, to blame, or to condone. They accept themselves as persons who get angry and accept this fact for what it is worth, without always having an impulse to snuff out their anger or to feel guilty about it.

The concept of acceptance, as used here, does not mean self-pity, smugness, or license to give way to any and all kinds of emotional outbursts. To accept oneself as one who has the right to be angry or afraid does not mean that every time one is angry or afraid one will automatically conclude that the anger is justified or the fear well grounded.

Freedom to feel is not to be confused with irresponsibility. This point is emphasized here because, in discussing the concept of emotional maturity with adolescents and adults, the senior writer has found that many persons have been so conditioned to the idea that emotions should be "controlled" that they seem to believe that it is unwise and even dangerous to question the idea that self-control in itself is a virtue.

To be compassionate with one who is angry means to know, in an emotional way, the nature of anger as it arises in oneself and the meaning it has for the one who is angry. To feel compassion for one who is lonely or hungry or jealous or sad or sexually aroused means that one has drawn on one's own resources for experiencing what these emotions, moods, and appetites mean.

Sharp differences in this ability to perceive the feelings of others can sometimes be observed when we associate with adolescents. Many adolescents can perceive distress when they come upon a child who is weeping or a crippled beggar who piteously asks for help. But individuals who can draw on a capacity for compassion do not need to meet distress in so naked a form to perceive it. They may be able to perceive it in a person who is silent and expressionless, who is not pointedly displaying loneliness or anxiety or signs of rejection. They may even be able to perceive that when the feelings of such a troubled person do burst forth they may look and sound more like anger than pain. They may be able to perceive, further, that this "anger" may be directed not against a tormentor, but against a friendly person, or against themselves.

The ability to pierce the disguises of feeling is one of the most hard-won properties of compassion.

How capable, we might ask, are young people of achieving compassion? We have little scientific data bearing on this question. We do not know what the "norm" is. But now and then one can observe adolescents who can see the distress that is concealed under the camouflage of bitterness, spitefulness, bullying, sarcasm, and cruelty in the behavior of their elders and peers.

Compassion is something that adolescents cannot learn from books. One does not mature emotionally at second hand. In this respect there is a difference between intellectual and emotional development. In the intellectual sphere, one can, to a large degree, appropriate to oneself what others have learned and put into words. One learns that the earth is round and does not have to go through the struggle, still less the persecution, of those who proved the earth was not flat.

But in their emotional development all children are pioneers. They can, as they grow older, catch certain overtones and undertones of anguish and hope, joy and sorrow, and anger and fear in the great literature, music, and paintings that have been bequeathed to them. But to realize the meaning of emotion, they must experience it firsthand, like learning to swim or ride a bicycle. They can never know what it is to *feel* simply by reading. They cannot know pain and suffering simply by seeing the expression of pain in a great painting. Love will forever be colorless to them until they have a chance to experience it.

The emotional maturity we speak of here as compassion is not won without a struggle. One cannot send proxies into the struggle and gain it through them. It is something distinctly intimate and personal. Some elements of compassion one can possess only at the price of pain; others one can possess only through having known the meaning of joy. But the full tide of compassion comes from all the streams of feeling that flow through human existence.

References

Albert, N., & Beck, A. T. Incidence of depression in early adolescence: A preliminary study. *Journal of Youth and Adolescence*, 1975, **4**, 301–307.

Allport, G. W. *Pattern and growth in personality*. New York: Holt, 1961.

Anderson, J. E., Harris D. B., et al. *A survey of children's adjustment over time*. Minneapolis: Institute of Child Development and Welfare, University of Minnesota, 1959.

Chess, S., & Thomas, A. Temperamental individuality from childhood to adolescence. Paper presented at *Annual Meeting of the Academy of Child Psychiatry*, 1975.

Cole, L. *Psychology of adolescence* (5th ed.). New York: Holt, 1959.

Collins, J. K., & Harper, J. F. Problems of adolescents in Sydney, Australia. *Journal of Genetic Psychology*, 1974, **125**, 187–194.

Deutsch, H. *The psychology of women* (2 vols.). New York: Grune, 1944–1945.

Elias, L. J. *High school youth look at their problems*. Pullman, Wash.: State College of Washington, 1949.

Erikson, E. H. *Childhood and society* (2nd ed.). New York: Norton, 1963.

Gurin, G. J., Veroff, J., & Feld, S. Americans view their mental health: A nationwide interview survey. *Joint Commission on Mental Illness and Health, Monograph Series* (No. 4). New York: Basic Books, 1960.

Havighurst, R. J., & Taba, H. *Adolescent character and personality*. New York: John Wiley, 1949.

Hollingworth, L. S. *Psychology of the adolescent*. Englewood Cliffs, N.J.: Appleton, 1928.

Jersild, A. T. *When teachers face themselves*. New York: Bureau of Publications, Teachers College, Columbia University, 1955.

Jervis, F. M., & Congdon, R. G. Student and faculty perceptions of educational values. *American Psychologist*, 1958, **13**, 464–466.

Kagan, J., & Moss, H. A. *Birth to maturity: A study in psychological development*. New York: Wiley, 1962.

Katz, P. A., Zigler, E., & Zalk, S. R. Children's self-image disparity: The effects of age, maladjustment, and action-thought orientation. *Developmental Psychology*, 1975, **11**, 546–550.

Kohlberg, L. The development of children's orientations toward a moral order. I. Sequence in the development of moral thought. *Vita Humana*, 1963, **6**, 11–33.

Kohlberg, L. Continuities in childhood and adult moral development revisited. In P. B. Baltes & K. W. Schaie (Eds.), *Life-span developmental psychology*. New York: Academic, 1973.

Lecky, P. *Self-consistency: A theory of personality*. New York: Island Press, 1945.

Lehman, H. *Age and achievement*. Princeton, N.J.: Princeton University Press, 1953.

Lustman, S. Yale's year of confrontation: A view of the master's house. *The Psychoanalytic Study of the Child*, 1972, **27**, 57–73.

Macfarlane, J. W. From infancy to adulthood. *Childhood Education*, 1963, **39**, 336–342.

McClain, E. W. An Eriksonian cross-cultural study of adolescent development. *Adolescence*, 1975, **10**, 527–542.

Mischel, W. *Introduction to personality* (2nd ed.). New York: Holt, 1976.

Neilon, P. Shirley's babies after fifteen years: A personality study. *Journal of Genetic Psychology*, 1948, **73**, 175–186.

Offer, D. *The psychological world of the teen-ager: A study of normal adolescent boys*. New York: Basic Books, 1969.

Owens, W. A., Jr. Age and mental abilities: A longitudinal study. *Genetic Psychology Monographs*, 1953, **48**, 3–54.

Owens, W. A., Jr. Age and mental abilities: A second adult follow-up. *Journal of Educational Psychology*, 1966, **57**, 311–325.

Peck, R. F., Havighurst, R. J., Cooper, R., Lilienthal, J., & Moore, D. *The psychology of character development*. New York: Wiley, 1960.

Piaget, J. Intellectual evolution from adolescence to adulthood. *Human Development*, 1972, **15**, 1–12.

Pope, C. Personal problems of high school pupils. *School and Society*, 1943, **57**, 443–448.

Protinsky, H. O., Jr. Eriksonian ego identity in adolescents. *Adolescence*, 1975, **10**, 428–432.

Rogers, C. R. A study of the mental health problems in three representative elementary schools. A study of health and physical education in Columbus public schools. *Monographs of the Bureau of Educational Research*, 1942 (No. 25). Columbus: Ohio State University Press.

Rogers, C. R. The actualizing tendency in relation to "motives" and to consciousness. In M. R. Jones (Ed.), *Nebraska Symposium on Motivation*. Lincoln: University of Nebraska Press, 1963.

Sanford, N. The uncertain senior. *Journal of the National Association of Women Deans and Counselors*, 1957, **21**, 9–15.

Saul, L. J. *Emotional maturity*. Philadelphia: Lippincott, 1947.

Scarr, S. Social introversion-extroversion as a heritable response. *Child Development*, 1969, **40**, 823–832.

Schaefer, E. S., & Bayley, N. Maternal behavior, child behavior and their intercorrelations from infancy through adolescence. *Monographs of the Society for Research in Child Development*, 1963, **28** (3, Serial No. 87).

Schonberg, W. B. Modification of attitudes of college students over time 1923–1970. *Journal of Genetic Psychology*, 1974, **125**, 107–117.

Schubert, D. S., & Wagner, M. E. A subcultural change of MMPI norms in the '60's due to adolescent role confusion and glamorization of alienation. *Journal of Abnormal Psychology*, 1975, **84**, 406–411.

Shirley, M. M. *The first two years: A study of twenty-five babies. Vol. 3. Personality manifestations*. Institute of Child Welfare Monograph Series, 1933: No. 8. Minneapolis: Univ. of Minnesota Press.

Shuey, A. M. Improvement in the scores of the American Council on Education Psychological Examination from freshman to senior year. *Journal of Education Psychology*, 1948, **39**, 417–426.

Srole, L., Langner, T. S., Michael, S. T., Opler, M. K., & Rennie, T. A. C. *Mental health in the Metropolis: The Midtown Manhattan study* (Vol. 1). New York: McGraw-Hill, 1962.

Stott, L. H. Persistent effects of early family experiences upon personality development. *Merrill-Palmer Quarterly*, 1957, Spring. (Special issue reporting seminar on child development.)

Sullivan, H. S. *Conceptions of modern psychiatry*. Washington, D.C.: William Alanson White Psychiatric Foundation, 1947.

Sullivan, H. S. *The meaning of anxiety in psychiatry and in life*. Washington, D.C.: William Alanson White Psychiatric Foundation, 1948.

Sullivan, H. S. *The interpersonal theory of psychiatry*. New York: Norton, 1953.

Super, D. E., Hummel, R. C., Moser, H. P., Overstreet, P. L., & Warnath, C. F. Vocational development, a framework for research. *Career Pattern Study Monograph One*. New York: Bureau of Publications, Teachers College, Columbia University, 1957.

Thomas, A., & Chess, S. *Evolution of behavior disorders in adolescence*. Paper presented at the annual meeting of the American Psychiatric Association, Anaheim, California, May, 1975.

Ullman, C. A. *Identification of maladjusted school children: A comparison of three methods of screening* (Public Health Monographs, No. 7). Washington, D.C.: U.S. Government Printing Office, 1952.

author index

Backman, C. W., 358, 383
Backman, M. E., 132, 142, 181, 198
Badgett, J. L., 198
Bailey, D. A., 133, 142
Bailey, M. M., 525, 533
Bailyn, L., 521, 530
Baird, L. L., 379
Baker, C. T., 203. *See also* Sontag, L. W.
Baldridge, B. J., 232. *See also* Kramer, M.
Balswick, J., 407, 548, 554. *See also* Robinson, I. E.
Balter, M. B., 455, 457, 460. *See also* Mellinger, G. D.
Baltes, P. B., 294, 299, 537*n.*, 554, 584
Balzer, R. H., 189, 202
Bamber, J. H., 217, 231
Bandura, A., 267, 268, 269, 273, 320, 339, 414, 421, 428
Barbee, A. H., 35, 51, 184, 202
Barclay, A. M., 126
Bardwick, J., 38, 49, 99, 124, 504, 523, 530
Barker, M. E., 495, 503
Barnett, R. C., 523, 530
Baron, R. A., 269, 275
Barrett, W. G., 232, *See also* Murray, H. A.
Barrowclough, B., 233. *See also* Vogel, G. W., 222
Barten, S., 77, 88
Barton, K., 199. *See also* Dielman, T. E.
Bartz, K. W., 401, 404
Baruch, G. K., 336, 337, 339
Baruch, R., 523, 530
Bath, J. A., 304, 339
Baumrind, D., 319, 320, 326, 339
Bayer, A. E., 401, 405
Bayley, N., 67, 68, 78, 79, 88, 108, 125, 173, 175, 176, 177, 178, 179, 180, 191, 192, 194, 196, 247, 252, 567, 585
Beach, F. A., 97, 124
Beck, A. T., 572, 584
Becker, W. C., 323*n.*, 325, 339, 415, 428
Beebe, G. W., 103, 126
Beech, R. P., 543, 554
Behnke, A. R. A., 89. *See also* Hampton, M. C.
Beilin, H., 512, 516, 530
Belenky, M., 555. *See also* Saltzstein, H. D.
Beling, G., 402, 405
Bell, R. Q., 78, 88

Bell, R. R., 110, 118, 124, 387, 405
Bell, S. M., 258, 273
Bellack, L., 208*n.*, 231, 260, 273
Belmont, L., 194, 198
Bengtson, V. L., 15, 18, 347, 379, 382. *See also* Kasschau, P. L.
Bennie, E. H., 333, 339
Benoit, C., 113, 124
Berens, A. E., 531. *See also* Horner, M. S., 524*n.*
Berg, J., 365, 384
Berger, A. S., 352, 379
Berger, B., 335, 339
Berger, B. M., 404, 405
Berkowitz, L., 261, 267, 269, 273
Berlyne, D. E., 189, 198
Bernstein, D. A., 270, 273
Berry, J., 532. *See also* Matthews, E. E., 528
Berry, K. L., 457. *See also* Braucht, G. N.
Berscheid, E., 88. *See also* Dion, K., 82
Bettelheim, B., 379
Bienstock, S. F., 105*n.*, 125
Binet, Alfred, 170–73
Binger, C., 391, 405
Birch, H. G., 91, 305, 343. *See also* Thomas, A., 77, 78*n.*, 305
Birns, B., 88. *See also* Barten, S.
Black, A. E., 339
Black, H. K., 391, 405
Blatz, W. E., 305, 339
Block, J., 28, 49, 379, 382, 383. *See also* Haan, N.
Block, J. H., 45, 49
Block, V. L., 313, 339
Bloom, B. S., 196, 199
Bloom, R., 442, 457
Blos, P., 468, 503
Blum, R. H., 457
Blumberg, L., 118, 124
Bohan, J. S., 38, 49
Boll, E. S., 551, 554
Bolles, M. M., 51, 125, 406. *See also* Landis, C.
Bond, H. M., 182*n.*, 199
Bonney, M. E., 358, 364, 366, 380
Bordin, E. S., 513, 526, 530
Bossard, J. H. S., 551, 554
Botkin, P. T., 167. *See also* Flavell, J. H.
Boufford, M. I., 99, 124
Bower, P. A., 142
Bowerman, C. E., 335, 340

Droege, R. C., 132, 142, 180, 181, 199
Dubanoski, R. A., 342. *See also* Marsella, A. J.
Dublin, C. C., 430. *See also* Silver, L. B.
Duck, S. W., 358, 360*n.*, 381
Dudycha, G. J., 165, 167
Dudycha, M. M., 165, 167
Duke, M. P., 412, 428
Dunphy, D. C., 351, 381
Dusseault, B., 183, 199
Dweck, S., 530. *See also* Astin, H. S., 522*n.*
Dymond, R., 28*n.*, 51
Dysinger, W. S., 497, 504

Earp, E., 183, 199
Eberly, D., 503. *See also* Havighurst, R. J., 483
Eckland, B. K., 502
Ehrhardt, A., 269*n.*, 275
Ehrmann, W., 117*n.*, 118, 124
Eichorn, D., 181, 182, 199
Eichorn, D. H., 79, 88
Einstein, A., 157
Einstein, S., 458
Eisenberg, L. A., 5, 19
Ekland, B. K., 477, 478, 479, 503
Elder, G. H., Jr., 167, 199, 320, 335, 339, 340, 351, 373, 380, 381, 406, 502, 504, 545*n.*, 553, 554, 555
Elias, L. J., 572, 584
Elinson, J., 458. *See also* Josephson, E., 442
Elkind, D., 33, 42, 50, 154, 155, 157, 167, 550, 554
Ellinwood, E. H., Jr., 447, 457
Elliott, D. L., 166. *See also* Almy, M. C., 149
Elliott, D. S., 394, 405
Elmer, E., 333, 341
Emmerich, W., 132, 142
Emprey, L. T., 510, 530
Engel, M., 34, 39, 50
Epperson, D. C. A., 308, 340
Erikson, E., 7, 19, 379, 381, 383, 468, 503, 508, 530, 563, 564, 584
Erikson, M. L., 409, 428
Erlenmeyer-Kimling, L., 191, 199
Ernest, E., 62, 88
Eron, L. D., 267, 269, 274
Erskine, H., 423, 428
Ervin, C. R., 405. *See also* Byrne, D., 388

Espenschade, A., 129, 130*n.*, 131*n.*, 133, 142
Evans, D. R., 255, 274
Evans, E. D., 382
Evans, R., 531. *See also* Hoyt, K.
Eysenck, H., 195, 199

Farris, J. A., 343. *See also* Stinnett, N., 312, 335
Fauquier, W., 141, 142, 366, 381
Faust, M. S., 106, 124
Fawcett, J., 430
Feinberg, M. R., 364, 381
Feingold, S. N., 532. *See also* Matthews, E. E., 528
Fejer, D., 442, 460
Feld, S., 584. *See also* Gurin, G. J.
Feldhusen, J., 183, 199
Feldman, K. A., 475, 482, 486, 488, 491, 493*n.*, 503, 504, 551, 554
Fendrich, J. M., 377, 381
Fenhagen, E., 412, 428
Fenigstein, A., 34, 50
Fenner, D., 506. *See also* Winchel, R.
Ferguson, L. R., 268, 274
Ferman, L. A., 551, 554
Feshbach, S., 257*n.*, 274
Festinger, L. A., 358, 381
Feuer, L., 15, 19
Fiedler, F. E., 140, 143
Fillmore, K. M., 219, 233
Final Report of the Commission of Inquiry into the Non-Medical Use of Drugs, 435, 457
Fine, B. D., 267, 275
Finney, J., 458. *See also* Jessor, R., 444, 445
Fisher, C., 222, 227, 228, 231, 232. *See also* Roffwarg, H. P.
Fishkin, J., 538, 554
Flanagan, J. C., 181, 199, 519, 530
Flapan, D., 158, 167
Flavell, J. H., 158, 167
Flory, C. D., 173, 174*n.*, 199
Follingstad, D., 457. *See also* Braucht, G. N.
Fontana, V. J., 333, 334, 340
Forbes, J., 274. *See also* Larsen, K. S.
Ford, C. S., 97, 124
Forehand, R., 343. *See also* Zegiob, L. E.
Forney, R. B., 435, 458
Forrest, D. J., 527, 532

Gordon, A., 169, 428, 443n., 444n., 457. *See also* Brook, J., 410, 411, 442, 443; Whiteman, M., 158, 159
Gordon, C., 15, 19
Gorham, W. A., 199. *See also* Flanagan, J. C., 181
Gornick, V., 530
Goslin, D. A., 380, 406, 554
Goss, A. M., 132, 143
Gotkin, E. H., 534. *See also* Super, D. E., 520
Gotkin, L. G., 200. *See also* Goldberg, M., 183, 185
Gottesman, I. I., 80n., 89
Gottfredson, G. D., 513, 531
Gowan, J. C., 185, 200
Graham, R. A., 504. *See also* Havighurst, R. J., 483
Grant, V. W., 396, 406
Graves, 316, 340
Gray, D. F., 41, 50
Green, B., 553. *See also* Adelson, J., 550
Green, S., 503. *See also* Bachman, J. G., 497, 498, 499, 500
Greenhouse, H. B., 220, 233
Gregg, C. F., 14, 18, 110, 124
Gregg, G., 333, 341
Gregory, A. J., 201
Greulich, W. W., 71, 89
Gribbons, W. D., 519n., 520, 521, 531
Grinder, R. E., 18, 50, 372, 381
Grinker, R. R., 422, 429
Grinspoon, L., 439, 458
Gronlund, N. E., 366, 381
Groobman, D. E., 467, 504
Gross, J., 231. *See also* Fisher, C., 227
Groth, M. J., 183, 200
Group for the Advancement of Psychiatry, 15, 19, 240, 252, 288, 298
Groves, W. E., 437, 445, 458
Gruenwald, P., 62, 89
Grumnon, D., 126
Gudeman, J., 459. *See also* McCord, W., 436
Guilford, J. P., 160, 161, 167
Gurin, G. J., 572, 573, 584
Gusfield, J., 436, 458
Guthrie, J. W., 505. *See also* Levin, H. M.
Gutmann, D., 504

Haan, N., 376, 377, 379, 382, 383. *See also* Smith, M. B.

Haberman, P., 458. *See also* Josephson, E., 442
Hackett, B. M., 339, 404, 405. *See also* Berger, B.
Hackman, J. R., 497, 504
Hadfield, J. A., 225, 231
Hagen, E., 171n., 172, 183, 203
Hall, C. L., 47, 50
Hall, C. S., 228, 229, 231
Hall, D. T., 511, 531
Hall, F. T., 336, 341
Haller, A. O., 358, 382
Halverson, C. F., Jr., 364, 384
Hamilton, G. V., 392, 396, 406
Hampton, M. C., 69, 89
Hansen, D. N., 295n., 299
Hansen, R. A., 192, 200
Hanson, R. C., 245, 247, 252
Hardeman, M., 166. *See also* Almy, M. C., 149
Harger, R. N., 435, 458
Harlow, H. F., 239, 246, 252
Harms, E., 458
Harper, J. F., 572, 584
Harper, L. V., 307, 341
Harris, D. B., 12, 19, 584. *See also* Anderson, J. E.
Harrison, R., 19, 298, 503. *See also* Frank, L. K.
Harroff, P. B., 119, 124
Harter, S., 249, 252
Hartley, E. L., 340, 503
Hartley, R. E., 336, 341
Hartup, W. W., 323, 341, 360, 361, 364, 365, 382
Hastings, P. K., 375, 382
Hauser, S. T., 512, 531
Havemann, E., 46, 50
Havighurst, R. J., 412, 428, 483, 504, 511, 531, 555, 567, 572n., 584, 585. *See also* Peck, R. F., 541
Hawley, P., 524, 531
Hays, J. R., 457. *See also* Bloom, R.
Heald, F., 72, 89
Healy, W., 251, 252, 411n., 429
Heilbrun, A. B., 48, 50
Heilbrun, A. B., Jr., 47, 50
Hein, R. N., 342. *See also* Lambert, W. E.
Helfant, K., 493n., 504
Hellersberg, E., 19, 298, 503. *See also* Frank, L. K.
Helson, R., 525, 531

Henry, N. B., 91
Herma, J. L., 531. *See also* Ginzberg, E., 516, 517
Herold, E. S., 386*n.*, 406
Herr, E. L., 530, 532
Herrnstein, R. J., 197, 200
Hershenson, D. B., 516*n.*, 531
Hertzig, M. E., 91, 343. *See also* Thomas, A., 77, 78*n.*, 305
Herzog, E., 337*n.*, 341
Hetherington, E. M., 313, 320, 326, 337*n.*, 338, 341, 415, 429
Hetzer, H., 13, 19
Heunemann, R. L., 89. *See also* Hampton, M. C.
Heyde, M. B., 520, 532
Hicks, N., 438, 439, 458
Hiernaux, J., 68, 89
Hiestand, D., 528, 531
Hill, D. T., 252. *See also* Sarason, S. B.
Hill, E., 371, 372, 381, 470, 503
Hill, K. T., 168. *See also* Kramer, J. A., 149
Hill, R., 386, 403, 406
Hindley, C. B., 178, 200
Hinsie, L. E., 267, 274
Hirschi, T., 411*n.*, 416, 429
Hitchcock, M. E., 402, 405
Hobbs, E. D., 154, 167
Hoch, P., 281, 298
Hochman, J. S., 441, 458
Hoffer, A., 450, 458
Hoffman, L. W., 50, 336, 337, 339, 340, 341, 428, 430, 481, 504, 525, 526, 531
Hoffman, M. L., 50, 307, 338, 339, 341, 415, 428, 429, 430, 551, 554
Hogan, N., 530. *See also* Davis, D. A.
Hogan, R., 445, 458
Hogarty, P. S., 201. *See also* McCall, R. B.
Hoge, D. R., 375, 382
Holland, J. L., 513, 514, 515, 531
Hollander, J., 517, 531
Hollingshead, A. B., 510
Hollingworth, L. M., 202. *See also* Pritchard, M. C.
Hollingworth, L. S., 7, 19, 98, 124, 183, 188, 200, 578, 584
Hollister, L. E., 460
Holmes, F. B., 270, 272, 274
Holstein, C. B., 538, 554
Holt, R. R., 209, 231

Homburger, E., 232. *See also* Murray, H. A.
Honzik, M. P., 178, 191, 194, 200
Hood, R., 418, 429
Hook, E. B., 75, 89
Hope, L. H., 198
Horan, K. M., 202. *See also* Pritchard, M. C.
Horner, M. S., 480, 481, 504, 524, 531
Horney, K., 284, 290–92, 298, 398, 406
Horowitz, F. D., 342
Horowitz, H., 135, 143
Hoshi, H., 66, 89
Houston, B. K., 297, 298
Hoyt, K., 528, 531
Huber, J., 532
Huesmann, L. R., 274. *See also* Eron, L. D.
Hume, D., 209, 232
Hummel, R. C., 586. *See also* Super, D. E., 563
Hurlock, E. B., 366, 367, 382
Husni-Palacios, M., 265, 271, 274
Hutchins, E., 477, 478, 506
Huxley, A., 449, 458

Ilg, F. L., 531. *See also* Gesell, A., 517
Inhelder, B., 151, 152, 154, 155, 156, 165, 167, 168, 394, 407, 550, 554. *See also* Piaget, J., 148*n.*
Inselberg, R., 401, 406
Insko, C. A., 407. *See also* Stroebe, W.
Institute for Social Research, 271, 274
Insull, W., Jr., 62, 89
Isaacs, A. F., 183, 201
Ivins, W., 402, 406
Izard, C. E., 359, 382
Izzo, L. D., 380. *See also* Cowan, E. L.

Jacklin, C. N., 38, 44, 45, 47, 51, 132, 135, 140, 143, 173, 181, 201, 268, 275, 294, 298, 357, 366, 382, 481, 505, 540, 555
Jackson, P. W., 161, 167
Jacob, P. E., 484, 485, 504
Jacobs, J. C., 183, 201
Jacobs, T., 414, 429
James, B., 110, 124
Jameson, S. H., 123, 125, 391, 406
Jarvik, L. F., 177, 191, 201
Jarvis, P. E., 167. *See also* Flavell, J. H.
Jencks, C., 197, 201

Jennings, H. H., 358, 362, 382

Jensen, A. R., 195, 201, 213, 217, 233

Jepsen, D. A., 527*n.*, 531

Jersild, A. T., 17, 18, 32, 44, 50, 85*n.*, 89, 105*n.*, 109*n.*, 125, 143, 153, 154, 168, 182, 184, 201, 227, 228, 232, 238, 250*n.*, 252, 256, 257, 260, 266, 270, 272, 274, 281, 298, 304, 317, 330, 341, 346*n.*, 382, 426*n.*, 429, 472*n.*, 473, 474, 476*n.*, 490, 491, 493*n.*, 494, 501, 504, 581*n.*, 584

Jersild, C. L., 232. *See also* Jersild, A. T., 227, 228

Jervis, F. M., 28*n.*, 50, 488, 491, 504, 577, 584

Jessor, R., 117, 118, 125, 436, 437, 444, 445, 458, 547, 552, 555

Jessor, S. L., 117, 118, 125, 437, 458. *See also* Jessor, R., 436, 444, 445

Johnson, A. H., 472, 504

Johnson, J., 340. *See also* Golightly, C.

Johnson, R., 274. *See also* Larsen, K. S.

Johnson, R. C., 51

Johnston, F. E., 96*n.*, 125

Johnston, L., 442, 458

Jones, H. E., 106, 125, 128, 136, 139, 140, 142, 143, 175, 201

Jones, K., 505. *See also* Perry, R. P.

Jones, M. C., 67, 90, 107, 108, 109, 125, 126

Jones, M. C. A., 12, 13, 19

Jones, M. R., 585

Jones, R. T., 441, 458

Jordaan, J. P., 516, 518, 520, 521, 527, 532, 534. *See also* Super, D. E., 518

Josephson, E., 432, 442, 457, 458, 459

Jourard, S. M., 83, 91, 357, 382

Joyce, C. S., 339. *See also* Allaman, J. D.

Jung, C., 561

Kaczkowski, H., 297, 298

Kagan, J., 45, 46, 47, 50, 51, 268, 274, 312, 323, 341, 342, 567, 584. *See also* Minton, C.

Kahl, J. A., 185, 192, 201

Kallman, F. J., 80*n.*, 89

Kandel, D. B., 326, 327, 341, 347, 353, 354*n.*, 382, 386, 390, 406, 434, 438, 442, 443, 453, 454, 459, 479, 504

Kaplan, D. M., 257*n.*, 274

Kapplin, D. A., 526, 530

Karmel, B., 477, 504

Karns, E. A., 506

Karson, E., 380. *See also* Devereaux, E. C.

Kasschau, P. L., 376, 377, 382

Katz, P. A., 562, 584

Kaufman, E., 454, 459

Kav-Venaki, S., 380. *See also* Devereaux, E. C.

Keasey, C. B., 540, 554

Keating, D. P., 149, 155, 168

Kelley, C. M., 434, 459

Kennedy, W. R., 476, 504

Keniston, K., 352, 374, 376, 377, 382, 456, 459, 554. *See also* Fishkin, J.

Kenkel, W. F., 387, 405

Kerley, S. A., 198

Kerpelman, L. C., 376, 382

Kessler, J., 422, 423, 429

Kessler, R., 459. *See also* Kandel, D. B., 434, 438, 442, 443

Keup, W., 460

Kiely, E., 380. *See also* Devereaux, E. C.

Kierkegaard, S., 281–82, 283*n.*, 298

Kifer, E., 197, 201

Kim, D., 75, 89

King, K., 336, 341, 401, 407. *See also* Robinson, I. E.

King, M., 274. *See also* Lewis, W. C.

Kinsey, A. C., 103, 111, 112, 114, 115, 117, 118, 119, 120, 121, 125

Klausmeier, H. J., 201

Kleck, R. E., 82, 83, 89

Kleindorfer, G. B., 505. *See also* Levin, H. M.

Kleitman, N., 220, 231, 232

Klinger, E., 217, 232

Klonoff, H., 459

Kluckhohn, C., 371, 382

Kniveton, B. G., 472, 505

Knott, V. B., 63, 89

Kogan, N., 161, 169

Kohlberg, L., 45, 46, 51, 374, 376, 382, 412, 429, 537, 538, 539, 540, 554, 576, 577, 584

Kolb, L. C., 81, 89

Komarovsky, M., 8, 19, 49, 51, 524, 532

Kopell, B. S., 460

Korman, A. K., 518, 532

Korn, S., 91, 343. *See also* Thomas, A., 305

Kowalski, R. S., 534. *See also* Super, D. E., 520

Kraines, R. J., 383. *See also* Troll, L., 376

Kramer, J. A., 149, 168
Kramer, J. C., 446, 459
Kramer, M., 226, 232
Kratcoski, J. E., 410, 429
Kratkoski, P. C., 410, 429
Kriger, S. F., 525, 532
Krogman, W. M., 64, 65n., 66n., 90
Kruglanski, A. W., 299. See also Ziv, A.
Kuhlman, C., 167
Kubie, L. S., 188, 201, 493n., 505
Kuhlen, R. G., 550, 554
Kvaraceus, W. C., 408, 423, 424, 425, 429
Kwalwasser, L., 533. See also Richardson, M. S., 523

Labouvie-Vief, G., 6, 19, 175, 202, 268, 275
Ladd, E. C., Jr., 15, 19
Lambert, W. E., 312, 342
Lamberth, J., 405. See also Byrne, D., 388
Landau, E., 399, 406
Landis, A. T., 51, 125, 406. See also Landis, C.
Landis, C., 43, 51, 123, 125, 394, 406
Landis, J. T., 400, 406
Landis, M. G., 400, 406
Landy, F. J., 270, 274
Langner, T. S., 299, 586. See also Srole, L., 573
Lantagne, J. E., 122, 125, 391, 406
Larsen, J. D., 231. See also Foulkes, D., 226
Larsen, K. S., 268, 274
Latham, A. J., 107, 125
Laufer, R. S., 18, 19. See also Bengtson, V. L., 15
Laughlin, F., 251, 252, 364, 382
Laurendeau, M., 155, 168
Lauten, D. A., 134, 143
LaVoie, J. C., 313, 316, 317, 342
Layton, B. D., 407. See also Stroebe, W.
Lazar, E., 201, 274, 341, 504. See also Jersild, A. T., 184, 260, 304, 317, 330, 493n.
Leary, T., 449, 459
Lebovici, S., 88, 90, 94n., 95n., 126
Lecky, P., 240, 252, 562, 569, 584
LeDain Report, 435, 446, 447, 448, 450, 451, 452, 453–56, 457
Lee, E. S., 196, 201
Lee, G., 552, 555

Lefkowitz, M. M., 274. See also Eron, L. D.
Lehman, H., 576
Lemkin, J., 312, 341
Lerner, M., 452, 460
Lerner, R. M., 347, 350n., 382
Lesser, G. S., 326, 327, 341, 347, 353, 354n., 382, 386, 390, 406, 479
Leuchtenberger, C., 439, 459
Leuchtenberger, R., 459. See also Leuchtenberger, C.
Levi, J., 533. See also Steinmann, A.
Levin, H. M., 499n., 505
Levine, J. A., 342. See also Minton, C.
Levine, S. V., 446, 459
Lewin, K., 241, 252
Lewis, E. C., 304, 339
Lewis, M., 245, 252
Lewis, R. A., 400, 406
Lewis, W. C., 259, 274
Libby, W., 208n., 232
Lieb, J., 460. See also Slaby, A.
Liebert, R. S., 374, 376, 382
Liebert, R. M., 269, 275
Lifton, R. J., 530
Lilienthal, J., 555, 585. See also Peck, R. F.
Lindzey, G., 382
Lipetz, M. E., 405. See also Driscoll
Lipset, S. M., 15, 19
Lloyd, D. D., 459. See also Levine, S. V.
Lloyd, R. C., 327, 342
LoCasio, R., 521, 532
Lochman, S. E., 89. See also Greulich, W. W.
Lohnes, P. R., 519n., 520, 521, 531
Long, D., 376, 379, 381
Longdon, W. H., 459. See also Levine, S. V.
Looft, W. R., 313, 316, 317, 342
Loomis, C. P., 358, 382
Lorenz, K., 267, 275
Lorge, I., 193, 201
Lourie, R. S., 430. See also Silver, L. B.
Lowrie, S. H., 387, 406
Luckey, E. B., 110, 115, 116n., 117, 118, 125, 514, 532
Lukoff, I. F., 347, 371, 382, 415, 428, 430, 443n., 444n., 457, 459, 478, 479, 505, 549, 552, 555. See also Brook, J., 410, 411, 442, 443
Lund, F. H., 132, 143

Mitani, S., 89. *See also* Gruenwald, P.
Mitchell, B. W., 89. *See also* Hampton, M. C.
Moberg, D., 547, 555
Mohs, K., 342. *See also* Marsella, A. J.
Money, J., 107, 109, 125, 269*n*., 275
Monge, R. H., 35, 51
Montagu, A., 97*n*., 125, 252, 406
Montesano, N., 517, 532
Moore, B. E., 267, 275
Moore, D., 555, 585. *See also* Peck, R. F.
Moore, D. R., 195, 201.
Moore, W. M., 63, 65, 90
Moran, B. K., 530
Moreno, J. L., 358, 383
Morgan, L. B., 470, 505
Morrill, W. H., 527, 532
Morrissey, R. F., 297, 299
Moser, H. P., 586. *See also* Super, D. E., 563
Mosher, L., 115, 125
Moss, H. A., 47, 51, 268, 274, 323, 341, 567, 584
Mowrer, O. H., 288, 298
Moynigan, D., 374, 375, 383
Muma, J. R., 361, 383
Munns, M., Jr., 311, 342
Murphy, G., 188, 201
Murray, H. A., 213, 232
Murray, J. P., 269, 275
Murstein, B. I., 219, 232
Musa, K. E., 40, 51
Mussen, P. H., 51, 67, 70*n*., 90, 91, 107, 108, 125, 126, 167, 176*n*., 198, 203, 274, 382, 429
Muuss, R. E., 97, 126
Myint, T., 523, 530

Nachmann, B., 513, 530. *See also* Bordin, E. S., 513
Naditch, M. P., 297, 299
Nadi, I., 342. *See also* Saad, Z.
Nass, G., 110, 115, 116*n*., 117, 118, 125, 386, 407
Nathanson, S., 527, 533
National Commission on Marijuana and Drug Use, 432*n*., 437, 438, 439, 441, 447, 452, 455, 456
National Institute of Alcohol Abuse and Alcoholism, 434, 460
Neale, J. M., 195, 200
Neilon, P., 567, 585

Neimark, E. D., 156, 168
Nelson, D., 340. *See also* Golightly, C.
Nelson, E., 547, 555
Nelson, J. M., 460. *See also* Weil, A. T.
Nelson, V. L., 203. *See also* Sontag, L. W.
Nesselroade, J. R., 294, 299
Nettler, G., 416*n*., 430
Neugarten, B. L., 383. *See also* Troll, L.
Newcomb, T. M., 340, 475, 486, 488, 493*n*., 503, 551, 554
Newton, N., 98, 126
Neyman, C. A., Jr., 199. *See also* Flanagan, J. C., 181
Niemi, R. R., 505. *See also* Perry, R. P.
Nishimura, T., 89. *See also* Gruenwald, P.
Norfleet. M. A., 186, 201
Northway, M. L., 365, 383
Nowicki, S., Jr., 268, 273
Nowlis, H. H., 440, 460
Nurco, D. N., 452, 460
Nye, I. F., 340, 401, 404, 531

Oakden, E. C., 157, 168
O'Connell, E. J., 78, 90
Oden, M., 176, 183, 187, 203
Offer, D., 39, 51, 218, 232, 267, 275, 289, 290, 299, 422, 430, 574, 577, 585
O'Hara, R. P., 516*n*., 519, 532, 534
Ohlin, L. E., 417, 428
Oiso, T., 89. *See also* Insull, W. Jr.
Ojemann, R. H., 493*n*., 505
Oliver, L., 530, 533
O'Neil, H. F., Jr. 295, 299
O'Neil, R., 553. *See also* Adelson, J., 550
Opler, M. K., 299, 586. *See also* Srole, L.
Oppenheimer, E. A., 518, 533
Orgel, S. Z., 82, 90
Orloff, H., 346, 383
Ornstein, P. H., 232. *See also* Kramer, M.
Orr, D. B., 199. *See also* Flanagan, J. C., 181
Osborne, R. T., 201
Osgood, C. E., 28, 51
Osipow, S., 521, 533
Osipow, S. H., 510, 513, 515*n*., 518, 522*n*., 523, 533
Osler, G., 239, 252
Osmond, H., 450, 458
Osofsky, J. D., 78, 90, 307, 342
Overstreet, P. L., 586. *See also* Super, D. E., 563

Owen, K., 297, 298
Owens, W. A., Jr., 175, 202, 576, 585

Pace, R. C., 551, 555
Packard, V., 117, 126
Panos, R. J., 497, 505
Papalia, D. E., 156, 168
Pařízková, J., 70, 90
Parke, R., Jr., 400, 407
Parker, C. A., 547, 551, 552, 555
Parry, H. J., 460. *See also* Mellinger, G. D.
Passow, A. H., 187*n.*, 188, 202
Patterson, L. E., 523, 533
Peck, R. F., 541, 555, 567, 585
Pederson, A., 380. *See also* Cowan, E. L.
Peisach, E., 192, 202, 380, 503. *See also* Brook, J. S., 347, 477, 478, 479
Pepinsky, H. E., 408, 409, 430
Perlman, D., 110, 126
Perrone, P. A., 513, 533
Perry, R. P., 476, 505
Perry, W. G., Jr., 486
Peterson, C., 504. *See also* Groobman, D. E.
Petre-Quadens, O., 220, 232
Philips, I., 198
Piaget, J., 46, 51, 148, 149–51, 152–58, 160, 165, 168, 352, 374, 383, 394, 407, 536, 537, 539, 550, 554, 555, 560, 575, 585
Pikas, A., 320, 342
Pinard, A, 155, 168
Pivik, T., 231. *See also* Foulkes, D., 226
Pomeroy, W. B., 103, 112, 125, 126. *See also* Kinsey, A. C., 111, 119, 120, 121
Pope, C., 268, 275, 572, 585
Porter, R. M., 487, 505
Powell, M. G., 299
Prendergast, P., 42, 51
President's Commission on Law Enforcement, 373, 383
President's Science Advisory Commission, 345, 351, 352, 383, 467, 477, 505
Preston, R. C., 154, 168
Pritchard, M. C., 193, 202
Prokopec, M., 59, 65, 66, 79, 90
Propper, A. M., 336, 342
Protinsky, H. O., Jr., 564, 585
Pytkowicz, A. R., 261, 275

Radin, N., 332, 342
Radler, D. H., 370, 383, 470, 505

Rainwater, L., 337, 342
Ramsey, G. V., 102, 103, 111, 126
Rand, W. M., 127
Ransford, H. E., 382. *See also* Kasschau, P. L.
Raph (Beasley), J., 185, 186, 202
Rardin, M., 231. *See also* Foulkes, D., 226
Rarick, G. L., 133, 142, 143
Rathus, S. A., 430. *See also* Senna, J.
Rechtschaffen, A., 221, 232
Redl, F., 422, 430
Reich, C. A., 352, 375, 383
Reimer, D. J., 409, 410, 411, 429
Reisman, D., 351, 383
Reiss, I. L., 110, 120, 126
Remmers, H. H., 370, 383, 470, 505
Rennie, T. A. C., 299, 527, 533, 586. *See also* Srole, L.
Report on the Committee on One-Parent Families, 337, 342
Revelle, R., 56, 89, 96*n.*, 124
Reynolds, D. J., 270, 273
Reynolds, E. L., 71, 72, 90, 100, 126
Reynolds, N. B., 489, 505
Rheingold, H. L., 247, 252
Ribble, S. A., 77, 90
Ricciuti, H., 273, 341
Rice, F. P., 256, 271, 275, 386, 400, 404, 407, 547, 551, 555
Richards, A. K., 258, 261, 274, 487, 503
Richardson, M. S., 507, 521, 523, 533
Richardson, S. A., 89. *See also* Kleck, R. E.
Ridberg, E. H., 341, 429. *See also* Hetherington, E. M., 320, 326, 415
Ritter, U., 459. *See also* Leuchtenberger, C.
Rivenbark, W. H. III, 30, 51
Roach, M. E., 40, 51
Roberts, D. E., 548, 549, 555
Robins, L. N., 453, 460
Robinson, I. E., 389, 407
Rodgers, R. R., 380. *See also* Devereaux, E. C.
Roe, A., 514, 525, 533
Roff, M., 361, 364, 365, 383
Roffwarg, H. P., 221, 222, 232
Rogers, C., 28*n.*, 51
Rogers, C. R., 299, 562, 572*n.*, 585
Rogers, E., 436, 460
Rohrbaugh, J., 547, 552, 555
Roll, S., 103, 127

Ronald, L., 89. *See also* Kleck, R. E.
Ronch, J., 88. *See also* Barten, S.
Ronda, T., 201
Rooks, E., 401, 407
Root, A. W., 95*n.*, 126
Rorschach, H., 213
Rosen, B. C., 308, 342, 512, 533
Rosen, J. J., 299
Rosenberg, F., 52, 468*n.*, 469*n.*, 505. *See also* Simmons, R.
Rosenberg, M., 52, 468*n.*, 469*n.*, 505, 549, 555. *See also* Simmons, R.
Rosenkrantz, P. S., 49. *See also* Broverman, I. K.
Rosenwood, L. M., 249, 252, 393, 406
Rosner, H., 394, 407
Ross, H. S., 188, 202
Rothbart, M. K., 312, 342
Rothenberg, B. B., 159, 169
Rottmann, L., 91, 407. *See also* Walster, E.
Routh, D. K., 180, 202
Rubin, Z., 393, 407
Rubovits, P. C., 195, 202
Rudisill, D., 411*n.*, 416, 429
Ruff, C. F., 299. *See also* Templer, D. I., 284
Ruff, W. K., 82, 90
Rutter, M., 247, 252
Ryan, F. R., 360*n.*, 383

Saad, Z., 332, 342
Saltzstein, H. D., 540, 555
Sanford, N., 42, 51, 485, 491, 505, 577, 585
Sanford, R. N., 208*n.*, 232
Sapiro, J. D., 452, 460
Sarason, I. G., 275. *See also* Pytkowicz, A. R.
Sarason, S. B., 244, 252
Saul, L. J., 579*n.*, 585
Sawrey, J. M., 143
Scarlett, G., 27, 51, 328, 342, 394, 407
Scarr, S., 567, 585
Schaefer, E. S., 325, 342, 343, 567, 585
Schaefer, R. A., 155, 168
Schaffer, L. F., 210, 211*n.*, 232
Schaie, K. W., 6, 19, 175, 198, 202, 537*n.*, 554, 584
Schatzoff, M., 127. *See also* Zacharias, L.
Scheier, M. F., 50. *See also* Fenigstein, A.
Scheur, P., 265, 271, 274
Schilder, P., 81, 90, 209, 232

Schlag, J. D., 220, 232
Schlossberg, N. K., 523, 533
Schlossberg, W. K., 528, 533
Schmeck, H. M., Jr., 63, 90
Schoeppe, A., 543, 554
Schonberg, W. B., 573, 585
Schonfeld, W. A., 68, 69, 71, 90, 93, 94*n.*, 95*n.*, 103, 107, 108, 109*n.*, 126
Schroeder, M. P., 336, 341
Schubert, D. S., 573, 585
Schwartz, A., 460. *See also* Slaby, A.
Schwartz, G., 372
Sclare, A. B., 333, 339
Scott, L. F., 371, 383
Scott, P. M., 343. *See also* Yarrow, M. R.
Scott, W. A., 51
Sears, P. S., 35, 51, 184, 202
Sears, R. R., 34, 52
Secord, P., 83, 91, 358, 383
Segal, S. J., 514, 533
Segal, S. S., 530. *See also* Bordin, E. S., 513
Sellin, T., 428
Sells, B., 361, 364, 383. *See also* Roff, M.
Senna, J., 411, 430
Sepulveda, P., 51. *See also* Prendergast, P.
Sewell, W. H., 497, 505, 506
Sexton, P. C., 134, 143
Shah, V. P., 497, 505
Shaikun, G., 232. *See also* Rechtschaffen, A.
Shainess, N., 99, 126
Shapiro, L. R., 89. *See also* Hampton, M. C.
Sharma, S., 198, 202
Sharp, W. H., 526, 533
Shaver, P., 506. *See also* Winchel, R.
Shaycroft, M. F., 199. *See also* Flanagan, J. C., 181
Sheerer, M., 247, 252
Sheldon, E. B., 522, 534
Shelov, M., 533. *See also* Richardson, M. S., 523
Sheppard, C. W., 435, 446, 450, 458
Sherman, M., 299
Shoben, E. J., Jr., 210, 211*n.*, 232
Short, J. F., Jr., 421, 430
Shouval, R., 380. *See also* Devereaux, E. C.
Shirley, M. M., 78, 91, 305, 343, 567, 585
Shuey, A. M., 576, 585
Shulman, A. D., 52. *See also* Silverman, I.

Shulman, S., 299. *See also* Ziv, A.
Shumsky, A., 540, 555
Shuttleworth, 59*n.*, 60, 89, 91, 126, 490, 505. *See also* Greulich, W. W.
Siegel, L., 430. *See also* Senna, J.
Siegel, A. E., 341
Siegel, R. L., 423, 428
Silver, L. B., 414, 430
Silverman, I., 38, 52
Silverman, S. S., 86, 91
Simmons, R., 34, 35, 52, 468, 469*n.*, 505
Simon, R. J., 410, 430
Simon, W., 126, 379, 388, 406. *See also* Berger, A. S.
Singer, J. L., 209, 210, 212, 213, 218, 232, 233
Singer, P. R., 232
Single, E., 459. *See also* Kandel, D., 434, 438, 442, 443
Sinha, V., 31, 52
Skeels, H. M., 190, 191, 193, 202
Skipper, J. K., Jr., 386, 407
Skodak, M., 190, 191, 202
Skolnick, P., 38, 52
Slaby, A., 438, 460
Slocum, W. L., 488, 505
Small, L., 517, 533
Smart, R. G., 442, 446, 457, 460
Smith, C. P., 50
Smith, E. J., 511, 533
Smith, G. F., 387, 407
Smith, J. W., 441, 457
Smith, M. B., 376, 379, 382, 383. *See also* Haan, N.
Smith, M. W., 172, 202
Smith, P. C., 232. *See also* Kramer, M.
Smith, R. B., 183, 202
Smith, W. M., 12, 19
Smoll, F. L., 133, 143
Soliah, D., 513, 530
Sollenberger, R. T., 95, 126
Sontag, I. W., 178, 203
Sorenson, J., 525, 534
Sorenson, R. C., 110, 114, 116, 117, 126, 389, 407
Sorokin, P. A., 245, 247, 252
Sparks, R., 418, 429
Spatz, D., 273. *See also* Anastasi, A.
Spear, P. S., 231. *See also* Foulkes, D., 222, 226
Special Task Force, Health, Education, and Welfare, 509, 533

Spencer, C., 358, 360*n.*, 381
Spielberger, C. D., 295*n.*, 296, 298, 299. *See also* O'Neil, H. F., Jr.
Spitz, R. A., 193, 247, 253
Spivack, S., 28*n.*, 36*n.*, 52, 299
Srole, L., 299, 573, 586
Staffieri, J. R., 82, 91
Stanfiel, J. D., 483, 506
Stanley, A. E., 120, 124
Starishevsky, R., 534. *See also* Super, D. E., 518
Starr, J., 351, 376, 383
Steadman, H. E., 231. *See also* Foulkes, D., 226
Steele, B. F., 332, 343
Stein, A. H., 525, 533
Stein, D. G., 299
Steiner, M., 19, 298, 503. *See also* Frank, L. K.
Steinmann, A., 524, 533
Stengel, E., 365, 383
Stephens, B., 156, 169
Stephenson, W., 28*n.*, 52
Stern, G. G., 482, 506
Stevenson, H., 429
Stewart, C. W., 548, 555
Stewart, C., 127
Stinnett, N., 312, 335, 340, 343. *See also* Graves, D.
Stolz, H. R., 56, 61, 71, 83, 91, 101, 126, 181, 203
Stolz, L. M., 56, 61, 71, 83, 91, 101, 126, 181, 203
Stone, C. L., 347, 383
Stott, L. H., 256, 275, 567, 586
Stout, R. T., 505. *See also* Levin, H. M.
Stouwie, R. J., 341, 429. *See also* Hetherington, E. M., 320, 326, 415
Strangeland, M., 255, 274
Stratton, G. M., 257, 275
Strauf, J., 530. *See also* Davis, D. A.
Strickland, B., 20. *See also* Zytkaskee
Strodtbeck, F. L., 421, 430
Stroebe, W., 392*n.*, 407
Strommer, M. P., 554, 555
Strutl, G. F., 132, 143
Stubbins, J., 513, 534
Sturt, M., 157, 168
Stycos, J. M., 113, 127
Suchman, E. A., 442, 445, 460
Suci, G. J., 51. *See also* Osgood, C. E.
Sudia, C. E., 337*n.*, 341

Sullivan, H. S., 33, 285, 286, 299, 562, 586
Suniewick, N., 530. *See also* Astin, H. S., 522n.
Super, D. E., 518, 519, 520, 529, 532, 533, 534, 563, 586
Sutherland, E. H., 416, 430
Svensson, A., 180, 181, 203
Swanson, E. M., 228, 231, 233. *See also* Foulkes, D., 226
Sykes, G. M., 418, 430
Symonds, J. D., 231. *See also* Foulkes, D., 222, 226
Symonds, P. M., 208n., 213, 214, 215, 216, 217, 233, 299
Szeminska, A., 168. *See also* Piaget, J., 148n.

Taba, H., 572n., 584
Taguiri, R., 358, 381
Takaishi, M., 58n., 64n., 91
Takeuchi, S., 89. *See also* Gruenwald, P.
Tannenbaum, A. J. 136, 143, 185, 186, 200, 202. *See also* Goldberg, M., 183; Passow, A. H., 187n.
Tannenbaum, P. H., 51. *See also* Osgood, C. E.
Tanner, J. M., 12, 19, 20, 58n., 59, 60, 61, 63, 64n., 65, 67, 68, 69, 70n., 71, 78n., 93, 94, 97, 101, 102, 125, 129, 144, 181, 203
Tasch, R. J., 153, 168, 252, 256, 257, 274, 472n., 473, 474, 504. *See also* Jersild, A. T., 250n., 501
Taschuk, W. A., 40, 52
Taube, I., 482n., 506
Taylor, J. A., 288, 299
Tec, N., 444, 460
Telford, C. W., 143
Templer, D. I., 284, 299
Terman, L. M., 36, 170, 171, 183, 184, 185, 187, 203
Thomas, A., 77, 78n., 91, 304, 305, 343, 568, 570, 574, 584
Thomas, C., 506. *See also* Yamamoto, K.
Thomas, D. L., 549, 555
Thomas, J. A., 166. *See also* Bynum, T. W.
Thomas, M. J., 511, 534
Thompson, B., 41, 52
Thompson, V. D., 407. *See also* Stroebe, W.

Thompson, W. R., 192n., 200
Thornberg, H. D., 350n., 352, 382, 383, 409, 430
Thorndike, R. L., 171, 172, 173, 178, 183, 203
Thurstone, L. L., 171, 203
Tiedeman, D. V., 516n., 534
Tinklenberg, J. R., 440
Toifo, R., 274. *See also* Eron, L. D., 267
Tomlinson-Keasey, C., 155, 169
Traub, A. C., 222, 233
Trautner, H. M., 326, 343
Traxler, A. E., 199
Trent, J. W., 482n., 506
Tresemer, D. W., 531. *See also* Horner, M. S., 524n.
Troll, L., 376, 383
Trost, M. A., 380. *See also* Cowan, E. L.
Truss, C. V., 438, 459
Tryon, C. M., 363, 384
Tsuchiya, K., 89. *See also* Insull, W., Jr.
Tuckman, J., 82, 90
Tuddenham, R. D., 330, 331n., 343
Turnure, C., 158, 159, 169
Tutt, N., 409, 410, 415, 430
Tweney, R. D., 180, 202
Tyler, L. E., 532. *See also* Matthews, E. E., 528

Ullman, C. A., 572n., 586
Ungerleider, J. T., 457
Updegraff, R., 202. *See also* Skeels, H. M., 193
Urberg,, K. A., 268, 275
U. S. Department of Labor, 522, 534

Vaillant, G. E., 453, 460
van der Werff ten Bosch, J. J., 57, 88
Van Dusen, R. A., 522, 534
Vaz, E. W., 373, 384
Vener, A., 127
Verden, P., 342. *See also* McCord, W., 325
Verinis, J. S., 103, 127
Veroff, J., 584. *See also* Gurin, G. J.
Vincent, C. E., 126
Vockell, E. L., 388, 407
Vogel, G., 232. *See also* Rechtschaffen, A.
Vogel, G. W., 221, 222, 231, 233
Vogel, S. R., 49. *See also* Broverman, I. K.

Voss, H. L., 394, 405
Vreeland, R., 482*n*., 506

Wagman, M., 268, 275
Wagner, M. E., 573, 585
Wagner, N. N., 275. *See also* Pytkowicz, A. R.
Wake, F. R., 119, 127
Wakefield, W. M., 316, 343
Walder, L. O., 274. *See also* Eron, L. D.
Waldrop, M. F., 364
Walker, R. N., 230. *See also* Ames, L. B., 213
Wallach, M. A., 161, 169
Walsh, R. H., 119, 127
Walster, E., 82, 88, 91, 388, 407. *See also* Dion, K.
Walters, J., 340, 343. *See also* Graves, D.; Stinnett, N.
Walters, R. H., 320, 339, 414, 421, 428
Ward, D. A., 383, 384, 509, 534, 586. *See also* Super, D. E., 563
Watson, J., 20. *See also* Zytkaskee, A.
Watson, R. J., Jr., 531. *See also* Horner, M. S., 524
Wattenberg, W. W., 71, 91
Watts, F. P., 483, 506
Watts, W. A., 376, 384
Waxler, C. Z., 343. *See also* Yarrow, M. R.
Weary, B., 532. *See also* Matthews, E. E., 528
Weatherley, D., 109, 127
Wechsler, D., 175, 203
Wegner, E. L., 497, 506
Weigert, A. J., 549, 555
Weil, A. T., 439, 460
Weiner, I. B., 326, 343
Weinstock, A., 346, 383
Weir, J. B. deV., 62, 91
Weisbroth, S. P., 540, 555
Weiss, J. M., 299
Weitz, L. J., 166. *See also* Bynum, T. W.
Well, A. D., 143. *See also* Strutl, G. F.
Wellman, B. L., 202. *See also* Skeels, H. M., 193
Wenburn, G. M., 457. *See also* Bloom, R.
Wenkart, A., 397, 407
Wertheimer, R. R., 364, 384
Wessen, W., 167
Wheeler, L., 524*n*., 534

White, R. W., 249, 253
Whitehouse, R. H., 58*n*., 64*n*., 91
Whiteman, M., 158, 159, 169, 202, 380, 428, 443*n*., 444*n*., 457, 503. *See also* Brook, J. S., 347, 410, 411, 442, 443, 477, 478, 479; Peisach, E., 192
Whiting, B., 268, 275
Whitman, R. M., 232. *See also* Kramer, M.
Whittaker, D., 376, 384
Whyte, W. F., 122*n*., 127
Wicas, E. A., 470, 505
Wieder, D. L., 355, 384
Wiesenthal, D. L., 52. *See also* Silverman, I.
Wigdor, B. T., 365, 383
Wiggins, R. G., 39, 52
Wikler, A., 441, 460
Wilkinson, K., 414, 430
Willenburg, E. P., 199
Willerman, L., 77, 78*n*., 91, 133, 144
Williams, A. F., 436, 437, 461
Williams, H. M., 202. *See also* Skeels, H. M., 193
Williams, V., 489, 506
Willoughby, R. H., 195, 200
Wilson, K., 522, 534
Winchel, R., 481, 506
Wineman, D., 422, 430
Wines, J. V., 100, 126
Winick, C., 459
Winkler, J. B., 270, 275
Winters, C. J., 525, 534
Wirtanen, I. D., 503. *See also* Bachman, J. G., 497, 498, 499, 500
Wittenberg, R. M., 365, 384
Wolfe, J. B., 89. *See also* Greulich, W. W.
Wolfgang, M., 428
Wolfson, K. P., 524, 534
Wolman, R. N., 274. *See also* Lewis, W. C.
Woods, R. L., 220, 233
Woodward, K. L., 334, 340, 343
Woodward, L. E., 533. *See also* Rennie, T. A. C., 527
Woodyard, E. S., 19. *See also* Jersild, A. T., 18
Worchel, P., 380. *See also* Byrne, D., 358
Wright, D., 552, 555
Wright, J. W., 167. *See also* Flavell, J. H.
Wuthnow, G., 547, 548, 555
Wurtman, R. J., 127. *See also* Zacharias, L.

subject index

Alcohol, 433–437; cultural factors associated with use of, 436; incidence of, 434; motivations for use of, 437; peer group support in adolescent's use of, 436–437; personality correlates of adolescent users of, 436–437; physiological effects of, 434–435; psychological effects of, 435; social factors associated with use of, 436

Aloneness, toleration of as aspect of maturity, 580

Amphetamines, 445–447

Androgens, 57, 101

Anger, 254–266; and compassion, 582; conditions that arouse, 255*ff*; deprecation of, 43–44; in fantasies, 260–261; mention of in self-assessment, 266; suppression of, 242. *See also* Aggression

Annoyances, in relations with parents, 313–314

Anxiety, 276–297; evidence of, 288–290; examples of, 277–280; and extreme stresses, 296–297; in parents, 314–315; and performance, 295–296; as a personality problem, 571; theories of, 281*ff*

Appearance: interplay of physical and psychological factors in, 81*ff*; personal, 81*ff*; physical, 81–88. *See also* Body image; Adipose tissues

Art, popularity of, 473

Aspirations, as related to "ideal self," 22–23

Assimilation, 149–150

Athletic ability, and popularity, 134*ff*; values attached to, 136*ff*

Attitudes: toward high school, 470–474; religious, 546*ff*; toward self, sex differences in, 38–39; toward work, 509

Authority, overt and covert attitudes toward, among delinquents, 420

Autobiographies, 26–27

Automobile: adolescents' interests in, 372–373; incidence of accidents with, 373

Autonomy, changes with age in, 322–324; moral, 536

Barbiturates, 447–448

Beliefs, religious, age changes in, 549*ff*

Biology, as a source of self-understanding, 492

Birth order, influence on intellectual development, 194–195

Body: build as related to sexual maturation, 67; image, 81*ff*

Boredom, 251

Breast development, 95, 100–101

Candor, role of in self-description, 30–31

Career: counseling, 526–528; development, 528–529

Career Pattern Study, 520

Case histories, factors leading to distortion in, 413

Change, capacity for, 569–570

Character, emphasis on in self-description, 32

Childhood difficulties, and delinquency, 412–413

Choice, necessity of, 10

Cognition, and emotion, 241–242

Cognitive aspects of moral development, 536*ff*

Cognitive development, 147*ff*; and ability to understand the motivations of others, 158–160; biological factors in, 149–150; concrete operations stage of, 151–152; consequences of, 156; and creativity, 160–161; formal operations stage of, 152–156; and insight, 161*ff*; sensorimotor stage of, 150; sex differences in, 156. *See also* Thinking; Intelligence; Mental growth

Collaboration, 285

College: outcomes of, 483*ff*; population, 483; youth, 482*ff*

Communes, 404

Communication, difficulty in between parent and adolescent, 316–317

Compassion, 518*ff*

Competition, 366–369

Competitiveness: as a defense against anxiety, 291; and low self-esteem, 368; as a source of anxiety, 287

Complaints, regarding school, 470–474

Compliance, as a defense against anxiety, 291–292

Compositions, as means of self-revelation, 26

Concrete operations, stage, of 151–152
Condensation, in dreams, 225
Confidants, parents as, 316–317
Conflict, in connection with dating, 391; in worries, 271. *See also* Anxiety
Conflicting and confusing cultural forces, 17–18
Conformity, 43–44, 369–371; intellectual, in college students, 485; morality based on, 541
Consistency: and change in rate of mental growth, 178–180; in sociometric ratings, 363–364; striving for, in view of self, 31
"Contact comfort" as source of affection, 246
Contraception, 113
Courtship ideals, 391–392. *See also* Dating; Love between the sexes
Creativity, 160–161, 576
Crime. *See* Delinquency
Crying, 258–259
Cultural aspects of emotional maturity, 578
Cultural factors in suppression of emotions, 243*ff*
Cultural forces in delinquency, 418*ff*

Dating, 385*ff*; behavior, activities engaged in, 386, 388–389; frequency of and ethnic differences, 387; sex behavior connected with, 118
Daydreams, 204*ff*; themes in, 210–211
"Death wish," 260–261
Defense mechanism, 279, 292–294
Defenses against anxiety, 290*ff*. *See also* Strategies
Delinquency, 408–428; age differences in, 410–411; environmental factors in, 416*ff*; ethnic differences in, 410; genetic factors and, 418–419; and hostility toward those who desire to help, 427–428; sex differences in, 410; theories relating to causes of delinquency, 416–418
Delinquents: exploitation of, 424–425; intelligence of, 412; parent–adolescent relations of, 414–415; persistence and change in, 425–427; personality traits of, 411*ff*; response to, 423–425; scholastic achievement of, 411–412

Democratic practices, 18
Denial, 293
Dependency on parents, outgrowing of, 321*ff*
Depression, 572
Deprivation, effects of on mental growth, 193; emotional effects of, 247
Desire, realization of through fantasy, 206*ff*
Detachment, as defense against anxiety, 291
Developmental asynchronies, 181–182
Deviant behavior, as related to religious beliefs, 553
Diaries, 26–27
Discrepancy between personal and social adjustment, 365
Displaced anger, 261–262
Displacement, 293; in dreams, 225
Divorce, 400
Dominant genes, 74–75
Doubt, religious, 551–552
Dreaming: effects of deprivation of, 222; patterns of, 222*ff*
Dreams, 219–230; and aggression, 228–229; content of, 226–227; physiological correlates of mental activity during, 220–222; and sexuality, 227–228
Dress and grooming, 86–87
Dropouts: from college, 483, 496–502; and intelligence, 497; personality dimensions of, 498; reasons given for leaving school, 499; self-esteem of, 498
Dropping out, effects of, 500; prevention of, 500–502
Drugs, 431–456; alcohol, 433–437; amphetamines, 445–447; barbiturates, 447–448; comments on the causes of use of, 454–456; heroin, 451–453; LSD, 448–451; marijuana, 437–445; multiple use of, 454; stages in use of, 453–454. *Also see specific drugs by name*

Early environment, as related to later careers of delinquents, 427
Early marriage, as related to early heterosexual involvement, 401
Economic unemployment, 13–14

Education: and adolescence, 465–502; of gifted youth, 187–188; for self-understanding, 491
Educational aspiration, 477*ff*
Educational expectations, 477*ff*; family influences on, 478–479; peer influences on, 479
Educational implications of mental pattern, 177–178
Educational level, and intelligence 193–194
Ego, 24, 283, 561; identity, 563–564
Egocentric, 151–152
Ejaculation, 94, 102–103, 112
Electroencephalograph, as an indicator of dreaming, 220
Emancipation from parents, 9, 321*ff*
Emotion: and cognition, 241–242; and drives, motives, and needs, 239–241; nature and development of, 237–297; neurological aspects of, 238–239; psychological attributes of, 238; release of through daydreams, 208
Emotional adjustment: and moral judgment, 540–541; of intellectually gifted, 183–184; of underachievers, 185*ff*
Emotional aspects: of being in love, 395*ff*; of religious doubt, 551–552; of the home, and intelligence, 194
Emotional maladjustment, and delinquency, 422–423. *See also* Problems; Personality
Emotional maturity, 6–7, 574, 578*ff*; and capacity for giving as well as taking, 579–580; compassion as an aspect of, 581*ff*; cultural aspects of, 578; psychological meanings of, 578–579
Endocrine glands, 57
Engagement, 390
Environment, and mental ability, 189*ff*. *See also* Socioeconomic status
Environmental factors, in delinquency, 416*ff*
Estrogens, 57
Ethnic differences, and dating behavior, 387–390; and delinquency, 410
Ethnicity: and intelligence, 195–197; and marijuana use, 442; and physical growth, 63–66; as related to occupational choice, 511–512

Expediency, morality based on, 541
Exploitation, of delinquents, 424–425
Eye movements, as an indication of dreaming, 220*ff*

Failure: and anger, 257–258; parental feelings of, 314; persisting fears of, 270–273
Faith, 9. *See also* Religion
Falling in love, 392*ff*
Family: changing role of, 334–338; background, and underachievement, 185–186; background, effects of on religious attitudes, 548–549; characteristics, awareness of, 311–312. *See also* Socioeconomic status
Fantasies, 204–219; as a reminder of unrealized aspirations, 206–207
Fantasy: adolescent, 210–212; experimental study of, 209–210; nature of, 210, 212; and problem solving, 208; vs. realism, in occupational choice, 516–517; and thinking, 207
Fat deposits, 69*ff*; psychological effects of, 71–73
Fate, as focal concern in delinquent subculture, 419–420
Fear, 270–273; concealment of, 243–244; as response to delinquents, 423; role of in compassion, 581*ff*; of success, 480–481, 524
Feeling, 238*ff*; expression of among friends, 355
Female career development: 521*ff*; and identity development, 523–524; personality factors in, 524–525; theoretical views regarding, 525–526
Femininity, acceptance of, 48–49
Fertility, menarche and, 96–97
"Focal concerns" in delinquent subculture, 419*ff*
Formal operational thinking: and cognitive syle, 156; and education, 156; and intelligence, 155–156
Formal operations, 575; stage of, 152–156
Free association: as an exploratory form of thinking, 229; as means of self-discovery and self-revelation, 25–26

Freedom: and anxiety, 281–282; effects, limits, and nature of, 4, 10

Freudian theory, 24, 560–561. *See also* Freud, S., *in author index*

Freud's theory of anxiety, 283–284

Friendships: 353, 355*ff*; and interpersonal attraction, 357*ff*; sex differences in, 357

Gang delinquency, 419*ff*

"Generation gap," 346–350

Genes, 73–75

Genetic background, need for knowledge of in studying delinquency, 418–419

Genetic and environmental factors, interaction between, 76*ff*

Genetic factors, 73*ff*; in intelligence, 189*ff*; significance of, 80–81; and stability in personality development, 565, 567–568

Genital development, psychological reaction to, 103–104

Genital organs, male: growth of, 94, 101*ff*; variation in timing of events, 94, 101*ff*

Genotypes, 74–75

Gifted youth, 182*ff*; characteristics of, 183*ff*

Gifts, as source of joy, 250

Goals, 8, 10–11; of adolescent development, 5–9

God, professed belief in, 547

Going steady, 389–390

Grievances, 262–263

Growth, course of physical, 55–88

Guilt: and fantasies, 214–216; parental feelings of, 315; repressed, as a source of anxiety, 287–288

Hair, growth, distribution, and texture of, 93–95, 101–102, 104

"Happiest day," experiences connected with, 250

Harsh environment, anxiety as a reaction to, 284

Healthy aspects of being in love, 397–399

Height: changes in, 58–65; and heredity, 78–79; stability in, 566

Heredity, 73*ff*; biochemical basis of, 76; and environment in background of delinquents, 418*ff*; and later careers of delinquents, 427; and mental ability, 189*ff*; and mental illness, 80

Heroin, 451–453

Heteronomous moral judgments, 536

Heterosexual behavior, 385*ff*

High school: adolescent attitudes toward, 470–474; policies regarding early marriages, 402–404

History, as a source of self-knowledge, 492

Homosexual activity, 120–122

Hope, 11; reviewing of, as aspect of maturity, 580

Horizontal décalage, 575

Hormones, 57

Hostility: and competitiveness, 369; of delinquents toward those who wish to help them, 427–428; irrational, 571; irrational, toward delinquents, 424–425. *See also* Anger; Anxiety

Id, 24, 283, 561

"Ideal self," 22–23, 29

Identification, 45–48

Identity: crisis, 564; diffusion, 564; formation, 45–48

Imagination, functions of, 205–208

Independence: parental characteristics and attitudes as related to adolescent, 325*ff*; and parental child-rearing practices, 319–320; steps toward, 322*ff*

Infatuation, 392

Inferiority complex, 561

Insight: into adolescence, 5; advantages of, 163–164; cognitive and noncognitive aspects of, 162–163; in college seniors as compared with freshmen, 485–487; difficulties in achieving, 164–166; into self, 161*ff*; and self-assessment, 31

Intellectual maturity, 575–576

Intelligence, 170*ff*; and academic achievement, 184–188; consistency and change in rate of growth, 178–180; of delinquents, 412; environmental factors in, 189*ff*; and ethnicity, 195–197; genetic factors in, 189*ff*; growth of, 173*ff*; and leaving

Monkeys, origins of affection in, 246–247

Moral character, 541–542

Moral development, 535*ff*; cognitive-developmental approach to, 536*ff*; stages of, 537–539

Moral judgment: and ability to take the role of another individual, 539–540; and behavior, 537, 539; effect of peers on, 536; and emotional adjustment, 540–541; sex differences in, 540; and sharing behavior, 537

Moral maturity, 576–577; consistency over time, 567

Moral qualities, emphasis on in self-description, 32

Moral realism, 536

Moral relativism, 536

Moral "types," 541

Mothering, effects of, 245–246; and sexual responsiveness in mature monkeys, 246–247

Mother's perception of child, 330–331

Motivations, for adolescent drinking behavior, 437; of others, ability to understand and cognitive development, 158–160

Motor abilities, development of, 129–133

Motor ability, sex differences in, 129–133

Motor performance, as related to: "good looks," 135; height, 135; intelligence, 135; popularity, 135; skeletal age, 135

Multiple drug use, 454

Neurological aspects of emotion, 238–239

"Neurotic anxicty," 277

Nocturnal emission, 102–103, 111–112, 119

Normal anxiety, 277

Obesity, psychological implications of, 72–73

Occupation, definition of, 509

Occupational advantage, as hoped-for outcome of college, 488

Occupational aspirations: 477*ff*; family influences on, 478–479; and parental values, 511; socioeconomic correlates of, 510–511

Occupational expectations, 477*ff*

Oedipal conflict, 312–313, 561

Orgasm, 118–119

Ossification, 67–68

"Outsider's" view, value of, 317

Parent–adolescent, interactions between, 304–307

Parent–adolescent relations, 303–338; and affection, 309*ff*; and adolescent's educational expectations and occupational aspirations, 477–479; attitudes and child-rearing practices of parent, 318–321; and early marriage, 401, 402; and delinquency, 414–416; impact of parent versus peers on adolescent behavior, 346–347; importance of, 308*ff*; and marijuana use, 443–444; objective and subjective aspects of, 307–308; outgrowing childhood dependency on parents, 321*ff*; parent–adolescent similarity in attitudes, 346–350; parental and adolescent use of alcohol, 437; parents as confidants, 316–317; postadolescent reassessment of parents, 330, 332; and student activism, 376–379

Parental abuse of children, 332–334

Parental acceptance, 309*ff*

Parental behavior, theoretical model of, 324–325

Parental child-rearing attitudes and practices: 318–321; effect of on child, 319–321, 325–327; socioeconomic correlates of, 332

Parental difficulties in "letting go," 329*ff*

Parental domination, methods of maintaining, 329–330

Parental satisfactions, 317–318

Parental values, and adolescent aspirations, 511

Parents: authoritarian, 319–321, 326–327; as objects of spite, 424; perception of roles of, 312–313; permissive, 319–321, 326–327; role of in arousal of anger, 256

Parents' attitudes toward dating, 386–387

Paternal absence, 337–338

Peer culture, 348, 351–353; and cultural factors, 353–354

Peer group: and adolescent's use of alcohol, 436–437; and marijuana use, 442–444

Peer relationships: competition in, 366–367; and conformity, 369–371; and peer culture, 348, 351–353; and social leisure-time interests and activities, 371–373; and youth movements, 373–379

Peers: friendships and relationships with, 353, 355–366; influence of, 311; influence of parents and, 346–347; and moral development, 536; relationships with, 344–379

Penis, growth of, 94, 101–103

Perception: as component of emotion, 238; of feeling, as related to compassion, 582–583; of parents, 307–308; of parents, acquiring realistic image of, 328; of parents, changes in, 311, 330–332; of parents, modifications of, 307–308, 328–329

Performance and anxiety, 295–296

Persistence and change in delinquent tendencies, 425–427

Personality, 559ff; correlates of adolescent alcohol use, 436–437; dreams as an aid to knowledge about, 223–224; and early marriage, 401–402; emphasis on in self-descriptions, 32; and female career development, 524–525; of marijuana users, 444–445; meaning of, 560; psychoanalytic theory of, 560–561; social learning theory of, 561–562; theories of, 560ff; and theory of self, 562–563; and vocational choice, 513–514

Personality characteristics, stability of, 565, 567–568

Personality development, 559ff; as affected by early and late physical maturing, 107ff; influence of cultural factors on, 564–565; influence of peers on, 564; and problems, 570–574; psychosocial stages of, 563–564; reaching for maturity and, 574ff;

stability and change in, 565ff; theories of, 560–565

Personality of dropouts, 498

Personality problems, 570–574; incidence of, 571ff; and delinquency, 421–423

Personality theories, 560ff

Personality traits, with delinquency, 411ff; of popular and unpopular adolescents, 360–363

Petting, 114–116, 118, 388–389

Phenotypes, 74, 75

Philosophy of life, influence of college on, 484

Physical abilities, 128–142

Physical ability, as related to mental ability, 134–135

Physical activity, decline in interest in, 132–133

Physical characteristics, and self-evaluation, 81ff

Physical development, 55–88; psychological repercussions of, 71–73 81ff

Physical education, ramifications of, 141–142

Physical growth: and anxiety, 281; ethnic differences in, 63–66; secular trend in, 62–63; sex differences in, 63–66; social class differences in, 65–66

Physical maturity, 6, 576

Physiological correlates of mental activity during dreams, 220–222

Pleasure, 249–250

Pleasures of the mind, 188–189

Political thought, development of, 544–545

Popularity: adult judgments of, 365–366; as related to athletic ability, 134ff; as related to dating, 391; stability in, 566. See also Sociometric tests

"Practical ability," 131–132

Preadolescence, influence of genetic factors during, 76–78

Preadolescent sex behavior, 110ff

Pregnancy, among early marrying girls, 401

Premenstrual syndrome, 99

Pride, in relation to anger, 257–258

Primary reaction patterns, 305–306

Problem solving: and delinquency, 421–422; through fantasy, 208*ff*
Projection, 292–293
Projective methods, 212*ff*; findings from, 16, 213*ff*
Proportions, bodily, changes in, 66, 67
Psychoanalytic theory, 560–561
Psychological attributes of emotion, 238
Psychological disturbance and vocational adjustment, 525–527
Psychological implications of physical ability, 139*ff*
"Psychological mother," 579
Psychosocial stages of personality development, 563–564
Psychosomatic illness, 265
Puberty, 92*ff*
Pubescent, 92–93
Pubic hair, 94, 101–103
Public opinion, as related to delinquency, 423*ff*

Q-sort, 28

Rationalization, 293
Reaction formation, 293
Realism, as an aspect of: maturity, 580; self-acceptance, 33
Recessive genes, 74–75
Regression, 294
Rejection: of delinquents by teachers, 423; by parents, 310–311; by peers, 358*ff*; of self, symptoms of, 37–38
Religion, 545–553; and adolescents, 545*ff*; beliefs and practices, 546*ff*; characteristics of adolescents who are religiously active, 552; consequences of for adolescent, 552–553; developmental changes in religious attitudes and beliefs, 549*ff*; emotional aspects of religious doubt, 551–552; influence of childhood experiences on religious attitudes, 548–549; nontraditional forms of, 548; reason, science and, 553
Religious beliefs, 546*ff*; and deviant behavior, 553; sex differences in, 547
Repression, 242, 292–294
Role-taking ability and cognitive development, 159
Running speed, changes in, 129–130

Scapegoats, delinquents as, 424–425
Schizophrenia, 80
School: academic, personal, and utilitarian aspects of, 487*ff*; adolescents who drop out of, 496*ff*; and disturbance in self-image of adolescents, 468–470; formal versus informal, 467–468; grievances and anger connected with, 256–257; high school youth and, 465*ff*; nature of, 467; as portrayed in adolescent fantasies, 216–217; as a problem, 572; role of in adolescence, 465–502; as source of fear, 270–271; as source of joy, 250; youth in college, 482*ff*
School achievement: and family characteristics, 497; and popularity, 135*ff*; and self-esteem, 469; and socioeconomic backgrounds, 477–478; family background and, 497; intelligence and, 497
School dropouts, 496*ff*; ability of, 497–498; family background of, 497–498
School subjects, attitudes toward, 470*ff*
Schooling, effects of on intelligence, 193–194
Security, desire for as incentive for going steady, 391
Self, 21*ff*; acceptance of, 34–37; anger directed against, 264*ff*; as "center" of personality, 560; components of, 22*ff*; "finding of," 7–9; insight into, 161*ff*; known dimensions and unperceived influences on, 22*ff*
Self-acceptance, 33*ff*; and competitiveness, 368; influence of early and late maturing on, 107–109; and mental health, 562; and self-rejection, balance between, 39*ff*; stability in, 566
Self-assertion, 372
Self-assessment, age trends in, 41, 42; limitations of instruments used for measurement of, 27–28, 30–31; major themes in, 31–32; mention of anger in connection with, 266
Self-concept, as related to vocational choice, 518*ff*; sex differences in, 482
Self-consistency, reinforcement through a striving for, 569
Self-deception, 23. *See also* Anxiety

Self-description inventories, 27–29
Self-determination, as related to anxiety, 281*ff*
Self-discovery, through dreams, 230; through reciprocated love, 393
Self-esteem: and achievement in school, 469; of dropouts, 498; and the religious environment of the adolescent, 549
Self-evaluation: intellectual ability, 197–198; and body image, 81*ff*
Self-examination: incentives for, 166; role of in studying adolescents, 4–5
Self-idealization, 23. *See also* Anxiety
Self-image, and the schools, 468–470
Self–improvement, adolescents' interests in, 474; as source of joy, 250
Self-insight, maturing of, 577
Self-regard, bolstering of through falling in love, 398; threats to as source of anger, 257–258
Self-rejection, 33*ff*; as related to obesity, 72–73
Self-scrutiny, in college seniors, 485–487
Self-understanding: as an announced goal by college students and instructors, 491; and promoting self-knowledge in others, 494–496; role of school in advancement of, 491*ff*
Self-views, factors related to, 32–34; stability and change, 34–36
Semantic differential, 28–29
Sensorimotor stage, 150
Separation anxiety, 284
Sex: in adolescent fantasies, 210–211, 214, 216–217, 219; and anxiety, 286; anxiety regarding, example of, 279–281; mention of in self-evaluation, 43–44. *See also* Heterosexual
Sex differences: in achievement motivation, 481–482; in aggression, 268–269; in attitudes toward self, 38–39; in automobile accidents, 373; in dating behavior, 387, 389; in delinquency, 410; in educational expectations and aspirations, 477; in fantasies, 214–217, 219; in friendships, 357; in manifest anxiety, 294; in marijuana use, 442; in mental ability, 180–181; in moral judgments, 540; in motor ability, 129–

133; in personality problems, 572; in physical ability, 128*ff*; in physical growth, 63–66; in religious beliefs, 547; in self-concept, 482; in sex activity, 115–119; in sexual attitudes, 389; in thinking, 156; in traits regarded as socially desirable, 363; in vocational choice, 523
Sex-role identity: biological correlates of, 45; cognitive view of, 45–47; and learning, 44*ff*; parental influences, on, 47–48; social learning theory view of, 46
Sex-role preferences, changes in, 49
Sex-typed activity, consistency over time, 566
Sexual attitudes: parent–adolescent disparity in, 119–120; in relation to attitudes toward self and others, 123–124
Sexual behavior: 14–15, 110*ff*; attitudes toward, 110, 112–113, 119–120, 123; attitudes toward and ethnicity, 110; correlates of, 116–118; in connection with dating, 388–389; in middle and late adolescence, 114–119; moral and emotional aspects of, 122–123; recent changes in, 112–113; sex differences in, 115–119; variations in, 116–119
Sexual characteristics, 93*ff*
Sexual desire, as related to being in love, 395–396
Sexual development, 92–124
Sexual intercourse, 114–119
Sexual maturation, 92–124
Sexual responsiveness, in motherless monkeys, 246–247
Sexuality, in dreams, 227–228
Sickness, as reported cause of school failure, 474–475
Skeletal age, 67–68
Skeletal growth, 67–69
Sleep and dream patterns, 222*ff*
Social acceptance and rejection, 358*ff*
Social attitudes and relationships, emphasis on in self-description, 32
Social class: and delinquent "subculture," 419; and differences in physical growth, 65–66. *See also* Socioeconomic status

Social issues, connected with sex practices, 120
Social reinforcement of personality traits, 561–562, 568–569
Social relations, anger in connection with, 255ff
Social system, and vocational development, 509–512
Socioeconomic status: and athletic ability and strength, 135, 139; and dating behavior, 387; and early marriage, 401; and educational expectations and aspirations, 477; of intellectually gifted, 183; and intelligence, 192; and occupational aspirations, 510–511; and parental child-rearing practices, 332; self-description, 32
Sociogram, 359–360
Sociometric tests, results of, 358ff
Speeding, 373
Stability in height, 566
Stability in personality development, genetic factors related to, 565, 567–568
Stereotype: feminine, 44ff; masuline, 44ff
"Stored-up" anger, 260
Storm and stress, 15–16
Strategies, in dealing with anxiety, 291–292
Strength, as related to: ethnicity, 132ff; height, 135; intelligence, 135; popularity, 134ff; school achievement, 135; sex, 132ff; skeletal age, 135; social status, 135
Strength, changes in, 128ff
Stress, and anxiety, 296–297
Stress, anxiety producing, 280–281; of adolescence, 13–18
Striving, 4
Superego, 24, 283, 561
Superior youth, 182ff
Suppression, of emotion, 242; of fear, 272–273
Sweat and sebaceous glands, 105
Symbolism, of dreams, 226

Teachers: perception of causes of student failure, 474–475; problems with, 572; ratings of as affected by prior information, 476–477; respect for, 489

Teachers' qualities, liked and disliked by students, 475–476; views concerning, 475ff
Television, and aggression, 269–270
Temperamental characteristics, stability in, 567–568
Temperamental qualities, 305–306
Tenderness, 395ff
Testes, growth of, 94, 101–102
Thinking: effects of alcohol on, 435; fantasy as a form of, 207ff; through free association, 229–230
Throwing, age changes in, 129–130
Time, conception of, 157–158
Tissues and organs, growth of, 69–72
Tolerance, effect of college on, 484–486
Trends in adolescent development compared with earlier generations, 11–13

Uncertainty, and manifest anxiety, 297
Unconscious aspects of personality, 23–25
Unconscious elements in anxiety, 276–279
Underachievers, 184ff
Unhealthy aspects of being in love, 397–399
Universality of formal operations, 154–155
Unknown dimensions underlying ideas and attitudes pertaining to self, 23–25

Value systems, development of, 542–544
Values: attached to athletic ability, 136ff; of college students, 484ff
Variability, in physical growth, 58ff
Vocabulary, "tribal," 371–372
Vocational adjustment and psychological disturbance, 526–527
Vocational choice: effects of intelligence on, 513; as an event, 512–515; fantasy stage of, 516; Holland's theory of, 514–515; influence of interests on, 513; personality correlates of, 513–514; as a process, 515ff; realistic stage of, 516; tentative stage of, 516